Rhetorical Criticism

LEXINGTON STUDIES IN POLITICAL COMMUNICATION

Series Editor: Robert E. Denton, Jr.,
Virginia Polytechnic Institute And State University

This series encourages focused work examining the role and function of communication in the realm of politics including campaigns and elections, media, and political institutions.

TITLES IN SERIES:

Governing Codes: Gender, Metaphor, and Political Identity, By Karrin Vasby Anderson and Kristina Horn Sheeler

Paving the Way for Madam President, By Nichola D. Gutgold

Maryland Politics and Political Communication, 1950-2005, By Theodore F. Sheckels

Images, Issues, and Attacks: Television Advertising by Incumbents and Challengers in Presidential Elections, By E. D. Dover

Democracy as Discussion: Civic Education and the American Forum Movement, By William Keith

Picturing China in the American Press: The Visual Portrayal of Sino-American Relations in Time *Magazine, 1949–1973*, By David D. Perlmutter

Lottery Wars: Case Studies in Bible Belt Politics, 1986-2005, By Randy Bobbitt

Post-9/11 American Presidential Rhetoric: A Study of Protofascist Discourse, By Colleen Elizabeth Kelley

Making a Difference: A Comparative View of the Role of the Internet in Election Politics, Edited by Stephen Ward, Diana Owen, Richard Davis, and David Taras

Seen and Heard: The Women of Television News, By Nichola D. Gutgold

Nuclear Legacies: Communication, Controversy, and the U.S. Nuclear Weapons Complex, Edited by Bryan C. Taylor, William J. Kinsella, Stephen P. Depoe, Maribeth S. Metzler

Conditional Press Influence in Politics, By Adam J. Schiffer

Telling Political Lives: The Rhetorical Autobiographies of Women Leaders in the United States, Edited by Brenda DeVore Marshall and Molly A. Mayhead

Media Bias? A Comparative Study of Time, Newsweek, the National Review, and the Progressive, 1975–2000, By Tawnya J. Adkins Covert and Philo C. Wasburn

Navigating the Post–Cold War World: President Clinton's Foreign Policy Rhetoric, By Jason A. Edwards

The Rhetoric of Pope John Paul II, Edited by Joseph R. Blaney and Joseph P. Zompetti

Stagecraft and Statecraft: Advance and Media Events in Political Communication, By Dan Schill

Rhetorical Criticism

Perspectives in Action

Edited by Jim A. Kuypers

LEXINGTON BOOKS

A division of
ROWMAN & LITTLEFIELD PUBLISHERS, INC.
Lanham • Boulder • New York • Toronto • Plymouth, UK

Portions of this book were previously published by: Pearson Education, Inc.

LEXINGTON BOOKS

A division of Rowman & Littlefield Publishers, Inc.
A wholly owned subsidiary of The Rowman & Littlefield Publishing Group, Inc.
4501 Forbes Boulevard, Suite 200
Lanham, MD 20706

Estover Road
Plymouth PL6 7PY
United Kingdom

British Library Cataloguing in Publication Information Available

Library of Congress Cataloging-in-Publication Data

Rhetorical criticism : perspectives in action / edited by Jim A. Kuypers.
     p. cm. — (Lexington studies on political communication)
  Includes bibliographical references and index.
  ISBN 978-0-7391-2773-5 (cloth : alk. paper) — ISBN 978-0-7391-2774-2 (pbk. :
alk. paper) — ISBN 978-0-7391-3617-1 (electronic)
  1. Rhetorical criticism. I. Kuypers, Jim A.
  PN4096.R52 2009
  809.5'1--dc22   2009007203

Printed in the United States of America

♾ ™ The paper used in this publication meets the minimum requirements of American
National Standard for Information Sciences—Permanence of Paper for Printed Library
Materials, ANSI/NISO Z39.48–1992.

To my family, Tammy, Bandit, and Blue
whose love and support are constant

Contents

Acknowledgements

I would like to thank my family for their unreserved and continued support of my writing. With gratitude I mention Virginia Tech, which paid my salary and also funded library services such as inter-library loan and Ebscohost, all absolutely necessary to the completion of this project. The value Virginia Tech places on research allows projects such as this book to be undertaken and completed. I also wish to thank my Department Head, R. L. Holloway, whose support during difficult times is exceptional.

Editor's Foreword

R*hetorical Criticism: Perspectives in Action* is designed to introduce students to the exciting art of rhetorical criticism. Since there are more than a few books about rhetorical criticism on the market, I thought I would share with you why and how this book was created. It all began as I was reading through the more popular criticism books—I began to feel something was missing. Over time it dawned on me: they simply were not as accessible to undergraduates as I felt they could be. This was a major concern of mine since I was introducing rhetorical criticism to undergraduates who had never before been exposed to the practice.

Fostering creativity was another concern. The more I read existing rhetorical criticism textbooks, the more I felt they presented material in a way that would encourage a formulaic approach to writing criticism. This is difficult to avoid; I know that one cannot escape completely from the bounds of formula when first teaching about rhetorical criticism. After all, one does have to begin teaching from some starting point, and the initial steps one takes are very much the same in every classroom. Still, I wanted to stress the very personal nature of criticism.

These two concerns—accessibility and creativity—led to the creation of the book you now hold in your hands, and several features differentiate it from others already on the market.

First, well-known perspectives and modes of rhetorical criticism are covered, but other less known yet important perspectives are presented as well. So in addition to finding chapters on Traditional Criticism or Dramatism, you will also find chapters on Mythic Criticism, Framing Analysis, Ideographical Criticism, Critical Rhetoric, Conceptually Oriented Criticism, and more.

Second, each chapter detailing a perspective is written by a nationally recognized scholar in that area. Thus, instead of one person writing a short synopsis of numerous perspectives, a noted expert with experience using that perspective has written the theoretical explanation. This approach allows students to discover quickly how personalities influence the practice of criticism, and even the teaching of criticism. Critics with well-developed voices wrote the chapters contained in this book; students will benefit from exposure to these voices, hopefully beginning the process of developing their own critical voice.

Third, each chapter also includes a short critical essay written by the chapter author. As I read through various books on criticism, I found plenty of previously published works included for students to read. The drawback here, though, is that these articles were written for the readers of a particular scholarly journal; they are not easily accessible to students, many of whom will not have had previous exposure to criticism. Because of this, these scholarly essays may actually defeat their purpose of providing useful examples of criticism for new critics to emulate. The critical essays contained in *Rhetorical Criticism: Perspectives in Action* were written specifically for this book with *student accessibility* in mind. Each essay provides a touchstone for students to use when crafting their own essays.

The potential danger with touchstones is that they can be so good that they trample over, rather then encourage, novice critics. The chapters in this book seek to avoid this. Criticism is an artistic process, yet far too often this personal nature of criticism remains a mystery to students. There are rules, but there are also instances when if followed they would stifle the critical process and produce sterile criticism. I believe strongly, though, that students benefit from knowing a basic structure around which they can organize their initial efforts at writing criticism. To this end, each of the chapters in this book loosely follows a pattern of theoretical discussion followed by an example essay. Before writing the example essay, each author was asked to loosely follow the D.A.E. organizational model for criticism (Description, Analysis/ Interpretation, and Evaluation). Some authors did and some did not. Since not all perspectives lend themselves well to the D.A.E. model, students will be presented with instances that deviate from this model and will he given reasons why this is desirable, thereby empowering them to make these decisions for themselves. In addition, some authors provide a standard academic version of a critical essay as their example, whereas some focused more on the interpretive aspects that their perspective encouraged.

Fourth, and stressing further the artistic and individual nature of criticism, each chapter contains the author's personal comments on the decisions he or she made while writing the essay. This allows students insight into the process of crafting a critical essay; in our case, essays written by noted experts in that area. Any writing project involves decisions about what to include or exclude, what to stress, and what to ignore. These personal comments allow students to see what questions and concerns guided the writing of the chapters they read.

Fifth, each chapter provides a "potentials and pitfalls" section that calls attention to the particular strengths and weaknesses the given rhetorical perspective possesses. Authors expose those aspects of the rhetorical artifact that their particular perspective highlights, thus stressing the artistic and insight producing aspects of the critical process. These comments shed light on how different perspectives both enable and discourage particular readings of texts.

Finally, authors provide an annotated recommended reading list for students who wish to study a particular perspective or mode of criticism in greater detail. Some authors prioritize the readings, thus helping students read in order those articles and books most helpful in beginning the process of writing criticism using a particular perspective.

Since some portions of this book were previously published, I would also like to thank the reviewers for their time and input on those portions: William Denman, Marshall University; Carolyn D. Holben, Matanuska-Susitna College; James Jasinski, University of Puget Sound; Jason MunseII, Wesleyan College; John M. Murphy, University of Georgia; Edward Schiappa, University of Minnesota; John Sloop, Vanderbilt University; John Tapia, Missouri Western State College; and Marsha Watson, University of Nebraska-Omaha.

It is my sincere hope that this book will encourage students to ask new questions about the rhetoric around them and that, in doing so, they will fulfill the critic's quest to produce both insight and understanding about the world in which we live.

Jim A. Kuypers
Virginia Tech
Fall 2008

1

What is Rhetoric?

Jim A. Kuypers and Andrew King

We imagine some of you asking, "What? Why study rhetoric? Isn't that just a tactic sneaky politicians use when they don't want to talk about the issues?" If you were thinking along these lines, you would not be completely wrong. The word rhetoric has had some negative meanings attached to it throughout the centuries. However, the full meaning of rhetoric is considerably richer than the everyday usage of the word suggests

Rhetoric has many meanings, some old, some new. To get at the heart of the definition let us first consider how the term rhetoric is most commonly used. When a politician calls for 'action, not rhetoric,' the meaning seems clear; rhetoric denotes hollow words and flashy language. It also connotes associations with deceit and tricks that mask truth and forthrightness. For example, former President Richard M. Nixon used the term rhetoric in this way in his 1969 inaugural address: "The simple things are the ones most needed today if we are to surmount what divides us and cement what unites us. To lower our voices would be a simple thing. In these difficult years, America has suffered from a fever of words; from inflated rhetoric that promises more than it can deliver; from angry rhetoric that fans discontents into hatreds; from bombastic rhetoric that postures instead of persuading." Although the type of rhetoric of which Nixon speaks is often worthy of study, it also leaves one thinking that it is certainly not the kind of language that an intelligent and civil person would willingly wish to use. Consider, too, these examples from political blog posts: "I think Obama's supporters have had too much Kool Aid to notice that their candidate is all *rhetoric* and no *action*."[1] Or this headline from a different blog: "Iran: Obama Rises Above Clinton's *Rhetoric* to Take *Action*."[2]

Rhetoric is also used to describe what some today consider embellished or over-ornamental language. The perception of excess has its roots in eighteenth and nineteenth century American oratorical practice. During these centuries before radio, television, and the Internet, public speeches were opportunities for audiences to be both informed and entertained; a certain lushness of language was exceeded, even expected. It was not at all uncommon for speeches to last several hours and for the speakers to use no notes. This 'spread eagle' style of American speaking was most evident in patriotic orations, and is well represented in George Caleb Bingham's painting, *Stump Speaking*. Albert Beveridge, in his 1898 speech

The March of the Flag, provides a common example of what we might consider embellished speech today:

> It is a noble land that God has given us; a land that can feed and clothe the world; a land whose coastlines would enclose half the countries in Europe; a land set like a sentinel between the two imperial oceans of the globe, a greater England with a nobler destiny.
>
> It is a mighty people that he has planted on this soil; a people sprung from the most masterful blood of history; a people perpetually revitalized by the virile, man-producing working-folk of all the earth; a people imperial by virtue of their power, by right of their institutions, by authority of their heaven-directed purposes—the propagandists and not the misers of liberty.[3]

Although the above examples are certainly forms of rhetoric, they but scratch the surface of rhetoric's deeply rich meaning. The study of rhetoric is an invention of early Western Civilization and has its roots in the fledgling democracies of ancient Greece.

A SYNOPTICAL SKETCH OF RHETORIC

The Greeks developed the original model of rhetoric, a systematic body of knowledge about the theory and practice of public speaking in the law courts, the governing assemblies, and on ceremonial occasions. Rhetoric was codified by Aristotle in his famous treatise, *The Rhetoric*, written somewhere around 335 BC. He defined rhetoric as the "power of discovering the means of persuasion in any given situation," a much more comprehensive and intellectually respectable meaning than today's common attributions of bombast and deception. The Sophists, wandering teachers and exiles in the ancient world, often taught rhetoric as a popular course designed to prepare ambitious youths for fame and success. The Greeks believed in the power of the spoken word and delighted in hotly contested debate; they even held oratorical contests as part of the Olympics. On the other hand, philosophers such as Plato condemned rhetoric, finding it a serious rival to Philosophy in the ancient educational system.

Later, the Roman republican government provided many opportunities for the practice of rhetoric in their popular assemblies, in provincial governing bodies, in their law courts, and in their huge civil service and military. The best-known Roman orator was Marcus Tullius Cicero (106-43 BC) who took over the Greek ideas of rhetoric and adapted them to the needs of a far-flung world empire. From modest origins he rose to the highest office in Rome, the Consulship, and was considered by many to be the greatest lawyer, speaker, and writer of his day. Fifty-eight speeches and nine hundred letters have come down to us; they still read well today and stand as models of powerfully persuasive oratory, biting wit, and incredible verbal skill. Cicero argued for an ideal rhetorician, an orator-statesman who would use rhetoric as a means of serving the people. A century later, Cicero's rhetorical teaching was codified by the first Imperial Professor of Rhetoric in Rome, Quintilian (AD 35-96), who was Rome's greatest teacher and codifier of rhetorical knowledge. Thus, the Greco-Roman world established a tradition of discourse that has been taught throughout Western history and continues to grow and to develop down to our own time.

Saint Augustine (AD 354-430) was largely responsible for early Christian uses of rhetoric, and his writings were used extensively by churchmen throughout the middle-ages. Augustine reasoned that since the Devil had full access to all of the available resources of rhetoric, others ought to study it if only for their own protection. The Church agreed, declaring that knowledge of its great power was essential for everyone, and both "in theory and practice the Christians forever influenced the development of rhetorical thought."[4] Likewise the influence of rhetoric on the spread of Christianity should not be underestimated. During the middle-ages rhetoric was at the heart of education. It was taught in the cathedral schools. It inspired the great university debates and disputations, and it set rules for the composition of sermons and royal proclamations. It even extended its domain over poetry and letter writing, and rhetorical modes of expression guided government bureaucracies.

In the Renaissance rhetoric became even more important, recapturing the high status it had enjoyed at the time of Cicero. Renaissance leaders revered Cicero as the ideal of the practicing rhetorician, the active agent in the service of the state and the people. Jean Dietz Moss noted "a widening wave of literacy extended beyond the church and the court to include as secular public, merchants, bankers, lawyers, artisans and others of the middle class."[5] In the fifteenth and sixteenth centuries, rhetoric dominated philosophy, literature, and politics. Early in the seventeenth century, the great Italian rhetorician Giambattista Vico took Descartes head on, writing that truth is discovered through the rhetorical process of Invention, and not through observation, as Descartes maintained.[6] Vico's work extended the intellectual scope of rhetoric to include the study of language and the evolution of society.

During the late eighteenth century there was a vast expansion of the middle class in Britain and North America. The tremendous growth of literacy was aligned with the growth of the press and the publishing industry. Like today's Internet, the printing press was a dynamo for the circulation and expansion of knowledge. As a result, rhetoric expanded beyond matters of political and legal conflict to areas of reading, criticism, and judgment. Vast fortunes were being made via the industrial revolution and upwardly mobile and newly rich individuals were eager to assimilate the speech, the ideas, and the manners of their higher status counterparts. The three greatest rhetorical theorists of the period were Hugh Blair, Richard Whately, and George Campbell. Each was a Christian minister, and each emphasized matters of ethics and of individual accountability in their rhetorical theory.

The nineteenth century was a time of huge industrial, political, and educational expansion in Europe and the United States. Parliamentary Democracy penetrated to many points of the globe. Nineteenth century practitioners of rhetoric cultivated the discipline as a form of individual intellectual training. They believed that knowledge of rhetoric would prepare any speaker or writer from age fifteen to age ninety to inform, persuade, or entertain any audience at any time on any occasion. The optimistic how-to-do-it rhetorical manuals of that day were an invitation to train in the privacy of one's own home for both self-improvement and social power. One example was the young Frederick Douglass studying his rhetoric book in secret in order to prepare for a career in public life that would lift him out of both slavery and poverty. Eloquence was seen as a means of gaining entry to the corridors of power. Books provided strategies for persuading others and provided models of great speeches for readers to imitate. A pantheon of great orators and their greatest speeches was established through books such as Chauncey A. Goodrich's *Select British Eloquence* in 1852. The book contained the speeches of the greatest British orators together with critical guides for study and tips on rhetorical emulation. Collections of great American orators soon followed and these became style models for the ambitious youth who saw the acquisition of rhetorical skill as a path to influence and wealth.

Although rhetorical treatises had been written since before Aristotle's day, academic departments did not come into being until the early twentieth century. There, scholars recovered the full range of the classical tradition and greatly expanded the study of rhetoric. Criticism became the major thrust of study, and theory was developed to explain the vast changes wrought by mass media, modern propaganda, and the immense social movements and revolutions of the first half of the century. In the latter half of the century and into the early twenty-first century, students of rhetoric moved far beyond the classical tradition. Traditionally scholars have focused on how exemplar speakers—gifted and influential individuals—used rhetorical arts to shape their world and affect social change. More recently scholars have inverted this relationship, and have begun to study the ways in which history and culture have shaped the practice of rhetoric itself. The very conditions in which rhetoric takes place are objects of study and they include who is allowed to speak in a public place, whose speech will be taken seriously, and the range of ideas that are considered debatable at any given time. Scholars have also emphasized the role of language or symbols in the process by which social influence occurs, and they have broken down the walls between visual, verbal, and acoustic messages. Rhetoric now includes far more than public speaking; focusing on understanding symbolic action, it embraces discourse in print, radio, television, and the Internet in many different forms and settings. Small wonder, rhetoric is now being studied across a whole spectrum of academic subjects and has become one of the central disciplines of our time.[7]

THE MEANINGS OF RHETORIC

Accordingly, at the start of the twenty-first century the study of rhetoric has expanded greatly, as have its definitions. We begin with a pragmatic introduction to some of those meanings.

Rhetoric has both an informative and persuasive element. For example, you might want to persuade someone to take a class with a certain professor; or, you might want to persuade your friends to vote for a particular candidate for public office. Both instances would use rhetoric. However, in order to effectively persuade, you must first provide information in the form of testimony, examples, stories, definitions, and the like. In short, you must use other than mere assertions as your arguments. In this sense, rhetoric involves the proper interpretation, construction, and use of supporting materials to back assertions and gain audience acceptance.

With this in mind, let us move to a working definition of rhetoric. When we use the term rhetoric in this chapter we mean: *The strategic use of communication, oral or written, to achieve specifiable goals.* There are two main ideas expressed by this definition. One involves the strategic, or intentional, nature of the language we use; the second involves knowing what goals we wish to reach through the language we use. This is an intentionally narrow definition of rhetoric, but we think using such is justified for now. After all, we need someplace to begin the inquiry, and it seems to us that a definition rooted in the most practical examples of intentional persuasion is a good place from which to launch our discussion.

The Strategic Nature of Rhetoric

We use symbols to communicate. These symbols essentially are something we use to represent something else. Words, spoken and written, are such symbols. Musical notes are such symbols as well. Certain gestures are symbolic representations of meaning, too. Of importance to us here is that words, spoken or written, are symbols whose meanings are more readily agreed upon than the meanings of other symbols used in communication. That is to say, a lion's share of those hearing or reading a particular word can come to some consensus concerning its meaning, whereas this does not hold true with other types of symbols. For example, the symbols used in art, architecture, dance, clothing, are all vague in their meanings; thus a communicator would have less control over their precise interpretation by a given audience. Unfortunately, the further we travel from the *intentions* of the communicator, the closer to the *inferences* of the audience we find ourselves. Since rhetoric works using symbols, the more variation in the symbolic meaning (the meaning of a *word* versus the architectural meaning of a doorway, for example) the less precision in the communication in general.

Nonetheless, rhetoric viewed from this broader aspect should be considered. For example, in the first edition of her book on rhetorical criticism, Sonja K. Foss wrote: "*rhetoric* means the use of symbols to influence thought and action. Rhetoric is communication; it is simply an old term for what is now called *communication*." In her second edition she refined that definition: "rhetoric means the action humans perform when they use symbols for the purpose of communicating with one another."[8] Rhetoric, for Foss, does involve action on the part of a communicator; it involves making conscious decisions about what to do. However, in part of her definition she stated: "Rhetoric is not limited to written or spoken discourse [any] message, regardless of the form it takes or the channel of communication it uses, is rhetoric." As such she wrote, "Speeches, essays, conversations, poetry, novels, stories, television programs, films, art, architecture, plays, music, dance, advertisements, furniture, public demonstrations, and dress are all forms of rhetoric."[9]

Foss presents a rather broad definition, one that clashes with a more pragmatic conception of rhetoric. As Marie Hochmuth Nichols wrote: "rhetoric is an act of adapting discourse to an end outside of itself. It serves many ends, from promoting decision to giving pleasure. It does not include ships, guns, an alluring sun, the dance, or the Cathedral of Chartres. It does not include rolling drums or the sound of marching feet; it does not include extralinguistic symbols of peace or the clenched fist of power. It does not deny that there are other symbolic forms for altering behavior, which often accompany or reinforce it."[10] Conceptions of rhetoric similar to that given by Foss minimize the point of view that as one moves further away from the use of symbols with generally agreed upon meanings (words) to the use of symbols with imprecise meanings (furniture, dance) one finds that the *intentions* of the rhetor play less a part in the rhetorical exchange and that the *impressions* of the receiver plays a greater role.[11] In this sense the meaning behind the rhetoric moves from the person crafting the message to the impressions of those receiving the message irrespective of the intentions of the original communicator.

This distinction was not lost on Hoyt Hopewell Hudson. In his landmark essay, "Rhetoric and Poetry," Hudson highlighted the differences between efforts aimed at rhetorical influence (rhetoric) and efforts aimed at symbolic expression (poetry). He began his comparison by citing numerous great poets in order to demonstrate the general focus of a poet: "The Poet . . . keeps his eye not on the audience or the occasion, but on his subject; his subject fills his mind and engrosses his imagination, so that he is compelled, by excess of admiration or other emotion, to tell of it; compelled, though no one hear or read his utterance."[12] In order to better discuss the differences, Hudson clearly marked where rhetoric begins and poetry ends: "For the moment, then, we shall say that poetry is for the sake of expression; the impression on others is incidental. Rhetoric is for the sake of impression; the expression is secondary—an indispensable means."[13]

This distinction is subject to exceptions, and here Hudson showed a graceful and discerning grasp of the differences between rhetoric and poetry, providing examples of how a poet might stray into the field of rhetoric. For example, a poet envisioning a speaker attempting to persuade listeners must use rhetoric—Mark Antony in Shakespeare's *Julius Caesar* and the speeches of the Fallen Angels in the first and second books of *Paradise Lost* are two such examples. He calls this imitative rhetoric, which may be studied for its own sake. A poet may at times consider the audience (a drama, for example), but there exist differences in the conception of the audience: "The poet thinks of a more general and more vaguely defined audience than the orator. The poet may even think of all mankind of the present and future as his audience."[14] Hudson even provided a loose scale to show the relationship between the most purely poetical—personal lyric and rhapsodic poem; then idyll, pastoral poetry; then narrative poetry, romance, the epic—to the more purely rhetorical—tragedy and comedy; finally didactic poetry, satire, odes, and epigrams. Hudson also demonstrated how an orator may cross over into the field of poetry: "Though the orator's end is persuasion, it is not hard to believe that there are moments in his discourse when this end is forgotten in his delight or wonder before some image which fills his inner eye. In such moments he has his eye on the subject, not the audience."[15]

The discussion above should point clearly to the differences between the more personally *expressive* use of ambiguous symbols—poetry, painting, dance, architecture—and the more publicly *impressive* use of symbols with generally agreed upon meanings—words spoken and written for the sake of persuasion. It is the latter that is the focus of this chapter and many of the chapters beyond. This is not to say that other forms of more ambiguous rhetoric cannot be studied, rather that we will take our first step on the firmer soil of rhetoric understood as strategic and intentional.

Rhetoric as Strategic, Goal-Oriented Communication

Coming back to the definition of rhetoric we gave above, we find that rhetoric is strategic because it is intentional. Communicators who wish to control the manner in which their messages are understood plan ahead. They think about what they are going to say and what impact their words are likely to have upon those listening to them. When they use rhetoric in this way they provide reasons for their listeners to agree with them. Just as importantly, rhetoric is intentional in the sense that it is employed only when words can make a difference. That is to say, rhetoric is *persuasive*. It seeks to influence our personal and collective behaviors through having us voluntarily agreeing with the speaker that a certain action or policy is better than another action or policy. Rhetors often think about their goals so that they are better able to plan what to say for a desired effect. Since there is no scientific certainty to human affairs, that is, we do not know for certain which policy will produce the absolute best results, rhetoric attempts to persuade listeners that one policy will *probably* be better than another. It is in this sense, then, that rhetoric is based upon probability—communicators try to convince us not that their proposed course of action is the only correct one, or that it will work with guaranteed certainty, but rather that it *probably* will reap greater success than competing solutions. The trick for the person trying to persuade is to make certain that the level of probability is high enough to convince the particular audience being addressed that a certain course of action will *probably* be better than another course of action.

Rhetoric works toward a goal. It may involve simply trying to have your audience believe a certain way, or it could work toward the enacting of one course of action or policy over another. In suggesting rhetoric is policy oriented we mean to say that it seeks to influence how those receiving the rhetoric act at either a personal or a public level. Policy at the personal level involves decisions about our beliefs or actions completely within our control: should I do this or do that? Beyond this, all of us also use rhetoric to influence those around us. For example, think of the last time you were together with a group of friends and you were trying to decide where to go for dinner. You most likely had several competing options and had to advance your good reasons for choosing one restaurant over another. The policy option resulting in action is simple: where to go eat? Your attempts at persuasion here involve more than just your actions, they involve deciding what to do for a group; the outcome is not solely under your control. At a more public level, consider the January 2008 words of Senator Barack Obama: "When I'm President, employers will be required to enroll every worker in a direct deposit retirement account that places a small percentage of each paycheck into savings."[16] The public policy here involves the mandatory contribution to a retirement account separate from Social Security tax contributions. Senator John M. McCain offered a competing policy option, one that would call "for workers to have the option of investing at least 20 percent of their Social Security payroll taxes in private accounts."[17] The public policy here involves allowing workers to shift a small portion of their social security taxes from Government controlled accounts to privately managed mutual funds. Which option one prefers depends on many factors, including the evidence each Senator presents to show how his plan would produce the best results for the greatest number of citizens, as well as the personal values of each citizen.

A more detailed yet common example of how rhetoric works shows that the good reasons rhetoric uses to persuade us very often incorporate the human qualities we use everyday when communicating with a goal in mind. Let us give you an example. A friend of ours was president of her neighborhood's homeowners association for several years. At one point during her tenure as president her neighborhood experienced a rash of mail thefts. The sheriff's department could do little; this was a rural setting, wooded, with little likelihood of catching whoever was stealing unless someone was willing to keep watch twenty-four hours a day. Our friend decided that the post office could be prevailed upon to install lock boxes in place of the old stand-alone type mailboxes. The post office agreed, but decided to place the new boxes in a wooded area alongside the road where there was no light during the evening hours. Our friend asked that they be placed in a more central, lighted area near the road; the postal worker said no. Not to be swayed, our friend began her use of rhetoric.

She used common examples in her efforts: Many of those who would be getting the mail would be women, driving alone or with their children. With daylight savings time soon to end they would be driving home at night after a day at work. Where the postal service wanted to place the mailboxes would necessitate the women getting out of their cars and walking away from them in order to get the mail. Our friend pointed out that all that it would take is one woman being attacked and then that particular postal worker would feel terrible. She also pointed out the very real possibility of the postal service being held responsible for any attacks that were facilitated by poorly placed boxes. The next day she had a phone conversation with the regional director of the postal service, and by the next week the new boxes were in, and in a new location so that no night driving mom would have to leave her car in order to collect the mail.

The persuasive effort used by our friend tells us a great deal about the nature of rhetoric. She used no extravagant arguments; rather she used everyday logic and reasoning (common sense), evoked a little emotion within her listeners, and ended up getting what was best for those in her neighborhood. It was not that her arguments had no weakness, or that they were scientifically reasoned out. Rather the arguments she used were constructed in order to convince the postal authorities that there was a high possibility that what she said would indeed happen. And that possibility was just high enough to persuade them to agree with her. So, this example shows how rhetoric is used everyday. Importantly, though, it also points out that rhetoric is concerned with contingent matters, too. Simply put, rhetoric addresses those problems that can be changed through the use of words. Put another way, the outcome of the situation is contingent upon what is said. So, for example, it was only because the possibility existed of having the location for mailboxes moved that rhetoric was able to effect a change.

As the above example shows, rhetoric is goal-directed. Our friend knew she wanted those mailboxes in a different location. She then thought of ways of constructing her arguments so that they would work with her particular audience; in this case, the postal workers who could change the location of the boxes. As you think about the goals communicators have in mind, it is important to remember another important aspect of rhetoric. When rhetoric is used, it is concerned with *informed opinion*. Most of us are not a mathematician trying to prove an equation; or a chemist following a formula. Instead we deal with human beings thinking on uncertain matters; we deal with their opinions. Humans act based upon what appears probable to them, and not always upon what they know for certain.

When we deal with questions of what we should do in a particular situation, there is no way to demonstrate using the scientific method that a certain course of action will be the best. Although *we* might know with certainty, those with whom we communicate may feel just as certain about a different course of action. What rhetors do, then, is try to persuade their listeners that their proposed course of action has the maximum probability of succeeding. Successful rhetors attempt to narrow the choices from which their audiences can choose. These audiences may have many choices for action; rhetoric helps them to decide which course is the best to take. Summing up such a position, Gerard Hauser wrote: "Rhetoric, as an area of study, is concerned with how humans use symbols, especially language, to reach agreement that permits coordinated effort of some sort. In its most basic form, rhetorical communication occurs whenever one person engages another in an exchange of symbols to accomplish some goal. It is not communication for communication's sake; rhetorical communication, at least implicitly and often explicitly, attempts to coordinate social action."[18] As Donald Cross Bryant so competently put it, rhetoric is not a body of knowledge, but a means of applying knowledge: "It does rather than is."[19]

The Moral Dimensions of Rhetoric

The foregoing example has illustrated the strategic and goal-oriented nature of rhetoric. Rhetoric always presupposes the existence of an audience. A rhetorician addresses a particular audience anchored in time, space, culture, and circumstance. Intellectuals who dismiss rhetoric and wish to present unvarnished truth are often people who do not understand the power of audiences. Like Plato, they believe that clear ideas, strong evidence, and a rational plan of reform are enough. They underestimate the influence of self-interest, fear of change, and the ways in which unequal power distorts communication.

The very practice of rhetoric has an impact upon the practitioners. But persuading others is always a matter of negotiating between the flux of local conditions and the enduring principles of political judgment. The mere exercise of deliberation helps nurture audiences by strengthening the norms of fairness. Communities do not exist prior to talk. They are built over time through communal understanding, argument, negotiation, and common action. Rhetorical practice is ethical in nature because it is advisory, and this advice has consequences for which the advice-giver is held accountable. It is not an ethically neutral act such as target shooting or throwing clay pots on a wheel. Participation in rhetorical discourse involves people in building citizenship and constructing community. And the decisions they make or the ideas they embrace can ruin or enrich their lives. Thus, rhetoric is an ethically significant practice that seeks to engage audiences in sound judgment; those judgments have consequences that we can judge to be good or bad.

Finally rhetoric sustains democratic culture. Rhetoric uses accepted beliefs to produce new beliefs and in so doing builds the stock of communal wisdom. It safeguards the stable beliefs that provide communal identity yet allows the community to manage change in ways that do not rend it apart and leave its people adrift.

A Larger Conception of Rhetoric

We mentioned earlier that the concept of rhetoric is expansive. In our discussion above we intentionally focus on a pragmatic conception of rhetoric. As will be reflected by some of the chapters in this book, rhetoric can be conceived in slightly larger ways. For instance, Charles Bazerman, wrote that rhetoric is the study

> of how people use language and other symbols to realize human goals and carry out human activities. Rhetoric is ultimately a practical study offering people greater control over their symbolic activity. Rhetoric has at times been associated with limited techniques appropriate to specific tasks of political and forensic persuasion. . . . Consequently, people concerned with other tasks have considered rhetoric to offer inappropriate analyses and techniques. These people have then tended to believe mistakenly that their rejection of political and forensic rhetoric has removed their own activity from the larger realm of situated, purposeful, strategic symbolic activity. I make no such narrowing and use rhetoric (for want of a more comprehensive term) to refer to the study of all areas of symbolic activity.[20]

"All areas of symbolic activity" certainly widens the scope of rhetoric's influence. Additionally, some have enlarged our understanding of rhetoric by making the argument that it does not have to be intentional for it to have a persuasive effect. As Kenneth Burke (1951) noted, rhetoric can work toward the promotion of " 'identification,' which can include a partially unconscious factor in appeal."[21] For example, a person might use symbols associated with wealth or class when writing news story. Upon exposure to these symbols, a reader might identify with the nuances of wealth or class without being fully aware of doing so.[22] Brooke Quigley explained that "the need to identify arises out of division; humans are born and exist as biologically separate beings and therefore seek to identify, through communication, in order to overcome separateness. We are aware of this biological separation, and we recognize additional types of separation based on social class or position. We experience the ambiguity of being separate yet being identified with others at the same time."[23] As Burke wrote, humans are "both joined and separate, at once a distinct substance and consubstantial with another."[24] Burke was interested in the "processes by which we build social cohesion through our use of language. His goal [was] that we learn to perceive at what points we are using and abusing language to cloud our vision, create confusion, or justify various and ever present inclinations toward conflict, war and destruction—or our equally-present inclinations toward cooperation, peace and survival."[25]

WHAT FUTURE FOR RHETORIC?

But despite our friend's success in the matter of the post boxes, is there still an important future for rhetoric? Some persons worry that the places for public deliberation are becoming smaller and fewer. They remind us that beyond the scope of the town meeting and neighborhood conclave, significant issues are selected and framed by the mass media, not local citizens. Experts debate these issues while the citizenry watches, sometimes enjoying the 'illusion' of participation but often feeling like powerless spectators. Such civic voyeurism, scholars such as Jurgen Habermas argue, could undermine the legitimacy of our institutions. After all, most Americans have never discussed public education, free enterprise, the income tax, or our immigration laws, yet they are imposed upon us by the dead hand of the past. These systems were largely developed before you were born, and are imposed upon you without your consent. Their direction is mostly in the hands of unaccountable public officials who enjoy lifetime tenure as unelected public servants. Policy details are complex, often known only to special interest groups.

Since many of our problems of race, ethnicity, poverty, and aging have been placed in the hands of government and state bureaucracy, they are effectively removed from the arena of public discussion. Further, the sheer number of issues and the volume of information concerning them are mind numbing and intimidating. Matters that were once seen to be province of ordinary citizens are now the property of specialized technical elites. We may fear that although these 'intellectuals' can organize data and design complex 'solutions,' they may understand very little about the fears, prejudices, and aspirations of ordinary people. Denied participation in civic debate, we become less skilled in managing discourse. Increasingly, we may view ourselves as mere masses manipulated by experts, not active citizens who are in charge of their own fate.

Finally, it can be argued that ever-increasing diversity and pluralism have destroyed the basic consensus that the practice of rhetoric requires. Rhetoric was born in the Greek polis, a small face to face homogenous community in which civic identity was girded by the premise that everyone shared a common destiny. Our society is becoming vast congeries of warring interest groups characterized by unbridgeable controversies and sedimented suspicion. Thus some critics argue that rhetoric is a method that only worked in the past and that it no longer has a place in twenty-first century life.

We argue that these criticisms predate the rise of a multicultural, technologically advanced, mega state; neither are these objections new. In one form or another they have been made for the past century. Despite numerous pronouncements about the death of rhetoric and civil culture, persuasive discourse persists. The practice of rhetoric is alive and well. Audiences and speakers are still engaged in building practical wisdom. Common dilemmas are still being attacked and resolved. Can Rhetoric still be powerful, useful, and moral? Roderick P. Hart and Courtney Dillard still think so:

> Is deliberation still possible? Some say no, others find the question fatuous. In defense of deliberation they point to democracies in which women were given the vote by men and in which blacks were enfranchised by whites. They find wars being stopped by college students, environmental laws being passed by the children of corporation executives, and Nelson Mandela's cause assisted by a distant band of college professors. They point to an American president being driven out of office by free press, a Russian president honored for dismantling a mighty Communist machine, and an Iraqi dictator stopped in his tracks.[26]

We simply cannot do without rhetoric. In fact, knowledge about the wise use of discourse has never been more necessary than it is today. Little wonder the study of rhetoric is enjoying a vast revival throughout our system of higher education. The chapters that follow will give you a sense of the variety and artistry of rhetorical discourse and of the cultural and historical faces that have shaped it. As you move through each chapter, you will find that the conception of rhetoric it advances modifies or moves beyond the working definition we provided above. This is as it should be. Take note of *how* the conception changes. Rhetoric is nuanced, and may be understood on many different levels. Each chapter that follows underscores this idea and will present a point of view that will add rich variety to the definition given above.

SUGGESTED READINGS

Bryant, Donald Cross. "Rhetoric: Its Function and its Scope." *Quarterly Journal of Speech* 39 (1953): 401-424.

Hauser, Gerard A. *Introduction to Rhetorical Theory* 2nd ed. (Prospect Heights, IL: Waveland Press, 2002).

Hudson, Hoyt Hopewell. "Rhetoric and Poetry." *Quarterly Journal of Speech Education* 10.2 (1924): 143-154.

[Nichols], Marie Hochmuth. "Rhetoric and the Humane Tradition" in *Rhetoric: A Tradition in Transition*, edited by Lloyd F. Bitzer and Edwin Black, 178-191. (Lansing, MI: Michigan State Univ. Press, 1974).

Smith, Craig R. *Rhetoric and Human Consciousness: A History* 2nd Ed. (Prospect Heights, IL: Waveland Press, 2003).

Wallace, Karl R. *History of Speech Education in America: Background Studies.* (New York City: Appleton Century-Crofts, 1954).

NOTES

1. Anthony, C.A. [pseud.], comment on "Obama, Clinton camps point to 'borrowed rhetoric,'" The CNN Ticker Political Blog, comment posted February 18, 2008, http://politicalticker.blogs.cnn.com/2008/02/18/obama-clinton-camps-point-to-borrowed-rhetoric/ [accessed February 19, 2008]. Emphasis in original.

2. Lee Ward, "Iran: Obama Rises Above Clinton's Rhetoric to Take Action," The Wiz Bang Blue Blog, entry posted on November 2, 2007, http://wizbangblue.com/2007/11/02/iran-obama-rises-above-clintons-rhetoric-to-take-action.php [accessed February 19, 2008]. Emphasis ours.

3. Speech contained in Ronald F. Reid, *American Rhetorical Discourse*, 2nd ed. (Prospect Heights, Illinois: Waveland Press, 1995), 657.

4. James L. Golden, Goodwin F. Berquist, and William E. Coleman, *The Rhetoric of Western Thought*, 4th Ed. (Dubuque, Iowa: Kendall/Hunt Publishing Company, 1989), 128–129.

5. Jean Dietz Moss, "Renaissance Rhetoric: An Overview," *Encyclopedia of Rhetoric* (Oxford U. Press, 2001), 681.

6. Giambattista Vico , *De Italorum Sapientia*, 1710.

7. For overviews of the development of rhetorical theory see the following: Hoyt Hopewell Hudson, "The Tradition of Our Subject," *Quarterly Journal of Speech* 17, no. 3 (1931): 320–329; Craig R. Smith, *Rhetoric and Human Consciousness: A History* 2nd Ed. (Prospect Heights, IL: Waveland Press, 2003).

8. Sonja K. Foss, "The Nature of Rhetorical Criticism," in *Rhetorical Criticism: Exploration and Practice* 2nd ed. (Prospect Heights, Illinois: Waveland Press, Inc., 1996), 4.

9. This and the immediately preceding quote, Foss, 6.

10. Marie Hochmuth Nichols, "Rhetoric and the Humane Tradition," in *Rhetoric: A Tradition in Transition*, ed. Walter R. Fisher (Michigan State University Press, 1974), 180.

11. As will be seen in the chapter on "Rhetorical Criticism as Art," one "receiver" of the rhetoric is the critic who examines the instance of rhetorical discourse. The further removed from agreed upon meaning the symbols under consideration are, the more power the critic has over deciding what they mean (over and above what the author of the rhetorical discourse intended them to mean). This can, and sometimes does, lead to abuses by the critic. For more on this see Jim A. Kuypers, "*Doxa* and a Critical Rhetoric: Accounting for the Rhetorical Agent through Prudence," *Communication Quarterly* 44, no.4 (1996): 452–462.

12. Hoyt Hopewell Hudson, "Rhetoric and Poetry," *Quarterly Journal of Speech Education* 10, no. 2 (1924): 145.

13. Ibid., 146.

14. Ibid., 148.

15. Ibid., 153.

16. Barack H. Obama, "Remarks of Senator Barack Obama: Reclaiming the American Dream, 29 January 2008," Obama '08 Website, http://www.barackobama.com/2008/01/29/remarks_of_senator_barack_obam_44.php [accessed February 20, 2008].

17. On the Issues, "John McCain on Social Security," On The Issues Website, http://www.ontheissues.org/2008/John_McCain_Social_Security.htm [accessed February 20, 2008].

18. Gerard A. Hauser, *Introduction to Rhetorical Theory,* 2nd ed. (Prospect Heights: Waveland Press, Inc., 2002), 2–3.

19. Donald C. Bryant, "Rhetoric: Its Function and its Scope," *Quarterly Journal of Speech* 39 (1953): 401–424.

20. Charles Bazerman, *Shaping Written Knowledge: The Genre and Activity of the Experimental Article in Science* (Madison: University of Wisconsin Press, 1988), 6.

21. Kenneth Burke, "Rhetoric—Old and New," *Journal of General Education* 5 (1951): 203.

22. Kenneth Burke, *A Rhetoric of Motives* (Berkeley: University of California Press, 1969).

23. Brooke L. Quigley, "'Identification' as a Key Term in Kenneth Burke's Rhetorical Theory," *The American Communication Journal,* 1, no. 3 (1998) http://acjournal.org/holdings/vol1/iss3/burke/quigley.html [Accessed February 21, 2008].

24. Burke, *Rhetoric of Motives*, 21.

25. Quigley.

26. Roderick P. Hart and Courtney L. Dillard, "Deliberative Genre," *Encyclopedia of Rhetoric* (Oxford: University of Oxford 2001), 213.

2

Rhetorical Criticism As Art

Jim A. Kuypers

The previous chapter provided a working definition of rhetoric. This chapter introduces you to another concept: the criticism of rhetoric. The purpose of this chapter is to show you how you can be a critic of rhetoric, how you can engage in the critical act.

When we critique instances of rhetoric, often called *rhetorical artifacts*, we are allowing ourselves to take a closer, critical, look at how rhetoric operates to persuade and influence us. Criticism has many broad applications, but in general it is a *humanizing* activity. That is to say, it explores and highlights qualities that make us human. As James Andrews et al. have written, criticism is "the systematic process of illuminating and evaluating products of human activity. [C]riticism presents and supports one possible interpretation and judgment. This interpretation, in turn, may become the basis for other interpretations and judgments."[1] For Donald Bryant, "common notions of criticism seem to involve or to imply some analytical examination of an artifact or artifacts, of some human transaction or transactions, toward the end of comprehension and realization of the potential of the object or event. Most notions of criticism extend also to appreciation and on to appraisal or judgment."[2] For our purposes, we are interested specifically in the analysis and evaluation of rhetorical acts. We are looking at how humans use rhetoric to bring about changes in the world around them.

T.S. Eliot is reputed to have said, "We do criticism to open the work to others." This is exactly what we are about when we perform rhetorical criticism. Rhetorical critics have varied reasons and purposes for producing criticism, but in general we engage in criticism for two broad reasons: *appreciation* and *understanding*. On this point Wayne Brockriede wrote, "By 'criticism' I mean the act of evaluating or analyzing experience. A person can function as critic either by passing judgment on the experience or by analyzing it for the sake of a better understanding of that experience or of some more general concept of theory about such experiences."[3] Simply put, we wish to enhance both our own and others' understanding of the rhetorical act; we wish to share our insights with others, and to enhance their appreciation of the rhetorical act. These are not hollow goals, but quality of life issues. By improving understanding and appreciation, the critic can offer new and potentially exciting ways for others to see the world. Through understanding we also produce knowledge about human communication; in theory this should help us to better govern our interactions with others.

Criticism as a Method

In its most basic form, a method is a particular manner or process for accomplishing a task. The researcher's task—humanist, social scientist, or scientist—is to generate knowledge. The method they use going about this task differs greatly, however. The use of rhetoric is an art, and as such it does not lend itself well to scientific methods of analysis. Criticism is an art as well, and as such is particularly well suited for examining rhetorical creations. Numerous critics have commented upon the Humanistic nature of the study of rhetoric. Marie Hochmuth Nichols, for instance, wrote that humane studies, of which the study of rhetoric fits prominently, are "concerned with the formation of judgment and choice." Such studies teach us that "technical efficiency is not enough, that somewhere beyond that lies an area in which answers are not formulary and methods not routine." Beyond "the area of the formula lies an area where understanding, imagination, knowledge of alternatives, and a sense of purpose operate."[4] That area is, of course, criticism.

The way the Sciences and the Humanities study the phenomena that surround us differ greatly in the amount of researcher personality allowed to influence the results of the study. For example, in the Sciences researchers purposefully adhere to a *strict* method (the scientific method). All scientific researchers are to use this same basic method, and successful experiments must be 100 percent replicable by others. Generally speaking, the researcher's personality, likes and dislikes, and religious and political preferences are supposed to be as far removed as possible from the actual study. Even the language scientists use to describe the results of their studies distances them from the results of those studies. For example, in scientific essays one normally finds a detached use of language, with researchers forcing themselves into the background by highlighting the working of the study itself: "This study found that. . . ."

In sharp contrast, criticism (one of many Humanistic methods of generating knowledge) actively involves the personality of the researcher. The very choices of what to study, and how and why to study a rhetorical artifact are heavily influenced by the personal qualities of the researcher. In the Sciences, the application of the scientific method may take numerous forms, but the overall method remains the same—and the personality of the researcher is excised from the study. In the Humanities, methods of research may also take many forms—criticism, ethnography, for example—but the personality of the researcher is an integral component of the study. Further personalizing criticism, we find that rhetorical critics use a variety of means when examining a particular rhetorical artifact, with some critics even developing their own unique perspective to better examine a rhetorical artifact.[5] Even the manner in which many critics express themselves in their writing brings the personal to the fore. Many write, "I found" instead of "This study found that . . ." This distinction was not lost on Edwin Black, who eloquently wrote:

> Methods, then, admit of varying degrees of personality. And criticism, on the whole, is near the indeterminate, contingent, personal end of the methodological scale. In consequence of this placement, it is neither possible nor desirable for criticism to be fixed into a system, for critical techniques to be objectified, for critics to be interchangeable for purposes of [scientific] replication, or for rhetorical criticism to serve as the handmaiden of quasi-scientific theory. [The] idea is that critical method is too personally expressive to be systematized.[6]

In short, criticism is an art, not a science. It is not a scientific method; it uses subjective methods of argument; it exists on its own, not in conjunction with other methods of generating knowledge (i.e., social scientific or scientific). As Marie Hochmuth Nichols articulated so well, "It is reason and judgment, not a [computer], that makes a man a critic."[7] Put another way, insight and imagination top statistical applications when studying rhetorical action.

THREE STAGES OF THE CRITICAL ACT

Superior criticism is not performed mechanically; there are, however, certain norms that critics follow when producing criticism. After all, good critics are trying to generate understanding and insight; they are not simply flashing their opinions about. In general, there are three stages involved in producing criticism: conceptual, communication, and counter-communication.

The Conceptual Stage

The conceptual stage takes place in the mind of the critic; it is an act of cerebration. It is a private act, and its purpose is to generate some type of insight concerning the rhetorical artifact. Since this is a very personal act—that is, not mechanistic—there is no standardized way critics go about flexing their cerebral muscles. What works for one critic might not work for another. Often, though, insight is generated in one of two very broad ways. The first is a type of spontaneous inception. Think of the *Eureka!* of Archimedes, or of the proverbial light bulb popping on inside your head. Critics often generate involuntary, almost instinctive reactions to rhetorical artifacts. This involves more than a simple reaction to the artifact, however, because critics are trained to observe, and their training has a bearing upon what they see in an artifact. In a sense, the experienced critic has assimilated particular ways of viewing rhetoric; these modes of seeing are part and parcel of the critic's personality. Some critic's may even come to see rhetorical artifacts in such a way that others recognize it as characteristic of that particular critic.

The other broad way a critic might generate insight is through a somewhat systematic examination of the rhetorical artifact. With this approach the critic uses some type of guide, formal or informal, that allows for an orderly progression through the rhetorical artifact. A more formal guide might take the form of *perspectives* on rhetoric, which we will discuss below. A more personal and informal guide could be a question the critic has about the workings of the world (often called a research question). Simply put, the critic starts with a question or two in mind, and then examines various rhetorical artifacts looking for answers to that question. For example, the authors of the chapter on Fantasy Theme Analysis state in their critical essay that they were guided by questions such as, "What do we expect from our Universities?" and "Why do we go to College?" With those questions in mind, they decided that using a type of criticism called Fantasy Theme Analysis would be a fruitful perspective to use when looking at different rhetorical artifacts. In this way the authors were guided by their initial research questions in both the decision about what approach to use and also in what to look for in the rhetorical artifacts they examined.

Whether a critic spontaneously generates an insight or searches a rhetorical artifact for information, it should be the critic, not the method or perspective, that is in control of the insights and knowledge generated. As Black wrote, "The critic's procedures are, when at their best, original; they grow ad hoc from the critic's engagement with the [rhetorical] artifact."[8] Of course, not all insights generated prove sound; some ideas are never meant to move beyond mere personal musing. In my experience, it is only a small minority of ideas that are birthed alive and well, waiting to grow. These ideas move to the next stage of the critical act: communication.

The Communication Stage

The second stage of the critical act is a quasi-public act of writing out the criticism in preparation for sharing it with others.[9] This stage of the critical act encompasses the private act of writing, sharing initial ideas with trusted friends and colleagues, and ultimately sharing with a wider audience. Your reasons for writing criticism will help to determine the particular audience for whom you write. For example, you could be writing a letter to the editor of your local paper concerning the rhetorical efforts of a politician running for office; you could be writing a term paper for your professor; or you could be writing with a specific scholarly journal in mind.

When sharing your criticism with others, it is not simply a matter of providing a detailed picture of your opinions. You are instead sharing *propositions* with those who will be reading your work. Propositions are only naked assertions, however, until you provide a very basic step: giving supporting evidence with which to back up those assertions. Craig R. Smith wrote that critics must hold themselves to high "standards of argumentation" when writing criticism. Specifically, he suggested that, "when we write criticism . . . we ought to confine ourselves to solid argumentation inclusive of valid arguments built on sufficient and high quality evidence produced from close textual readings and masterings of context."[10] In short, critics must *invite* their audiences to agree with them. This is accomplished through stating their case and then providing evidence for their audience to accept or reject.

When writing you must always keep in mind the audience with whom you will share your criticism. Recall that part of the purpose of criticism is to enhance the understanding and appreciation of others concerning the rhetorical artifact. On this point Black wrote: "The critic proceeds in part by translating the object of his criticism into the terms of his audience and in part by educating his audience to the terms of the object. This dual task is not an ancillary function of criticism; it is an essential part of criticism."[11] For example, consider the speeches given by presidential candidates George Bush and Al Gore on December 13, 2000. After an incredibly tight general election, the election of the next president settled down to a series of contested recounts in Florida. Fewer than 1000 votes separated the candidates, and after approximately one month of tense political and legal conflict, the United States Supreme Court put an end to what had become a series of seemingly endless recounts. By the slimmest of margins, Bush took Florida and won the 2000 presidential election.

Both George Bush and Al Gore were expected to speak after this historical decision, and they did. I can honestly say of both of these speeches that they were rhetorical home runs and that I liked them. Fair enough, but so far we have only my opinions. I might go one step further, however, and make specific assertions concerning the speeches. I could say that Al Gore's speech worked well because it attempted to achieve several objectives: heal wounds, keep the door open for a presidential run in 2004, and remove a possible sore loser stigma. I could then say that George Bush's speech worked well since it, too, attempted to achieve several objectives: reach out to Democrats, having Bush perceived as a gracious, not arrogant, winner, and to assure the nation of the proper transfer of political power.

At this point you would find yourself with additional information, but still I have only provided you with *unsupported assertions*. I have merely given you my opinions about the speeches. I move into the realm of criticism when I provide the support for these assertions of mine; when I provide you with evidence that asks you to agree with me, or that makes you aware of some aspect of the speeches that you had previously overlooked (the sharing of insights). For example, I could provide specific sentences from both speeches that I feel support my assertions. In terms of Vice President Gore's attempt to keep the door open for a 2004 presidential race I could highlight this statement: "I do have one regret: that I didn't get the chance to stay and fight for the American people over the next four years, especially those who need burdens lifted and barriers removed, especially for those who feel their voices have not been heard. I heard you and I will not forget."[12] In terms of then-Governor Bush's attempt to reach out to partisan Democrats I could highlight this statement: "Our nation must rise above a house divided. Americans share hopes and goals and values far more important than any political disagreements. Republicans want the best for our nation, and so do Democrats. Our votes may differ, but not our hopes."[13] From these examples I would then share my reasoning about the connection I see between the examples and my assertions.

The main point to be remembered from this is that critics are trying to argue for a certain understanding of the rhetorical artifact. In this sense they are actually using rhetoric to try to gain acceptance of their ideas. The best critics simply do not make a judgment without supplying good reasons for others to agree with them. On this point Bernard L. Brock, et al., wrote, "[S]tatements of tastes and preference do not qualify as criticism. [Criticism is] an art of evaluating with knowledge and propriety. Criticism is a reason-giving activity; it not only posits a judgment, the judgment is explained, reasons are given for the judgment, and known information is marshaled to support the reasons for the judgment."[14]

The idea of rhetorical criticism being a form of argument is not new. Wayne Brockriede wrote in 1974 that useful rhetorical criticism must function as an argument to be effective criticism.[15] In his landmark essay, Brockreide advanced five interanimated characteristics of an argument:

(1) an inferential leap from existing beliefs to the adoption of a new belief or the reinforcement of an old one; (2) a perceived rationale to justify that leap; (3) a choice among two or more competing claims; (4) a regulation of uncertainty in relation to the selected claim—since someone has made an inferential leap, certainty can be neither zero nor total; and (5) a willingness to risk a confrontation of that claim with one's peers.[16]

More significant arguments will have a greater number and strength of the five above characteristics than less significant arguments. This is to say, the five qualities of arguments given above are on a sliding scale of sorts. The fewer of the five, or in weaker form, the less the criticism is effective argument. The greater the number of the five, or in stronger form, the more likelihood the criticism is effective argument. As Brockriede wrote, "When a critic only appreciates the rhetoric or objects to it, without reporting any reason for his like or dislike, he puts his criticism near the nonargument end of the continuum. On the other hand, when an evaluating critic states clearly the criteria he has used in arriving at his judgment, together with the philosophic or theoretic foundations on which they rest, and when he has offered some data to show that the rhetorical experience meets or fails to meet those criteria, then he has argued."[17]

The propositions and claims used by a critic are generally advanced through the use of different *perspectives* on criticism. Because a rhetorical artifact is a multi-dimensional, complex, and nuanced event, there exists no one best way of viewing it (although some ways can be better for certain artifacts than others). Moreover, no one effort to describe or evaluate the artifact will yield all the knowledge that there is to know about that artifact. Although slowly changing, the lion's share of academic criticism today takes its structure from a particular perspective. Perspectives allow critics to view the rhetorical artifact from different angles. Since the 1960s there has been an incredible expansion of perspectives critics have used to better understand the rhetoric that surrounds us. By one count, over 60 formally recognized perspectives have been catalogued,[18] with many more being used and with some critics even blending perspectives. Later in this book you will be exposed to many popular perspectives designed for generating insight and understanding about a rhetorical artifacts.

Using an established perspective to produce criticism has both strengths and weaknesses. One particular strength is that adopting a perspective allows you to see an artifact differently than if no perspective had been adopted. In a sense, using a perspective allows you to see the world in a particular way. A perspective will highlight certain features of a rhetorical artifact not featured by another perspective. Adopting a particular perspective also allows you to stay focused because, when properly used, the perspective *guides* rather than dictates your analysis. This can be particularly useful for novice critics who often are at odds with the enormous range of options any one rhetorical artifact offers for analysis.

On the flip side of the coin, adopting a particular perspective will introduce certain biases into the criticism. A perspective is partial, and encourages you to view the world in a certain manner. So while some aspects of a rhetorical artifact are highlighted, others are screened out. The potential problem with this, as Lawrence Rosenfield wrote, is that a "critic who comes upon a critical object in a state of mind such that he has a 'set of values' handy (or, indeed, any other system of categories) does not engage in a critical encounter so much as he processes perceptual data."[19] Thus a critic who follows too closely the dictates of a particular perspective runs the risk of producing stale and lifeless criticism. That critic is simply looking for what the perspective suggests should be looked for. In short, improperly used, a perspective would be allowed to *dictate* rather than guide what a critic does in the analysis.

The perspectives presented in this book represent a wide array of critical possibilities. Some are well know and practiced; others are less known but extremely potent in their potential. As you become familiar with these perspectives, you will see how they differ in the type of material they allow a critic to focus on, as well as the type of material they exclude. A central question remains, however: *How does a critic choose which perspective to use?* The choice will be guided by several factors. First, the critic's personal interest will play a crucial role in determining which perspective to adopt. As you study the perspectives detailed in this book, you will find that some appeal to you while others do not. This attraction or repulsion is natural, so your first clue to which perspective to use should be your personal interest in that perspective. Second, and just as important, a critic must consider the unique characteristics of the rhetorical artifact being examined. As already mentioned, perspectives focus a critic's attention upon certain aspects of a rhetorical artifact. A critic should take this into consideration when choosing a particular perspective to use since any given perspective will not fit every rhetorical artifact. Some, even when there is a sound fit, might need modification. More experienced critics may choose to combine perspectives, modify perspectives, or develop a completely novel perspective, and this is something we will look at in the chapter on Eclectic Criticism—the choice is the critic's to make. Of course, the greater your understanding of the nuances of different perspectives, the greater your ability to discern the intricacies of individual rhetorical texts; thus, the greater the likelihood of producing productive criticism.

Advancing your propositions through different perspectives also makes an important contribution to the development of a critical vocabulary for both you and other critics to use. You will be contributing to both the understanding of human communication and the development of rhetorical theory. In one sense, you will be accumulating knowledge for others to draw upon. Ultimately, though, I agree with Stephen E. Lucas who wrote, "In the last analysis, our scholarship will be judged, not by the perspectives from which it proceeds, but by the quality of the insight it produces."[20]

The Counter-Communication Stage

Once the criticism is actually performed the final stage of the critical act, counter-communication, is entered. This is a public act, and at this stage the critic shares openly with others. For instance, your criticism could take the form of a letter to the editor of the local paper. If published, it will allow others the opportunity to share your thoughts and possibly to respond. In more academic settings, students will submit their essays and receive feedback from their professors and possibly their classmates; professors and some students will have written their essays for a conference presentation or for submission to a scholarly journal. The idea is to share your criticism with some segment of the public with the hope that it will provoke some type of feedback; the best criticism attempts just this.

Feedback can take many forms, as can the public exchanges about the critic's ideas. Students will receive comments from their professor, and professors receive comments from their reviewers. If published, an essay then receives wider responses. The point is, once released to this public realm, a critic's work takes on a life of its own. Feedback, positive or negative, should be viewed as what it is: evidence of the critic entering into a larger conversation. A problem critics often encounter, though, is a reply of *de gustibus non est disputandum*, there is no disputing taste. In other words, you might hear from others that your point of view is simply subjective, and that their point of view is equally valid. However, if you paid attention to providing the good reasons mentioned above, then the exchange does not necessarily boil down to "I'm right, you're wrong," but arguing who can see the fullness of the rhetorical artifact better. As Brockriede wrote, "Critics who argue are more *useful* than critics who do not."[21] Along these same lines Black wrote: "the critic can only induce us, and therefore it is we, the readers of criticism, who demand the critic's compliance with certain of our expectations. We expect the critic to see things for us that we are unlikely to see for ourselves until the critic has called them to our attention."[22]

What we are about during this stage of the critical act is none other than entering into dialogue about matters of importance. The exchange and discussion of ideas is crucial to criticism; only the best criticism provokes this. Actually, the cry of many critics might well be, "Love me, hate me, but don't ignore me." Remember that good criticism *is* an act of rhetoric.

Key Issues in Criticism

When you begin to write your criticism, it will be helpful to know about five key issues with which all critics must wrestle at some time or another. These issues are longstanding and have various resolutions, with different critics taking different approaches to the same issue. For now it is enough to know the important questions these issues invite you to ask, not that you have the answers. By conscientiously thinking about these issues, you will be in a better position to produce deliberate and well-informed criticism.

One important issue involves the most basic element in criticism: *what to include in your writing*. Generally speaking your essay should contain three components: a description, an analysis, and an evaluation. Every critical essay should have these components, but each essay will present them in a slightly different manner (as will be seen in critical essays contained in the chapters that follow).

Description refers to both a description of the rhetorical artifact and, in more academic settings, a description of the theoretical background used in the essay. A description of the artifact is crucial if your readers are to be able to follow you. The way you describe the artifact may well be the only exposure they have to it, so you must take care in presenting as accurate a picture as possible. In more formal instances of criticism—term papers, conference presentations—a discussion of the theory being used to perform the criticism is also expected. On this point, William L. Nosthstine, et al., wrote, "'Theory' has become virtually the singular objective of criticism . . . contributing to theory *is* regarded as the fundamental goal of [rhetorical] criticism."[23] James Jasinski noted that the "two most common patterns in the [communication] literature are (a) theory provides a [perspective] that is utilized in critical practice (theory serves criticism) or (b) criticism contributes to theorization through its heuristic capacity, through illustration and hypotheses testing, and through the reflexive implementation of theoretically-derived [perspectives] (criticism serves theory)."[24] Most academic readers want to know in which rhetorical theories your perspective is grounded, exactly how you are using the theory to guide your analysis, and how your analysis has added to the pool of theoretical knowledge. This allows them to learn from your examples and also adds to the theoretical body of knowledge, an ever-growing element of academic criticism. This drive toward generation of theory is so strong for some critics that the very quality of criticism is judged by the contributions to the growing mass of rhetorical theory. For others, theory is a means to an end: the generation of insights into a rhetorical artifact with the ultimate goals of producing understanding and appreciation. Thus for now, particularly among scholarly journals, the fascination with theory rules the day; there are signs of changes, however, and these will be highlighted in the chapters on Eclectic Criticism and Conceptual Criticism.

When you describe the artifact and the perspective used to examine it you will also want to relay the importance of the artifact, the study, or both. In short, at some point you will want to justify what you are doing. Given the countless appeals for our attention each day, readers may well ask, "Why is this important for me to know?" Although *you* might think what you are doing is important, not everyone else will think the same way. It is up to you to share with others the reasons why they should invest their time and energy to read what you have written.

After you share with your readers what you will be examining (the rhetorical artifact), how you will be going about that examination (rhetorical theory), and the importance of what you are doing, you move on to the actual analysis of the rhetorical artifact. This section of your essay will generally consume the most space. When I write analysis I mean both analysis *and* interpretation. They are not the same, but neither are they completely separate. In one sense, analysis is discovering *what is in* a rhetorical artifact and interpretation is determining *what it means*. Analysis asks us to explain how the rhetorical artifact works; it provides a sketch of sorts, showing how the artifact is put together: what are its parts, how do they go together, and what the whole looks like. The type of analysis depends upon the temperament of the critic, but also upon the perspective guiding the criticism.

Interpretation is a contested term in criticism. Some critics hold that rhetorical criticism should involve a minimum of interpretation. For example, Barnett Baskerville wrote that the central concern of critics (at that time primarily speeches), are fairly straightforward in their meaning. They are "seldom abstruse or esoteric . . . A speech, by its nature, is or should be immediately comprehensible, hence the interpretive function of the critic is seldom paramount."[25] Not all critics agreed with Baskerville on the nature of interpretation. Thomas R. Nilsen, for example, wrote that "if within the meaning of the speech are included the many attendant responses, the more subtle understanding and conceptions evoked by the speech and their possible consequences, then interpretation is a much needed function of the critic."[26] Critic Michael Leff pointed out that it is with "the act of interpretation by which the critic attempts to account for and assign meaning to the rhetorical dimensions of a given phenomenon."[27] Such interpretations can focus on the external or internal dynamics of a rhetorical artifact. External interpretations focus on how the rhetorical artifact interacts with the situation that surrounds it, and internal interpretations focus on how different parts of the rhetorical artifact act together in forming a whole.

A recent speech by Senator Barack Obama during the 2008 Democratic primary season demonstrates the dual functions of analysis and interpretation. Increasingly in early 2008, Senator Obama was enduring criticism about his association with Reverend Jeremiah Wright, the leader of Trinity Unity Church of Christ. In response, Senator Obama delivered a speech, "A More Perfect Union," in which he responded to Wright's ardent anti-Americanism, including statements indicating America deserved 9/11.[28] An analysis could discover many things about this speech, including Senator Obama's use of analogy. Take, for example, this passage:

> I can no more disown [Reverend Wright] than I can my white grandmother—a woman who helped raise me, a woman who sacrificed again and again for me, a woman who loves me as much as she loves anything in this world, but a woman who once confessed her fear of black men who passed by her on the street, and who on more than one occasion has uttered racial or ethnic stereotypes that made me cringe. These people are a part of me. And they are a part of America, this country that I love.[29]

Analysis allows us to see this passage as analogy; beyond this, analysis ends and interpretation begins. Just what does this analogy mean? One interpretation of the meaning of this passage could be that Senator Obama was trying to show that racial tensions exist and are active in America; that whites and blacks have suspicions, anger, and even hatred inside. Along these lines, consider this statement made in response to the speech:

> [He] challenged Americans to learn something about their country, to seek to understand those whose emotions seem threatening, wrong-headed, even un-American. He asked whites to understand that the anger behind Rev. Wright's comments, while paralyzing, was also valid, the result of decades and centuries of real discrimination and oppression suffered by African Americans. And he asked blacks to understand that whites who resent affirmative action and whose fears of crime lead them to stereotype blacks should not be dismissed as racists, because their concerns and fears are real and valid, too.[30]

Of course, analogies are a form of argument, thus can invite alternate interpretations. Take, for instance, another interpretation of the Senator Obama's speech, one that asserted that one plank in Senator Obama's defense was the idea of moral equivalence:

> Sure, says Obama, there's Wright, but at the other "end of the spectrum" there's Geraldine Ferraro, opponents of affirmative action and his own white grandmother, "who once confessed her fear of black men who passed by her on the street, and who on more than one occasion has uttered racial or ethnic stereotypes that made me cringe." But did she shout them in a crowded theater to incite, enrage and poison others?
>
> "I can no more disown (Wright) than I can my white grandmother." What exactly was grandma's offense? Jesse Jackson himself once admitted to the fear he feels from the footsteps of black men on the street. And Harry Truman was known to use epithets for blacks and Jews in private, yet is revered for desegregating the armed forces and recognizing the first Jewish state since Jesus' time. He never spread racial hatred. Nor did grandma.
>
> Yet Obama compares her to Wright. Does he not see the moral difference between the occasional private expression of the prejudices of one's time and the use of a public stage to spread racial lies and race hatred?[31]

In the end, these examples might make it seem as if analysis and interpretation are two separate steps. That is not the case at all. The very first step a critic takes, deciding what the rhetorical artifact actually is, is itself an interpretive act. For instance, is Senator Obama's speech an apology, an attack, or a statement of policy? We separate out these steps for the sake of discussion. As you write criticism, become aware of how analysis and interpretation interanimate each other. On this point Michael Leff wrote:

> The act of interpretation mediates between the experiences of the critic and the forms of experience expressed in the [rhetorical artifact]. To perform this act successfully, critics must vibrate what they see in the [rhetorical artifact] against their own expectations and predilections. What critics are trained to look for and what they see interact in creative tension; the two elements blend and separate, progressively changing as altered conceptions of the one reshape the configuration of the other.[32]

Through the analysis and interpretation section of your essay, you share your insight and understanding of the artifact, and you actively make a case for your conclusions, which leads to the final component of a criticism essay: evaluation.

Evaluation of the rhetorical artifact boils down to the judgments you make about it. However, judgment is more than the expression of like or dislike. It necessitates first that you know the thing that you are studying; it also necessitates that your judgments are shared with the goal of enriching both understanding and appreciation. Judgments may certainly be made, and appreciation or disdain expressed, but they must be made after two conditions are met: one, the fair-minded description of the inner workings of the rhetorical artifact have been presented for the world to see; and two, the standards of judgments you use are provided for all to see. In short, the expression of judgment is conjoined with the reasons you think the way you do. The standards of judgments made will differ depending upon the type of perspective used and also upon your personality. As you acquire information on each perspective, notice what type of information the perspective allows you to gather about the rhetorical transactions. This is a clue about the types of value judgments that particular perspective allows. Usually these will revolve around differing combinations of ethics, effects, truth, or aesthetics involved with the rhetorical transaction.[33] The standards of judgment you use will flow from the perspective you use to examine the rhetorical artifact; thus, how the terms above will be understood is directly related to the perspective you will use.

Another important issue facing critics is the seemingly easy decision concerning *which perspective to use in their critical endeavor.* Simply put, how will a critic go about producing criticism? As you read additional chapters in this book, you may well find that a certain perspective appeals to you. You may not be certain why it does, but you seem to gravitate toward it. The perspective seems natural for you to use. As you use it, you become increasingly familiar with its nuances and potentials. Some critics are well known for producing insightful and nuanced work using a particular perspective. For example, Andrew King is well known for using Burkean theory in his work; Marilyn Young's work using the situational theory is another such example; mythic criticism and the names Rushing and Frentz are no strangers.

Perspectives are not to be used as formulas, however. Although they do suggest a particular way of viewing the world, as the critic you must direct the criticism. When critics first begin to use a perspective, they often apply it *rigidly* to the rhetorical artifact. As critics become more knowledgeable about the perspective they use they often become more *flexible* in its application, allowing for personal insight and interests to guide the criticism. The personality of the critic begins to blend with the perspective used. The best criticism involves this. As Michael Leff has written, "Interpretation is not a scientific endeavor. Systematic principles are useful in attempting to validate interpretations, but the actual process of interpretation depends on conjectures and insights particular to the object [rhetorical artifact] at hand."[34]

Regardless of the perspective chosen, a critic must be cautious in its application. Perspectives are to help a critic, not direct the criticism; a successful critic's ideas blend in with those of the perspective. Perspectives are not molds to be forced upon a rhetorical artifact—mechanistic and rigid criticism. Black puts this idea, and the consequences, in proper perspective:

Because only the critic is the instrument of criticism, the critic's relationship to other instruments will profoundly affect the value of critical inquiry. And in criticism, every instrument has to be assimilated to the critic, to have become an integral part of the critic's mode of perception. A critic who is influenced by, for example, [Burkean Dramatism] and who, in consequence of that influence, comes to see some things in a characteristically dramatistic way—that critic is still able to function in his own person as the critical instrument, and so the possibility of significant disclosure remains open to him. But the would-be critic who has not internalized the pentad, who undertakes to "use" it as a mathematician would use a formula—such a critic is certain (yes, *certain!*) to produce work that is sterile. An act of criticism conducted on mechanistic assumptions will, not surprisingly, yield mechanistic criticism.[35]

Some critics, myself included, take the process of assimilation one step further by blending and developing their own framework from which to proceed with criticism. This type of criticism is often called *eclectic* criticism. This type of criticism will be discussed in chapter 19; it involves "the selection of the best standards and principles from various systems of ideas."[36]

Yet another issue involves *how one should approach a rhetorical artifact* (what Ed Black calls rhetorical transactions). This is to say, should one begin with a theoretical orientation or should one begin with the artifact itself?[37] Black described this distinction as *etic* and *emic* orientations. One using an etic orientation "approaches a rhetorical transaction from outside of that transaction and interprets the transaction in terms of pre-existing theory." In contrast, one using an emic orientation "approaches a rhetorical transaction in what is hoped to be its own terms, without conscious expectations drawn from any sources other than the rhetorical transaction itself."[38] A pure etic or emic orientation is, of course, impossible. One should think of them being on a sliding scale of more or less. The more one adopts an etic orientation, the less of an emic orientation is used, and the opposite holds true as well.

Both orientations have strengths and weaknesses. An etic orientation allows for a fuller development of rhetorical theory. The major end of criticism would be to develop and advance rhetorical theory, thus adding to our overall knowledge concerning human communication. An emic orientation would allow for a more nuanced description of the rhetorical artifact, and also provides more room for the critic's personality and intuition to play a part in the criticism. A weakness with the etic orientation is that critics may very well find exactly what they expect to find, even if its not really there in the rhetorical artifact; in short, the rhetorical artifact is forced into a mold. A weakness with the emic orientation can arise because critics may "aspire to so sympathetic an account [during the descriptive and interpretive phases of criticism] that the critic's audience will understand that object as, in some sense, *inevitable*."[39] On this point Leff wrote, "the critic at some point . . . in the interpretive process comes to form a conception of the object as a whole, a conception so strong as to appear inevitable. This conception . . . is something other than the actual expression in the text; otherwise, there would be no interpretation. Consequently, while still engaged in the interpretive act, the critic constructs a meaning for the object, an hypothesis or model that explains what it is."[40] The difficulty in this process lies with the "good faith" of the critic. After so sympathetic account of the rhetorical artifact, the critic will be hard pressed to return to a more objective role during the evaluative phase of criticism.[41]

Yet another concern involves *the notion of criticism as an objective or a subjective endeavor*. It is clear that criticism is not a scientific act; the very best criticism involves the personality, insights, and imagination of a critic. Yet for all that, there are critics—I among them—who maintain that a certain degree of objectivity is necessary for honest, productive criticism. When I use the term "objective," I do not mean that critics ought to possess or are capable of possessing a scientific detachment from the object of criticism. This would surely produce a sterile criticism devoid of its lifeblood: the critic's intermingled intuition, insight, and personality. What I am suggesting is that the critic approach the artifact under consideration with a fair and open mind, with a *detached curiosity*. In this sense the critic sets aside personal politics or ideological "truths" and approaches the artifact with a sense of curiosity. The artifact under consideration ought not to be altered to fit the prejudgments of the critic, but be allowed to voice its inner workings to the world. The work of the critic is to make certain that this voice is intelligible to and approachable by the public.

This does not detract from the critic bringing to bear an individual stamp upon the criticism produced; nor is it the antiseptic application of theory upon an unsuspecting rhetorical artifact. It suggests instead that the critic must learn how to appreciate the inner workings of a text, even if personally the critic finds that text to be repugnant, or wishes it to be other than it is. In this sense, the critic is being "objective," or disinterested, when approaching and describing a text.[42] My notion of objectivity is somewhat similar to the notion of "appreciation" put forth by Lawrence W. Rosenfield. I position "objective" criticism between a politically partisan criticism and detached scientific objectivity; Rosenfield positions "appreciation" between ideologically driven criticism and scientific objectivity. For Rosenfield, appreciation is "founded on an inherent love of the world, while [scientific] objectivity, the effort to establish distance on the world (for whatever laudable ends) sometimes betrays an essential distrust of the world, a fear that one will be contaminated in some manner if one is open to its unconcealment."[43]

Although I agree heartily with Rosenfield that, "Partisan involvement may be a civic virtue, but insight derived therefrom must be continually suspect,"[44] other critics disagree with me, as you will find while reading some of the chapters that follow. For these critics, the act of criticism involves a more active attempt at persuasion in all three phases of criticism—description, analysis/interpretation, and evaluation. Very often the direction of this persuasion takes its cue from the political ideology of the critic. For example, Robert Ivie defined productive criticism as "a detailed and partisan critique."[45] According to Ivie, a critic "intentionally produces a strategic interpretation, or structure of meaning, that privileges selective interests . . . in specific circumstances."[46] The purpose of criticism is made clear: those who engage in rhetorical criticism are, or should be, advocates: "criticism, as a specific performance of general rhetorical knowledge, yields a form of scholarship that obtains social relevance by strategically reconstructing the interpretive design of civic discourse in order to diminish, bolster, or redirect its significance. [Criticism] is a form of advocacy grounded in the language of a particular rhetorical situation."[47]

Often some attempt at political fairness is made, although the result is still the politicization of the critical act. For example, Michael McGee wrote: "When interpellating 'the critic' and 'criticism,' the first thing a rhetorician should do is to identify her political orientation. Her syllabus should contain a paragraph describing the trajectory of her course. Her book should have a Chapter that aligns her politics with that politics practiced in the workaday world by political parties competing for control of the State. She must be fair, describing the politics of those who disagree with her in a light that leans more toward portraiture than caricature"[48] However, regardless of the attempt, I am inclined to agree with Rosenfield when he asserts that a difficulty with ideological criticism is that the "very notion of commitment to an ideology, no matter what its value system, implies a kind of immunity to those experiences of the world which in any way contradict the ideology."[49] Further clarifying this politicization of criticism, McGee stated, "That which [ideologically driven] critics do today is proactive, openly political in its acknowledgment of its bias and its agenda to produce practical theories of culture and of social relations (including political relations)," and thus appears to embrace the very action Rosenfield described above.[50]

Although summarizing a much larger conversation on this topic, the positions advanced are clear. On the one hand we have critics striving to keep personal politics from the initial stages of the criticism—most notably, during the description and analysis phases of the critical act. This position presupposes that part of the purpose of criticism is to produce knowledge that disputants can draw upon when making decisions about how to live—academic critics should not be partisan agents of social change. On the other hand we have academic critics allowing their personal politics to guide them during all three stages of criticism. This position presupposes that critics begin by seeing the world differently than the public they seek to persuade, and that the job of the critic is to produce partisan social change in the direction of that critic's choosing.[51] A good example of this contrast is found when looking at the chapters on traditional criticism and feminist criticism.

The chapters that follow will give you a sense of the variety and artistry of rhetorical criticism. As you move through each chapter, you will find that the way the author(s) practice criticism both modifies and moves beyond the definition I share with you in this chapter. This is as it should be. Take note of *how* the nature and scope of criticism changes in each chapter. Criticism is not a sterile endeavor, and you will find that some of the chapters resonate more strongly with you than do others. Just like rhetoric, criticism is nuanced, and may be understood on many different levels. Each chapter that follows underscores this idea and will present a point of view that will add rich variety to your overall understanding of the critical act.

SUGGESTED READINGS

Black, Edwin. *Rhetorical Criticism: A Study in Method.* (Madison, WI: University of Wisconsin Press, 1978), pp. ix–xv, 1–9.

Brockriede, Wayne. "Rhetorical Criticism as Argument." *Quarterly Journal of Speech* 60 (April 1974): 165–174.

Jasinski, James. "Criticism in Contemporary Rhetorical Studies" in *Sourcebook on Rhetoric* (Thousand Oaks, CA: Sage Publications, Inc., 2001) 125–144.

Kuypers, Jim A. "Must We All Be Political Activists?" *The American Communication Journal* 4.1 (2000). http://acjournal.org/holdings/vol4/iss1/special/kuypers.htm.

Rosenfield, Lawrence W. "The Experience of Criticism." *Quarterly Journal of Speech* 60.4 (1974): 489–496.

Sillars, Malcolm O., "Persistent Problems in Rhetorical Criticism" in *Rhetoric and Communication: Studies in the University of Illinois Tradition.* Edited by Jane Blankenship and Herman G. Stelzner, 69–88. (Urbana, Il; University of Illinois Press, 1976).

NOTES

1. James Andrews, Michael C. Leff, and Robert Terrill, "The Nature of Criticism: An Overview," *Reading Rhetorical Texts: An Introduction to Criticism* (Boston: Houghton Mifflin Company, 1998) 6.

2. Donald C. Bryant, *Rhetorical Dimensions in Criticism* (Baton Rouge: Louisiana State Univ. Press, 1973) 25.

3. Wayne Brockriede, "Rhetorical Criticism as Argument," *Quarterly Journal of Speech* 60 (April 1974): 165.

4. Marie Hochmuth Nichols, *Rhetoric and Criticism* (Baton Rouge: Louisiana State University Press, 1963) 7.

5. See "The Experiential Perspective" in Bernard L. Brock, Robert L. Scott, and James W. Chesebro, eds. *Methods of Rhetorical Criticism: A Twentieth-Century Perspective* 3rd ed. (Detroit: Wayne State University Press, 1989) 85–95.

6. Edwin Black, *Rhetorical Criticism: A Study in Method* (Madison, WI: University of Wisconsin Press, 1978) x–xi.

7. Marie Kathryn Hochmuth, "The Criticism of Rhetoric" in *A History and Criticism of American Public Address* vol. 3, Marie Kathryn Hochmuth, ed. (New York City: Russell & Russell, 1954) 13. Hochmuth later changed her name to Marie Hochmuth Nichols.

8. Edwin Black, "On Objectivity and Politics in Criticism," *American Communication Journal* 4.1 (2000) http://acjournal.org/holdings/vol4/iss1/special/black.htm. [Accessed March 21, 2009].

9. This is not to say that one could not orally delivery criticism. Certainly a critic could prepare a response as a speech or public presentation. One could even prepare criticism for a podcast. Since the majority of academic criticism is written, my primary focus is on that form in this chapter.

10. Craig R. Smith, "Criticism of Political Rhetoric and Disciplinary Integrity," *American Communication Journal* 4.1 (2000) http://www.acjournal.org/holdings/vol4/iss1/special/smith.htm. [Accessed March 21, 2008].

11. Black, *Rhetorical Criticism*, 6.

12. For a transcript of this speech see: Al Gore, "Vice President Al Gore Delivers Remarks," CNN.com. http://www.cnn.com/ELECTION/2000/transcripts/121300/t651213.html. [Accessed March 31, 2008]. For an audio recording of the speech, go here: Al Gore, "2000 Presidential Concession Speech," *American Rhetoric Online Speech Bank*, http://www.americanrhetoric.com/speeches/algore2000concessionspeech.html. [Accessed March 31, 2008]. Of course, we now know that Al Gore declined to run again for president. That does not preclude, however, that he kept that option open. If one takes into account the massive amount of speculation concerning the potential for Gore to run in 2004 and even in 2008, one sees that Gore actually succeeded in leaving that door open.

13. George W. Bush, "Governor George W. Bush Delivers Remarks," C-Span (December 13, 2000). http://www.cnn.com/ELECTION/2000/transcripts/121300/bush.html. [March 31, 2008]. For an audio recording of the speech, go here: George W. Bush, "2000 Victory Speech," *American Rhetoric Online Speech Bank*, http://www.americanrhetoric.com/speeches/gwbush2000victoryspeech.htm. [Accessed March 31, 2008].

14. Brock, Scott, and Chesebro, 13.

15. Brockriede, 165–174.

16. Ibid., 166.

17. Ibid., 167.

18. For instance, see Ronald Matlon and Sylvia Ortiz, *Index to Journals in Communication Studies through 1995* (Annandale: National Communication Association, 1997).

19. Lawrence W. Rosenfield, "The Experience of Criticism," *Quarterly Journal of Speech* 60.4 (1974): 491.

20. Stephen E. Lucas, "Renaissance of American Public Address: Text and Context in Rhetorical Criticism," *Landmark Essays on American Public Address*, Martin J. Medhurst, ed. (Davis, CA: Hermagoras Press, 1993): 199.

21. Brockriede, 173.

22. Black, "On Objectivity."

23. William L. Nosthstine, Carole Blair, and Gary A. Copeland, *Critical Questions: Invention, Creativity, and the Criticism of Discourse and Media* (New York: St. Martin's Press, 1994) 34.

24. James Jasinski, "The Status of Theory and Method in Rhetorical Criticism," *Western Journal of Communication* 65.3 (2001) 252.

25. Barnett Baskerville, "The Critical Method in Speech," *Central States Speech Journal* 4.1 (1953) 2.

26. Thomas R. Nilsen, "Interpretive Function of the Critic," *Western Speech* 21.2 (1957) 70. Essay reprinted in Thomas R. Nilsen, ed., *Essays on Rhetorical Criticism* (New York: Random House, 1968) 86–97.

27. Michael Leff, "Interpretation and the Art of the Rhetorical Critic," *Western Journal of Speech Communication* 44 (1980) 342.

28. Examples of this can be found here: Brian Ross and Rehab El Buri, "Obama's Pastor: God Damn America, U.S. to Blame for 9/11," *ABC News*, March 13, 2008. http://abcnews.go.com/Blotter/Story?id=4443788 [Accessed March 21, 2008].

29. The speech, entitled, "A More Perfect Union," may be found here http://blogs.wsj.com/washwire/2008/03/18/text-of-obamas-speech-a-more-perfect-union/?mod=googlenews_wsj and here http://www.barackobama.com/2008/03/18/remarks_of_senator_barack_obam_53.php [Accessed March 21, 2008].

30. James Carney, "Obama's Bold Gamble on Race," *Time* March 18, 2008. http://www.time.com/time/nation/article/0,8599,1723302,00.html Last accessed March 19, 2008.

31. Charles Krauthammer, "The Speech: A Brilliant Fraud," *Real Clear Politics*, March 21, 2008. http://www.realclearpolitics.com/articles/2008/03/questions_for_obama_1.html [Accessed March 30, 2008].

32. Leff, 345.

33. For detailed examples of these see, Karlyn Kohrs Campbell and Thomas R. Burkholder, *Critiques of Contemporary Rhetoric* 2nd. Ed. (Belmont, CA: Wadsworth Publishing Company, 1997) 109–127.

34. Leff, 343–344.

35. Black, *Rhetorical Criticism*, xii. The Pentad is explained in chapter 11.

36. Pauline Kael, *I Lost It at the Movies* (Boston: Little, Brown, 1964) 309.

37. This is not a new problem in rhetorical theory. See Michael Leff, "Interpretation and the Art of the Rhetorical Critic," *Western Journal of Speech Communication* 44 (1980): 337–349.

38. Edwin Black, "A Note on Theory and Practice in Rhetorical Criticism," *Western Journal of Speech Communication* 44 (1980): 331–332.

39. Black, "A Note on Theory and Practice in Rhetorical Criticism," 334.

40. Leff, 345.

41. For a different take on the etic/emic orientation that includes a methodological suggestion for emic criticism, see W. Charles Redding, "Extrinsic and Intrinsic Criticism," *Essays on Rhetorical Criticism* Thomas R. Nilsen, Ed. (New York City, NY: Random House, 1968), 98–125.

42. The preceding two paragraphs can be found in Jim A. Kuypers, "Must We All Be Political Activists?" *The American Communication Journal* 4.1 (2000) http://acjournal.org/holdings/vol4/iss1/special/kuypers.htm. [Accessed March 31, 2008].

43. Rosenfield, 494.

44. Ibid., 492.

45. Robert L. Ivie, "A Question of Significance," *Quarterly Journal of Speech* 80.4 (1994).

46. Robert L. Ivie, "Productive Criticism," *Quarterly Journal of Speech* 81.1 (1995).

47. Robert L. Ivie, "The Social Relevance of Rhetorical Scholarship," *Quarterly Journal of Speech* 81.2 (1994).

48. Michael Calvin McGee, "On Objectivity and Politics in Rhetoric," *American Communication Journal* 4.3 (2001) http://acjournal.org/holdings/vol4/iss3/special/mcgee.htm. [Accessed March 31, 2008].

49. Rosenfield, 494.

50. McGee.

51. How and why we practice rhetorical criticism is an ongoing conversation. Those seeking to better understand the changing nature of our critical practices have a wonderful resource in the following

special collection of essays published in 1957, 1980, 1990, and 2001 respectively. Taken together they present a wonderful opportunity for students of rhetoric to better understand criticism's changing nature. See, "Symposium: Criticism and Public Address," edited by Ernest Wrage, in *Western Speech* 21 (1957). These essays were later reprinted along with five others in Thomas R. Nilsen, ed., *Essays on Rhetorical Criticism* (New York: Random House, 1968). See also, "*Special Report*: Rhetorical Criticism: The State of the Art," edited by Michael C. Leff, *Western Journal of Speech Communication* 44.4 (1980); "Special Issue on Rhetorical Criticism," edited by John Angus Campbell, *Western Journal of Speech Communication* 54.3 (1990); and "*Special Issue*: Rhetorical Criticism: The State of the Art Revisited," *Western Journal of Speech Communication* 65.3 (2001).

A critical exchange focusing on the purposes of rhetorical criticism is found in the *American Communication Journal*: "Criticism, Politics, and Objectivity, edited by Jim A. Kuypers 4.1 (2000) http://www.acjournal.org/holdings/vol4/iss1/index.htm, "Rhetoric, Politics, and Critique," edited by Mark Huglen, 4.3 (2001). http://www.acjournal.org/holdings/vol4/iss3/index.htm, and the final essay in the exchange, Jim A. Kuypers, "Criticism, Politics, and Objectivity: *Redivivus*," 5.1 (2001) http://www.acjournal.org/holdings/vol5/iss1/special/kuypersresponse.htm [All accessed March 31, 2008].

Another resource on the historical changes in rhetorical criticism is the special issue of *Rhetoric Review* dedicated to Ed Black. See Interdisciplinary Perspectives on Rhetorical Criticism, *Rhetoric Review* 25.4 (2006).

3

On Objectivity and Politics in Criticism

Edwin Black

In his invitation to participate in this colloquium, the editor wrote: 'These are opinion pieces, so it is your thoughts on these matters our readers will be interested in.'

It is my thoughts that readers will be interested in? What a luxury! Does it mean that I don't have to be 'objective?' That I can write whatever I please, without restraint, without discipline, without discretion? Well, not quite. I still want to avoid appearing to be an ass. And so, out of concern for my reputation (subjective), I will try to present something that will make sense to an intelligent reader (objective). Which, in turn, suggests that the polarities of subjective and objective are not always antithetical. Sometimes they may be complementary.

I can certainly understand how the issue of objectivity in criticism arises. Scientific inquiries always seek to minimize the influence of the investigator by their methods of research and their requirement of replicability. This quest for objectivity has become, along with other attributes of scientific inquiry, an intellectual standard that some people apply indiscriminately. It's a mistake. Objectivity is not universally desirable.

No one, to my knowledge, has represented criticism as scientific. At most (or least?), it has been characterized as 'pre-scientific' — a condescending representation that assumes, quite gratuitously, that human mental activity is a pyramidal hierarchy with something called 'science' hovering halo-like above its apex and a grotesquely conceived 'criticism' buried somewhere in its nether region. The conception itself is pre-scientific in the historic sense in which anything medieval can be called pre-scientific.

If we want to know about criticism, we look to people who have practiced it, who have engaged its problems and have somehow resolved some of them in tangible acts of criticism. And what accomplished critic has ever claimed that criticism should only be objective? Criticism is not supposed to be always objective. It is, of course, supposed to be always intelligent. More to the point, it is supposed to be always fair. Sometimes fairness requires objectivity and sometimes it doesn't. Therefore, the relationship between objectivity and criticism is not constant; it is variable.

This essay originally appeared in The American Communication Journal 4.1 (Fall 2000). Reprinted with permission from the *American Communication Journal*.

In my use of the term 'criticism,' I cannot extricate it from its origin in the Greek term 'krisis,' which translates into 'judgment.' The critic exercises judgment. In fact, in Greek the term for 'judge' and the term for 'critic' were the same term. Let's play with that ambiguity a bit:

We do not demand that a judge in a courtroom be uniformly 'objective.' We demand that the judge be fair. If the judge's being fair requires, at some phase of the judicial process, neutrality or detachment or distance—all, qualities associated with objectivity—then those are what we expect. On the other hand, if the judge's being fair requires, at some other phase, empathy or compassion or introspection—all, qualities associated with subjectivity—then those are what we expect. What is important is that the judge be whatever is required for being fair. Exactly the same obtains with the critic.

Sometimes, at some stages of the critical process, it is important to be as objective as it is possible to be. There are critical problems that require for their solution a puritanical self-control—a disciplined indifference to one's own proclivities and one's own local conditions. That is especially true of rhetorical criticism, which can be at its most valuable when it focuses on odious rhetors—bigots, demagogues, habitual liars—the understanding of whom may require critics to suspend their repugnance temporarily and, for a period, try to see the world with the cold neutrality of a sociopath. But such acts of objectivity are only intermittent, and never an end in themselves.

Of course, the analogy between the critic and the courtroom judge can be taken only so far. A critic's being fair in criticism is not wholly the same as a judge's being fair in a courtroom. Conventional procedures of law prescribe to a considerable extent the claims and counterclaims to which a judge is obliged to attend in order to be fair. Such a prescriptive order is not available to the critic. The critic's procedures are, when at their best, original; they grow ad hoc from the critic's engagement with the artifact. And because the critic has to generate not only a judgment of the artifact, but also the procedure by which the judgment was reached—because, in short, the critic's responsibilities are legislative as well as judicial—the critic may have to be subjective more often than the judge in the court. That is because critics, unlike judges, cannot lay responsibility for their judgments on any code for which the critics themselves are not individually responsible.

The critic's subjectivity is also the consequence of the critic's having no powers of enforcement. The critic cannot compel our compliance with the critic's judgment. The critic can only induce us, and therefore it is we, the readers of criticism, who demand the critic's compliance with certain of our expectations. We expect the critic to see things for us that we are unlikely to see for ourselves until the critic has called them to our attention. That means that we expect the critic to tell us things that we do not already know. Because the critic's perceptions are supposed to be valuable and uncommon (otherwise, why would we bother to read about them?), there is much in critical activity that ought to be subjective in the sense of being individual, novel, unconforming, sometimes even shocking.

So, far from encouraging critics to be objective all the time, I hold rather that a critic can be excessively objective. Indeed, excessive objectivity is a failure that occurs with unfortunate frequency in criticism.

Impersonal criticism is, by definition, objective. Objectivity, therefore, is manifested in more than just a passive facticity. Objectivity inheres in the substitution of any apriori method for the critic's own perceptions and judgments. It follows, then, that the application in criticism of a political or ideological program that is not the critic's own invention is an exercise in objectivity. And such exercises frequently display the deformities common to excessive objectivity in criticism, which are predictability and pedantry and wearisome uniformity. That is why excessively objective criticism—criticism that is without personality—is so repressive to write and so deadly to read.

Political judgments are certainly relevant to criticism, and political presuppositions are probably unavoidable in criticism. But politicized criticism—criticism that is in the service of an ideology—is another matter. The problem has been that so much of politicized criticism is heavy-handed and closed to discovery. The impetus of politicized criticism is to exploit its subject for the ratification of itself.

In 1844, Karl Marx said, 'The essential sentiment of criticism is indignation; its essential activity is denunciation.' Marx's view is reflected in much of the dyspeptic criticism written by his acolytes, even those who are many levels removed from the Master: the echoes of echoes of echoes. A critical agenda that confines itself to indignant denunciation seems to me awfully constricted. Criticism has richer possibilities.

Good criticism is always a surprise. It is a surprise in the sense that you can't anticipate what a good critic will have to say about a given artifact.

I don't think that the expression of conventional opinions constitutes interesting criticism. By 'conventional opinions' I mean to refer not just to the views of the Rotarian in Peoria; I mean to refer also to the pieties of any coterie whatever. The inventory of opinions that defines a political movement—no matter whether progressive or regressive, rational or psychotic, popular or insular—must become, at least to the adherents of that movement, conventional. It must in order to function as the ideological adhesion for a collective identity. Even anarchists have an orthodoxy.

Although it seems impossible for any of us to live a civic life without subscribing to some body of received doctrine, that doctrine, even if the critic conceives it vividly and believes it ardently, is not the stuff of enlightening criticism. Whatever its merits may be, it is derivative, and it intercedes between the critic and the object of criticism by effecting trite observations and stock responses in the critic.

T.S. Eliot wrote that 'the readers of the Boston Evening Transcript sway in the wind, like a field of ripe corn.' They're not the only ones. We all have episodes of marching in the parade or dancing in the chorus. It is gratifying sometimes to move in synchrony with others. But we just shouldn't try to be professional critics while we're in the ripe corn mode.

It seems to me reasonable to demand of any writer: Surprise me. If the writer can't deliver, the writer can be dismissed, no matter whether what is written is critical or political or fictional or anything else. Note that the demand is not, 'please me;' nor is it, 'comfort me.' It is not a demand for conformity to any sort of bias in the reader. It is simply a demand that a writer have something to say. And repeating the pieties of an ideology is not having something to say. I think it was Truman Capote who once said of a fellow novelist's work, 'That isn't writing; that's typing.' The same can be said of echoic ideologues.

So that these remarks are at least the semblance of an argument instead of being simple dogma, let me try to be clear about their premise. They are predicated on a proposition having to do with the relationship between criticism and its reader. The proposition is that although criticism is generically epideictic, since it engages in praise and blame, it is not functionally epideictic. That is, I am assuming that you do not read criticism solely in order to have your own opinions confirmed, but that you read criticism in order to be brought to see something that you hadn't noticed on your own. If, on the other hand, it is personal confirmation that you want—if you want to be reassured and to have your intellectual passions licensed—you don't then sit down and read criticism. You seek an epideictic occasion—some sort of rally or ceremony where co-believers can celebrate their articles of faith. Really good criticism is too singular to be confirmatory.

We don't want to read criticism that tells us nothing that we didn't already know. We don't want to read criticism that reiterates yet again what we have heard before.

Certainly there is nothing wrong with a critic's having political convictions. It is unavoidable. Only an idiot is without political convictions—in rare cases, maybe a holy idiot, but an idiot all the same. The very term, 'idiot' is from the Greek word for 'non-political person.' We don't want to read rhetorical criticism written by an idiot, which really means that we don't want to read rhetorical criticism that has no political dimension to it. It may be possible to write apolitical but still luminous criticism of pure music or of nonrepresentational painting, but it is hard to imagine apolitical rhetorical criticism that isn't desiccated. So, yes, rhetorical criticism is likely to have a political dimension and it ought to.

The inhibiting complication is that although the critic's political convictions may merit respect, they are not necessarily going to be any more interesting or intelligent or original than the general run of political convictions. Just being a critic doesn't qualify one to have anything to say about politics that has not already been said—and maybe better said—many times. So, I think that unless the critic has something fresh and knowledgeable to say, the critic should just shut up about politics. If the critic does that, then the political convictions of the critic will be presuppositional. That is, the critic will observe, judge and argue from some political convictions rather than to them. The critic's politics will be implicit rather than explicit. Even so, the contours of the critic's political convictions will be clear enough from the criticism.

In the end, there are no formulae, no prescriptions, for criticism. The methods of rhetorical criticism need to be objective to the extent that, in any given critique, they could be explicated and warranted. But it is important that critical techniques also be subjective to the extent that they are not mechanistic, not autonomous, not disengaged from the critics who use them. The best critics have so thoroughly assimilated their methods that those methods have become their characteristic modes of perception.

The only instrument of good criticism is the critic. It is not any external perspective or procedure or ideology, but only the convictions, values, and learning of the critic, only the observational and interpretive powers of the critic. That is why criticism, notwithstanding its obligation to be objective at crucial moments, is yet deeply subjective. The method of rhetorical criticism is the critic.

4

The Rhetorical Situation

Kathleen Farrell and Marilyn J. Young

In "The Rhetorical Situation" Bitzer defines that term as "a complex of persons events, objects, and relations presenting an actual or potential exigence which can be completely or partially removed if discourse introduced into the situation can so constrain human decision or action as to bring about the significant modification of the exigence."[1] Further, he writes, in "any rhetorical situation there will be at least one controlling exigence which functions as the organizing principle: it specifies the audience to be addressed and the change to be effected." The rhetorical audience, then, is that which can alleviate the exigence. There are three main parts to the rhetorical situation, then. The *exigence* we have defined above. The *audience*, which is that group of persons who have the power to modify in some way the exigence, is the second component. Bitzer also wrote of *constraints*, which are an important consideration in that they can influence both what can be said and what should not be said:

> [Constraints are] made up of persons, events, objects, and relations which are parts of the situation because they have the power to constrain decision and action needed to modify the exigence. Standard sources of constraint include beliefs, attitudes, documents, facts, traditions, images, interests, motives and the like; and when the orator enters the situation, his discourse not only harnesses constraints given by the situation but provides additional important constraints—for example his personal character, his logical proofs, and his style.[2]

Thus, as an example, when President Franklin Roosevelt addressed Congress following the Japanese attack on Pearl Harbor, he was responding to that attack as the controlling exigence. The attack would seem to require a response in kind—a declaration of war. Yet, Roosevelt was constrained by the Constitution, which grants Congress the responsibility for declarations of war. The attack, then, required Roosevelt to ask Congress to declare war on Japan; in that way, the controlling exigence—the attack—entailed the necessary audience—Congress—and the action to be taken—the declaration of war.

Yet it was not enough for Roosevelt to merely address Congress, for even with a declaration of war, Roosevelt needed the support of the American people. It is also true that the public needed to hear from the President. In light of this, his speech was designed to respond to two exigencies: the need for a declaration of war and the need of the people to hear from their leader.[3]

Bitzer's ideas about the rhetorical situation are best understood when considered in relation to his notions of public knowledge, where he articulates his understanding of the role of the public in rhetorical practice. When he refers to the "public" Bitzer is not referring to the audience, although these concepts may overlap. Bitzer's construction of the public is a community of persons who share values, interests, and outlook. Publics form around specific values, ideas, policies, and proposals. Yet Bitzer recognizes that these publics are fluid, that specific publics can form, disband, and re-form in a different configuration. Further, there can be "sub-publics" within a larger public, such as ethnic or some political groups within a particular community. These persons are inter-dependent and possess the power to validate community truths and values. It is this group that has the power to "authorize" decisions and actions—not in any formal way as with Congress, but in the sense that some decisions become part of the public sense of truth and value.[4]

Part of the function of the public in a situation such as December 7, 1941, is to authorize the president to seek declarations of war in times of attack. In a way this is the actualization of the notion imbedded in the U.S. Constitution: "with the consent of the governed." That consent is offered formally through Congress, but it is also granted informally through the notion of public assent, a concept that is most successful when public knowledge is informed and has coalesced.

American democracy works because we believe it will and we therefore defer to its precepts. In that sense, democracy is a process of communication, and it is the role of the public through discourse to communicate—formally and informally—its assent to the actions of our leaders. For example, at the conclusion of World War II, in the face of strong public sentiment to "bring the troops home," Roosevelt could not guarantee our allies the presence of an American occupying force in Europe; Churchill's proposal for an alliance of the "English speaking peoples" fell on deaf ears; and American women, who had been the backbone of the workforce during the war, were expected to return home and make room for returning soldiers. The public authorization for the war effort and its exigences no longer existed; decisions had to reflect that new truth.

In the case of the Japanese attack on Pearl Harbor, the situation—and the exigence—was relatively clear, as was the fitting response. When things are not so clear, the development of public knowledge becomes critical; before assent can be communicated, the public must accumulate enough knowledge to

1. agree on the situation itself;
2. understand the options open for a fitting response;
3. debate the costs and benefits of those options.

If these elements do not materialize, the notion of public assent cannot entail the notion of consent, but rests instead on ignorance.

Bitzer's ideas are grounded in the notion that all rhetoric is "situated." That is to say, rhetorical discourse derives its meaning from the situation in which it is created. Absent that situation, meaning is often lost. Think about the "great speeches" in American history; how many of them make real sense outside the time in which they were spoken? Certainly, there are speeches that may come alive while one is studying the era in which they were salient, and many "great" speeches have passages that ring though the ages. Usually, though, these are passages that can be given new life by applying them to a current situation. Nevertheless, by far the majority of speeches given in this country during its existence have fallen into obscurity, not because they were not good examples of the art and craft of speechmaking, but because they no longer speak to us.

Even those speeches that carry powerful impact over time derive much of that strength from the situation they address. Martin Luther King's "I Have A Dream," for example, draws its power from the situation of segregation, the March on Washington, the imagery King employs, the vigor of his delivery, and the fact that his dream had yet to be realized. The Gettysburg Address, also full of imagery and poetry, nonetheless is memorable at least in part because of the situation in which it was conceived: a commemoration of the deadliest battle in American history, a great civil war testing the strength of the union, and a challenge that tried the principles of equality and liberty on which that union was founded, as well as the fact that we need to continuously renew our commitment to those ideals. On the other hand, Lincoln's second inaugural, considered one of the best inaugural addresses ever given, is nonetheless remembered only in part, rather than in whole. Like most great addresses, those passages that one recalls are those the public has "authorized" by moving them into public knowledge.

In Bitzer's view, the situation in which rhetoric is called forth encompasses more than the context of the speech or the events that gave rise to the occasion for the speech. It includes all of the elements that influenced the moment: the events, the individuals involved, the circumstances, and the relationships among these factors. Thus, returning to Roosevelt's request for a Declaration of War, the situation would consist of Roosevelt himself and the attack on Pearl Harbor; but it would also include the Congress and the Constitution, the negotiations that had been going on between the US and the Japanese, the ongoing war in Europe, the widespread isolationism of most Americans prior to the attack, and so on. In analyzing a speech using the situational perspective, the critic must take into account the totality of the situation and must consider the role or roles played by each element. For sake of discussion, we offer these suggestions as guiding questions in a situational analysis:

- What are the elements that constitute the particular situation? Intitially, this list should be inclusive, even exhaustive; elements can be omitted later if analysis demonstrates their role to be negligible.
- What role or roles did each element listed play?
- What is the dominant element, or exigence that will govern the response?
- In terms of the response to the situation, was the exigence modified and the response "fitting"?

These questions are not exhaustive steps in a method to be applied as a sort of "cookie cutter." They do, however, provide a beginning point for analysis that focuses on the significance of the situation. As with any critical effort, it is the rhetorical artifact that will determine how the critical narrative develops. Situational analysis is seldom used as a stand alone tool to evaluate a rhetorical artifact; more typically, it enriches other analytical methods by providing a deeper understanding of context in all its dimensions. Only by understanding the full context of a rhetorical event can the critic comprehend and evaluate the artifact itself.

POTENTIALS AND PITFALLS

The beauty of situational theory is that it allows the critic to account for outside forces that impact a rhetorical event in ways that other methods do not. If we recognize that all rhetoric is situated—that it is dependent for meaning on the time, place, and circumstances in which it occurs—then situational theory allows us to view rhetoric as an organic phenomenon. We are then able to view differently those rare instances of discourse that transcend the situation and live on in national memory. Situational theory also allows us to examine the choices a speaker makes in constructing a particular discourse. Those choices are ultimately influenced by the situation in which the discourse arises—whether ceremonial or as a result of crisis. It also combines naturally with a number of other critical perspectives, allowing the critic to construct a richer, more robust analysis.

There are criticisms of the situational perspective; some see it as mechanistic. Additionally, the idea of the exigence is viewed by some theorists as robbing the rhetor of invention,[5] because, in Bitzer's view, the exigence calls forth rhetoric to craft a fitting response and if the response is not deemed fitting the response is not rhetorical. While this is a pretty shallow view of situational analysis, it does cause some to reject its utility as a critical tool.

There is also the possibility that the critic might overlook elements that are not part of the situation but that would illuminate the rhetorical artifact, such as logical elements, rhetorical devices, or fallacies. Finally, the critic must not lose sight of the fact that the rhetor is responsible for what is said, regardless of the forces that impinge on his or her rhetorical choices.

SITUATIONAL PERSPECTIVE TOP PICKS

Bitzer, Lloyd F. "The Rhetorical Situation." *Philosophy and Rhetoric,* 1 (1968): 1–14. This is the essay where Bitzer first explains situational analysis.

——. "Rhetoric and Public Knowledge." In *Rhetoric, Philosophy, and Literature: An Exploration,* edited by Don Burks, 67–94. (West Lafayette: Purdue University Press, 1978). In this essay Bitzer discusses his theory of public knowledge: how cultural truths are absorbed by groups and used to acknowledge new information and authorize action in response to rhetorical situations.

——. "Functional Communication: A Situational Perspective." In *Rhetoric in Transition: Studies in the Nature and Uses of Rhetoric,* edited by Eugene E. White, 21–38. (University Park: Pennsylvania State University Press, 1980). Bitzer responds to his critics and offers some modifications of his theory.

——. "Rhetorical Public Communication." *Critical Studies in Mass Communication* 4.4 (1987): 425–428. Bitzer discussed public communication, focusing on "journalists as a new and important class of rhetors."

Grant-Davie, Keith. "Rhetorical Situations and Their Constituents." *Rhetoric Review,* 15 (Spring 1997): 264–279. Grant-Davie argues that the roles of rhetor and audience are dynamic and interdependent. Audience as a rhetorical concept has transcended the idea of a homogenous body of people who have stable characteristics and are assembled in the rhetor's presence.

Kuypers, Jim A., Marilyn J. Young, and Michael K. Launer. "Of Mighty Mice and Meek Men: Contextual Reconstruction of the Iranian Airbus Shootdown." *The Southern Communication Journal* 59.4 (1994): 294–306. The authors use criticism informed by a situational perspective to examine the rhetoric surrounding the incident in 1988 when United States forces shot down an Iranian passenger airliner in the Persian Gulf.

Patton, John H. "Causation and Creativity in Rhetorical Situations: Distinctions and Implications." *Quarterly Journal of Speech,* 65 (1979): 36–55. Patton notes that exigences, although necessary conditions for rhetorical discourse, are not, in themselves, sufficient conditions. Underlying this argument is the assumption that "rhetoric is essentially historical," and that it is through invention and creativity that the rhetorical situation is appropriately addressed, producing the "fitting response" that every rhetor seeks.

Smith, Craig R. and Scott Lybarger. "Bitzer's Model Revisited." *Communication Quarterly,* 44:2 (1996): 197–213. The authors discuss responses to Bitzer's theory and describe Bitzer's own attempts to refine it. What is most significant to Smith and Lybarger, however, is that Bitzer, in his refinements, opened the door to a more complex view of perception and situation.

Young, Marilyn J. "Lloyd F. Bitzer: Rhetorical Situation, Public Knowledge, and Audience Dynamics" in *Twentieth Century Roots of Rhetorical Criticism,* edited by Jim A. Kuypers and Andrew King, 275–301. (Praeger, Westport, CT: Praeger, 2001). Young reviews the criticism of Bitzer's work and argues that most of his critics have underestimated the power of the theory of situation. Bitzer's theory gains power and becomes more complete when considered in conjunction with his ideas about public knowledge.

NOTES

1. Lloyd F. Bitzer, "The Rhetorical Situation," *Philosophy and Rhetoric* 1 (1968), 6. According to the Merriam Webster Dictionary online, http://www.merriam-webster.com/, "exigence" [exigency] is "that which is required in a particular situation." [Accessed April 3, 2008].

2. Bitzer, 8.

3. See, Franklin Delano Roosevelt, "A Day That Will Live in Infamy," at http://www.americanrhetoric.com. [Accessed April 3, 2008].

4. Lloyd F. Bitzer, "Rhetoric and Public Knowledge" in Don M. Burks, ed., *Rhetoric, Philosophy, and Literature: An Exploration* (West Lafayette: Purdue University Press, 1978), 67–94.

5. For instance, Richard Vatz, argues that, in explicating his theory of situation, Bitzer has not accounted for the creativity of the rhetor. In making his argument, Vatz provides some of the grounding for the role of perception within a rhetorical situation. See Richard E. Vatz, "The Myth of the Rhetorical Situation," *Philosophy and Rhetoric,* v. 6 (1973), 154–161; and Richard E. Vatz, "The Mythical Status of Situational Rhetoric: Implications for Rhetorical Critics' Relevance in the Public Arena," *Review of Communication* 9. 1 (2009): 1–5.

5

The "Traditional" Perspective

Forbes I. Hill

Traditional criticism is usually taken to mean criticism guided by the theory of rhetoric handed down from antiquity.[1] Although this theory takes several different shapes and forms, they are mostly variations on a theme—that while rhetoric describes reality and does not create it, our perceptions of the real world can be changed by persuaders who insist that their own perceptions are more accurate or, at least, more advantageous to themselves or to the public interest. The tools for changing other peoples' understanding of reality are arguments that can be analyzed by a rhetorician; arguments are presented in language, which in most cases is believed to have more impact when it keeps perspicuity but is made attractive with artfully plotted phrasing. Normally the arguments are marshaled in a compelling order and presented to the listeners by speakers who have mastered the art of paralinguistic features (varying volume, or rate of speaking, for example) and the art of kinesics (using the body to convey meanings and emotions). This is a pragmatic conception of rhetoric.

Some critics have used traditional theory to explain advertisements, propaganda, docudramas, and even novels and films, especially those with a covert propagandistic purpose. This is, of course, not a new idea. In the early 1920s, Hoyt Hopewell Hudson advocated broadening the paths of rhetorical study to include pamphleteering, newspapers, editorial writing, radio broadcasting, advertising, propaganda, and others.[2] In short, whenever there are direct attempts at persuasion, the traditional perspective may prove useful.

TRADITIONAL CRITICISM

The traditional perspective assumes that criticism entails both explication of what went on when speakers engaged listeners or readers, and evaluation of how well the speakers performed the task of changing these receivers' understanding of reality. These twin tasks, explication and evaluation, together comprise the rhetorical critique. In its simplest form, it is a critique of the assumed interaction of a speaker with his audience or an author with his readers at a particular point in time. But in their more complex forms rhetorical critiques may be used to explicate and evaluate the performance of several speakers or writers engaged in a campaign or perhaps a social movement; for example, a study of the changing rhetorical arguments in the campaign for abortion reform during the twentieth century.

Aristotle, often considered the fount of traditional criticism, was no doubt thinking of the interaction of an individual with a particular audience when he set out the elements which we today use for analysis: "A discourse involves three factors: the speaker, the matter about which he speaks, and the persons to whom he is speaking."[3] If we add to this, as most rhetoricians do, the occasion on which the speech is given, it is still a simple plan for a critique. This plan may be made more inclusive by using slightly more complex terms that are near synonyms for the four factors. In place of the term speaker, for example, we often use *source*, by which is meant ghost writer, public relations agent, campaign committee, or advertising team. In place of matter about which one speaks, modern writers use the term *message*; that is, whatever matter is formulated for transmission to others. In place of persons who are addressed, even Aristotle used the term *audience*. The audience is understood as the group of people who have similar reactions to the message, and in some modern cases these auditors are not even in the same space as the person presenting the message; they may be reading the message in a book or receiving it by radio or television. For occasion the term *context* is now used. Traditional criticism is highly contextual; it looks at source, message and audience as they interact within a given span of time.

Ultimately, the traditional perspective's "point of view," Herbert Wichelns wrote, "is patently single. It is not concerned with permanence, nor yet with beauty. It is concerned with effect. It regards a speech as a communication to a specific audience, and holds its business to be the analysis and appreciation of the orator's method of imparting his ideas to his hearers."[4] Even if one expands this notion of audience to include a number of related groups of people, targets of a persuasive campaign for example, he is still dealing with *effect*—that is, analysis and appreciation of the method used by strategists planning the campaign to impart their ideas to these people over this limited period of time.

Wichelns's concern with effect follows Aristotle's statement "the audience is the end—the reason for making the discourse."[5] Aristotle believed that all natural activities are directed toward some end state: *telos* in his language; hence his philosophy is said to be teleological. He thought that the telos of any activity was its purpose for being and defined its essential nature. This orientation is basic to traditional criticism. Some utterances may be entirely self-expressive; crying "ouch" when one touches a hot stove, for example. Rhetorical utterances, however, are not primarily expressive; they are made holding in the forefront of the mind the impact they will have on other people. They are the product of strategic choices about how the speaker wants auditors to respond.

An account of the audience logically comes first when one is composing a critique of a rhetorical event. Nevertheless, it is in practice difficult to start a highly contextualized critique such as the one a scholar writes, without answering the question, When does this audience come into being and under what conditions? Reconstructing the audience is inseparable from determining the context of a rhetorical production.

What follows is an overview of how one might begin a criticism that uses the traditional perspective. I do not wish to imply that all critical efforts of this nature follow this exact pattern. The majority of traditional critiques do, however, touch upon the following five areas. These are: recreation of the context; recreation of the audience; description of the source of the message; the analysis of the message; and the evaluation of the discourse.

Recreating the Context of Rhetorical Events

What is the context in which the speech occurred? Context is often divided into two parts: the physical setting for the event or events, the so-called *mise en scene*, and the social and political context out of which the need for using rhetoric arose. An oft-cited example in traditional criticism is Abraham Lincoln's Gettysburg Address. Why did President Lincoln go to speak at Gettysburg? One reason is that the State of Pennsylvania had planned a ceremony dedicating a cemetery right on the battlefield where many thousands had fallen. Near the field, but somewhat removed from the burial operations, a platform was erected on which sat numerous important political figures. The audience, numbering some twenty thousand, stood near rows of graves in the crisp November sun. Is this mise en scene important? Definitely so in this case The fact that Lincoln was facing the field of battle and the graves is a controlling factor over the speech: "We are met on a great battlefield of that war; we have come to dedicate a portion of that field as a final resting place."

Consider President Clinton's first apology to the Nation after the Lewinsky scandal broke. The setting was important enough to his purpose for the President to make specific refeences to it in his speech: "This afternoon, in this room, in this chair, I testified before the Office of Independent counsel and the Grand Jury."[6] Often, however, the setting is not so important. If a contemporary president makes a statement from a news studio in a large city, a description of the scenery may actually get in the way of creating an adequate critique. The studio might be anywhere; the important question, aside from whether or not he's in prime time, is what was the political situation that this administration thought required a presidential speech?

While the actual scene is often described, the social or political context must also be described. For example, Lincoln could have turned down the invitation to appear at Gettysburg. He was not the featured speaker; the ceremony was centered on a great oration to be delivered by another. Lincoln was in a busy period of his presidency, overwhelmed by the various duties of the office and by the cares of his family life. He chose to go to Gettysburg because of the importance of the occasion: it was the celebration of a battle where many lives had been lost. It was also an opportunity to make news in anticipation of the coming presidential campaign. But above all, it was time for him to put his spin on the significance of the war, to prepare for the postwar period of reconciliation. He dropped everything to take an exhausting train journey to the battlefield.[7] This is the political context of his speech.

For the critic, creating the political context is often a difficult task. Out of all the events in the life of the speaker and the history of the times, which are those that determine the rhetorical situation? Answering this question becomes even more difficult the further removed one's rhetorical artifact is from the present day. The critic simply cannot reproduce a complete account of an era as the jumping off place for his critique. For example, it is obviously important to President Roosevelt's War Message that the Japanese made a surprise attack on Pearl Harbor. However, is it also important that Japan had an alliance with Germany, that the Japanese imperialists had been occupying territory throughout Asia for many years, that American political and business interests in Asia were compromised, that a large peace movement had prevented America's planning for war, that people were psychologically unprepared for war, and that many people were distracted by the military victories of Germany? A narrative about all these factors could overwhelm a critic's account of the War Message itself. Probably the important factors in this case have to do with how complacent Americans were and how startled they became at the unexpected attack, along with their sense that the attack was completely undeserved. These are the factors that Roosevelt assumed and developed in his message. The effect various factors have upon the message should usually be the principal criterion for their inclusion in the section of an essay that recreates context.

Constructing Audiences for Rhetorical Events

Those receiving a message are collectively known as the audience. Traditional rhetoric regards them as free agents who make largely rational choices about the matters at hand. Their choices are influenced by their emotional states, but are not infinitely malleable. Traditional rhetoricians divide audiences into three kinds: either they are jurors in a court of law, who decide about a public or private action that took place in the past (forensic discourse), or they are legislators who decide about some course of action to be taken in the future (legislative discourse), or they are spectators who come to experience a celebration or commemoration of some person or event—that is, a ceremony in the present (epidiectic discourse). Aristotle, at least, emphasized the audience's function as decision-makers; even the auditors at a ceremonial speech, who primarily serve as spectators at a performance, in the final analysis are judges of the expedience and inexpedience of decisions made by those who are praised or blamed at the occassion.[8]

One must discover, then, which of these kinds of audience a speaker was asking to make a decision. Often this choice is obvious as in the case of Roosevelt's War Message, which ends: "I ask that the Congress declare that since the unprovoked and dastardly attack by Japan on Sunday, December 7, 1941, a state of war has existed between the United States and the Empire of Japan." But what can be said of the Gettysburg Address? What decision did Lincoln expect his audience to make? To care about the honored dead? They already cared—cared enough to have come in most cases from far away. Even those who read his speech in the newspapers undoubtedly cared at a time when everyone had a relative who fought in the war.

Lincoln also recommended a course of action, that we "take increased devotion to the cause for which they gave their last full measure of devotion." Does this phrase's orientation to the future make the speech deliberative? After a careful examination of text and context Gary Wills judged it to be a speech that changed people's attitude toward the war: no longer were they to be caught up in the blood and guts of the fray, or even the contentiousness that brought on the war. They were to transcend such matters, which go unmentioned in the address, to see the war as a necessary phase in the nation's progress toward a more perfect Union. If we accept this interpretation, then it is clearly a ceremonial speech. It does not aim at a decision about some imminent course of action. By praising the common sacrifice of all those who struggled in the battle of Gettysburg, it aims to change people's whole belief system from one that dwells on the strife to one that is oriented to the making of peace. Use of praise and blame to forge the auditors into an audience that agrees on common values, such as peace and progress, is what ceremonial addresses are all about.

The choice of the kind of audience at which the discourse is aimed is in this, as with other cases, not obvious. Making that choice requires careful examination of the text as well as the context. This examination is complicated when rhetorical productions are designed to change the perceptions and beliefs of more than one group of people, as is often the case in modern times. Take President Clinton's August 17, 1998 speech of apology to the Nation as an example. This speech addresses several distinct groups, and is in response to numerous competing political and social contexts. In antiquity one could conceive of the audience as those citizens in the popular assembly, mostly male native born speakers of a common language actually listening to the speech. With the advent of mass media and 24 hour news coverage, however, the concern with audience takes on especial importance for the critic.

Back to Roosevelt's War Message. Ostensibly addressed to Congress, it was heard on the radio by millions; its brevity and simplicity is a clue that it was intended to be a deliberative speech aimed at a decision by the larger audience of Americans. The War Message, heard in schools and churches and public buildings throughout the country, may have been one of the last speeches where members of the media audience were in contact with each another. President Clinton's apology went out over the major news networks during prime time; its message was intended to speak to everyone who heard it. However, then as now, an address by a great public figure is heard by an audience totally fragmented—a collection of individuals. Does this make a difference? Traditional criticism seems forced to answer this question in the negative. Here is a rationalization for this position.

Any analysis of the audience is a construct. Let us say that a speaker's audience is the U.S. House of Representatives: 435 members from 50 states. That is a diverse group, and even in the age of maximum information one can hardly know empirically what the range of individual opinions is, especially since there are always some curmudgeons that defy classification. A rhetorical strategist needs to make a profile: most are not young, none are poor (2008 rank and file Congressional salary is $169,300 per year—in the top 5 percent income bracket); almost all affect some kind of Judeo-Christian religious belief; almost all are committed Democrats or Republicans; most desire to be reelected; none of them reveal the whole truth about themselves. This profile is based on a minimum of real data. It is what Aristotle would call *probability*, that is, what one would reasonably expect about people elected every two years as Representatives. Since some improbable things actually happen, we also expect that several members do not fit the profile, but we ignore them. Given the right subject, e.g., war with Iraq, the Congress can be forged into something that approaches a unity; they can become a true audience. Even though bickering about Iraq is now (2008) commonplace, the House (296–133) and Senate (77–23) willingly voted to authorize President Bush to use U.S. military force to make Iraq comply with U.N resolations.

Though the media audience is fragmented, can we construct it in this same way we constructed the Congress? We have some data about them: there are polls, both formal and informal, and sometimes focus groups. The polls are often broken down demographically: regions of the country are separated; the young are separated from those in their prime and the elderly; the wealthy from the middle class and the poor; women from men. Aristotle provides some probable statements characterizing these groups. He states that the young are sanguine and expect life to become better for them; the elderly are more skeptical having often experienced failure. The wealthy expect to control affairs; the poor tend to expect disappointment.[9] Although Aristotle did not characterize women as distinct from men, modern pollsters do tabulate data for women and contrast that to men. Such hints about the ages and fortunes of people provide us with materials to refine polling questions and to better interpret polling data.

From polling data and Aristotle's character sketches, a critic can construct a profile of the fragmented media audience. The profile, if carefully made, will probably be nearly as accurate as one's profile of a divided Congress. The critic operating from a traditional perspective should search biographies and accounts of journalists to find out how the speaker conceived of the audience so that he can contrast the speaker's construction with potentially more accurate ones.

Describing the Source of the Message

Traditional rhetoricians have historically thought about the source as a singular person—an orator skilled in the art of speaking. The roster of speakers who fulfilled that vision is almost, but not quite, congruent with the list of great statesmen. A few exceptions can be noted, Thomas Jefferson was not much of a speaker, but for his time he was an exception. Most orators wrote their own speeches, perhaps with a little editorial help. From this point of view it makes sense to ask questions such as, What was the nature of the orator's unique personal charm? What was his education? And what were the orator's peculiar qualifications as thinker and stylist? What obstacles did the orator overcome on the road to rhetorical celebrity? Such questions are the stuff of rhetorical biography. It is still a pleasure to read a short biographical essay—one which touches the peaks of a man or a woman's speaking career. When done well, it makes the reader consider himself a close watcher of a great career.

Historical figures may still be treated this way. Imagine a retrospective of Franklin D. Roosevelt: his home schooling directed by an imperious mother, his editorship of the *Harvard Crimson*, his mediocre performance in law school, his dashing entrance into politics, his marriage to the woman who became a truly remarkable public figure in her own right, his overcoming a crippling illness to reestablish an impossible political career, his use of that remarkable voice to compensate for an inability to move around the platform, his discovery of radio, his adventurous spirit and yes, his confidence that bordered on arrogance making him at times a divisive figure. Such an essay can never go out of date.

As exciting as a rhetorical biography can be, though, it is only a small part of a traditional critique. Going back to antiquity one finds the personality of a speaker thrust strangely into the background. Dionysius of Halicarnassus, who left us a number of well developed critiques, illuminates the life of the speaker in only a sentence or two. What he develops instead is the speaker's construction of a public image, his *ethopoeia*; he avoids any implication that he is constructing a true character.

In *Rhetoric,* Aristotle presents copious materials from which a discourse should be composed: lines of argument, directions for logic, systems of values, and clues as to how to bring auditors into emotional states, such as anger. When he comes to talk about the speaker, he presents only a minimum theoretical framework for developing *ethos.* The three sources of ethos, he says are good sense, good character, and good will, since people disbelieve speakers either because they think them senseless, or of such bad character that they do not give their true opinions, or they lack good will toward the auditors so that even being sensible and honest they do not say what they think. That is all that Aristotle says about the speaker.

In recent times a speaker is likely to serve as a spokesman for an organization: he is a cabinet member or public relations officer of an agency or corporation. The message he delivers is not his own; even if the speaker drafted it, numerous others in the organization have edited it and revised to the point where it has become a car put together by a committee. And the text of the message is probably given out to the newspapers before the speech is delivered. Take the July 13, 2003 comments made by National Security Advisor Condolezza Rice. She spoke to both *Fox News Sunday* and *Face the Nation.* During these talks she stated: "the president took the nation to war to depose a bloody tyrant who had defied the world for 12 years."[10] Rice was speaking for President Bush and his administration, not for herself.[11]

Under these circumstances it no longer makes sense to ask about the speaker's education, or his unique language choices. The question is, what kind of a committee of writers put together the message? What interests did they represent? For a president this often means State versus Defense, for example. How did the writers work together and interface with the spokesman? The question about *ethopoeia* is still relevant: what does the text show about how they built a favorable public image for the spokesman? How did committee and spokesman construe what would build credibility? Covering these factors are what we now mean by describing the source.

It is still relevant to ask, did the spokesman deliver the message with conviction? With a flair? Did he show great energy? Was he serious or lighthearted? Did he dominate the audience and seem to reach into their hearts? Appropriate delivery is itself a source of credibility.

Think of President Clinton's voice when he declaimed, "I did not have sexual relations with that woman, Miss Lewinsky." Think of President Bush's vocal and physical expression of great determination as he insisted that Afghanistan must give up al Qaeda terrorists. These are important elements of the traditional critique.

Analyzing the Message

The traditional perspective begins its consideration of the message by asking about the text—a written document that recreates what a speaker said to that audience on that particular occasion. If one is going to consider questions of proof or of rhetorical style, it is desirable to have an accurate account of the verbal utterance of the moment, or, at least, of what the author intended a reader to read.

Often a good text is available; some independent agent has made an audio or video recording. We should be alert if the recording or document is available only from the source. Texts are often edited; it is well-attested that Congressmen may revise the Congressional Record at any time until the printing presses start to move. Often a speaker will be asked to write out his remarks for publication after the presentation. The importance of finding a reliable text is well-exemplified by this example: the text published by the *Boston Globe* of Professor George Wald's signature utterance, *A Generation in Search of a Future*, furnished to the newspaper by the speaker does not contain the lines italicized here:

> Nobody is the aggressor any more except those on the other side. *And this is why that, that Neanderthal among Secretaries of State—Rusk—went to such [applause]—went to such pains, went to such pains, stuck by his guns, because in him, uhh, stubbornness and density take the place of character, [laughter] uhh, went to such pains to insist as he still insists that in Vietnam we are repelling an aggression. And if you're repelling an aggression, anything goes.*

This characterization of Dean Rusk is grotesquely unfair; he never held that if you are repelling an aggression, anything goes, and he did not resemble Neanderthal man. Professor Wald apparently had second thoughts when he edited this passage out of the version he gave the press. The independent recording put out by Cadmon Records gives what he said unedited.[12] It also shows why the unedited version is important: Wald received by far the most vociferous reaction to these statements of anything else in his speech. They resonated wildly with an audience of 1960s radicals who were united in their hatred of established authority figures like the Secretary of State. What you know from other sources about Wald's audience is amply confirmed.

Another example details how important it is to obtain the primary document and not rely on secondary sources or press accounts. On November 8, 1997 President Clinton spoke at a fundraiser sponsored by a homosexual advocacy organization, the Human Rights Campaign. At one point in his speech he was interrupted by a member of the audience who yelled, "People with AIDS are dying." The president responded with what appeared to be a spontaneous addition to his planned remarks: "People with AIDS are dying. But since I've become President we're spending 10 times as much per fatality on people with AIDS as people with breast cancer or prostate cancer." If one were only to rely on reports of the press, one would never know that the president uttered these highly controversial words.

For instance, the *Los Angeles Times* wrote that as he "spoke, Clinton was interrupted twice by AIDS activists . . . Clinton said, 'I'd have been disappointed if you hadn't been here tonight. People with AIDS are dying. But since I became president, we're spending 10 times as much on AIDS research and treatment programs.' "*The New York Times* wrote that the president faced one man who "cried out, 'People with AIDS are dying!' The crowd hushed him, but Mr. Clinton chuckled. 'I'd have been disappointed if you hadn't been here tonight,' he said. He added, 'People with AIDS are dying, but since I became President we're spending ten times as much' combatting the disease." Not one major paper reported the rest of the President's controversial sentence. The full text is only available from the White House.[13]

Historical speeches pose an even more difficult problem. The text of the Attic orations derives from copies made by the orators as examples for use in the schools of rhetoric. Naturally the orators transmitted to the schools only the fairest texts of what they said. Speeches in the eighteenth and early nineteenth century House of Commons and House of Lords were mostly recreated by reporters who stood closely packed in the galleries where they were not supposed to make transcriptions of the proceedings. The Lincoln-Douglas debates were collated from newspaper reports by Lincoln; it is small wonder that his speeches look more finished in the received text than Douglas's. The traditional critic will often need to make a caveat about most speeches: 'I don't vouch for every word of the text; I worked with the best text available.'

The traditional perspective considers the message itself under the headings of *invention*, *disposition*, and *style*. By invention is meant the finding of appropriate materials for the discourse. This is usually done by checking through an inventory of stock materials—topics—looking to see whether the speaker has used all available means of persuasion, as Aristotle put it. Topical thinking is a type of systematic brainstorming using predefined categories. Although developed in ancient times, more recent applications are available. For example, John Wilson and Carroll Arnold developed 16 topics for the contemporary student. These include the "existence of nonexistence of things"; "degree or quantity of things, forces, etc."; "spatial attributes"; "attributes of time"; "motion or activity"; "form, either physical or abstract."[14] By disposition is meant the arranging of these materials in a structure as well plotted as the order of battle when skilled generals make a plan for victory. Structure can be influenced by many factors, although it is generally agreed upon that your audience, topic, and purpose play a deciding role. By style is meant the use of the right language to make the materials of exposition and argument clear and convincing. We will now consider each of these in turn.

Invention. When a critic seeks to investigate invention, he is dealing with both artistic and inartistic proofs. Artistic proofs are the invented proofs. They are created by the speaker, the arguments that he uses to try to persuade the audience. They are usually, if somewhat inaccurately, grouped under the headings of logos, ethos, and pathos. Inartistic proofs are not created by the speaker, but instead exist on their own: contracts, wills, or other documents, for example.

In relation to *logos*, the critic should look to see whether the appropriate commonplace arguments, deduced from the list of topics, have been used. Logos refers in general to logic based on reason. This is not a scientific logic, but rather a rhetorical logic, one based upon probability. Those creating arguments need to construct them based on common notions of what is probable. To prosecute a company for spreading toxic waste, one looks for the green water and brown air in the neighborhood; the prosecutor seeks out people who claim to be sick and compares them to those in comparable areas who are not sick. He points to the prevalence of cost cutting among companies who look at the bottom line and the absence of witnesses and regulators and the arrogant behavior of company executives. These are the commonplaces of environmental claims, and failure to use them should be construed as not making the most effective speech possible. A critic would look for such commonplaces.

Although there are many ways to examine the logic used in a speech, one particularly important aspect to be examined is the concept of the enthymeme. The essence of the enthymeme is that some parts of the logical argument are omitted when the speaker or writer can predict that the auditors will supply them. Take this example from Richard Nixon: "The American people cannot and should not be asked to support a policy which involves the overriding issues of war and peace unless they know the truth about that policy. Tonight I would like to answer some of the questions that I know are on the minds of many of you listening to me."[15]

This is a typical example of an enthymeme that builds the speaker's credibility and that also requires the listener/reader participation in supplying a crucial missing term. Presented as a traditional syllogism this would look like this:

Premise: All policies that the American people should be asked to support are policies about which they will know the truth.
Premise: The policies which I reveal when I answer your questions are policies that the American people should be asked to support.
Conclusion: The policies which I reveal when I answer your questions are policies about which you will know the truth.

Nixon's actual statement is making the claim that he will tell the truth about his policies. He says that people should not be asked to support them unless they will know the truth about them. Although I supplied all three parts of the syllogism, Nixon never actually explicitly claims that he is going to tell the truth. The second premise I give is actually not stated by Nixon; rather, one is tempted to supply it, and if the listener supplies it, the very activity of completing the logical structure starts the process of the listener assenting to the argument. As Lloyd Bitzer wrote: "Enthymemes occur only when speaker and audience jointly produce them. . . . Because they are jointly produced, enthymemes intimately unite speaker and audience and provide the strongest possible proofs."[16] That process will be completed unless the auditor checks himself and looks at it. He is more likely to yield to the process because the formal logic behind this argument is good enough, though the second premise is unsupported and probably false.

Persuasive discourse is constructed so that there are a number of ethos claims like this one. Ethos is basically an interpretation by the audience of qualities possessed by a speaker as the speaker delivers his message. Thus, by the way a speaker argues, an audience makes judgements about his intelligence, character, and good will. A speaker becomes unpersuasive if he has to claim directly, "I am not a crook" or "I did not have sexual relations with that woman." If he needs to state it in this bald way, he has already lost credibility. An exposition of how a speaker establishes ethos is a significant part of a traditional critique. Sometimes the discourse will contain a narrative of the discovery of the right course of action. Such a narrative shows the good sense of the spokesman and his advisors who did not make decisions off the top of their heads, but only after consideration and reflection. The way in which a speaker supports his arguments and organizes his materials can impact the assessment of his intelligence. Very often his character—moral qualities—can be assessed by how qualities such as justice, courage, generousity, and so on are exhibited in his arguments.

Finally, a speaker could also show goodwill by finding common ground with the readers/listeners. The speaker who comes to campus tells us, "I remember when I was a student; like so many of you I didn't have enough time in the day to do everything. I worked part time in the dining room and stole away to the quietest corner of the library every night. But hard as that was, it was worth it." Speakers also indulge in a little subtle flattery: "you who have a university education easily recognize that group behavior differs from individual behavior." Commenting on such statements is part of a traditional critique as it relates to ethos.

The first step in dealing with *pathos* in the critique is identifying the emotional states that dominate the discourse. The speaker's words will *invite* us to feel a particular way. Sometimes this is obvious. In the case of Roosevelt's *War Message* the emotional states are anger and confidence. The anger springs from our sense of betrayal by an inferior people from whom we are entitled to receive respect. The confidence comes from our feeling of unity and our sense of righteousness. Roosevelt amplified the sneakiness of the attack and the innocent lives lost to bring people into a greater state of anger, and he represented himself as speaking for all our people who recognize the facts of Japanese aggression which are so obvious that they speak for themselves. When auditors are angry enough they minimize feelings of fear; they become ready to accept with confidence hardships and sacrifices: hence the above listed *pathe* are the stuff of War Messages.

Another example is seen in the commercials for the Christian Children's Fund. These commercials begin with images of children in truly impoverished conditions. Many of the children are shown playing in what might be raw waste and garbage; many have flies around their eyes, and walk with distended bellies. This is quickly contrasted with images of those children helped by this charity: better clothing, healthier looking, etc. All this in the background reinforces the same verbal message by the speaker. Your emotional register goes from pity and perhaps guilt to hope. A critic would look for these emotional appeals and determine their effectiveness toward moving us along toward doing whatever it is the speaker wishes us to do. In the case of the Christian Children's fund, sponsor a child.[17] Not all appeals to emotiion will be so easy to detect; the critic must step back and carefully look for these.

Disposition. The critic must also ferret out dispositon, or the speech's organization *as it relates to persuasion.* In almost no case is a discourse arranged randomly, though occasionally a speech writer will try to make it appear random. Roosevelt's War Message, Stelzner points out, falls almost into two halves, separated by the sentence "As Commander in Chief of the Army and Navy I have directed that all measures be taken for our defense." All material prior to that sentence is in the past tense and the Japanese empire is the actor. What follows that sentence is in the present tense; the President, Congress and the people become the actors.[18] Such is the disposition of this celebrated speech.

Take Lincoln's Address at Cooper Union for another example; it divides into three parts: first a forensic section in which the speaker refutes the belief that Congress could not constitutionally legislate as to slavery in the Federal territories; then a shorter constructive section on the idea that Republicans are the ones who perpetuate the constitutional doctrines of the Founding Fathers, it's the Southerners who have made a radical change; then the shortest section, a little deliberative speech to Republicans exhorting them to act with restraint while refusing to compromise their basic ideals. Accusation to constructive defense to exhortation (in long, shorter, and shortest sections) is the pattern for disposition in the Cooper Union Address. There ought to be some discernible rationale, as in the cases cited, for the disposition of the materials of the discourse. It is the task of the critic to figure out that rationale.[19]

Style. Traditional criticism treats the style of the discourse as part of the persuasive force of the arguments. Style must be, however, both appropriate to subject and audience. In most cases clarity is assumed as the cardinal virtue of style. Clarity is achieved with factors such as using common words, avoiding jargon, creating metaphors that make matters vivid, using active verbs, and avoiding more than the minimum of adjectives. The speaker who uses such locutions as "the optimum moment of contact" is probably not persuading as well as one who says "timing's important; there's a right moment for everything." That is, of course, unless the audience is composed of those predisposed to accept a specific technical vocabulary. When Thomas Paine refutes the argument that America has flourished under her former connection with Great Britain by writing that, "We may as well assert that because a child has thrived upon milk that it is never to have meat," he chooses a metaphor that is both concrete and familiar.[20] Observations of this sort are the meat of traditional criticism in relation to clarity of style.

Yet working against this preference for the unmodified common word is the notion that style should make an impression—that statements should have a certain heft to give an idea presence. That is also a precept of traditional rhetoric; the style of public address is never colloquial, though it may be deliberately kept simple. So the speechwriter is to make a certain admixture of long words and a few unusual ones; he is occasionally to look for a unique way of phrasing something even amid the clichés.

Clarity and impressiveness are also to be gained from figures of syntax: parallel structure of clauses and sentences and the devices that reinforce it. When Lincoln declaimed, "Fondly do we hope, fervently do we pray that this mighty scourge of war may speedily pass away," he created a syntactical structure that speaks seriously; it is hard, however, to sing it to a merry tune. The contrast of hope and pray (antithesis) would be entirely broken up if he had said, "Fondly do we hope and we also pray fervently." Fondly and fervently, too, must be in the same grammatical position in each clause; then the alliteration works to reinforce the structure. The rhyming of pray and away (epistrophe) is also important to the structure. Traditional rhetoric views this artistry in structuring prose as a significant part of rhetorical effectiveness. These rhetorical figures of speech are more than window dressing, they are an important part of the persuasive process.

Summary. When looking at the message, a critic will look to see whether the discourse is deliberative, forensic, or epidiectic. Deliberative discourse is concerned with the future, and its auditors are asked to make judgments about future courses of action. Forensic discourse is concerned with past acts, and its auditors are asked to make judgments concerning what actually happened in the past. Epidiectic discourse is set in the present, and concerns speeches of praise or blame. Its auditors are being asked to make judgments concerning how well the speaker accomplishes his goals.

Generally a critic looks for three items in a text: invention, disposition, and style. Under invention, a critic looks to see how well the speaker created his rhetorical appeals; were all the available means of persuasion used? Both artistic—logos, ethos, and pathos—and inartistic proofs will be examined. A critic wil also look hard at the disposition, or organization of a speech, to determine its impact upon persuasive effect. Finally, a critic will look at the style of the speech. How might the language choices made impact the persuasive effort?

Evaluating the Discourse

Aristotle lays down the rule that a discourse should be judged by whether it uses sound method: "it is not the function of rhetoric to persuade but to observe the available means of persuasion for situations like this one, just as in all the other arts. For example, the function of medicine is not to make healthy, but to bring the patient as far toward health as the case permits. For sometimes it is impossible to bring health, but one must give sound treatment."[21]

If he follows this rule, the critic goes through a checklist of the available lines of argument to see if any are omitted that might persuade this audience on this subject; he considers the possible ways of disposing the narrative and arguments to see if the best way has been used; he looks at the stylistic devices that clothe the arguments to see if there are others more appropriate to the situation. If everything is done, he is ready to render a judgment: this must be the best discourse—or, possibly, it falls short in the following ways. Regardless, there is a certain concern with the aesthetics involved with the speech making process: How well were the arguments constructed? Was the message well organized? And was the style used appropriate for the specific audience?

In practice, almost no critic is wholly satisfied with this kind of purely internal critique. Almost invariably critics add some kind of external measure. The legislature did not pass the bill.

The jury did not convict. The voters did not elect the candidate. The president gave a speech on the economy, and the stock market rose or fell. These *effects* are the simplest indicators of success, but we know that they are often misleading. Sometimes legislators have commitments that make it impossible for them to respond even to the most finely crafted speech. Some juries will nullify the law because of their sympathy for the defendant even though the presentation of the case has been artistically satisfactory.

We may look to somewhat more indirect measures as well. The legislature took up the bill next session or the one after, and without much additional debate passed it. The jury did not convict, but all the editorial writers agreed that they should have. The stock market immediately reacted like a bear to the president, but two weeks later the bull market began, and it ran a long course. Take, for example, Susan B. Anthony, who was the center of controversy throughout most of her life, but never lived to see woman's suffrage. When the suffrage amendment finally passed, she was honored as the ancestor of all suffragettes. These historical results are, perhaps, more just indications of the success or failure of a persuasive campaign than a decision made in the midst of the struggle. George Orwell's critique of the totalitarian tendencies of the modern state did not result in the overthrow of any totalitarians, but it has become a standard against which states are judged; the use of Orwellian language is almost universally taken as the sign of approaching danger.

Thus a critic using the traditional perspective will discuss the speech's internal dynamics, but also touch upon its impact upon its audience. Rhetoric, viewed from a traditional perspective, is used for a purpose, it is intentionally created, and this is taken into consideration when a critic offers an evaluation. A thoughtful discussion of the historical context and some speculation on the influence of the discourse forms the conclusion of a traditional critique.

CRITICAL ESSAY

Much of the writings of those who used traditional criticism assumed a general knowledge concerning the classical roots of the rhetorical theory that underpinned the criticism. The essay that follows proceeds along the same path. Instead of a fully developed review of literature this essay instead focuses upon putting into practice traditional criticism as outlined above. You should be aware, however, that if you are writing for an academic audience that you most likely will need to take time to define your terms and outline your theoretical perspective.

When reading this essay, look for the reconstruction of context, the construction of audience, a discussion of the source (speaker), and an analysis of the message (look in particular for a discussion of Invention, Disposition, and Style). Finally, look for an evaluation of the rhetorical artifact.

CRITICAL ESSAY: MR. DOUGLASS'S FIFTH OF JULY*

Following the Compromise of 1850 the abolitionist movement, somewhat dispirited by the failure to block the Fugitive Slave Law, renewed its efforts to publicize the evils of slavery. In

---

* Unless otherwise noted, all quotations from this speech come from the following source: Frederick Douglass, "Speech at Rochester July 5, 1852." In *Negro Orators and their Orations*, ed. Carter Godwin Woodson (Washington, D.C.: The Associated Publishers, Inc., 1995), 197–223.

Rochester, New York, which was a center of anti-slavery activity, the Rochester Ladies Anti-Slavery Society decided to mark Independence Day 1852 with their own celebration featuring an address by their neighbor, the famous abolitionist speaker, Frederick Douglass. The celebration was held on July 5th since the 4th fell on a Sunday, and the custom of that era prohibited secular events on the Sabbath.

The Rochester Ladies rented Corinthian Hall, where five to six hundred people assembled, having paid 12 cents each as entry fee.[22] After the opening prayer and a reading of the Declaration of Independence, Mr. Douglass made his presentation: "What, to the Slave, is the Fourth of July?" His recitation, according to Frederick Douglass's paper, was "eloquent and admirable, eliciting much applause throughout." Before the meeting was adjourned, "A Request was . . . made that the Address be published in pamphlet form, and seven hundred copies were subscribed on the spot." It was also published in Frederick Douglass's paper on July 9 and many times subsequently. Perhaps we should now consider it an American classic. It is especially appropriate to make a critique like this using the standards of traditional rhetoric because Mr. Douglass and many in his audience were familiar with these standards.

The Audience

In constructing Douglass's audience, let us first ask, who is to make a decision about what? Those immediately before the speaker were abolitionists, their sympathizers, and their friends. Many of them were followers of William Lloyd Garrison, with whom Douglass had recently made a rancorous break. Douglass demanded that they condemn slavery—not just in an intellectual way, but with an emotional fierceness that would keep them agitated until it was abolished. What the audience might have expected on the Fourth of July was a speech praising our ancestors, our country, and our people. In an astonishing reversal Douglass gives them a discourse of uninterrupted blame: a true epideictic speech of vituperation.

If the audience before him consisted of anti-slavery zealots, it was nevertheless not of one mind about how slavery was to be ended. A special group of auditors were strict Garrisonians, who believed that the Constitution supported slavery, and since it did, it should be wiped away, and a new Republic without the South should be established to avoid any contact with the evil of slavery. Others present took a more centrist position, and some may have been opponents of slavery only in the sense that they thought it an evil whose spread should be prevented. The auditors were united enough in their anti-slavery sentiments that Douglass could give a speech so critical of the Republic that no patriot would sit still for it. A different audience, even in the North, might have driven him from the platform.

But what of the reading public, the ones who got the speech from the papers and pamphlets? At first the address was carried only by the abolitionist papers; there Douglass could be assured of a favorable response. Soon it was published as a pamphlet, probably circulated mostly to abolitionists and those to whom they were proselytizing. The pamphlet certainly had no circulation in the South. Three years later an extract containing the most impassioned parts of the Fourth of July oration was made an appendix to Douglass's second autobiography, *My Bondage and My Freedom*. In this form it enjoyed a national circulation. A measure of acceptance by the larger audience was guaranteed by the indubitable fact: the American Revolution did not bring freedom to the slave. On the other hand, there must have been an ample number of readers irritated by the insult to our great national holiday. We can reasonably conclude that the oration aimed at energizing the friendly rather than converting the hostile.

The Spokesman

By 1852 Frederick Douglass was well known as a speaker: he had traveled throughout the northeast and the middle states as a full-time agitator for the Massachusetts Anti Slavery Society from 1841 to 1845. Born in 1817, he spent the first twenty-one years of life as a slave. Nevertheless, he learned to read and write as a child. In his autobiographies he tells the story of getting an important book, *The Columbian Orator*, used in the schools as a source of precepts exemplified by extracts from speeches and dramas. In 1838 he escaped from the plantation, making his way north to Massachusetts. He changed his name from Frederick Augustus Washington Bailey, but after publication of the first autobiography, *Narrative of the Life of Frederick Douglass, an American Slave*, his cover was blown; he could have been arrested as an escaped slave. He fled to England, where he lectured on temperance and abolition until his freedom was bought from his old master in 1847. In England he became the most glamorous spokesman for the anti-slavery cause, the one who spoke from firsthand experience and with great fervor and eloquence. On his return, "a series of enthusiastic reception meetings was held to honor him; he completely dominated the annual meeting of the American Anti-Slavery Society, held on May 11, 1847; and two weeks later his co-workers installed him into the Garrisonian establishment by electing him president of The New England Anti-Slavery Society."[23]

Douglass's first autobiography went through four editions in the year of its publication. Loren Reid explains its success based on its appearance at a time when the narrative form was becoming increasingly popular, as evidenced by the sales of novels and travelogues, and by the popularity of evangelical sermons that relied more on Biblical narrative than direct argument.[24]

The sponsors of the Fourth of July celebration in 1852 knew what they were doing when they made Frederick Douglass their main speaker. He was at the height of his oratorical powers in 1852, a physically impressive figure, obviously strong and vital with a large head of hair, not yet gray, and a resonant baritone voice. He could be counted on to give a good show, as he had many times before. It hardly needs to be said that the whole ceremony was built around that good show the orator was expected to give. In the nineteenth century, as Gary Wills has remarked, the orator at a public celebration was intended to be a virtuoso performer who presented a long speech replete with rhetorical flourishes. Anything less would disappoint the people who came to celebrate.[25] Douglass was conscious of his obligation to perform: "I have been engaged in writing a Speech," he wrote Gerritt Smith after the fact, "for the 4th. July, which has taken up much of my extra time for the last two or three weeks. You will readily think that the Speech ought to be good that has required so much time."[26]

Disposition and Summary of the Speech

Douglass's exordium is given over to a conventional expression of modesty: "He who could address this audience without a quailing sensation, has stronger nerves than I have. I do not remember ever to have appeared as a speaker before any assembly more shrinkingly, nor with greater distrust of my ability, than I do this day." In this case, as in most such expressions in 18th and 19th century orations such expressions must be taken ironically. The speaker could not have failed to know that he was among the dozen most celebrated orators of his time.

Douglass organized the central section of this address on the principle of contrast between *then* and *now*. The first third of this section consists of conventional praise for what happened in the past. He does what any 4th of July orator would be expected to do: celebrate the birth of the nation. This occasion is to you "what the Passover was to the emancipated people of God." It is "easy now to flippantly descant on how American was right and England wrong, but when your fathers first talked this way, they were accounted plotters of mischief, agitators and rebels, dangerous men." They petitioned the Throne, but the British government kept its course, with "the blindness which seems to be the unvarying characteristic of tyrants since Pharaoh and his hosts were drowned in the Red Sea." One can view this section like a classicist, as an historical narration; or one may see it as the first part of the section that is usually called the proof (which follows naturally assertions). In either case, the reason for praising the courage of the Fathers is to prepare for a contrast with contemporary politicians, and the reference to the Passover and to Pharaoh is meant to cue us to the denunciation of slavery to come. Typically in conventional speeches these historical narrations are used for foreshadowing.

Suddenly Douglass switches gears: he no longer speaks about then but now and announces his subject: "AMERICAN SLAVERY." He identifies himself as a speaker for the bondman, who knows that America is false to the past, false to the present, and solemnly binds herself to be false to the future. "What have I, or those I represent, to do with your independence. . . . The sunlight that brought life and healing to you has brought stripes and death to me. This Fourth is yours not mine. You may rejoice; I must mourn. . . . I do not hesitate to declare, with all my soul, that the character and conduct of this nation never looked blacker to me than on this 4th of July!" The rest of the proof is taken up by a development of the blackness of character and conduct of the nation.

The arguments used to justify slavery are mere rationalizations, not even worthy of serious refutation. He makes outstanding use of the figure paralepsis, claiming not to be refuting these arguments, while in fact making a summary refutation of each.[27]

"Must I undertake to prove that the slave is a man? Of course not; it is beyond doubt: you hold him responsible for crimes like other humans. Laws in most Southern states forbid teaching him to read. No one makes such laws about the beasts of the field. When the dogs in your streets, when the fowls of the air, when the cattle on your hills, when the fish of the sea and the reptiles that crawl shall be unable to distinguish the slave from a brute, then will I argue with you that the slave is a man!" He claims not to make the arguments that he has made. Is not man entitled to liberty? That's not a matter to be debated by Republicans, to be settled by logic and argumentation. "How should I look today, in the presence of Americans, dividing and subdividing a discourse, to show that men have a natural right to freedom?" With a magnificent *ad hominem*, Douglass concludes that he cannot argue this (though he has) because: "There is not a man beneath the canopy of heaven who does not know that slavery is wrong for him."

Is it not wrong "to make men brutes, to rob them of their liberty, to work them without wages, to keep them ignorant of their relations to their fellow men, to beat them with sticks, to flay their flesh with the lash, to load their limbs with irons, to hunt them with dogs, to sell them at auction, to sunder their families, to knock out their teeth, to burn their flesh, to starve them into obedience and submission to their masters?" Such a system is obviously wrong; "I have better employments for my time and strength than such arguments would imply," Douglass avers, but, of course his list of these oppressions of slavery has made the strongest of arguments.

Is slavery sanctioned by God? "There is blasphemy in the thought. That which is inhuman cannot be divine! Who can reason on such a proposition? They that can, may: I cannot." But he *has* reasoned. Thus with repeated *paralepsis*, Douglass minimizes the justifications for slavery into insignificance. He concludes his refutation, "What to the American slave is your 4th of July?" A day which reveals to him, more than all other days, the gross injustice and cruelty to which he is the constant victim. The extent of the gross injustice and cruelty is now to be exemplified through several examples.

There is the internal slave trade, thought somehow to be more respectable than the African slave trade. Douglass uses his unique ethos; he claims to be have been born amid the sights and scenes of the trade. He lived in Baltimore near the market. After the auction the flesh-mongers gathered up their victims by dozens and drove them in chains to the general depot. A ship had been chartered to convey the forlorn crew to Mobile or to New Orleans. From prison to ship they must be driven in the darkness of night due to the anti-slavery agitation, but as a child he heard the rattle of their chains and their cries.

There is the Fugitive Slave Act, through which Mason and Dixon's line has been obliterated; New York has become Virginia, and the power to hold, hunt, and sell men, women, and children remains no longer a mere state institution but is now an institution of the United States. In court two witnesses testify that this individual is the escaped slave; he may not testify on his own behalf or bring witnesses, and at the end of the proceeding he is taken in chains back to slavery. By way of amplification, this law stands alone in the annals of tyrannical legislation.

There is the attitude of the clergy who support the Fugitive Act. Using the traditional topos (topic) of inconsistency between their behavior and their pretensions, Douglass charges: "if the Fugitive Slave Law concerned the right to worship God according to the dictates of their own consciences, a general shout would go up from the church demanding repeal, repeal, instant repeal." But the church of our country does not esteem the law as a declaration of war against religious liberty. In supporting the law the church has made itself the bulwark of American slavery, and the shield of American slave hunters. Let us "welcome infidelity, welcome atheism, welcome anything in preference to the gospel as preached by our Divines." Douglass attacks by name a number of prominent pastors who defended the Act. He concludes that the church is superlatively guilty, since the common sense of every man at all observant of the actual state of the case knows this truth: "There is no power out of the church that could sustain slavery an hour, if it were not sustained in it." What a difference between the attitude of the American church toward the anti-slavery movement and that occupied by the churches in England toward the movement in that country. There the question of emancipation is a highly religious question. It is demanded in the name of humanity and according to the law of the living God. An all out attack on the American church is a daring move by Frederick Douglass; he made himself the enemy of the churches, for they claimed, of course, to be upholding law and order.

In his peroration Douglass does find some hope. For the first time he explicitly invokes the Declaration of Independence, "the genius of American Institutions." It is at the head of the obvious tendencies of this age. "No nation can now shut itself up from the surrounding world, and trot round in the same old path of its fathers without interference. The time was when such could be done. . . . But change has now come over the affairs of mankind. Walled cities and empires have become unfashionable. The arm of commerce has borne away the gates of the strong city. Intelligence is penetrating the darkest corners of the globe. God speed the year of jubilee The wide world over."

It is plain that from the disposition of the material in an order where one part follows another that there is a logical structure to Douglass's oration. The arguments are vividly sketched rather than developed, and the figure, *paralepsis*, is used to justify not giving them a full development. What is more notable is the use of the *pathe*, which are not just sketched but are amply developed.

Pathos and Ethos

Fundamental to the effect of this speech is pity: pain at a destructive evil when it comes on those who do not deserve it. We feel it when we think that we could easily suffer in the same way as the objects of our pity. Identification with the sufferer is a necessary condition of pity. The slave in this oration does not deserve to be shut out from the independence ceremony; we are celebrating independence, but he is not independent. He "is engaged in all manner of enterprises common to other men, digging gold in California, capturing the whale in the Pacific, feeding sheep and cattle on the hillside, living, moving, acting, thinking, planning living in families as husbands, wives and children, and, above all, confessing and worshipping the Christian's God, and looking hopefully for life and immortality beyond the grave." We can see ourselves in his position: what would it be like for us to be always subject to sale, instant separation from our families, perhaps never to see them again? The slave dealer socializes with the buyers; he is "ever ready to drink, to treat, and to gamble. The fate of many a slave has depended upon the turn of a single card; and many a child has been snatched from the arms of its mother by bargains arranged in a state of brutal drunkenness."

We who are free and believe in virtue and family are those who can feel the injustice of undeserved disaster, particularly as we are not so close to the disaster ourselves as to be filled with dread (which drives out pity). The black person is the type of those pitiable; he is never at ease; if he has committed no crime, it hardly matters; whether he is honest and industrious or the opposite, it does not make him safe. He is subject to the whim of the master; what happens to him is not tied to merit; it usually comes undeserved. No good thing occurring to a slave is ever sure for more than a minute, so good fortune is hard for him to enjoy. The listeners' pity for the slave becomes a basis for anger, the pain that is felt at an unjustified debasement of ourselves or those near to us. Anger must be directed against persons; in this case, against the slave drovers, the legislators, and the clergy. Douglass visualizes anger against the practicing slave merchants: "I see clouds of dust raised on the highways of the South; I see the bleeding footsteps; I hear the doleful wail of fettered humanity on the way to the slave markets, where the victims are to be sold like horses, sheep, and swine, knocked off to the highest bidder. There I see the tenderest ties ruthlessly broken, to gratify the lust, caprice and rapacity of the buyers and sellers of men." By definition those we get angry with are those who devalue their victims, as when they treat those we identify with as horses or swine. We get especially angry when the signs of victims' suffering are brought before the eyes (and ears) as when the "fettered marchers' footsteps bleed," and we hear them wail. Being separated from friends and family is pitiable as when slaves are sold far away. If the debasement is public, as at a market, the victims' suffering provokes greater anger, and the injustice of it is greater because the targets of our anger are motivated only by lust, caprice, and rapacity.

Legislators became fully complicit in this debasement of the slave with the Fugitive Slave Act. They put the power of the United States behind the right to hold, hunt, and sell men, women, and children as slaves. They made the fugitive a bird for the sportsman's gun and make the "broad republican domain a hunting ground for men. Your lawmakers have commanded all good citizens to engage in this hellish sport." The law makes mercy to the fugitive a crime and pays judges to try them. Again, anger is justified because the legislators have debased those we now identify with, making them animals to be hunted by sportsmen and forbidding making them subject to acts of humanity and mercy. Yet, these legislators have no regrets; while they enforce this law, they celebrate a tyrant-killing, king-hating, people-loving, democratic, Christian America.

The clergy, too, are targets of anger. They are indifferent to what is happening to the slaves, so they also, in effect, debase them. "If the law abridged the right to sing psalms, to partake of the sacrament, or to engage in any of the ceremonies of religion, it would be smitten by the thunder of a thousand pulpits. A general shout would go up from the church demanding repeal, repeal, repeal!" The fact that the church of our country (with fractional exceptions) does not esteem "the Fugitive Slave Law as a declaration of war against religious liberty, implies that the church regards religion simply as a form of worship, an empty ceremony, and not a vital principle, requiring active benevolence, justice, love and good will toward man. It esteems sacrifice above mercy, psalm-singing above right doing." The religious leaders consider what is happening to the slaves insignificant; in their preoccupation with the forms of religion, they belittle real humans.

Lastly there is the role of shame in the address. Shame is a pain that is felt at doing bad things that bring a person into ill repute. It is obviously most felt by people who have pretensions to virtue, like you Americans, who are tyrant-killing, king-hating, people-loving Christians. You are ready to carry democracy to all the countries of the world, so long as it does not imply freedom for the slave. Even your inferiors, like the savages or the subjects of Kings and tyrants are not guilty of practices more shocking and bloody than are the people of these United States at this very hour. Those who stand outside the system, like God and the crushed and bleeding slave, cannot help but denounce this shamefulness, "in the name of humanity which is outraged, in the name of liberty which is fettered, in the name of the constitution and the Bible, which are disregarded and trampled upon." Acts of cruelty, such as supporting the slave trade are particularly shameful, taking advantage of weakness, playing the coward in the face of the slave merchant, enacting laws that protect his shameful dealing.

Frederick Douglass's use of pathos is supplemented by his peculiar ethos. He lived through slavery: who is to tell him that his view of suffering by the slaves is not accurate? This is especially true of the section on the slave market:

> To me the American slave trade is a terrible reality. When a child, my soul was often pierced with a sense of its horrors. I lived on Philpot Street, Fell's Point, Baltimore, and have watched from the wharves the slave ships in the Basin, anchored from shore, with their cargoes of human flesh, waiting for favorable winds to waft them down the Chesapeake.
>
> The flesh-mongers gather up their victims by dozens and drive them chained to the general depot in Baltimore. When a sufficient number have been collected here, a ship is chartered for the purpose of conveying the forlorn crew to Mobile or to New Orleans.
>
> In the deep darkness of midnight, I have been often aroused by the dead heavy footsteps and the piteous cries of the chained gangs that passed our door. The anguish of my boyhood heart was intense; and I was often consoled, when speaking to my mistress in the morning, to hear her say that the custom was very wicked; that she hated to hear the rattle of the chains and the heart rending cries. I was glad to find one who sympathized with me in my horror.

This kind of eyewitness account, buttressed by the reluctant testimony of the slave mistress herself, is hard to deny. The emotions of pity, shame, and anger, are fully exploited in these ways.

Douglass does not criticize the Revolution; rather, he identifies with the ideals of the founding fathers. Washington could not die until he had broken the chains of his slaves. The fathers in their admiration of liberty lost sight of all other interests. They believed in order, but not the order of tyranny. The Constitution they framed is a "GLORIOUS LIBERTY DOCUMENT." Douglass also picks up considerable credibility from his familiarity with the Bible. Asking him to praise the Fourth of July is like the Hebrews being asked to sing a song of Zion after having been removed to a foreign land (Psalm 137: 1–6). The preachers who justify the fugitive slave law are like the scribes and Pharisees "who pay tithe of mint, anise and cumin" while ignoring the weightier matters of the law, judgment, mercy, and faith (Matthew, 23:23).

Theirs is a religion for oppressors, tyrants, man-stealers and thugs, not that "pure and un-defiled religion" which is from above, and which is "first pure, then peaceable, easy to be en-treated, full of mercy and good fruits, without partiality and without hypocrisy" (James 1:27). And in a striking *apostrophe* the American church might well be addressed in the language of the prophet Isaiah, "Yea! When ye make many prayers, I will not hear. YOUR HANDS ARE FULL OF BLOOD; cease to do evil; learn to do good" (Isaiah 1:13–17).

Douglass even identifies his position with the Constitution. It is the fundamental law. It is a slander on the memory of the Fathers to believe that it guarantees slavery. In his per-oration Douglass identifies his views with progress: "intelligence is penetrating the darkest corners of the globe . . . oceans no longer divide, but link nations together." All the good things of the Bible and history and those that are coming to us, he identifies with his cause when building ethos.

Rhetorical Style

A traditional rhetorician would describe the language of this address as grand style. The emo-tional tone is enhanced by a fullness in the development of relatively simple themes. Here is a series of *parallel* phrases in which Douglass develops the statement that the 4th of July is a day which reveals to the slave, more than all other days, the gross injustice and cruelty to which he is the constant victim.

> To him, your celebration is a sham; your boasted liberty an unholy license; your national greatness swelling vanity; your shouts of liberty and equality hollow mockery; your prayers and hymns, your sermons and thanksgivings, with all your religious parade and solemnity are to him mere bombast, fraud, deception, impiety and hypocrisy—a thin veil to cover up crimes which would disgrace a nation's savages. There is not a nation on the earth guilty of practices more shocking and bloody than are the people of these United States at this very hour.

One can easily point to the rhetorical hyperbole of this series—could even an intelligent slave think that all the celebration is utterly false, that there is no pious feeling to the hymns and sermons nor anything but self deception to the feeling of national pride? Could the edu-cated black man not have known of the shocking and bloody practices of the French troops in the Napoleonic wars or the Australia of the prison ships? We understand, of course, that this flamboyance is part of the show, and while there's more than a grain of truth to it, there's also a grain of salt.

It is justified because it is told from the point of view of the slave, though certainly not in the language of the slave. There is the exploitation of *anaphora*, the repetition of the same word or phrase at the beginning of each clause, along with the hint of a rhyme in vanity, mockery, hypocrisy, and bloody—just enough there to constitute *epistrophe*, the repetition of the same phrase at the end of each clause. More than that, however, how many words does it take to say that much of the pageantry on the 4th is hypocritical, something that we all have occasionally felt at the end of an overlong ceremony? The excess of near synonymy is there to build the rhythm into a solemn march, abruptly broken by the conclusion of that last sentence with the finality of "at this very hour."

One of the characteristics of grand style is the freedom in the use of rhetorical figures of speech. These figures, such as anaphora and epistrophe, are useful in lectures and expositions, but figures of thought such as hyperbole and paralepsis are the language of feeling. Rhetorical questions are of this sort, particularly when used in a sequence that builds, like this one:

> Would you have me argue that man is entitled to liberty? That he is the rightful owner of his own body? Must I argue the wrongfulness of slavery? Is that a question for Republicans? Is it to be settled by the rules of logic and argumentation, as a matter beset with great difficulty, involving a doubtful application of the principle of justice, hard to be understood?

This sequence in particular is an example of how a series of rhetorical questions get a listener into the mindset of yea or nea-saying.

Besides rhetorical questions there is the use of paralepsis as principle for structuring the section refuting the imagined justifications of slavery. By claiming not to refute these justifications he belittles them almost out of existence. Taken all in all, the style of this speech is exciting, as befits this kind of occasion.

Evaluation

If we take the purpose of this speech to be vituperation, bringing people into a state of wrath and fury at the institution of slavery, a greater success at using the resources of the traditional perspective could hardly be imagined. It is a real case of strategic employment of all the available means of persuasion. As an educational tool, to be sure, it falls short. The view of slavery is without depth or nuance. All that is presented are chains, beatings, and moanings. It is stereotyped; it is the propagandist's eye view of the institution. Douglass's purpose, however, was *arousal*, not *education*. One would like to think that he could have accomplished both purposes, but that is not what he set out to do.

It seems to have been almost a total failure in convincing the Garrisonians. Though Douglass quoted Garrison favorably three times and closed with a complete rendition of one of his anti-slavery poems, they were not mollified; they continued to hold the view that the Constitution must be re-written and the union reestablished without the South.

The many reprintings of this famous address indicate the extent to which it has intrigued readers over the years. For us it is a window onto a long lost stage dominated by men whose states of feeling are far different from ours. But it fully exploits the precepts of traditional rhetoric.

PERSONAL COMMENTS ON THE ESSAY

This essay could have taken forms different than that written above. For example, I decided to make the essay more of a journey through the stages of traditional criticism than a regular style academic paper. I did this because I thought it would make traditional criticism more accessible for those new to criticism to read. I wanted a bit more of a conversation and less of the usual academic paper. Traditional style criticism is not lacking in sophistication, so a more accessible journey through the stages seemed better than putting up a bunch of lists for you to follow.

It is not unusual for those drawn to traditional criticism to also be drawn to history. I am very certain this shows in many of the examples I have used in this essay. This reflects my personal interests in American political history, as does my choice for a rhetorical artifact to analyze for my essay. Frederick Douglass's 5th of July oration was one of hundreds of such orations I could have chosen to study. I decided upon this one since it is the most famous, and is most likely to be familiar to you; moreover, I simply like this speech. My decision to use this particular speech was also influenced by my liking for Douglass's orations in general. The efforts of almost any speaker could have been analyzed, however.

POTENTIALS AND PITFALLS

I am certain that you noticed in the above examples for speakers that I used a contemporary speaker. This represents both a potential and pitfall of traditional style criticism. Far too often those teaching traditional style criticism give the impression that it is only useful for explicating historical texts. Nothing could be further from the truth. Traditional criticism will serve you well even if you decide to look at a contemporary speaker such as President Obama, President Bush, James Dobson, or Dr. Laura. The choice of rhetorical artifact is up to you. What differentiates traditional style criticism from the other critical perspectives to which you will be exposed has to do with the type of information that is generated.

Another potential pitfall involves formulaic criticism—also known as cookie-cutter criticism. This is often the result if one simply uses theory as a checklist, looking for instances of each and every concept covered, and then writing it down to share. This is simply not criticism. Yes, there is some of this type of criticism written by those using a traditional perspective; it has been, after all, practiced longer than any other perspective covered in this book. Be that as it may, it is also a common pitfall associated with numerous critical perspectives. For example, genre criticism has often come under just such a criticism. Even so, we have examples of genre criticism approaching the sublime, just as we do with traditional criticism. The possibility for formulaic criticism rests more with the critic than with the perspective used. To avoid formulaic criticism you need to learn as much about the perspective you intend to use as possible. A good place to start is with the Top Picks I list below. There you will find excellent examples of criticism that is reflexive, not stale.

TRADITIONAL CRITICISM TOP PICKS

Cooper, Lane. *The Rhetoric of Aristotle, an expanded translation with supplementary examples for students of composition and public speaking* (New York, London: D. Appleton and Company, 1932). The gold standard translation for this text. It went unchallenged for decades until Kennedy's book was published in 1991. Either one will work well. See George A. Kennedy, *Aristotle on Rhetoric: A Theory of Civic Discourse* (New York: Oxford University Press, 1991).

Hitchcock, Orville A. "Jonathan Edwards." In *A History and Criticism of American Public Address*, William Norwood Brigance, editor (New York City: McGraw-Hill Book Company, Inc., 1943): 213–237. The essay represents a classical application of traditional criticism.

Hochmuth [Nichols], Marie Kathryn. "The Criticism of Rhetoric." In *A History and Criticism of American Public Address*, vol. 3, Marie Kathryn Hochmuth, ed. (New York City: Russell & Russell, 1954). A solid definition of rhetoric as conceived during the reputed heyday of Traditional criticism. The essay compliments well a functional approach to communication studies and rhetorical criticism.

Howell, Wilbur Samuel and Hoyt Hopewell Hudson. "Daniel Webster." In *History and Criticism of American Public Address.*, vol. 2. William Norwood Brigance, ed. (New York City: McGraw Hill

Book Company, Inc., 1943). An excellent essay that shows the possibilities of Traditional Criticism when it moves beyond analysis of a single speech and occasion. Puts the lie to the assertion that Traditional Criticism is only concerned with single speeches and immediate effects.

Thonssen, Lester, A. Craig Baird, and Waldo W. Braden. *Speech Criticism*, 2nd ed. (New York: The Ronald Press Company, 1970). You may well find a copy of this once common text in your school's library. In it you will find detailed explanations of the concepts outlined in the chapter above.

The following is a short selection of more contemporary essays that draw upon the traditional perspective in greater or lesser degrees. They show the dynmic possibilities for using the perspective today.

Gross, Alan G. "Renewing Aristotelian Theory: The Cold Fusion Controversy as a Test Case." *Quarterly Journal of Speech* 81 (1995): 48–62.

Henry, David. "The Rhetorical Dynamics of Mario Cuomo's 1984 Keynote Address: Situation, Speaker, Metaphor." *Southern Speech Communication Journal* 53 (1988): 105–120.

Hogan, J. Micheal and L. Glen Williams, "Defining 'the Enemy' in Revolutionary America: From the Rhetoric of Protest to the Rhetoric of War," *Southern Communication Journal* (Summer 1996): 277–289.

Holcomb, Chris. "'Anyone Can Be President': Figures of Speech, Cultural Forms, and Performance." *Rhetoric Society Quarterly* 37.1 (2007): 71–96.

Ritter, Kurt and David Henry. *Ronald Reagan, the Great Communicator* (Westport, CT: Greenwood Press, 1992).

Zagacki, Kenneth. "Eisenhower and the Rhetoric of Postwar Korea." *Southern Communication Journal* (Spring 1995): 233–246.

NOTES

1. Traditional critisim is often called Neo-Aristotelian criticism.

2. See, Hoyt Hopewell Hudson, "De Quincy on Rhetoric and Public Speaking," in *Studies in Rhetoric and Public Speaking in Honor of James Albert Winans by Pupils and Colleagues*, ed. A. M. Drummond (New York: The Century Co., 1925), 133–152; and Hoyt Hopewell Hudson, "The Field of Rhetoric," *Quarterly Journal of Speech Education* 9.2 (1923): 167–180.

3. *Rhetoric,* I 3, 1358a 37–1358b 1.

4. Herbert Wichelns is routinely given credit for broadening the communication discipline's rhetorical horizons to include written as well as oral discourse in his 1925 essay, the "Literary Criticism of Oratory." However, in "Hoyt Hopewell Hudson's Nuclear Rhetoric," Jim A. Kuypers convincingly argues that Hudson is deserving of this credit. Kuypers cites Hudson's 1921 essay, "Can we Modernize the Study of Invention?" where Hudson implied the use of topics for "speech or argument." The "Field of Rhetoric" contains more explicit definitions. In this essay Hudson fully defined the term rhetoric, which included the study of written as well as oral discourse. Because rhetoric is the "faculty of finding, in any subject, all the available means of persuasion," the rhetorician is "a sort of diagnostician and leaves it to others to be the practitioners; the rhetorician is the strategist of persuasion, and other men execute his plans and do the fighting. In practice, however, and in any study of the subject, this distinction can hardly be maintained, since the person who determines the available means of persuasion . . . must also be, in most cases, the one to apply those means in persuasive speech and writing." See Herbert A. Wichelns, "The Literary Criticism of Oratory" in *Studies in Rhetoric and Public Speaking in Honor of James Albert Winans by Pupils and Colleagues*, ed. A. M. Drummond (New York: The Century Co., 1925), 209; Hoyt Hopewell Hudson, "Can We Modernize the Theory of Invention?" *Quarterly Journal of Speech Education* 7.4 (1921): 326; Hoyt Hopewell Hudson, "The Field of Rhetoric," *Quarterly Journal of Speech Education* 9.2 (1923): 169–170; Jim A. Kuypers, "Hoyt Hopewell Hudson's Nuclear Rhetoric" in *Twentieth-Century Roots of Rhetorical Criticism*, eds. Jim A. Kuypers and Andrew King (Westport, CT: Praeger, 2001), 701–702.

5. *Rhetoric*, I iii, 1358a 3–4.

6. William J. Clinton, "Address to Nation, August 17, 1998."

7. Garry Wills, *Lincoln at Gettysburg: The Words That Remade America* (Touchstone Books, 1993).

8. *Rhetoric*, II 18, 15-17.

9. *Rhetoric*, II 2-12.

10. Thomas Eichler, "Rice Downplays Significance of Iraqi Uranium Claim," http://www.usinfo .state.gov. July 13, 2003.

11. Some have called such utterances part of an "administrative text." For a fuller explanation see Jim A. Kuypers, Marilyn J. Young, and Michael K. Launer, "Of Mighty Mice and Meek Men: Contextual Reconstruction of the Shootdown of Iran Air 655," *Southern Communication Journal* 59.4 (1994): 294-306; and Jim A. Kuypers, *Presidential Crisis Rhetoric and the Press in a Post Cold War World* (Westport, CT: Praeger, 1997), 3-8.

12. Cadmon Records, TC 1264.

13. Elizabeth Shogren, "Clinton, In Historic Speech, Urges Acceptance of Gays," *Los Angeles Times* (November 9, 1997): A20; James Bennet, "Clinton is Greeted Warmly as He Speaks to Gay Group," *The New York Times* (November 9, 1997): A30.

14. John F. Wilson and Carroll C. Arnold, *Public Speaking as a Liberal Art*, 5th ed. (Boston: Allyn and Bacon, 1983), 83–88.

15. Nixon, November 3, 1969.

16. Lloyd L. Bitzer, "Aristotle's Enthymeme Revisited," (1959) *Quarterly Journal of Speech*, 45 (1959): 408.

17. I wish in no way to minimize the work of the Christian Childrens Fund. This is an outstanding charity. See http://www.christianchildrensfund.org/ for details.

18. Jane Blankenship and Hermann G. Stelzner, eds. *Rhetoric and Communication: Studies in the University of Illinois Tradition* (Urbana: University of Illinois Press, 1976).

19. H. L. Mencken disagrees with Lincoln's assessment: "The Gettysburg speech was at once the shortest and the most famous oration in American history. Put beside it, all the whoopings of the Websters, Sumners and Everetts seem gaudy and silly. It is eloquence brought to a pellucid and almost gem-like perfection, the highest emotion reduced to a few poetical phrases. Lincoln himself never even remotely approached it. It is genuinely stupendous. But let us not forget that it is poetry, not logic; beauty, not sense. Think of the argument in it. Put it into the cold words of everyday. The doctrine is simply this: that the Union soldiers who died at Gettysburg sacrificed their lives to the cause of self-determination that government of the people, by the people, for the people, should not perish from the earth. It is difficult to imagine anything more untrue. The Union soldiers in the battle actually fought against self-determination; it was the Confederates who fought for the right of their people to govern themselves." H. L. Mencken, *A Mencken Chrestomathy* (New York: Vintage Books, 1949), 222–223.

20. Thomas Paine, 1776 .

21. *Rhetoric*, I 1, 1355b, 10–16.

22. In 2008 dollars that is somewhere between $3.00 and $5.00.

23. Gerald Fulkerson, "Exile as Emergence: Frederick Douglass in Great Britain, 1845–1847," *Quarterly Journal of Speech* 60 (February 1974): 69–82.

24. Ronald F. Reid, *American Rhetorical Discourse* 2nd ed. (Prospect Heights, IL: Waveland Press, 1995).

25. Wills, *Lincoln at Gettysburg*.

26. (Douglass to Gerritt Smith, July 7, 1852 quoted in Blassingame, 1982).

27. Paralepsis is one of over 100 rhetorical figures, stylistic devices used by speakers to acheive a certain effect. In this particular instance, a paralepsis emphasizes something either by mentioning it cursorily or by neglecting to mention it altogether.

6

Close Textual Analysis: Approaches and Applications

Stephen Howard Browne

Close Textual Analysis (CTA) refers to an interpretive practice, the aim of which is to explain how texts operate to produce meaning, effect persuasion, and activate convictions in public contexts. To this end CTA attends in detail to the interplay of ideas, images, and arguments as they unfold within the spatial and temporal economy of the text. The rewards of such an approach may be glimpsed, for example, if we think of Martin Luther King's masterful "I Have a Dream" speech of 1963. Here, following the address from its first words, deliberate and restrained, we would note the mounting intensity, the shape and direction of its metaphors, and follow the movement of the text to its thunderous conclusion. The general conviction underlying such an approach is that rhetorical texts are active, dynamic, and complex; explaining how they work accordingly requires a keen sensitivity to the play of language itself.

Practitioners of CTA generally view their art less as a method per se than as a disciplined search for the linguistic particulars that eventually comprise the whole of a given rhetorical performance.[1] Students and scholars working in this vein are thus particularly attuned to the nuances, echoes, and subtle gestures that exist in the object of their study. It thus requires a sensibility cultivated by broad reading across the humanities, and asks that we bring to the task a literary critic's sharp eye for textual detail. A cultivated and disciplined engagement with history, literature, and philosophy will go a long way toward preparing the rhetorical critic for such work. Above all, however, a basic love of the human language, in all its glories and all its messiness, is requisite.

Although CTA may be put to work across a broad range of genres—critics have used it to better understand orations, films, visual rhetoric, pamphlets, and poetry—one key premise drives virtually all such analysis. This premise holds that the rhetorical force of a text can never be presumed as given or fixed; rather, its rhetorical force is the result of a complex set of symbolic forces set into play at the moment of utterance. The critic working from this perspective accordingly seeks to identify and account for this process. In the following pages, we will explore the main principles guiding the practice of CTA; place this approach within certain historical and disciplinary contexts; consider a brief case study; and note several lines of argument raised by critics of CTA. We turn first to four principles upon which the practice of CTA rests.

Principle 1: Rhetorical Texts are Sites of Symbolic Action

What does this "mean"? By way of an answer, it will help here and throughout this chapter to have beside you a copy of Barack Obama's Philadelphia speech of March, 2008.[2] As you look it over and perhaps recall reading or viewing it previously, you might ask one of two questions: either "what does this speech mean?" or "what is it doing?" The first question encourages us to think of texts as containers of ready-made semantic units that may be extracted from the text as needed. Put another way, the speech itself may be said to offer a guide for answering the question "what is this text about"? "Well," you might reply, scanning through the paragraphs, "it means just what it says; let me quote a few lines and you'll get the gist of the matter." In one sense, of course, this is a perfectly reasonable response. It does not, however, offer a very close look at how the speech functions as a text, or more specifically, as a rhetorical text. Why? Because the response fails to take into account the symbolic action, or the language-in-motion that defines the dynamics of the rhetorical performance. Close textual critics thus tend to view such texts as verbs, so to speak, *and to ask not what a text means but what it does*. If you happened to see the speech on television or YouTube, or if you have now read it for the first time, pause for a moment and ask yourself: "what does this text do?"

Once this question is posed at the outset, a world of interpretive possibilities opens into view. Imagine for a moment the nearly infinite ways in which a text may be said to act. It may: disclose or camouflage, seduce, exalt, debase, deface, deflect, direct, invite, distance, defer, deny, destroy, create, recreate, form, deform, reform, silence, provoke, tickle, numb, transcend, descend, portend, threaten, demur, announce, renounce, or pronounce. Texts may inaugurate, promise, plead, deny, decry, dissemble, lie, waffle, tempt, dissuade, disabuse, or deter. They may call out, call for, call on, call in, call to, or call a cab. The point is surely evident by now, but however basic the insight, such a view of textual action attunes us to the manifold ways in which we can understand what, precisely, is rhetorical about a given text: the decisive and distinctive manner in which it acts in the world.

Principle 2: Form and Content Cannot be Divorced

If CTA is particularly alive to the active nature of rhetorical texts, it is similarly sensitive to the interplay of form and content shaping that action. Close textual critics accordingly seek to correct a lingering tendency, dating well back into antiquity, to view properties of form—images, tropes, the "style" of a given rhetorical production—as somehow distinct from the essential content of its message. In its most reductive expression, this tendency suggests that we invent something to say—what it is we really want to get across to our auditors or readers—and then trick out the message with appealing drapery, the better to arrest attention or gratify the aesthetic appetite of our audience. This view of style is not uncontested, however, and theorists of language since the early twentieth century have taught us that such a view is illusory, and that if we are to make plausible sense of how rhetoric works, we need to reunite what has been put asunder. Form and content belong together. To invoke King's address again, consider how integral his use of figures and other imagery is to the meaning of his message. At a minimum, they may be said to arrest attention, establish pace and meter, and to make concrete otherwise abstract principles of justice and redemption.

Our second principle seems to be mere common sense, but in fact presents us with difficult issues from the outset. For example: while it is the case that form and content cannot be separated, they are not the same thing. And if form and content are not the same, then how are they different from one another? In order to answer that question, we need a working definition of each. Here, too, we need to acknowledge that both terms are notoriously slippery and the objects of considerable academic debate. For the purposes of this chapter, let us take "form" to refer to those linguistic resources that give conspicuous structure to otherwise abstract formulations. To play with this definition for a moment, note how abstract it is. It needs form! So let's put it another way, with apologies to William Butler Yeats: "form is to content as the dancer is to the dance." Here the abstract is given heightened intelligibility by embodying itself in a concrete and dynamic image. Form and content need each other. By extension, we may take content to refer to that dimension of a message reducible to the level of a proposition. Let us turn to the Obama text again for an example of how this principle plays out in practice:

> I can no more disown him [Wright] than I can disown the black community. I can no more disown him than I can disown my white grandmother—a woman who helped raise me, a woman who sacrificed again and again for me, a woman who loves me as much as she loves anything in this world, but a woman who once confessed her fear of black men who passed by her on the street, and who on more than one occasion has uttered racial or ethnic stereotypes that made me cringe.

Now, what can we say about the interplay of form and content in this passage? With respect to its content, we can ask: "what is the basic proposition here?" We might answer: "The fact that Reverend Wright has his faults, like all of us, is insufficient grounds for disowning him." To leave it at this, however, is to miss the rhetorical force imported to the proposition by virtue of the form in which it is expressed. We would want also to note, for example, the parallel constructions initiating the first several lines: "I can no more disown him . . . I can no more disown him." Not only do they establish the metrical cadence of the passage, but rather ingeniously invoke the Obama campaign's mantra of personal empowerment. We observe, too, how the proposition is inscribed into a narrative account of the candidate's grandmother, who comes to represent a kind of universal type—human, warts and all—with whom we can identify and whose image is thereby made to soften the specter of Reverend Wright. Form and content in this way are seen to sponsor each other.

Principle 3: Text Informs Context, and Vice Versa

The emphatic emphasis CTA places on the text as such invites the suspicion that we may have here too much of a good thing. That is, does it not stand to reason that the more closely we look at an "object," the further we remove ourselves from the context in which that object appears? And does this not bracket out information essential for understanding such texts, especially in their rhetorical aspect? We will attend to this question in greater detail later; here it is sufficient to stress that if indeed contextual considerations are made to drop by the wayside, then of course we have a real problem. The good news is that nothing of the kind is entailed from the practice of CTA. On the contrary, it is inconceivable that a satisfactory interpretation of rhetorical texts is possible without taking all relevant features of context into consideration.

Still, we are left with the question as to how a given text is best attuned to its context. Once again, the answer is contingent upon a matter of definition: what, after all, is a "context"? Is it the immediate exigence to which the text responds? Certainly that plays a part, but what about those rhetorical performances which seems less beholden to such pressing forces—meditations, say, in the manner of Ralph Waldo Emerson or Elizabeth Cady Stanton? And in what sense can we say that contexts are bound by fixed conceptions of space and time? The Declaration of Independence, for example, continues to be expropriated for all manner of rhetorical purposes, not only in the US, but in revolutionary Viet Nam, Poland, and the nations of South

America. At a minimum, then, we need to adapt a very elastic sense of what qualifies as relevant context, make a sound case for stipulating one rather than another, and set about the task of informing our textual analysis with systematic reference to its semantic environment.

One particularly useful approach to this interpretive work is to acknowledge that while each text is distinctive on its own terms, it yet partakes in and deploys an indefinite range of other texts and discursive modalities. Another way of thinking about this phenomenon is to view contexts as themselves texts of a kind, from which a speaker or writer borrows on an as-needed basis. For a brief example of how this works rhetorically, let us turn again to the Philadelphia speech. Clearly we have an immediate exigence: popular disapproval of comments made by Obama's minister, thought to have been racially charged and in violation of basic norms of civil and political discourse. The speech is self-evidently an effort to allay such anxieties as the Reverend Wright stirred up. But there is more to the matter than that, because part of the text's rhetorical achievement is to resituate, or recreate, another and more compelling context in which the speech itself hopes to be understood. For evidence of this process, we turn, as always, to the text itself. What other texts or discursive modes does the speaker import into his own speech? A quick glance gives us the answer:

U.S. Constitution
Declaration of Independence
Hebrew Bible/Old Testament/New Testament
Personal narrative
Sermon
Testimony
Memoir
Novel
Supreme Court decision
Anecdote

The point is clear: texts work rhetorically by responding to exigencies, yes, but they work as well by reconstituting their own interpretive contexts. On reflection, we can see how this process moves both ways: contexts inform texts, and texts inform contexts. Thus it is not unrealistic to predict that Obama's speech will itself enter into the vast storehouse of rhetorical resources and become available to ensuing speaker as they seek to effect change in the world. The speech, that is, emerges from one context, realigns itself and eventually becomes part of an even greater context.

Principle 4: Rhetorical Texts Exhibit Artistic Density

Our fourth principle may best be considered an extension and summary of the foregoing discussion. Like the others, it seems perhaps uncontroversial, even obvious. In fact, however, the principle of artistic density cuts to the heart of CTA. How does it do this, and why does it matter? To get at these questions we need to step back for a moment and see where CTA came from, the company it keeps, and how it distinguishes itself from other reading practices.

The discipline we now associate with communication departments in the U.S. originated in large measure by breaking away from the academic study of English. The major argument justifying this new development was that "speech communication" attended to related but significantly different phenomena: not literature as such, but the products of human beings moved to express themselves to persuasive ends in largely oral and public contexts. This interest could of course claim a heritage dating well into western antiquity, but had gradually been subsumed under the auspices of literary study. Early twentieth-century champions of the revitalized discipline thus sought to distinguish their work from that of literary critics, who were concerned to explain aesthetic properties of poems, novels, plays and the like. Rhetorical critics, on the other hand, laid claim to those speech activities that were self-evidently more instrumental, time-bound, and broadly political in character: orations, parliamentary debates, and sermons, for example. As the discipline grew and flourished throughout the century, this emphasis on the pragmatics of human communication tended to bracket out, and sometimes repudiate altogether, the aesthetic dimensions of rhetorical practice.[3]

Why this apparent indifference or even hostility to the aesthetic? For many, the answer was programmatic: the very identity of our discipline required that we sustain the differences separating rhetorical studies from literary criticism. For others, it had to do with certain political investments in situating rhetorical acts within their material and ideological milieu. To preoccupy one's self with aesthetic concerns was to forget or elide the dynamics of power that superintend all rhetorical productions.

Now, there are legitimate reasons for such anxieties, but students of CTA tend to reject the premises upon which they are based. Above all, such reasoning presupposes that we cannot in principle have it both ways, and that a zero-sum game seems to be in play when we consider either the rhetorical or the aesthetic. That is, to engage the one is to discount the other. On reflection, however, we must ask: is this really the case? Can we not ask after the ways in which the aesthetic can be put to rhetorical purposes? Indeed we can, if only by simply reminding ourselves that rhetoric is, after all, an art, and that such an art may be glimpsed by attending to techniques of production. Surely it affects no damage on King's "I Have a Dream" oration to acknowledge its artistic achievement; more positively, a full accounting of that achievement goes a long way toward explaining its enduring rhetorical legacy. And this, in the end, may be taken as the basic rationale for CTA: by submitting texts to close inspection, we are able to see better the ways in which rhetoric works at its most fundamental levels of operation. Put another way, it is difficult to see how we can understand the whole of King's speech or any other text without attending to its parts. Ultimately, we arrive at the technical process through which that whole is rendered coherent and compelling.

Taken together, our four principles should prepare us for a sensitive and instructive reading of Obama's Philadelphia speech. We will turn to the text shortly, but here might be a place to indicate what CTA is not. This will help clear further misconceptions from our path, and free us from the weight of unwanted and unwarranted concerns. We have already alluded to several of these: skilled textual critics do not turn a blind eye to context; do not reduce the "meaning" of texts to the propositions advanced by the text's author; do not entertain the aesthetics of the text in the manner of "art for art's sake." In addition, it is worth stressing that CTA, for all its attention to the "how" of textual production, does not satisfy itself with a mere naming and listing of such techniques. The aim rather is to provide a comprehensive account of how the parts cohere into a whole greater than the sum of those parts. Further, CTA is clearly more than an advance version of textual appreciation; on the contrary, it arms the critic with material with which to render judgment as to efficacy, ethics, success, and failure. Important also is the position that CTA is not a "method" as such, if we mean by that term a specific how-to program for textual analysis. This is not to imply that it is simply impressionistic. It is rather to insist upon a rigorous and evidence-bound explication that nevertheless leaves ample room for the play of critical insight and authorial voice. Finally, it is useful to remind ourselves again that CTA involves a great deal more than paraphrasing what is expressed in the text; it seeks rather to ask, as we did with reference to our first principle, "what is this text doing?"

CRITICAL ESSAY

Now let us turn to our case-in-point. In the following, I offer one interpretation of Barack Obama's March 18, 2008 speech in Philadelphia. The analysis is designed as an exercise in CTA, and aims to illustrate several—certainly not all—features of this approach. Among the questions I ask of this text: from what family of rhetorical acts does it take inspiration? That is, can we identify one or more generic antecedents that seem to guide the speaker's treatment of his theme? We are then led to ask what this theme is, and how it superintends the symbolic action of the text as it unfolds. We want to ask further about the internal structure of this move-ment, and how this structure assists in the production of the speaker's message. Similarly, what kinds of images, metaphors, and other dimensions of style animate Obama's arguments and give them conspicuous form? Mindful, too, of contextual forces at play in the text, we will need to identify both the immediate exigence to which the speech responds, and the ways in which it seeks to transform the contexts in which it asks to be interpreted. A number of other questions germane to be asked and answered, of course, and no pretense is made here to a final or even authoritative exposition of the text. Far from it, I encourage the reader to contest, elaborate, or otherwise engage this particular rendering. The presumptive payoff is a deeper understanding of how texts work to induce conviction and impel audiences to action.

Analysis of the Text

The unprecedented nature of Obama's campaign for the Oval Office all but ensured the most intense kind of public and media scrutiny. The first African American making a serious bid for the office, running against the female with realistic chances for nomination, taking place in a time of war on two fronts, a faltering economy, and widespread concern over the nation's capacity to deliver health care to its own citizens. Within such a heated environment, partisan supporters can be almost as dangerous as the official opposition, as Obama, Clinton, and Mc-Cain were each to discover from their respective camps. No supporter raised as great a fire-storm, however, as the Reverend Jeremiah Wright, pastor of Chicago's Trinity United Church of Christ and longtime spiritual guide to the Illinois senator. The Reverend was known for ad-dressing his congregation in language of exceptional intensity, color, and, sometimes, provoca-tion. One such sermon, in which he expressed his disappointment with US race relations with the recurrent phrase "Goddamn America," was captured on video, frequently replayed across a variety of media, and was very soon the object of widespread condemnation.

All campaigns run into stumbling blocks, of course, and although some are undone by such episodes, most manage to survive and push on to their fated ends. But for many this was a different matter. At stake was not just the candidate's affiliation with the intemperate pas-tor, but the persistent questions haunting the nation's past and present race relations. Senator Obama had offered the prospect—however idealized—of a "post-race" America, in which an African American might run for the highest office in the land and be judged, in the words of Martin Luther King, "not by the color of his skin but by the content of his character." Now this promised appeared to be on the verge of collapse. Obama and Clinton were still neck and neck in the polls, conservative talk show hosts were banging their drums of disapproval, and it soon became obvious that the candidate had to say something. On the morning of March 18, before a nationally televised audience, Senator Barack Obama stepped to the podium across the street from Philadelphia's famed Constitutional Hall and delivered, to that point, the most important speech of his life.

The situation was thus novel in many respects, but that does not mean that the speaker was bereft of resources. On close reading, we discover that, consciously or not, he drew on a rich and enduring rhetorical genre known as the "jeremiad."[4] The term takes as its referent the imposing figure of the prophet Jeremiah in the Torah and Christian New Testament. For thousands of years, the prophet has served as a model for a particular type of rhetoric, marked by lamentation over the fallen state of a chosen people, the dangers of failing the terms of a sacred covenant, and the urgent need to restore one's self and one's community into a proper relationship with God and the world. It is not a rigid model, and had been put to different uses in different ways throughout the history of the genre. But its key components—covenant, violation, and atonement—have remained relatively stable over time. On review of Obama's text we see that there is no need to impose this model; the speech rather gives evidence of this tradition at every step. We may then allow the text to teach us, so to speak, how to understand its rhetorical task by taking up its own cues. To this end, the following analysis is organized according to each of the three functions noted above.

The very first words out of the speaker's mouth alert us to the centrality of promise to American collective identity: "We the people, in order to form a more perfect union." By thus invoking the inaugural lines of the U.S. Constitution, Obama reminds his audience that they, like their forebears, are bound together in a civically-sacred trust. That document announced to the world the arrival a unique moment in the world, when plain white men—not yet blacks, Native Americans, or women—entered into an "improbable experiment in democracy." We are hence called to be mindful that the ideal of perfection is just that—an ideal—and more over an ideal which remains to be fully met. But the very notion that a nation could be founded under the promise to nevertheless keep striving toward such a goal remains a fact of striking historical significance, and it gives shape and direction to all that follows.

One of the hallmarks of early colonial jeremiads was their belief that the new immigrants were a select people who had endured great hardship to enter upon a "journey into the wilderness." The scriptural resonance to the Israelite exodus from slavery into freedom is unmistakable, and underscores the sense that Americans were embarked upon a journey of their own. John Winthrop's sermon on board the *Arbella* perfectly captures this sense of simultaneous righteousness and anxiety that was to mark American exceptionalism for centuries to come. "For we must consider that we shall be as a city upon a hill. The eyes of all people are upon us, so that if we shall deal falsely with our God in his work we have undertaken, and so cause him to withdraw his present help from us, we shall be made a story and a by-word through the world."[5] Winthrop understood that the success of that journey was very much a matter of literally keeping the faith, of staying on the right path. In context, of course, Obama's appeal to this imagery is secular and civic, but the rhetorical work it affects is analogous. And where the Pilgrims were severely reminded of their departures from the path, their failure to keep the covenant, so America needs its own reminder. Here was a nation blessed by freedom, bounty, and democratic government, but whose promise to form a more perfect union was stained by the "original sin of slavery, a question that divided the colonies and brought the convention to a stalemate until the founders chose to allow the slave trade to continue for at least twenty more years, and to leave any final resolution to future generations."

Now we see the first instance of a structural dynamic that will direct the course of the speech generally. Put simply, it works by first introducing a positive—in this case, America's promise to work toward an ideal. Here we see the concept of *covenant* at work. Obama then asserts a negative example (slavery) of how that promise has been broken—hence the *violation* of that covenant. The former assumes expression in the celebratory or affirmative mode—hence the location of Obama's address beside Constitution Hall in Philadelphia's historic section. The latter gets articulated in the form of accusation or lament—hence the speaker's insistence on acknowledging those moments when American's have failed their own aspirations.

On the path, off the path; but now what? In keeping with the jeremiad's purposes, the speaker is obliged not to leave matters there, but to alert his audience that a choice now presents itself: either the people can opt to remain off the path, or chose to return and keep struggling toward their professed ideal. The people, in short, have the means to redeem themselves if only they would, and it is the work of the speaker to animate them toward acting on that choice alone. Here then we see the third function of the jeremiad—the means to *atonement*. The Constitution itself contained the language upon which such action could be authorized, but ultimately, he stresses, "What would be needed were Americans in successive generations who were willing to do their part—through protest and struggle, on the streets and in the courts, through a civil war and civil disobedience and always at great risk—to narrow the gap between the promise of our ideals and the reality of their time." This commitment acting upon choice is the key to redemption itself, but it presupposes yet another promise, and that is to act together, as a community or people collectively striving toward that more perfect union. In the speaker's words, "we cannot solve the challenges of our time unless we solve them together—unless we perfect our union by understanding that we may have different stories, but we hold common hopes; that we may not look the same and we may not have come from the same place, but we all want to move in the same direction—toward a better future for our children and our grandchildren."

We are now only five paragraphs into the text, but already the basic coordinates have been set. Its overarching theme—the need to act together to form a better version of America—is activated within a given genre—the jeremiad—and unfolds through successive stages of covenant, violation, and atonement. Thus form, content, and purpose collaborate to produce an artistic whole in a process that will be recapitulated throughout the performance, in a manner suggesting variations on an orchestral motif. We now consider this dynamic at work in the second and central phase of the speech.

Barack Obama was not born in Chicago, but even as young man he made the city his political home. Shortly after earning his law degree from Harvard University, he took up residence in Hyde Park, whence he launched a systematic and very successful campaign to insinuate himself into the complex network of Chicago politics. If every step was not calculated, most were, and before long this son of a white American mother and Kenyan father had moved to the forefront of that city's center of power. Along the way, Obama encountered and fell under the spiritual tutelage of the Reverend Jeremiah Wright, a prominent leader in the black community and, by all accounts, a spellbinding speaker. As we noted above, he could on occasion cross a line thought by many to be taboo by vehemently denouncing America and its benighted record on race relations. When one such performance hit the airwaves, Obama was severely criticized for associating with the pastor and called upon to address the issue. He did so briefly by denouncing Wright's more excessive language, but made clear that he continued to hold his mentor in high regard. This effort did little to allay the controversy, and at length Obama undertook to settle the matter once and for all—hence the Philadelphia speech.

How the speaker manages the Jeremiah Wright issue is perforce key to the address as a whole. To better understand it, let us return to our pilgrims for a moment. One of the striking characteristics of their sermons is the way in which seemingly all events of note are relegated to the status of an example or manifestation of God's disposition. Are crops bountiful and children healthy? Evidence of divine pleasure. Are famine and sickness in the village? Evidence of divine wrath. Was a two-headed calf born on the Dooley's farm? Divine warning. In short, the later day Jeremiahs sought to convince their flock that virtually everything could be properly understood and acted upon not with reference to the event itself, but to an overarching narrative in which any given phenomenon is but an episode. Its meaning was not inherent to the event, but in the greater story still unfolding. For Winthrop and his fellow shipmates, for example, the meaning of their journey was not limited to a group of malcontents, or land hunger; it had to be comprehended terms appropriate to the age-old narrative of slavery, exodus, freedom, and redemption

Now, what does all have to do with Obama's response to the Wright matter? On closer inspection, we see that the jeremiad provides the speaker with a means to render the controversy into a minor but noteworthy episode in America's own story and its march toward a more perfect union. By transforming the "meaning" of Reverend Wright from a media-generated bogey man into an allegory of America writ large, Obama strips him out of the hands of his critics and re-inscribes Wright into a more meaning-full and instructive lesson than could otherwise have been the case. Taking up our organizing principles, we can plot the process by which this transformation is effected

Covenant (affirmation of the positive)

> The man I met more than twenty years ago is a man who helped introduce me to my Christian faith, a man who spoke to me of our obligation to love one another; to care for the sick and lift up the poor. He is a man who served his country as a U.S. Marine; who has studied and lectured at some of the finest universities and seminaries in the country, and who for over thirty years led a church that serves the community by doing God's work here on Earth—by housing the homeless, ministering to the needy, providing day care services and scholarships and prison ministries, and reaching out to those suffering from HIV/AIDS.

Violation (exposing and condemning the negative)

> But the remarks that have caused this recent firestorm weren't simply controversial. . . . Instead, they expressed a profoundly distorted view of this country—a view that sees white racism as endemic, and elevates what is wrong with America above all that we know is right with America. . . . As such, Reverend Wright's comments were not only wrong but divisive, divisive at a time when we need unity; racially charged at a time when we need to come together to solve a set of monumental problems.

Atonement (restoration and redemption)

> But I have a firm conviction—a conviction rooted in my faith in God and my faith in the American people—that working together we can move beyond some of our old racial wounds, and that in fact we have no choice if we are to continue on the path of a more perfect union.

Close textual analysis takes as a given that texts have direction, that they unfold within a temporal economy established by the text itself. Obama's oration is doubly interesting because it not only has direction, but is also about direction. We have charted this fact above by observing how the speaker avails himself of certain features native to the jeremiad. It will come as no surprise, then, that this ancient rhetorical genre is activated and sustained through conspicuous word choice, which is to say its "style" collaborates in effecting the intended message. Again, this sense of style in no way views such word choice as ornamentation or afterthought. On the contrary, it is constitutive of the message itself, which may be grasped by attending to the Judeo-Christian imagery at work throughout the text and its appeal to the path as its leading trope.

We have already made reference to a number of scriptural allusions. It may be useful at this point to pause and consider them in the aggregate. A quick list of resonant terms and phrases is suggestive:

Original sin
Promise
Bondage
Faith (repeatedly)
Love one another
God's work
Foot of the cross
David and Goliath
Moses and Pharaoh
Christians in the lion's den
Ezekiel's field of dry bones
Vessel of hope
Do unto others as we would have them do unto us
Let us be our brother's/sister's keeper

Mindful that such usage is meaningful only within the contours of the text itself, we nevertheless glimpse the point. Obama's appeal to scriptural imagery functions to underscore not only his own ethos as a man of faith, but it also enriches the rhetorical force of the message itself. Taken together, we may observe that each allusion invokes different facets of the covenant binding the nation to its historical mission. Broken or repaired, forgotten or remembered, this covenant weaves through the speech as it presumably weaves through America's own journey toward the full realization of its promise. Hence the Hebrew Bible/Christian Old Testament imagery of original sin, bondage, and faltering faith is transformed within the text into New Testament emphasis on love, charity, and redemption. This sense of forward movement is punctuated further by recurrent appeals to the image of the path and its clustered associations. Thus:

Travel across the ocean
The long march of those who came before us
Path to understanding
Path of a more perfect union
That path means embracing the burden of our past

However briefly, the above rendering suggests how the formal and ideational content of the text work together to create an artistically coherent message. The overall argument—that America has within itself the moral capacity to renew its commitment to form a more perfect union—is mobilized through a series of structural and stylistic resources, which together offer the speaker's audience a reason to believe and to act on such belief.

We are now in a position to revisit the four principles of CTA inaugurating this essay. Each asks a certain kind of question the critic needs to grapple with in coming to terms with his or her particular text. Let us take them up individually in the order presented.

1. *The text is a site of symbolic action.* Such a principle prompts us to then ask: "What does a text DO"? By way of an answer, and with reference to Obama's speech, we can now say that *texts act by summoning rhetorical resources (i.e., the jeremiad) to impose meaningful order on the world and, if successful, to make that order a compelling basis for conviction.*

2. *Form and content cannot be divorced.* Here we must ask: "How do they collaborate to create meaning and effect persuasion"? Obama's address teaches us that *form (i.e., metaphors, allegories, etc.) imparts to content conspicuous intelligibility, and content (i.e., reasons for forgiving Reverand Wright) imparts to form propositional argument.*

3. *Texts inform contexts, and vice versa.* If this is the case, then we need to ask: "How do texts recreate or restructure context"? On reflection, we are led to see *that texts borrow from other texts and discursive traditions to re-order the terms in which they hope to be interpreted.* Thus Obama, for example, invoked founding state papers, the Bible, and sermons to re-orient his critics from one view toward another.

4. *Rhetorical texts exhibit artistic density.* That said, we may well ask: "how is such artistic density manifested, and to what end?" The Obama speech illustrates that *texts reveal their own techniques of production, and to the extent that these techniques yield a coherent and compelling product, they invite attention and assent.*

POTENTIALS AND PITFALLS

No interpretive practice can presume to be complete or satisfactory on every count, and CTA is no exception. Through the years, it has both attracted and provoked some of the discipline's most able critics. This essay has sought to demonstrate the gains to be had from this approach, but it would be incomplete without some attention to its limits. Several of these have been mentioned, notably, the alleged tendency to bracket out contextual dynamics. Still, at least two persistent concerns remain about the assumptions upon which CTA is built and the tendencies it encourages in practice: its reliance on an ideal critic/audience construct, and its privileging of canonical texts. In the following, I briefly develop each critique but leave counter-arguments to the reader's discretion.

The first criticism of CTA takes us to near ground zero in the work of interpretation. In effect, it asks: what are we really saying when we claim that a unit of language means this or that? We have already discarded the notion that meaning resides objectively and inherently in the unit itself; and we have stressed that, for rhetorical criticism at least, it is best to attend to what language does in a given context. But we are not out of the woods yet, and need to press further on the question. When, as the author of this essay, I claim that such and such a passage in Obama's speech means or does something, what am I really saying? Am I making a claim about what the audience supposedly thinks? Inasmuch as I have no access to its mental activity at the moment of performance, I can make no such claim. Or am I attributing certain intentions to the speaker, as in: "This is what Obama really means here." Again, I have no grounds for arguing along these lines: who knows what his intentions were? And even if we did know, what would it have to do with the ways in which his listeners and readers made their own sense of the oration?

In the face of such questions, CTA (but not CTA alone) finds itself exposed to the criticism that it posits an ideal reader and an ideal audience. That is, the critic implicitly operates from a privileged position, as if to say, "I offer to you the reader the preferred interpretation of this text." True, the critic is obliged to argue for his or her rendering and be otherwise held to the highest standards of scholarship. But if we cannot plausibly ascribe intention to the speaker, or reception to the audience, then is not the critic in effect saying: "this is how I think the text works"? And if that is the case, on what basis can we generalize beyond the critic's self-reporting?

The second line of criticism advanced against CTA is more politically-charged but no less insistent. It holds that practitioners of the art tend almost invariably to seize upon texts of unquestioned cultural significance and artistic achievement. There are exceptions to this argument, but then there can be no mistaking the fact that CTA in general concerns itself with canonical texts. In rhetorical studies, for example, critics associated with the practice have featured the Declaration of Independence, Jefferson's First Inaugural Address, Lincoln's major addresses, Elizabeth Cady Stanton's "Solitude of Self," FDR's First Inaugural Address, and King's "I Have a Dream" speech.[6] These are, of course, perfectly understandable as fit objects of interpretation. So what is the problem? In the view of some critics, lavishing such attention upon the masterpieces of American discourse unwittingly reproduces a suspect standard of what gets to count as a masterpiece, or, more pointedly, privileges the very concept of masterpiece, itself—these critics argue—a gendered and presumably outdated category. Why not use CTA to study vernacular expressions, forgotten texts, those without the cultural cache of a Jefferson or Lincoln? One might respond that in principle nothing is stopping critics from looking at quotidian texts; but in practice, the lion's share of attention is directed at the presumptively "great" rhetorical productions of American history. In doing so, is not CTA complicit in silencing or otherwise bracketing out the many marginal voices of our cultural heritage?

Close textual analysis came of age in the field of communication studies during the 1980s, and was closely associated with the work of several rhetoricians at the University of Wisconsin. The discipline, like many in the humanities, was undergoing significant transformations, especially with respect to what was called the politics of interpretation. Critics and theorists were increasingly concerned to expose the epistemological and methodological assumptions underlying their scholarly work. Operating within this climate, CTA came under considerable scrutiny for reproducing certain habits that were thought to be suspect; we have noted above two such lines of critique. A third, and for our purposes final, such argument continues to challenge its practitioners, and is in fact an extension of the concern over idealizing and canonizing the text as an object of inquiry. Put simply, this critique asks us to reconsider what it is that texts—much less textual criticism—can really tell us about the power of language and the language of power.

So what is the explanatory force of a given text? One way to get at this question is to ask another: is a text a cause or an effect? For those skeptical of CTA, the answer tends to focus on the latter. That is, the text is an effect. The line of argument runs something like this: humans are decisively shaped by the material, social, and ideological forces within which they act. Consequently, what they produce—including texts—are themselves the result or effect of these forces. To claim that a text is unique, or the hallmark of individual genius, or otherwise independent of the political milieu in which they are produced is to remain trapped in an idealized and delusory model of interpretation. Here the claim is not that texts are incapable of instigating action in the world; it is rather that texts alone can never be accorded such a primary role. They can only be, again, the effects of power relations already extant and operating in a given historical moment. Close textual critics will want to ask themselves whether such reasoning makes sense, and if so, how their own practice systematically acknowledges the point.

Is CTA politically naive? Does it tend to extract the text from the very interstices of power that gives rise to texts in the first place? Or can we have it both ways, that is, justify the focus on a single text even as we place it in situ and within the material conditions of its own making?

These are all legitimate questions, but, again, they are perhaps best addressed by those now considering the possibilities and limits of CTA for the first time. At a minimum, we may conclude that we have in CTA a robust and systematic resource for the interpretation of rhetorical texts; that it offers a means of understanding how texts work by engaging them carefully and with great detail; and that it sets on display the very human drama of language in action.

PERSONAL COMMENTS OF AUTHOR

I first came to the study of close textual analysis as a graduate student at the University of Wisconsin. There I encountered a small but remarkable group of critics who combined deep historical and philosophical learning with a keen interest in discovering how texts manage to do what they do. Then as now, such close attention to texts seemed the ideal means to open windows to other vistas and distant horizons. By peering intently at Booker T. Washington's "Atlanta Exposition Address," for example, I learned not only how metaphors operate to invite interpretation, but about race relations in the New South, the importance of pageantry to regional identification, and styles of African American leadership. For this reason, CTA offered a venue for bringing into focus wide-ranging interests—indeed, kept me from ranging *too* widely and without direction.

After more than two decades in the field of rhetorical criticism, one's interests are bound to grow and change. And while I now pursue other avenues of inquiry, including rhetoric and public memory, social movements, and rhetoric in the Early Republic, one constant has remained firmly in place: the conviction that rhetorical texts are just as worthy as any other genre of close, patient, and imaginative interpretation.

CTA TOP PICKS

Benson, Thomas W. "The Rhetorical Structure of Frederick Wiseman's *High School*." *Communication Monographs* 47 (1980): 233–61. Benson presents a fine-grained analysis of the famed documentary filmmaker's masterpiece, with special emphasis on the play of form and content.

Black, Edwin. "Gettysburg and Silence." *Quarterly Journal of Speech* 80 (1994): 21–36. A subtle but provocative reading of Lincoln's address, Black's essay is sharply attuned as much to what Lincoln did not say as much as to what he did say.

Browne, Stephen H. "Encountering Angelina Grimke: Violence, Identity, and the Creation of Radical Community." *Quarterly Journal of Speech* 82 (1996): 55–73. Browne examines the first public statement by the early abolitionist, and finds evidence of a radical consciousness coming into being.

Campbell, Karlyn Kohrs. "Stanton's 'Solitude of Self': A Rationale for Feminism." *Quarterly Journal of Speech* 66 (1980): 304–12. Campbell explores Stanton's speech as a statement on the human condition, which in turn operates as a summons to enlightened political action.

Leff, Michael. "Textual Criticism: The Legacy of G. P. Mohrmann." *Quarterly Journal of Speech* 72 (1986): 377–89. Leff explains the rationale for textual analysis and provides concrete examples of how it works.

Lucas, Stephen E. "Justifying America: The Declaration of Independence as a Rhetorical Document" in Thomas W. Benson, ed., *American Rhetoric: Contexts and Criticism* (Carbondale, Il: Southern Illinois

University Press, 1989): 67–131. A tour de force essay combining close textual analysis, deep historical learning, and sharply observed insights into the founding text.

NOTES

1. In addition to essays notes in "top picks," the following articles are representative of some of the notable works of close textual analysis: Michael C. Leff and Gerald P. Mohrmann, "Lincoln at Cooper Union: A Rhetorical Analysis of the Text," *Quarterly Journal of Speech* 60 (1974): 346–358; Kenneth Burke, "The Rhetoric of Hitler's Battle" in *The Philosophy of Literary Form* (Berkeley: University of California Press, 1971): 191–220; Amy R. Slagell, "Anatomy of a Masterpiece: A Close Textual Analysis of Abraham Lincoln's Second Inaugural Address" *Communication Studies* 42 (1991): 155–71; Michael C. Leff, "Things Made by Words: Reflections on Textual Criticism," *Quarterly Journal of Speech* 78 (1992): 223–31; and Martin J. Medhurst, "Reconceptualizing Rhetorical History: Eisenhower's Farewell Address," *Quarterly Journal of Speech* 80 (1994).

2. Transcripts are readily available online. One such transcript can be found at the National Public Radio website: http://www.npr.org/templates/story/story.php?storyId=88478467 [Accessed March 25, 2009]. Unless otherwise noted, all quotations of this speech derive from this source.

3. For summaries of the early 20th Century growth of the communication discipline see: Thomas W. Benson, "The Cornell School of Rhetoric: Idiom and Institution," *Communication Quarterly* 51 (2003): 1–56; Jim A. Kuypers and Andrew King, eds., *Twentieth-Century Roots of Rhetorical Studies* (Westport, CT: Praeger, 2001); and Theodore Otto Windt, Jr., *Rhetoric as a Human Adventure: A Short Biography of Everett Lee Hunt.* (Annandale, VA: Speech Communication Association, 1990).

4. See especially Sacvan Bercovitch, *The American Jeremiad* (Madison: University of Wisconsin Press, 1978); and James R. Darsey, *The Prophetic Tradition and Radical Rhetoric in America* (New York: New York University Press, 1999).

5. For an examination of Winthrop's sermon, see Stephen Howard Browne, "Errand into Mercy: Rhetoric, Identity, and Community in John Winthrop's 'Modell of Christian Charity'" in James R. Andrews, ed., *Rhetoric, Religion, and the Roots of Identity in British Colonial America* (East Lansing: Michigan State University Press, 2007), 1–36.

6. Representative essays treating these texts include Lucas, "Justifying America": Stephen Howard Browne, *Jefferson's Call for Nationhood: The First Inaugural Address* (College Station: Texas A&M University Press, 2003); Gary Wills, *Lincoln at Gettysburg: The Words that Remade America* (New York: Simon and Schuster, 2005); Suzanne Daughton, "Metaphorical Transcendence: Images of the Holy War in Franklin Roosevelt's First Inaugural," *Quarterly Jounral of Speech* 79 (1993): 227–46; and Drew Hansen, *The Dream: Martin Luther King and the Speech that Inspired a Nation* (New York: Ecco, 2003).

7

Generic Elements in Rhetoric

William Benoit

To help understand a complex and variegated world, we often make use of generalizations that are sometimes referred to as stereotypes. We can use a generalization such as "Ashley's a conservative" to draw reasonable, but not certain, conclusions about Ashley. If we want to know whether Ashley supports private school tuition vouchers, the best way to find out the answer to this question is to ask Ashley, or locate a statement by Ashley about her position on vouchers. These options, however, are not always available. In the absence of better ways to answer our question, we can use Ashley's political leanings to make an educated guess about her position: Because many conservatives support vouchers, Ashley, who we know is a conservative, probably supports vouchers too. Knowing something (support for private school vouchers) about most members of a group (conservatives) allows us to make educated guesses about other members of that group (Ashley). Similar generalizations about groups of discourse or "genres" can also be helpful.

Generic rhetorical criticism is based on the idea that observable, explicable, and predictable rhetorical commonalities occur in groups of discourses as well as in groups of people. A critic using the generic approach would first identify a distinctive group or category of discourse, a genre: for example, presidential nominating convention keynote speeches, presidential inaugural speeches, graduation commencement addresses, or eulogies. Then, the critic adopts an *inductive* approach, examining numerous past instances of this genre to develop a description or generalization of its characteristics. It is also important for the critic to explain *why* speeches of this kind ought to have the commonalities found in the analysis. Take presidential nominating convention Keynote Speeches as an extended example.[1] These speeches are designed to sound a "key" note or set a tone for the convention. The Keynote is designed to celebrate the ideals of the party and the fitness of the nominee to represent the party in the general election campaign and, ultimately, to win the office of the presidency. All Keynote Speeches are given in a similar situation: the Republican or Democratic presidential nomination convention. The result of this process, the description of the rhetorical characteristics of a genre (keynotes, for instance), can be used in at least three important ways.

First, generic descriptions can be used as part of a rhetorical theory that describes rhetorical practices according to genre. Rhetorical theory can describe also offer prescriptions about how it ought to be conducted. Inductive generic descriptions can provide an empirical foundation for descriptive rhetorical theory. For example, we might want to describe the practice of campaign rhetoric (keynote speeches) or political rhetoric (state of the union addresses) or ceremonial rhetoric (commencement addresses, eulogies). If so, the generalizations discovered through a generic analysis could be very useful to theory building.

Second, generic descriptions can be used by practitioners, by rhetors that seek advice about how to develop a speech that falls in that genre. Those who are confronted with a need to invent a particular kind of discourse can be guided by systematic descriptions of past instances of that kind of discourse. If you need to write a eulogy, for example, it could be very useful to know what other eulogists have said in the past. A description of the practice of past eulogies could give you ideas, a starting point, and perhaps even "models" to imitate.

Third, rhetorical critics can apply what we have learned about a genre to help understand and evaluate other, as yet unexamined, instances of that genre. That is, we can compare a new instance of a genre to past practices. On March 20, 2003, President Bush announced the beginning of "Operation Iraqi Freedom," the war in Iraq. We can learn something about this speech by comparing it with other presidential speeches announcing military action. We could compare the 2003 speech with one or more other, earlier, speeches, but it would be more efficient to compare it with the results of a generic rhetorical criticism that described a group of similar speeches.[2]

It should be obvious that the fundamental assumption of genre criticism is that rhetorical artifacts examined by a critic to establish a genre, or to develop the inductively-derived generic description, will resemble in important ways other rhetorical artifacts that fall into that genre. The power of generic criticism is that, if this assumption is reasonable, critics, practitioners, and theorists can learn something about some rhetorical artifacts by examining other similar rhetorical artifacts. Rhetorical critics, schooled in the humanistic tradition, do not ordinarily make this idea explicit, but the basic argument is that the texts studied in a generic rhetorical criticism are a sample of a larger population of texts and that the results of generic rhetorical criticism can be generalized to other similar discourses. Of course, the generalizations derived from the discourses studied to identify and define the genre must be applied cautiously to other discourses. Discourses that belong to the same class or genre and therefore have *some* similarities could be different in other important ways. For instance, Ashley may be one of the few conservatives who does not favor school vouchers.

Furthermore, the generic description is inherently limited by the characteristics of the artifacts examined to develop the description. Genre criticism can only describe—and not improve on—the actual practice of discourse. This means that if rhetors that have created discourse in a genre have not yet discovered the best or most effective approach for that kind of rhetoric, the generic description cannot include the optimum approach.[3] It also means that as our culture changes through time, discourses that were effective or appropriate in the past—the discourses studied to describe the genre—may be ill-suited to understanding future discourses given in different times. The remainder of this chapter is divided into two sections. First, I provide an overview of the theory and practice of generic rhetorical criticism. Second, I provide a sample essay that highlights how one may use generic rhetorical criticism.

The Theory and Practice of Generic Rhetorical Criticism

A common thread in this literature is that genres are a class, set, or group of related discourses. For example, Walter Fisher argues that "a genre is a category" and "genres are generalizations."[4] Similarly, Jackson Harrell and Wil Linkugel explain that "At base, genre means class. A genus is a class or group of things. The decision to classify a particular group of things as a genus rests on recorded observations which indicate that one group of entities shares some important characteristic which differentiates it from all other entities."[5] This statement contains an important implicit claim: A genre, or each member of a genre, is distinct from other genres.[6] A Keynote is one kind of campaign speech and these speeches are different in some ways from nominating convention Acceptance Addresses,[7] presidential television spots,[8] or presidential debates.[9] Because these are all forms of presidential campaign discourse, they probably share some features in common, but if they are distinct genres they must have distinguishing differences.

Some genre studies seem to adopt a *situational* base, such as examination of gallows speeches[10] or Inaugural Addresses.[11] Other instances of generic criticism seem to focus on *purpose*, including investigations of agitation and control,[12] redemption,[13] and polarization.[14] Still other genre studies focus on the rhetorical characteristics of groups of *rhetors* include studies of early Afro-American feminists,[15] radical-revolutionary speakers,[16] radical, liberal, and conservative rhetors,[17] the religious right,[18] or the radical right.[19] Finally, some genre studies focus on characteristics of the *medium* of discourse, such analysis of political pamphlet[20] or songs.[21] There can be no question that a great deal of interesting scholarship of extremely diverse nature had been conducted under the rubric of generic rhetorical criticism. It can be difficult to explore this literature, because critics do not always label their work "generic criticism" even though we might consider it as such. In reviewing this body of literature, three areas seem to me to stand out: the relationship between situation and genre; the relationship between purpose and genre; and the relationship of genre to other elements. To each of these we now turn.

Situation and Genre

Rhetorical scholars have described recurrent forms of discourse since at least as early as Aristotle's *Rhetoric* which identified three broad genres of rhetoric: forensic (legal), deliberative (legislative), and epideictic (ceremonial).[22] Edwin Black offered one of the earliest, if not the earliest, conceptual discussion of the assumptions of rhetorical genre:

> First, we must assume that there is a limited number of situations in which a rhetor can find himself. . . . To be sure, there may be accidental factors peculiar to a given situation; but our assumption is that there will be a limited number of ways in which rhetorical situations can be characterized, and that the recurrent characteristics of rhetorical situations will make it possible for us—if we know enough—to construct an accurate and exhaustive typology of rhetorical situations.[23]

Black assumes that the number of rhetorical situations—and therefore, the number of potential genres—is limited. This makes the task of identifying genres and locating a sufficient number of texts to study more practical than if there were an infinite number of rhetorical situations. Black continues his description:

> Second, we must assume that there is a limited number of ways in which a rhetor can and will respond rhetorically to any given situational type. Again, there may be accidents of a given response that will prove singular, but on the whole—we assume—there will be only a finite number of rhetorical strategies available to a rhetor in any given situation, and his playing his own variations on these strategies will not prevent the critic from identifying the strategies as characteristic of the situation.[24]

This assumption, that there are a limited number of potential responses, means that the texts of a genre are likely to share common features (which the critic can identify and describe).

The alternate, an unlimited number of responses, could mean that every member of a genre could be completely different. Finally, Black discusses the possible uses of generic rhetorical criticism:

> Third, we must assume that the recurrence of a given situational type through history will provide the critic with information on the rhetorical responses available in that situation, and with this information the critic can better understand and evaluate any specific rhetorical discourse in which he may be interested.[25]

So, understanding past instances of a genre may provide insight into other examples of that kind of rhetorical message. Of course, the artifacts which participate in or belong to a genre will not be identical in all regards, but for generic criticism to be a useful method of criticism, the similarities must be important.

The emphasis on understanding genre as rooted in a particular situation is popular in the literature.[26] Harrell and Linkugel agree that genres are situationally based: "We think that rhetorical genres stem from organizing principles found in recurring situations that generate discourse characterized by a family of common factors."[27] Similarly, Campbell and Jamieson's oft-quoted definition stipulates a situational base for rhetorical genres:

> Genres are groups of discourses which share substantive, stylistic, and situational characteristics. Or, put differently, in the discourses that form a genre, similar substantive and stylistic strategies are used to encompass situations perceived as similar by the responding rhetors. A genre is a group of acts unified by a constellation of forms that recurs in each of its members. These forms, in isolation, appear in other discourses. What is distinctive about the acts in a genre is the recurrence of the forms together in constellation.[28]

The term "constellation" is especially well-chosen, suggesting that the recurrent elements appear in a recognizable configuration or pattern.

Purpose and Genre

A second thread in the literature grounds genres in the rhetor's purpose.[29] Carolyn Miller points out that "genres have been defined by similarities in strategies or forms in the discourse, by similarities in audience, by similarities in modes of thinking, by similarities in rhetorical situations." Her recommendation is that "a rhetorically sound definition of genre must be centered not on the substance or form of a discourse but on the action it is used to accomplish."[30] In my opinion, there is overlap between situational and purposive approaches to genre, but they are not entirely identical.

Certainly the rhetor's purpose and the rhetorical situation frequently coincide. For example, eulogists face a situation in which a person has died. When a person dies, the survivors will never again be able to see or talk with the deceased, a cause for sadness. A death also reminds everyone concerned in a very direct fashion that they are mortal. Hence it is appropriate for a eulogist to praise the departed, to ease the transition, and to try to help auditors deal with their grief and heightened sense of mortality. As Jamieson and Campbell explain it, "In Western culture, at least, a eulogy will acknowledge the death, transform the relationship between the living and the dead from present to past tense, ease the mourners' terror at confronting their own mortality, console them by arguing that the deceased lives on, and reknit the community."[31]

Here, the situation and the rhetor's purpose are completely compatible, and it is difficult to see or draw a distinction between the situation and the rhetor's purpose.

However, I believe that it is not always the case that a rhetor's purpose is consistent with the situation. For instance, consider a eulogy for someone killed by a gunshot wound. If the eulogist felt strongly about gun control, he or she might choose to include such an appeal in the eulogy; if the eulogist did not feel strongly about gun control, he or she would likely not discuss gun control. An appeal for gun control is not a necessary part of such a eulogy. If a eulogist failed to praise the deceased, the eulogy would seem odd and incomplete if not wrong, but if a eulogist failed to include a plea for gun control, the speech would not seem incomplete. Although the particular situation may be seen to authorize such an appeal for gun control (unless the deceased were a staunch 2nd Amendment supporter), it does not require it; rather, the rhetor's purpose (advocating gun control) would determine whether to include this idea in the eulogy.

To extend this analogy one step further, consider Rick Kahn's plea at Senator Paul Wellstone's memorial service: "We are begging you to help us win this Senate election for Paul Wellstone." In these cases, the rhetor's purpose produced discourse that was in part irrelevant to if not incongruent with the immediate situation. Nothing in this eulogy's situation authorized this topic. Although a listener might happen to agree in principle with the appeal to vote for a Democrat, such an appeal has nothing to do with the deceased or the eulogy itself. It seems inappropriate; a plea to vote for a Democrat probably detracted from the ceremony for some of the audience.

As a final argument for the importance of distinguishing between situation and purpose, consider any rhetorical discourse that occurs in a controversy. Those rhetors who supported and opposed prohibition spoke and wrote in essentially the same situation. Similarly, the situation confronting pro-choice and pro-life advocates is exactly the same. These groups of rhetors—and it would be easy to add additional groups in this list—produced contradictory rhetorical artifacts, and the primary reason for those differences was their purpose, not differences in the situation. Of course, one could argue that opponents' perceptions of the situation are different, but Lloyd Bitzer at least argues that the situation is "objective and publicly observable historic facts in the world we experience."[32] Thus, the rhetors' purpose can be a source of generic similarities in rhetorical messages, and, while purpose may overlap with situation, conceptually they are distinct concepts.

Genre: "Act" at the Intersection of Scene, Purpose, Agent, and Agency

The third thread in the literature highlights the interanimated nature of situation and purpose with three other considerations. There is no question that situation and purpose do, or should, influence the production of discourse. However, in actuality, five factors jointly influence the production of rhetorical discourse. Kenneth Burke's notion of ratios[33] helps clarify the relationships between these factors.[34] Ratios are comprised of two terms from Burke's pentad—act, scene (situation), agent (rhetor), agency, and purpose. Ratios essentially describe the influence of the first term on the second. Given that in this chapter we are discussing the production of discourse, or acts, "act" is the second term in each of these four ratios:

- Scene-act: The situation in which a discourse is produced exerts an influence on that discourse.

- Purpose-act: The rhetor's purpose, goal, or intent influences the discourse he or she produces.
- Agent-act: The nature of the rhetor influence the discourse he or she produces.
- Agency-act: The means, including the communicative medium, influences discourse.

The scene-act ratio corresponds to situationally based approaches to genre (e.g., gallows speeches, Inaugural Addresses). The purpose-act ratio relates to genre approaches based on the rhetor's purpose (e.g., polarization, resignation[35]). The agent-act ratio pertains to genres focused on rhetor (e.g., radical, liberal, and conservatives). Finally, the agency-act ratio corresponds to studies of kinds of discourse (e.g., pamphlets, song). All four of these ratios or factors can influence the production of discourse and can serve as the basis for a genre.

Situations are opportunities for discourse, which rhetors may choose to exploit to further their own purposes. This can help explain why discourse that occurs in similar situations, such as the eulogies discussed above, would share important similarities. However, some rhetors have different purposes, which can also influence the discourse they produce, even when they face similar situations. Think of the gun control example given above.

However, I believe that critics are certainly capable of identifying or creating groupings of discourse that share a common source (such as situation, purpose, rhetor) but which ordinary people have not conceptualized at any level. A little imagination can devise diverse categories that could be used to divide discourse into a variety of groupings.

Generic Description: An Inductive Approach

I want to stress that there is no single way to write a genre criticism. It is important for a rhetorical critic who wants to write a generic rhetorical criticism to read a variety of genre studies before attempting the task. Still, some observations are worth making. There are two fundamental approaches to genre criticism: generic description (inductive) and generic application (deductive).[36] Generic description begins with a generalization and applies it to specific members of the genre. Generic application begins with a genre that has already been described; it applies the characteristics of that genre deductively to another instance of that genre in order to explain or evaluate it.

When a critic suspects the existence of a genre, he or she may use generic description to examine particular instances of a possible genre for common features. There are three basic steps in this process: (1) identify the defining characteristic (e.g., the situation, purpose, or kind of rhetor that constitutes the genre); (2) carefully scrutinize examples of the possible genre to identify similarities; (3) explain the observed similarities in terms of identifying characteristics (identifying the "internal dynamic" of the genre). Each of these steps is discussed below.

Identifying Defining Characteristics. If the critic believes that he or she may have found a useful genre, he or she must identify the defining characteristic(s) of that candidate genre. For example, the defining characteristic could be the situation/scene in which the rhetorical artifacts occur (Keynote Speech or eulogy), the rhetor's purpose that prompts the rhetorical discourses (celebrating the party's presidential nominee or helping the bereaved confront their own mortality), salient characteristics of the rhetor/agent (Republicans or women), or the medium/agency (speech, television spot, or political debate) that shapes the artifacts. One cannot select artifacts at random to discover genres; the critic must be able to clearly define the candidate genre in order to select appropriate particular rhetorical artifacts, instances of the category, for analysis.

For example, President Bush's speech of March 20, 2003 is an example of a speech announcing a war. However, it may not be clear whether speeches about the search for Bin Laden and Al Queda are about *war* (perhaps the struggle against terrorism is not the same as a war against a country). The genre critic needs to make a clear decision about which messages to include in a study. However, given a clear understanding of the defining characteristics of the candidate genre, the critic can select appropriate texts for scrutiny.

Having identified the defining characteristics of the candidate genre, the critic must acquire several instances of the discourse in question for analysis. The critic must be prepared to read, watch, and/or listen to the artifacts repeatedly, closely, and carefully, in order to determine whether these texts have rhetorical commonalities and what those similarities are. Two important questions arise in this phase of generic description: what to look for, and how many discourses to examine.

Unlike most other rhetorical perspectives, generic rhetorical criticism helps the critic decide *which* artifacts to examine but does not prescribe *how* to analyze artifacts. For example, a critic employing the generic approach could look for common metaphors in war speeches. A genre critic might look to see whether such speeches displayed similar rhetorical visions or fantasy themes, or used narrative in similar ways. Thus, generic rhetorical criticism helps the critic decide which rhetorical artifacts to examine, and it tells the critic to look for commonalities, but it does not help the critic know what sorts of similarities to look for. The whole idea of genre criticism is that rhetorical artifacts in the past can be studied and that the results of this study will tell us about future artifacts of the same kind (or other past artifacts that were not included in the initial study). Thus, it is very important for the critic to select the appropriate artifacts to study; inclusion of artifacts that do not really belong to the genre will produce a flawed study.

In my opinion, a critic using the generic approach should be familiar with several methods of rhetorical criticism, and with rhetorical theory generally. It is useful to know what features might be important in a genre. When the critic utilizing the generic approach is repeatedly reading the artifacts of the candidate genre, he or she may notice that certain kinds of metaphors are used frequently. Or, the critic could notice that the rhetors seem to be engaging in a certain narrative form frequently. Critics using the generic approach who are generally familiar with numerous rhetorical perspectives are probably more likely to notice important rhetorical similarities than critics who are not widely read.

Generic description, as noted above, is an inductive approach. This means that it is subject to the tests of inductive argument. The most important test is whether a sufficient number of instances—in this case, enough rhetorical artifacts—have been examined.[37] There is no simple answer to this question: The number of instances a critic should examine to establish the nature of a genre depends in part upon the complexity and variety of artifacts examined. The greater the complexity of the artifacts in the possible genre, the more variety in the artifacts, the greater the number of instances that ought to be studied to have confidence in the study's conclusions. The number of artifacts needed also depends on how prominent the common rhetorical features appear in the artifacts. The more obvious and important the rhetorical similarities, the fewer artifacts may be needed to persuasively establish the genre. If few artifacts are available and they are difficult to acquire, readers may accept a critic's decision to examine fewer of them.

Identifying Similarities. Once the texts to be analyzed have been identified and located, the generic rhetorical critic must examine them carefully to identify rhetorical similarities. If the critic discovers seemingly important similarities in the texts under scrutiny, he or she should organize those commonalities and locate clear examples from the discourses that can be used to illustrate the features of the genre. For example, if I were to simply say that war speeches often include metaphors that would not be as clear as if I gave examples of metaphors from such speeches.

It is possible that any randomly selected group of speeches will show similarities simply through the operation of coincidence. Most speeches are supposed to have introductions, main bodies, and conclusions, but that does not mean they all belong to the same genre. I suspect this may in part account for Campbell and Jamieson's statement that "a genre is composed of a constellation of recognizable forms bound together by an internal dynamic."[38] Harrell and Linkugel write about the "organizing principles found in recurring situations that generate discourse characterized by a family of common factors."[39] The point is that the common rhetorical features that are discovered through generic description must be explained by the genre's identifying feature. Take, for example, a Keynote Speech. They are designed to encourage viewers to support the nominee; because of this, it makes perfect sense for a Keynote to praise the party's nominee. Similarly, the two presidential nominees face off in the general election campaign, so it is reasonable for a Keynote Speaker to attack his or her nominees' opponent. Thus, the nature of the situation facing rhetors who deliver keynote addresses can explain the presence of certain rhetorical features of those addresses.[40] This raises the question of sub-genres; would it be useful to distinguish between keynote speeches during a seriously contested nomination and keynote speeches to an essentially unified party?

Explaining Observed Similarities. Because coincidental similarities are possible, it is important to explain the similarities found in the rhetorical texts. Those who base genres on rhetors' purposes must be able to link those purposes to the common features of the rhetorical artifacts in those genres. For example, the similarities found in messages of redemption (following Kenneth Burke) should be related to that purpose.[41] We should be able to explain why common features of discourse that is designed to polarize[42] issues and ideas should be expected to occur in artifacts with that purpose. Rhetors who engage in rhetoric designed to agitate or control[43] should produce messages that can be better understood through a consideration of that purpose.

Those who base genres on the nature of groups of rhetors must be able to link the common rhetorical features to the character of those rhetors. For instance, we ought to be able to account for similarities in messages produced by rhetors with similar political beliefs (e.g., radical, liberal, conservative) by considering those beliefs.[44] If those who belong to the religious right[45] produce similar messages, the critic using the generic approach should be able to show how their political/religious beliefs explain the existence of those similarities. We might wonder again about the possibility of "sub-genres": Are Republican keynotes different from Democratic ones?

Generic Application: A Deductive Approach

The process of generic application can occur only after someone has already conceptualized a genre. Most commonly, genres would be developed through generic description: inductively describing the nature of a conceptually related group of speeches. However, it is possible that one could generate a generic description theoretically, rather than through an examination of instances of that genre. Regardless of how the genre was conceptualized, generic application includes three basic steps.

First, a genre must have already been described. The critic pursuing generic application must identify the nature of the genre ("Keynote Speeches") and then describe the salient features of that genre. What would discourses in the genre be likely to look like, or to have in common?

Second, an artifact that is a member of the genre is identified and shown to participate in, or belong to, the genre described in the first step. For example, one might choose to apply the genre of Keynote Speeches to President Ford's 2000 Keynote Speech. In this step, the critic refers to the defining features of the genre (in this case, situational) and demonstrates that the new artifact belongs to the genre. This is an important step, because, as Robert C. Rowland correctly observes, "If a work is inappropriately placed in a given category the analysis of it inevitably will be flawed."[46]

Sometimes this will be quite simple. If "Keynote Speeches" is considered to be a genre, it should be sufficient to note that the artifact under consideration is identified as one. In other cases it could require an argument. If the genre is defined by the rhetors' purposes, the critic may need to provide evidence of the rhetor's likely purpose in the new artifact. If the genre is defined by situation, it is possible that the critic may need to provide a rationale for the claim that the rhetor and/or the salient audience perceived the situation as the critic suggests. It must be clear to the reader of the rhetorical criticism that it is reasonable to view the new artifact as a member of the genre.

Finally, we are ready to begin making arguments about the "new" artifact based on the claim that it is a member of the genre. Here, evidence for these arguments can be based on the description of the genre as a standard for evaluation as well as on the message itself. It is possible to draw a variety of conclusions in a generic application. For example, the critic might measure the new artifact against the standards articulated in the genre: based on past examples, is the new artifact well or poorly conceived? Did the rhetor include the proper elements and were they developed effectively?

If the artifact shares the common features that comprise the genre, there is no problem for the critic. The "internal dynamic" explains why these features ought to occur in the kind of genre identified by the defining characteristics. Of course, if the new artifact follows the strictures of the genre but appears to have been a failure, the critic has some explaining to do.

Even more complex is when the artifact violates the expectations established during generic description. What can the critic utilizing the generic approach conclude if the artifact does not conform to the characteristics of the genre? Although there can be numerous reasons which account for deviations from the genre, there are four which deserve special attention. First, it is possible that the "new" artifact doesn't really belong in the genre. The critic should make certain that the discourse being examined in fact fits the defining characteristics of the genre. It is conceivable that the critic would decide either that the artifact doesn't really belong in the genre after all, or that the defining characteristics need to be revised.

Second, the artifact could be a generic hybrid,[47] which means it "belongs" to two genres at once. If so, it could contain some of the rhetorical features specified in each of the genres that contribute to the rhetorical hybrid. If the critic has reason to believe that this discourse is not unique, that other messages may well resemble this one, the critic may propose the existence of a hybrid.

Third, it is possible that the rhetor who created the artifact under examination made mistakes. Perhaps the rhetor did not understand the implications of the situation. Perhaps the rhetor did not examine previous artifacts or deliberately chose to ignore them. It is possible that the rhetor did not correctly analyze the audience or chose to ignore them. The critic using the generic approach, however, should make arguments about why the differences between the artifact and the common features of the genre were mistakes if that is the claim being advanced.

Fourth, it is also possible that the rhetor is experimenting and improving the genre rather than making errors. Rhetors may not have yet discovered the optimum discourse, and the rhetor being analyzed here may have developed an idea or ideas about how to invent a better discourse. Ironically, if the audience has developed expectations, it is possible that they will not like the changes even if a more objective analysis concludes that the changes made by the rhetor are improvements. Here again, if the rhetorical critic believes that the differences between the artifact and the common features of the genre are an improvement, the critic must explain why the changes should be considered improvements.

CRITICAL ESSAY

This section will illustrate the basic features of generic rhetorical criticism through analysis of presidential Inaugural Addresses. Every four years, America elects a president. The first duty of the newly elected President is to take the oath of office and give an Inaugural Address. I want to conduct a brief generic description of Inaugurals given from 1961 through 1997. Then I will use the results of that investigation to perform a generic application to George W. Bush's 2001 Inaugural Address. I could have included earlier inaugural addresses, but these should be sufficient to illustrate this approach. I could have included the 2001 Inaugural in the sample, but omitting it allows me to also to illustrate the process of generic application by applying the results of the generic description to Bush's text. My goal in the essay that follows is not so much to present a standard academic essay, but rather to demonstrate the process of both generic description and generic application.

CRITICAL ESSAY: AN ILLUSTRATION OF THE PROCESS OF GENRE CRITICISM: INAUGURAL ADDRESSES

The critic employing the generic approach should begin by examining the literature. Most rhetorical criticism of Inaugural Addresses focus on particular speeches and so they are not genre studies.[48] Still, rhetorical criticism of individual Inaugurals could be very helpful to the critic seeking to understand the genre of Inaugural Addresses. I was able to locate two studies of Inaugural Addresses as a genre.[49] Given that my analysis here is designed simply to illustrate the process of generic criticism, I will not review this work. However, in a standard academic essay, this literature should be reviewed and also drawn into the evaluation section, discussing points of similarity and difference between your analysis and previous research on speeches in the genre.

Nature and Context of Inaugural Addresses

Inaugural Addresses are an instance of situational genre. They are speeches that are given in a particular situation: the occasion in which an elected President assumes office. These speeches are also given by a particular rhetor, the President; but the situation in which Inaugurals are given distinguishes this kind of speech from other presidential discourses, such as campaign speeches or State of the Union Addresses. By definition, Inaugurals are points of transition. They mark the end of a presidential campaign, one contested by the winner and the loser(s), as well as by their supporters. Just as a presidential nomination Acceptance Address can be expected to appeal for unity after a contested primary, it is reasonable to expect that an Inaugural Address ought to attempt to unify the country.

Inaugurals also mean change from the old administration to the new administration or movement from the first to the second term of a re-elected president. At the same time an Inauguration signals a beginning, the start of a new administration. Because of this, Inaugural Addresses might be expected to discuss change and to sketch out the principles that will guide the Administration. It also means that second Inaugurals, initiating a President's second term in office, might offer less emphasis on change and more stress of continuity.

Generic Description: Analysis of Inaugurals from 1961–1997

I repeatedly read transcripts of these Inaugurals; when I had videotapes of these speeches, I watched them repeatedly. I looked for commonalities and, not surprisingly, I found several. Common themes in these speeches were: Change, Appeals for Unity, Identification of the Enemy, Values and Ideals, Goals, and Religious References. Some similarities, such as Change and Appeals for Unity, were expected. Others, such as Identification of the Enemy, were unexpected. I will illustrate each theme with excerpts from these addresses.

Acknowledgment of Change. John F. Kennedy succinctly noted that "The world is very different now" from the time of our founding fathers. Lyndon B. Johnson noted that "Even now, a rocket moves toward Mars. It reminds us that the world will not be the same for our children, or even for ourselves in a short span of years." He also observed that "Change has brought new meaning to that old mission" of world peace. Richard M. Nixon's first Inaugural acknowledged that "The spiraling pace of change allows us to contemplate, within our own lifetime, advances that once would have taken centuries." His second Inaugural implied change, observing that "we stand on the threshold of a new era of peace in the world." He also noted a "shift from old policies to new." Jimmy Carter's Inaugural quoted his high school teacher, Julia Coleman: "We must adjust to changing times and still hold to unchanging principles." He also observed that "This inauguration ceremony marks a new beginning." Ronald Reagan's first Inaugural noted how important the "orderly transfer of authority" that occurs when a new president is inaugurated. His second Inaugural acknowledged that "So much has changed" since George Washington was President. In 1989, George Bush declared that "a new breeze is flowing . . . the totalitarian era is passing. . . . There is new ground to be broken and new action to be taken." Bill Clinton observed in his first Inaugural that our founding fathers "knew that America, to endure, would have to change. Not change for change's sake, but change to preserve America's ideals." He also noted that "When George Washington first took the oath I have just sworn to uphold, news traveled slowly. . . . Now the sights and sounds of this ceremony are broadcast instantaneously to billions across the world." He also noted that "We have changed the guard." Clinton's second Inaugural noted that over the last century, "America became the world's mightiest industrial power." We "harness[ed] the Industrial Revolution" and now we face the "Information Age." This is important, because "as times change, so government must change." Thus, each of these Inaugurals commented on past and current changes in America and the world.

Appeals for Unity. Kennedy argued for the importance of unity: "United, there is little we cannot do in a host of cooperative ventures. Divided, there is little we can do—for we dare not meet a powerful challenge at odds and split asunder." He also suggested that we should "let both sides explore what common problems unite us instead of belaboring those problems which divide us." Johnson argued that "Our fate as a nation and our future as a people rest not only upon one citizen, but upon all citizens." Nixon, in his 1969 Inaugural, noted that "we are torn by division, wanting unity." His second speech explained that "I pray for your help so that together we may be worthy of our challenge." Carter's Inaugural Address asked, "Let us learn together and laugh together and work together and pray together." Reagan in his 1981 speech indicated that he would unify the country by adopting their goals: "Your dreams, your hopes, your goals are going to be the dreams, the hopes, and the goals of this administration, so help me God." His second speech asked that "with heart and hand, let us stand as one today." He ended by declaring that we are "one people under God." Bush explained that "we need compromise; we have had dissension. We need harmony; we have had a chorus of discordant voices" and he declared that "We will work hand in hand." He argued that in "crucial things, unity. . . is crucial." Clinton's first Inaugural asked "Congress to join with me. But no President, no Congress, no government, can undertake this mission alone. My Fellow Americans, you, too must play your part in our renewal." He added, "we recognize a simple but powerful truth—we need each other." Clinton's 1997 Inaugural declared that "There is work to do, work that government alone cannot do." Clearly, these Inaugurals included appeals for unity.

Identification of the Enemy. In 1961, the Communists were an obvious enemy, and one mentioned by Kennedy. However, he also called for "a struggle against the common enemies of man: Tyranny, poverty, disease, and war itself." Johnson turned inward to find an enemy, talking about poverty, hunger, and illiteracy, explaining that "injustice to our people, . . . waste of our resources, was our real enemy." Nixon's first Inaugural also turned inward to find an enemy: "American has suffered from a fever of words; from inflated rhetoric that promises more than it can deliver; from angry rhetoric that fans discontents into hatred; from bombastic rhetoric that postures instead of persuasion." The theme of internal enemies continued in 1977, as Carter explained that "we will still fight out wars against poverty, ignorance, and injustice—for those are the enemies against which our forces can be honorably marshaled." The enemy in Reagan's first Inaugural was the economy: "We suffer from the longest and one of the worst sustained inflations in our national history. It distorts our economic decisions, penalizes thrift, and crushes the struggling young and the fixed-income elderly alike. It threatens to shatter the lives of millions of our people." Poverty and war were enemies in 1985: "Every blow we inflict against poverty will be a blow against its dark allies of oppression and war. Every victory for human freedom will be a victory for world peace." For Bush, an important enemy was drugs: "The most obvious area now [where we must rise up united and express our intolerance] is drugs." The economy returned to the forefront in Clinton's first Inaugural: Our economy "is weakened by business failures, stagnant wages, increasing inequality, and deep divisions among our people." "We have drifted, and that drifting has eroded our resources, fractured our economy, and shaken our confidence." In his second Inaugural, the enemy was "prejudice and contempt" which "cripple both those who hate and, of course, those who are hated." While the enemy was sometimes external and sometimes internal, these Inaugurals identified enemies.

Identification of Values and Ideals. Peace and freedom were important values in Kennedy's Inaugural. Johnson discussed three key ideals: justice, liberty, and union. Nixon's first Inaugural stressed peace, freedom, justice, and mentioned "Goodness, decency, love, kindness" as well. His 1973 speech stressed peace and freedom and mentioned civility, decency, and dignity. Carter spoke of the American dream, liberty, equal opportunity, compassion, justice, peace, humility, and mercy. Reagan's 1981 Inaugural talked about liberty, freedom, and hope. His second Inaugural stressed freedom, dignity, and opportunity. Bush emphasized freedom and discussed moral principle, unity, diversity, generosity, kindness, and gentleness. Clinton's 1993 Inaugural discussed life, liberty, the pursuit of happiness, fairness, and responsibility. In 1997, Clinton spoke of liberty, diversity, peace, freedom, and the human spirit. These Inaugurals appealed to values that were likely to resonate with the American public.

Delineation of Goals. Kennedy explained that he wanted to "assist free men and free governments in casting off the chains of poverty," to help empower the United Nations, to seek peace (including arms control agreements). Johnson, in keeping with his three ideals, wanted to improve justice, overcome "tyranny and misery," and "turn our unity of interest into a unity of purpose." Nixon's 1969 speech mentioned the "goals of full employment, better housing, excellence in education; in rebuilding our cities and improving our rural areas; in protecting our environment and enhancing the quality of life." However, he also spent a great deal of time talking about achieving peace. His second Inaugural again talked about achieving peace with honor. Carter's Inaugural discussed equality of opportunity, enhancing freedom abroad, eliminating nuclear weapons, providing jobs, strengthening the family, increasing respect for the law, and restoring pride in government. Reagan's first Inaugural goals were to decrease inflation, create jobs, and thwart terrorism. His second speech revealed that he wanted to "permanently control Government's power to tax and spend." He explained that "From new freedom [from government intervention] will spring new opportunities for growth, a more productive, fulfilled, and united people, and a stronger America." He echoed Carter's call for elimination of nuclear weapons while maintaining a strong defense. Bush observed that "There are the homeless, lost and roaming. There are the children who have nothing; no love, no normalcy. There are those who cannot free themselves of enslavement to whatever addiction—drugs, welfare, the demoralization that rules the slums. There is crime to be conquered, the rough crime of the streets. There are young women to be helped who are about to become mothers of children they can't care for and might not love." Clinton's first Inaugural set as a goal "To renew America." He noted that "we must meet challenges abroad as well as at home. . . . The world economy, the world environment, the world AIDS crisis, the world arms race—they affect us all." Clinton's second Inaugural suggested that we should be "teaching children to read; hiring people off welfare rolls; coming out from behind locked doors and shuttered windows to help reclaim our streets from drugs and gangs and crime." These passages show how these speeches articulated goals for the next four years as president.

Religious References. Kennedy's speech ended by "asking His blessing and His help, but knowing that here on earth God's work must truly be our own." Johnson mentions God four times, once explaining that "But we have no promise from God that our greatness will endure. We have been allowed by Him to seek greatness with the sweat of our hands and the strength of our spirit." Nixon ended his first Inaugural "sustained by our confidence in the will of God and the promise of man." His 1973 Inaugural ask for citizens "prayers that in the years ahead I may have God's help." Carter quoted from the Bible near the beginning. Reagan's first Inaugural declared that "together, with God's help, we can and will resolve the problems which now confront us" (note that this passage also discusses unity). Reagan's 1985 Inaugural ended with, "God bless you and may God bless America." Bush took his oath of office with the same Bible used by George Washington, and then told the audience that "My first act as President is a prayer." Clinton ended his first Inaugural by declaring that "with God's help, we must answer the call." His second Inaugural closed with this appeal: "May God strengthen our hands for the good work ahead—and always, always bless our America." So, religious references occurred in these speeches.

Summary. Examination of these Inaugurals revealed features both expected and unexpected. First, these speeches openly acknowledge change and transition. Second, appeals to unity were common, as were descriptions of the goals for the next four years. There were recitations of values and ideals as well. These are reasonable features of an Inaugural Address. However, analysis of these texts also revealed themes that were not expected. First, these speeches tend to identify a common enemy. This makes sense, because one way to unite a group is to fight against a common enemy. Thus, this theme reinforces the unification appeals. Second, these speeches, like the majority of American political discourse, contained religious references. The only question I raise is whether this feature occurs because these discourses are Inaugural Addresses specifically or presidential addresses generally.

I want to acknowledge that these speeches had other features as well. For example, Carter offered an interesting contrast when he noted that "We must adjust to changing times and still hold to unchanging principles." Still, in my opinion the themes identified above are the most prominent and important similarities for the genre of Inaugural Addresses, given the situation in which these addresses occur. I would also like to note that not every speech discussed each theme as extensively as other speeches. Furthermore, some seemed to me to do a better job at developing these themes. Finally, some speeches seemed to do a better job relating their goals to values and ideals that would guide implementation of those goals.

As I mentioned earlier, if this were intended as more than an illustration of the process of generic rhetorical criticism, I would at this point return to the literature on Inaugurals and discuss points of similarity and difference between my findings and theirs. I would also spend more time teasing out specifics. For example, I would talk more about the common values and ideals. Still, this brief application should give readers the basic idea of how generic description is conducted.

Generic Application: George W. Bush's 2001 Inaugural Address

The above generic description of recent Inaugural Addresses identified six common themes: acknowledgment of change, appeals for unity, identification of common enemy, identification of values and ideals, delineation of goals, and religious references. Using generic application, I will next examine George W. Bush's 2001 Inaugural Address to see whether it conforms to the common themes found above.

President Bush began by acknowledging the change: He explained that "with a simple oath we affirm old traditions and make new beginnings," acknowledging that the inauguration is a transition. He then observed that "sometimes our differences run so deep, it seems we share a continent but not a country." Then he noted the importance of unification: "Our unity, our union, is the serious work of leaders and citizens and every generation. And this is my solemn pledge: I will work to build a single nation of justice and opportunity." The enemy Bush identified was terrorists, which seems eerily prophetic in the wake of the terrorist attack on the World Trade Center and the Pentagon about nine months later: "We will confront weapons of mass destruction so that a new century is spared new horrors. The enemies of liberty in our country should make no mistake: America remains engaged in the world." Values discussed include civility, courage, compassion, and character, opportunity ("everyone deserves a chance"), freedom, and hope. In addition to building a strong defense, his goals were to "reclaim America's schools," "reform Social Security and Medicare," and "reduce taxes to recover the momentum of our economy." Finally, Bush ended his speech by saying, "God bless you all, and God bless America." So, Bush's Inaugural Address conformed to the standards set by previous Inaugurals.

In evaluating his speech, I would say it enacted these themes generally well. One minor weakness was that he promised unity without working very hard in his speech to give citizens a reason to unite behind him. That is, I do not think it is enough for the President to *pledge* unity, particularly after the bitterly contested election of 2000 and the fact that some people believe Bush actually lost the popular vote to Gore.[50] Bush ought to have offered citizens a reason to join with him. Second, he could have easily used the common enemy of terrorism as a justification for unity. The common enemy should have served as an explicit justification for unification. Third, I would have tried to relate the values and ideals he articulated more closely to his goals. In other ways, though, his speech was acceptable.

Once again, if this were intended as a complete rhetorical criticism, I would discuss the relationship of this analysis to prior research on Inaugurals. Similarly, I would spend more time discussing specifics, especially details of the historical context that existed at the time of the inaugural. However, this essay was designed to outline how generic description and application proceeds.

PERSONAL COMMENTS ON THE ESSAY

I could have made other choices in examining these speeches. For example, I could have looked for the use of emotional appeals, or metaphors, or myths in Inaugural Addresses. However, I tried to let these texts "speak" to me, trying to see what stood out, rather than explicitly searching for particular rhetorical elements such as metaphors. I believe it is important to try to identify the "internal dynamic," explaining *why* these common features make sense for discourses written for, and presented in, these situations. Furthermore, it should be clear that my analysis reflects a scene-act perspective: The observed common rhetorical features are (I argue) a result of the nature of the situation in which these texts emerged: the newly elected president's first formal address to the country.

POTENTIALS AND PITFALLS

Generic rhetorical criticism has many advantages. First, it is well-designed for attempting to understand the nature of rhetorical practice. What do speeches announcing a war, or Inaugural Addresses, or diatribes, or resignation speeches, look like? What features do they have in common and why should these commonalities exist? Generic description can help rhetorical theorists and practitioners alike. Furthermore, generic application can help rhetorical critics understand and evaluate new examples of speeches that belong to a given genre, once generic description has occurred.

The rhetorical critic must keep in mind that the generic method offers advice on which speeches to study, but not on precisely how to study them. As I suggested before, another critic could look at Inaugural Addresses (or any other genre) looking for metaphors, or myths, or fantasy themes. Any particular method of rhetorical criticism can be used to guide the critic's analysis of the speeches in a genre.

One limitation of generic analysis is that the method lumps good messages with mediocre and bad ones.[51] The inductive method of generic description suggests that the critic locate a sufficient number of examples of the potential genre. It never suggests that the critic only examine successful messages or place the best texts in one subgrouping and the failures in another. As discussed in the preceding section, it is conceivable that a rhetoric creating a Keynote speech in the future could try something new, something better than any previous Keynote. Unless we believe that the best possible examples of discourse in a genre have already been created, there is always room for improvement.

It can also be objected that generic rhetorical criticism ignores the nuances of individual rhetorical discourses. This criticism applies more to rhetorical criticism that focuses too heavily upon description. By its very nature inductive generic description searches for commonalities among the instances of the genre, ignoring differences between individual instances of the genre. Because the critic who is conducting generic description is attempting to discover what these texts have in common, the differences are truly irrelevant. Of course, subsequent generic application should focus on the individual nuances of the specific instance of the genre under examination. For example, Keynote Speeches from 1960–1996 attacked in 48 percent of their utterances. But Barbara Jordan's Democratic Keynote in 1976 contained only a single attack.[52] A critic using the deductive generic approach could argue that Jordan failed to include enough attacks on the opposing party. Understanding the particular nuances of this speech might shed some light on her reluctance to attack. So, while generic description must by nature ignore the nuances of individual members of the genre, generic application can and should take particulars into account.

Generic rhetorical criticism takes advantages of the fact that, while no two discourses are identical, discourses do fall into groups or genres that have important similarities. Knowing the nature of these groups, and their common rhetorical characteristics, can be useful to rhetors, theorists, and practitioners alike. Of course, critics must never lose sight of the fact that there *are* differences even between members of the same genre, and critics must realize that genres can develop over time and potentially improve over past practice. Still, intelligent use of the method of generic rhetorical criticism can provide powerful insights into the nature of rhetorical discourse.

GENERIC RHETORICAL CRITICISM TOP PICKS

Benoit, William L., Joseph R. Blaney, and P. M. Pier. "Acclaiming, Attacking, and Defending: A Functional Analysis of Nominating Convention Keynote Speeches, 1960–1996." *Political Communication* 17 (2000): 61–84. This essay takes a more explicitly content analytic approach, but it is still concerned with identifying important common features of this message form.

Campbell, Karlyn K. and Kathleen H. Jamieson, eds. *Form and Genre: Shaping Rhetorical Action*. (Falls Church, VA: Speech Communication Association, 1978). This volume pulls together essays from a diverse array of scholars addressing the nature of genre.

Clark, Thomas D. "An Analysis of Recurrent Features in Contemporary American Radical, Liberal, and Conservative Political Discourse." *The Southern Speech Communication Journal* 44 (1979): 399–422. This essay is interesting because unlike most genre studies, Clark contrasts three different (although related) groups of discourse.

Condit, Celest M. "The Function of Epideictic: The Boston Massacre Orations as Exemplar." *Communication Quarterly* 33 (1985): 298–298. Classic treatment of a genre that is often overlooked.

Jamieson, Kathleen H. and Karlyn K. Campbell. "Rhetorical Hybrids: Fusions of Generic Elements," *Quarterly Journal of Speech* 68 (1982): 146–157. Genres are not always static. This essay discusses the merging of two genres into a single new genre.

Ware, B. L. and Wil A. Linkugel. "They Spoke in Defense of Themselves: On the Feneric Criticism of *Apologia.*" *Quarterly Journal of Speech* 59 (1973): 273–283. One of the earlier studies of genre and a classic treatment of the important genre of apologia.

NOTES

1. William L. Benoit, Joseph R. Blaney, and P. M. Pier, "Acclaiming, Attacking, and Defending: A Functional Analysis of Nominating Convention Keynote Speeches, 1960-1996," *Political Communication* 17 (2000): 61-84.

2. For rhetorical criticism of justifications of war, see Kathleen M. German, "Invoking the Glorious War: Framing the Persian Gulf Conflict through Directive Language," *Southern Communication Journal* 60 (1995): 292-302; Robert L. Ivie, "Presidential Motives for War," *Quarterly Journal of Speech* 60 (1974): 337-345; Mary E. Stuckey, "Remembering the Future: Rhetorical Echoes of World War II and Vietnam in George Bush's Public Speech on the Gulf War," *Communication Studies* 42 (1992): 246-256.

3. William L. Benoit, "In Defense of Generic Rhetorical Criticism: John H. Patton's "Generic Criticism: Typology at an Inflated Price," *Rhetoric Society Quarterly* 10 (1980): 128-135.

4. Walter R. Fisher, "Genre: Concepts and Applications in Rhetorical Criticism," *Western Journal of Speech Communication* 44 (1980): 291.

5. Jackson Harrell and Wil A. Linkugel, "On Rhetorical Genre: An Organizing Perspective," *Philosophy & Rhetoric* 11 (1978): 263.

6. Thomas D. Clark, "An Analysis of Recurrent Features in Contemporary American Radical, Liberal, and Conservative Political Discourse," *The Southern Speech Communication Journal* 44 (1979): 400–401.

7. William L. Benoit, William T. Wells, P. M. Pier, and Joseph R. Blaney, "Acclaiming, Attacking, and Defending in Nominating Convention Acceptance Addresses, 1960–1996," *Quarterly Journal of Speech* 85 (1999): 247–267.

8. William L. Benoit, "The Functional Approach to Presidential Television Spots: Acclaiming, Attacking, Defending 1952–2000," *Communication Studies* 52 (2001): 109–126

9. William L. Benoit and Allison Harthcock, "Functions of the Great Debates: Acclaims, Attacks, and Defense in the 1960 Presidential Debates," *Communication Monographs* 66 (1999): 341–357.

10. Bower Aly, "The Gallows Speech: A Lost Genre," *Southern Speech Journal* 34 (1969): 204–213.

11. Karlyn K. Campbell and Kathleen H. Jamieson, "Inaugurating the Presidency," *Presidential Studies Quarterly* 15 (1985): 394–411; Halford R. Ryan, "Roosevelt's Fourth Inaugural Address: A Study of its Composition," *Quarterly Journal of Speech* 67 (1981): 157–166.

12. John W. Bowers, Donovan J. Ochs, and Richard J. Jensen, *The Rhetoric of Agitation and Control*, 2nd ed. (Prospect Heights, IL: Waveland Press, 1993).

13. A. Cheree Carlson and John E. Hocking, "Strategies of Redemption at the Vietnam Veterans' Memorial," *Western Journal of Speech Communication* 49 (1988): 14–26.

14. Andrew A. King and Floyd D. Anderson, "Nixon, Agnew, and the 'Silent Majority': A Case Study in the Rhetoric of Polarization," *Western Speech* 35 (1971): 243–255; Richard D. Raum and James S. Measell, "Wallace and his Ways: A Study of the Rhetorical Genre of Polarization," *Central States Speech Journal* 25 (1971): 28–35.

15. Karlyn K. Campbell, "Style and Content in the Rhetoric of Early Afro-American Feminists," *Quarterly Journal of Speech* 72 (1986): 434–445.

16. James Chesebro, "Rhetorical Strategies of the Radical-Revolutionary," *Today's Speech* 20 (1972): 37–48.

17. Thomas D. Clark, "An Exploration of Generic Aspects of Contemporary American Campaign Orations," *Central States Speech Journal* 30 (1979): 122–133.

18. Bernard K. Duffy, "The Anti-Humanist Rhetoric of the New Religious Right," *The Southern Speech Communication Journal* 49 (1984): 339–360.

19. Dale G. Leathers, "Belief-Disbelief Systems: The Communicative Vacuum of the Radical Right" in *Explorations in Rhetorical Criticism*, eds. G. P. Mohrmann, Charles J. Stewart, and Donovan J. Ochs (University Park, PA: Pennsylvania State University Press, 1973), 124–137).

20. Carl R. Burgchardt, "Two Faces of American Communism: Pamphlet Rhetoric of the Third Period and the Popular Front," *Quarterly Journal of Speech* 66 (1980): 375–391.

21. David A. Carter. "The Industrial Workers of the World and the Rhetoric of Song," *Quarterly Journal of Speech* 66 (1980): 365–374.

22. Aristotle, *The Rhetoric*, trans. W. Rhys Roberts. (New York: Modern Library, 1954).

23. Ed Black, *Rhetorical Criticism: A Study in Method* (Madison: University of Madison Press, 1965; reprint, University of Madison Press, 1978), 133.

24. Ibid., 133.

25. Ibid., 133.

26. See Lloyd F. Bitzer, "The Rhetorical Situation," *Philosophy & Rhetoric* 1 (1968): 1–14; William L. Benoit, "The Genesis of Rhetorical Action," *Southern Communication Journal* 59 (1994): 342–355.

27. Harrell and Linkugel, 263–264 (italics omitted).

28. Karlyn K. Campbell and Kathleen H. Jamieson, *Form and Genre: Shaping Rhetorical Action* (Falls Church, VA: Speech Communication Association, 1978), 20.

29. Situational factors and evidence from the text and rhetor can be used to make a argument about the rhetor's likely purpose.

30. Carolyn R. Miller, "Genre as Social Action," *Quarterly Journal of Speech* 70 (1984): 151.

31. Jamieson and Campbell, "Rhetorical Hybrids: Fusions of Generic Elements," *Quarterly Journal of Speech* 68 (1982), 147.

32. Bitzer.

33. Kenneth Burke, *Counter-Statement* (Berkeley: University of California Press, 1968; originally published in 1931); Kenneth Burke, "Dramatism," *International Encyclopedia of the Social Sciences* 7 (1968): 445–452; Kenneth Burke, *A Grammar of Motives* (Berkeley: University of California Press, 1969; originally published 1945); Kenneth Burke, "Questions and Answers about the Pentad," *College Composition and Communication* 29 (1978): 330–335. See too, volume 1, issue 3 of the *American Communication Journal*. There you will find essays on each of the following topics: "motive," "sacrifice and moral hierarchy," "identification," "the pentad," and the cycle of "guilt, purification, and redemption." http://acjournal.org/holdings/vol1/iss3/curtain3.html [Accessed March 21, 2009].

34. William L. Benoit, "Beyond Genre Theory: The Genesis of Rhetorical Action," *Communication Monographs* 67 (2000): 178–192.

35. Howard W. Martin, "A Generic Exploration: Staged Withdrawal, the Rhetoric of Resignation," *Central States Speech Journal* 27 (1976): 247–257; Gerald L. Wilson, "A Strategy of Explanation: Richard M. Nixon's August 8, 1974, Resignation Address," *Communication Quarterly* 24 (1976): 14–20.

36. Harrell and Linkugel; Robert C. Rowland "On Generic Categorization," *Communication Theory* 1 (1991): 143.

37. David L. Vancil, *Rhetoric and Argumentation* (Boston: Allyn and Bacon, 1993); George W. Ziegelmueller and Charles A. Dause, *Argumentation: Inquiry and Advocacy* (Englewood Cliffs, NJ: Prentice-Hall, 1975).

38. Campbell and Jamieson, *Form and Genre*, 21.

39. Harrell and Linkugel, 263–264 (italics omitted).

40. William L. Benoit and J. J. Gustainis, "An Analogic Analysis of the Keynote Addresses at the 1980 Presidential Nominating Conventions," *Speaker and Gavel* 24 (1986): 95–108.

41. Carlson and Hocking.

42. King and Anderson; Raum and Measell.

43. Bowers, Ochs, and Jensen.

44. Chesebro; Clark; Leathers.

45. Duffy.

46. Robert C. Rowland, "On Generic Categorization," *Communication Theory*, 1 (1991), 129.

47. Jamieson and Campbell, "Rhetorical Hybrids."

48. Ronald H. Carpenter, "In not-so-Trivial Pursuit of Rhetorical Wedgies: An Historical Approach to Lincoln's Second Inaugural Address," *Communication Reports* 1 (1988): 20–25; Suzanne M. Daughton, "Metaphoric Transcendence: Images of the Holy War in Franklin Roosevelt's First Inaugural," *Quarterly Journal of Speech* 79 (1993): 427–446; Barbara A. Harris, "The Inaugural of Richard Milhous Nixon: A Reply to Robert L. Scott," *Western Speech* 34 (1970): 231–234; Anthony Hillbruner, "Archetype and Signature: Nixon and the 1973 Inaugural," *Central States Speech Journal* 25 (1974): 169–181; Michael Leff, "Dimensions of Temporality in Lincoln's Second Inaugural," *Communication Reports* 1 (1988):

26–31; Stephen E. Lucas, "Genre Criticism and Historical Context: The Case of George Washington's First Inaugural Address," *Southern Speech Communication Journal* 51 (1986): 354–370; Martin J. Medhurst, "American Cosmology and the Rhetoric of Inaugural Prayer," *Central States Speech Journal* 28 (1977): 272–282; Ryan; Robert L. Scott, "Rhetoric that Postures: An Intrinsic Reading of Richard M. Nixon's Inaugural Address," *Western Speech* 34 (1970): 46–52; Vito N. Silvestri, "Background Perspectives on John F. Kennedy's Inaugural Address," *Political Communication and Persuasion* 8 (1991): 1–15; Amy R. Slagell, "Anatomy of a Masterpiece: A Close Textual Analysis of Abraham Lincoln's Second Inaugural Address," *Communication Studies* 42 (1991): 155–171; Martha Solomon, "'With Firmness in the Right': The Creation of Moral Hegemony in Lincoln's Second Inaugural," *Communication Reports* 1 (1988): 32–37; David Zarefsky, "Approaching Lincoln's Second Inaugural Address," *Communication Reports* 1 (1988): 9–13.

49. Karlyn K. Campbell and Kathleen H. Jamieson, "Inaugurating the Presidency," in *Form, Genre, and the Study of Political Discourse*, edited by Herbert W. Simons and Aram A. Aghazarian (Columbia: University of South Carolina Press, 1986), 203–225.

50. There remain over 1.5 million uncounted absentee ballots. Until they are counted, we will never know for certain who "won" the popular vote.

51. Benoit, "In Defense."

52. Benoit, Blaney, and Pier.

8

Criticism of Metaphor

Thomas R. Burkholder and David Henry

On August 28, 1963, Martin Luther King, Jr., began his speech on the steps of the Lincoln Memorial in Washington, D.C.: "Five score years ago, a great American, in whose symbolic shadow we stand today, signed the Emancipation Proclamation. This momentous decree came as a *great beacon light of hope* to millions of Negro slaves, who had been *seared in the flames of withering injustice*. It came as a *joyous daybreak to end the long night of their captivity*."[1] Rhetorical scholars recognize immediately the "trope" or figure of speech present in this passage—and throughout King's speech—that contributed to making "I Have A Dream" both memorable and of continuing scholarly interest—metaphor.[2]

Most undergraduate students probably encounter metaphor and its companion figure, simile, in introductory public speaking or English composition courses. Usually, those figures are discussed as means of embellishing the style of written compositions or speeches. For example, Stephen E. Lucas asserts that "speakers can use imagery . . . to make their ideas come alive." Two means of generating imagery, he explains, are metaphor and simile.[3] Likewise, David Zarefsky points out that "analogy is a powerful form of reasoning: a comparison can help people to accommodate a new idea or new information by deciding that it is similar to what they already know or believe. Comparisons can be made vivid by using similes and metaphors."[4]

Zarefsky's comment suggests how metaphor and simile are alike: both are comparisons of one thing to another. Technically, the difference between metaphor and simile is that similes always include either *like* or *as* while metaphors do not. Thus, saying that "lowering the drinking age to eighteen is *like* giving a stick of dynamite to a baby"[5] is a simile, while saying that "teenagers drinking *is* dynamite in the hands of babies" is a metaphor. Imagine other ways of expressing the same idea. Instead of using a metaphor or simile, one might say: "Lowering the drinking age to eighteen would be dangerous." The meaning is virtually the same, but with the metaphor or simile, the statement gains its vivid, forceful quality. Thus, regardless of whether the figure is technically a metaphor or a simile, it functions to embellish the style of a written or spoken message by making ideas vivid. In that sense, distinctions between the two figures matter little.

Despite those important stylistic or ornamental functions of metaphor and simile, critics are most interested in their *rhetorical* functions, in their capacity to influence the thoughts and actions of readers and listeners. That is especially true of metaphor, which rhetorician Kenneth Burke has called one of the four "master tropes."[6] In this chapter, we explore the rhetorical functions of metaphor. Then, we suggest how the criticism of metaphor might proceed. Finally, we illustrate criticism of metaphor through analysis of former New York Governor Mario Cuomo's famous Keynote Address to the 1984 Democratic National Convention.

HOW METAPHORS WORK

A metaphor consists of two terms that draw a comparison between two things, people, places, situations, events, etc., that belong to "different classes of experience."[7] One of those two terms, usually called the *tenor* or *focus,* is *relevant* to or *continuous* with the topic under discussion. The other term, usually called the *vehicle* or *frame,* is *discontinuous* with, or of a different class of experience from, that topic.[8] When the two terms, the *tenor* (or *focus*) and the *vehicle* (or *frame*), are brought together by a speaker or writer to form a metaphor, readers or listeners are invited to see the comparison between the two.

For example, while discussing means of coping with the pressures and stresses of contemporary life, the popular TV psychologist, Dr. Phil McGraw, tells his audience, "Life is a full-contact sport and there's a score up on the board."[9] The discussion is about life's problems, so the term "life" is the *tenor* of the metaphor because it is *continuous* with the topic under discussion. The term "full-contact sport" is the *vehicle* of the metaphor because it is *discontinuous* with that topic; in other words, it is from a different class of experience.

McGraw's metaphor serves obvious stylistic functions. It is vivid and memorable because we usually do not think of life as a sport; however, it serves potentially more powerful *rhetorical* functions as well. Listeners are invited to consider the similarities between "life" and "a full-contact sport." In doing so, their thoughts—their perceptions or understanding of life—are altered, and perhaps their everyday actions are changed. The potential for such changes in thought and action is evident when we consider an alternative metaphor. A television advertisement for a popular Italian restaurant, Macaroni Grill, says that "Life is delicious." If we follow that metaphor, the way we think about life and plan our everyday actions will be very different from "a full-contact sport."

Rhetorical Functions of Metaphor

Rhetorically, metaphors ask readers or listeners to comprehend one thing, represented by the *tenor,* "in terms of" another, represented by the *vehicle.* When that happens, certain relevant and important characteristics of the *vehicle* are "carried over" to the *tenor,* thus providing a new understanding of that term.[10] According to Malcolm O. Sillars and Bruce E. Gronbeck, "metaphor, because it draws an analogy among situations that are unrelated (e.g., 'the war on drugs,' 'a marriage of convenience,' 'loan sharks'), is a way to create new thought through language use. Thus, it is central to making sense through language."[11] That sense-making, however, depends upon whether or not readers or listeners can make the link; that is, on whether they understand what elements or characteristics of the *vehicle* appropriately "carry over" to the *tenor.* Martha Cooper provides an additional example that explains this rhetorical function of metaphor:

> Probably the classic metaphor is, "man is a wolf." This statement encourages the audience to associate the characteristic(s) of a wolf with man. Stated more directly, the pattern is simply "man is like a wolf." The metaphor *works like* an enthymeme in that the audience is asked to participate

by supplying the characteristics of a wolf and drawing the comparison between wolves and man. The metaphor, by suggesting an association, triggers a pattern of thinking in which comparisons are chained out.[12]

When readers or listeners make the association that Cooper explains, when they complete the association in their minds, their perception or understanding of humans is changed.

That intended change in perception, however, occurs only when the appropriate characteristics of the *vehicle*, "wolf," are carried over to the *tenor*, "man." After all, wolves walk on four feet. Their bodies are covered with fur. They have tails, an acute sense of smell, long teeth, and sometimes they howl at the moon. Although possible, it is doubtful that the speaker or writer who says, "man is a wolf," intends for "man" to be seen in terms of those wolf-like characteristics. On the other hand, wolves are strong, powerful, cunning predators. They are fiercely territorial. They are dangerous to other animals and sometimes to each other. It is almost certainly wolf-like characteristics such as those that the speaker or writer intends for listeners or readers to "carry over" to humans. Thus, listeners or readers must "get it"; they must complete the enthymeme for the metaphor to have its intended effect.

Such rhetorical functions of metaphor grow from what anthropologist J. David Sapir calls "the simultaneous likeness and unlikeness of the two terms." According to Sapir, "by replacing a term continuous to a topic with one that is discontinuous or by putting the two in juxtaposition, we are compelled . . . to consider each term in relationship to the other."[13] Thus, to complete the association presented by the metaphor, "man is a wolf," listeners or readers must be aware simultaneously of how men and wolves are both alike and different. In the process of completing the association, the differences are discarded and the likenesses emphasized. Or, in Burke's words, the metaphor "brings out the thisness of that, or the thatness of this."[14] Michael Leff explains that the thought process involved "works in two stages; the juxtaposition of the two terms first causes the vehicle to assume a pattern of foreground associations, and then this pattern serves to direct our understanding of the tenor." The "mutual attraction of terms belonging to different classes," Leff writes, "causes a response that decomposes the elements associated with these terms and then recombines them into a new structure of meaning."[15] In the case of our example, "man is a wolf," when the process is complete the metaphor has performed its *rhetorical* function and listeners or readers begin to think of man in terms of the appropriate characteristics of wolves.

Cooper's assertion that metaphors function like enthymemes, arguments in which the audience participates in forming the conclusion, is especially important for rhetorical critics. If the function of metaphor depends on cooperation between the rhetor (the writer or speaker) and the audience (the readers or listeners) to produce meaning, then both must be part of the same "speech community." That is, they must at minimum share knowledge and experiences that allow the rhetor to form, and the audience to complete, the enthymeme. Ideally, in addition to knowledge and experience, they must also share beliefs, attitudes, and values that would permit the audience to complete the argument as the rhetor intends. Imagine audience members who have no knowledge whatsoever of the *vehicle,* wolf. For them, the metaphor, "man is a wolf," would do little to alter their understanding of the *tenor,* man. Or, imagine an audience whose beliefs, attitudes, and values related to "man" have been previously influenced by a competing metaphor, such as the Christian teaching that "man is a temple for the Holy Spirit." Even though that audience may understand the appropriate characteristics of wolves that the rhetor wishes them to carry over to man, they may be extremely reluctant to do so. As Leff explains, "metaphor draws its materials from communal knowledge, achieves its effects through the active cooperation of the auditor, and assumes its form in relation to a particular context."[16] Thus, if rhetor and audience are from different speech communities, the metaphor is likely to have little rhetorical, or even ornamental, effect.

Metaphor in Political Discourse

Sometimes the associations between the metaphoric *tenor* and the *vehicle* are relatively simple and straightforward, as in the examples provided thus far. But in other cases, those associations can become extremely complex and powerful, altering our understanding of significant issues and events. According to Leff, "Since metaphoric structure limits and organizes our perception of a situation, it seems to establish the ground for viewing that situation; it creates a perspective and hence defines the space in which we encounter the situation. A metaphoric meaning localizes our attention," says Leff, "it produces a frame within which we can synthesize our reactions to the ongoing flow of events in time."[17] In other words, metaphors can determine how we think about issues and the actions we take with regard to those issues. That function of metaphor is arguably most obvious and potentially most powerful in political discourse.

"Politics" and its companion subject "government" are extremely complex issues. When we think of "politics" we may think of politicians, of the citizens whose votes determine the outcomes of elections, or we may even think of the "political process" within which politicians and citizens act. Yet as complex as that process and the relationships between those individuals are, this is just the beginning.

We "do" politics at the local, state, national, and international levels. At least at the first three, politics involves executive, legislative, and judicial functions. Elected officials are joined in those functions by tens of thousands of public employees, staff members, researchers, aides, advisers, law enforcement officers, military personnel, diplomats, and the like. Those individuals, even more so than elected officials, are the "elites"[18] of politics—highly skilled or trained individuals often with considerable experience in dealing with myriad social, economic, legal, environmental, medical, and foreign policy issues, to name only a few. In the area of foreign policy, the complexity of "politics" is magnified by similar systems and processes in the nations with which the United States must deal. Obviously, the details of "politics" are far too complex for any single individual to grasp fully. That fact holds significant implications for political discourse, the persuasive efforts to influence thought and action within the political system. To cope with the almost unending complexity of government, political discourse relies heavily on metaphor.

In one important sense, metaphors are essential simply for understanding complex political issues. Psychologist Jeffrey Scott Mio asserts that "metaphors can act as both filters that screen out much of the available information, leaving only the core ideas consistent with the metaphors, and as devices to collapse disparate information into smaller, more manageable packets."[19] That is, by drawing comparisons between complicated political issues (the *tenor*) and more familiar, relatively simple events or ideas (the *vehicle*), metaphors in political discourse render those complicated issues understandable. Thompson provides a typical example:

[T]he flow of revenue to the Federal government is determined by, among other things, macroeconomic policy, international trade and capital flows, and the perturbations of the business cycle. The pattern of expenditures is influenced by social entitlements, continuing programs, new defense or civilian programs, and the vagaries of disaster relief. Individuals have experience with budgets, but they are typically simple enough affairs—income determined by one's salary and perhaps investments, and expenditures largely determined by the necessities of survival at the level to which one has become accustomed. In several fundamental ways the federal budget is not just a personal or household budget writ large. But for the typical citizen, and even for the relatively sophisticated policy maker, thinking about the federal budget typically begins with the metaphor of a household or business budget: *'[I]f the government were a company, it would have gone bankrupt years ago'; 'In government, just like your own home, you can't spend money you don't have.'*[20]

Thus, for both policy-making elites and for average citizens, the federal budget (*tenor*), becomes understandable in terms of the more familiar and considerably less complex budgets of a business or family (*vehicle*).

In perhaps a more important sense, metaphors in political discourse influence not only understanding but also actions—the policies enacted in response to public issues or problems. Talking about and envisioning the issue of illegal drugs as "a problem of addiction" or as a "symptom of social dysfunction" would lead to policies that focus on the role of social workers, counselors, and medical personnel, while declaring "war" on drugs would shift the focus to law enforcement and punishment or perhaps even to the military.[21]

So important is this rhetorical function of metaphor in political discourse that competing political forces—candidates for office, political parties, liberals, conservatives—struggle for a sort of "metaphoric superiority." The metaphor that gains widest acceptance, within the government, in the public at large, or both, often determines the outcome of political contests. During the Vietnam conflict, for instance, supporters of U.S. military action in Southeast Asia, known metaphorically as "hawks," frequently offered the domino theory to justify continued military efforts. On the other side of the issue, opponents of military action, known metaphorically as "doves," came to label the Vietnam conflict as a "quagmire" from which the U.S. should extricate itself. Neither the domino theory nor the quagmire, of course, explained fully the extremely complex social, economic, political, and military situation that existed in Southeast Asia. Nevertheless, both elite policy makers and ordinary U.S. citizens came to see that geographic region as either a line of dominoes waiting to fall or as a quagmire. Eventually, the quagmire metaphor gained wider acceptance than the domino theory and the U.S. withdrew its military forces from South Vietnam.

Thompson points out that metaphors function in exactly the same way in domestic politics. "As much as they would like to, policy makers are unable to control the range of metaphors available or the uses to which they are put," he explains. "Opponents and interest groups in domestic politics compete vigorously to establish the winning metaphor in policy debates and, without too much exaggeration, campaigns can be seen as struggles over metaphors."[22] How one voted in the 2004 U.S. presidential election, for example, may have been determined by whether one saw George Bush as "Baby Bush" or "The man in the arena."

Critics must also keep in mind that these potentially powerful rhetorical functions of metaphor are not without potential risks. One of those risks is that use of metaphor may so oversimplify complex issues or problems that proposed remedies are themselves oversimplified to the point of ineffectiveness. As already noted, Mio explains that metaphors "screen out much of the available information, leaving only the core ideas." Unfortunately, the key to resolving complex political issues often lies in managing details rather than in core ideas.

Metaphors may also be a "double-edged sword" that can work both for and against the interests of rhetors who use them. Put differently, although metaphors may produce desired rhetorical effects, they can also entrap the rhetors who use them. As we explained earlier, declaring "war" on drugs leads to policies that feature intensified law enforcement efforts and perhaps even the use of U.S. military forces to interdict drug shipments and to arrest and punish drug dealers. The metaphor also has significant rhetorical power to rally public support for those efforts. Nevertheless, the U.S. simply cannot "win" a war on drugs in the sense of "winning" a war against another nation; that is, "drugs" can never be forced to sign an "unconditional surrender" and submit to an "army of occupation" to enforce the terms of that surrender. So, although officials who declare "war" on drugs may enjoy some short-term rhetorical success in the form of public support for their programs, and those programs may produce some dramatic results, the metaphor may also create expectations for the outcome of that "war" that are simply unattainable. Continuing frustration with the drug problem in the U.S. may be a result.[23]

Perhaps the greatest of those risks occurs when metaphors become "literalized"; that is, when we stop thinking of one thing *in terms of* another and begin to think of it as literally *being* the other. As Robert L. Ivie explains, "we are in the presence of a literalized metaphor when we act upon the figurative as if it were real, not recognizing that two domains of meaning have been merged into one despite their differences."[24] Ivie's analysis of Cold War rhetoric revealed a cluster of metaphoric images that were commonly used to characterize both the U.S. and the Soviet Union. "Summarized briefly, these vehicles illustrate the rhetorical essentials of the logic of confrontation," he notes. "The nation's adversary is characterized as a mortal threat to freedom, a germ infecting the body politic, a plague upon the liberty of humankind, and a barbarian intent upon destroying civilization." Equally vivid were the metaphors that depicted the U.S. Ivie continues: "Freedom is portrayed as weak, fragile, and feminine—as vulnerable to disease and rape. The price of freedom is necessarily high because the alternatives are reduced symbolically to enslavement and death."[25] The problem, says Ivie, was that these metaphors became literalized in a way that severely and unnecessarily limited the policies available to the U.S. According to Ivie, these metaphors "evolved over four decades into powerful conventions of public discourse that diminish the political imagination, undermine the incentive to envision better alternatives, and thus reduce the scope of practical options available to leaders of both nations. . . . Yet, the stuff of which these durable motives are made is mere metaphor."[26] In other words, Cold War rhetors were also trapped by their language.

Similarly, in his analysis of Cold War rhetoric, Edwin Black suggests that the pervasiveness of the "cancer of communism" metaphor in the rhetoric of the most radical elements of the right in U.S. politics may have brought the world to the brink of nuclear war. Noting that the "cancer of communism" metaphor is "simply not present in 'liberal' or leftist discourses," Black argues that "it seems to crop up constantly among Rightists—Rightists who sometimes have little else in common besides a political position and the metaphor itself." Further, Black suggests that the "cancer of communism" metaphor may have been "literalized," to use Ivie's term, in a way that risked nuclear annihilation. According to Black, what we little understand is that when a radical rightists

refers to America, he refers to a polity already in the advanced stages of an inexorable disease whose suppurating sores are everywhere manifest and whose voice is a death rattle. . . . The patient is *in extremis.* It is in this light that risks must be calculated, and in this light the prospect of nuclear war becomes thinkable. Why not chance it, after all? What alternative is there? The patient is dying; is it not time for the ultimate surgery? What is there to lose? In such a context, an unalarmed attitude toward the use of atomic weapons is not just reasonable; it is obvious.[27]

Ivie and Black are not alone in warning of the perils of literalizing metaphors of disease and illness. Steven Perry's analysis of the "infestation metaphor" in the rhetoric of Adolf Hitler helps to explain how significant segments of the German population of the 1930s and 1940s were persuaded to turn violently against their own Jewish brothers and sisters. Perry explains:

Though there was unquestionably a very real current of anti-semitism in central Europe at the time of National Socialism's rise, the Jews nonetheless were not popularly perceived as enemies of the German nation. Hitler had to shape and channel popular anti-semitism; particularly, he had to explain how it was that the heretofore *scorned* Jew was actually a dangerous and foreign threat to the very foundation of the German nation. The use of infestation metaphors provided Hitler with the answer. Such metaphors were suitably de-humanizing, and, even more important, they provided a figurative explanation of the Jewish threat: The Jew was like the disease-causing microbe, the internal parasite, or the secretly-administered poison, wreaking an invisible but ultimately fatal havoc on the national body. Hence, it was not as though the Jew had somehow suddenly metamorphosed from a worthless but harmless object of scorn into a full-blown national threat. Rather, the Jew had always posed such a threat, and the German masses had only needed a savior, a Hitler, to rise and show them the real working of the insidious, invisible Jewish plague."[28]

Thus, Perry suggests, was Hitler able to persuade Germany to follow him into the holocaust.

In sum, metaphors work by drawing comparisons between two things, people, places, situations, events, etc. In doing so, they can embellish the style of written and oral messages alike. More important, they also have the capacity to perform powerful rhetorical functions, altering the thoughts and actions of readers and listeners. Additionally, although metaphors are potentially powerful figures of speech, their use also entails potential risk. We turn now to how rhetorical critics might make use of this knowledge of metaphor.

CRITIQUING METAPHOR

We view rhetorical criticism as a primary means for creating knowledge in the humanistic study of communication. Further, we believe strongly that for criticism to fulfill that function, it must be an "organic" or inductive process. That process ends by bringing together textual, contextual, theoretical, interpretive, and evaluative elements in a finished critique. It begins, however, with a close, exhaustive reading of the rhetorical artifact under consideration, the end of which is largely descriptive at the initial stage. When that descriptive analysis is complete, the discourse is placed within its historical and cultural context and the rhetorical problems or obstacles to success faced by the rhetor must be explained. Based on a thorough understanding of both text and context, critics select or invent a theoretical framework or analytical tool, such as a theory of metaphor, that both guides the completed analysis and suggests criteria or standards for interpretation and evaluation. Only when the above is complete can the textual, contextual, theoretical, interpretive, and evaluative elements be brought together.[29]

Thus, we believe that to talk about "metaphor criticism" as a distinct form or type of rhetorical criticism is both misleading and potentially counterproductive. Rather, we see metaphor as one of many analytical tools available to critics, a theoretical framework that can guide rhetorical analysis. Put differently, critics should "do" metaphor criticism only when careful descriptive analysis of the text in question reveals that metaphor is a significant—perhaps *the most* significant—rhetorical element in that text. To reverse that process, to start with a theory of metaphor and then apply it indiscriminately to whatever text happens to be in question, renders the entire critical process fraudulent.[30] That process, then, must begin with a thorough, close reading of the text under consideration; if it reveals that metaphor is a salient rhetorical element in the text, relevant theory can become a useful analytical tool.

When metaphor is a significant element of the text, critics should determine whether a single major metaphor is developed throughout the text or whether a series of metaphors are present. If a series of metaphors are present, critics should determine whether they operate independently or whether they cohere into a single vision or image. For example, a close reading of Martin Luther King Jr.'s 1963, "I Have A Dream," reveals that three major, interrelated metaphors dominate the text: 1) the "promise" set forth in the Declaration of Independence "that all men would be guaranteed the unalienable rights of life, liberty, and the pursuit of happiness" (the *tenor*) characterized metaphorically as a "check" or "promissory note to which every American was to fall heir" but that had yet to be paid in full (the *vehicle*); 2) King's goal of a free and just society if only the check were to be cashed (*tenor*), characterized metaphorically as his "dream" (*vehicle*); and 3) King's vision of the "great nation" the United States could become (*tenor*), characterized metaphorically as freedom "ringing" throughout the land (*vehicle*).[31]

Those three major metaphors in King's speech cohere into a single vision in that they "move" chronologically from the past—the promise set forth in the Declaration of Independence—to 1963—conditions of oppression for black Americans as a result of the failure of the United States to "cash the check"—and into the future—the vision of freedom ringing throughout the land. Moreover, the metaphors cohere even further in that they also move from bad (the social and economic conditions faced by black Americans) to good (the free and just society King envisioned).

Critics should determine as well whether minor or secondary metaphors are present in the text and, if so, how they interact with the major metaphor or metaphors. Once again, secondary metaphors appear throughout King's "I Have A Dream" speech. Some stand alone to create vivid images in the minds of listeners. For instance, social conditions (*tenor*) are depicted metaphorically when King explains that black Americans are "still sadly crippled by the manacles of segregation and the chains of discrimination" (*vehicle*). Economic conditions (*tenor*) are depicted when he says that black Americans are living "on a lonely island of poverty in the midst of a vast ocean of material prosperity" (*vehicle*). However, other secondary metaphors function to reinforce the past-present-future and bad-to-good relationship between the major metaphors: "Now is the time to lift our nation from the quicksands of racial injustice to the solid rock of brotherhood," said King. "The whirlwinds of revolt will continue to shake the foundations of our nation until the bright day of justice emerges," he continued.

When major and secondary metaphors have been identified, critics might productively ask: What elements or characteristics of the *vehicle* does the rhetor intend for the audience to carry over to the *tenor*? How do those elements or characteristics function to alter audience understanding of the *tenor*? How is that altered understanding related to the *purpose* or *purposes* the rhetor wishes to achieve? How do the metaphors interact with other rhetorical strategies present in the text? Finally, how might the use of metaphor best be interpreted or evaluated?

We hope this brief description suggests at least a general direction for critiquing metaphor. Now, we turn to an example of metaphor criticism that incorporates all of the elements of a finished critique that we mentioned earlier: contextualization; a theoretical framework or analytical tool; application of that theory to illuminate the text; and interpretation and evaluation.

CRITICAL ESSAY

The text we have selected for analysis in our example of metaphor criticism is the keynote address delivered on July 16, 1984, to the Democratic National Convention in San Francisco by New York's then-Governor Mario Cuomo. Although the speech was delivered nearly twenty-five years ago, it is especially well suited for this example. Even a cursory reading of

Cuomo's speech reveals that metaphor is a significant—perhaps *the most* significant—rhetorical element in that text. Thus, the speech is not only a model of rhetorical excellence, but its analysis also provides beginning rhetorical critics with a clear example of a text that warrants metaphor criticism.

CRITICAL ESSAY: MARIO CUOMO'S KEYNOTE ADDRESS TO THE 1984 DEMOCRATIC NATIONAL CONVENTION[32]

Immediate reactions to New York Governor Mario Cuomo's keynote address to the 1984 Democratic National Convention were extremely positive. Delegates in the convention hall were lavish in their praise. "'He's reaching an emotional chord that hasn't been touched since John Kennedy,' said Lucille Maurer, a Maryland legislator from Silver Spring."[33] "It was a perfect speech," added Virginia state party chairman Alan A. Dimondstein. "He talked about the middle class. We're talking about a man who stood up and expressed the feelings of the majority of people in America."[34]

Media pundits were likewise kind in their assessment of the speech. Hedrick Smith of the *New York Times* observed that Cuomo "built a speech like a lawyer making a case,"[35] and then added: "Beforehand, [Cuomo's] aides had said the keynote was 'not a stemwinder, not a podium-pounder' but a carefully constructed indictment of the Reagan legacy. Yet with eyes welling with tears and a powerful rhythmic delivery, the Governor repeatedly roused the Democrats to foot-stomping applause and roaring partisan chants."[36] Howell Raines, also of the *New York Times,* noted the "persistent, preacherly rhythm" of Cuomo's speech.[37] Lou Cannon and Helen Dewar of the *Washington Post* observed that "the delegates . . . listened in rapt attention to the New York governor and interrupted him with applause 42 times."[38]

Interesting as those comments are, they do little to explain the rhetorical force of Cuomo's speech. That is, although those comments describe Cuomo's delivery of the speech and the positive reactions of both the delegates and the press, they do not reveal the elements within the text that had the capacity to produce those positive reactions. The rhetorical force of the speech, we believe, grew from the Governor's use of metaphor to attempt to refute President Ronald Reagan's own metaphoric depiction of the United States as a "Shining City on a Hill," and then to depict the people of the United States as a "family" that must reject Reagan's policies and elect a Democrat as president.

The Context: Obstacles to Rhetorical Success

Cuomo suggested the purpose of his keynote address in the third paragraph of the speech when he said that he would "deal immediately with questions that should determine this election and that we all know are vital to the American people."[39] But a simple enumeration of campaign issues was obviously not his ultimate aim. Instead, he sought to unite Democrats and other voters to elect Walter Mondale and Geraldine Ferraro president and vice president of the United States. At the end of the address he said:

> And, ladies and gentlemen, on January 20, 1985 . . . we will have a new president of the United States, a Democrat born not to the blood of kings but to the blood of pioneers and immigrants.
>
> And we will have America's first woman vice president, the child of immigrants, and she . . . will open with one magnificent stroke, a whole new frontier for the United States. Now, it will happen.
>
> It will happen—if we make it happen; if you and I can make it happen.

In his effort to achieve that purpose, Cuomo faced significant rhetorical problems growing from the generic obstacles encountered by all keynote speakers as well as from obstacles unique to his specific situation.

Generic Obstacles. The opening of a political party's national convention is an identifiable, regularly recurring ceremony that requires that a speech be given to fulfill expectations for the occasion. Thus, Wayne N. Thompson called keynote addresses "a subgenre of ceremonial speaking,"[40] making them epideictic in Aristotelian terms and suggesting that their method should be praise and blame.[41] But the purpose of keynote addresses goes beyond traditional aims of epideictic speaking. As Edwin A. Miles observed, the "keynote speech has two primary purposes: to raise the enthusiasm of the delegates to a high pitch and to rally the voters of the nation to the party's standard."[42] That is, in addition to any purely ceremonial functions, the pragmatic aim of keynote addresses is to help the party's nominee win the coming presidential election. Cuomo's purpose reveals just that aim.

The keynote address, then, is a rhetorical hybrid. It employs epideictic means—praise and blame—appropriate to the ceremonial occasion in order to achieve deliberative ends, election of the party's candidate. Thus, Miles explained that highly-partisan audiences in the convention hall came to expect keynote speakers' "language . . . to be bombastic, for custom demands that he 'avoid no extravagance of speech, either in praise or blame' in glorifying the brilliant accomplishments of his own party or in lamenting the dismal failures of the opposition."[43]

Unfortunately, perhaps, for contemporary speakers, widespread television coverage of keynote addresses has been problematic. Keynoters encounter not only the partisan, immediate audience, but also a large and diverse audience watching the televised speech at home. Some members of that larger audience are equally partisan, but most vary in their conviction and many support the opposition.[44] Those dual audiences present keynote speakers with a dilemma. According to Thompson, "whereas emotional partisans of a speaker's own party expect a vigorous attack on the opposition, neutrals and members of the other political party are likely to find strong attacks irritating and offensive."[45]

Cuomo faced those obstacles generic to the keynote situation as he addressed the 1984 Democratic National Convention. But like any other keynote speaker, he also faced obstacles growing from the specific problems that developed as Democrats prepared to meet in San Francisco in mid July.

Specific Obstacles. On the eve of Cuomo's address, Democrats were dispirited and divided. Political commentators Jack W. Germond and Jules Witcover noted that many convention delegates (and probably many other Democrats as well!) despaired of Mondale's chances of defeating Ronald Reagan in November.[46] But the delegates' spirits were buoyed significantly, "when the word of Gerry Ferraro's selection [as Mondale's vice-presidential running mate] filtered out on the Wednesday night before the convention was to open." The delegates' reaction to Ferraro, according to Germond and Witcover, was "akin to pulling the living room drapes back and letting the sunshine in . . . [W]hat shook the Democrats out of their doldrums was the evidence in Mondale's decision that he was not the storefront Indian he seemed to so many of them to be—dull, unimaginative, the cardboard New Dealer who dared to be cautious," they explained.[47]

Despite the excitement over the selection of Ferraro, opinion polls indicated that the Democratic ticket was in trouble. As Robert Strauss, former head of the Democratic National Committee, explained: "If [Mondale and Ferraro] try to win a popularity contest with Ronald Reagan, they're not going to make much headway. The people of America like Ronald Reagan too well."[48] Strauss was right. The day after Cuomo's speech, the *Los Angeles Times* reported a

Gallup poll indicating that "based on in-person interviews with a national sample of registered voters . . . Reagan-Bush beats Mondale-Ferraro, 53 percent to 39 percent. When Reagan and Mondale alone are pitted against each other, Reagan's margin is 55 percent to 36 percent." Among women voters, the same poll revealed, "the contest would be a virtual toss-up, with 47 percent choosing Reagan-Bush compared to 45 percent for Mondale-Ferraro. Among men, the GOP ticket leads 59 percent to 34 percent."[49]

Whether those figures signaled distrust of Mondale, approval of Reagan's political agenda and policies, or simple affection for the amiable president, they did not look good for the Democratic candidates. Moreover, coupled with the generic obstacles faced by all keynote speakers, they constituted significant rhetorical problems for Cuomo. To overcome those problems, Cuomo relied in large part on the strategic use of metaphor.

Metaphor as Rhetorical Strategy

Cuomo's reliance on metaphor was consistent with expectations for epideictic speaking's elevated style. Nevertheless, consideration of the nonornamental capacities of metaphor is essential for understanding its functions in Cuomo's keynote address. That metaphor serves more than embellishment has been demonstrated by scholarship in interaction theory and adapted in critical studies illustrating the significant interplay between metaphor and topical invention, wherein metaphor "frames rhetorical situations" while "topics order the elements within the frame."[50] Figures that frame situations support George Lakoff and Mark Johnson's thesis that metaphor is "primarily a matter of thought and action and only derivatively a matter of language," instrumental to our understanding of reality, and advantageous to people in power who "get to impose their metaphors."[51] The power to create a new order by imposing a metaphor that "redescribes reality," Paul Ricoeur argues, is contingent on first "creating rifts in an old order."[52] Moreover, the creation of dissonance is promoted when the similarities selected for a metaphorical frame are experiential rather than objective similarities. As Lakoff and Johnson point out, objectivists may be correct to suggest that "things in the world" constrain our conceptual systems, but that matters only if the "things" are experienced.[53] Metaphor's capacity to displace one "reality" with another by focusing on experiential themes is central to Cuomo's speech.

Textual Analysis: Cuomo's Use of Metaphor

Cuomo's ultimate objective was to promote a vision of the American people as a "family." Movement toward that goal proceeded through three phases. First, consonant with the dictates of Ricoeur's theory of metaphor, Cuomo aimed to raise doubts about the accuracy of a favored Reagan figure, that of America as a "shining city on a hill."[54] Next, he moved to the articulation of the American family alternative. Finally, Cuomo offered his own family's experience as an embodiment of the metaphor's reflection of the American reality.

Since the creation of a new perception of reality is enhanced by an initial denigration of an old conception, Cuomo began his appeal with a revision of a favorite Reagan metaphor:

> Ten days ago, President Reagan admitted that although some people in this country seemed to be doing well nowadays, others were unhappy, even worried, about themselves, their families and their futures.
>
> The president said that he didn't understand that fear. He said, "Why, this country is a shining city on a hill."

And the president is right. In many ways we *are* "a shining city on a hill."

But the hard truth is that not everyone is sharing in this city's splendor and glory.

A shining city is perhaps all the president sees from the portico of the White House and the veranda of his ranch, where everyone seems to be doing well.

But there's another city, another part of the city, the part where some people can't pay their mortgages and most young people can't afford one, where students can't afford the education they need and middle-class parents watch the dreams they hold for their children evaporate.

In this part of the city there are more poor than ever, more families in trouble, and more and more people who need help but can't find it.

Even worse: There are elderly people who tremble in the basements of the houses there.

And there are people who sleep in the city streets, in the gutter, where the glitter doesn't show.

There are ghettos where thousands of young people, without a job or an education, give their lives away to drug dealers every day.

There is despair, Mr. President, in the faces that you don't see, in the places that you don't visit in our shining city.

In fact, you ought to know Mr. President, that this nation is more a "Tale of Two Cities" than it is just a "Shining City on a Hill."

The "Tale of Two Cities" metaphor was designed to "displace" Reagan's vision of reality, the "Shining City on a Hill," with a new vision. Significantly, Cuomo's contrasting metaphor did not force his listeners to see America from *either* the perspective of the Shining City *or* the perspective of its opposite—perhaps a "wasteland." Rather, America was *both* the Shining City that Reagan saw *and* a much more dismal place. Cuomo built the remainder of his anti-administration appeal on the foundation of the two-cities theme as he proceeded through a series of paired consequences he described as inevitable results of Reagan's programs. Republican policies, he argued, "divide the nation: into the lucky and the left-out, the royalty and the rabble. The Republicans are willing to treat that division as victory. They would cut this nation in half, into those temporarily better off and those worse off than before, and call it recovery." The Democrats' task, he continued, was to work for the election of a "new President of the United States." The challengers' success in 1984, Cuomo maintained, was contingent on supplanting one vision of the nation with another.

The objective, he intoned, was first to "make the American people hear our 'tale of two cities,'" and then to "convince them that we don't have to settle for two cities, that we can have one city, indivisible, shining for all its people." The metaphorical framing of his theme allowed Cuomo to figuratively allege objectionable consequences of the president's policies without alienating an increasingly patriotic electorate overwhelmingly enamored of the incumbent. At the same time, by raising doubts about the opposition's ideas, he fulfilled one of the functions of the keynote speech—blaming the opposition.

Praise of the Democratic Party stemmed from the subsequent introduction of the family metaphor. The family metaphor addressed the concerns of both the immediate convention observers and the "middle America" target audience. For partisans, the figure of the family served two purposes. At one level, Cuomo's enunciation of party achievements differentiated what he termed realistic, principled Democrats from their Republican counterparts. Cuomo contended, for instance, that whereas GOP policies preclude the metaphoric "wagon train" of American progress from reaching the "frontier unless some of our old, some of our young, and some of our weak are left behind," Democrats believe that "we can make it all the way with the whole family intact." This is, he continued, attested to by "wagon train after wagon train" of success, ever since Franklin Roosevelt "lifted himself from his wheelchair to lift this nation from its knees." Democrats led the way, in Cuomo's view: "To new frontiers of education, housing, peace. The whole family aboard. Constantly reaching out to extend and enlarge that family. Lifting them up into the wagon on the way. Blacks and Hispanics, and people of every ethnic group, and Native Americans—all those struggling to build their families and claim some small share of America."

The principles that underlay Cuomo's description of the party surely meshed with the personal facts influential in the target audience's thinking—family, mutual support, equality, and progress. Cuomo made explicit the link between such values and the ideals of the middle class when, late in the speech, he extended the family theme from the past and present to the future. "We can have a future that provides for all the young of the present," he asserted in a subtly worded play on the guiding family metaphor, "by marrying common sense and compassion." Success will depend, he suggested, on continued recognition of the importance of the party's "progressive principles. That they helped lift up generations to the middle class and higher: gave us a chance to work, go to college, to raise a family, to own a house, to be secure in our old age, and before that to reach heights that our own parents would not have dared dream of."

Although it is unlikely that many members of the larger public would take issue with the desirability of the middle class family ideals he described, Cuomo clearly believed that his perspective of the American "city" and "family" differed sharply from that of citizens who consistently expressed favor with President Reagan's performance. Consequently, he sought to revise the dominant perception of the country's status. Cuomo spoke of Republican policies guided by a philosophy that dictated that government "can't do everything," so it should settle for taking care of "the strong and hope that economic ambition and charity will do the rest. Make the rich richer and what falls from the table will be enough for the middle class and those trying to make it into the middle class." Left to their own survival skills in a nation governed by such a philosophy are the "retired school teacher in Duluth," the "child in Buffalo," the "disabled man in Boston," and the hungry in Little Rock. An alternative, Cuomo maintained, was the Democratic principle of mutuality that underlay a government committed to the "good of us all, for the love of this great nation, for the American family, for the love of God."

What distinguished his pronouncement of this litany of stock political god-terms was Cuomo's personalization of them, for the ideas were not merely lines in a speech but convictions produced of a lifetime. Thus, when he moved into his peroration he reinforced the metaphorical base of his message. In so doing he offered his own experience as a warrant for a shift in the focus of public attention, away from a now tarnished "shining city on a hill" and toward recognition of a strong future via the "American family." The philosophy of mutuality that had moved Democrats to protect the retired, the young, the disabled, and the hungry, he claimed, "is the real story of the shining city. It's a story I didn't read in a book, or learn in a classroom. I saw it, and I lived it. Like many of you." Then, Cuomo's own family became the symbol of the American story:

> I watched a small man with thick calluses on both hands work 15 and 16 hours a day. I saw him once literally bleed from the bottoms of his feet, a man who came here uneducated, alone, unable to speak the language, who taught me all I needed to know about faith and hard work by the simple eloquence of his example. I learned about our kind of democracy from my father. And, I learned about our obligation to each other from him and from my mother. They asked only for a chance to work and to make the world better for their children and they asked to be protected in those moments when they would not be able to protect themselves. This nation and this nation's government did that for them.

110 Thomas R. Burkholder and David Henry

And that they were able to build a family and live in dignity and see one of their children go from behind their little grocery store in South Jamaica on the other side of the tracks where he was born, to occupy the highest seat in the greatest state of the greatest nation in the only world we know, is an ineffably beautiful tribute to the democratic process.

With the choice of the family metaphor, Cuomo not only offered an alternative to the dominant Reagan trope, but also provided through his own experience a case for the efficacy of the alternative.

Conclusion

Assessed for its effect, Gov. Mario Cuomo's keynote address to the 1984 Democratic National Convention merits a largely negative evaluation. His aim had been to rally support for the Democratic candidates, Walter Mondale and Geraldine Ferraro. But despite his best effort, Ronald Reagan and George H. W. Bush rolled to an impressive victory in November, carrying forty-nine states with 525 electoral votes to Mondale's 10—the largest electoral-college margin in history.[55] However, given Reagan's enormous personal popularity, it is probably unfair to expect any keynote address, no matter how brilliant, to carry the election for Mondale and Ferraro.

Judged by an aesthetic standard, however, Cuomo's speech is worthy of praise as a highly-skilled effort to overcome significant rhetorical problems. Clearly, his rhetorical strategy met the situational and audience challenges posed by the keynote setting. By first raising doubts about the accuracy of Ronald Reagan's vision of America as a "shining city on a hill," Cuomo united his diverse listeners around the shared values and experiences common to both target audiences. He did so by packaging his theme of progressive pragmatism or traditional Democratic principles in the metaphorical container of the family, thereby offering an appealing alternative to the president's preferred but allegedly misleading trope.

Convention speakers faced with similar demands thus might be well advised to give due attention to the potential of figurative language as a powerful force for framing complex issues and engaging multiple audiences. The demonstrated capacity of metaphor to challenge established images and present attractive alternatives suggests the prospective value of such endeavors.

PERSONAL COMMENTS ON THIS ESSAY

Cuomo's keynote address to the 1984 Democratic National Convention provides fertile ground for rhetorical analysis. Thus, although we believe our critique that focuses on Cuomo's use of metaphor yields significant insight into how the speech was intended to work, we also know that our metaphor analysis does not exhaust the text. Other critical approaches grounded in other rhetorical theories could have produced equally insightful analyses.

For example, a close reading of Cuomo's speech reveals the presence of another figure of speech that Kenneth Burke has also labeled one of the four "master tropes"—irony.[56] Interestingly, Cuomo's use of irony grows out of the metaphors he develops in the speech. More specifically, by contrasting Ronald Reagan's metaphor of the United States as a "Shining City on a Hill" with his own metaphor of the United States as a "Tale of Two Cities," Cuomo portrays Reagan as an "ironic victim" who is blind to the true condition of the country and out of touch with the needs of the people.[57] So, rather than focusing exclusively on Cuomo's use of metaphor, critics could focus on his use of irony or even on the interaction between the two.

Likewise, although we chose to examine Cuomo's speech as a single rhetorical act bounded by a relatively narrow historical context, it could also be viewed as a member of a group or class of similar rhetorical acts—the *genre* of political convention keynote addresses.[58] Taking that approach, critics might carefully describe the keynote genre, develop from that description a set of standards or criteria that might be used to evaluate individual speeches that form the genre, and then apply those criteria to Cuomo's speech.

We are not suggesting that any one of these three critical approaches—metaphor, irony, genre—is inherently superior or inferior to the others. Quite the contrary; we believe that the richness of Cuomo's speech allows for significant, insightful analysis from any of these approaches, and probably others as well. In other words, careful descriptive analysis of Cuomo's speech indicates that metaphor, irony, and genre are all three major rhetorical elements of the text. Critics might productively exploit all three, but it would be a mistake to assume that there is one—and *only* one—approach to the speech. In the case of our critique, we chose metaphor criticism because in this chapter we wanted to illustrate that approach.

POTENTIALS AND PITFALLS

Appropriately used, metaphor criticism has the potential to reveal the rhetorical functions of language—of tropes and figures of speech—frequently imagined to be primarily ornamental. Although texts rich in metaphor may be aesthetically pleasing, metaphor analysis can reveal their capacity to alter thought and action and to influence—for good or ill—the policy decisions made by individuals and even by entire nations. Our critique of Cuomo's speech is one example of such analysis.

Earlier we suggested that critics should engage in metaphor criticism only when close analysis reveals that metaphor is a dominant element of the text in question. Thus, we believe that the major "pitfall" of metaphor analysis would be to use that theoretical perspective when it is not warranted by the text.

For example, on July 29, 1998, U.S. Supreme Court Associate Justice Clarence Thomas, a politically conservative black American, addressed the National Bar Association (NBA), a largely-liberal organization of black American lawyers. In that speech, Thomas sought to answer criticisms from many members of the NBA, as well as from the public, that his conservative judicial philosophy and many of his judicial rulings were somehow inappropriate for a black American jurist. Thomas's speech is rhetorically interesting and is especially important both socially and historically as a defense of black American conservatism. A close reading of Thomas's speech reveals that it contains many metaphors: "The hope that there would be expeditious resolutions to our myriad problems has evaporated"; "the stench of racial inferiority still confounds my olfactory nerves"; "the opaque racial prism of analysis"; "some who would not venture onto the more sophisticated analytical turf are quite content to play in the minor leagues of primitive harping"; "the lingering stench of racism "; "the battle between passion and reason"; "the caldron of ridicule"; and others. However, those metaphors appear in isolation and do not cohere in a rhetorically significant fashion.[59]

Likewise, George W. Bush's justifications for the U.S. invasion of Iraq in March, 2003, are extremely important historically and they are also interesting rhetorically. However, although close textual analysis of Bush's major speeches reveals various isolated metaphors, once again they do not cohere in a rhetorically significant fashion. Rather, Bush's discourse on Iraq is dominated by mythic images of "Good—versus—Evil" that provide fertile ground for rhetorical analysis but not for metaphoric criticism.[60] Thus, despite the fact that metaphors appear in both the speech by Thomas and that by Bush, and the fact that these speeches are important both historically and rhetorically, we do not view metaphor criticism as a productive approach to these texts.

METAPHOR CRITICISM TOP PICKS

We believe the following essays are exemplars of metaphor criticism that should be familiar to all beginning rhetorical critics:

Ausmus, William A. "Pragmatic Uses of Metaphor: Models and Metaphor in the Nuclear Winter Scenario." *Communication Monographs* 65 (1998): 67–82. The "nuclear winter" metaphor was a dominant trope in the campaign against atomic weapons in the late twentieth century. Ausmus examines the invention and evolution of the metaphor in two articles by Carl Sagan.

Black, Edwin. "The Second Persona." *Quarterly Journal of Speech* 56 (1970): 109–19. Black's essay illustrates how rhetors can invite listeners to assume roles or personas—to think of themselves in particular ways—that heighten the persuasiveness of speeches. He illustrates that strategy through analysis of the "Cancer of Communism" metaphor in the Cold War rhetoric of the radical Right in U.S. politics.

Condit, Celeste M., Benjamin R. Bates, et al. "Recipes or Blueprints for Our Genes? How Contexts Selectively Activate the Multiple Meanings of Metaphor." *Quarterly Journal of Speech* 88 (2002): 303–325. The authors evaluate why "recipe" did not successfully replace "blueprint" as the dominant metaphor in 1990s public discourse about genetic research. Drawing from Josef Stern's *Metaphor in Context,* they assess context as a central variable in the construction of multiple meanings in rhetorical transactions.

Daughton, Suzanne M. "Metaphorical Transcendence: Images of the Holy War in Franklin Roosevelt's First Inaugural." *Quarterly Journal of Speech* 79 (1993): 427–446. FDR combined religious and military "metaphoric clusters," Daughton contends, to create a controlling image of a holy war aimed concurrently to curb public anxieties and move them to action.

Henry, David. "The Rhetorical Dynamics of Mario Cuomo's 1984 Keynote Address: Situation, Speaker, Metaphor." *Southern Speech Communication Journal* 53 (1988): 105–20. This essay forms a partial basis for our critique of Cuomo's speech that appears earlier in this essay. It is an insightful treatment of the interaction between the speaker's background, the rhetorical situation, and the choice of metaphor as a key persuasive strategy.

Ivie, Robert L. "Metaphor and the Rhetorical Invention of Cold War 'Idealists.'" *Communication Monographs* 54 (1987): 165–82. This critique is a compelling analysis of metaphoric depictions of both the United States and the Soviet Union in the rhetoric of the Cold War.

Leff, Michael. "Topical Invention and Metaphoric Interaction." *Southern Speech Communication Journal* 48 (1983): 214–229. Leff takes issue with conventional treatments of rhetorical precepts, in which argument falls discretely within the province of invention and metaphor within the rubric of style. Grounding his analysis in the teachings of interaction theory, he explores metaphor's inventional potential through a close reading of Loren Eisley's essay, "The Bird and the Machine."

Osborn, Michael. "Archetypal Metaphor in Rhetoric: The Light-Dark Family." *Quarterly Journal of Speech* 53 (1967): 115–26. In this groundbreaking work, Osborn explores the universal appeal and persuasive potential of archetypal metaphor. He illustrates those characteristics of archetypal metaphor with a discussion of metaphors of light and darkness.

Osborn, Michael. "Rhetorical Depiction" in *Form, Genre, and the Study of Political Discourse,* edited by Herbert W. Simons and Aram A. Aghazarian, 79–107. (Columbia, SC: University of South Carolina

Press, 1986). This essay extends Osborn's award-winning scholarship on light-dark metaphor. Rather than a replicating of his earlier work, Osborn advances a theory of depiction amenable to the criticism of mediated as well as verbal discourse.

NOTES

1. The text of King's speech appears in James R. Andrews and David Zarefsky, *Contemporary American Voices: Significant Speeches in American History, 1945–Present* (New York: Longman, 1992), 78–81. All quotations from King's speech are from this source. Emphasis ours.

2. Andrews and Zarefsky.

3. Stephen E. Lucas, *The Art of Public Speaking*, 7th edition (Boston: McGraw-Hill, 2001), 266.

4. David Zarefsky, *Public Speaking: Strategies for Success,* 3rd edition (Boston: Allyn and Bacon, 2002), 276.

5. Zarefsky, 276.

6. Kenneth Burke, *A Grammar of Motives* (Berkeley: University of California Press, 1969), 503.

7. Michael Leff, "Topical Invention and Metaphoric Interaction," *Southern Speech Communication Journal* 48 (1983): 217.

8. Leff, 216–217; J. David Sapir, "The Anatomy of Metaphor" in *The Social Uses of Metaphor: Essays on the Anthropology of Rhetoric,* ed. J. David Sapir and J. Christopher Crocker (Philadelphia: University of Pennsylvania Press, 1977), 7.

9. Marc Peyser, "Paging Dr. Phil," *Newsweek,* September 2, 2002, 55.

10. Burke, 503–504.

11. Malcolm O. Sillars and Bruce E. Gronbeck, *Communication Criticism,* 2nd Edition (Prospect Heights, IL: Waveland Press, 2001), 102.

12. Martha Cooper, *Analyzing Public Discourse* (Prospect Heights, IL: Waveland Press, 1989) 111. Emphasis ours. For a review of enthymeme see chapter five of this text. See too, Lloyd L. Bitzer, "Aristotle's Enthymeme Revisited," *Quarterly Journal of Speech*, 45 (1959): 399–408.

13. Sapir, 9.

14. Burke, 503.

15. Leff, 217.

16. Ibid., 219.

17. Ibid., 219.

18. Seth Thompson, "Politics Without Metaphors is Like a Fish Without Water" in *Metaphor: Implications and Applications,* ed. Jeffery Scott Mio and Albert N. Katz (Mahwah, NJ: Lawrence Earlbaum, 1996), 191.

19. Jeffery Scott Mio, "Metaphor, Politics, and Persuasion" in *Metaphor: Implications and Applications,* ed. Jeffery Scott Mio and Albert N. Katz (Mahwah, NJ: Lawrence Earlbaum, 1996), 130.

20. Seth Thompson, 187.

21. Ibid., 190.

22. Ibid., 191.

23. For a parallel study in which a president's choice of metaphors established unrealistic public expectations in policy, see David Zarefsky, *President Johnson's War on Poverty: Rhetoric and History* (Tuscaloosa and London: University of Alabama Press, 1986), especially 21–37.

24. Robert L. Ivie, "Cold War Motives and the Rhetorical Metaphor: A Framework of Criticism" in *Cold War Rhetoric: Strategy, Metaphor, and Ideology,* ed., Martin J. Medhurst, Robert L. Ivie, Philip Wander, and Robert L. Scott (East Lansing: Michigan State University Press, 1997), 72.

25. Ivie, 71–72.

26. Ibid., 71.

27. Edwin Black, "The Second Persona," *Quarterly Journal of Speech,* 56 (1970): 114–117.

28. Steven Perry, "Rhetorical Functions of the Infestation Metaphor in Hitler's Rhetoric," *Central States Speech Journal,* 34 (1983): 232.

29. For a full explanation and illustration of the critical process, see Karlyn Kohrs Campbell and Thomas R. Burkholder, *Critiques of Contemporary Rhetoric,* 2nd Edition (Belmont, CA: Wadsworth Publishing, 1997) especially chapters 1–5.

30. Campbell and Burkholder, 17–20.

31. The text of King's speech appears in James R Andrews and David Zarefsky, *Contemporary American Voices: Significant Speeches in American History, 1945–Present* (New York: Longman, 1992), 78–81. All quotations from the speech are from that source.

32. Portions of this analysis appeared in David Henry, "The Rhetorical Dynamics of Mario Cuomo's 1984 Keynote Address: Situation, Speaker, Metaphor," *Southern Speech Communication Journal* 53 (1988): 105–120, and are used by permission of the Southern States Communication Association. Other portions appeared in Thomas R. Burkholder, "Irony Through Metaphor: Burkean Master Tropes in Mario Cuomo's Keynote Address to the 1984 Democratic National Convention," paper presented to the Speech Communication Association Convention, San Diego, CA, November, 1996.

33. Quoted in Lou Cannon and Helen Dewar, "Gov. Cuomo Rouses Dispirited Delegates," *Washington Post,* July 17, 1984, A1.

34. Quoted in Cannon and Dewar, A8.

35. Hedrick Smith, "Cuomo Would Attack Record, Not Reagan," *New York Times,* July 17, 1984, A1.

36. Smith, A15.

37. Howell Raines, "Democrat Calls on Party to Unify and Seek Out 'Family of America,'" *New York Times,* July 17, 1984, A1.

38. Cannon and Dewar, A8.

39. Mario Cuomo, "Keynote Address," delivered to the Democratic National Convention, July 16, 1984, Associated Press transcript reprinted in *Congressional Quarterly Weekly Report* 42 (July 21, 1984), 1781–1785. All quotations from Cuomo's speech are from that source.

40. Wayne N. Thompson, "Barbara Jordan's Keynote Address: Fulfilling Dual and Conflicting Purposes," *Central States Speech Journal* 30 (Fall 1979): 272.

41. Aristotle, *Rhetoric and Poetics,* trans., W. Rhys Roberts and Ingram Bywater (New York: The Modern Library, 1954), 1358a33–1358b10.

42. Edwin A. Miles, "The Keynote Speech At National Nominating Conventions," *Quarterly Journal of Speech* 46 (February 1960): 26.

43. Miles 26. See also: Craig R. Smith, "The Republican Keynote Address of 1968: Adaptive Rhetoric for Multiple Audiences," *Western Speech* 39 (1975): 32–39.

44. Wayne N. Thompson, "Purposes," 272.

45. Wayne N. Thompson, "Barbara Jordan's Keynote Address: The Juxtaposition of Contradictory Values," *Southern Communication Journal* 44 (Spring 1979): 224.

46. Jack W. Germond and Jules Witcover, *Wake Us When It's Over: Presidential Politics of 1984* (New York: Macmillan, 1985), 380.

47. Germond and Witcover, 380.

48. Quoted in Smith, A15.

49. *Los Angeles Times,* July 17, 1984, I7.

50. Michael C. Leff, "Topical Invention and Metaphoric Interaction," *Southern Speech Communication Journal* 48 (1983): 218 and 223. Also instructive are: Michael Osborn, "Archetypal Metaphor in Rhetoric: The Light-Dark Family," *Quarterly Journal of Speech* 53 (1967): 115–126; Michael Osborn, "The Evolution of the Archetypal Sea in Rhetoric and Poetic," *Quarterly Journal of Speech* 63 (1977): 347–363; and William Jordan, "Toward A Psychological Theory of Metaphor," *Western Speech* 35 (1971): 169–75; Pradeep Sopory and James Price Dillard, "The Persuasive Effects of Metaphor: A Meta-Analysis," *Human Communication Research* 28 (2002): 382–419; Celeste Condit, et al., "Recipes or Blueprints for Our Genes? How Contexts Selectively Activate the Multiple Meanings of Metaphors," *Quarterly Journal of Speech* 88 (2002): 303–325; and Josef Stern, *Metaphor in Context* (Cambridge: The MIT Press, 2000).

51. George Lakoff and Mark Johnson, *Metaphors We Live By*, Chicago: University of Chicago Press, 1980), 153, 156, and 157.

52. Paul Ricoeur, *The Rule of Metaphor,* trans., by Robert Czerny (1975; Toronto: University of Toronto Press, 1977), 22.

53. Lakoff and Johnson, 154.

54. William F. Lewis makes passing reference to the wisdom of Cuomo's tack in his assessment of Ronald Reagan's reliance on, and success with, the narrative form in his presidential discourse. See: "Telling America's Story: Narrative Form and the Reagan Presidency," *Quarterly Journal of Speech* 73 (1987): 280–302.

55. Germond and Witcover, 537.

56. Burke, 503

57. See Thomas R. Burkholder, "Irony Through Metaphor: Burkean Master Tropes in Mario Cuomo's Keynote Address to the 1984 Democratic National Convention," paper presented to the Speech Communication Association Convention, San Diego, CA, November, 1996.

58. For a discussion of generic criticism and the genre of political convention keynote addresses see John M. Murphy and Thomas R. Burkholder, "The Life of the Party: The Contemporary Keynote Address" in *New Approaches to Rhetoric,* eds. Patricia A. Sullivan and Steven R. Goldswig (Thousand Oaks, CA: Sage, 2004), 129–148.

59. Clarence Thomas, "I Am a Man, a Black Man, an American," July 29, 1998.

60. For an analysis of Bush's major addresses that picks up on themes such as "good—versus—evil" see, Jim A. Kuypers, *Bush's War: Media Bias and Justifications for War in a Terrorist Age* (Lanham, MD: Rowman and Littlefield, 2006).

9

The Narrative Perspective

Robert Rowland

During the spring and summer of 2007, public attention focused on the Virginia Tech massacre, rising gas prices, and six trapped Utah miners. The public also was fascinated and horrified by the Minneapolis Interstate bridge collapse. At the same time, the public was not focused on other issues that would seem to be at least as important: the growing subprime mortgage crisis and the growing Federal budget deficit are two examples of issues that were very important, but generated little interest. Nor is 2007 unique. The single subject that received the most public attention the previous spring was high gasoline prices followed by stories of British officials stopping a terrorist plot to blow up airplanes flying to the U.S. What explains public fascination with gas prices, Virginia Tech, the Utah miners, and so forth, while the public is less interested in other important issues such as the Federal debt? The obvious answer is that some events generate public attention and are easily understood and interpreted as stories with compelling characters and an interesting plot, while the subprime mortgage crisis and the budget deficit lack those characteristics.

It is widely recognized that narrative is a human universal found in all cultures and at all times in human history.[1] There is strong evidence in cave paintings and other artifacts that humans have told stories for tens of thousands of years. Whereas ancient humans told stories around the fire and in the caves where they lived, modern humans use all forms of human communication to tell stories. The popularity of narrative easily can be demonstrated by looking at the daily television guide, a listing of movies at the local theater, or a glance at the best seller list. Television is dominated by shows such as the *Desperate Housewives*, *House*, and *C.S.I.* that tell stories. It has always been that way. Forty-five years ago the shows might have been *Gunsmoke, Leave it to Beaver*, or *I Love Lucy*, but narrative always has dominated the medium. And even on programs that at first glance seem to be news or issue oriented, narrative is very common. *Sixty Minutes* is a news show, but the focus of each episode is on using narratives about real people to explore an issue or other topic. That same point could be made about many nonfiction programs.

Films and books are also dominated by narrative, both fictional and in the form of biography. So is much popular music. From Cole Porter, to Led Zeppelin, to the present day, great songs often have told stories. A number of authors in a variety of disciplines have noted that narrative is common not only in popular entertainment, but also as a means for explaining phenomena on the most esoteric subjects. From the law, to economics, to even the hard sciences, these scholars have recognized the importance of narrative.[2] Scholars in rhetoric and communication also have recognized the significance of narrative. No scholar, however, has done more to reveal the importance of narrative than Walter Fisher.[3]

What makes narrative so important? The short answer is that we all like stories and we find them a useful tool for understanding the world. In the remainder of this chapter, I lay out in more detail why we like stories so much and how they work to explain our world. I begin by describing narrative form and explaining the functions that narrative fulfills for the consumer of the narrative—the audience. I also describe a number of approaches that have been taken to analyzing narratives in rhetoric and describe in some detail Fisher's "narrative paradigm." After describing current perspectives on narrative, I present a critical essay in which I develop a system for interpreting narratives and analyze a story concerning American children abducted to and detained in Saudi Arabia to illustrate how a rhetorical analyst can break down the form and function of a social narrative. I conclude this chapter by evaluating the strengths and weaknesses of the narrative approach and citing recommended essays for further reading.

DESCRIBING NARRATIVE FORM AND FUNCTION

What is a narrative and how is it different from other rhetoric? The most basic answer to this question is that narratives are stories and stories function differently than purely descriptive or argumentative rhetoric. It is one thing to make a strong argument for invading Iraq. It is quite another to tell a story about oppression in Iraq in which real or hypothetical people are treated brutally in order to support an implicit claim that the United States should preemptively attack Iraq.

Narrative Form

What are the component parts of any story? Any story contains characters, a setting, a plot, and a theme. Stories are not about statistics. They are about the actions of *characters* (mostly people, but sometimes animals and other beings) in relation to other characters and the environment. The main action of a story centers on one or more protagonists. We sometimes call the protagonist the hero or heroine. If there is a protagonist, there must also be an antagonist (or villain) whose narrative function is to create conflict in order to carry the story forward. Oftentimes the antagonist will be a person who fights against the protagonist, although in some cases the antagonist may be the natural environment or even some weakness inside the hero. From Old Testament narratives such as the story of David and Goliath to the present day in great popular film series such as *Star Wars* and *Indiana Jones*, the focus of the narrative is on the conflict between the protagonist and the antagonist.

The examples of the stories above illustrate the most fundamental principle concerning the relationship between the protagonist and antagonist. The protagonist and the antagonist must be of approximately equal power in a credible and compelling narrative. *Star Wars* would not have been a good film if Darth Vader had been opposed by one of the robots. But when Luke Skywalker and Han Solo joined forces, the battle was more equal and George Lucas was able to tell a series of compelling stories. The point is that if the difference in power between the protagonist and the antagonist is too great, the plot of the narrative will not be interesting because the ultimate outcome will be a foregone conclusion. *Jaws* would have been a much less successful film and novel if the killer fish had been a crazed sturgeon, rather than a giant shark.

The point that effective stories revolve around the conflict between protagonist and antagonist and that this relationship must be based on near parity also illustrates the difference between effective and true stories. In the real world, people often fight against insurmountable odds and have essentially no chance of success. Or a person may face an antagonist so weak that there is no question about his or her ultimate success. The point is that what makes a story true and what makes it compelling for the audience are related, but very different concepts.

An almost limitless set of characters and character types can serve as the protagonist (or antagonist) in narrative. Sometimes the protagonist will be a great hero, even an angel or god. In others cases, the protagonist will be an ordinary person who does great deeds. In still other narratives, the protagonist may be one of us, or even inferior to us in ability or intellect.[4] In some stories there may be multiple protagonists and antagonists. The plot will move back and forth among each of their stories and the overall message of the story will be woven together out of the different narratives. It would seem that anyone can be a protagonist in a given narrative. There even was a quite short-lived TV series in which the "hero" was a college professor.

Although it might seem that there are so many possible types of protagonists that there is no means of cataloguing them, in fact, from a rhetorical perspective protagonists fall into two basic types. The protagonist can be one of us and serve the rhetorical function of creating a sense of commonality with the audience or the protagonist can be greater than us and serve as a model for action. When the hero is one of us, his or her rhetorical function is to create what the great critic and theorist Kenneth Burke called a sense of identification or consubstantiality.[5] This type of protagonist is a regular person who shows us what it is like to live his or her life. In other stories, the protagonist is not one of us, but instead a hero who serves as a model for action. Throughout American history, the Founding Fathers have served this kind of rhetorical function. They provided models for how citizens ought to act in a democratic society. We continue to tell stories about them in a radically different time (Jefferson didn't have much to say about global warming after all), because they serve as heroic models and we still need such models.

The contrast between protagonists who create identification with the audience and protagonists who serve as models to be imitated points to one other conclusion about the way that the protagonist functions in rhetorical narratives. As a general rule, narratives that are designed to produce understanding or sympathy will have protagonists who are ordinary people like us. But if the function of the narrative is to motivate great action, the protagonist generally will be a hero.

Stories rarely involve just a hero and a villain. There often are a host of other characters, including friends, acquaintances, bystanders, and so forth. Although there are so many different types of characters in narrative rhetoric that it would be impossible to catalogue all of them, it is possible to identify several narrative functions that they often fulfill. Supporting characters assist the protagonist or serve as obstacles to be overcome. In that way they function to support the primary conflict between the protagonist and antagonist. Supporting characters also may be used to illustrate narrative themes or create sympathy in the audience. In a film about World War II, a supporting character may be killed or wounded early in the narrative to illustrate for the audience the inhumanity of the Japanese soldiers. Finally, supporting characters may comment on the action, either to create comic relief or to critique the actions of the protagonist and antagonist.

The second basic component that defines any story is *setting*. The story takes place somewhere. That place and time can be literally anywhere and anytime. In fact, there are some science fiction and fantasy stories that take place in a universe very different from our own. The point is that narrative can take us anywhere that the storyteller can imagine and describe.

The important rhetorical point about setting in narrative is that stories can transport us out of our here and now and put us in places very different from our own world. As I write this chapter, I am sitting in Lawrence, Kansas, a progressive (for Kansas) college town in the American Midwest. But through narrative, a skillful rhetor could transport me to Auschwitz, the battle of Gettysburg, or any other place or time in or out of human history. As a consequence, narrative can be used to break down barriers to human understanding. It is difficult for early 21st century Americans to understand the horrors of the Holocaust. But through narrative, Elie Wiesel and others have taken us to Auschwitz and made us see the horrors of the death camps.[6]

The third component of narrative form is *plot*. Plot can be defined as the action of the story. Although literary theorists have built any number of theories about plot types in fiction, and historians have developed theories for explaining historical narrative, from a rhetorical perspective there are two important points to be made about plot. First, the function of the plot is to keep the attention of the audience and reinforce the theme or message in the story. In order to keep the attention of the audience, plots generally build to a climax and include multiple points of conflict. The plot builds to a climax that resolves the conflict between hero and villain because the story would not be very interesting if the biggest obstacle were overcome in the first few minutes of the film or the first few pages of the novel. Similarly, the plot must be varied enough and include enough action to keep the audience focused on the story. Obviously, the action required to keep audience attention will vary with the audience.

The second point in relation to plot in rhetorical narratives is, as Lewis O. Mink notes, that what makes a good plot and what makes a true story are sometimes different things.[7] In a gripping mystery novel, for instance, every detail may be a crucial clue. It may be enormously meaningful that the trash truck arrives in the first scene early on Wednesday morning. In real life, however, the only meaning may be that Wednesday is trash day. Nor do real-life conflicts always move in a gradual pattern of escalating conflict to a final climax that resolves the conflict. In the real world, the greatest point of conflict may occur at the beginning of the plot, not the end. Thus, rhetorical critics need to recognize that narrative form may be more easily adapted to present some messages over others, and that some "true" stories are unlikely to be interesting stories for an audience.

The final component of narrative form is *theme*—the message of the narrative. In some narratives, the theme may be quite explicit. In other instances, the theme may be implied, but not explicitly stated. On the surface, George Orwell's classic novel *Animal Farm* is a fantasy story about animals taking over an English farm. Underneath the surface, the novel is usually treated as an allegorical attack on communism and the Soviet Union. The animal characters and the plot concerning them are meant to reflect Orwell's view that the Russian revolution quickly led to tyranny and oppression of the Soviet people by Stalin and others. The larger point is that some narratives require more understanding of context and rhetorical type in order to identify the theme than do other narratives. The rhetorical analyst needs to keep in mind that in stories where the theme is not explicitly stated there may be considerable variation in audience interpretation of that theme.

The discussion of theme in rhetorical narratives is also important because it points to a difference between narrative in literature and narrative in rhetoric. Although much literature is rhetorical in the sense that it supports a persuasive message, and some narrative rhetoric is also literature in that sense that it may possess great aesthetic power, what makes a good theme in the two related contexts is somewhat different. The theme of a literary narrative may be literally anything—the nature of love, the meaning of beauty, what it means to be left-handed. In great novels or films, the theme may be quite complex and very subtle. The theme may point to the conflicts that human beings feel about love or honor or family or any other subject. In contrast, rhetorical critics are primarily interested in narratives that attempt to persuade an audience to believe a conclusion or reinforce an audience that already has a given perspective. This persuasive function of rhetorical narrative in turn usually requires a theme that is either explicit or clearly implied. If the theme is subtle or overly complex, the audience may miss it.

Consequently, great literature often fails as rhetoric because the theme is too complex for the mass audience. On the other hand, great rhetorical narratives often are inferior literature. Harriet Beecher Stowe's novel about the horrors of slavery, *Uncle Tom's Cabin,* is generally not considered to be great literature. The characters are based on simple stereotypes and show little subtlety. But there is no question that Stowe's novel had an immense rhetorical impact on popular attitudes about slavery in the North in the years leading up to the War Between the States. Similarly, Upton Sinclair's attack on the meat packing industry, *The Jungle,* may not be thought of as one of the greatest American novels, but the very lack of subtlety that a literary critic might decry, helped it influence Congress to regulate the industry.

In summary, the four primary components of narrative form are characters, setting, plot, and theme. The first three components define what narrative form is and together they create the theme, which is what the narrative means. To this point, I have focused on narrative rhetoric that tells a complete story in order to make a point. In some cases, however, the rhetor may not retell a complete narrative, but only give the audience a scene from that narrative or tap into a narrative that is well-known to the audience. In these variants of narrative form, the rhetor relies upon the capacity of the audience to fill in the meaning of the narrative from the scene that is presented or pull out of the well-known narrative the appropriate meaning.

After considering the formal components that define narrative rhetoric, it is appropriate to consider the rhetorical functions that narrative fulfills. If the components of narrative *form* describe what narrative is and means, the components of narrative *function* describe what rhetorical narrative does to an audience.

Narrative Function

There are two related but somewhat different sets of functions fulfilled by narrative form: epistemic and persuasive. Epistemology is the study of how we come to know. Clearly, narrative is one such means. We often use narrative, as Mink suggests, as a "primary cognitive instrument" for comprehending the world.[8] Thus, we make sense of the demand for U.S. intervention in Iraq by translating the situation into a story. One dominant story line is that Saddam Hussein was a brutal dictator, a modern day Hitler, who viciously oppressed his own people and was seeking weapons of mass destruction in order to threaten the world. In this narrative, President Bush and others who supported military action against Iraq, are treated as heroes who are willing to fight in order to rid the world of this terrible dictator. Others see the situation through a very different narrative lens. They agree that Hussein was a bad leader, but put much of the blame for the present situation on failed U.S. policy in the past. In this view, U.S. support during the Iran-Iraq war (1980–1988) propped up Hussein and we are now reaping the terrible harvest of that decision. In this narrative, the United States is not heroic, but an arrogant and selfish bully that is trying to control the world. The invasion of Iraq was not an act of heroism, but a foolish attempt to enforce American domination over another nation.

The point that I am making with the discussion of the two possible narratives concerning Iraq is that people use narrative as a way to understand the world. The narrative acts as a lens that helps the individual discover who are the heroes and villains of the story, what their motivations are, and so forth. Walter Fisher has written extensively about how narrative functions as an epistemic worldview.

While people use narrative to understand the world, they also sometimes create narratives in order to persuade others to accept a narrative worldview. This rhetorical function is fulfilled by stories in four key ways. The first function of narrative is to keep the *attention* of the audience. I made the point earlier that popular culture is chock full of narrative. The reason that there is so much narrative on television, at the movies, in books, and elsewhere is that humans like stories. You would have to look long and hard in the television guide to find a show on a topic such as "Dartmouth experts talk statistics." But virtually every channel runs fictional or nonfictional stories about people and their lives.

Popular reaction to the events of 9/11 illustrates the power of narrative to energize an audience. Previous to 9/11, experts on terrorism were well aware that there was a serious risk that terrorists might use weapons of mass destruction on U.S. targets. Although the risk was known, there was little public attention to it because the testimony of the experts did not fit into what the public found to be a credible narrative. Airplanes flying into tall buildings was perceived to be the stuff of summer adventure movies, not real life. After 9/11, however, there was a powerful narrative to go with the warnings of the experts. That narrative energized the audience and support for action to deal with the terrorist threat increased dramatically.

Thus, narratives that the audience perceives to be credible are a powerful means of getting and keeping the attention of an audience. It is important to note, however, that the key issue in terms of persuasiveness is not the truth of the narrative, but its credibility. Prior to 9/11, a narrative about terrorists using weapons of mass destruction against the United States was not perceived to be credible, no matter how many experts supported it. On the other hand, a narrative may be perceived to be credible when there is little support for it. It is widely believed, for instance, that the nuclear power accident at Three Mile Island was a major disaster. In fact, the best data suggests that there was very little radiation released and that many of the safety systems worked effectively.[9] However, the strong data I have mentioned in no way undercuts the powerful social narrative describing Three Mile Island as a nuclear disaster. In summary, narrative is a compelling means of getting and keeping the attention of an audience. To serve this function, the narrative need not be true, but it must be perceived to be credible.

The second rhetorical function of narrative is to create a sense of *identification* between the audience and the narrator or characters in the narrative. Great novels such as Harper Lee's *To Kill a Mockingbird* played a role in the civil rights movement because they helped create a sense of identification between white and black Americans. Lee's novel and many other stories showed the audience that the black characters in the books were people just like them. Similarly, narrative can allow us to see the world through the eyes of a Palestinian terrorist and understand what might drive him or her to blow up buses filled with Israeli citizens. One of the most powerful functions of narrative is to generate in the reader/viewer/listener the understanding that "I'm like him or her."

The third rhetorical function of narrative is to *break down barriers* to understanding by transporting us to another place or even time. This function is similar to the identity-related function, but deals with place, time, and culture, rather than personal identity. People understand the world based on their own experiences and culture, meaning that they often find it difficult to understand a radically different culture or time. Narrative works better than other forms of rhetoric for ripping us out of our time and culture and placing us in another culture. For example, contemporary Americans may have great difficulty understanding the strict social regulation of women's role in the mid-nineteenth century. While history can describe women's roles in that period, narrative is a much more powerful vehicle for bringing home the restrictions women then faced. By placing us in the time and culture of nineteenth century American life, we better understand the social dynamics.

The final persuasive function of narrative is to serve as a rhetorical means of *tapping into values and needs* in order to create a strong emotional reaction. A story about the death of an innocent child or the horrors of the Holocaust can tap into our emotional nature in a way that statistical data and other forms of argument cannot do. A statistical study proving that several hundred children die a year because of improperly installed car seats, for example, lacks the emotional punch of a narrative about the death of a single baby because of such improper installation. The narrative produces this emotional reaction because the story links directly to a basic value such as life or a basic need, such as the need for security. The story in effect enacts the value or need in the context of a particular set of characters.

After identifying the form and function of narrative rhetoric, it is important to consider approaches that rhetorical critics have taken to the study of narrative. In the next section, I summarize various approaches to narrative, paying special attention to Walter Fisher's seminal analysis of the "narrative paradigm."

APPROACHES TO NARRATIVE RHETORICAL CRITICISM

With the rebirth of the study of rhetoric early in the twentieth century, rhetorical critics tended to follow the example of Aristotle in building their theories of rhetoric and methods for analyzing it. Critics who were influenced by Aristotle, often called neo-Aristotelian or Traditional critics, usually focused on the three modes of proof identified by Aristotle, (logos, ethos, and pathos), which broadly speaking defined rational argument, appeals to credibility, and rhetoric that produced an emotional reaction. In this system, there was little room for the analysis of narrative and neo-Aristotelian critics tended to focus on rational forms of persuasion.

As recently as forty years ago, there was not a sizable literature identifying narrative approaches to rhetorical analysis. Walter R. Fisher and Richard A. Filloy were getting at this point in a 1982 essay on "Argument in Drama and Literature: An Exploration," where they noted that "Argument has been conceived traditionally in terms of clear-cut inferential structures, a judgment that limited the study of narrative forms of persuasion."[10] They went on to argue that many works of narrative, including novels such as *The Great Gatsby*, and plays such as *Death of a Salesman,* make arguments. Although Fisher and Filloy cited a number of modern critics, including Kenneth Burke and Wayne Booth, who had focused on narrative forms of rhetoric, their main point was that critics had not recognized the importance of narrative or the capacity to build narrative arguments. In retrospect, it is astonishing that critics had not recognized the importance of narrative as a means of persuasion and a method for understanding the world.

In this crucial essay, Fisher and Filloy saw a need for a method to test "one's interpretation of a dramatic or literary work."[11] They outlined a four step process in which the critic first determines "the message, the overall conclusions fostered by the work." At a second step, the critic tests the message by evaluating the "reliability" of the narrator, the words and actions of the other characters and the descriptions of the scenes in the story. At a third step, the analyst considers the outcomes of the story as a means of asking "whether the story rings true as a story in itself." Finally, the critic should test "(a) whether the message accurately portrays the world we live in and (b) whether it provides a reliable guide to our beliefs, attitudes, values, and/or actions."[12] Fisher and Filloy applied their method to critique the implicit argument in both *The Great Gatsby* and *Death of a Salesman*.

The Narrative Paradigm and Rhetorical Criticism

Although Fisher and Filloy provided a method for analyzing argument in narrative, they did not focus on larger issues concerning the way that narrative functions persuasively. In fact, their approach remained quite close to traditions in the discipline that emphasized rational communication. The final step in their narrative methodology essentially called upon the critic to do an argumentative analysis of the claim in a given story. Under this approach, the narrative essentially was transformed into an argument and then tested by the standards appropriate for rational argumentation. Fisher, however, had realized that narrative was more than just a type of argument. It also was a basic form of human communication, what he would call "paradigm" for understanding all communication.

In a series of essays and an important book, Fisher laid out the characteristics of the narrative paradigm; he developed the paradigm as an alternative to traditional rationality, which he believed provided little guidance for citizens concerned with issues of public moral conflict. He argued that traditional rationality privileged the perspectives of experts and created a situation in which ordinary citizens felt disempowered.[13] His solution was to argue that human beings were essentially storytellers, what he called "homo narrans."[14] He based this judgment on the fact that narrative is a human universal found in all cultures, concluding that all communication "whether social, political, legal or otherwise, involves narrative."[15] He later argued that "There is no genre, including technical communication that is not an episode in the story of life."[16] In his book on the narrative paradigm, he made the claim that all communication is narrative quite strongly, stating "All forms of human communication need to be seen fundamentally as stories."[17]

Instead of traditional rationality, Fisher argued for the value of narrative rationality. He argued that narrative rationality is a human universal since everyone knows what makes a good story, and that as a consequence standards of narrative rationality provided a way around the elitism inherent in what he called the "rational world paradigm."[18] Fisher embraced two principles for testing narrative reason: *narrative probability* and *narrative fidelity*. He defined narrative probability as a standard for testing "what constitutes a coherent story."[19] He later explained that narrative probability involved three related tests of coherence: structural coherence, which involves testing the internal consistency of the narrative, material coherence, which involves "comparing and contrasting stories told in other discourses," and characterological coherence, which tests the consistency of action by the characters.[20] In addition to narrative probability, Fisher argued that the critic should apply the standard of narrative fidelity, which tests "whether the stories they experience ring true with the stories they know to be true in their lives."[21] He later added that standards of formal or informal logic also could be applied at this point *"when relevant."*[22]

According to Fisher, the narrative paradigm was superior to other approaches to understanding human communication for two reasons. First, he based this view on the claim that narrative is a universal form of communication. As I noted earlier, he argued that all communication is a narrative of one type or another. Second, he argued that the standards of narrative rationality provided a way around elite domination by experts and a method of choosing between empowering and disempowering stories. He went on to argue that the standards of narrative rationality provided the critic with a means of identifying stories that recognize "the truths humanity shares in regard to reason, justice, veracity, and peaceful ways to resolve social-political differences." He cited stories by Lao-tse, Buddha, Zoroaster, Christ, Mohammed, as well as works by political leaders such as Lincoln, Gandhi, and Churchill as meeting these standards.[23]

The narrative paradigm drew a great deal of critical attention. Many critics and theorists praised Fisher and the paradigm for illuminating the way that narrative functions in human communication. Others argued that the narrative paradigm was unclear or overly broad. Barbara Warnick and I both argued that the parameters of the paradigm were unclear, that the standards of narrative rationality were not adequately specified, and that there was a difference between a credible and a true story.[24] I also claimed that narrative was better understood as a mode of discourse as opposed to a paradigm and that it was important to distinguish between works that actually told stories and works that described a topic or made arguments.[25] Later, I argued that Fisher's criticism of traditional rationality was overstated and that the standards of narrative rationality could not be applied to works of fantasy or science fiction, because those genres were judged by criteria different from realistic fiction.[26]

Although there was considerable debate about the value of the narrative paradigm and how expansive a definition of narrative form should be applied, there was no disagreement about the importance of studying narrative. Fisher's various essays had highlighted the importance of narrative as a form of human communication.

Applications of the Narrative Paradigm

Fisher's work on narrative awakened rhetorical critics to the crucial importance of narrative. The result was a huge increase in narrative criticism, much of it clearly inspired by Fisher's approach. The narrative criticism that was produced fell into two main categories. A number of critics borrowed from Fisher's terminology, especially the standards of narrative rationality, as the primary method of their critique. Other critics used an inductive approach to narrative analysis to discover the specific narrative pattern at the heart of a given story.

An example of the first category of narrative criticism is Ronald H. Carpenter's analysis of "Admiral Mahan, 'Narrative Fidelity,' and the Japanese Attack on Pearl Harbor."[27] Carpenter uses Fisher's terminology to critique the narrative power of works of Alfred Thayer Mahan on naval power. Mahan was a U.S. Navy officer, who wrote extensively on naval history and strategy. According to Carpenter, the Japanese government was influenced by Mahan's work because it possessed strong narrative fidelity that made his story "'ring true' for the Japanese prior to the attack on Pearl Harbor."[28] Another example of a critique that drew heavily on Fisher's terminology was Thomas A. Hollihan and Patricia Riley's, "The Rhetorical Power of a Compelling Story: A Critique of a 'Toughlove' Parental Support Group."[29] In this essay, Hollihan and Riley analyzed the narratives found in a "toughlove" support group that advocated parents taking extremely strong stands against adolescent children who behaved badly. They concluded that the "toughlove" narrative "met the needs" of group members and "fulfilled the requirements for a good story" including both narrative fidelity and probability. Hollihan and Riley went on to argue that the "toughlove" story was a dangerous one because it could encourage parents "to get a quick-fix to their problems by ejecting their children from the house when far less drastic actions would be more appropriate."[30]

Numerous other examples of works utilizing terminology drawn from Fisher's analysis of the narrative paradigm could be cited. In general, these essays used a two-step critical process, first breaking down the narrative into coherent themes and then applying the standards of narrative rationality in order to assess those themes. It is important to recognize that Carpenter,

Hollihan and Riley, and other critics tended to use Fisher's terminology for a purpose quite different than that originally proposed by Fisher. Fisher touted the narrative paradigm and the standards of narrative rationality as an alternative to traditional rationality. Critics such as Carpenter and Hollihan and Riley used the standards of narrative rationality as a way of explaining why a particular audience found a given narrative to be persuasive. It also should be apparent that the narrative paradigm did not provide critics with a complete roadmap for how to identify the themes and strategies in a given narrative. This led a number of rhetorical critics to develop inductive approaches to narrative analysis.

Under the inductive approach, the critic does not apply a preexisting theory of narrative, but instead discovers the implicit narrative pattern in a given story. Many examples of scholars taking this approach could be cited. Thomas Rosteck analyzed narrative form in Martin Luther King's final speech. Martha Solomon and Wayne J. McMullen argued that the film *Places in the Heart* was an "open text" that possessed a number of conflicting ideological themes. James Jasinksi identified the narrative argument found in the film *The Big Chill*. Sally J. Perkins discovered the narrative structure found in two feminist plays about the sixteenth century feminist Queen Christina of Sweden. Robert Rowland and Robert Strain argued that Spike Lee's film, *Do the Right Thing*, possessed an underlying narrative form similar to Greek tragedy.[31]

William F. Lewis's essay, "Telling America's Story: Narrative Form and the Reagan Presidency,"[32] is a typical example of the inductive approach. In the essay, Lewis argues that much of Reagan's political and rhetorical persuasiveness can be traced to his success as a storyteller. Lewis identifies two different kinds of stories that are found in Reagan's rhetoric: anecdotes and myths. Anecdotes are small stories that Reagan used to keep the interest of his audience. In contrast, myth "informs all of Reagan's rhetoric."[33] Lewis shows how Reagan used both kinds of stories to generate support for his program and explains why the American people found Reagan's narratives to be so compelling, even though according to Lewis they often were inaccurate.

Lewis's analysis of the narratives at the heart of Reagan's rhetoric brilliantly illuminated much of the reason for Reagan's popularity. At the same time, Lewis's analysis also illustrated the difficulty with the inductive approach to narrative analysis. While Lewis and the other inductive narrative critics have discovered the narrative patterns present in a number of important speeches, films, and so forth, their approach provides little guidance to how the critic should approach the next narrative analysis. Inductive critics do a detailed analysis of the narrative and pull out of that analysis the narrative theory that applies to the particular work of rhetoric. In effect, they build a new theory of how to approach narrative in every essay. This doesn't provide much guidance for future criticism. Thus, there is need for a general approach to narrative analysis that provides the critic with tools for discovering the narrative pattern in any given story. In the following section, I develop such an approach.

NARRATIVE ANALYSIS—A SYSTEMATIC PERSPECTIVE

The narrative critic needs a perspective that is both clear and also allows him or her to explore the complexity present in any given narrative; thus, the critic needs something that is both systematic and also flexible. The best means of achieving both these ends is to apply a critical approach that moves in a three-step process from the *form* of the narrative to the *functions* fulfilled by the particular story, and finally to an *evaluation* of how effectively the narrative functions persuasively with a given audience.

The first step in this process is to identify the four formal elements that define all stories: characters, setting, plot, and theme. In relation to characters, it is important to think not only about who the characters are, but what they represent and their function in the story. For example, both James Stewart and John Wayne made a number of films about the American West. However, their characters tended to represent different messages. Stewart often played an everyman. He was an average American caught in a difficult conflict doing his very best. In playing such a role, Stewart sent the message that any American could be a hero in the right circumstance. Wayne, in contrast, played a more traditional hero. He was the tough as nails lawman or cavalry officer who personified strength and courage. Both Wayne and Stewart played heroes, but different types of heroes.

After identifying the protagonist(s), it is important to identify the antagonist and supporting players and consider their role in the story. The antagonist may be a person or persons, or perhaps something in nature. Discovering the fundamental conflict between the protagonist and the antagonist will provide the critic with a major clue concerning the plot structure and also the theme of the narrative. Similarly, it is important to consider the roles played by supporting characters in the story and how they are depicted. Role identification of supporting characters can help the critic identify the underlying message in the story.

After identifying the main characters and their role in the narrative, the critic should focus on the setting of the story. In many cases the setting will be both a particular place and also by implication other places of relevance to the audience. So, a film such as *Erin Brockovich* is set in a particular place, but in another sense the setting is anywhere there is a problem caused by corporate misconduct. In narratives in which the plot functions to break down barriers to understanding a different culture or time, the setting will be specific to that culture or time. In that situation, the narrative works not so much to say it could happen here, but to rub the nose of the audience that it "did happen" there.

The next step is to identify the plot. The plot of the narrative often moves in a pattern of rising action in which more and more difficult problems occur, leading to the final crisis in which the issue is resolved. The critic should list the main events in the story and consider what those events and the order in which they happened reveal about the message of the story. The primary function of the plot is to keep the attention of the audience, but careful analysis of the plot may reveal the underlying message of the narrative.

Finally, based on the analysis of characters, setting, and plot, the critic should be able to identify the theme or themes in the story. Here, it is important to recognize that narratives often work by implication and that explicit calls for specific action are rare in narrative rhetoric. In fact, there are many stories in which the underlying narrative form supports a different theme than that enunciated by the narrator. For example, a liberal activist might preface a story about the ballot count in Florida in the 2000 presidential election by saying that his or her goal was to provide information on what went wrong and not to cast blame at a particular person or party. But the story this person told might clearly blame the Bush campaign for manipulating the system. It is important to remember that the theme in the story is in all aspects of the narrative and not just explicit conclusions drawn by the narrator.

In summary, the first step in narrative analysis is to identify the characters and the roles they play, the setting in which the action occurs and any more general implied setting, the plot pattern present in the narrative and what that plot pattern implies about how the audience should react. From this information, the critic should be able to identify the themes in the story and the actions requested of the audience.

In the second step, the critic tests the degree to which the narrative fulfills the four rhetorical functions I identified earlier. Initially, this means considering whether and how the narrative energizes the attention of the audience. Is the story compelling for the audience? The critic also should consider whether the narrative is designed to create a sense of identification between the audience and characters (or the narrator) in the story. Questions to consider include: Who does the author want us to like or admire? Does the author create a sense of identity between the reader/viewer/listener and the protagonist or other characters? Third, the critic should consider whether the story is designed to bring the message home by placing the audience in a setting very different from their own lives. If the story is set in Des Moines, the answer is probably no. But if the story is set in a sweat shop in Malaysia, the story may well be designed to show ordinary Americans what life is like in a developing nation. Finally, the critic should consider whether the narrative taps into basic values or needs in order to produce an emotional reaction in the audience. In testing this rhetorical function of narrative, it is important to remember that the story does not directly tug on the heartstrings of the audience. Instead, it uses the incidents in the story to tap into values and needs shared by audience members in order to produce the emotional response.

The last step in narrative analysis is to take the findings of the first two steps and make a coherent argument about the functioning of the particular story. Here, the critic links together the formal and the functional analysis to make an argument about how the story functions (or why it fails to function) for a given audience. At this stage, the critic should ask three final questions. First, the critic should consider whether the formal elements of the narrative are compelling. Is the plot interesting? Are the characters appealing (and in the case of the antagonist revolting)? Does the author transport us to the setting of the story? Second, the critic should summarize the degree to which the story fulfills the four rhetorical functions of narrative. If the story fulfills all four that is a sign that it is a powerful and coherent narrative. If it fails to fulfill any of the functions that suggests strongly that it failed as a story. If, on the other hand, it fulfills some of the functions, but not all, the critic must consider the importance in the particular context of the functions that were fulfilled.

Finally, the critic should consider the credibility of the story for the audience. I mentioned earlier that the truth and credibility of a story are very different things. The early rock and roll song, "Wake Up Little Susie" by the Everly Brothers, illustrates this point. In the song, little Susie and her date fell asleep in the movie theater and woke up at four in the morning. While that was in fact what happened (at least in the song), they knew that no one would find that story credible. They would be "in trouble deep" with their parents and their friends would say "ooh-la-la" because both the parents and the friends would assume that little Susie and her boyfriend had been having a sexual encounter. While they in fact had just fallen asleep in the theater (it must not have been much of a date or a film), no one would believe that story. As this example illustrates, it is important to consider whether the narrative is a credible one for a given audience.

Earlier, I noted problems with the standards of narrative rationality (narrative probability and narrative fidelity) developed by Walter Fisher in his discussion of the narrative paradigm. Although those standards may have limited value for evaluating the accuracy or truth of a narrative, they are immensely useful for making judgments about the credibility or believability of a narrative. The standards of narrative probability and fidelity get at two aspects of narrative credibility. Humans tend to believe stories that are coherent and stories that are consistent with personal experience. Thus, we expect people to behave in a consistent fashion and we interpret events through the lens of our own experience in the society. In the song about little

Susie, for example, the story that the couple had fallen asleep was not coherent; it did not fit with our understanding about how people behave on dates; the contrary story that little Susie and her date were off at a lover's lane was quite consistent with experience in the society of the 1950s. That is why their friends said "ooh-la-la." The critic can use standards of narrative fidelity and probability to make a strong case that explains whether or not the story had credibility for a given audience.

At the end of the third step, the critic should be able to make a coherent argument about the rhetorical effectiveness of the narrative for a given audience. It is important to note that this judgment is always in relation to a particular audience. What seems coherent to an early 21st century American audience might seem ludicrous to an audience in Japan or elsewhere. An example may make this point clear. It widely has been reported that many in the Arab world believe that Israel organized the 9/11 attacks and that several thousand American Jews did not show up for work at the World Trade Center on 9/11. In fact, there is exactly no data supporting this story. However, a significant portion of the Arab world apparently finds it to be credible. This audience has been exposed to extremely harsh anti-Israeli rhetoric for many years in the context of the Israeli-Palestinian conflict. In this context, what would seem obviously absurd to almost any American, apparently seems quite credible.

Summary of a Systematic Perspective on Narrative Analysis

Step 1—Form Identification
   A. Identify characters, character types and what they represent.
   B. Identify the place in which the narrative is set and what it represents.
   C. Sketch the plot pattern and identify points of conflict.
   D. Reason from the characters, setting, and plot to the stated or implied theme.
Step 2—Functional Analysis
   A. Does the narrative energize the audience?
   B. Does the narrative create a sense of identification between characters or the narrator and the audience?
   C. Does the narrative transport the audience to a place or time different from contemporary life?
   D. Does the narrative tap into basic values or needs of the audience?
Step 3—Linking Formal and Functional Analysis
   A. Are the formal elements and the plot compelling?
   B. Does the narrative effectively fulfill narrative functions?
   C. Is the narrative credible for a particular audience?

In the last few pages, I have explained an approach to narrative analysis that can be applied systematically to any narrative. It also can be used to critique speeches and essays that tap into societal narratives. However, I have not provided an approach to testing the epistemic function of narrative. How can the critic apply rhetorical standards in order to test the accuracy of a given narrative? The short answer is that rhetorical standards are of very limited value in making such a judgment. The story of little Susie again illustrates this point. The ultimate question concerning Susie and her date is whether they in fact fell asleep in the theater. This is a factual question and not one where standards of rhetorical coherence are especially useful. Like little Susie's friends and parents, I find it unlikely that two teenagers out on a date would fall asleep in the theater. I find the competing story that they went someplace and had sex to be much more coherent. But coherent and true are not the same thing and sometimes people behave in inconsistent ways. A story about a popular president risking his presidency and his legacy by having sex with a young White House intern would have to be viewed as incoherent. So would a story about hanging chads and butterfly ballots deciding a presidential election. But these incoherent stories did occur. The point is that rhetorical critics are in a good position to judge the persuasiveness and credibility of a narrative, but the tools of the critic are not well-designed for judging the accuracy of the story.

CRITICAL ESSAY

In this section, I illustrate the systematic perspective on narrative criticism by analyzing a narrative concerning children abducted and held in Saudi Arabia. In a number of instances, Saudi men have married American women and, after the marriage failed, abducted their children to Saudi Arabia, where the children have been held against their will. A recent Congressional hearing told the stories of several mothers who have had their children taken from them and their efforts to get them back.

CRITICAL ESSAY: A NARRATIVE ANALYSIS OF STORIES OF CHILDREN ABDUCTED TO SAUDI ARABIA

On June 12, 2002, Representative Dan Burton, the chairman of the House Government Reform Committee, held a hearing on "U.S. Citizens Held in Saudi Arabia."[34] In the first minutes of that hearing Representative Burton made the following statement:

> Managing our relationships in the Middle East is one of the most difficult challenges faced by every administration. It's been a problem for every president and every secretary of State since World War II. With all of these massive strategic interests hanging in the balance, it's no wonder that sometimes the problems of average, everyday people get swept aside.
>
> Humphrey Bogart said—and I usually don't quote movies in this hearing, but it's one of my favorite movies, "Casablanca"—Humphrey Bogart once said, "The problems of two little people don't amount to a hill of beans in this world." Great statement. Sometimes that's just the way it is and there's nothing you can do about it.
>
> But there are also times when we have to set aside all those big global issues and do the right thing by the people we're elected to serve. There are times when someone has to say, "Timeout. Let's stop and take a good, hard look at what we're doing." And that's the purpose of this hearing. We need to take a timeout and take a hard look, a good, hard look at our relationship with Saudi Arabia.
>
> The specific problem that I'm talking about is that Saudi men who kidnap their American children and take them away to Saudi Arabia must be taken to task. We've seen cases where these men have violated court orders, taken their children away against their will, and kept them away from their mothers for years, if not decades.
>
> Despite the fact that arrest warrants have been issued for some kidnappings, the Saudi government has refused to lift a finger to help resolve these cases. In fact, the Saudi government has created a safe haven for these child abductors in a country where women and children are treated like property.
>
> Maybe the saddest thing of all is that our government, our State Department, has done very little to help bring these children home. In one of the cases we're going to talk about today, a mother

went to the U.S. embassy in Riyadh after her two children. She was trying to rescue them from her abusive father—from their abusive father—and the embassy kicked them out. And after she was kicked out, she was arrested and put into prison in Saudi Arabia. I don't understand that.

One of the reasons I decided to hold this hearing is that I was so appalled at the lack of effort we've made to take the Saudis to task for letting these things happen. We have a lot at stake with Saudi Arabia. We need their cooperation. But at what price? If we're not willing to stand up and fight for American citizens whose children have been kidnapped, then what kind of priorities do we have?

Today we're going to hear the stories of three mothers who had their children snatched away from them. Three things stand out in each of these stories: One, the brutal treatment of women in Saudi Arabia; the incredible courage of these women who did everything they could to rescue their children; and finally, the total lack of effort by our State Department to challenge the Saudi government.

These stories are all so powerful that I'd like to talk about each one of them in detail. But I'm not going to do that, because I can't tell their stories nearly as well as they can. But I do want to mention a few key facts.

Pat Roush has been living this nightmare for 16 years. In those 16 years, she has seen her two daughters one time for two hours. Her ex-husband came to the United States in 1986, kidnapped their two young daughters in violation of a court custody order, and took them to Saudi Arabia. An arrest warrant was issued here in the U.S., but the Saudi government did absolutely nothing.

The year before that, when Pat went to Saudi Arabia to try to salvage their marriage, her husband beat her so badly that two of her ribs were broken and the Saudi police didn't do anything then either.

Over the last 16 years, U.S. ambassadors have come and gone in Riyadh. Some have tried to help and some have not. But it's clear that the Saudis were never told by senior officials that this was a problem that was going to affect the relationship between our two countries.

In 1986, the U.S. ambassador was told by his boss that he had to maintain impartiality in the Roush case. Why? Pat Roush's husband broke the law. An arrest warrant was issued. Why should we maintain impartiality? To me, that attitude goes right to the heart of this problem. Ambassador Ray Mabus deserves special credit in this case. In 1996, he started a new policy: No one from this man's family was allowed to get a visa to come to the United States, it caused a big problem for them.

Unfortunately, after a year, Ambassador Mabus returned to the United States and his policy was discontinued. If this policy had been kept in place, it might very well have put the pressure on them to return these children to their mother. I'm very disappointed that that didn't happen.

We were told just this week that Pat's youngest daughter, Aisha, who is now 19, was recently forced into a marriage with a Saudi man. Pat's older daughter, Alia, was forced to marry one of her cousins a year ago.

Now let me say a few words about Monica Stowers. In 1985, she went to Saudi Arabia with her husband and two young children. When she arrived, she realized for the first time that her husband had a second wife and another child. She didn't know about that. Their marriage fell apart after six months. Her husband divorced her and had her deported without her children.

In 1990, Monica heard that her ex-husband was abusing her children. She went back to Saudi Arabia. She took her children and went to the U.S. embassy to ask for help. Did they put her on the next plane to America? No. At the end of the day, they told Monica that she had to leave the embassy. She pleaded with them not to kick her out. She told them that she would be arrested for overstaying her visa. But the counsel general had the Marine guards carry them out. Sure enough, she was arrested. That actually happened.

Can you imagine that? An American citizen is in a crisis, a mother and her young children, and the embassy staff tell the Marines to drag them out of the embassy so they could be arrested. That actually happened.

Monica is not here today. For most of the last 12 years she has stayed in Saudi Arabia to protect her children. She can leave any time she wants, but her husband refuses to allow their daughters to go. Her ex-husband tried to force her daughter into a marriage when she was only 12 years old. And Monica will not abandon her. While Monica can't be here to testify, her mother, Ethyl Stowers, is here to speak on her behalf, and we're very glad to have her here.

The third story we're going to hear about today is about Miriam Hernandez-Davis and her daughter Dria. They're both here to testify today. The reason they can both be here today is not because anybody in the United States government came to their rescue. The reason that Miriam's daughter is here today is that Miriam was able to scrape together $180,000 to pay two men to smuggle Dria out of Saudi Arabia.

Even though Miriam's husband kidnapped their daughter in 1997, and even though the FBI issued an international warrant for his arrest, she got almost no help from the State Department or our embassy.

The courage of these women, Pat Roush, Monica Stowers, and Miriam Hernandez, and their kids, is just incredible to me. You've all endured terrible pain as a result of what's happened, and it's a real honor to have all of you here today.

These are not isolated incidents. These are three examples of a much bigger problem. The State Department has a list of 46 recent cases involving as many as 92 U.S. citizens who have been held against their will in Saudi Arabia.

The root cause of this problem is the Saudi government. They have refused to respect U.S. law and U.S. arrest warrants. The law in Saudi Arabia lets Saudi men keep American women and children in Saudi Arabia even when they're in violation of court orders, even when arrest warrants have been issued, and even when they've abused their wives and their children. And that's just wrong.

We can't let this go on. Our relationship with Saudi Arabia is important, but this just can't be allowed to continue. The only way we're going to resolve this problem and get these kids home again is by elevating this issue, letting the American people and the people throughout the world know about it. This has to be raised with the Saudis at the highest levels. The Saudis have to be made to understand that if they let this go on, their relationship with us is going to suffer. And I don't think that's happened yet.

I'm preparing a letter to the president. I'm going to ask all of my colleagues on the committee to sign it. We're going to ask the president to raise this issue with Crown Prince Abdullah to try to get it resolved. Just a couple of month ago, President Bush raised the case of Laurie Berenson with the president of Peru. Lauri Berenson was twice convicted of terrorist activities in that country. Surely the Roush family and the Stowers family deserve at least as much.

We in Congress have to do our part as well. We've got to continue to hold hearings like this and write letters and do whatever we can to keep the pressure on. My colleague, Mr. Lantos, who I'm sure will be here in a few moments, held hearings and had Pat Roush testify way back in 1987 — 15 years ago. He deserves a lot of credit for constantly pushing human rights issues, and we all need to keep doing it.

Approaching Burton's Statement from a Narrative Perspective

At first glance, Representative Burton's statement does not look much like the narratives that dominate popular culture in film, fiction, and television. Underneath the surface, however, Burton skillfully uses narrative to support a political agenda in regard to U.S. policy toward Saudi Arabia. The stories that he tells clearly are at the core of that agenda in two ways. They reflect his anger at both the Saudis and U.S. officials who fail to confront them and they also reflect his attempt to pressure the government to change its policies. The aim for the rhetorical critic in looking at this statement is, therefore, to find a way to pull apart Burton's remarks in order to explain the various ways in which it works.

My starting point for approaching Burton's story is a comment by Walter Fisher: "what makes one story better than another" can be explained based on two "features" of the story—"formal and substantive."[35] Fisher is getting at two fundamental goals of narrative analysis, to identify how the story works on an audience and the characteristics of narrative form and content that allow it to produce that impact. Narrative critics have identified a number of functions that can be fulfilled by stories. Fisher focused his attention on the way that stories can be used to serve an epistemological or knowledge generation function in educating an audience. He referred to the capacity of stories to "give order to human experience and to induce others to dwell in them."[36] There are other purposes served by narrative as well, including the capacities to create a sense of shared identification and to tap into shared values.[37] Most narrative critics have focused their analysis on the function fulfilled by a particular narrative or set of narratives and consequently have not laid out a complete list of possible functions. However, the previous treatments of narrative can be placed into four main functional categories:

1. Narrative may function to attract the attention of the audience;
2. Narrative may be used to help the audience come to understand a position and therefore create new social knowledge;
3. Narrative can create a sense of shared identity between the audience and people described in the story;
4. Narrative can produce strong emotional responses by tapping into the values and needs of the audience.

In approaching Burton, it is important to identify the rhetorical functions served by the narrative he tells.

How can those functions be identified? The answer to this question at first may seem paradoxical; the critic should begin with narrative form, rather than narrative function. Before the critic can discover the functions served by the narrative, he or she must first uncover the defining characteristics of the story itself. Just as a cook begins with a list of ingredients, the narrative analyst must pull out of the story, the defining ingredients of the narrative. Where should the critic start in this effort? Since Fisher and Filloy focused on how drama and literature often serve an argumentative function, critics have recognized that narrative themes come out of the interaction of characters (including the narrator), the setting, and the plot.[38] Thus, the narrative analyst should begin by identifying the rhetorical forms (characters, setting, plot, and theme) that define the story and move from there to a consideration of rhetorical function. At that point, the critic can turn from "what" the narrative form was, to an analysis of "how" the form of the narrative influenced its capacity to achieve one or more of the possible narrative functions.

The fundamental concern here is to identify the linkage between rhetorical form and function—to figure out how the characters, plot, setting, and theme engage the audience (or fail to do so). In order to achieve that aim, it is important to move in a systematic way from the particulars of rhetorical form (characters and character types, setting, plot characteristics, and implied theme) to a consideration of how (or whether) those particulars fulfilled one or more rhetorical functions. In general, narratives engage an audience in ways that are tied to the form of narrative. An interesting plot may grab the attention of the audience. The characters of the narrative may provide role models to emulate or, alternatively, the protagonist in the story may be an ordinary person with whom the audience will identify. In that case, the audience members may be influenced by the story because they can imagine it happening to them or someone close to them. The setting of a narrative may transport the audience to a reality very different from the one in which they live. And finally, the combination of plot, characters, and setting may produce a narrative theme that in turn taps into the fundamental values or basic human needs of the audience and consequently produces an emotional response.

After the linkage between narrative form and function has been identified, the rhetorical critic can assess the persuasive value of the narrative. Here, the key goal is to consider whether the narrative will be perceived as a "coherent story" that will "ring true" for the audience.[39] Three rules of thumb are particularly useful in that regard. In general, persuasive narratives will contain formal characteristics (plot, setting, characters, and theme) that the particular audience will find interesting. (This is the principle that explains why so many television shows focus on emergency room doctors, homicide cops, or high-profile prosecutors and so few on college professors). A second rule of thumb is that narratives which effectively fulfill the four functions I have described are more likely to influence an audience than narrative that do not fulfill those functions. Finally, narratives that possess "formal coherence,"[40] or credibility for a particular audience because they draw on aspects of that audience's world are more likely to have persuasive impact than those that do not. Thus, by moving from form, to function, and then to how the form influenced the function, the critic can explain what was in the narrative, how it worked (or failed to work) on an audience, and draw an overall conclusion about the impact of the story. In the following section, I apply this approach to narrative criticism to the statement of Representative Burton.

Narrative Form and Function in Burton's Statement

Representative Burton's statement combines narrative with appeals to basic American values and rational argument. In the conclusion, he builds the argument that "The root cause of this problem is the Saudi government." He also appeals to values of justice and concern for the innocent when he attacks the Saudi government for failing to "respect U.S. law." Burton's ultimate claim is that the Congress should call on the President to pressure the Saudi government to release the abducted children. Implicitly, Burton assumes that a threat from the President to Saudi leaders that failure to release the children could cause "their relationship with us to suffer" would be sufficient to motivate the Saudis to act.

Although Burton relies upon an appeal to basic values and rational argument in the conclusion of his statement, the dominant strategy is clearly narrative. Burton uses the stories of three American women—Pat Roush, Monica Stowers, and Miriam Hernandez-Davis—to build the case that the U.S. government has failed its citizens and must take remedial action. In Burton's narrative (or three related mini-narratives) the protagonist in each case is the American mother. All three women are depicted as strong and loving mothers who have sacrificed mightily for their children and suffered greatly. Pat Roush tried to salvage her marriage and suffered broken ribs as a consequence. She has worked for sixteen years to protect her children. Monica Stowers stayed in Saudi Arabia for "most of the last 12 years to protect her children." And Miriam Hernandez-Davis "scrape[d] together" $180,000 of her own money in order to save her daughter Dria. These three women are in a sense everywoman. They married a man who turned out to be someone other than the person they thought they were marrying. But they refused to give in and instead fought and sacrificed for their children.

There are three different, but related, antagonists in Burton's narrative. At one level, the husbands who took the children, abused them by forcing them into marriage or other acts, and prevented them from leaving Saudi Arabia play the role of antagonist. In Burton's narrative, the husbands and their abuse are not described in any detail. They figure far more prominently in the testimony of the women later in the hearing. At a second level, the antagonist is the Saudi government that Burton so strongly attacks in the conclusion. In his brief retelling of Roush's story, Burton states that in response to both the kidnapping of Roush's children and physical abuse that broke "two of her ribs" "the Saudi police didn't do anything." Although Burton clearly views Saudi government as tyrannical and Saudi society as uncivilized, the focus of his fury is on the U.S. government itself. The most important antagonist facing Roush, Stowers, and Hernandez-Davis is a U.S. government apparently more concerned with trouble-free relations than with the rights of American citizens. In relating Roush's story, Burton cites an American ambassador who "was told by his boss that he had to maintain impartiality in the Roush case." Burton then asks "Why? Pat Roush's husband broke the law. An arrest warrant was issued. Why should we maintain impartiality?" Later, he tells about how when Monica Stowers and her children sought help in the American embassy, "the counsel general had the Marine guards carry them out." Burton clearly finds this action to have been a shocking violation of American value. At the end of his retelling of it, he adds "That actually happened."

In Burton's narrative, the primary antagonist is the United States government itself. Burton describes a government that has lost its values, a government that is more concerned with placating the Saudis than with taking care of its own citizens. In Burton's narrative, the government has become utterly spineless. The one government official who wasn't gutless in Burton's story was Ambassador Ray Mabus who tried to pressure the Saudis into releasing Pat Roush's children. In Burton's narrative, Mabus plays a heroic role, but in another sense his personal story supports the larger point that American policy has become quite weak. While Mabus's policy "might very well have put the pressure on them to return those children [of Pat Roush] to their mother," after he returned to the United States, "his policy was discontinued."

The only other characters in Burton's narrative are the children who have been abducted. Burton does not discuss them in any detail. Their role is simply that of innocent victim. These innocent children have suffered not only from being taken from their mothers, but also from being abused by their fathers. Both daughters of Pat Roush were forced into arranged marriages. The children of Monica Stowers also were abused. The only child who has been saved is Dria, the daughter of Hernandez-Davis. And Dria is safe not because of the action of the United States, which provided Ms. Hernandez-Davis with "almost no help," but because Hernadez-Davis spent her own money to get her child back.

The primary setting of Burton's narrative is of course in Saudi Arabia. Saudi government and society are described as uncivilized. They do not respect law. Worse, they do not protect innocent women and children from abusive husbands. It is a society in which the child of Monica Stowers can be forced into a marriage at the age of twelve. While the primary setting of the story is in Saudi Arabia, there is a sense in which the story is set in a soulless bureaucracy that no longer understands the difference between policy and principle. In Burton's narrative only the mothers and Mabus understand that the lives of innocent children must be protected at all cost. Burton implies that the bureaucrats in the Department of State and elsewhere in the government have lost track of both the power of the United States and fundamental American values.

The primary plot devices in Burton's narrative are betrayal and commitment. The women and their children are betrayed first by their husbands, but in a more fundamental sense they are betrayed by their own country. In Burton's narrative the husbands are almost faceless. He describes their actions as terrible, but as typical of their society. His real fury is reserved for the U.S. government, which has failed its citizens by kowtowing to the Saudis. In sharp contrast to the government, the three mothers have acted with courage and commitment. At the end of

136   *Robert Rowland*

telling their stories, Burton's feeling about them comes through quite clearly: "The courage of these women, Pat Roush, Monica Stowers, and Miriam Hernandez, and their kids, is just incredible to me. You've all endured terrible pain as a result of what's happened, and it's a real honor to have all of you here today." There clearly is a relationship between the two plot devices. Burton's narrative is based on the premise that if the government had not betrayed the women and their children, but had acted with anything like the commitment shown by the mothers, the kids would have been saved.

There are two primary themes in Burton's narrative. One theme simply concerns the women and their children. In Burton's narrative these innocent people have been abused because of their betrayal by their husbands (and fathers) and also by their own country. The other theme in Burton's narrative is implicit. While Burton explicitly attacks the State Department for failing to fight for the abducted children, by implication, he argues that while weakness and betrayal go together so too do courage and commitment. If we just have the courage to stick by our principles as the mothers have done and Ray Mabus did, we will be able to force the Saudis to let the kids go.

The analysis of the forms in Burton's narrative makes it quite clear that the story fulfills all four functions of narrative. First, the narrative is well designed to grab the attention of the audience. At the end of the statement, Burton notes that the three stories "are not isolated incidents." He adds that "The State Department has a list of 46 recent cases involving as many as 92 U.S. citizens who have been held against their will in Saudi Arabia." The statistic that Burton cites is not nearly as compelling as the three narratives. It would be easy to ignore the statistic and reason that given the crucial importance of Saudi Arabia in the world oil market, we really are doing all that we can do. Later in the hearing Deputy Assistant Secretary of State for Near Eastern Affairs Ryan C. Crocker testified that

we [the State Department] have no higher priority than the safety and security of our citizens. I believe our record shows a consistent and sustained engagement on child custody cases in line with this priority. But, as noted above, we operate in accordance with the laws of our two governments, laws that do not mesh well on civil and social issues.[41]

After hearing the stories of Roush, Stowers, and Hernandez-Davis, Crocker's statement comes across as mere rationalization. The stories of the three women send the message that when the welfare of small children who are American citizens is at stake the government of the United States of America, the strongest nation by far on the planet, could act strongly.

Burton's story also fulfills the second and third functions of narrative rhetoric. Burton uses the three stories to create identity between the audience and the three mothers and their children. Implicitly, he tells us that this could happen to your sister or your daughter or granddaughter. He also draws on the power of narrative to transport us to a different place or time. This function is most clearly fulfilled in his description of how Monica Stowers fled with her children to the American embassy and then was kicked out by American marines on the order of the counsel general. Although Burton's description is brief, one image comes through quite strongly—an American bureaucrat ordering Marine guards to escort a mother and small children out of the Embassy to be arrested by the Saudi police. Here, Burton takes us to two uncivilized places—Saudi Arabia that does not respect the law or the rights of women and children and an American embassy that no longer fights for American citizens.

Burton's narrative also clearly taps into basic American values such as justice, freedom, and honor and also basic human needs concerning family and children. The narrative produces two strong emotional reactions, anger and guilt. It produces anger at the government for selling out our own citizens and guilt that we haven't done more over the years to help the women and their family. There is just a hint of that guilt in one of Burton's final remarks, "We've got to continue to hold hearings like this and write letters and do whatever we can to help keep the pressure on. My colleague, Mr. Lantos held hearings and had Pat Roush testify way back in 1987—15 years ago." Burton seems to be implying that 15 years is an awfully long gap between hearings and that Congress needs to do more.

Although Burton's retelling of the stories of the three women and their children is brief, it is also quite powerful. In the preceding sections, I made the point that his narrative brings life to what otherwise might seem one more complex foreign policy dispute. The setting, characters, and plot produce a powerful theme that transforms a foreign policy dispute into a call for justice. Burton also effectively fulfills the functions of narrative, especially in relation to shared identity. Clearly, he creates a sense of identification between the women and their children on the one hand and other Americans on the other. He also uses the power of narrative scene to take us out of our here and now to force us to see that similar actions could happen to members of each of our families.

Burton's story also has great narrative credibility. The story possesses internal coherence and also rings true with what we know about treatment of women and children by Islamic fundamentalists. The story is coherent in two senses. First, the Saudi husbands and their government consistently act to deny the women and their children any rights. The three narratives hang together perfectly in that regard. Second, the story is coherent in its depiction of an American State department more interested in geopolitics than protecting the rights of American citizens. Finally, the story clearly rings true. In the aftermath of September 11, 2001, it was discovered that 15 of the 19 hijackers were Saudis. Consequently, this story fits common attitudes about how Islamic fundamentalism threatens American freedom and security. It is important to note that for many Americans the story would have had considerably less narrative fidelity if the hearing had been conducted prior to September 11th, at a time when the dominant perception was that Saudi Arabia was a crucial ally that also helped keep the world oil market stable.

In summary, Burton's narrative powerfully sets forth the case that the United States should use all of our power and moral authority to pressure the Saudi government to release children of American mothers and Saudi fathers to the custody of the American mothers and allow them to leave the country. The previous analysis does not, however, tell us if such a policy in fact would be a good idea. Burton's narrative is by its very nature one-sided; it also favors the rights of the mothers over the fathers. We have no rhetorical means of testing whether the stories he tells are accurate. Nor do we know whether U.S. pressure would be effective in gaining release of the children. Burton's powerful narrative avoids questions about culture and consequences of action. Citizens of the United States would be outraged if a foreign government pressured this nation to act because it perceived our culture to be immoral in some way. Surely the Saudi's are no different. It is quite possible that pressuring the Saudis might be counterproductive.

It is also possible that larger issues involving oil supplies and stability in the Persian Gulf simply require that the United States look the other way on this issue. I find that position distasteful and immoral, but the effect of U.S. pressure on the stability of the Saudi regime is certainly a relevant question. The key point is while the standards of narrative criticism are quite useful in revealing how Burton's narrative effectively presents a particular perspective, they do not provide much guidance in determining whether that narrative is either factual or would be the basis of good public policy. Those questions are at their base not rhetorical in nature.

PERSONAL COMMENTS ON THIS ESSAY

The key decision that I made in approaching the Burton story was to let the rhetorical analysis emerge from the form and function of the narrative. One of the perils of rhetorical analysis is the danger that the critic will use a rhetorical method as a set of blinders, rather than as a kind of powerful critical magnifying glass, to explain how the rhetoric functions. Thus, an argumentation critic might always find rhetoric to be dominated by argument. Any rhetorical theory and the terminology associated with it can be turned into a similar set of blinders that essentially shapes the critical process. At the same time, all good criticism is based on the application of rhetorical theories to illuminate the underlying structure and function of a work of rhetoric.

To avoid the danger that a critical (rhetorical) terminology can become a set of blinders, but still produce theory-based criticism, my approach is always to begin by identifying the defining formal characteristics of the rhetoric in question, to move from that analysis of form to a consideration of rhetorical function, and then to consider how rhetorical theory illuminates the linkage between rhetorical form and function. The three-step approach developed in the essay is designed to achieve that aim and in the process apply a kind of theoretical glass cleaner to the critical lenses that I used.

In actuality, there was a key step in the analysis of the essay that came before the three steps I identified. The step that came first was the identification of narrative form in Burton's testimony. If his testimony had been driven by a kind of legalistic case, then an argumentative, rather than a narrative analysis, would have been more appropriate. Alternatively, Burton, who is among the most conservative members of Congress, might have presented a statement shaped by his ideology. In such an instance, ideological analysis would have been the order of the day. In this case, however, Burton's statement was shaped by the stories of the three women. Once I recognized the narrative elements dominating the statement, the appropriate analytical steps became clear.

In sum, rhetorical critics need a wide-ranging knowledge of rhetorical theory and methodology, but along with that knowledge, they need a healthy skepticism about those theories as well. That skepticism helps critics avoid a situation in which a theory no longer illuminates rhetorical action, but becomes a set of blinders.

POTENTIALS AND PITFALLS OF NARRATIVE CRITICISM

The analysis of a variety of approaches to narrative analysis and the presentation of a systematic approach to narrative criticism suggests several potentials and pitfalls associated with the rhetorical analysis of narrative. The most significant potential is the importance of revealing the power of narrative in our society. There is no question that narrative is an extremely powerful rhetorical form. If the battle is between strong statistics on one side and a compelling narrative on the other, there is little doubt that at least in the short run, the narrative will be more influential. Humans love stories and stories are powerful means of making connections with others and tapping into basic values and needs. The immense power of narrative makes it especially important that critics uncover how narratives function in particular instances. While a number of theorists (myself included) have critiqued the narrative paradigm, the field of rhetorical criticism owes an enormous debt to Walter Fisher for pointing out so forcefully the importance of narrative.

Although narrative criticism can be quite useful, it is not without pitfalls, three of which are particularly important. First, narrative criticism is most easily and appropriately applied to rhetoric that is clearly a story. However, much rhetoric draws on stories that are in some sense out there in the society. A speaker or writer might refer to a story about the Founding Fathers or a story about Paris Hilton or Monica Lewinski and assume that the audience would fill in the details. The problem is that it is difficult for the critic to know how the audience fills in those details or exactly what gets filled in. There is also a fine line between an example included as support material in a speech or essay and a developed narrative. While the line between these two types of rhetoric is a fine one, the line is also important. There is a difference between a Member of Congress citing the example of Pat Roush and the more developed story told by Burton. Narrative criticism is much more applicable to the developed story, as opposed to the implied reference or short example. The critic can distinguish between these two rhetorical types by considering whether the story in any rhetoric is developed in such a way that it fulfills any or all of the persuasive functions of narrative that I identified earlier. If it does fulfill those functions, the story usefully can be treated as narrative. If it fails to fulfill those functions, it may be more appropriate to consider it an extended example.

A second pitfall of narrative criticism relates to the variability in how human beings interpret stories. Narrative critics need to recognize that different people prefer very different types of narratives. A glance at the bestseller list for fiction supports this judgment. Some of us love fantastic novels about space or romantic stories about dashing men and ravishing women. Others like murder mysteries or historical novels. Personally, I prefer the intellectual (often balding) hero, with a subtle sarcastic wit, but that may just be me. My point is that human beings seem to prefer very different types of stories. If that is true in relation to fiction, it probably is true about other types of narratives as well. I made this point earlier when I noted that many in the Arab world found the story that Israeli intelligence had orchestrated the September 11th attacks to be quite credible, when nearly all Americans found that story to be absurd. Consequently, rhetorical critics need to ground their analysis of a narrative in the attitudes of a given audience and recognize that stories which they find to be credible may not be credible to others.

The final pitfall of narrative analysis relates to variation in narrative type. Narrative criticism works best on stories that support a clear theme and that are grounded in the real world as we know it. Narrative analysis of works of fantasy, science fiction, or allegory is more difficult because the critic must not only discover the underlying narrative pattern, but also translate the message out of the category of science fiction or fantasy into the category of realistic narrative.[42] An example may make this point clear. Janice Hocker Rushing has interpreted the first two *Alien* films from a psychological perspective, concluding that in the films "the patriarchy has induced the feminine to fight itself" creating a situation in which "the feminine is actually subverted."[43] My own reading of the films would focus on how the protagonist (Ripley) is both feminine and powerful and also how the films send a strong message that power and money often produce corrupt decision-making.

However, I think it would be very difficult to determine one "correct" interpretation of these films because they are works of science fiction set in a time and place quite far from our reality. There inevitably will be much more variation in the interpretation of works of science fiction, fantasy, and allegory than of realistic narratives, such as that of Burton. This point is easily illustrated in relation to allegory, a type of narrative in which the author uses a story set in a place very different from the contemporary world to imply a judgment about our world. Even when a work of allegory has a very clear theme, such as George Orwell's attack on communism in *Animal Farm*, interpretation is more difficult than in realistic narratives. Allegorical interpretation requires a translation process in which the critic translates the allegory into a realistic narrative prior to analyzing it. This translation stage adds complexity to the interpretive process. Thus, the third pitfall of narrative criticism is that the perspective works most effectively on realistic narratives that lay out a clear conclusion. If the narrative genre is not realistic or if the message is complex and confused, narrative critics may be forced to lay out a series of alternative interpretations of the story.

Storytelling is one of the hallmarks of human culture. From the time that humans developed the capacity to use symbols, we have told stories. And stories are among the most powerful forms of persuasion. Yet, until relatively recently, rhetorical critics shied away from analyzing narratives and focused instead on rational argumentation and other rhetorical forms. While argument is clearly important, narrative plays a crucial role in every human culture. Rhetorical critics need a systematic way of explaining how narratives work to persuade audiences. The approach developed in this chapter is a starting point that the critic can use to break down both the forms present in a given narrative and how those forms function in relation to an audience.

NARRATIVE ANALYSIS TOP PICKS

Fisher, Walter R. "Narration as a Human Communication Paradigm: The Case of Public Moral Argument." *Communication Monographs* 51 (1984): 1–22. This essay is the original statement of the narrative paradigm and the most influential article about narrative published to date in a communication journal.

Fisher, Walter R. *Human Communication as Narration* (Columbia, SC: University of South Carolina Press, 1987). In his book, Fisher fleshes out all aspects of the narrative paradigm.

Hollihan, Thomas A. and Patricia Riley. "The Rhetorical Power of a Compelling Story: A Critique of a 'Toughlove' Parental Support Group." *Communication Quarterly* 35 (1987): 13–25. Hollihan and Riley provide one of the clearest applications of principles of narrative rationality to a real world story.

Lewis, William F. "Telling America's Story: Narrative Form and the Reagan Presidency." *Quarterly Journal of Speech* 73 (1987): 280–302. Lewis essay is among the best examples of the inductive approach to narrative analysis. It is accessible and clearly argued.

Rowland, Robert C. and Robert Strain. "Social Function, Polysemy and Narrative-Dramatic Form: A Case Study of *Do the Right Thing*." *Communication Quarterly* 42 (1994): 213–228. Rowland and Strain illustrate the advantages of the inductive approach, but also the difficulty with the approach as a method of criticism.

NOTES

1. See Hayden White, "The Value of Narrativity in the Representation of Reality," *Critical Inquiry* 7 (1980): 6.

2. For example, Wallace Martin, *Recent Theories of Narrative* (Ithaca, NY: Cornell University Press, 1986), 7.

3. In a number of essays and an important book, Fisher explored what he called the "narrative paradigm," for human communication. See especially Walter R. Fisher, "Narration as a Human Communication Paradigm: The Case of Public Moral Argument," *Communication Monographs* 51 (1984): 1–22; Walter R. Fisher, *Human Communication as Narration* (Columbia, SC: University of South Carolina Press, 1987).

4. Northrop Frye has built an entire theory of narrative around the level of heroic power present in the protagonist. See Northrop Frye, *Anatomy of Criticism: Four Essays* (Princeton, New Jersey: Princeton University Press, 1957).

5. See Kenneth Burke, *A Rhetoric of Motives* (Berkeley: University of California Press, 1969).

6. See Elie Wiesel, *Night*, trans. Stella Rodway (New York: Avon Books, 1958).

7. Lewis O. Mink, "Narrative Form as a Cognitive Instrument" in *The Writing of History: Literary Form and Historical Understanding*, ed. Robert H. Canary and Henry Kozuchi (Madison: University of Wisconsin Press, 1978), 129–130.

8. Mink, 131.

9. See *Report of the President's Commission on the Accident at Three Mile Island: The Need For Change: The Legacy of TMI* (Washington: Government Printing Office, 1979); Robert C. Rowland, "A Reanalysis of the Argumentation at Three Mile Island," in *Argument in Controversy: Proceedings of the 7th SCA-AFA Conference on Argumentation*, ed. Donn Parson (Annandale, Virginia: SCA, 1991), 277–283.

10. Walter R. Fisher and Richard A. Filloy, "Argument in Drama and Literature: An Exploration" in *Advances in Argumentation Theory and Research*, J. Robert Cox and Charles A. Willard eds. (Carbondale, IL: Southern Illinois University Press, 1982), 343.

11. Fisher and Filloy, 360.

12. Ibid.

13. Fisher, "Narration as a Human Communication Paradigm," 4–9, Fisher, *Human Communication as Narration*, 67.

14. Fisher, "Narration as a Human Communication Paradigm," 6.

15. Ibid., 7.

16. Walter R. Fisher, "The Narrative Paradigm: An Elaboration," *Communication Monographs* 52 (1985): 347.

17. Fisher, *Human Communication as Narration*, xi.

18. Fisher, *Human Communication as Narration*, 75; Fisher, "Narrative as a Human Communication Paradigm," 8–9.

19. Fisher, "Narration as a Human Communication Paradigm," 8.

20. Fisher, *Human Communication as Narration*, 47.

21. Fisher, "Narration as a Human Communication Paradigm," 8.

22. Fisher, "The Narrative Paradigm: An Elaboration," 350.

23. Fisher, "Narration as a Human Communication Paradigm," 16.

24. See Barbara Warnick, "The Narrative Paradigm: Another Story," *Quarterly Journal of Speech* 73 (1987): 172–182; Robert C. Rowland, "Narrative: Mode of Discourse or Paradigm," *Communication Monographs* 54 (1987): 264–275.

25. In addition to "Narrative: Mode of Discourse or Paradigm?" see "On Limiting the Narrative Paradigm: Three Case Studies," *Communication Monographs* 56 (1989): 39–53.

26. See "On Limiting the Narrative Paradigm," and Robert C. Rowland, "The Value of the Rational World and Narrative Paradigms," *Central States Speech Journal* 39 (1988): 204–217.

27. Ronald H. Carpenter, "Admiral Mahan, 'Narrative Fidelity,' and the Japanese Attack on Pearl Harbor," *Quarterly Journal of Speech* 72 (1986): 290–305.

28. Carpenter, 291.

29. Thomas A. Hollihan and Patricia Riley, "The Rhetorical Power of a Compelling Story: A Critique of a 'Toughlove' Parental Support Group," *Communication Quarterly* 35 (1987): 13–25.

30. Hollihan and Riley, 23, 24.

31. See Thomas Rosteck, "Narrative in Martin Luther King's *I've Been to the Mountaintop*," *Southern Communication Journal* 58 (1992): 22–32; Martha Solomon and Wayne J. McMullen, "*Places in the Heart*: The Rhetorical Force of an Open Text," *Western Journal of Speech Communication* 55 (1991): 339–353; James Jasinski, "(Re)Constituting Community Through Narrative Argument: *Eros* and *Philia* in *The Big Chill*," *Quarterly Journal of Speech* 79 (1993): 467–486; Sally J. Perkins, "The Dilemma of Identity: Theatrical Portrayals of a 16th Century Feminist," *Southern Communication Journal* 59 (1994): 205–214; Robert C. Rowland and Robert Strain, "Social Function, Polysemy and Narrative-Dramatic Form: A Case Study of *Do the Right Thing*," *Communication Quarterly* 42 (1994): 213–228.

32. William F. Lewis, "Telling America's Story: Narrative Form and the Reagan Presidency," *Quarterly Journal of Speech* 73 (1987): 280–302.

33. Lewis, 282.

34. *U.S. Citizens Held in Saudi Arabia*, Hearing of the House Government Reform Committee, June 12, 2002. Available online, Congressional Universe, Lexis-Nexis.

35. Fisher, "Narration as a Human Communication Paradigm," 16.

36. Ibid., 6.

37. In relation to the creation of shared identity, see Fisher, "Narration as a Human Communication Paradigm," 14–15. In relation to the capacity of narrative to produce a strong emotional response see Lewis.

38. See Fisher and Filloy, 360.

39. Fisher, "Narration as a Human Communication Paradigm," 8.

40. Ibid., 16.

41. Ryan C. Crocker, "Statement of Ryan C. Crocker Deputy Assistant Secretary for Near Eastern Affairs," *U.S. Citizens Held in Saudi Arabia*, Hearing of the House Government Reform Committee, June 12, 2002. Available online, Congressional Universe, Lexis-Nexis.

42. See Rowland, "On Limiting the Narrative Paradigm: Three Case Studies."

43. Janice Hocker Rushing, "Evolution of 'The New Frontier' in *Alien* and *Aliens*: Patriarchal Co-optation of the Feminine Archetype," *Quarterly Journal of Speech* 75 (1989), 10.

10

Kenneth Burke's Dramatic Form Criticism

Floyd Douglas Anderson, Andrew King, and Kevin McClure

Messenger:	Unwounded of his enemies he fell
Manoa:	Wearied with slaughter, then, or how? Explain.
Messenger:	By his own hands
Manoa:	Self violence! What cause
	Brought him so soon at variance with himself
	Among his foes?
Messenger:	Inevitable cause—
	At once both to destroy and be destroyed.

John Milton, *Samson Agonistes*

THE MASTER OF FORM: THE IMPORTANCE OF BEING BURKE

Kenneth Burke (1897–1994) was the leading American rhetorical theorist of the twentieth century. Scholar, editor, poet, novelist, critic, and essayist, Burke's career spanned seven decades. He left behind a school of critics and theorists, and an academic society dedicated to the development and extension of his ideas. In addition, Burke produced a huge body of books, scholarly treatises, and critical essays that are still eagerly read. In a very real sense Burke is still a living presence. His methods are being used by hundreds of scholars and his ideas evoke lively debate among students of rhetoric, literature, and the social sciences.

Unlike so many of the fashionable scholars of the modern academy, Burke is not a European intellectual or a French expatriate. Born in Pittsburgh, Burke was a college dropout who spent much of his adult life on his small farm. Always on the margins of university life he wandered from school to school as a visiting lecturer. He was part of Greenwich Village bohemian artistic life during the 1920s, a freelance radical intellectual during the Great Depression of the 1930s, a failed poet and sometime literary critic during World War II. His greatest period of productivity from 1945 to 1950 established him as a brilliant critic whose works were thought to be rich in intellectual insight, but often demanding and occasionally impenetrable.

During the 1960s Burke was "discovered" by academic departments in major research universities. As a result of this fame, Burke was constantly in demand speaking on hundreds of campuses, large and small from 1960 to 1980. Just before the close of this peripatetic or wandering time, the National Kenneth Burke Society was established in 1978. By the time

143

of his death in 1994, Burke had become an institution. Graduate seminars and undergraduate honors courses on Burke and Burkeanism were given throughout the nation's colleges. New interpretations of his work were constantly being published and signed copies of his books became coveted objects for professors and students. A few persons even began to refer to him as "the master" and other Burkeans began to debunk his reputation as a cult figure and "wise man" on the grounds that hero worship would discourage the reading of his works and stop the future development of his ideas. Over a decade after his death, Burke is still considered the most creative and influential rhetorician of our time.

Burke's Wonderful Life

Burke had a wonderful life. He grew up in a leafy residential area of Pittsburgh. His turn-of-the-century youth was spent in a home with large leisurely rooms full of books, pictures, and magic lanterns. Pittsburgh had not yet become the sprawling metropolis it is today and Burke and his childhood friends roamed the woods and the fields. The countryside was still close to the city's edge in those prosperous and optimistic years before World War I. He was a member of his high school literary group at a time when American high schools routinely had large literary societies. He matriculated at Ohio State and quarreled with the soon to be great James Thurber. Bored with undergraduate life he went on to New York City and attempted (sometimes successfully) to sit in on Graduate Seminars at Columbia University. During the 1920s he was in the seething heart of Greenwich Village, and was first the assistant editor and then briefly chief editor of *The Dial*, perhaps the most famous literary magazine of its time. Early in the decade of the 1920s, he bought a farm in New Jersey and his summers were spent truck farming; during the winter he and his growing family remained in Greenwich Village where he pursued a literary career. Burke labored as an editor and produced a steady stream of critical essays, poems, and reviews. He placed his hopes in a collection of poems, *The White Oxen* and a novel, *Toward A Better Life*.[1] They were labored, introspective works, arid, intellectually rigorous and muscular. But they lacked pace, wit, movement, and poetic imagery. By 1930 it was evident that Burke would make his mark as a critic and not as an imaginative writer.

During the Great Depression 1930–1941, Burke began to be an outsider in American intellectual circles. He criticized his fellow American intellectuals, so many of whom affectionately called Vladimir Lenin 'The Little Father' and Joseph Stalin our 'Uncle Joe.' Burke pointed out that 'the Little Father' and 'Uncle Joe' had put to death millions of kulaks, small entrepreneurs, and former Czarist minor officials. In 1938 he wrote "*The Rhetoric of Hitler's Battle*," an article exposing Hitler's philosophy and plans at a time when some isolationists and German-American Bundists were hopeful that Hitler would mellow in office. Others assured us that we had nothing to fear from a community as highly civilized and prosperous as the German Reich.[2] Burke feared neither Right, Left, or Center. From his small Jersey farm he gave notice that he would not suffer fools gladly no matter what their pedigree or ideology.

During the 1940s and 1950s Burke was able to secure a series of temporary university posts. During that time he wrote some of his most famous works: *Grammar of Motives* in 1945, *Rhetoric of Motives* in 1950, and *The Rhetoric of Religion* in 1960. These three works are the heart of the Burke corpus. They contain his matured theory and his two major analytical methods, Dramatism and Logography. During the 1960s Burke was hailed as an original thinker and a major critic of literature, political discourse, and popular culture. By 1980 a cadre of his followers had formed the Kenneth Burke Society. By the 1990s there were Burkean literary critics, media critics, Sociologists, and of course Burkean rhetoricians. There were even a few

Burkean economists. When the news came of his death in the late autumn of 1994, my graduate students felt as if they had lost a good friend. All but two had never seen him or spoken with him, but they had heard his tapes, read his books, and discussed his ideas. Most of all they had been impressed with his mission. Although he had no academic degrees, Kenneth Burke was more a professor than most of us who teach in colleges and universities today. He had a mission and he professed something.[3]

Burke's Big Ideas

Burke had two or three very big ideas. They gave his life meaning and purpose. One of Burke's earliest big ideas was that of *Symbolic Action*. We do not directly engage our environment. We act upon it symbolically. Through language, mathematics, art, and other symbol systems we interpret the world, harness the environment and even reconfigure nature. Because of symbol systems (particularly language) we can preserve the past, accumulate culture, build human knowledge, and plan for the future. Symbols make our societies into "learning societies" and these knowledge communities are the source of all of our power over the world.

Yet symbols also have a dark side. Because we have language we have the unique ability to say "no" to the world as we find it. We can change nature to satisfy human desires, often without even a feeble idea of the consequences of our actions. In large areas of the world we have interfered in the plant cycle and brought about record yields. In some of these same areas we have unwittingly let half of our topsoil blow away and we have poisoned the ground water. We have hurled the skyscrapers into the heavens in a celebration of our dominance over the planet but in the United States alone we have paved over 50,000 square miles of fertile land, removing it from food production forever. We often know the short-term gains of our actions but are surprised by the unexpectedly horrific consequences of the long term. We are also goaded by symbols, victimized by our myths, seduced by our own stories. Burke reminds us that symbols are shortcuts to realms of experience; they arouse emotion and desire, and that is why artists use them; because they arouse us so powerfully, hustlers, dictators, mass advertisers, political figures, preachers, and salesman also employ symbols. We are constantly being urged by these practitioners of symbolic actions to join something, vote for someone, purchase something, embrace new ideas, and change our beliefs and practices, and to transform our lives and ourselves in small and large ways.

The second major contribution to which we draw attention is *Perspective by Incongruity*. This was Burke's major method of the 1930s. Burke used this method to bring new and fresh insight to the analysis of conventional problems. He did so by juxtaposing unfamiliar or even opposed terms, metaphors, or images. Burke's image of radicals who were "violent in the pursuit of peace" is an example. Burke's most famous example is the one he took from Thorstein Veblen, the idea of "trained incapacity" by which Burke noted that special insight in one area might end up blinding one to insight in another area. Burke's idea of insight by breaking familiar patterns and increasing inventional power through a kind of self-induced intellectual vertigo is one that is found throughout his work. The term "symbolic action" is itself an example of perspective by incongruity.

The third contribution is simply called *Dramatism*. Burke was fascinated by action. He wanted to know how language was used to get things done. He was less interested in the "truth or accuracy of a statement than in its strategic power." One of the most common ways in which humans made sense of the world was through the language and form of drama. He believed that people viewed their political contests, their sports activities, and their marriages much as they viewed a theatrical production. Burke argued that ordinary humans naturally processed their worlds through dramatic categories. Life was drama. Theatre was a secondary product distilled from the dramatic experiences of life; dramatism was the way in which people interacted with their language. Burke did not analyze language as a means of conveying information or truth, but as a vehicle of action. Every human action exhibited the dramatic elements of a who (agent), a where (a scene), a why (purpose), a how (agency—means or strategies or instruments) and a what (acts). In any particular drama one or more terms were dominant. This may be seen by a quick review of paired terms. Thus a drama might be characterized by scene-act ("Given these circumstances what else could I do?") or agency-act ("technology determines my actions") or agent-act ("Given a person like Stalin what could we expect but acts of oppression?") or purpose-act ("Because I strove to help others I became a physician") or act-act ("He hit me so I hit him").

Burke saw drama everywhere. It is true that new presidential administrations try to get a good drama going as quickly as possible. Sporting teams thrive on conflict between players. Businesses advertise their 'story.' Corporate leaders are in search of a good script. Ordinary people look for 'defining moments' in their lives as if they were living out a scenario, and clergy tell their followers about dramatic reversals of fortune and about finding appropriate 'roles' and new 'voices.' Our lives are saturated with the language of the drama.

CRITICAL ESSAY

This essay demonstrates the power of Burke's conception of dramatism by analyzing a segment of the political career of Senator Edward Kennedy of Massachusetts. If politics is drama, the Kennedy family seems especially dramatic, and its fortunes correspond to the rise and fall of a Greek Tragic House. Teddy Kennedy's *rise* to heir apparent to his brother's shattered presidency, his tragic *fall* with the death of Mary Jo Kopeckne at Chappaquiddick, his *mortification* during the 1980 presidential campaign, and his *redemption* through suffering enact the ancient communal drama of the scapegoat.* Kennedy's campaign reaffirmed the high political ideals of the community even as it brutally crushed his personal aspirations for the nation's highest office. Burke notes that we often see our public leaders within the classic form of the myth of the Questing Hero. One of our basic dramatic "forms" is that of the hero who rises to greatness, suffers a terrible fall, experiences suffering and ostracism, and as a result of his trials "dies" to his old character, and emerges as a purified redeemer of the community. This journey of fall, guilt, suffering, death (either physical or spiritual) rebirth and return to serve the community lifts a public figure out of mundane politics, and imparts a transcendent quality. Even a partial fulfillment of this dramatic form gives iconographic power to an otherwise ordinary individual. Since ancient times communities in troubled times have sought out a scapegoat. Unable to blame themselves for bad times, mistakes, or poor decisions, they have blamed a scapegoat and either killed or driven out the victim in order to purify themselves. According to Burke, this pattern is repeated over and over as troubled communities seek to purge themselves of guilt and restore their social health and sense of worth.

---

*This is known as the guilt-redemption cycle, which Burke considered at the heart of all rhetoric. Ultimately, the motivation of a person (agent) is to purge guilt that arises from breaking society's hierarchy. Guilt is greater than just a sense of doing something wrong; it instead encompasses feelings such as anxiety, shame, and similar emotions. For a detailed explanation of how this works, see Rise Jane Samra, "Guilt, Purification, and Redemption," *American Communication Journal* 1.3 (1998) http://acjournal.org/holdings/vol1/iss3/burke/samra.html

Mindful that politics is above all, drama and wishing to make the dramatistic analysis as emphatic as possible, our analysis is presented in three acts, corresponding to the conventional format of a staged play. *Act One* reviews Kennedy's glory days and his fall from grace during the Chappaquiddick incidents through his early 1980 primary election defeats. *Act Two* recounts his efforts to achieve personal and political redemption through the processes of mortification and self-immolation by waging a losing campaign for political principle. *Act Three* explains how he used the occasion of his speech at the 1980 Democratic National Convention to effect catharsis and to dramatically symbolize his new rebirth and identity. Senator Kennedy died as a career candidate and was reborn as an empty vessel, an instrument to serve the community's idealism. Let the play begin!

Act One: From Camelot to Chappaquiddick—Paradise Found and Lost

"The drama of the self in quest," writes William H. Rueckert, "is an extraordinarily complex life-long ritual of death and rebirth, rejection and acceptance, purification and change, disintegration and reintegration; essentially, it is the drama of moral choice."[4] Edward Moore Kennedy's "drama of the self in quest" began with his birth in Boston, Massachusetts in 1932. The fourth son as well as the youngest and final child of nine of a wealthy and socially prominent Catholic family, he enjoyed in his childhood all the advantages and opportunities that wealth and influence provide. After graduating from Milton Academy in 1950, he entered Harvard, but dropped out for two years while serving in the U.S. Army. He then returned to Harvard and graduated in 1956. In 1959 he earned a law degree at the University of Virginia and while in law school, he met, courted, and married Joan Bennett, the debutante daughter of a wealthy and socially prominent Catholic family. Following the election of his brother John to the presidency, Edward, thirty and fresh out of law school, succeeded him as United States Senator from Massachusetts. During John F. Kennedy's presidency and throughout the 1960s, Edward (Ted), along with the entire Kennedy family, enjoyed the spotlight of an enamored media and American public. This short-lived period of triumph was later called Camelot after the contemporaneous highly popular Broadway musical of that name, which had popularized the Arthurian legend in American public consciousness. Unfortunately, this brief triumphal period was followed by two tragic assassinations, John F. Kennedy in 1963 and Robert F. Kennedy in 1968. Moreover, Teddy Kennedy's later actions eventuated in his own fall from grace both in the media and with the American public.

"If the sixties had been a decade of triumph and disaster for the Kennedy's," John Davis writes, "the seventies would witness a steady erosion of the family's image as one by one certain disturbing allegations out of the family's immediate past would come to light."[5] These "disturbing allegations," sometimes about his deceased brothers John or Robert (both, for example, were rumored to have had affairs with actress Marilyn Monroe), were all too often about Teddy; rumors of excessive drinking, fast and reckless driving, compulsive womanizing, habitual adultery, and wild sexual orgies.[6] Early in his senatorial career Teddy Kennedy earned the reputation "as a 'man of the Senate'—hard-working, dedicated, competent (or at least presiding over a staff with such qualities, though choosing talent wisely is in itself a talent)."[7] His image "as the 'Good Senator' in public life" now increasingly came to be contrasted with "the image of the 'swinger' and 'playboy' in private life." In fact, Lewis Lapham likened him to a Minotaur. Teddy, he thought, seemed to represent "the worst as well as the best that could be found in a man."[8] Lapham himself acknowledged that many of the rumors about Teddy's personal life, like rumors generally, probably had little or nothing to do with his actual behavior or character. That they were widely reported in the press and other media, however, suggests that many people took them to be truthful accounts of his behavior and character. Teddy Kennedy's "drama of the self in quest," at least in many people's eyes, had become the drama of a man making wrong moral choices. Camelot, whatever its shining moments, apparently also had a darker side.

Teddy fell prey to what Burke called 'diminished identity' or 'identity deficit.' Burke has noted that identity is symbolically constructed. Others confer it upon us, and, like image or reputation, it can be strengthened or weakened, gained or lost. Thus retired persons often experience a loss of status when they no longer perform prestigious jobs, or former office holders may resent the loss of power and complain that they no longer feel like themselves. Novelists whose books are no longer bought, athletes who hit a long slump, or television evangelists who fall from grace all experience a status dilemma or an identity deficit. Teddy had experienced a similar loss of identity. In 1980 Ted Kennedy's candidacy no longer seemed to invite people to join Camelot. The younger brother of the martyred president reminded people of a hero who had been marred or spoiled, of someone who might have achieved greatness, but had somehow missed the heroic measure.

As Kenneth Burke reminds us, in the Judeo-Christian religion all people are born into a fallen state, burdened by "original sin." The linguistically created social order, the dramatistic equivalent of the "Covenant" in the Judeo-Christian tradition, prescribes what people would be and how they should act; it provides them with their ideals (social, sexual, familial, intellectual, political and economic) and with a variety of alternative selves from which to chose; it offers a complete set of values in terms of which people can find themselves and measure success and failure, or good and evil. Built into this preexisting hierarchical Covenant are hundreds of "thou-shall-nots"[9] and "thousands of moral, social, familial, economic, and religious negatives.[10] But people are incapable of keeping all the commandments, and of obeying all the "thou shalts" and "thou shalt nots," of the Covenant and in some way they will fail or disobey. The "linguistic commandments," as C. Allen Carter points out, "set unattainable standards. The result is broken laws, concomitant guilt, and a need for purgation."[11]

The earliest publicly known occasion of Teddy's failure to abide by an institutional "thou-shall-not" was his having used a stand-in on a Spanish examination at Harvard in 1951, which resulted in his temporary suspension.[12] While in law school at the University of Virginia he had at least four encounters with the Charlottesville police because of his reckless driving.[13] In one of the encounters he attempted to avoid a speeding ticket by outdistancing a police car, but was discovered by the officer parked on a side road with the lights out and "doubled up" and hiding in the darkness behind the steering wheel.[14] These are regrettable "sins," but surely no one of these acts was of such magnitude as to demand great personal atonement through sacrifice and suffering.[15]

Growing up in the patriarch Joseph Kennedy's home, Teddy must have internalized at a very early age the family's "macho role model," in which "the male dominance principle and the double standard were the ruling modes."[16] These modes seem to have been most attractively personified for Teddy in the figure of his older brother, Jack, who became Teddy's sexual role model. Both Jack and Teddy "had difficulty in relating with any emotional depth to a woman, or seeing her as other than a sex object or a field for conquest."[17] Emulating his older brother, Teddy, too, became "cool" about sex and began a lifelong pattern of pursuing women as sexual conquests. He had "no pretenses about romantic love or emotional involvement [and made] his sexual approaches to attractive girls with a matter-of-fact directness and absence of personal commitment that sometimes startled them." Long after the women's movement had ushered in a new awareness on sexual matters, one in which predatory, "chauvinistic womanizing" was no longer seen as "cool," Teddy not only continued to pursue women as conquests, but to do so in a very public way.[18] According to Max Lerner, the description of the lifestyle of the test pilots in Tom Wolfe's *The Right Stuff* as "hard drinking, hard driving" and engaged in "the private pursuit of manliness" fit Teddy Kennedy's lifestyle perfectly.[19]

Teddy's behavior during the 1969 Chappaquiddick incident—when he drove a car off Dyke Bridge on tiny Chappaquiddick Island, was unable to rescue his passenger, Mary Jo Kopechne, and then waited ten hours before contacting the authorities—raised significant lasting public questions about his character.[20] Although he later spoke to the nation in a carefully crafted television address in which he portrayed himself as a helpless victim of circumstances beyond his control, a spin that enabled him to evade personal responsibility for his behavior,[21] doubts about his character and conduct lingered in public consciousness. From Chappaquiddick on he was viewed by many not only as a reckless driver, a heavy drinker, and compulsive womanizer, but also as someone unable to take responsibility for his actions and as a cowardly person who panics and runs away from problems. These lingering negative perceptions prevented him from being a presidential candidate in 1972 and 1976.[22] Perhaps when he entered the presidential race in fall 1979 he believed that Chappaquiddick was no longer an issue.

But after a decade, Chappaquiddick refused to go away. It "was lying there," in the words of Tom Wicker, "not so much like a time bomb but as a cancer on his candidacy."[23] President Carter in a veiled reference to the incident during a "town meeting" in New York City was the first to make Chappaquiddick a campaign issue. "He himself," Carter observed, "had never 'panicked' during moments of crisis." The next day Carter sent Kennedy a handwritten note assuring him that he had been discussing "high moments of state," that his remarks were not meant as a personal attack on Kennedy, and that he had not, perish the thought, uttered the dreaded "C" word. "But fairly or unfairly, the black cat of Chappaquiddick was out of the bag."[24] A media feeding frenzy set in immediately. "It seems as though any newspaper that wants to be considered credible," Charles B. Seib wrote, "feels obliged to undertake still another rehashing of Chappaquiddick." In Washington, Seib pointed out, both the *Post* and the *Star* published their versions of the scandal.[25] Columnists and editorial writers, too, seemed compelled to weigh in on Chappaquiddick. At the *New York Times*, for example, three different columnists—William Safire[26] (representing the right) and also Tom Wicker[27] and Anthony Lewis[28] (with center-left perspectives)—expressed their concerns about Chappaquiddick, or as Safire preferred to call it "Waterquiddick.[29] *Reader's Digest*, in the February 1980b issue, printed the most widely read Chappaquiddick exposé, an exhaustive and damning rehash of what was already well known, titled "Chappaquiddick: The Still Unanswered Questions."[30] Television news anchors got in on the act as well. "The tough Kennedy [television] interview," Seib observed, had become "the thing."[31] First Tom Jarriel on ABC and then Roger Mudd on CBS questioned Kennedy not only about Chappaquiddick but also about other aspects of his personal as well as his political life. Because it was well known that Mudd was a personal friend of Teddy and other Kennedy family members, the critical and somewhat skeptical nature of his questions and commentary surprised and shocked many viewers and seemed to surprise Kennedy himself. In response to Mudd's questions about Chappaquiddick, Teddy did accept a limited degree of responsibility.

> I've been impacted by a number of tragedies in my life. . . . Those circumstances which I didn't have control. I could feel the sense of regret and the sense of sadness and the sense of loss. But this was a circumstance in which I did have a responsibility, and that—in that sense it was quite different from life's other experiences.[32]

For many, however, Kennedy's limited acceptance of responsibility for the death of Kopechne was too little and much too late to be seen as possible atonement or redemption.

Conservative writer Richard Brookhiser was no doubt speaking for many people of diverse ideological persuasions when he wrote: "Chappaquiddick raises a host of other issues—panic, cowardice, calculation, perjury, obstruction of justice, manslaughter."[33] Even writers on the left, who were generally sympathetic with Kennedy's positions on the issues, seemed compelled to bring up Chappaquiddick. For example, Alexander Cockburn and James Ridgeway praised Kennedy's as "the decent program" but still wondered which of the two Democratic candidates for president was worse: "is it the man who did not go to the police for ten hours worse than the man who played politics with the hostages for over two hundred days."[34] If Kennedy really had believed that, after a decade, Chappaquiddick had been forgotten he was greatly mistaken.

Damaging as Chappaquiddick was to Teddy's public image, the so-called "Joan factor" was equally harmful. The "Joan factor" was the notion developed by the news media and widely believed by the public that her husband's conspicuous womanizing and simultaneous neglect of wife and family had driven Joan Kennedy to alcoholism.[35] Asked about the state of his marriage during his television interview with Roger Mudd, Kennedy's response was so feeble and fumbling that he actually reinforced and fueled the widespread negative perception.

> *Senator Kennedy*: Well, I think it's a—we've had some difficult times, but I think we've—have—we've I think been able to make some very good progress, and its—I would say that its—its—its—I'm delighted that we're able to—to share the time and the relationship that we—that we do share.
> *Mudd*: Are—are you separated, or are you just—what—how do you describe the—the situation?
> *Senator Kennedy*: Well, I don't know whether there is a single—a single word that should—have for a description of it. Joan's involved in a continuing program to deal with the problem of—of alcoholism, and—and she's doing magnificently well, and I'm immensely proud of . . . the progress that she's made. . . . It's the type of disease that one has to continue to—to work on, and she continues to work on, and the program that's been devised is—is in Boston.[36]

Many were unimpressed with Kennedy's proclaimed pride in his wife's progress in overcoming alcoholism. Gail Sheehy, for example, expressed skepticism in a *New York Times* column: "Teddy Kennedy props up a wife who suffers from alcoholism to endorse him in public, though the strain on her delicate balance must be great."[37] Ellen Goodman reported seeing a like-minded bumper sticker in Cambridge, Massachusetts: "Vote for Jimmy Carter, Free Joan Kennedy."

The Kennedy campaign had its credibility undermined by fresh revelations in *Time* and elsewhere about Teddy's continued philandering. "When his marriage began to turn bad," *Time* reported, "there were reports of dalliances with New York socialite Amanda Burden, skier Suzy Chaffee, Washington socialite Lee Huftly and Margaret Trudeau, among others."[38] Despite the Kennedy campaign's efforts at damage control, the "Joan Factor" remained a serious and continuing problem.

In addition to Teddy's publicity perceived "guilt" stemming from character factors, he may also have felt some personal "familial guilt" arising from his unfulfilled political ambitions for the presidency as inculcated by his father and brothers, and by virtue of his having inherited the "head of the family" mantle. The guilt occasioned by surviving his brothers and the challenge of having to measure up to Martyrs suggests the strong possibility of additional categorical guilt within Teddy—perhaps a deep sense of guilt for failing to live up to inherited expectations coupled in some way perhaps with sibling rivalry. Steven Roberts speculated that "Teddy was running against his brothers—against the Kennedy legend—and the legend seems to be beating him": Could he have some deep, internal doubts about himself? Is there not even a possibility of a suicidal impulse? Is there some deep-seated fear that [he] cannot measure up to John or Robert, or to the office they sought or, ultimately, to the public's notion of what he is, or should be? The wild driving, the womanizing—could they all be an elaborate, unconscious way of saying: Let this cup pass from me."[39]

Entering the 1980 presidential primary campaign Teddy Kennedy was perceived by many— probably a majority—of the American public to be a "polluted" and "guilty" man, a man who was unwilling, perhaps unable, to control his own unruly impulses—unwilling to slay his own "vile beasts within"—and to obey the commandants set forth in the Social Covenant. He was clearly much in need of the expiation made possible by redemptive symbolic action and a corresponding rhetoric of rebirth.

Burke notes that the basic religious form is the journey from selfish personal ambition to unselfish love of others and service to the community. The individual must "die" to self in order to be redeemed. This powerful form is not only played out in religious life, but other areas such as the art, sports, science, the military, business, and especially politics have borrowed this form. American business is full of saviors, science is full of charismatic geniuses, art is full of godlike creators. Burke finds it especially important in politics, an activity that he calls 'secular piety' or a form of 'secular prayer.' Politics uses religious forms because it is about joining like-minded interests to build community and to oppose all those interests they consider threatening. Political leaders constantly stress unity and the practice of politics frames personal and communal identity in ways that are both material and spiritual. Political leaders constantly use religious language, speak of great crusades, pronounce personal vows, embark on missions, see visions of the future and like the prophets of old foretell utopian dreams.

Burke often noted that even the most secular and material things become invested by a divinity. Thus a simple business audit may be expressed as a vindication of our integrity, or a sporting event is called a test of moral character, a military victory is called the 'will of God' while a particular model of car is advertised as an instrument of human freedom. Likewise a university education is said to confer social mobility and human dignity on its constituents. Religious expressions, attitudes, and symbols have migrated to the secular world. In the section that follows, we will constantly remind the reader that even as drama came out of early religion, that much contemporary political drama may be seen as religious ceremony with secular vestments.

Curtain: End of Act One

Act Two: Teddy's Redemption—Slaying the Vile Beasts Within

When Teddy Kennedy began his presidential campaign in fall 1979, he and practically everyone else believed that he would have little trouble taking the nomination away from the sitting president whose poll ratings, hovering near twenty percent, were "as low as any incumbent's have ever been."[40] The American hostages were still in Iran, the economy was in a deepening recession with unemployment approaching 8 percent,[41] inflation was soaring, and several of the most influential constituent groups of the Democratic Party were alienated from President Carter and disagreed with his policies.[42] In fact, a majority of the American people seemed to blame Carter for many of the nation's most serious problems. An NBC/AP telephone opinion survey, for example, found that 66 percent of the people nationwide considered Carter a weak leader. The poll also found that "most Americans blamed [him] for every aspect of the country's worsening economic condition." For example, 78 percent of the people thought he "was at least 'partly to blame' for continued inflation; 68 percent said he was 'partly to blame' for higher prices on energy; and 61 percent faulted him for gasoline shortages."[43] The left-wing of the Democratic Party, in particular, was unhappy with Carter's "centrist" ideals and policies and tended to regard him as a "conservative infidel,"[44] a deserter of the party's liberal principles and a betrayer of its traditions. With the polls registering Carter's growing unpopularity and with his public approval rating hovering close to an all time low of 20 percent,[45] several major figures, representing the diverse constituent groups of the Democratic Party, fearing a debacle in the 1980 election, began urging Teddy to seek the Democratic presidential nomination. Teddy was "the last Prince of Camelot,"[46] a fact that seemed to make it inevitable that he make a run for the presidency. "The press, the polls, other politicians, and most of the people," Morton Kondracke reported, "have come to believe that some irresistible force, some historical or genetic inevitability, was operating to make Kennedy a candidate for president."[47]

With President Carter being made the scapegoat for virtually all the nation's problems by press, media and public alike, presidential hopefuls in both political parties also began to scapegoat him. Ronald Reagan and the other Republican presidential candidates scapegoated Carter and his policies as the root causes of the nation's diverse problems. Teddy Kennedy, on the other hand, despite his strong record of support for Carter's policies in the Senate, scapegoated the President from the left. Carter's abandonment of traditional Democratic principles and policies, he maintained were responsible for the nation's diverse problems. "The high-unemployment, high-interest economic policy didn't work for William McKinley," Teddy repeatedly told audiences, "it didn't work for Herbert Hoover, and it won't work for Jimmy Carter. . . . Its time to put a real Democrat in the White House." Throughout the primary Teddy described Carter as "a pale carbon copy of Ronald Reagan" and as a "clone" of Reagan,[48] and after it became clear that Reagan would win the Republican presidential nomination, he began telling audiences that, "Mr. Carter has created Ronald Reagan."[49] "His explanation: by bemoaning the limitations of the presidency as he sees it, Carter encouraged Americans to look for someone who proposes simplistic solutions to problems."[50]

Conventional wisdom maintained that Carter was "hopelessly weak" and had little to no change of winning re-election to a second term whereas Kennedy "couldn't be beat."[51] Public opinion polls bolstered this viewpoint. In late summer, 1979, a Gallup poll showed Carter's support among Democrats at 21 percent compared to 54 percent for Kennedy.[52] The same poll showed Carter behind both potential Republican challengers, while Kennedy was far ahead of both Reagan and Ford.[53] Other polls seemed to suggest "that Chappaquiddick was fading as a factor in people's minds."[54] And a poll conducted by Lewis Harris revealed that 71 percent of the American people doubted that President Carter had the competence to be president, whereas 67 percent thought Teddy Kennedy had the right leadership traits for the job.[55] If conventional wisdom and the polls were right, things looked good for the "last Prince of Camelot" in his "historically inevitable" quest for the presidential nomination.

Both the assumption that Carter couldn't win and the assumption that Kennedy couldn't lose proved to be entirely wrong. There were several reasons. The first reason was President Carter's ability to take advantage of his incumbency, as well as his ability to exploit the Iranian situation (and later the Afghanistan situation) and the plight of the hostages to further himself politically. His inability to secure the release of the hostages was initially one of his greatest political liabilities, but by the late fall 1979 his handling of the crisis had actually strengthened his standing in the polls. "A rally-round-the-president-in-a-foreign-crisis syndrome came into effect as Carter scored an unprecedented rise of more than 30 points in his Gallup approval rating."[56] Both Gallup and Harris polls showed "a dramatic reversal" in the Carter-Kennedy race, with Carter leading Kennedy, and by 8 points (48–40) in the Gallup poll.[57]

A second reason why the conventional wisdom that Teddy could not lose turned out to be wrong was his own weakness as a political campaigner, particularly his ineffectiveness as a political stump speaker. "From virtually the moment that his presidential campaign seemed certain last fall," write Thomas Oliphant, "he has been measured against standards—most involving myths about his late brothers—and found by some to be a stumbling, inarticulate bumbler."[58] In the past Oliphant pointed out, "on the few occasions he had been on national television—usually reading carefully drafted speeches—there has never been a problem. The myth of yet another 'Kennedy' was always reinforced."[59] Reading aloud a carefully written manuscript was one thing. Delivering off-the-cuff remarks on the stump was another matter altogether. Morton Kondracke also found Teddy's extemporaneous speaking ineffective: "He couldn't get his syntax straight or make eye contact. . . . He seemed to lack fire and made . . . his listeners doubt whether he really wanted to be president."[60] In one campaign appearance after another he "sometimes seemed to lose his concentration" half way through his speech and simply wandered through the rest of it, uttering mechanical, "rambling, almost incoherent sentences."[61] Not only did Teddy lack facilty in extemporaneous speaking but many of the speaking techniques that he did employ—shouting and pounding his fists on the lectern, for example—came across poorly on television.

No doubt the most important reason why the conventional wisdom that Kennedy was unbeatable turned out to be false was the lingering public doubt—constantly played up by the news media—about his personal character, about his alleged fast-driving, hard-drinking, swinging, playboy lifestyle, about Chappaquiddick and the "Joan factor." Nor were attacks on Kennedy's character written only by conservative writers and published only in conservative journals of opinion. Even some liberal and left-of-center writers and publications questioned Teddy's motives and character. In slightly more than a month after he had formally announced his candidacy, Kennedy had plunged in the opinion polls and, far from being unbeatable, his campaign was generally considered hopeless—a view that was verified soon after by his lop-sided defeats in all of the early primaries.[62] His candidacy had been destroyed by what *Time* called "the smoldering resentment against his personal excesses in earlier years."[63] Tom Pettit, on an NBC *Nightly News Report*, had a similar view. "Kennedy has gone nowhere," he stated, "a victim of anti-Kennedy sentiment which cannot be exorcised."[64] "The prince of American politics [had] become a frog."[65] Until his crushing two to one defeat by President Carter in the January 21 Iowa primary, Teddy had never lost an election.

The rhetorical situation that Kennedy confronted following his early primary defeats, given the widespread public perceptions of him as a "guilty" and "polluted" person, was one which called for a rhetoric of redemption. But the drama of redemption requires victimage, a scapegoat, and a kill. For Kennedy, this meant offering himself as the sacrificial scapegoat and enduring the resulting public humiliation and mortification associated with conducting a losing campaign. Only through public humiliation and suffering, as well as through the "slaying" of the "vile beasts within," could Kennedy create the cathartic responses necessary for effecting his public, and perhaps also his private redemption. Hence, Kennedy's redemptive campaign was only the appropriate or "fitting response" to his rhetorical situation.[66]

In one primary election or caucus after another Teddy shrugged off defeat "with enough humor and grace to win the admiration of political opponents."[67] But his humiliation was not limited to electoral defeats. He encountered the Chappaquiddick issue everywhere he went and he frequently faced hostile demonstrators, many of them carrying placards calling him a "Killer."[68] He appeared at a rally with Mayor Jane Byrne in Chicago, a city that "used to revere his brother John," and was jeered by a sizable minority of the audience. He later confided to a friend that this "had left an ugly scar."[69] It must have also left a scar, especially in light of his strong record on women's issues, when Iris Mitgang, Chair of the National Women's Political Caucus, called him a "known womanizer" whose private life raised serious questions about his fitness for the presidency.[70] Having his marital problems and his personal sexual behavior constantly, openly, and widely discussed and condemned in the media must have left a deep scar indeed. This aspect of his campaign resembled, according to George Will, "a public penance and a stoning. All campaigns involve mortification of the flesh, but Kennedy's has involved spiritual mortification too."[71] Another humiliation came when his campaign began to falter and he found "that professed 'old friends' in the Senate and the nation's statehouses would not even return his phone calls." This "shocked him into the realization of just how lonely it was to be a loser."[72]

By carrying on in the face of one humiliating defeat after another, by remaining good humored in defeat, and by taking the political opprobrium heaped on him and still keeping his dignity, Teddy not only refuted many of the lingering doubts about his character but even won the respect and admiration of many people. On some basic level he understood the power of the dramatic form. He knew that to gain a new political identity, he would have to play the drama all the way to the end. He could not be drawn into a single harsh word about the friends who had pleaded with him to enter the race and then, scared, did nothing to help him: John Culver of Iowa, for example, or Birch Bayh of Indiana.[73] Even one of the advisors to Ronald Reagan was quoted as saying of Kennedy's behavior in defeat: "You have to admire him for it. He is not a whiner."[74]

At the time, the results of Teddy's redemptive campaign were essentially positive, enabling him to gain at least some measure of public redemption and possibly some measure of private redemption as well. He won five of his last eight primary contests,[75] and a total of ten primaries overall, including the delegate rich New York primary. These wins suggest that the humiliation and mortification he experienced during the fall campaign and during his early primary election defeats had afforded him a sufficient measure of public redemption to permit him to prevail in the later primary contests. Kennedy's comeback enabled him to win a total of 1,235 convention delegates, but Carter's total of 1,982 was 316 more votes than were required to win the presidential nomination. Kennedy had lost the nomination but he had "effectively divided the party." *Newsweek*'s political writers theorized that his loss of the presidential campaign was "the moral equivalent of victory." Although Teddy had been forced to endure "a string of early humiliations" he did so "with little bitterness, he has remained true to his social goals and his dignity in the face of adversity has begun to persuade some people that [he] is more than a playboy politician who once drove off a bridge."[76] In suffering a self-imposed political death by conducting a losing campaign for principle, Kennedy was perceived to be saying "no" to his own "vile beasts within." The atonement afforded by his symbolic death, however, opened the possibility of rebirth. The electorate, too, was caught up in the drama. By participating in the form they now saw Kennedy in a new role. His old public identity as shallow playboy was dead. In dying to his old identity, he began to be reborn as the selfless guardian of the embattled Democratic liberal heritage.

Curtain: End of Act Two

Act Three: Teddy's Rebirth—Paradise Regained

"All year," *Time* commented, "the irony has been that the further Kennedy seemed from the nomination, the better he performed and was received by the voters. There seemed to be some form of liberation in losing."[77] This irony also seemed to be true in the case of Teddy's speech before the Democratic National Convention, August 12, 1980 at Madison Square Gardens. His presentation of this speech—which represents the cathartic climax, the final purgative-redemptive moment of his campaign—was a masterful "purification ritual" and a "ritual of rebirth."[78] Teddy portrayed himself as a "cleansed" and reborn man.

Teddy began on an appropriately self-deprecating note (an opening tactic often employed by public speakers, but especially suitable for a vanquished and defeated political candidate). His purpose, he avowed, was "not to argue for a candidacy but to affirm a cause . . . the cause for which the Democratic Party has stood in its finest hours . . . since the days of Thomas Jefferson, the cause of the common man—and the common woman."[79] It was the cause of Woodrow Wilson and the "New Freedom," of Franklin Delano Roosevelt and the "New Deal," and of John F. Kennedy and the "New Frontier" and to "fair and lasting prosperity" that had been the motivation behind his own presidential campaign, Teddy told his listeners. But that historic "cause and commitment" now seemed endangered by the increasingly conservative mood of the country. There was even some in his own party (he did not name President Carter, but his listeners understood his meaning) who shared this conservative mood, who had strayed from the party's historic purposes, and who had sought "refuge in reaction."[79] "We cannot," Teddy pleaded, "let the great purposes of the Democratic Party become the bygone passages of history."[80]

But before developing his theme further, Teddy launched an attack on the Republicans, especially their presidential nominee, Ronald Reagan, who probably more than anyone else personified the growing conservative mood of the county. In his attack, Teddy symbolically eviscerated Reagan. In what was described as "a lyrical sequence of scorn,"[81] Teddy quoted past statements made by Reagan to support the charge that he was "no friend" of labor ("Unemployment insurance is a prepaid vacation plan for freeloaders"); "no friend" of the cities ("I have included in my morning and evening prayers every day the prayer that the Federal Government does not bail out New York"); "no friend" of the elderly ("Social Security should be made voluntary"); nor was he "a friend: of the environment ("Eighty percent of air pollution comes from plants and trees").[82] Attacking Reagan enabled Kennedy to unite, at least temporarily, the diverse factions—his own delegates as well as Carter's—of the deeply divided Democratic Party around their common opposition to a dreaded foe. "During a national election," Burke points out, "the situation places great stress upon a division between the citizens. But often such divisiveness...can be healed when the warring factions join the common cause against an alien enemy (the division elsewhere thus serving to reestablish the principle of continuity at home)."[83]

Teddy now got back to his theme, "a trumpet for the liberalism that was being derogated by many in his own party."[84] He depicted his campaign as a crusade to resist the growing conservative tide and to defend traditional liberal principles against those, both inside and outside his party, who would derogate them. To amplify the enduring quality of Democratic values in opposition to changing political "fashions," Teddy employed an extended fashion metaphor. "The commitment we seek is not to outworn values but to old values that will never wear out. Programs may sometimes become obsolete but the idea of fairness always endures."[85] Unlike fashions which come into style and go out of style, human wants and needs endure. "The poor," for example, "may be out of political fashion, but they are not without human needs. The middle class may be angry, but they have not lost the dream that all Americans can advance together."[86] Despite changing political fashions, Teddy assured his listeners, his presidential quest had championed the enduring "old values": economic justice, fairness, hope—"new hope"—for a better life. "And someday, long after this convention, long after the signs come down, and the crowds stop cheering, and the bands stop playing," Teddy wished to be remembered as the defender of enduring, traditional Democratic principles and values. "We kept the faith," he assured the faithful, "but the work goes on, the cause endures, the hope still loves, the dream shall never die."[87] His presentation of these lines—which Devlin has described as representing "not only the essence of the speech but also what the campaign was supposed to be about"[88] —brought cheering and applause but also tears to many eyes. He had achieved a moment of transcendence. Burke posits that after suffering and symbolic death, one may be born anew. And in the drama of political salvation, one becomes the perfect emblem of the community, a purified vessel of its aspiration, hopes, and vision.

As he concluded, Teddy ought to dramatically symbolize his rebirth and new identity. He did so by quoting lines from Tennyson's *Ulysses*, lines he said his "brothers quoted and loved—and that have special meaning to me now":

> I am part of all that I have met . . .
> Tho much is taken, much abides . . .
> That which we are, we are—
> One equal temper of heroic hearts . . . strong in will
> To strive, to seek, to find, and not to yield.[89]

In identifying his own redemptive journey with that of Ulysses, Teddy suggested to his listeners the nature of his new identity. Just as the aging wanderer Ulysses returned from his years of journey and struggle a chastened but a wiser man, Kennedy had returned with a sense of new hope and renewed faith, ready "to strive, to seek, to find and not to yield."[90]

As Teddy spoke "nearly each of the text's 150 well paced sentences drew shouts, laughter, or applause."[91] He was interrupted a total of fifty-one times by applause, and on five occasions there was sustained applause and prolonged chanting of the "We want Kennedy."[92] Tears filled the eyes of most convention delegates. Many of Teddy's supporters wept throughout his presentation. "Often we sailed against the wind," Teddy intoned, "but we always kept our rudder true. There were so many of you who stayed the course and shared our hope. You gave your help, but even more you gave your hearts. . . . When I think of you I recall the poet's words, and I say: 'What golden friends I had.'"[93] This intonation brought sustained applause but also profuse weeping. "Both pitiful weeping and mirthful laughter," Burke writes, are "akin to love," but "they are not identical with it."[94] In fact, "tragic catharsis through fear and pity operates as a *substitute* for catharsis through love."[95] "One's state of identification or communion with the object of one's pity is nearly like the kind of identification or communion one feels for a love object." What Burke calls "perfect catharsis" arises from "a sense of universal love" and, like other forms of perfection, it is humanly unattainable.[96] "Insofar as such a condition is not attained," Burke says, "the next best thing is a sense of radical pity that lies on the slope of tearful release."[97] The catharsis effected by Teddy's speech, then, was not "perfect catharsis," it did not engender feelings of "universal love," but if not "perfect" it was "the next best thing." Kennedy and his audience (both the convention delegates and the much larger television audience), who pitied him and wept for him, were "cleansed by a bath of pitiful tears, a benign orgastic downpour."[98]

The dramas enacted during political campaigns also afford audience members with opportunities to take pleasure in "sympathetic mediations" on the varied misfortunes and sufferings of political figures. For example, in pitying Kennedy, less exalted (and less fortunate) Americans could be "to that extent exalted"; identifying with Kennedy in his fallen state enabled them to be "overtly charitable" while simultaneously feeling "covertly superior." For Kennedy's supporters, those who loved him and shared his ideology, feeling consubstantial with him was easy. His political opponents, both inside and outside the Democratic Party, had greater difficulty identifying with him. But, Burke points out, "pity solves this problem too. For Aristotle observes that we pity undeserved suffering, and thus we could in imagination pity even our worst enemy, if we imagined him undergoing heavier punishment then even we would wish on him."[99] When Kennedy's campaign had faltered and he began to suffer public humiliation, many of his political opponents took "unseemly glee" in his "difficulties, something akin to the pleasure children sometimes take pulling the wings off flies."[100] At this point pity took over. As Kennedy's "punishment" seemed to be even greater than they "would wish on him," his opponents were enabled to pity him—George Will, William Safire, and some of Ronald Reagan's advisors were among those who did so[101]—for they could at once be openly and broadly generous toward Kennedy while covertly feeling themselves to be his moral better. This, too, provides a kind of "cleansing." In identifying with Kennedy in his fallen state, both his supporter and his opponents were taking pleasure in "sympathetic mediations" on his suffering. In granting him expatiation and forgiveness for his "sins" they were simultaneously gaining vicarious purging, cleansing, and expiation from their own "sins." They were alienating "from themselves to [Kennedy] their own uncleanliness."[102]

At the conclusion of her husband's speech, Joan Kennedy appeared on the stage and embraced him, suggesting to many that their marriage too had been renewed.[103] As Teddy hugged his wife, the convention's most tumultuous demonstration erupted. Ignoring repeated calls to order by Chairman Thomas "Tip" O'Neill, Teddy's supporters danced, sang, and chanted: "We want Teddy!"[104] O'Neill gave up as the convention band began playing "medleys of *For He's a Jolly Good Fellow*, McNamar's Band, and *Happy Days Are Here Again*."[104] On the convention floor many delegates talked enthusiastically about how much Teddy's speech had moved them. *Time*, for example, quoted Gary Brandt, a 6-ft. 2-in., 230-lb. welder from Ohio. Wiping tears from his eyes, Brandt said of Teddy, "He could have turned the damned country around. If he'd talked that way during the campaign, this would have been his convention."[105] Morton Kondracke wrote that "Kennedy had a brilliant day in the sun, delivering what may be one of the best political speeches of our time, one that served as a catharsis for his sullen supporters and may get the bulk of them working for the Democratic ticket in the fall."[106] L. Patrick Devlin, expressing the view of many academic critics, wrote: "Here was a candidate—the champion of rejected ideas and rejected himself—able to resurrect the Kennedy legacy in the impressive instance of the convention speech."[107] Perhaps Teddy's friend and ex-college roommate, former California Senator John Tunney, best described the nature of the 1980 Kennedy campaign. It was, according to Tunney, "a campaign of atonement."[108] He added: "That campaign and that speech spell the end of the Chappaquiddick era. It was something that had to be done."[109]

Curtain: End of Act Three

Epilogue

Our analysis demonstrates that Teddy Kennedy achieved some degree of public redemption by suffering the mortification and symbolic self-immolation associated with waging a losing campaign for political principles. As a drama of political purification it involved scapegoating, self-atonement, and purification. Kennedy's 1980 presidential primary campaign was selected to serve as our representative dramatic form because it is widely considered an exemplar of the rhetoric of self-atonement. Burke teaches us that such a rhetoric is eventuated by a fall from grace and is characterized by sacrifice, suffering, humiliation, mortification and purgation, all designed to slay the "vile beasts within." But symbolic self-slaying also leads to transcendence and rebirth. As Milton's Samson was able to slay his enemies through his own self-destruction, so Kennedy's symbolic death enabled him to slay the doubts, charges, and accusations hurled against him by his enemies. By offering himself as a victim and suffering the resulting mortification with good cheer Kennedy gained some measure of public expatiation for his publicly perceived shortcomings. His self-victimage resulted, at least for the moment, in rhetorical transformation and symbolic rebirth.

Several conclusions follow from our drama. First, the selection of Kennedy's 1980 presidential primary campaign as our typical political drama as a rhetoric of self-victimage was shown to be an efficacious choice. Second, a redemptive rhetoric of public mortification was found to be the only appropriate—or "fitting"—response to the rhetorical situation with which Kennedy found himself confronted following his early primary defeats. Waging a losing campaign for political principles enabled him to achieve some degree of public redemption. Third, it was dramatic form that drew its spectators into the play. As Burke would say, we became collaborators inside the form. Kennedy's story became our story.

We have illustrated the utility of Burke's major analytical tools through the study of a single political campaign. Following Burke we treated the campaign as a drama that began with guilt and a dream of salvation. It was a drama of ritual death and dying, but it is also a drama of ritual transcendence and rebirth. And it is a drama that ends with the attainment and maintenance of a state of redemption, of a new identity, and a strengthened sense of community. Our analysis was also a reminder of the power of form. Burke's genius was to see that these common forms are repeated endlessly in human events that dramatic form allows us to participate in the larger events of our communities. Form gives shape and meaning to what might otherwise appear to be a shapeless mass of sequential events. And it allows students of form a special insight into the power and the limits of the various life scripts in which we are caught up as players. Our last admonition is to go and read Burke. His ideas provide insight into the constant rhetorical struggle that characterizes everyday life.

PERSONAL COMMENTS ON THE ESSAY

Writing an essay illustrating Kenneth Burke's rhetorical perspectives is a daunting task. First of all, Burke has so many ways of analyzing rhetoric that we were afraid the article might turn into a catalog of examples. Thus we chose to use a few of his major ideas with the assumption that students would benefit from broader applications and fewer working parts. We wanted the reader to understand that Burke believes that drama is not a metaphor for life but the stuff of life itself. We frame our world in dramatic terms with plot, scene, character, dialogue, climax, and resolution. The categories of drama come out of the structure of our mind and are part of our sense making apparatus.

We chose Ted Kennedy because the Kennedy family appears to be a modern variant of a Greek Tragic House. They exhibit the flawed greatness that we have always associated with tragedy. Once we had explicated the terms of Burke's drama, the case study of Teddy Kennedy's misfortune almost wrote itself. Our problem was to know how much to include, and we wound up cutting nearly thirty pages from the original chapter.

We found it hard to gain a balance. The first article merely outlined the dramatic terms and the bulk of the article was critical application. Our editor wisely suggested there was too little theory, too little Burke, and too much exposition. Our second draft expanded theory and method and cut half of the application. This time our editor suggested the piece was too theo-retical. It seemed to have embraced method for the sake of method rather than finding insights into the language of politics in contemporary America. Finally, we attempted to balance theory and application by condensing our explanation of the method and making our application to the case study more pointed and direct. We believe we were successful in our third and final draft in reaching this balance. Burke was a great theorist but he had contempt for mere theory unless it had a strong practical application. He wanted his theoretical applications to give people the tools that would allow them to understand the world around them and to make decisions on the basis of that understanding.

We also wanted the reader to understand Burke's views in the context of his life and moral outlook. We believe we have been able to do so. We hope that this chapter will create greater interest in the life and work of Kenneth Burke. Finally, we are deeply grateful to the editor who gave us the opportunity to write this piece.

POTENTIALS AND PITFALLS

Kenneth Burke warned us that politicians and advertisers who were trying to manipulate us surrounded us. He provided us many rhetorical tools that we could use for our defense. Some critics think he gave us too many. I must also admit that some of Burke's books and articles are hard to read, and that occasionally his ideas are dense and complex. He tends to analyze persuaders with exhausting thoroughness. He seems to have a hidden agenda and he uses ex-amples from Goethe, Shakespeare, Coleridge, The New Testament, Matthew Arnold, and from ancient philosophy, examples that assume his readers are quite well read.

But if Burke demands a bit of work from the reader he gives us much more in return. Using only three terms (Division, Identification, and Hierarchy) Burke teaches us to analyze social movements. Using a simple set of dramatic ratios (the Pentad) he gives us the tools to under-stand and critique a speech, a campaign, a social movement, a piece of literature, or a revolu-tion. Further, Burke was a reformer whose entire life was dedicated to making the world a better place, and his theoretical applications are infused with the idea of moral choice. Burke's critical tools are particularly good at unmasking hidden meanings and coded phrases. In short, while Burke demands our full attention, he provides us with powerful and insightful strategies for dealing with the world.

DRAMATIC FORM CRITICISM TOP PICKS

Burke, Kenneth. "Dramatism" in *International Encyclopedia of the Social Sciences*, vol. VIII., edited by David L. Sills, 445–452. (New York City: The Macmillan Company and Free Press, 1968). Here in Burke's own words is the best description of Dramatism ever penned. It defines the key words and illustrates basic concepts. The article is one of the most lucid pieces of criticism ever written, and it is one of the best short articles Burke wrote in his seventy-year career. I would recommend it to anyone who wanted to use an off-the-shelf version of Dramatistic theory.

Burke, Kenneth. "Anthony on Behalf of a Play" in *Philosophy of Literary Form*, 329–343, 3rd ed. (Berkeley: University of California Press, 1974). This article uses the famous speech of Mark Anthony from Shakespeare's Julius Ceasar to illustrate the explanatory power of dramatism. Burke's analysis gives the reader a much deeper appreciation of Shakespeare's profound understanding of the dynamics of human communication. Burke uses the device of having Anthony reveal his tactics in composing and delivering the speech in a series of brilliant 'asides' to the reader. The reader is given a blow-by-blow account of one of the most successful pieces of persuasion ever written.

Burke, Kenneth. "The Rhetoric of Hitler's Battle" in *The Philosophy of Literary Form*, 164–190, 3rd ed. (Berkeley: University of California Press, 1974). Three years before Hitler declared war on Europe, Burke wrote this profound article warning us about the kind of horrors the Nazi dictator had in store for the world. This article makes use of the scapegoat and prefigures Burke's expansion of his method from Dramatism to Logography. It has long been considered the most brilliant short example of Burke's critical method at work. Thus, it is often assigned to students as an introduction to Burke.

Crable, Bryan. "Burke's Perspective on Perspectives: Grounding Dramatism in the Representative Anecdote." *The Quarterly Journal of Speech* 86 (2000): 318–333. Bryan Crable's article shows the wide uses that can be made of Dramatism. It adds one of Burke's most potent concepts, the Representative Anecdote, and applies the method in a great variety of situations. Crable is one of the best Burke scholars in the nation and he has a very vivid way of putting things.

Cathcart, Robert S. "Instruments of His Own Making: Burke and Media" in *Extensions of the Burkean System*, edited by James Chesebro, 287–308. (Tuscaloosa, Alabama: Alabama University Press, 1993). Robert Cathcart's article shows extensions of Burke from traditional rhetorical analysis to media settings. Cathcart uses the insights of various theorists to apply Burke to film, television, advertising, and computers.

Griffin, Leland M. "A Dramatistic Theory of Social Movements" in *Landmark Essays in Kenneth Burke*, edited by Barry Brummett, 199–220. (Davis, California: Hermagoras Press, 1993). Griffin, the inventor of movement studies in discourse, writes about his excitement at having found Burke's Dramatism. Griffin had spent thirteen years searching for a perspective that would be comprehensive enough to deal with a large number of messages produced by a large number of people in a big loosely organized movement. Although this is an early example of the uses of dramatism, it is one of the most interesting and imaginative.

NOTES

1. Kenneth Burke, *Toward a Better Life* (University of California Press, 1966).

2. Kenneth Burke, "The Rhetoric of Hitler's Battle" in *The Philosophy of Literary Form* (University of California Press Berkeley, 1969). First published 1945.

3. William Rueckert, "A Field Guide to Kenneth Burke—1990" in *Extensions of the Burkeian System*, edited by James W. Chesebro (University of Alabama Press, 1993), 13.

4. William H. Rueckert, *Kenneth Burke and the Drama of Human Relations* (Minneapolis: University of Minnesota Press, 1963), 45.

5. John H. Davis, *The Kennedys: Dynasty and Disaster, 1848–1983* (New York: McGraw-Hill, 1984), 609.

6. Max Lerner, *Ted and the Kennedy Legend: A Study in Character and Destiny* (New York: St. Martin's Press, 1980), 145–153.

7. Richard Brookhiser, "The Last Kennedy," *National Review*, March 21, 1980, 340.

8. Lapham, 38.

9. Rueckert, 131.

10. Ibid., 132.

11. C. Allen Carter, *Kenneth Burke and the Scapegoting Process* (University of Oklahoma Press, 1996).

12. Lerner, 43.

13. Ibid., 48.

14. Ibid.

15. For a description of the factual basis of Kennedy's "swinger" image, see Lerner.

16. Ronnie Dugger, "The Trashing of Teddy," *The Nation*, June 21. 1980, 746.

17. Lerner, 150.

18. For discussions of Teddy Kennedy's sexual attitudes and behavior, see especially Lerner, 145–153; also see Hirsch, 111, 203; and Dugger, 744–746. For a feminist perspective on Teddy's womanizing and extramarital relationships see Suzannah Lessard, "Kennedy's Woman Problem–Women's Kennedy Problem," *Washington Monthly*, December 1979, 10–14.

19. The irony was that, despite his image as a "swinger" and "Chauvinistic womanizer," Kennedy had one of the strongest voting records in the Senate on Women's issues. See Dugger, 744.

20. See John Barron, "Chappaquiddick: The Still Unanswered Questions," *Readers Digest*, February 1980, 66–72, 219–242.

21. Edward Kennedy "Speech of July 25, 1969," *New York Times*, July 26, 1969, A10. For a useful pentadic analysis of Kennedy's Chappaquiddick address see David A. Ling, "A Pentadic Analysis of Senator Edward Kennedy's Address to the People of Massachusetts July 25, 1969," *Central States Speech Journal* 21 (1970): 81–86.

22. Davis, 575–601.

23. Tom Wicker, "Reprieved by 'Jaws,'" *New York Times*, November 9, 1979, A35.

24. "Jimmy Strikes Back," *Newsweek*, October 8, 1979, 26.

25. Charles B. Seib, "Enough of Chappaquiddick," *Washington Post*, November 16, 1979, A21.

26. William Safire, "Waterquiddick," *New York Times*, November 12, 1979, A21.

27. Tom Wicker, "Reprieved by 'Jaws,'" A35.

28. Anthony Lewis, "Lower the Gate," *New York Times*, November 15, 1979, A31.

29. Safire, "Waterquiddick," A21.

30. Hersh, 66–72, 219–242.

31. Seib, "Enough of Chappaquiddick," A21.

32. "Teddy." Correspondent Roger Mudd. *CBS Reports*, CBS. November 4, 1979.

33. Brookhiser, "The Last Kennedy," 341.

34. Quoted in Dugger, 744.

35. For a fuller discussion of the "Joan Factor," see Marcia Chellis, *Living With the Kennedys: The Joan Kennedy Story* (New York: Simon and Schuster, 1985), 143–147. Another helpful work is Lester David, Joan: *The Reluctant Kennedy* (New York: Warner, 1975); also see "The Vulnerable Soul of Joan," *Time*, November 5, 1979, 19.

36. "Teddy," 4–5.

37. Quoted in Ellen Goodman, "Joan: Nobody's Victim Anymore," *Boston Globe*, February 21, 1980, 17.

38. "The Kennedy Challenge," *Time*, November 5, 1979, 20; also see Carl Rowan, "Kennedy Candidacy Masochistic Move," *Fort Wayne Journal Gazette*, November 2, 1979, 2A; Rowan professes dismay that *Time* would print the names of the women with whom Kennedy had been involved, but he then proceeded to pass along *Time*'s list to the thousands of readers of his syndicated column.

39. Steven Roberts, "Ted Kennedy: Haunted By The Past," *New York Times Magazine*, February 3, 1980, 74 and 55.

40. Morton Kondracke, "Superman Crashes," *New Republic*, December 21, 1979, 7.

41. "Teddy's Long-Shot Scenario," *Newsweek*, May 12, 1980, 54.

42. Kondracke, 7.

43. Thomas E. Cronin, "Looking for Leadership 1980," *Public Opinion*, February/March 1980, 15.

44. William Safire, *Lend Me Your Ears, Great Speeches in History* (New York: W. W. Norton, 1997; revised and expanded edition), 933.

45. "Teddy's Long-Shot Scenario," 54.

46. Kondracke, 7.

47. Dugger, 742.

48. Kondracke, 7.

49. Alexander Cockburn and James Ridgeway, "Into the Abyss," *Village Voice*, August 13–19, 1980, 10; "Ted Knew His Chances Were Slim," *Chicago Tribune*, August 17, 1980, sec 3:11.

50. "Vowing Defiance to the End" *Time*, July 21, 1980, 21.

51. "Vowing Defiiance to the End," 21.

52. Kondracke, 7.

53. Ibid.

54. Ibid.

55. Ibid.

56. Ibid.

57. Cronin, 17.

58. Thomas Oliphant, "Why Is that Man on Television Always Shouting," *The Boston Globe*, May 2, 1980, 2.

59. Oliphant, 2.

60. Safire, "Lend Me Your Ears," 933.

61. Kondracke, 8.

62. James Reston, "What Makes Teddy Run?," *The New York Times*, June 11, 1980, A31; also see Kondracke, 8.

63. "Kennedy Goes Out In Style—And Looks Ahead," *Time*, 25 August 1980, 25.

64. *NBC Nightly News*, February 26, 1980.

65. Will, "Kennedy May be Wrong but He's No Amateur," C7.

66. We borrow the phrase "fitting response" from Lloyd Bitzer, "The Rhetorical Situation," *Philosophy and Rhetoric* 1 (1968): 1–14. Although we do not employ Bitzer's situational method, we believe an analysis based on it would draw the same conclusion we have, namely that Kennedy's redemptive campaign represented the only appropriate response.

67. "Kennedy Goes Out In Style," 25.

68. Rowan, 2A.

69. "Kennedy Goes Out In Style," 25.

70. "Kennedy Private Life Questioned; He is Called 'Known Womanizer,'" *New York Times*, September 22, 1979, 7.

71. Will, "Kennedy May be Wrong But He's No Amateur," C7.

72. "Kennedy Goes Out In Style," 25.

73. Lewis, A23.

74. "What Makes Teddy Run? Liberal Convictions, and A Refusal to Admit Defeat," 21.

75. "Teddy's Long-Shot Scenario," 54.

76. "Teddy's Long-Shot Scenario," 54.

77. "Kennedy Goes Out In Style," 25.

78. Burke, *Attitudes Toward History*, 317–318.

79. Edward M. Kennedy, "Principles of Democratic Party: Common Hopes for the Future," *Vital Speeches of the Day*, August 12, 1980, 714.

80. Kennedy, 714.

81. "Madison Square Garden of Briars," 16.

82. Kennedy, 716.

83. Kenneth Burke, *Language as Symbolic Action, Essays on Life Literature and Method*, (Berkeley and Los Angeles; University of California Press, 1968), 51.

84. Safire, Lend Me Your Ears, 933.

85. Kennedy, 714.

86. Ibid.

87. Ibid.

88. L. Patrick Devlin, "An Analysis of Kennedy's Communication in the 1980 Campaign," *Quarterly Journal of Speech* 68 (1982): 417.

89. Kennedy, 716. Also see Alfred Lord Tennyson, "Ulysses," *Works* (London: Macmillian, 1891), lines 65–70. In Kennedy's quotation of *Ulysses* he left out some telling passages in which the aging wanderer Ulysses admits his weakness and lost strength to his followers. Apparently Kennedy did not wish his audience to think he had been weakened or had lost strength by his campaign struggles.

90. Kennedy, 716. Also see Tennyson, "Ulysses," lines 65–70.

91. "Madison Square Garden of Briars," 16.

92. Devlin, 416.

93. Kennedy, 716.

94. Kenneth Burke, "Catharsis Second-View," *The Centennial Review* 5 (1961):108.

95. Ibid., 108.

96. Ibid., 109.

97. Ibid.

98. Burke, "On Catharsis or Resolution," 344–345.

99. Burke, "Catharsis Second-View," 109.

100. Will, "Kennedy May be Wrong . . . ," C7

101. Will, C7; Seib, A21; and "What Makes Teddy Run?" 21.

102. Burke, *A Grammar of Motives*, 406.

103. Ironically, however, they were divorced shortly after this.

104. "Madison Square Garden of Briars," 16.

105. Ibid.

106. Morton Kondracke, "The Dream is Dead," *The New Republic*, 23 August 1980, 6.

107. Devlin, 416.

108. "Kennedy Goes Out In Style," 25.

109. Ibid.

11

Pentadic Criticism: The Wheels of Creation

Andrew King

Introduction

Burke defined rhetoric the strategic use of language to change attitudes or to induce action. He developed pentadic criticism to make visible the ways in which persuaders use language to change our beliefs and influence our actions. Burke understood that our forms of language and forms of experience were interlocked and that spokespersons in advertising, government, public relations, and media knew how to use these persuasive forms. He worried, though, that much public persuasion is unconscious, and that we embrace appeals uncritically without understanding their implications. Burke argued that the master form was the common story, a form that was generated by the structure of our minds. Burke developed a critical method based on that form. The method he invented is simple and complex, flexible yet straightforward, both prosaic and poetic. Its purpose is to help defend us against the tremendous flood of persuasive messages that assault us every moment of our waking lives.

Burke's term for persuasion is identification. Because persuasion is often thought of as acceptance of a new idea or program, Burke felt he needed a stronger term to describe the goals of the mind-changing industry in our society (advertising, sales, politics, etc.). Persuasion in a consumer-orientated mass society involves emotion, life-style choices, and systematic appeals to deeply held values. Thus, Burke adopted the name Identification as a term more descriptive of the goals of public rhetoric. Identification suggests more than mere like-mindedness; it connotes individuals "acting together" and sharing common feelings, "sensations, concepts images, ideas, and attitudes."[1] Burke's critical method is designed to give us a deep awareness of the nature and resources of identification and a discerning eye for its costs and consequences.

What is it?

Pentadic Criticism is an academic success story. Kenneth Burke birthed this famous method in the last year of World War II in the pages of his 1945 blockbuster book, *A Grammar of Motives.*[2] Despite its eventual celebrity, the new approach was not an immediate hit. Perhaps because of the enormous popularity of a long established method called The New Criticism, the use of Burke's insights spread slowly. Marie Hochmuth Nichols, a legendary professor who also worked to popularize the work of I. A. Richards and Kenneth Boulding, gave Pentadic Criticism a major boost.[3] She brought Burke to the University of Illinois where he expounded his approach to a group of brilliant graduate students, many of whom went on to become heads of major academic departments.

She also wrote two very influential articles explaining Burke's methods and theories in a fluent and lucid manner.[4] It was not until 1965, after two decades of relative neglect that Pentadic Criticism began its meteoric rise. It eclipsed some modes of criticism and displaced others, generating a huge literature about its theory and practice during its long rise to the zenith. Today a large and diverse group studies it. This group includes both rhetorical and literary critics, philosophers, social scientists, and even theologians. Once it was only used as a tool for textual analysis, but its uses have grown to include methods of composition, of psychological, sociological, and philosophical analysis. This chapter will confine its attention to the core mission of Pentadic Criticism: the development of a kind of verbal karate that can help people resist the floodtide of persuasive messages that assault them and to develop persuasive messages of their own.[5] What follows is far from exhaustive, but it will give the reader a strong hint of the kinds of help that Burke has to offer.

Where Does it Come From?

The founder of Pentadic Criticism, Kenneth Burke, did not so much "invent" it as revamp and expand a scheme inherited from earlier critics. Like most perspectives it is a combination of earlier ideas. From Aristotle's *Poetics* he took the ideas of dramatic form and the power of stories in human history.[6] Aristotle affirmed the centrality of human story telling to the formation and maintenance of community. Our stories lie at the root of our identity. It has been said that we can know a people by the kinds of stories they tell. Aristotle was also a great name-giver and classifier. The philosopher believed that we need a good set of labels if we are to talk sensibly and at length about anything. Accordingly he constructed a useful vocabulary, labeling all the parts of narrative structure. With a common set of categories critics could better decide what made narratives strong or weak, beautiful or ugly, effective or clumsy. He left us names for the central features of the common story, names such as *plot, character, spectacle, dialog*, and *concept*. Burke renamed these parts with the words act, agent, scene, agency, and purpose.[7]

From the great Roman poet, Horace, Burke took the notion of generative categories. Generative categories are the building blocks of creativity. They not only provide the skeleton and structure of a story, they serve as a stimulus to invent new ideas, to clothe the bones with new nerves, tendons, and sinews. Two thousand years ago in a still admired essay giving advice to would-be writers, Horace used a series of basic questions as building blocks in playwriting and story telling. In his famous work, *Ars Poetica*, Horace advised his readers on a method of composing stories, a method so universal that it did not matter whether the writers were fifteen or ninety, libertines or monks, intellectuals or merchants.[8] All they had to do was apply his categories to a subject and they could produce a text. Horace believed that all stories were the product of the answers to a series of basic questions. Who are the main characters? What is the place in which they are set? What is the nature of their conflict or problem? What is the era in which the story is set? What is their purpose? What are the means they use to solve their problems and what obstacles do they face? And what kind of resolution can be made?

Horace argued that if you answered those questions in an imaginative way you would produce the germ of a story. Modern journalists honor Horace when they tell us that the way to write a complete news story is to answer the basic questions: What happened? Who did it? Where and under what circumstances was the action done? When did it happen? How was the thing done? Why was it done? Burke borrowed these questions and updated them. He maintained that the questions could be used to gain a complete understanding of any human action and the motives from which it arose. Burke does not use the term motive in the legal or formal sense. It is simply a name we give to our acts, a strategic symbolic summing up of an action. Since my purpose is not to provide a philosophical scheme but an explanation of a critical perspective, I will eschew an extended discussion of these claims.

From the language scholar and co-author of *The Meaning of Meaning*, Ivor Armstrong Richards, Burke took the idea of the importance of form in art.[9] Burke was interested in the aesthetic appeal of form, particularly narrative form.[10] Form invites our participation; it arouses our desires and promises to fulfill them. Everyone knows the power of form in sports, religion, and in the military; these three are great repositories of form. Ritual forms give us a sense of order, piety, shared community, and emotional closure. Burke has made us acutely aware of the power of narrative form, a form that dominates our orientation toward the world. Burke noted that comedians make use of our socialization to conventional forms. We expect jokes will have a punch line; we expect that football squads will punt on fourth and long; we expect that mazes will have a center; that heroes will (usually) win out in the end. Form invites our participation; we become caught up in it. Artists and writers use form to draw us into their works; propagandists and advertisers use musical, visual, and verbal forms to gain our compliance. Burke's Pentadic Criticism focuses on the widespread use of dramatic form. Dramatic form is one of the most common ways that we interpret events. It is one of the great human lenses we employ to discover meaning in our environment. Dramatic form, Burke tells us, is much bigger than theatrical performance; it is embedded in the structure of our minds. Thus, *dramatic form exists logically prior to our experience.* It is like an actor waiting in the wings to come on stage and interpret for us what it is that we are seeing and hearing as we move through the world. In this sense dramatic form is literal, not metaphorical. The scheme of dramatic form is not a metaphor derived from a study of lots of drama or years of going to conventional theatre and watching plays. In fact, the contrary is true. The movies, plays, stories, and news events are endless reincarnations of dramatic form.

Why is it Important?

Frightened by growing alliance of big commerce and big media, Burke began to worry about the future of self-government in North America. Despite his associations with leading figures of the Left, Burke was basically an old-fashioned Jeffersonian American who believed that issues and ideas ought to come from the bedrock of the people, not from mandarin intellectuals and technical operatives. His little farm in Andover, New Jersey, was close to his ideal, a place where groups of people met for free discussion of just about everything under the Sun, but especially the local, state, and federal policies of their government. But how could this model thrive or even survive in an America now dominated by corporations, giant research universities, and government bureaucracies? How will autonomous American citizens survive surrounded by agents and institutions who were trying to manipulate them? Advertising, propaganda, slanted news, corporate public relations; political action groups, social movements, cults, together with Hollywood and the mass media have saturated the environment with persuasive images and words. During the Great Depression, Burke witnessed the rise of Hitler, Mussolini, Franco, and Stalin, demagogues who manipulated millions of followers through demonic messages greatly amplified by nearly absolute control of public media.

But even in the open societies of Democratic Britain and the United States, he noted that large masses of Western citizenry suffered from fear, confusion or deep cynicism as a result of the great ocean of programmatic messages from every corner. After the great stock market crash of 1929, and the ruin of millions of families, our economic system seemed to have failed. Back-to-the-Land Agrarians, Technocrats, Communists, Fascists, Single Taxers and other disaffected groups emerged from the wreckage. Spokespersons who had formerly been dismissed as cranks and utopians were getting a hearing. Burke noted that many of his fellow citizens were confused, uprooted, and fearful. He believed without guidance they would not know how to discover the content and the consequences of these competing ides. Unlike European thinkers whose answer was guidance by a class of intellectuals, Burke thought that people ought to be able to analyze and understand public questions on their own. In particular they ought to be able to discover the personal agendas and disguised advantages that people often hide beneath idealistic rhetoric. In the old American sprit of self-help and individualism, Burke offered a perspective that would unmask personal motive and separate personal advantage from high-sounding public promises.

Burke had begun his career wanting to be a famous literary figure. Throughout the 1920s he associated with famous American and British writers in Greenwich Village. He translated the work of Thomas Mann, reviewed the work of many of the leading writers of the day as editor of *The Dial*, then one of America's foremost literary magazine.[11] But by the early 1930s Burke was ready to face the fact that he was not a gifted novelist and that his real talent lay in another direction. He was more suited to the role of literary critic and social theorist. He believed that the role of the artist was crucial in society and that the artist to a much greater extent than the psychologist and the social worker could perform a therapeutic role in society. Embracing a tradition running back to Aristotle, Burke believed that the writer could be a kind of physician of society. He was a pioneer in raising environmental awareness, an early voice warning about the polarization of class and race, and about the unsustainability of our agricultural system and industrial system.[12] For the last five decades of his existence, all of his efforts were dedicated to giving people the analytic tools to resist manipulative persuaders and to seek a more poetic vision of society.

Advertisers, propagandists, and hustlers of all kinds like to have us respond rapidly and uncritically to their messages. They want us to act, without stopping to reflect deeply on the full meaning of their message. But a critical perspective means that we stop to do some analysis; and this time of reflection prevents the rapid stimulus-response kind of action so dear to mass marketing persuasion. My brother Charles, a former creative director of one of the world's largest ad agencies, joked that he wanted people who saw the ads to respond like Pavlov's spinal dogs. He wanted them to rush to buy the product, not to engage in an analysis of its claims and benefits. Criticism not only delays our reactions to messages, it may modify our reactions; it can allow us to reframe the message in an alternative way, or adopt other attitudes toward it or perhaps think about the intentions of the maker of the message, or to the long term consequences of acting upon such a message. In thinking deeply about their attractions to the language and imagery various products, one might also discover some useful things about one's mind and heart. Thus the practice of criticism not only helps us make better choices, it may also be transformational.

How Does it Work? or, the Naming of the Parts

The Dramatistic Pentad is not about finding the underlying and absolute truth of a situation. Rather it is a method of discovering why people do what they do. Language is not analyzed for its truth, but for its strategic uses. As Clarke Rountree puts it, Dramatism is useful for "explaining what he, she or others, say about his, her or their own past present, and future actions of the past present and future actions of others."[13] According to Burke, language is a mode of symbolic action, most often as a way of presenting one's self to others. As I noted earlier Burke does not say that our daily lives resemble a drama. He says life is a drama. Thus we perceive the world in dramatic terms with plots, antagonists, protagonists, settings, motives, and so on. We are hardwired for drama. No wonder our news stories, no matter how chaotic and enigmatic in their shape, are put into dramatic form by the mass media. It is our primary way of making sense of the world. Often the dramatic frame features a battle over meanings, perspectives, and values.

The Pentad is made up of five parts that are universally found in all narratives. Each of these parts is phrased as a question. Answering these questions will determine which of the five parts dominates the others. The critic will make this decision. He or she will do so by answering the basic questions about an action described in the text. Who did it? Where and when and under what constraints? With what means and modes? Alleging what purpose? According to Burke, the answers to these questions will circumscribe the range and variety of reasonable interpretation.

The Five Rhetorical Elements of the Dramatistic Pentad are act, scene, agent, agency, and purpose. Burke praises them for their universal application to discourse. He says their "participation in common ground makes for transformability."[14]

Act

Act is associated with dramatic action. It answers the question what is the action? What is being done? What is going on? It is associated with the philosophy of realism. These people believe that the truthfulness of any belief rests upon the closeness of its correspondence with reality. Discourse that emphasizes the primacy of action have a deep hold on us. We admire devotees of action, and even when doing nothing would be a sensible course, or when there is little agreement about what to do, we still admire the leader who rushes headlong into an act. And we do so even when we suspect it may be a bad thing to do. We have a fear of too much reflection. We hold Hamlet in contempt because it takes him so long to act; we love action-heroes who act without hesitation or reflection. Long ago Edmund Burke noted that a big noisy destructive government policy was more admired than a wise quiet temperate policy. Too much reflection and analysis frightens people. We tend to associate thoughtful decision making with passivity, a state that fills red-blooded Americans with fear. (Burke's most succinct statement of Act is found on pages 64–69 of his *Grammar of Motives*.)

Scene

Scene is the dramatistic term for the context of the act. Texts that emphasize the power of the surrounding environment or the coercive power of circumstances feature the philosophical doctrine of determinism. Many adventure stories that show people battling the elements or the power of nature emphasize scene. People who believe in situational ethics argue that circumstances are more important in determining our deeds than our received moral codes. Those who argue that crime is a result of slum living and can be solved by slum clearance are making an argument that emphasizes scene. I have known advertising executives who believed that effective advertising practices could be learned only in New York. During the middle of the last century some editors came to believe that the greatest American literature could only be written in the American South. Thomas Jefferson believed that only independent local farmers could maintain sustainable agriculture. Persons have often attributed magical properties to place. Ancient people often believed that special places like oracles, sacred grove, or aligned hilltops possessed special power. Others attribute power to labyrinths, caves, or even buildings with special atmospherics. Many early religions adopted the idea of a sacred center. In the inner sanctum only the gods could dwell, in the second circle high priests, and on the profane margins the worshippers. In romantic novels, the outer scene seems sympathetic to the inner state of the characters. Duels are fought against the background of a storm, and lovers break up in the dead of winter. (Burke's richest definitions of Scene can be found on pages 127 to 132 of his *Grammar of Motives*.)

Agent

This is the term for the person or persons who perform the actions. American folklore has honored people with strongly assertive personality. We assume that strong leadership is vital for success in business and sports. Those who speak of the indispensable person are emphasizing the importance of the agent in human affairs. Much has been written about the charismatic leader who triumphs in spite of obstacles, setbacks, and enemies. Texts that emphasize the agent feature the philosophical viewpoint of idealism. Ronald Reagan was fond of talking about great American heroes. His celebrations of these people emphasized the power of an individual's inner resources against adverse circumstances. For Reagan the agent was always more powerful than the scene in which he or she was set. Character triumphed over circumstance. In his famous 1986 address to the nation on the Challenger disaster, Reagan emphasized the character of the astronauts above all.[15] He did not dwell on the failure of the technology or question the purpose of the program. He identified the astronauts with the American pioneer spirit and linked their deaths to a deeper resolve for the conquest of space. (Burke's clearest description of Agent can be found on pages 171–175 of his *Grammar of Motives*.)

Agency

The dramatistic term for the means the agent used to do the deed is agency. It is the method, the technique, the apparatus, or the institution we use to get the thing done. Spokesmen for technology tend to emphasize a technological fix for all of our problems. Bureaucrats tell us that the system is the solution. A well-known ski manufacturer used to say that the secret was in the design. A well-known bodybuilder used to tell people that his method was the only one that produced big results. Those who emphasize agency as the dominant term in their messages tend to espouse a philosophy of Pragmatism. This is the Philosophy that the most important aspect of any idea is its ability to produce good results, preferably ones with great cash benefits. In other words, a good idea is one that is useful to the believer in the idea. We are bombarded with courses selling us special methods of building our bodies, transforming our personalities, or becoming immensely wealthy. We are promised seven ways to save our marriages, three dynamic verbal techniques for successful negotiation, or a special technique to increase intelligence or expand memory. (Burke's most compelling explanation of Agency can be found on pages 275 to 278 in his *Grammar of Motives*.)

Purpose

Purpose answers the questions why! Moralists often emphasize this question in their messages. Purpose has to do with the justification for the action. Its driving focus is on the value of objectives, goals, and courses of action. Those who strongly emphasize purpose tend toward a philosophy of mysticism. Messages emphasizing purpose feature ends rather than means. Purposive thinkers and writers often speak of acts as small parts of a much larger system. We must protect our family as a part of helping the community. Helping the community furthers the greatness of the nation. The greatness of the nation is necessary to advance civilization. There is a natural tendency for messages centered on purpose to move toward transcendence. Cicero advised Roman youth to study rhetoric in order to enter the Senate. In entering the Senate, they preserved the Republic. In preserving the Republic they carried the Roman message of order and prosperity to the newly conquered peoples of the Empire. In embodying the Roman message they served the gods who had clearly favored the spread of the Roman Way throughout the world. (Burke's most illuminating discussion of Purpose occurs in his Grammar of Motives, pp. 292–297.)

The Ratios

Because each of these elements is interconnected in a dramatic structure of action, Burke calls them a *grammar of motives*. In any one discourse, one of these elements usually dominates the others and this ratio allows us to name or characterize the action. The predominance of one term over the others gives each drama a characteristic shape. That shape is what gives the drama its bite, its attitude, its persuasive bias. Since a text or a speech represents a persuasive act, I will pair each term with act: Thus, Scene-Act, Agent-Act, Agency-Act, Purpose-Act, and even Act-Act. In theory one might use more than twenty ratios by simply pairing each term with every other term in sequence. This level of complexity is seldom necessary for actual critical practice, however.

Scene-Act Ratio

The place or the circumstances define the meaning of the act. Example: Considering the violence of urban life we should expect city dwellers to commit more crimes. Example: Given the slovenly nature of government oversight, Enron was inevitable. Example: A beautiful and revitalized downtown area will attract creative people to settle here from across the nation. Example: Given the distractions of Paris, it was hard to get much work done. In each of the above examples, the scene dominates our understanding. The scene is also sometimes used to justify power. Leaders sometimes point to dangerous situations in order to justify expanding their powers. On the other hand Clarence Darrow pleaded for clients on the grounds that they could not help themselves, having been mercilessly shaped by bad heredity and a bad environment. Karl Marx believed that class conflict was a situation (scene) that would gradually ripen into revolution. During my military service I was told again and again that available forces on the ground and the local terrain determine military tactics. We are often told that a failed plan might have worked in a different place. Soldiers are told that they must fight harder to defend their homeland and that fighting on native soil will bring a special zeal to their efforts.

Philosophical Position: Texts that emphasize scene downplay free choice and emphasize situational determinism. They tend to emphasize the power of circumstances over individual choice. Clarence Darrow excused the behavior of many criminals by arguing that they were victims of bad heredity and merciless environment. Speakers who routinely advise accommodating to circumstances rather than trying to change them emphasize the deterministic power of scene.

Agent-Act Ratio

The actor is the most important factor in the execution of an act. Example: Given a monster like Hitler we should have expect millions of people would be exterminated. Example: Only Albert Einstein could have made this discovery. Example: Everything depends upon the quality of our military leaders. Example: From a proven winner like Arnold Schwarzenegger you can expect miracles in whatever he tries to do. Thus an agent-act ratio comes into play whenever we connect character and behavior. Dynastic historians wrote histories centered on the personalities of various kings. Persons who look for charismatic leaders to solve their problems tend to speak in this mode.

Philosophical Position: Texts or speeches that emphasize the Agent reflect idealism. Idealism emphasizes ambitions, values, and meanings. It assets that individuals are motivated by desires, emotions, and ambitions. Character is seen as far more important than the force of circumstances or the existence of resources or special techniques.

Agency-Act Ratio

The methods of tools used to perform an act. Example: Only Tuck Business school methods can produce a company like Dyganamics. Example: The success of Beckham was a result of his secret training methods. Example: Only advances in technology can bring economic growth to this region. Example: Advanced training and trade craft have made the British MI 6 the greatest spy agency in the world. As Charles Kneuuper used to say: "Give a child a hammer and everything will be treated like a nail."[16] Or as an Indy driver once said: "Victory is 80 percent car, 15 percent team, and 5 percent driver." As a famous bodybuilder used to say: "There are many ways to build a mighty grip, but only the Jowett Crusher Grips can give you a way to outgrip professional athletes." For those who speak from an agency supreme perspective the system is always the solution.

Philosophical Position: Texts or speeches that emphasize agency demonstrate pragmatism. Pragmatism is the doctrine that the best idea or solution is one that produces the best outcome. Methods are judged by their consequences. The best idea is the one with the biggest cash value.

Purpose-Act

One might describe this ratio in the following manner: In order to get X you have to do Y. In order to win the war, we must adopt the methods of our enemy.[17] Example: If we want to produce great thinkers, we must subject our students to rigorous intellectual training. Example: If Capitalism is to function successfully, it must allow people to fail. Example: If I am to be a good example I must act openly and honorably. Example: I may have made several bad mistakes, but I had the very best intentions. Everyone remembers the IRA members who said they regretted killing innocent people but that such things had to be done for the sake of the cause. Another version of the Purpose-Act is the generic: "You cannot make an omelet without breaking a few eggs." The Problem is that ends often become means. Temporary methods often sabotage one's goals. Stalin promised an end to food shortages in the Soviet Union, but his method of achieving that goal brought the death of four million kulaks.

Philosophical Position: Since Purpose is merely another name for the goal of an act, speeches or texts that emphasize purpose suggest the concerns of mysticism. Such texts tend to move toward the transcendent. Decisions are always seen in terms of a larger program.

In an extreme example of this kind of rhetoric means are subordinated to ends. One might be urged to break local laws for the sake of a higher or divine law. It is well to recall the revolutionary excuse for violence: They tell us that they must break a few eggs to make an omelet.

Act-Act Ratio

The world is filled with Act-Act ratios: "I had to hit him because he hit me first." Remember all the Domino theories from the cold War: If we don't beat them in the Pacific we will soon be fighting them in San Francisco and finally in Boston. Example: All success formulas are pushed to their conclusion. We began by seeking to heal the body. We will end by demanding that medicine provide eternal life in renewable bodies. Perhaps the most striking example of the Act dominated by policy was the Cold War's mutually assured destruction: Don't push me too far, or I will kill us both.

Philosophical Position: Texts that emphasize act suggest realism. Realism is the philosophy that says that it doesn't really matter what People are. What is important is what they do. Abstractions like "the People" or "the national character" or "the common good" are seen as silly abstractions. There is no such thing as the public; they do not believe in the "common good." People act through special interests; for them Presidents or political parties are just empty agents who act on behalf of one interest group or another. Behavior is what counts and most high-minded rhetoric is seen as a mask or a justification for self-interested action.

We could cite more ratios but the five above are enough to illustrate the two-fold power of the Pentad.[18] Suffice to say that the Pentad can generate discourse from a variety of perspectives, and provide a lively sense of the limits of any single perspective and the necessity of viewing messages from several points of view. And in looking at the feasibility and effectiveness of any public proposal the Pentadic ratios allow us to critique it from a multiplicity of views. For instance, does an agent appear to understand the scene in which he or she operates? Are the agencies or methods selected by the agent appropriate to the scene? Is the agent capable of dealing with the situation, does he or she have character, expertise, support? Is the purpose used to justify acts that seem to undermine it in Orwellian fashion, such as militarizing the state to achieve order, or using censorship to prevent the spread of subversive ideas?

Use of the Pentad

Clarke Rountree and others have cautioned critics about using the pentad as a cookie cutter.[19] Despite its seemingly tidy structure, the Pentad is a heuristic device. Scenes, for example, can shrink or grow. In his famous speech on the Grenada invasion, President Reagan began talking about the difficulties on the island as an immediate threat to the safety of Americans, but he gradually expanded the scene to include meddling by Cuba and finally a larger plot by the Soviet Union.[20] Burke himself spoke of the plasticity of terms. Technology, formerly classified as agency in our culture had (in his judgment) become an agent, a self sustaining interest group with an agenda of accelerated technological change.[21] A leader like Castro may be presented as a forceful Agent in his youth, but presented as an icon (scene) in his dotage. The assigning of ratios is an imaginative exercise, not a stodgy formula.

SAMPLE APPLICATIONS

Example One: Agrarian Concerns

The Slow food Movement, the Farmer's Market Movement, and the Neo-Agrarians are all social movements touting the need for sustainable agriculture and an organically produced food supply. Their rhetoric has a heavy scenic component. Like Thomas Jefferson and Wendell Berry they argue that we must encourage local small individual farmers over corporate agriculture.[22] They argue that individual owners act responsibly while corporate farms over-produce, exhaust the soil, cut down tree breaks and let the precious topsoil blow away. While they destroy rural communities by displacing individual owners, they are also quick to abandon the countryside once they have exhausted the soil and the water supply. These people use many scenic words such as community, local, American earth, husbandry, organic, and home place. Like Wes Jackson they speak of the magic of "becoming native to the place" in their quest for a responsible and sustainable agriculture.[23] These repetitive patterns of good words Burke called "clusters" and therefore we should expect to find some opposite words, bad words that he called "agons." In the rhetoric of the Neo-Agrarian opponents have a different group of scenic terms routinely applied to them: inorganic, rootless, unsustainable, wasteful, global, etc.

This strategic emphasis on scene has great strengths. In the time of the environmental movement we are familiar and mindful of our natural surroundings. On the other hand, an extreme form of this emphasis might degenerate into extreme determinism. We might be told that only soldiers who have experienced combat should be allowed to make military policy and civilians should not be permitted to interfere since "they have not been there" and do not understand the essence of the matter. Opponents of scenic rhetoric might argue that in its strongest forms it reflects a philosophy of naive materialism.

Example Two: Stressing the Agent

Numerous students of Martin Luther King's speaking have noted that he tended to emphasize the agent. He frequently emphasized the need for soul power and the nonviolent discipline over the power of the scene to provoke demonstrators to violence. He featured an agent-scene ratio and his perspective comes down to this: Given the right kind of demonstrator, the scene can be transformed from one of hatred and exclusion to one of acceptance and forgiveness. President Jimmy Carter also emphasized agent or character. In his speeches he constantly reminded people of his background as a Christian, a nuclear physicist, an engineer, a peanut farmer, a father, a former governor, and a military officer. His personal political message was this: Given this broad range of roles, I have deep understanding and competence in a broad arena. For some listeners this litany of roles evoked identification and confidence. For others the wide list of disparate roles may have failed to produce a unifying leadership image. Carter's famous Conservation of Energy speech is a good example of bad dramatistic choices. Carter appeared in the White House in a sweater turning down the thermostat as an example of conservation of energy. He went on to blame the oil companies, several Arab nations and the American people for bringing on the crisis. His message was that we lacked the stuff of our pioneer ancestors and that we had acted in a self-indulgent and undisciplined manner. We were now suffering for our actions and must endure a lower standard of living and endure limitations imposed by the federal government on driving speeds and availability of supplies. In this way Carter used agency in a negative way. No one enjoys being blamed for a bad situation and Carter's approval ratings plummeted.

Example Three: Stressing Agency

Proponents of traditional education used to blame declining reading and math scores on the invention of television. Now they blame the supposed declines in analytical thinking on computer games. Newspaper editors increasingly speak of a loss of rigor in investigative reporting and blame it on the speed of new technologies that privilege rapid news delivery over responsible reporting. Promoters of athletic machines argue the technological superiority of their product as a means of producing larger and more powerful muscles. Others attempt to sell us new methods of nonlinear creative thinking as superior methods of problem solving. The most extreme example of this is the idea of the "technological-fix" or the notion that new forms of advanced technology can solve all human problems.

Burke taught us that motives weren't fixed things, but "a term of interpretation, and beings such it will naturally take its place within the framework of our Weltanschauung as a whole."[24] According to Burke "Motives" are the names we give to our actions. We may use a weighted vocabulary to talk about our building of a suburban development as our contribution to the American Dream of owning one's own home, or we may call it a great opportunity for personal profit. In each case our discourse would reflect a purpose-act ratio. One can envisage a developer using both vocabularies of motive to different audiences on different occasions.

The important point here is that our orientation determines how we characterize events and therefore our motives toward events. Charles Kneupper notes how rival orientations can be at war in our discourse:

> For example, if two persons were to observe the actual event in which lumberjacks cut down trees in a forest and one describes the event as "progress" while the other describes it as "the destruction of natural resources," then significant differences of orientation and motives are implied. Both descriptions are strategic interpretations of reality. As Burke notes, "strategies size up situations, name their structure and outstanding ingredients and name them in a way that contains our attitude toward them." The "progress" observer has a favorable/supportive attitude toward the cutting witnessed. . . . [T]he "destruction of natural resources" observer has an unfavorable altitude.[25]

Kneupper's example notes that people are disposed to act in different ways toward the same events. And when we want to influence people's responses we will pick out certain factors that appeal to an audience and minimize or obscure factors that may not be received well. As Burke has noted, this is really a power play, a way to define or redefine a particular event. Whoever is able to define the event wins the day in any given situation. Much is at stake in rival dramatic schemes. Some people routinely define the world as a tragedy. Burke tells us tragedy usually ends in victimage, death, sacrifice, and grief. Others define events as comedy. In a comic play there is always room for another alternative or point of view. It is a more open form. The late Morris Udall of Arizona once told me that the way to break through partisanship in the House of Representatives was to use humor. In this way he avoided the brutal partisan train wrecks of polarized parties. Burke was an enemy of polarization. He often noted polarized alternatives generally ended badly, in violence, horror, and death. Pentadic Criticism was his way of breaking the gridlock. The pentad suggests a variety of perspectives, standing places, and attitudes. It is generative, heuristic, creative, and frame breaking.

FINDING THE DOMINANT TERM: GRAPPLING WITH THE TEXT

But how does one search and find the most important Pentadic term? This is done during a close reading of the text. Like an accountant doing an audit, one looks for patterns. Patterns are determined by frequency of repetition. To discover the pattern is to locate the speaker's perspective. Which words are repeated more than others? Some texts are heavy on description or scene; others seem to focus more on the methods (agency) by which things are done, and some concentrate on the character of the person or people in the text. Yet others may deal with the justification of the actions described in the text (purpose). David Ling studied Senator Ted Kennedy's Chappaquiddick speech and discovered that most of the words used to characterize Kennedy's actions related to the scene. Describing the accident in which Mary Jo Kopeckne died; Kennedy blamed the lack of lighting, the narrowness of the bridge, and the darkness of the road without guardrails. He noted that the car filled with water rapidly, and that he was disoriented by the murky water, the cold, and the suddenness of events. In other words, the scene produced the accident and Ted Kennedy and Mary Jo Kopeckne were both victims of the situation; they were overpowered by circumstances.[26] And when circumstances (Scene) produce an accident, it really is nobody's fault. Listeners who expect a leader to be conspicuously active might forgive one who is a victim of circumstances but they may be disappointed with a leader who was unable to triumph over a bad situation. In Reagan's famous Challenger Disaster speech in which he memorialized the lost astronauts, he characterized them as pioneers who had sacrificed themselves so that the world might move forward to the conquest of space. All of his imagery favored the agents not the agency (technology) or the scene (outer space). The speeches of bureaucrats typically emphasize agency (procedures) over the other Pentadic terms. An audience of reformers who are enamored of purpose (moral objectives) might find this kind of speech as extremely boring. An audience of bureaucrats, however, might find speeches emphasizing procedure and ritual deeply satisfying, if not inspiring.

So the crux of the matter is that the texts (the speeches, the stories, the descriptions of things) represent what Burke called "multiple versions of reality." We see things in different ways and these different ways are reflected in our choice of words. Audiences and readers respond to these different ways of seeing, these different perspectives, and they may embrace or reject them. They may find these perspectives good or bad, useful or useless, beautiful or ugly, noble or despicable. Making the perspective visible through the application of the pentad to the text allows us to see why the discourse affects us in a particular way. It also helps us to evaluate a text in terms of its power to move an audience and to talk intelligently and at length about that power. By analyzing a text in terms of its images and emotions, we reconnect it to the social, cultural, and political contexts that surround it.

CONCLUSION

In short, perspective matters. Burke notes that a patient might report a dream to "a Freudian analyst or a Jungian or an Adlerian, or to a practitioner of some other school. In each case the "same dream will be subjected to a different color filter, with corresponding differences, in the nature of the event as perceived, recorded, and interpreted."[27] Burke's point is that we can identify competing perspectives in a critical self-conscious way and come to some understanding of their power and their limits. And by imagining the same matter from other than our own perspective, we can come to a more rounded and objective understanding of matters. In short, gaining perspective is at the heart of Pentadic Critical method. Perspective shows that provisional truth lies on several sides, but that some perspectives have serious limitations.

Long ago, Marcus Aurelius, perhaps the most humane of the Roman emperors, used a similar method to make important decisions. Withdrawing temporarily from the scene of action, he would visualize the execution and outcome of several possible courses of action. This gave him a sense of distance, humility, and made him consider the larger community and the long-term consequences of history. Using this method he became wiser, kinder, and more humane.

As with Marcus Aurelius, this method produces a confrontation of several perspectives or what Burke often referred to as a perspective of perspectives.[28] While we remain living human beings we can never transcend the limits of our bodies or our language. We can never get outside or above a message and examine its truth or falsity, its goodness or badness in a godlike way, or after the manner of a disembodied sage. However, we can get pretty near the knuckle if we use the Pentadic method as a guide. By identifying the perspective of a piece of discourse and then looking at it from several other perspectives we can go far in discovering whether it is wise or foolish, moderate or extreme, helpful or destructive, self interested or altruistic. And we can live sanely, humanely, and wisely in an environment in which we are assaulted by mountebanks and arch-charlatans bewildering in doctrine and number.

POTENTIALS AND PITFALLS

One of the weaknesses of Burke's method is that it can be used as a cookie cutter. That is, if applied to a speech, a story, even a joke, its categories will yield results. It can be used almost mindlessly. As critics we need to remind ourselves that Burke's goal was to bring deeper understanding, to shake us out of our usual ways of looking at things and to shake us up by giving us a set of fresh categories. Burke spent much of his life as an outsider, an attacker of established formulas. Thus it would be ironic to treat his pentad as a static, orthodox, tried and true method. Despite the formulaic nature of his five-pointed system, one needs to understand that the concept are simply tools for analysis, aids to understanding the power and appeal of messages. It is also well to remember that Burke was more interested in having us resist the power of rhetorical messages than in constructing them ourselves.

BURKEAN TOP PICKS

Bello, Richard. "A Burkean Analysis of the 'Political Correctness' in Confrontation in Higher Education." *Southern Communication Journal* 61 (1996): 243–52. One of the very best studies of how Political Correctness went from a God Term to a Devil Term for many embattled academics.

Blankenship, Jane, Marlene G. Fine, and Leslie K. Davis, "The Republican Primary Debates: The Transformation of Actor to Scene," *Quarterly Journal of Speech* 69 (1983): 25–36. A very imaginative treatment of the Pentad and the ways in which one term can merge with another is seen in this essay.

Brummet, Barry. "A Pentadic Analysis of Ideologies in Two Gay Rights Controversies." *Central States Speech Journal* 30 (1979): 250–61. Burke treats ideology as a vocabulary that justifies the possession of power. Brummet performs a brilliant analysis of rival claims to power in this essay.

Burke, Kenneth. "Dramatism" in *Drama in Life: The Uses of Communication in Society*, edited by James E. Combs and Michael Mansfield, 7–17. (New York: Hastings House, 1976). The master himself has written a street-level, worm's-eye view of Dramatism that provides a concrete set of examples. His exposition will satisfy the advanced critic as well as the neophyte.

——. "The Rhetoric of Hitler's Battle" in *The Philosophy of Literary Form*, 191–222. (Baton Rouge: Louisiana State University Press, 1941). In 1938 Burke wrote a prophetic analysis of Hitler's *Mein Kampf*. This is perhaps the most lucid and penetrating article Burke ever produced.

Enos, Theresa (ed.). *Encyclopedia of Rhetoric and Composition* (New York: Routledge, 1996). One of the very best sources for practical applications of Burke's basic critical vocabulary can be found in this volume. See Tillie Warnock, "Burke" 90–92; Bill Bridges, "Terministic Screens," 722–23 and "Pentad," 499–501; James W. Chesebro, "Dramatism," 200–01; Pat Youngdahl and Tilly Warnock, "Identification," 337–40; H. L. Ewbank, "Symbolic Action," 710–11.

Ling, David. "A Pentadic Analysis of Senator Edward Kennedy's Address to the People of Massachusetts," *Central States Journal* 21 (1970): 81–86. Certain articles are classics and one that will live as long as Burkean studies is this one by David Ling. Presidential candidates are supposed to appear as active agents for us, but Ted Kennedy presented himself as a tragic victim. Ling shows that Kennedy's pentadic choice was a fateful one.

Rountree, III., Clarke J. "Charles Haddon Spurgeon's Calvinistic Rhetoric of Election: Constituting an Elect." *Journal of Communication and Religion* 17 (1994): 33–48. There is much misunderstanding of the idea of predestination in intellectual circles. Rountree uses Burke's ideas about hierarchy and the pentad to explore the confusion over some of the most basic religious concepts in Western civilization.

NOTES

1. Kenneth Burke, *A Rhetoric of Motives* (New York: Prentice-Hall, 1950).

2. Kenneth Burke, *A Grammar of Motives* (New York: Prentice-Hall, 1945).

3. For a full discussion of Nichols's contributions, see: John H. Patton, "Marie Hochmuth Nichols's Voice of Rationality in the Humane Tradition of Rhetoric and Criticism," in *Twentieth Century Roots of Rhetorical Studies*, eds. Jim A. Kuypers and Andrew King (Westport, CT: Praeger, 2001), 123–142.

4. Marie Hochmuth, "Kenneth Burke and the 'New Rhetoric'" *Quarterly Journal of Speech* 38 (1952): 133–144. See also Marie Hochmuth, "Burkean Criticism," *Western Speech* 21 (1957): 89–95.

5. For the clearest statement of Burke's foundational theory of dramatism, see Kenneth Burke, "Dramatism," in *International Encyclopedia of the Social Sciences*, vol. III, ed. David L. Sills (New York: Macmillan and the Free Press, 1968), 445–452.

6. Aristotle's belief in the centrality of the Polis to civilized conduct and culture is too well known to be cited here. For a brilliant discussion of the Aristotelian relationship between narrative culture and community see Gabriel Lear, *Happy Lives and the Highest Good: An Essay on Aristotle's Nichomachean Ethics* (Princeton: Princeton University Press, 2004).

7. Burke, *A Grammar of Motives*, xv.

8. See Helena Detmer, *Horace: A Study in Structure* (New York: Olms-Weidmann, 1983) and also R. K. Hack, "The Doctrine of Literary Forms," *Harvard Studies in Classical Philology* 27 (1916): 1–65.

9. On this subject, I. A. Richards wrote three deeply influential books: *The Meaning of Meaning: A Study of the Influence of Langue Upon Thought and the Science of Symbolism* w/C/K. Ogden (1923), *Principles of Literary Criticism* (1924) and *Practical Criticism*, (1929). His studies in psychology and semantics laid the foundation for the close readings of texts that dominated literary criticism for decades after.

10. Burke discusses the power of form in many places. The sections on "Formal Appeal" and "Rhetorical Form in the Large" in *A Rhetoric of Motives*, 65–78. Also see "Literature as Equipment for Living" in *The Philosophy of Literary Form*, 2nd ed (Baton Rogue, LSU Press). 293–313.

11. For a full discussion of Burke's association with literary figures and his editorship of *The Dial*, see Jack Selzer, *Kenneth Burke in Greenwich Village: 1915–1931* (Madison: University of Wisconsin Press, 1996) and Jack Selzer and Anne George, *Kenneth Burke in the 1930s* (South Carolina Press, 2007).

12. In 1937 Burke speculated about the future importance of "one little fellow named Ecology." For a full statement of Burke's long association with the movement see "Kenneth Burke on Ecology," in *A Synthesis: Extensions of the Burkean System*, ed. James Chesebro (Tuscaloosa: University of Alabama Press, 1993), 251–268.

13. Clarke J. Rountree, III, "Coming to Terms with Kenneth Burke's Pentad," *American Communication Journal* 1, no. 3 (May 1998). http://www.acjournal.org/holdings/vol1/iss3/burke/rountree.html (accessed September 17, 2008).

14. Burke, *Grammar of Motives*, xix

15. Ronald Reagan, "Address to the American People on the Challenger Disaster," found at www.AmericanRhetoric.com.

16. Charles Kneupper, "Dramatistic Invention: The Pentad as Heuristic Procedure," *Rhetoric Quarterly* (Spring 1977): 129–135.

17. Kneupper, 131.

18. Sonja Foss presents many rich examples of Pentadic Criticism in the eleventh chapter of her *Rhetorical Criticism: Exploration and Practice* (Long Grove, Illinois: Waveland Press, 2004).

19. Rountree, *American Communication Journal*.

20. See, for instance, http://www.spartacus.schoolnet.co.uk/USAreagan.htm. (accessed September 18, 2008).

21. Personal conversation with Kenneth Burke at New Harmony, Indiana Convention, July 10, 1990.

22. He has authored one of the most enduring books in American eco-criticism. See Wendell Berry, *The Unsettling of America* (Sierra Club Books, 1977). For a sense of Burke's contributions to ecology see, Tarla Rai Peterson, "The Will to Conservation: A Burkean Analysis of Dust Bowl Rhetoric and American Farming Motives," *Southern Communication Journal* 52 (1986): 1–21.

23. Wes Jackson, *Becoming Native to This Place* (Lexington: University of Kentucky Press, 1994).

24. Burke, *Grammar of Motives*, 130.

25. Kneupper, 131.

26. All materials quoted from David A. Ling, "A Pentadic Analysis of Senator Edward Kennedy's Address to the People of Massachusetts, July 25, 1969," *Central States Journal* 21 (1970): 84.

27. Burke, Language as Symbolic Action, 45.

28. This is Burke's ultimate vantage point. It has roots in the ancient practice of rhetorical exercises that one reads about in Seneca, Marcus Aurelius, and in the spiritual exercises of Pierre Hadot. In preparing to argue a position or make an important decision, the ancients were wont to visualize the matter from several different points of view (from the victim's point of view, from that of the accused, from the vantage of the judge, from that of the victim's family, the accuser's family, the verdict of history, etc.).

12

Framing Analysis

Jim A. Kuypers

If you have ever had a picture framed, you know that the frame you chose emphasized some elements of the picture at the expense of others. Similarly, if you were to reframe the picture, you would notice that the very elements previously emphasized—colors, patterns, composition—would subsequently be de-emphasized by the new frame. Instead, a different combination of elements would be highlighted. Similar to pictures, ideas and events—facts—are also framed. When we frame in a particular way, we encourage others to see these facts in a particular way. Framing in this sense can be understood as taking some aspects of our reality and making them more accessible than other aspects.

The tremendous power of frames to shape the manner in which we interpret certain issues and situations is readily discernable in a study by Paul M. Sniderman, Richard A. Brody, and Philip E. Tetlock. These researchers used mandatory testing for HIV (human immunodeficiency virus) as the issue for their study. They found that the effect "of framing is to prime values differentially, establishing the salience of the one or the other. [A] majority of the public supports the rights of persons with AIDS [acquired imuno-deficiency syndrome] when the issue is framed to accentuate civil liberties considerations—and supports . . . mandatory testing when the issue is framed to accentuate public health considerations."[1] Thomas Nelson and colleagues provide another powerful example of frames. Using a local news story about a Ku Klux Klan march as their issue, these researchers presented audiences with either one of two stories: "One framed the rally as a free speech issue, and the other framed it as a disruption of public order. Participants who viewed the free speech story expressed more tolerance for the Klan than those participants who watched the public order story."[2]

Frames are so powerful because they induce us to filter our perceptions of the world in particular ways, essentially making some aspects of our multidimensional reality more noticeable than other aspects. They operate by making some information more *salient* than other information; therefore, they "highlight some features of reality while omitting others."[3] We rarely notice this process, especially the omission of information, because our public attention is highly selective; we too often rely upon and accept information that is easily accessible. Our judgments about the world are in part due to what standards come to our minds, but also are related to information that is easily accessible.

William Gamson asserted that a "frame is a central organizing idea for making sense of relevant events and suggesting what is at issue."[4] In noting that facts remain neutral until framed,

Gamson argued that they "take on their meaning by being embedded in a frame or story line that organizes them and gives them coherence, selecting certain ones to emphasize while ignoring others."[5] Framing, then, is the process whereby communicators act—consciously or not—to construct a particular point of view that encourages the facts of a given situation to be viewed in a particular manner, with some facts made more or less noticeable (even ignored) than others.

When highlighting some aspect of reality over other aspects, frames act to define problems, diagnose causes, make moral judgments, and suggest remedies. They are located in the communicator, the text, the receiver, and the culture at large. Frames are central organizing ideas within a narrative account of an issue or event; they provide the interpretive cues for otherwise neutral facts. Framing is, however, a normal part of the communication process. We need ways to negotiate the massive amounts of information that comes to us everyday. Large and complex ideas and events figuratively cry out for framing since they have so many elements demanding attention. Because of this, framing analysis is a particularly useful way to understand the impact of rhetoric. Although framing analysis can be used to better understand any rhetorical artifact, I feel it is particularly suited for understanding the effects of mediated communication. Considering that we receive the vast majority of information about our world from local and national news outlets, I intend to focus the remainder of this discussion on framing analysis and the mainstream American press, by which I mean print, broadcast, and online news.

FRAMING AND THE PRESS

To better understand framing and news, we first need to locate framing analysis within the family of methods, primarily social scientific, used to study the press. Specifically, we will look at how the press set an agenda by focusing the attention of the public on some issues and not others: agenda-setting. After this we will look at how the press induces its audiences to interpret the news in a particular manner: agenda-extension.

The Agenda-Setting Function of the Press

Part of the strength of agenda-setting theory is that it affirms that the press does strongly influence political decision-making; moreover, it clearly demonstrates that the media are especially influential in telling the general population what to think about. For example, Maxwell E. McCombs and Donald L. Shaw found that voters learn about an issue "in direct proportion" to the attention given that issue by the press.[6] They asked if the key issues in a political campaign, as reported by the general public, correlated with actual news media content. They found that the press provided voters with the "major primary sources of national political information"; more importantly, however, they found that voters tended to share what the press defined as important.[7]

Other studies have confirmed these results; for example, Sheldon Gilberg et al. found that the press could set our government's agenda, even to the point of influencing the content of a State of the Union address.[8] The influence of the press in this regard is highlighted by McCombs and Shaw: "the press is an independent force whose dialogue with other elements of society produces the agenda of issues considered by political elites and voters. Witness the major role of the elite press as a source of information among major decision makers. Through its winnowing of the day's happenings to find the major events, concerns, and issues, the press inadvertently plays an agenda-setting influence role."[9]

Following the logic of agenda-setting theory, we can say that the press shape what the public "perceives" as "political reality." Moreover, the press also shapes how political elites understand what voters and opinion leaders are thinking about. In a sense, a relationship develops between the press, its sources, and the public audience that determines "what is *accepted* as the public agenda."[10] Unfortunately, research data suggests that this relationship is unidirectional—press content affects public concern, but public concern does not affect news content.[11] Press influence of public knowledge takes on more importance when we consider the degree to which we rely upon the press for information about our local communities, our country, and the world. The further information is removed from our day-to-day experiences the more we must rely on the news media to provide us with the information we desire. Because of this, the "news media exercise a near monopoly as sources of information and orientation."[12]

From Agenda-Setting to Agenda-Extension

Communication researchers Judith S. Trent and Robert V. Friedenberg wrote that "the media set public priorities just by paying attention to some issues while ignoring others. They determine what issues are important and in this way play an important role in structuring our social reality."[13] This structuring of our perceptions of the important news we receive is well known to those who study mass communication; early in the 1980s researchers interested in this area began to discover an evaluative component to media news. They postulated that the press provide contextual cues that enable audience members to evaluate that which was under consideration. Although the press must provide a proper context in which to understand the news, reporting the news so a *press-supported context* will be produced moves beyond agenda setting and involves the influencing of public opinion. I call this extra dimension of press reporting *agenda-extension*.[14]

Agenda-setting can be described as the role the press play in focusing the public's attention on a particular event or issue over another, primarily by how much attention the media gives to that event or issue. In the mid-1990s, however, some scholars using agenda-setting theory began to focus on the persuasive aspects of news coverage. This new area of endeavor was called second level agenda setting, and it posits that the press can focus pubic attention on particular attributes within an event or issue. This notion of second level effects allows us to see how the press would be elevating one attribute over another in the mind of the public. Since a particular attribute on an issue would be foremost in the public eye, it seems likely that the public would use that particular attribute to evaluate a politician's actions. The public becomes primed to evaluate the president, for example, by how well he handles the particular issue covered by the press. The more the press covers an issue, the more the public will evaluate the president's success or failure in relation to the content of press coverage. As important as this work is, it stresses only *what* attributes are highlighted, not how or to what effect.

Anne Johnston, surveying work in agenda-setting research, shed light upon the agenda-extension process.[15] She stated that news stories not only provide their audiences with the important topics to think about, but they also provided "contextual cues or frames in which to evaluate those subjects."[16] Gladys Engel Lang and Kurt Lang, who argued that this type of agenda-extension was operating during the Watergate hearings, provide one of the earlier examples of this.[17] They found that agenda-extension begins when media gatekeepers decide to publish a particular story because station managers, producers, or editors often frame issues by *how they decide to tell a particular story*. Although deciding what story to tell (gatekeeping) is the first step in all news reporting, the press takes a second step when determining how much attention to give to the story (agenda-setting), and a third step when they determine how to tell the story (agenda-extension). As pointed out by Doris Graber, it is at this "point where ordinary agenda-setting activities can most readily turn into deliberate agenda-building [agenda-extension]."[18]

By continually focusing on an issue, the press thrusts it into the forefront of national thought. But how is the public asked to view the press-generated issue? Looking at how it is framed one way to answer this question. In the Watergate example, Lang and Lang noted that coverage was first framed in terms of the election campaign. The nation became obsessed, however, as soon as the press switched frames, moving from the framework of the 1972 presidential campaign to the framework of continual Washington corruption. Shanto Iyengar and Adam Simon also show how framing can induce audience members to interpret events in a particular manner. Sharing the results of their study on the first Gulf War, these researchers found that "content data (showing that network news coverage was preoccupied with military affairs and highly event oriented) and survey data are coupled to show that respondents reporting higher rates of exposure to television news expressed greater support for a military as opposed to a diplomatic response to the crisis, because the press framed the events in the Gulf episodically as a series of military actions."[19]

It is at this point that the notion of agenda-extension moves beyond second level agenda-setting in that it posits that the press not only focuses attention on particular attributes of an issue, making some portions more salient than others, it does so in such a manner that a particular political interpretation is advanced. More to the point, second level agenda-setting examines *what* attributes are stressed, agenda-extension—as will be seen below—asks *how* those attributes are stressed to influence audience reaction. Using an agenda-extension perspective, one moves beyond frequency of reporting to examine the manner in which the papers reported the issues—thus one may look for bias.[20] Framing analysis is one way to see the agenda-extension process.

Neutral Role of the Press

Providing contextual cues for proper interpretation is an important part of press responsibility. A problem occurs, however, when the press place their partisan context over a neutral one needed by the people or government. In America we generally think that the press should have objective sources for the news we need to make informed decisions. We also generally believe that the press should be fair in its treatment of all sides of an issue. Journalism ethics researcher Louis A. Day suggested that reporters must "clearly distinguish between fact and opinion."[21] When writing for the public, journalists must place news stories into "perspective" by providing "relevant background."[22] This involves being objective, fair, and truthful. According to Mitchell Stephens, objectivity involves both impartiality and the reflection of the "world as it is, without bias or distortion of any sort."[23] In short, the news as a true image of the world. A laudable goal, but difficult to put into practice.

The notion of agenda-extension allows researchers to determine if something other than the above-idealized norms operates within press stories. By framing an issue, the press have a decision to make: They can frame it to reflect their view of the world; they can frame it to reflect what they think their audiences wish to hear; or they can, as accurately as possible, frame it to impart the meaning of those speaking/writing upon it. The last of these choices seems to adhere best to the requirements of a fair and responsible press. According to Day, media practitioners should "strive to keep their personal preferences and opinions out of news stories. . . . [They should be] concerned with facts and impartiality in the presentation of those facts."[24] Framing analysis can help us determine if journalists are living up to these standards.

Comparative Framing Analysis

So far this chapter has provided a brief overview of concepts of agenda-setting and agenda-extension. I think it safe to say that the power of the news media to establish the relevance of some issues and events over others and thus control the content and direction of public discussion is great. In particular we discussed agenda-extension—the idea that the press does more than tell us what to think about, it tries to tell us *how* to think about an issue. A rhetorical version of framing analysis is one tool that allows us to detect how this process of telling us how to think works. Framing involves how the press organizes the context through which the public views its news. At its heart this is a rhetorical process, and this is why I believe framing theory can be especially fruitful when adapted to a rhetorical perspective.

Recall that some facts are emphasized by frames and others are not; it is this presence or absence of certain facts that can reveal the implicit aspects of news coverage. A fruitful way to detect frames is by comparative analysis. Robert M. Entman provided a good example of how to conduct such a study when he comparatively analyzed the narratives within news stories about the KAL 007 and Iran Air 655 shoot downs.[25] Although big news at the time, few now recall that in 1983 Soviet Migs shot down a Korean jumbo jet that had flown into Soviet airspace, and that in 1988 the *U.S.S Vincennes*, while operating in the Persian Gulf, shot down an Iranian passenger jet. All aboard both planes perished. Because of their similar nature, these incidents could have been reported on in a similar fashion. Entman thought that because of this, any differences in the information that comprised the frames would be easier to detect. According to Entman, "frames reside in the specific properties of the news narrative that encourage those perceiving and thinking about events to develop particular understandings of them."[26] Specifically, the above properties of which Entman wrote reside in the press narrative accounts of events; they are composed of key words, metaphors, concepts, symbols, visual images. They may also include names given to persons, ideas, and actions.[27] These elements will consistently appear within a narrative and "convey thematically consonant meanings across . . . time."[28] Thus, framing makes some ideas more salient than others, while making some ideas virtually invisible to an audience. Often the best way to detect this is to examine more than a single news story.

Once the framing process is initiated, often by the interaction of sources and journalists, the established frame guides both audience and journalist thinking. Entman called this type of frame an "event-specific schema" since it was a frame generated in response to a specific event. Once in place, event-specific schema encourages journalists to "perceive, process, and report all further information about the event in ways supporting the basic interpretation encoded in the schema."[29]

How was this accomplished? In terms of agenda-setting, the mere occurrence of reporting must be taken into account. Entman used news items appearing in *Time*, *Newsweek*, *CBS Evening News*, the *Washington Post*, and the *New York Times*. During the two-week period following the KAL 007 shoot down, the *New York Times* printed 286 stories and the *Washington Post* printed 169 stories. During the two-week period following the shoot down of Iran Air 655 the *New York Times* printed 102 stories and the *Washington Post* printed 82 stories. Thus, the actual coverage helped to determine the importance of the event. So, the importance of the issues has been established, but what frame was generated? He found that the destruction of

KAL 007 was framed as a moral outrage, whereas the destruction Iran Air 655 was framed as a technical problem.

These and other findings reported by Entman demonstrated how frames impose a specific interpretation onto events. They often obscure contrary information that may be presented in a particular case. Entman found that "for those stories in which a single frame thoroughly pervades the text, stray contrary opinions are likely to possess such low salience as to be of little practical use to most audience members."[30] In terms of the two shoot downs, this meant that although it was perfectly acceptable for political elites to describe the KAL shoot down as a brutal attack, it was far less likely for them to describe it in terms of a tragedy; the frame had been set: the Soviets were evil and at fault. To think of the shoot down in terms of tragedy runs against the frame and would mitigate the culpability of the Soviets. In contradistinction, the Iran Air 655 shoot down was framed as a technical problem. To call it other than an accident or tragedy, or to suggest American Gulf policy was at fought, would run counter to the established frame.

Comparative analysis also works for rhetorical analyses. Critics operating within a framing perspective are looking for cues of how language choices made by communicators (in our case, the press) push our thinking in particular directions. In *Presidential Crisis Rhetoric and the Press in a Post-Cold War World*, I performed a comparative analysis of the rival frames used by the Clinton administration and the printed press when discussing crisis situations in North Korea, Bosnia, and Haiti.[31] Specifically, I used both framing and agenda-setting theory from a rhetorical perspective to discover how the Clinton administration framed the situations and how the press framed the situations as a response to the administration's statements. I examined the *Washington Post* and the *New York Times* during a ten-day period following each of President Clinton's public statements concerning the above crises.

In order to discover frames, I began by analyzing President Clinton's statements for narratives. Simply put, what stories were being told? Next, I specifically looked for the various framing devices that may have been used: key words, metaphors, concepts, and labels (names). Having accomplished this, I repeated the analysis on the news stories and editorials. Three questions guided my investigation: (1) How did Clinton frame the crisis situations in Haiti, North Korea, and Bosnia? (2) When responding to Clinton, how did the press frame the respective situations? (3) Did the frames of the president and the press ever coalesce to present an unified contextual whole?

I reasoned that unless a reader had firsthand access to transcripts of the Clinton administration's utterances, all public knowledge about the crises were filtered through the frame of the press. However, I also found that while the *content* of presidential messages was being reported, the *framing* of the original message was often not conveyed. In short, the press often relayed the words of the president, but not the original frame. Another way of looking at this is to say that the press reframed the words of the president to fit the press's own framing of the issues and events. This moves beyond reporting of political opposition or the providing of commentary.

For example, during the North Korean situation, the press framed the crisis in a manner that highlighted the potential drama of the North Korean's withdrawal from the nuclear nonproliferation treaty. The Clinton administration framed the crisis in a manner that stressed calm negotiation and the budding reconciliation of North and South Korea. Unless you had read the speech transcripts, you would only be exposed to the press frame. For another example, in 1995 President Clinton declared he would send 20,000 U.S. troops to Bosnia for peacekeeping missions. The press was predisposed to accept his decision to send troops.[32] Because of this, perhaps the most important frame the administration advanced—that the mission was acceptable to the American people and relatively risk free—was actually adopted in whole by the press. Such was not the case in other areas. For instance, the press framed the issue of congressional support for the mission differently than the Clinton administration framed it. According to the press, the Republican-controlled Congress was openly hostile and partisan in its deliberations. This frame was so well structured that it made contrary opinions, such as the president's, irrelevant. At a time when calm deliberation and consensus were extremely important for the U.S. government to project, the press was advancing a contradictory impression of the continuing discussion between Congress and the White House over U.S. involvement in Bosnia. In this manner, then, *the press was intentionally miscommunicating the direct assertions of the president of the United States.*

As another example of oppositional framing, consider that when President Clinton took office in 1993 the country was threatened with a flood of Haitian refugees. Candidate Clinton had promised to end the policy of sending Haitians intercepted at sea back to Haiti. Just prior to taking office, though, he was informed that over 100,000 Haitians were preparing to leave Haiti and make their way by boats and rafts to Florida. He reversed his campaign promise and adopted the repatriation policy already in place. Eventually this turned into a year-long crisis for the Clinton administration. I found that the press framed the situation as a domestic issue, and the administration framed it as a foreign policy issue. The Clinton administration stressed a foreign policy that had as its focus the return of democracy to Haiti and the aversion of a massive humanitarian tragedy. The press frame stressed a domestic focus that highlighted its perception of an "inhumane" administrative policy of returning all Haitian boat people to Haiti. Although the press did report what the administration said, the frame of the press replaced the original frame used by the Clinton administration. Not restoration of democracy, but rather the domestic, legal issue of the administration's policy became the focus. In such a setting the administration was presented, not as a source of news but as one side of a partisan battle with the press.

In another project, *Bush's War: Media Bias and Justifications for War in a Terrorist Age*, I investigated how the mainstream media relayed to the public what President Bush said about the War on Terror.[33] In terms of a comparative analysis, my central questions were, What did Bush say, and what did the press say he said? I examined important speeches given by President Bush between September 11, 2001 and November 2005. For comparative purposes, I looked at all reports concerning each of the President's speech found in *The New York Times, The Washington Post, USA Today, ABC News, CBS News*, and *NBC News*. The general flow of the analysis was to first look for any themes that the president stressed in his speeches, and then to see how he framed those themes. A theme is the subject of discussion, or that which is the subject of the thought expressed. The frame, of course, is suggesting a particular interpretation of the theme. I then repeated this same process with the news reports and articles, looking for what themes the press highlighted and how they framed those themes. Since the press reports usually spread out over several weeks, this analysis also allowed for discovery of how themes and frames develop over time. So, for instance, reading Bush's speech might yield several different themes: good versus evil, patience, and the economy. After determining these, I would go back and look for key words, phrases, concepts, labels, etc. that shed light on how these themes were framed; that is, how did the president wish for them to be understood? This process was then repeated for each news article and broadcast. I looked for themes repeated over time, and then for evidence of how those themes were framed over time as well. As David Levin wrote, "The reason themes [are] taken as a measure of the presence of frames [is] the difficulty of finding a completely developed frame in a single press release. [Frames] are built across a series of news media articles, and not all elements are present in any single article."[34]

What I found was that the news media echoed the president's themes and the framing of those themes immediately following 9/11. Themes such as the "nature of the enemy" and "safety" were reported, and the way the president framed these themes was relayed as well. The press was not uncritical during this period, however; both critics and oppositional points of view were presented. However, the press did not interject its *own point of view* into the hard news coverage; instead it reported what the president said (both the themes and the framing of those themes) and what others said about the president's speeches. Just eight weeks later, however, the president spoke to the United Nations. By this time the press had changed its manner of reporting, and was actually framing Bush as an enemy of civil liberties. Important to this time period, the press was also ignoring several major themes relayed by President Bush: themes such as "good versus evil" and "civilization versus barbarism," important parts of the president's speech and reasoning, were not relayed by the press. Those themes that were relayed, "nature of the war" and the "economy" were framed in such a way that the president's original meaning was lost. As each year passed, this oppositional framing continued and increased.

The results of this study demonstrate the insight producing power of a rhetorical version of framing analysis. Numerous social scientific studies of the period following 9/11 argue that the news media relayed uncritically the assertions of the president, and that this uncritical passing of information on the American public facilitated our war with Iraq.[35] For example, Kevin Coe, et al., looked at 15 speeches by President Bush between January 2001 to March 2003 (start of Iraq war). They looked for the binary opposites: good/evil and security/peril. They next looked at editorials published in 20 U.S. newspapers within two days from each speech. They found that both the speeches and the editorials contained references to these binaries. Because of this, they reasoned, the news media "echoed" the words of the President. This "echoing," they argued, acted to provide him with unprecedented support: "it seems highly likely that the press, through consistent amplification of the president's communications, contributed to the president's remarkable successes with Congress between September 11 and the Iraq War and to the Republican Party's 2002 election triumph."[36] From a rhetorical point of view, however, Coe and colleagues found only *content*. They did not analyze or interpret the *context* in which the binaries were found. They mistook the presence of *themes* as evidence of a particular *frame*. What is left out of many of the studies suggesting a permissive press is information on *how* the discovered themes are framed. The news media may well relay what the president says, but it does not necessarily follow that the president's framing of those themes is accurately conveyed prior to the press offering commentary or criticism from others. Thus we often find the echo of the *theme*, but not of the *frame*.

CRITICAL ESSAY

For my critical essay I have written about Minister Louis Farrakhan's speech at the 1995 Million Man March. I am interested in Minister Farrakhan's rhetoric because he delivers a message pointedly different from other black leaders. The Million Man March garnered tremendous media coverage as well, so I thought his speech would have generated a good deal of press coverage. In the simplest terms, I thought I would conduct a framing analysis of Farrakhan's speech, and then look for *all* mainstream print press articles about the speech published during the two weeks following the speech. I would then examine those articles for frames, eventually comparing the frames generated by Farrakhan and those generated by the press.

Rarely does a newspaper article provide the entire text of a speech, so by comparatively analyzing the speech and subsequent news coverage we can more easily detect any differences in frames. By looking at all the press coverage we can make generalizations at the national level. This will also allow us to see if the national press presents a cohesive frame of the speech or if it instead allows for multiple interpretations.

CRITICAL ESSAY: PRESS FRAMING OF MINISTER LOUIS FARRAKHAN'S MILLION MAN MARCH SPEECH

On October 16, 1995 Minister Louis Farrakhan[37] spoke to approximately 600,000 Americans—primarily black men—gathered in front of the Capitol Building.[38] The subject of his speech was atonement and reconciliation. The speech was the culminating moment of the march and was delivered over the course of approximately 2 and 1/2 hours.[39] The Cable News Network reported that over 2.2 million households tuned in to watch parts of the speech. Commentators have put forth numerous reasons for the march, but the basic reason, according to the man who called it into being, Louis Farrakhan, was for atonement and reconciliation.

In this essay I examine Louis Farrakhan's speech and the subsequent press coverage using a rhetorical version of framing analysis. In doing this, I proceed in two main sections: a discussion of framing analysis and the analysis of Farrakhan's speech and the press coverage it generated.

THEORETICAL CONSIDERATIONS: QUESTIONS OF AGENDA-SETTING, AGENDA-EXTENSION, AND FRAMING ANALYSIS

In 1963 Bernard C. Cohen made a then arresting observation: the press "may not be very successful in telling its readers what to think, but it is stunningly successful in telling its readers what to think about."[40] This is the gist of agenda-setting theory. In its simplest form, this theory affirms that the press does influence political decision-making and that the media are especially influential in telling the general population what to think about. Maxwell E. McCombs and Donald L. Shaw stated that "Through its winnowing of the day's happenings to find the major events, concerns, and issues, the press inadvertently plays an agenda-setting influence role."[41] Agenda-setting confirms that there is a direct correlation between the amount of press coverage and the public's perception of the importance of certain issues. As Judith S. Trent and Robert V. Friedenberg state: "[T]he media set public priorities just by paying attention to some issues while ignoring others. They determine what issues are important and in this way play an important role in structuring our social reality."[42]

Many researchers have since moved beyond Cohen's understanding. The press still tells us *what* to think about; however, they also tell us *how* to think about it. Doris Graber stated that this is the "process whereby news stories influence how people perceive and evaluate issues and policies."[43] I have called this agenda-extension: "it posits that the media not only focus attention on particular attributes of an issue, making some portions more salient than others, it does so in such a manner that a particular political agenda is advanced. Simply put . . . agenda-extension allows us to see *how* those attributes are stressed to influence audience reaction."[44]

Obviously this moves beyond agenda-setting since it involves the influencing of public opinion. Framing analysis provides one way of seeing how this process occurs. A frame is, according to William Gamson "a central organizing idea for making sense of relevant events and suggesting what is at issue."[45] Although facts remain neutral until framed, they "take on their meaning by being embedded in *a frame or story line* that organizes them and gives them coherence, selecting certain ones to emphasize while ignoring others."[46] An example of how this works is found in the results of a study by Gladys Lang and Kurt Lang about the Watergate hearings. In their analysis, Lang and Lang discovered that news coverage of the Watergate break in was initially framed as part of the 1972 election campaign; this led the public to associate it with partisan politics. However, once the press switched frames, moving from the campaign to a new frame of continual Washington corruption, the nation became obsessed—and a presidency tumbled.[47] Frames can possess such power because they alter how we interpret the reality around us. As Entman stated, to frame is to take "some aspects of a perceived reality and make them more salient in a communicating text, in such a way as to promote a particular problem definition, causal interpretation, moral evaluation, and/or treatment recommendation for the item described."[48]

Thus frames define problems, diagnose causes, make moral judgments, and suggest remedies. They operate by making some information more salient than other information; therefore, they "highlight some features of reality while omitting others."[49] To detect this process, Thomas E. Nelson, Rosalee A. Clawson, and Zoe M. Oxley conducted a study that used a local news story about a Ku Klux Klan march as the controlled frame. They presented audiences with either one of two videotaped stories. The first story stressed a free speech frame. Viewers were presented with a theme that stressed both Klan members and protesters wanting to share their respective messages. Quotes shared in the taped stories included a protester showing a sign reading: "No free speech for racists." Another quote came from a Klan supporter who said: "I came down here to hear what they have to say and I think I should be able to listen if I want to." Images shown included the chanting of protesters and a Klan leader speaking into a microphone. Finally, four interviews were presented, three of which were Klan supporters wishing to hear the Klan message. The second story stressed a disruption of public order frame. Viewers were presented with a theme that stressed that Klan marches tend to be disorderly and potentially violent. Quotes given included an observer saying: "Here you have a potential for some real sparks in the crowd." Another quote came from a reporter who said: "The tension between Klan protesters and supporters came within seconds of violence." Images shown included police officers in front of Klan members protecting them from the crowd. Finally, three interviews were presented, each of which mentioned the violence and disruption of public order. The results of the study are instructive: "Participants who viewed the free speech story expressed more tolerance for the Klan than those participants who watched the public order story."[50] This study demonstrates that the power of frames to sway opinion is great, even with such an emotion-provoking subject.

Robert M. Entman provides another example of the power of framing. He comparatively analyzed the narratives within news stories about the 1983 KAL 007 and the 1988 Iran Air 655 shootdowns.[51] The first involved the Soviet Union shooting down an Korean Jumbo Jet which had flown over Soviet airspace; all 269 persons on board perished. The second incident involved the *U.S.S. Vincennes* shooting down an Iranian Airbus over the Persian Gulf; all 290 persons perished. Entman felt that the incidents could have been reported upon in a similar fashion by the American press. He also felt that any differences in information that comprised the frames used by the press would be easy to detect given the similarities of the incidents. He examined reports from a variety of media: *Time*, *Newsweek*, *CBS Evening News*, the *Washington Post*, and the *New York Times*.

In order to detect frames, Entman looked for key words, metaphors, concepts, symbols, and visual images. He argued that frames are fashioned by particular words and phrases that consistently appear within a narrative and "convey thematically consonant meanings across time."[52] He found that the KAL shoot down was framed as a moral outrage, whereas the Iran Air shoot down was framed as a technical problem. Although the differences in the frames were striking, Entman stressed the implications of the frames used: "for those stories in which a single frame thoroughly pervades the text, stray contrary opinions are likely to possess such low salience as to be of little practical use to most audience members."[53] So although it was perfectly acceptable for political elites to describe the KAL shootdown as a brutal attack, it was far less likely for them to describe it in terms of a tragedy; the frame had been set: the Soviets were evil and at fault. To think of the shootdown in terms of tragedy runs against the frame and would mitigate the culpability of the Soviets.

For the remainder of this critical essay, I perform a framing analysis on Louis Farrakhan's speech delivered at the Million Man March. I do this by first reading the speech to find the main themes highlighted by Farrakhan. Themes suggest the presence of frames,[54] so I next determine how these themes are framed by looking for key words, concepts, labels (names), metaphors, and phrases that help contextualize remarks. The basic question answered is: How did Farrakhan frame the issue? After answering this question, I look for the main themes highlighted within all mainstream printed press news coverage in a two-week period following Farrakhan's speech. The basic question answered is: How did the press, responding to Farrakhan, frame the issue?[55] Finally, I detail how the frames produced by Farrakhan and the press failed to produce a unified contextual whole.

How Did Minister Farrakhan Frame the Issue?

Farrakhan's speech presents his audience with a complex blending of religion and politics. Early in his speech he asserted that there is "hostility now in the great divide between the people. Socially the fabric of America is being torn apart and it's black against black, black against white, white against white, white against black, yellow against brown, brown against yellow. We are being torn apart." He had seen the divisions between blacks and whites in America. He sees the place to begin to heal the divisions between the races is within black communities across the country. His speech is framed in such a manner that the major problem is depicted as the racial division brought on by a lingering white supremacy. Both blacks and whites must work to eliminate this. These ideas are expressed within two main themes: *responsibility* and *a more perfect union*.

Responsibility. The divisions can be overcome in part by blacks *and* whites accepting responsibility for their share in black America's problems. At the personal level, blacks must follow God and stop hurting each other. Farrakhan implores black men to "accept the responsibility that God has put upon us, not only to be good husbands and fathers and builders of our community, but God is now calling upon the despised and the rejected to become the cornerstone and the builders of a new world." White supremacy harms both blacks *and* whites. Blacks have become fractured and put down; Whites have "whitened" history and religion, producing a "sick" worldview. Both races must evolve out of white supremacy as part of the movement toward the more perfect American Union. Never does Farrakhan imply that the races cannot live together, rather he suggests that they each have their work to do before coming together to form the more perfect union he envisions.

In constructing his notion of white responsibility, Farrakhan brings up the "Willie Lynch" speech.[56] Farrakhan shares this story to help explain the divisions black Americans must overcome. The story also grounds his later arguments about white America's responsibility for the black condition. Farrakhan recites the speech of Willie Lynch, allegedly a white slave-holder who is said to have delivered this address in 1712 on how to control black slaves. In its essence, the speech advises slaveowners to sow discord and distrust among their slaves as a method of control. Light-skinned slaves were to be pitted against dark-skinned slaves. House servants were to be pitted against field hands. Young were to be pitted against old, and so on and so forth. Importantly, Farrakhan does not use the speech to say that all whites are racists; neither does he say that all black problems result from white supremacy. He instead offers listeners the opportunity to incorporate his conceptualization into their process of atonement: "the real evil in America is not white flesh, or black flesh. The real evil in America is the idea that undergirds the set up of the western world. And that idea is called white supremacy." Farrakhan makes it clear that every black man in America must accept a personal portion of responsibility for the condition of black America today: "Who is it that has to atone? [Audience]: Me. Who went wrong? [Audience]: Me. Who got to fix it? [Audience]: Me. Who should we look to? [Audience]: Me."

A More Perfect Union. Throughout the speech runs a theme of movement toward a more perfect American union. This ultimate social union comes first from a union of the differences within the black communities across the nation. On this matter Farrakhan stated: "There's a new Black man in America today. A new Black woman in America today. [F]rom this day forward, we can never again see ourselves through the narrow eyes of the limitation of the boundaries of our own fraternal, civic, political, religious, street organization or professional organization." Before black healing can occur, however, the government (white) must atone for its past wrongs, namely, white supremacy. This is the unfinished business facing whites. Whites must look to the past of slavery and atone. Once this happens, however, blacks must accept this, forgive, and move on. While waiting for the government to atone, black Americans must also atone.

Farrakhan frames the march as part of a larger process of atonement. He outlines eight specific stages of growth: point out the fault, acknowledge the fault, confess the fault, repent, make amends, forgiveness, reconciliation, and perfect union. During this process black Americans must look to themselves as a source of strength; they must not look to whites or the government for help until this process is completed. However, the process of which Farrakhan speaks involves more than only atonement: Blacks must accept blame for their troubled communities. Both whites *and* blacks must accept blame for white supremacy. Blacks must also join organizations that promote black unity. As a people they must organize to help themselves. This involves spiritual renewal: join a church, synagogue, temple, and take the pledge.

The pledge is the cornerstone of Farrakhan's envisioned change. The men in the audience are led by Farrakhan in a pledge to renounce violence of any kind except in self-defense; to go home and build up their communities; to stop the use of illegal drugs; and to support black owned and operated businesses. Ultimately, however, blacks must come together first, and the government must ask for forgiveness. To overcome the remnants of white supremacy, Farrakhan suggests that blacks "don't have to bash white people," rather all they have to "do is go back home and turn our communities into productive places. All we gotta do is go back home and make our communities a decent and safe place to live. And if we start dotting the Black community with businesses, opening up factories, challenging ourselves to be better than we are, White folk, instead of driving by, using the "N" word, they'll say, look, look at them. Oh, my God. They're marvelous. They're wonderful. We can't, we can't say they're inferior anymore."

How Did the Press, Responding to Minister Farrakhan, Frame the Issue?

There were three primary themes throughout the national press coverage of this speech.

Overwhelmingly, the press coverage focused on the *character* of Farrakhan. The press framed coverage of Farrakhan's speech as a critique of his character. The press prejudged Farrakhan, and used this judgment to define his character during the march. Two other themes of note were discovered: the *message* of Farrakhan and the march and *comparisons* between Martin Luther King Jr. and Minister Farrakhan.

Farrakhan's Character. Simply put, the press framed Minister Farrakhan as a racist, sexist, bigoted, Jew-hating "homophobe." However, these allegations were not based upon Farrakhan's speech at the Million Man March. Instead, reporters and columnists shared their prior opinions of Farrakhan. In this sense, the reporters were reporting not what Farrakhan said, but rather upon their own preconceptions. For example, *The Boston Globe* stated that "the Black Muslim minister, who has often made remarks denounced as racist, sexist, and anti-Semitic."[57] *The New York Daily News* stated that "Farrakhan's past slurs against Jews recently expanded to add Arabs, Vietnamese, and Koreans to the list of 'bloodsuckers' of the black community."[58]

Whereas news stories tended strongly to suggest that Farrakhan is a racist, sexist, and so on, editorials and opinion essays came right out and stated this was the case. For instance, columnist Tom Teepen wrote: "All honor to the many black leaders who refused on principle to participate because Farrakhan is a career bigot—racist, anti-Semitic, homophobic, and woman-baiting [*sic*]."[59] The *New York Daily News* editorially stated that Farrakhan's "hateful history" and "vile anti-white, anti-Semitic bent" are everything, and that it was this "context" through which readers should view his speech.[60] The *Chattanooga Free Press* editorially asserted that although Farrakhan "toned down his racism" for his speech, he was a "vicious hater and power seeker."[61] Columnist Dan Schnur personalized the accusations when he wrote that "Like [Mark] Fuhrman and David Duke, Farrakhan is a racist. He is a bigot. His own demons, his own hatred, will drive him back into the shadows of public discourse."[62] Lars-Erik Nelson wrote that "It's all too easy to denounce Farrakhan's bigotry. His remarks about Jews are vicious and uncivilized. And he surrounds himself with black-shirt, Gestapo Wanna-be bodyguards and thugs."[63]

These judgments were based solely on the press's prior opinion of Minister Farrakhan, and not on what he actually said during the march. Because Farrakhan was framed as so vile a man, the press had to ask if one could separate the message from the messenger because, in the eyes of the press, Farrakhan was obviously a "flawed messenger for racial unity."

The Message of the March v. Farrakhan's Message. The press actually reported on two messages. One was the message from the march and the other was what the press said Farrakhan's message to the marchers was. The message of the march was of unity and brotherhood. Farrakhan's message, which the marchers were to have separated from the messenger, was racist. The press version of the message of the march sent is well expressed by *The Tampa Tribune*: "The message of self-reliance, family values and community uplift could have come from a Christian Coalition flier or a Pat Buchanan speech. But it didn't. It came from Monday's Million Man March for black men."[64] Editorially speaking the *Daily News* stated that the men came "for a day of atonement and reconciliation" but that they "and the millions who share their quest for a better life deserve better than Farrakhan's self-aggrandizement."[65] *The New York Times* stated that the black men who attended the rally heeded a "call for personal atonement and racial solidarity" but then went on to report that Farrakhan's speech compounded "the controversy that led up to the rally over whether the message of uplift could be heard effectively beyond Mr. Farrakhan's own record as an aggressive black separatist leader."[66] Ignoring Farrakhan's stress on the eight steps to atonement, *The Washington Post* stated that although "Farrakhan called the Million Man March a day of atonement for black men, his address often focused on the historic sins of white America."[67]

Farrakhan's message to the marchers was framed in opposition to that of the march itself. The press focused on two main areas: white supremacy and Farrakhan's separatism. For example, the *Chicago Sun-Times* wrote that Farrakhan "urged blacks to unify while railing against what he said was an American society that is oppressive, dominated by whites and intolerant of anyone of color. '(The) idea of white supremacy is you should rule because you're white,' Farrakhan said. . . . 'That makes you sick, and you produce a sick society and a sick world.'"[68] The *Asheville Citizen-Times,* implying that Farrakhan was addressing white America only, stated: "'White supremacy,' he said, is the root of America's suffering. 'That makes you sick,' Farrakhan said, 'and you produce a sick society and a sick world.'"[69] Many examples contained even less detail. *The Boston Herald,* for example, simply stated, "Farrakhan denounced 'white supremacy' as 'the real evil in America.'"[70]

Concerning the issue of separatism the press depicted Farrakhan as wishing for the racial segregation of black and whites, and for being a "divisive" leader: black and white America are to simply to "go and do their own thing," according to press interpretations of Farrakhan. For instance, *The New York Times* provided a common example of this when it wrote that Farrakhan sounded an "aggressive and divisive note, calling for African-American leadership in building 'a more perfect union' but also attacking Lincoln, the Founding Fathers, President Clinton and 'the power and arrogance of white America.' [The] appeal was by blacks to blacks and, if not explicitly separatist, spelled out no clear role for white people."[71] Along similar lines, columnist Jane Ely stated that "Minister Farrakhan and his appeal for racial separatism have contributed way too much to the chasm of bile and distrust that has widened understanding among races and, especially in recent days, threatened to heat to a boil that could ever scar the base that is America. Worse, through his stern refusal to even soften his dangerous rhetoric of hate and dissention, Farrakhan clearly has shown his intent to pursue his relentless way as far as he can in separating the races and fomenting their distrust of one another."[72]

The Tampa Tribune asserted that the crowd would be "unlikely to accept the separatist, anti-Semitic philosophy of Farrakhan."[73] The *Los Angeles Times* stated that despite "the many issues that divide him from most Americans—including his racist comments, advocacy of black separatism and his nationalist hybrid of Islamic scripture—Farrakhan's message of self-reliance and independence from white America strikes a responsive chord that many find lacking in other black leaders."[74] Columnist Thomas Eagleton echoed the separatist framing of his fellow journalists when he wrote, "When [Farrakhan] talks about black men taking responsibility for their own well-being, accepting responsibility and caring for their families, he's as conservative as Clarence Thomas. When he talks about God sending the idea of the march to and through him, he is off on a flight of egotistical fancy. When he attacks the founding Fathers, Abraham Lincoln and the 'power and arrogance of white Americans,' he puts on his separatist, nationalist hat."[75]

Little was mentioned of Farrakhan's sophisticated explanation of atonement. Although atonement was often given as the reason for the march, Farrakhan had been separated from the march. Because of this, he had been separated from the message of atonement.

Personality Comparisons. Finally, the press forced comparisons between Minister Farrakhan and Reverend Martin Luther King, Jr. Framing here was concise: King's speech was short and inclusive; Farrakhan's was long and exclusive. King focused on unity; Farrakhan focused on separatist black nationalism. King was good; Farrakhan was bad.

For example, editorially speaking, the *Daily News* stated: "At his best, Farrakhan led the assembled in a pledge to care for their families and their communities. . . . But even then, his goal seemed to be his own inauguration as the leader of black America. Contrast that with the greatest moment in civil rights history the 1963 march on Washington. There the Rev. Martin Luther King Jr. spoke briefly but left the nation with an enduring dream. For it to be realized, there must be a healing of the races. Despite repeating his call for dialogue with Jews, Farrakhan's vile anti-white, anti-Semitic bent disqualifies him."[76] The *Chicago Sun-Times* boldly summed up the Million Man March this way: "Oh, that the message from Minister Louis Farrakhan had risen to the occasion. Unfortunately, he failed. Would that he had taken a lead from the 'I Have Dream' speech of Dr. Martin Luther King Jr. and raised his voice in an uplifting tone. Farrakhan spoke 150 minutes of divisiveness, contrasted with the 19 minutes of 'bring us together' oratory of Dr. King. By all measurements, less was better."[77] The *Plain Dealer* expressed brief but similar sentiments: "Farrakhan's long speech was almost anticlimactic. It was not the emotional equivalent of Dr. Martin Luther King Jr.'s 'I Have a Dream' speech 32 years ago."[78]

The *St. Louis Post-Dispatch* summed the framing of the press well when it wrote, "America has left behind the hallowed memory of Martin Luther King when blacks and whites assembled to share King's vision of all races walking hand in hand. King's 'I Have a Dream' speech would have sounded out of place at the Million Man March. Farrakhan is not the new Dr. King."[79]

Did the Frames Converge to Present A Unified Contextual Whole?

From the above examples I think it safe to say that at no time did the themes of the press accurately match those presented by Farrakhan. The press simply chose not to relay Farrakhan's message, relaying instead press preconceptions of Farrakhan. Moreover, the press took an extraordinary negative view of Farrakhan. Of 40 opinion essays, only 2 were positive concerning *the event*; 8 took a more or less objective view of *the event*; however, a full 30 were negative, focusing exclusively upon *Farrakhan's character*. Editorials were similarly written. 5 of the 7 were distinctly negative *toward Farrakhan*, with 2 taking a more objective view of *the event*. So while Farrakhan garnered the lions share of attention from the March, his character was assassinated.

Recall frames act to define problems, diagnose causes, make moral judgments, and suggest remedies. Both Farrakhan and the press presented frames that contained these elements. Farrakhan spoke at length to the divisions between and within black communities across the nation. He relayed the Willie Lynch story to highlight the importance of overcoming these divisions for black healing and unity. He would have blacks and whites in America walk separate paths on the road to forgiveness and eventual unity. Whereas Farrakhan saw lingering white supremacy *and* problems in black communities as preventing better socioeconomic progress for blacks, the press heard *only* his comments about white racism. According to Farrakhan, blacks must look first to themselves, atone, and then forgive. Whites must do the same, with blacks accepting white atonement. The press ignored this story, and instead casted Farrakhan as pushing for black separatism, even though he did not advocate this in his speech.

Farrakhan saw that the healing of black hurts must come from two main sources. First, blacks must atone for their own sins, and then walk away from the actions that have hurt black communities across the nation. Second, they must also accept the government and white atonement for white supremacy. Only when these actions are taken can healing occur. The press mentioned atonement, but separated it from its spiritual dimensions and from the notion of a white supremacy that hurts both blacks and whites. When white supremacy is mentioned, it is used to impugn Farrakhan's character, casting him as a demagogue trying to call white America names.

The press brought with it judgments made prior to Farrakhan's speech. The framing of Farrakhan's character—"Farrakhan the bigot"—was so strong that it prevented the press from covering his speech any other way. Thus the press relayed its prejudgments as news about the march. Whereas Farrakhan's march message was a complex blend of spiritual and secular action, the press only relayed that message through a secular interpretation. This interpretation was tainted by the press's own prejudgment of Farrakhan the press's own vision for racial unity, exemplified through a mythic portrayal of Martin Luther King, Jr.

Implications of Press Framing

Following World War II the Commission on Freedom of the Press issued a report titled *A Free and Responsible Press*. The basic premise of the report was that "the power and near monopoly position of the media impose on them an obligation to be socially responsible."[80] This idea of social responsibility is summed by Theodore Peterson: "Freedom carries concomitant obligations; and the press, which enjoys a privileged position under our government, is obliged to be responsible to society for carrying out certain essential functions of mass communication in contemporary society"[81] Among the standards listed by the commission were five that bear particular note:

1. The press must provide "a truthful, comprehensive, and intelligent account of the day's events in a context which gives them meaning."[82]
2. The press must serve as a "forum for the exchange of comment and criticism."[83]
3. The press must project "a representative picture of the constituent groups in society."[84]
4. The press must assume responsibility for "the presentation and clarification of the goals and values of the society" in which it operates.[85]
5. The press must provide "full access to the day's intelligence."[86]

The overwhelming majority of mainstream papers in America assert that they subscribe to the sentiments expressed by the Commission on Freedom of the Press; this is seen in their own statements of principle and codes of ethical conduct. For example, *The Washington Post* asserts it still adheres to the 1935 principles penned by then publisher Eugene Meyer. Four of Meyer's principles have special relevance to this study: "The first mission of a newspaper is to tell the truth as nearly as the truth can be ascertained. The newspaper shall tell ALL the truth so far as it can learn it, concerning the important affairs of America and the World. The newspaper's duty is to its readers and to the public at large, and not to the private interests of its owners. The newspaper shall not be the ally of any special interest, but shall be fair and free and wholesome in its outlook on public affairs and public men."[87]

The American Society of Newspaper Editors statement of principles has been in existence since 1922. Articles 1 and 4 are particularly relevant to this study:

ARTICLE I: The primary purpose of gathering and distributing news and opinion is to serve the general welfare by informing the people and enabling them to make judgments on the issues of the time.

ARTICLE IV: Every effort must be made to assure that the news content is accurate, free from bias and in context, and that all sides are presented fairly. Editorials, analytical articles and commentary should be held to the same standards of accuracy with respect to facts as news reports. Significant errors of fact, as well as errors of omission, should be corrected promptly and prominently.[88]

The Society of Professional Journalists hold similar views: "Members of the Society of Professional Journalists believe that public enlightenment is the forerunner of justice and the foundation of democracy. The duty of the journalist is to further those ends by seeking truth and providing a fair and comprehensive account of events and issues. [Moreover, journalists must examine] their own cultural values and avoid imposing those values on others."[89] The Associated Press Managing Editors Code of Ethics states in part that: "The good newspaper is fair, accurate, honest, responsible, independent, and decent. The newspaper should strive for impartial treatment of issues and dispassionate handling of controversial subjects."[90]

These codes of conduct express clear norms. As I have stated in a different venue, "The press *voluntarily* commits to providing the American public with the *full details* of important issues within an *unbiased context*. In short, the press says it acts to serve *all Americans* regardless of political position."[91] The papers in this study represent the mainstream print news; they voluntarily subscribe to the codes of conduct cited above; they offer themselves as unbiased and objective sources of news. However, this study has shown that the mainstream press injected its favored political ideology into the very information it gave to the public as objective news. As Gary C. Woodward stated, "political journalism is—against its own high standards—a flawed enterprise," because it cannot live up to its stated goal of objectivity.[92]

In this sense then, the mainstream press failed miserably in carrying out its own stated goals of objectivity. In the present case, it violated numerous tenants of its own norms of reportorial practice. Some of the more egregious examples of these violations included failure to provide "a truthful, comprehensive, and intelligent account of the day's events in a context which gives them meaning." More specifically, the press failed to accurately portray the march and the content of Farrakhan's speech. The press also failed to "assure that the news content is accurate, free from bias and in context, and that all sides are presented fairly." Farrakhan's words were not relayed accurately, nor in a context free from bias. Instead, the press imposed its own system of pre-held values upon Farrakhan, and reported that as news. In short, the press "imposed" its "own cultural values on others." Finally, the press utterly failed to "strive for impartial treatment of issues and dispassionate handling of controversial subjects."

PERSONAL COMMENTS ON THE ESSAY

This above critical essay could have taken many different turns. That is the nature of criticism. Specifically, I could have included more discussion of theory. I made a decision to limit the number of studies cited in a general manner and instead focused on detailing several studies I thought of particular interest. I could also have spent more time discussing agenda-setting theory. I decided against that, however. The purpose of that material was to provide an introduction to the notion of agenda-extension, and not to focus on agenda-setting. Ultimately, my goal was to streamline the theoretical material and focus on the actual analysis. Thus the theory section was acting to function as an orientation for my readers; it was not a full literature review. Rather it acted to highlight and provide examples of the major ideas necessary to support the analysis of this essay.

In terms of the actual analysis, other decisions could have been made. For example, at one point I thought it might be of interest to omit the section analyzing Farrakhan's speech and instead comparatively analyze the mainstream press and the black American press coverage of the speech. I thought of that after reading this statement by the American Society of Newspaper Editors: "The typical newspaper journalist is still a liberal, college-educated, white-male baby boomer."[93] Such a comparison might have brought up interesting contrasts between black owned and operated press outlets and mainstream journalists. Ultimately, though, I felt that contrasting the original utterances of Farrakhan with the mainstream press coverage would present results in which different frames would be most easily detected. Additionally, this study could also have focused upon broadcast coverage. How did the major news networks— NBC, ABC, and CBS—frame the speech? How did the two major cable news channels—FOX and CNN—frame the speech? One could also have included weekly news magazines such as *Time, Newsweek,* and *U.S. News and World Reports.* Regardless, each of these changes would have wrought a different essay.

One decision researchers must frequently make concerns what results to share from the actual analysis. Often decisions must be made about relevance; also, one can become so bogged down in details that the overall picture is lost. For example, during this analysis I identified several minor themes I did not include in the actual essay. I reported in the essay, "Two other themes of note were discovered: the *message* of Farrakhan and the March and *comparisons* between Martin Luther King Jr. and Minister Farrakhan." What I did not report was that I also had identified a minor theme in which an exchange between Minister Farrakhan and President Clinton was reported. One reason for not including this information was simply space; including that information would take several pages. Also, it was redundant in terms of the final evaluation I would make. I felt I already had enough information in the essay to justify my conclusions. Finally, it was not as interesting to me as the material on Farrakhan and King.

In terms of the evaluation section of the essay, I thought that using press generated norms of conduct to evaluate their reportorial practice (as revealed through the framing analysis) would be interesting and fair. I did not wish to complicate the essay by developing a theoretical explanation of press ethics, rather I wished to advance a standard of practice from which then to judge press conduct. By including the actual press norms, I was also providing an explicit example of the norms of judgment I was using in order to evaluate the press. Criticism should offer evaluations, but they should flow from the analysis and also be readily available for readers to see.

POTENTIALS AND PITFALLS

Framing analysis is especially well-suited for comparative analyses. Those using this approach to criticism will find that by comparing and contrasting frames that clear results are to be had. It is also an approach to criticism that is particularly well-suited for determining the worldviews of those producing the discourse being studied.

Careless critics often find what they set out to find. Framing analysis might well exacerbate this tendency if a critic is not careful in its application. It is very easy to "discover" a frame and then impose it upon the remainder of the rhetorical artifact. Critics must be especially careful to examine the entire rhetorical artifact before determining what frames are operating. That is to say, do not assume a particular frame is operating and then go look for it. The best framing analyses allow the rhetorical artifacts to speak for themselves.

FRAMING ANALYSIS TOP PICKS

D'Angelo, Paul. "News Framing as a Multiparadigmatic Research Program: A Response to Entman." *Journal of Communication,* 52.4 (2002): 870–888. An outstanding exploration of the concept of framing. D'Angelo argues that there are three broad paradigms of framing, and that researchers ought to be flexible in how they define frames.

Entman, Robert M. "Framing: Toward Clarification of a Fractured Paradigm." *Journal of Communication* 43 (1993): 51–58. This is a well-written introduction to the concept of framing. Entman is particularly effective at bringing together disparate nuances of framing to facilitate a more cohesive understanding of the concept.

Gamson, William A. "News as Framing: Comments on Graber." *American Behavioral Scientist* 33 (1989): 157–161. This essay provides a brief and extremely well written definition of the concept of framing. It is a must read for any student serious about using framing analysis.

Kuypers, Jim A. "Framing Analysis from a Rhetorical Perspective" in *Doing News Framing Analysis: Empirical and Theoretical Perspectives*, edited by Paul D'Angelo and Jim A. Kuypers. (NY: Rutledge, in press). This chapter contrasts a rhetorical version of framing analysis with the social scientific conception.

Kuypers, Jim A. *Bush's War: Media Bias and Justifications for War in a Terrorist Age* (Lanham, MD: Rowman and Littlefield, 2006). This book provides a detailed conception of framing analysis for rhetorical studies, and focuses especially on the differences between themes and frames. It examines numerous speeches by President Bush given between September 2001 and November 2005, and also the subsequent print and broadcast news reports about the speeches. It provides details on how the news media can report the same themes as the president while concomitantly using different frames.

Nelson, Thomas E., Clawson, Rosalee A., and Oxley, Zoe M. "Media Framing of Civil Liberties Conflict and its Effects on Tolerance." *American Political Science Review* 91.3 (1997): 567. This well-conducted study provides detailed examples of the construction of frames used for social scientific research. In so doing, this study also helps guide rhetorical scholars in discerning differences among frames residing in rhetorical artifacts.

NOTES

1. Paul M. Sniderman, Richard A. Brody, and Philip E. Tetlock, *Reasoning and Choice: Explorations in Political Psychology* (Cambridge, England: Cambridge University Press, 1991), 52.

2. Thomas E. Nelson, Rosalee A. Clawson, and Zoe M. Oxley, "Media Framing of Civil Liberties Conflict and its Effects on Tolerance," *American Political Science Review* 91.3 (1997): 567.

3. Robert M. Entman, "Framing Toward Clarification of a Fractured Pardigm," *Journal of Communication* 43 (1993): 53.

4. William A. Gamson, "News as Framing: Comments on Graber," *American Behavioral Scientist* 33 (1989): 157.

5. Gamson, 157.

6. Maxwell E. McCombs and Donald L. Shaw, "The Agenda-Setting Functions of the Mass Media," *Public Opinion Quarterly* 36 (1972): 177.

7. McCombs and Shaw, 185.

8. Sheldon Gilberg, Chaim Eyal, Maxwell E. McCombs, and D. Nichols, "The State of the Union Address and the Press Agenda," *Journalism Quarterly* 57 (1980): 584–588.

9. Maxwell E. McCombs and Donald L. Shaw, "Agenda-Setting and the Political Process" in *The Emergence of American Political Issues: The Agenda-Setting Function of the Press*, ed. Donald L. Shaw and Maxwell E. McCombs (St. Paul, MN: West Publishing Co., 1977), 151.

10. McCombs and Shaw, "Agenda-Setting and the Political Process," 152.

11. For instance, see Roy L. Behr and Shanto Iyenger, "Television News, Real-World Cues, and Changes in the Public Agenda," *Public Opinion Quarterly* 49 (1985): 38–57.

12. Maxwell E. McCombs and Sheldon Gilberg, in "News Influence on Our Pictures of the World" in *Perspectives on Media Effects*, eds. Jennings Bryant and Dolf Zillman (Hillsdale, NJ: Lawrence Erlbaum Associates, Publishers, 1986), 11.

13. Judith S. Trent and Robert V. Friedenberg, *Political Campaign Communication: Principles and Practices*, 5th ed. (Lanham. MD: Rowman & Littlefield Publishers, Inc., 2004), 135.

14. I first used this term in 1997. See Jim A. Kuypers, *Presidential Crisis Rhetoric and the Press in the Post-Cold War World*, (Westport, CT: Praeger, 1997).

15. Anne Johnston, "Trends in Political Communication: *A Selective Review of Research in the 1980s*" in *New Directions in Political Communication: A Resource Book*, ed. David L. Swanson and Dan Nimmo (Newbury Park, CA: Sage Publications, 1990), 329–362.

16. Johnston, 337.

17. Gladys Engel Lang and Kurt Lang, "The Media and Watergate" in *Media Power in Politics*, ed. Doris A. Graber (Washington, D.C.: Congressional Quarterly Press, 1984), 202–209.

18. Doris A. Graber, *Mass Media and American Politics*, 7th ed. (Washington, D.C.: Congressional Quarterly Press, 2005) 165.

19. Shanto Iyengar and Adam Simon, "News Coverage of the Gulf Crisis and Public Opinion: A Study of Agenda-Setting, Priming, and Framing," *Communication Research* 20.3 (1993): 365. Italicized in original.

20. For a good example of using agenda-setting to determine coverage of candidates issues see, Dalton, Russell J., Paul Allen Beck, Robert Huckfeldt, and William Koetzle, "A Test of Media-Centered Agenda Setting: Newspaper Content and Public Interests in a Presidential Election," *Political Communication* 15 (1998): 463–481. Of note is that these researchers found that no bias was seen in the papers covered simply because the papers covered the issues brought up by the candidates.

21. Louis A. Day, *Ethics in Media Communication* (Belmont, CA: Wadsworth Publishing Company, 1991), 35.

22. Day, 35.

23. Mitchell Stephens, *A History of News: From the Drum to the Satellite* (New York: Viking Penguin, 1988), 264.

24. Day, 32.

25. Robert M. Entman, "Framing U.S. Coverage of International News: Contrasts in Narratives of the KAL and Iran Air Incidents," *Journal of Communication* 41.4 (1991): 6–27.

26 Robert M. Entman, "Framing U.S. Coverage," 7.

27. One other important aspect of framing involves how the press uses labels or names. Zhongdang Pan and Gerald M. Kosicki suggested that word choice often "signifies the presence of a particular frame" (Zhongdang Pan and Gerald M. Kosicki, "Framing Analysis: An Approach to News Discourse," *Political Communication* 10.1 (1993): 55–75). They cited the descriptions of Saddam Hussein given by American reporters during the Gulf War. Hussein was described as the "Iraqi dictator," a description that placed him in the same category, in the minds of Americans, as Hitler, Mao, Stalin, Castro, and other loathsome totalitarians. Contrast this with describing him as the "Iraqi leader," "Iraqi president," or the "Iraqi commander in chief." From this example we can see that the lexical choices made within the various framing devices (names used to describe an individual), act to frame the news story in such a manner that a dominant reading is suggested.

For another example, consider some American press descriptions of Yugoslavian President Slobodan Milosevic given during the NATO bombing of Serbia. He was described as an "evil dictator, " "a cruel and determined enemy," and "a brutal dictator" to name only three. Frequent comparisons were made with Adolf Hitler as well: "Adolf Hitler had a 'final solution.' Slobodan Milosevic has 'ethnic cleansing.' Each leader's term gives a brilliant, if not positive, spin to his massacres" (Ben Kauffman, "As You Were Saying . . . Evil Euphemisms Must Not Pass Our Lips Unexamined," *Boston Herald* May 2, 1999, A28). Others in the press described Milosevic as the "Yugoslavian leader," "Yugoslavian president," or the "Yugoslavian commander in chief." Consider how these different terms complicate considerations about Milosevic's legitimacy.

Naming works for American leaders as well. Former Senate Majority Leader Trent Lott has been referred to as "hater," "homophobe," "narrow-minded," "extremist," "prejudiced," and "right-wing radical" (Jim A. Kuypers, *Press Bias and Politics: How the Media Frame Controversial Issues* (Westport, CT: Praeger, 2002), 147–167). Contrast these labels with those given to President Clinton following his speech "One America": "passionate," "congenial," and "up there with President Abraham Lincoln and Martin Luther King Jr." (Kuypers, *Press Bias*, 53–88). As can be seen from these examples, the labels the press uses to describe a politician or social leader will help to establish a frame from which to understand remarks from that politician.

Although it may seem ironic, labeling can also work by lack of labels. The manner in which the American news media reported the 2001 scandal involving Democratic Congressman Gary Condit demonstrates that frames can in part be defined by what information is left out. Condit received enormous press attention because of his numerous alleged affairs, including one with Chandra Levy, an intern with whom he had an affair and who also mysteriously dissappered. Standard reportorial practice is to identify members of Congress with their party affiliation. However, between May and July 2001 the major networks (ABC, CBS, and NBC) reported 179 stories on Condit, but mentioned his party affiliation only 14 times: only 8 percent of the stories labeled Condit as a Democrat. In the majority of those 14 stories, Condit was labeled as a "conservative" Democrat linked to the "right-wing" of the party. However, Condit's voting record placed him, after "12 years in Congress [with] a 48 percent rating from the American Conservative Union and a 52 percent score from the liberal Americans for Democratic Action" (Media Research Center, "Avoiding Gary Condit's Democratic ID," (July 12, 2001). http://www.mrc.org/realitycheck/2001/20010712.asp)

28. Entman, "Framing U.S. Coverage," 7.

29. Ibid.

30. Ibid., 21.

31. Kuypers, *Presidential Crisis Rhetoric*.

32. See Kuypers, *Presidential Crisis Rhetoric*, 200.

33. Jim A. Kuypers, *Bush's War: Media Bias and Justifications for War in a Terrorist Age* (Lanham, MD: Rowman and Littlefield, 2006).

34. David Levin, "Framing Peace Policies: The Competition for Resonate Themes," *Political Communication* 22 (2005): 89. This argument is also made by Kuypers in *Bush's War*.

35. See, for example, W. Lance Bennett, Regina G. Lawrence, and Steven Livingston, *When the Press Fails: Political Power and the News Media from Iraq to Katrina* (University of Chicago Press, 2007); Kathleen Hall Jamieson and Paul Waldman, *The Press Effect: Politicians, Journalists, and the Stories that Shape the Political World* (Oxford: Oxford University Press, 2003); Paul Waldman, *Fraud: The Strategy Behind the Bush Lies and Why the Media Didn't Tell You* (Naperville, IL: Sourcebooks, Inc., 2004).

36. Kevin Coe, David Domke, Erika S. Graham, Sue Lockett John, and Victor W. Pickard, "No Shades of Gray: The Binary Discourse of George W. Bush and An Echoing Press," *Journal of Communication* 54.2 (2004): 248–249.

37. Minister Louis Farrakhan is the national representative of Elijah Muhammad and the Nation of Islam. For additional information on Minister Farrakhan and the Nation of Islam, see the Nation of Islam web site (http://www.noi.org) and the *Final Call* (http://www.finalcall.com/)

38. This number is contested. March organizers suggest over 1 million and U.S. Park service representatives suggest fewer than 600,000 attended.

39. Louis Farrakhan, "Million Man March Speech." Transcript from Minister Louis Farrakhan's remarks at the Million Man March <http://www-cgi.cnn.com/US/9510/megamarch/10-16/transcript/index.html>. Since there were no page numbers in this document, I have included none in citations. All Farrakhan quotes come from this speech.

40. Bernard C. Cohen, *The Press and Foreign Policy* (Princeton: Princeton University Press, 1963), 13.

41. McCombs and Shaw, "Agenda-Setting and the Political Process," 151.

42. Trent and Friedenberg, 135.

43. Graber, *Mass Media*, 287.

44. Kuypers, *Press Bias,* 10.

45. Gamson, 157.

46. Ibid.

47. Lang and Lang, 202–209.

48. Entman, "Framing: Toward Clarification," 52. Italicized in original.

49. Ibid., 53.

50. Nelson, Clawson, and Oxley, 567.

51. Entman, "Framing U.S. Coverage," 6–27.

52. Ibid., 7.

53. Ibid., 21.

54. See Kuypers, *Bush's War*; Levin.

55. All papers contained in the Lexus/Nexus database were included for this portion of the study. I examined editorials, opinion essays, and news articles. In all, there were 107 articles: 60 were news articles, 40 were opinion pieces, and 7 were editorials. Editorials and opinion essays were initially treated separately from hard news stories. No substantial differences in themes or frames were detected. Hard news stories followed the same general themes and frames as editorials and opinion essays. The major difference was that an editorial writer would directly assert an opinion; a hard news writer would do so anecdotally or by quoting another.

56. The Willie Lynch speech is considered by most to be a late 20th century forgery. For information on the speech see the web site on this topic provided by the University of Missouri-St. Louis Thomas Jefferson Library Reference Department: http://www.umsl.edu/services/library/blackstudies/lynch.htm. The library states that the "document was written in the mid to late 20th Century." See http://www.umsl.edu/services/library/blackstudies/narrate.htm> for an analysis of the speech.

57. Zachary R. Dowdy, "Black Men Hear Appeal to Action," *The Boston Globe* (October 17, 1995): A1.

58. William Goldschlag, Dave Eisenstadt, and Raphael Sugarman, "Farrakhan Foes Quick to React Minister Should Atone, They Say," *Daily News* (October 17, 1995): 23.

59. Tom Teepen, "Separating Message From Messenger at the Million Man March," *Star Tribune* (October 21, 1995): A18.

60. Editorial, "Minister Me Holds Court," *Daily News* (October 17, 1995): 32.

61. "The Washington March," *Chattanooga Free Press* (October 17, 1995).

62. Dan Schnur, "The March Wasn't Really Necessary," *The San Fransico Chronicle* (October 18, 1995): A23.

63. Lars-Erik Nelson, "Farrakhan Preached A Positive Message," *Daily News* (October 18, 1995): 31.

64. William March, "March Meaning: Enormous Turnout Raises Questions About Political Direction of Blacks," *The Tampa Tribune* (October 19, 1995): Nation/World 1.

65. Editorial, "Minister Me Holds Court," *Daily News* (October 17, 1995): 32.

66. Francis X. Clines, "The March On Washington: Overview," *The New York Times* (October 17, 1995): A1.

67. David Maraniss, "A Clear Day, A Cloud of Contradictions; At Event Designated for Reconciliation, Its Organizer Stresses White America's Sins," *The Washington Post* (October 17, 1995): A19.

68. Charles Pereira, Doug Mills, Mark Wilson, and Brian Jackson, "'We Are One' 400,000 Black Men Join Show of Atonement, Unity," *Chicago Sun-Times* (October 17, 1995): A1.

69. "Million Man March Largest Black American Gathering Since 1963," *Asheville Citizen-Times* (Asheville, NC) (October 17, 1995): A1.

70. Andrew Miga, "On the March!: Black Unity Rally Draws Thousands to Nation's Capital," *The Boston Herald* (October 17, 1995): A1.

71. R. W. Apple Jr., "The March On Washington: News Analysis: Ardor and Ambiguity," *The New York Times* (October 17, 1995): A1.

72. Jane Ely, "Clinton Had a Powerful Message, Too," *The Houston Chronicle* (October 18, 1995): 22. Both sentences are the original text.

73. William March, "March Meaning; Enormous Turnout Raises Questions About Political Direction of Blacks," *The Tampa Tribune* (October 19, 1995): Nation/World 1.

74. Sam Fulwood, III, "Blacks Ponder Next Steps After Historic Rally," *Los Angeles Times* (October 18, 1995): A1.

75. Thomas Eagleton, "The March Others Could Not Produce," *St. Louis Post-Dispatch* (October 22, 1995): B3.

76. Editorial, "Minister Me Holds Court," *Daily News* (October 17, 1995): 32.

77. "Kup's Column," *Chicago Sun-Times* (October 18, 1995): 64.

78. Jonathan Tilove, "March Seems a Holiday after Summer of Tension," *The Plain Dealer* (October 17, 1995): A1.

79. Thomas Eagleton, "The March Others Could Not Produce," *St. Louis Post-Dispatch* (October 22, 1995): B3.

80. See Fred S. Siebert, Theodore Peterson, and Wilbur Schramm, *Four Theories of the Press* (Urbana: University of Illinois Press, 1956), 5.

81. Siebert, Peterson, and Schramm, 74.

82. Ibid., 87.

83. Ibid., 89.

84. Ibid.

85. Ibid.

86. Ibid.

87. "Eugene Meyer's Principles for The Washington Post," *The Washington Post* http://www .washpost.com/gen_info/principles/.

88. American Society of Newspaper Editors Statement of Principles. "ASNE's Statement of Principles was originally adopted in 1922 as the 'Canons of Journalism.' The document was revised and renamed 'Statement of Principles' in 1975." The full document can be obtained at <http://www.asn e.org/kiosk/archive/principl.htm>

89. Code of Ethics, Society for Professional Journalists, http://spj.org/ethics_code.asp.

90. For the complete listing of the Associated Press's code of ethics, see http://www .asne.org/ideas/codes/apme.htm>

91. Kuypers, *Press Bias,* 202.

92. Gary C. Woodward, "Narrative Form and the Deceptions of Modern Journalism," in *Political Communication Ethics: An Oxymoron?* ed. Robert E. Denton, Jr. (Westport, Connecticut: Praeger, 2000), 127.

93. "The Newspaper Journalists of the '90s," A Survey Report of the American Society of Newspaper Editors, April 1997, p. 5.

13

Fantasy-Theme Criticism

Thomas J. St. Antoine, Matthew T. Althouse, and Moya A. Ball

In the final game of a tied series, the Marauders and the Blue Sox struggle in an epic battle for the championship. With the score tied in the bottom of the ninth, there are two outs, and a base runner is on second. A designated hitter for the Marauders, Spikes O'Reily, steps to the plate, taps the soil from his cleats with his bat, and loosens his swing. The pitcher, ace reliever Cannonball Braden, makes eye contact with the catcher. The two Blue Sox players exchange nods, and Braden launches the ball from the mound. Before the streaking fastball can pass over the plate and into the catcher's glove, O'Reily manages to swing his bat into the ball's path. The ball is struck, races past the first baseman's glove, and rolls into right field. As the fielder stops the ball, the base runner at second, Pokey Howard, rounds third and sprints toward home. Howard begins the slide. Simultaneously, the catcher stretches for the ball, which is rocketing from right field. From within the cloud of blinding dust produced by Howard's slide, the umpire makes the close call: "Safe!" Of course, fans of the winning Marauders from the City of Champions are jubilant. They praise the speed of the base runner, the timely batting of Spikes O'Reily, and—of course—the perceptiveness of the umpire. The fans of the losing team from Baseballville, however, are livid and decry the umpire's call. Given the importance of the championship game, they cannot believe that an official's incompetence cost the Blue Sox their rightful claim to the title.

FANTASY-THEME CRITICISM: AN INTRODUCTION

If you can imagine how fans might tell interpretive stories about this hypothetical scenario, you can appreciate the scope and the goals of Ernest Bormann's fantasy-theme analysis. This method is used to look at how a group dramatizes an event and at how that dramatization creates a special kind of myth that influences a group's thinking and behaviors. In this context, the word "fantasy" does not refer to a fiction created by a group. Instead, a fantasy is a technical term that is the key to understanding the social reality of a group. Bormann explains that the word "fantasy" can be traced back to its Greek root "phantastikos" which means to be able to present or show to the mind, to make visible.[1] For instance, fans of the losing Blue Sox from Baseballville may have at the core of their stories the fact that their team failed to win. However, explanations of the loss will be shaded by the way they manipulate stories about the event. Consequently, in the process of talking about the loss, their discussions may lead to a number of colorful speculations. "The ump was a bum," "The ump was partial to the other team," or "The ump was paid off." Possibly, these reflections may not be accurate, but they "make visible" a shared social reality for the fans. What is more, these imaginings are narrative manifestations that provide a rhetorical critic with a special perspective on the beliefs and values of a given group of people.

The purpose of this chapter is to provide a guide for using and appreciating fantasy-theme analysis, which illuminates the worldview shared by a rhetorical community. In Ball's words, fantasy-theme analysis can be used to address questions like, "How does communication function to divide individual from individual, group from group, and community from community? How does communication function to create a sense of community, integrating individuals and groups into large, cooperative units? How does communication function to interpret reality for symbol using beings?"[2] During the past several decades, scholars have used Bormann's fantasy-theme analysis to examine a myriad of topics, including group decision making, corporate communication, and political cartoons, to name a few. Regardless of the subject matter, these studies share some basic assumptions that are outlined in this chapter. In particular, the first part of this chapter surveys fundamental concepts associated with fantasy-theme analysis and with symbolic-convergence theory, which provides the theoretical chassis on which Bormann's method rests. The second part of the chapter provides a case study. In this section, we examine fantasy themes that have guided perceptions of higher education in the United States during the twentieth century.

Fundamental Concepts

To conduct a fantasy-theme analysis, a critic must understand at least four basic terms: fantasy theme, chaining, fantasy type, and rhetorical vision. Arranged here from the most basic unit to the most intricate, these concepts help us understand how imaginings shared in interpersonal and small-group contexts may evolve into ways of thinking at a cultural level.

Fantasy Theme. The term fantasy theme refers to a narrative construal that reflects a group's experience and that helps a group understand that experience. Sonja K. Foss states that a fantasy theme is "a word, phrase, or statement that interprets events in the past, envisions events in the future, or depicts current events that are removed in time and/or space from the actual activities from the group."[3] Although a fantasy theme can incorporate verifiable facts, it is a dramatization, which means it is creative and imaginative. As Bormann explains, "When people dramatize an event, they must select certain characters to be the focus of the story and present them in a favorable light while selecting others to be portrayed in a more negative fashion."[4] Therefore, it follows that individual groups may form unique perspectives on a single event in the past and create distinctive prognostications about their respective futures.

In light of such thinking, it is not surprising that fans from the City of Champions and from Baseballville create dissimilar fantasy themes about the championship game. Reflecting back on the event, fans of the Marauders praise the heavy hitter who produced the final run batted in: "Spikes O'Reily is the best player on the face of the planet! Without question, he's destined for the Hall of Fame!" To make these assessments, the fans may not be objective by comparing the batter's statistics with those of other active players or with those of anyone enshrined in the Hall. However, their approximations do provide a socially-constructed and accepted perspective for their community. Simultaneously, fans of the losing Baseballville Blue Sox call Spikes O'Reily "the luckiest man alive," an estimation that may not be entirely true. The batter may be, in fact, highly skilled. Yet, the rhetorical assertion that he is "lucky" fosters a shared sense of veracity for the disappointed community of Baseballville.

Chaining. When fantasy themes are shared and are elaborated, group fantasy chains may occur. Chaining happens when dramatizations that resonate with a community "catch on." Put differently, fashionable fantasy themes created by small groups may propagate through media including, but not limited to, public speeches, interpersonal interaction, and television. In face-to-face exchanges, evidence of chaining becomes manifest when people in a group become excited about discussing the theme, and they elaborate it. Further, as Bormann, Knutson, and Mulsof note, "The members respond in an emotionally appropriate way. That is, they express emotions such as happiness, sadness, anger, and pleasure in a way that fits into the initial mood of the dramatization."[5] In mediated communication, evidence of chaining may become manifest when creators of texts borrow, adapt, and disseminate frequently-used, dramatized images and ideas.[6] Of course, not all fantasy themes find acceptance and chain out; indeed, some face disinterest and rejection. Yet, when they do stir attention, successful fantasy themes cause emotional responses reminiscent of the ones evoked by previous stories. Consequently, because of the sharing of fantasy themes, the initial dramatizations of a few people may lead to a shared symbolic reality for many.

For instance, media in Baseballville may discuss vigorously the unfairness of their team's loss. The debate is broached by talk-radio personalities and leads to editorializing on local TV sports shows. Phrases such as "constant bias" and "injustice for the underdogs" are used. Consequently, when hearing these broadcasts, people familiar with the Blue Sox may become irked by the game's outcome and may contribute to dramatizing conversations, even though they might not be avid fans who actually watched the game. That is, casual fans and other interested parties for whom the dramatizations resonate may get caught up in fantasizing about the matter of "their team" getting bested because of "bias" and "injustice." What is more, common perceptions that result from chaining foster a group's sense of togetherness. In a rhetorical community, shared fantasy themes make available motives that impel people to beliefs and to actions that are grounded in a "social reality filled with heroes, villains, emotions, and attitudes."[7]

Fantasy Type. Simply put, a fantasy type is an umbrella term for a cluster of recurring, related fantasy themes. According to Bormann, a fantasy type is a "stock scenario repeated again and again by the same characters or by similar characters."[8] This kind of scenario can include recognizable plot lines, scenes, situations, and representations of people. To illustrate the concept, William Benoit et al. compare a fantasy type to "a saga, which is also called a myth, is another form of often repeated expressions that carries special meanings to the group members for whom they are intended."[9] Also, Foss illustrates the concept with the example of Watergate, which has led to the creation of terms like "Billygate to describe Jimmy Carter's brother's Middle-Eastern affairs, Irangate to describe the Iran-contra affair during Ronald Reagan's administration, and Whitewater to describe Bill Clinton's involvement in a failed real estate venture."[10] Once established, fantasy types enable the use of shorthand allusions to a community's shared stories. Consequently, the utilization of fantasy types provides the critic with evidence of shared fantasy themes.

In Baseballville, fans expect their Blue Sox to be defeated, although they wish this situation would change. More specifically, the squad has a long-standing reputation for losing in close games. So, when they were bested by the Marauders from the City of Champions, fans from Baseballville exclaimed, "It figures! The umpire strikes again!" On the surface, this may seem like a benign comment. However, if the phrase "The umpire strikes again" has recurred over the years, it may represent a fantasy type that brings to mind a number of related fantasy themes. When fans hear the phrase uttered, they might recall a story about an umpire's peculiar expanding and contracting strike zone in the 1983 series. Also, they might recollect the tale about a fair ball called foul that resulted in a lost, pivotal game in the 1994 season. Moreover, because fans are conditioned to see close games lost, the fantasy type provides a serviceable frame of reference for explaining the Blue Sox defeat against the Marauders.

Rhetorical Vision. A rhetorical vision refers to a composite drama that is made up of related fantasy themes that have been clustered into specific fantasy types. When linked together into a rhetorical vision, confederate fantasy themes reveal a coherent, unified, and holistic picture of a community's shared beliefs. Moreover, rhetorical visions feature recognizable characters and plots that, when alluded to in a variety of contexts and discussions, can trigger responses similar to those observed in the original interaction that spawned it.[11] Bormann claims that within a rhetorical vision a critic may be able to detect a "master analogy" that "pulls the various elements together into a more or less elegant and meaningful whole. Usually, a rhetorical vision is indexed by a key word or slogan [such as] The New Deal, The New Frontier, Black Power, The Cold War, The New Left, The Silent Majority, and The Moral Majority."[12] Bormann claims that words such as these call forth recollections of stories that resonate with specific communities.

For instance, Thomas G. Endres examines narratives of young, unmarried mothers, who must deal with the disadvantages and social stigmas of their situation. In their stories, he discerns rhetorical visions concerning being "down and out" (e.g., the mothers feel negatively about themselves and victimized by close friends, acquaintances, and family members), trying to "make the best" of their circumstances (e.g., the mothers learn to ignore social stigmas associated with having a child outside of a marriage and learn to visualize a positive future), and attempting to become a "young, upwardly mobile mother" (e.g., the mothers replace feelings of victimage with feelings of empowerment).[13] Based on the results in Endres's study, one might speculate that if some details of these visions were introduced to a group of young, unmarried mothers, they would identify with and respond emotionally to the ideas presented.

In the case of the Marauders, the words "Iron Dynasty," a master analogy for a rhetorical vision, may evoke affective reactions from people in the City of Champions. They might immediately be reminded of certain fantasy types that elucidate their team's championships during the 1970s. Further, those fantasy types illuminate the team's recent, successful run for the championship against the Blue Sox. One such fantasy type might include "clutch heroes," like Pokey Howard. In fans' minds, this player's deft base running exemplifies how the Marauders always perform their best at critical moments. Another fantasy type evoked by mention of "Iron Dynasty" might be "dramatic finishes," a category of fantasy themes about compelling climaxes in important games. In the present case, fans from the City of Champions are reminded of how the Sox gained an early lead. However, the story ended spectacularly because of Spikes O'Reily's timely run-batted-in. In all, remembrances of stories like these support a coherent rhetorical vision, "a unified putting-together of the various scripts that gives participants a broader view of things."[14]

How to Conduct Fantasy-Theme Criticism

With an understanding of its basic concepts, one can address the business of conducting fantasy-theme criticism. Put simply, to do a fantasy-theme analysis, one needs to examine discourse for fantasy themes, chaining, rhetorical visions, and fantasy types. Yet, to accomplish these tasks, a critic should proceed with caution, being aware of an important point associated with examining rhetoric for dramatizations: it matters how audiences communicate. With many frequently-used methods of rhetorical criticism, the goals of analyses are to apprehend key characteristics of a message or to discern the appeal of a message's source. However, fantasy-theme analysis places emphasis on the audience—not on the message or on the message's source—and their reactions to and utilizations of dramatizing messages. With this thought in mind, a critic is ready to conduct a fantasy-theme analysis by finding evidence of dramatized messages, by categorizing those messages, and by constructing rhetorical visions.

Finding Evidence. To find evidence of dramatized messages, or fantasy themes, a critic must first find an appropriate topic for analysis. Ball recommends considering communicative events such as "a decision-making group, a rhetorical controversy, a social group, a support group, a rhetorical community, a policy-making unit, a political campaign, a social movement, or the like that is intellectually intriguing, about which there are questions to be answered." Certainly, a critic may select virtually any topic for analysis. However, a critic must be ready to argue (1) for the topic's social significance and (2) for its role in some kind of persuasive process. Once a topic is selected, rhetorical texts concerning the topic must be found. Therefore, a critic may gather videotapes of meetings, transcripts of speeches, interviews, and similar artifacts that may reveal dramatizations. Within these artifacts, a critic searches for "evidence of shared narratives, dramatic communication, imagery, figures of speech, and the like,"[15] while remembering the definition of a fantasy theme: it is an imaginative and dramatic message used to interpret an audience's past, present, or future, as revealed by the given texts. Bormann reminds us that for a message to be dramatic, "The action is set in a time and place other than the here-and-now of the group."[16]

For instance, in transcripts of conversations, a critic might look for words that trigger a chaining event. At a recent meeting of the Baseballville Booster Club, one person says, "I sure hope we have a better season next year." To this, another person replies, "Yes, we do not want a repeat of 'The Game.'" With mention of "The Game," other group members enthusiastically add interpretive recollections of the less-than-satisfactory results of the lost championship game: "Our lousy manager, Sparky Croft, should have brought in our all-star reliever, Cannonball Braden, sooner." "We could never win at the Marauder's Indian Rivers Stadium! We can be a horrible road team." Or, "I still can't believe that rotten call the umpire made!" Again, because of individuals' emotional responses to a remembrance of "The Game," critics might speculate that they have found evidence of fantasy themes.

Categorizing Messages. Once critics find evidence of dramatizations in a group's discourse, they must categorize and count the themes to make determinations about a group's attitudes and values. This requires a careful look at a text's characteristics. For visual media, like a film, a critic may need to examine it scene by scene. For speeches, each sentence in a transcript may need to be scrutinized. Formulating categories requires hard work, however, many scholars agree that the themes found may be categorized according to settings, to characters, and to actions. For instance, Karen Foss and Stephen Littlejohn found data that fit into these three categories in the 1983, made-for-TV movie called *The Day After*. The film deals with the pressing, Cold War concern of nuclear holocaust, which prompted approximately 100 million Americans to watch the event on ABC. In their study, Foss and Littlejohn demonstrate that themes relating to characters were few. Instead, scenic elements and plotlines dominate the film. In the shattered remains of American civilization, characters appear helpless as they labor to cope with prominent themes, including attempting to survive deadly radiation and pollution (scenic elements) and endeavoring to find limited service and resources (plotline).

With this reading of the film, Foss and Littlejohn do more than the important work of finding and counting themes revealed in the discourse. With this reading, the authors of the study establish the "manner in which the film addressed various thematic components"—a critical accomplishment that illuminates America's mood in the early 1980s concerning the threat of nuclear war.[17]

In the process of categorization, a critic may also search for fantasy types. Like fantasy themes, fantasy types can be difficult to identify, especially for outsiders to a group who have not participated in a community's creation of meaning through dramatization. Nevertheless, through careful study, special "scripts" in a culture become evident, exhibiting recurrences of "particular fantasies with similar plot lines, scenes, characters, or situations."[18] For instance, a critic examining the discourse of talk radio in the City of Champions hears "Babe Ruth" and "Spikes O'Reily" uttered in the same sportscaster's breath. In this case, Ruth represents an archetypal fantasy with which O'Reily is now associated. That is, Ruth's legend is well known by many baseball fans. Because a clear comparison is being made, commentators are suggesting, for instance, that O'Reily swings a bat with the same ferocity as Ruth. Consequently, the fantasy type used provides people with a way to interpret the actions of and to set expectations for the Marauder's heavy hitter. Although not all fantasy-theme analyses search for and identify fantasy types, their discovery can substantially reinforce a critic's study.

Constructing Rhetorical Visions. After categorizing fantasy themes and types found in discourse, a critic searches for a rhetorical vision. There is no easy, formulaic way to accomplish this task, as the complexities of a vision may be many. Additionally, more than one rhetorical vision may be functioning within a given community at one time. However, Ball provides some hints concerning thoughts a critic might consider when reaching this step of a critical study. In a rhetorical vision, there will be "heroes and villains, key personae, characterizations, attitudes about work, praising and blaming, valorization of some emotions and not others, behavior that is praised and behavior that is censured, insiders and outsiders, and a multitude of beliefs and values that, ultimately, become warrants for argument and action."[19]

Although finding rhetorical visions in discourse may appear daunting, there are some precedents that may prove useful. As noted previously, a critic may find a master analogy (e.g., "New Deal") embedded in the dramatized discourse. Additionally, prior fantasy-theme analyses suggest that many rhetorical visions correspond to three genres—the pragmatic, the social, and the righteous. As Bormann, Knutson, and Mulsof explain, a pragmatic rhetorical vision "is shared by people who seek practical and utilitarian views." In a pragmatic rhetorical community, people extol the virtues of science, of effectiveness, and of common sense. Pragmatic people value goals and accomplishments. The social rhetorical vision "celebrates interpersonal relationships and the development of good families at the concrete level as well as in the utopian envisioning of the future achievement of the family of humankind's residing at peace on the spaceship earth." Not surprisingly, these visions feature idealistic notions of harmony and freedom, as relationships are paramount concerns. Finally, righteous rhetorical visions may be shared by those "who take part in a consciousness that is dedicated to some overarching cause or position."[20] For instance, in a certain community, soldiers killed in battle might be eulogized as brave men who wanted to "do the right thing" for their country, despite individual consequences: a "higher calling" guided the soldiers' gallantry.

In Baseballville, an examination of newspaper articles and radio talk show transcripts reveal two complementary visions about the city's team: the Blue Sox as "hard-luck losers" and as "lovable losers." About the first vision noted here, a critic finds that the team is subject to numerous scenic impediments. Unfortunate injuries to key players, poor managerial decisions, mystical curses conjured by the trading of star players—excuses like these have kept the home team from "winning the big one," although they have experienced some moderate successes. About the second vision, a critic finds evidence of character-based fantasy themes that suggest the exceptional personal attributes of players in the team's history. Generally, players are represented as altruistic, heroic, and charismatic. Because of these characteristics, Baseballville takes great pride in the team and believes they embody the persona of the city. Consequently, in their narratives about the Blue Sox, residents of Baseballville expect the team should win a championship eventually, as "good things happen to good people." Both visions appear to be social in nature, as they relate to community and to feelings of interpersonal connection. In all, by identifying rhetorical visions such as these, a critic can speculate about the values and behaviors of the rhetorical community that cheers for the Blue Sox.

About Symbolic-Convergence Theory

At this point, it is valuable to pose this question: Why is fantasy-theme analysis an important, critical tool? Simply put, it helps us see how stories shape reality and, therefore, how people may act in relation to that socially-constructed reality. Yet, a more complete answer to this question rests with an understanding of symbolic-convergence theory. Although fantasy-theme analysis is the tool for rhetorical criticism associated with Bormann's work, symbolic-convergence theory is the theoretical mold in which that tool is forged. The theory underscores the human tendency to share dramatized narratives, which leads to the potential for persuasion. According to Bormann, rhetoric does not always occur through rational means. Argument, evidence, refutation—these are all parts of a traditional perspective on rhetoric. However, Bormann argues that through the sharing of fantasies, "private symbolic worlds incline toward one another" and "come more closely together, or even overlap."[21] It is this overlap created by shared dramatizations that results in a "convergence" that makes shared attitudes, values, and actions possible.

To illustrate symbolic convergence, let us consider yet another hypothetical, but not unlikely, story about baseball. In the City of Champions, a decision must be made about its sports venue, Indian Rivers Stadium. Should it be demolished to make way for a new, state-of-the-art facility for the Marauders, or should it be restored to its former glory? In favor of a new stadium is the owner of the Marauders, Briefcase Michaels, who is generally perceived as a well-meaning and likable fellow. Yet, as an astute capitalist, he is motivated by financial gain. Therefore, with a corporate backer, he generates a profitable plan for a new facility that features luxury boxes and a four-star restaurant that overlooks the playing field. Michaels' conceptualization of "SuitCorp Park" is thoughtful and financially sound. Despite this resounding logic of his plan, some fans view it skeptically, as they venerate tradition and the sense of continuity embodied by Indian Rivers. The stadium is situated in an old, established neighborhood in the city. So, the park is a landmark for the community, which is more important to many nearby residents than the conveniences of a new stadium. Therefore, as Bormann might speculate, fans are, to some degree, predisposed to consider the SuitCorp Park proposal in relation to symbolic resources created by dramatized stories of Indian Rivers. Consequently, to make a decision about the present, fans might rely more on fantasies about the past than on rationality. In the following sections, this example concerning the future of Indian Rivers Stadium will be revisited to illustrate three characteristics of symbolic-convergence theory.

It is a General Theory. Broadly speaking, a general theory deals with tendencies of humans that are readily recognized by actual participants in communicative events. Put differently, a general theory makes sense to "ordinary people." In the case of symbolic-convergence theory, it is general because of its emphasis on our propensities for sharing narratives. Who could deny that dramatized story telling is an important part of phenomena such as interpersonal relationships, cultural cohesion, and public speeches? Because of its versatility and applicability, Bormann labels symbolic-convergence theory general, as it is "transhistorical and transcultural" and as it is able to "account for broad classes of events."[22]

If symbolic-convergence theory suggests the universality and persuasive potential of sharing dramatized stories, what might the citizens of the City of Champions say about the situation concerning Indian Rivers Stadium? To save their stadium from the economic interests of Suit-Corp, fans of the Marauders may tell dramatized stories about Indian Rivers' past. The venue, which is located east of the Mississippi River, has served as the site of late-inning comebacks, of heart-pounding playoff games, and of legendary championship victories. Although the structure is nearly a century old and in need of repair, critics of plans for SuitCorp Park argue that the advantages of luxury boxes and elegant restaurants cannot replace feelings of nostalgia. Certainly, in other cities, this kind of thinking may not spare an old sports stadium from destruction, as newness, progress, and luxury tend to be valued. Yet, in the City of Champions, many residents say the stadium should remain to preserve the past and to provide inspiration for the team's future. The point here is that symbolic-convergence theory does not hold that all communities share the same fantasy themes. Instead, it simply posits that people do share fantasies, and those fantasies may create a common consciousness that provides the premises upon which collective decisions are made.

Moreover, because it is a general theory, symbolic-convergence theory is valuable because it suggests a "plausible pattern of communication."[23] That is, from a rhetorical perspective, the theory proposes a broad means by which meaningful change in a community can occur and be studied. Bormann believes that a successful persuasive campaign may hinge on dramatic stories; the use of alluring, resonating fantasy themes can entice "converts."[24] These themes encourage people to participate in a shared consciousness that fosters a sense of inclusiveness. Thus, before a referendum for renovations to Indian Rivers Stadium is due for a vote, proponents may (perhaps unknowingly) utilize principles of symbolic-convergence theory. They may assume that the stadium embodies traditions that people in the City of Champions revere traditions that belong to "everyone" in the metropolis. Therefore, to encourage citizens to participate in the preservation of the stadium, proponents may borrow phrases from an old, local folksong about baseball called "Swingin' Shaun Austin." Consequently, the slogan, "What would Swingin' Shaun say?" is born and becomes popular because it resonates with residents' sense of shared narratives.

It is a Grounded Theory. To understand symbolic-convergence theory as a grounded theory, one should know that it is an empirically-based undertaking that relies on both humanistic and social-scientific investigations. In a manner of speaking, all criticism is empirically based insofar as it relies on the presentation of evidence such as excerpts from speeches and transcripts of meetings. However, many forms of rhetorical criticism emphasize the insights of the critic to produce the conclusions of studies. Symbolic-convergence theory, on the other hand, emphasizes audience responses to generate the results of studies. Thus researchers often employ social-scientific methods for theory development. Bormann explains the grounded nature of symbolic-convergence theory by writing, "Thus, we begin with humanistic rhetorical qualitative analysis to analyze messages, shift to the social science methods for the study of audience response, and then return to humanistic critical analysis to explain in depth the way rhetoric functions in terms of response."[25] By saying that social-scientific methods are important to his thinking, Bormann is not claiming that every fantasy-theme analysis requires the use of surveys or experimental observations. Rather, he is claiming that social-science research enhances the critical power of symbolic-convergence theory and, consequently, of fantasy-theme analysis.

Social science plays an important role in Bormann's thinking because he bases symbolic-convergence theory on research conducted in the quantitative realm of small-group communication. In fact, Bormann's work is influenced significantly by the research of Robert Bales. In his book titled *Personality and Interpersonal Behavior*, Bales asserts that groups create fantasy chains for two reasons. First, communicators in small groups may harbor common psychodynamic issues. Consequently, when topics of interest are raised, the potential for sharing fantasies emerges. Second, dramatizing messages may occur when a group works on a common project that produces problems. If these problems result in tension between group members, they may employ imaginative language to soothe matters. In both cases presented here, Bales' conclusions are based on observations of participants in actual interactions.[26] What is more, because of the assumptions of social-scientific methodology, the results produced by Bales' research purport (1) to lead to some degree of predictability of human behavior and (2) to allow for replication, meaning that the conclusions of one study can be reproduced in others.

Bormann took Bales's thinking about sharing group consciousness and applied it to rhetoric. Of course, to make this leap, Bormann needed to avoid the temptation to merely "re-label" the phenomenon of public discourse with terminology about small-group interaction. Therefore, over decades, scholars have conducted numerous studies about symbolic-convergence theory to strengthen the link between dramatizations and public discourse, including hundreds of studies conducted and supervised by Bormann at the University of Minnesota. Based on these efforts, he concluded that the phenomenon of group fantasizing affects and is applicable to persuasive events on a public scale.[27]

It is an Epistemic Theory. If a theory of communication is epistemic, simply stated, it suggests that discourse creates reality. Of course, this statement does not imply that the use of the words "pink elephant" conjures a physical one out of thin air. Instead, it implies that words can change the way people relate to the world and to one another. Words can, according to an epistemic approach to communication, create beliefs, affect perceptions, and motivate actions, especially in the absence of certainty. As Pierre Thevenez elucidates, "Man acts and speaks before he knows. Or, better, it is by acting and in action that he is enabled to know."[28] If this statement is meritorious, then human knowledge is not final, as people continue to act and to speak. Hence, knowledge evolves over time through the processes of human interaction. In the case of symbolic-convergence theory, Bormann takes the notion of rhetoric as epistemic and relates it to the public sharing of fantasies. Thus, he claims the sharing of dramatized communication can socially construct the reality of a community.

One might argue that the myth of Indian Rivers Stadium as "the greatest venue in baseball" is an epistemic construct, created by participants in a rhetorical community that chains fantasy themes. Fans of the Marauders are fond of saying, "Indian Rivers is the toughest place in which an opposing team can play. It's loud. It's crazy. It's intimidating. No one wins an important game against us at the Rivers!" Indeed, the Marauders have won pivotal games and have made spectacular plays on their home field. However, according to statistics, it is not truly the toughest place to play. The team that boasts the most wins at home is the Green Wave of Coastal City, and the team with the best winning percentage at home is the Red Streaks of Central City. In both categories, the Marauders rank second and third respectively. Nevertheless, because of fantasies perpetuated by people in the City of Champions and by sports commentators, Indian

Rivers boasts a special ethos that impels fans to cheer loudly and to heckle opposing players mercilessly. That is, the myth has created the "reality" that encourages fans to be loud. What is more, because of the stadium's myth, people are mounting a very "real" campaign to curtail SuitCorp Park and to preserve Indian Rivers.

CRITICAL ESSAY

Although we must now leave Baseballville and the City of Champions behind, we take with us our appreciation of fantasy-theme analysis to explore rhetorical visions of higher education in America. Many students attend college thinking that it is the "smart thing to do" or the "best preparation for the future and for a career."[29] The nation's leaders often propose that enabling more people to attend college will solve many social problems, including economic inequality or a lack of responsible citizenship. Moreover, throughout the twentieth century until today, higher education has been promoted as a democratic institution that provides opportunities for individuals from all social classes. Americans agree that higher learning is critically important, yet there is ambiguity about the nature and purpose of a college education. Many Americans emphasize the professional and practical benefits of higher education. Other Americans, however, emphasize more abstract benefits of an education including the duty that college graduates have to their communities.

In the critical essay that follows, we examine such differences and related dramatizations of higher education in public discourse. We address questions such as "What do we expect from our universities?" and "Why do we go to college?" In considering these questions, we find that two different views, or what Bormann calls rhetorical visions of higher education, emerge. One rhetorical vision, which we call the communal idealist vision, depicts a college education as an intellectual enterprise that values service to others and learning for the sake of learning. The competing vision, called the individual utilitarian vision, interprets higher education as a practical experience that prepares students for worldly success. Public discourse about higher learning is important because it shapes expectations for colleges and universities. Moreover, those expectations are influential in determining, to name just a few considerations, whether students attend college, how schools are evaluated, and what kind of public and private resources are made available to educational institutions.

CRITICAL ESSAY: INSTITUTIONS OF HIGHER LEARNING AND FANTASY THEMES

Fantasy theme analysis is based on the phenomenon of group fantasizing. Groups often talk about "characters, real or fictitious, playing out a dramatic situation in a setting removed in time and space from the here-and-now transactions of the group."[30] These messages are fantasy themes, and they often carry over into public discourse. As Ernest G. Bormann notes, "the dramatizations which catch on and chain out in small groups are worked into public speeches and into the mass media and, in turn, spread out across larger publics, serve to sustain the members' sense of community, to impel them strongly to action."[31] In other words, public messages often help listeners to assign meanings to the events and ideas that shape their everyday lives. Similar fantasy themes can be sorted into categories of related themes, clusters called fantasy types. Once a critic accomplishes the work of identifying fantasy themes and types, he or she can assemble them into a coherent rhetorical vision. A rhetorical vision is "a unified putting-together of the various shared scripts that gives the participants a broader view of things."[32] That is, people who share a group of fantasies and fantasy types may also share a unified perception of social reality.[33]

To create and live in a unified social reality, people participate in dramatizations that chain out in a rhetorical community, allowing participants to assign meaning to and make sense out of important experiences, characters, and ideas in the life of that community. Thus, fantasy theme analysis is "a form of rhetorical criticism that highlights the way groups construct shared symbolic realities."[34] Essentially, this process of dramatizing sanctions groups of people to work together in understanding their world. Moreover, group fantasizing allows layers of meaning to build, one on top of another. Imagine, for example, the deposits of calcium that form around a grain of sand as a pearl is formed in an oyster. Similarly, fantasies layer meaning around an event or a concept, which allows the perceptions of a rhetorical community to expand.

Fantasy theme analysis can help us to understand organizations, including schools, businesses, and governments. If a rhetorical vision contains a group's view of symbolic reality, it will then provide members of an organization with emotions, values and attitudes, heroes and villains, and hence, their motives for action. Bormann explains, "when a person appropriates a rhetorical vision he gains with the supporting dramas constraining forces which impel him to adopt a life style and to take certain action."[35] The influence of the rhetorical vision on organizations is best understood from the perspective of institutional theory. According to this theory, for an organization to be legitimated, its structures and practices must be seen as consistent with the values of the society within which the organization exists.[36] Organizational structures and actions, whether rational or not, are often constructed symbolically to show that the organization meets the demands of public opinion. W. Richard Scott summarizes the environment's influence on organizations by stating, "Cultural controls can substitute for structural controls. When beliefs are widely shared in categories and procedures taken for granted, it is less essential that they be formally encoded into the organizational structure."[37]

Through the chaining of fantasies, rhetoric can influence and reaffirm the values held by an audience, and those values will influence organizations. For example, an organization's methods of guaranteeing legitimacy are often used as criteria to judge the organization.[38] Thus, opinions about higher education establish expectations and criteria for evaluating those institutions, and fantasy theme analysis of public discourse about higher education provides the critic with evidence that the audience has dramatized those opinions. Accordingly, if the public views a college education as career preparation, schools will not be seen as successful unless graduates obtain well-paying jobs. Likewise, the individualistic views of higher education and communal views of higher education can be connected to conditions with which contemporary colleges and universities must deal.

To consider the role of public discourse in creating expectations for higher education, the critic should identify evidence of fantasy themes chaining out and clustering into fantasy types. The fantasy-theme analysis should then consider the implications of these fantasy types and their formation of a rhetorical vision of higher education. A rhetorical vision will suggest what the purposes of education ought to be. As a result, the vision will reflect the community's ideas on issues such as what students should learn in college, what majors ought to be offered, or what a graduate can expect to do after college.

To accomplish the tasks listed in the above paragraph, we assembled a cross section of twentieth and early twenty-first-century discourse about higher education. The rhetorical artifacts examined here were chosen to provide a diversity of positions about the purposes of higher education and to represent the thinking of a variety of rhetors, including educators, politicians, and business leaders. We began by reviewing the indices of the periodical *Vital Speeches of the Day* and identifying speeches about higher education. We also included edited anthologies of speeches and essays on higher education and books that elaborate on the attitudes toward higher education that were seen in *Vital Speeches of the Day*. Finally, we unearthed a few surveys and empirical studies that verified the fantasies found in the discourse were embraced by the general public. In all, the rhetoric examined provided us with evidence that the individual utilitarian and communal idealist visions of higher education had, indeed, chained out.

The Individual Utilitarians in Higher Education

Twentieth and early twenty-first century discourse on higher education contains evidence of two very different sets of fantasy types chaining out to create opposing visions. We explore first the individual utilitarian vision, which favors an experiential education encouraging immersion in society. This vision emphasizes the discovery of useful knowledge, practical education, and the economic benefits of learning. Unlike the idealist vision, utilitarians see education as a means of achieving some other end outside the academic realm. The individual utilitarians speak positively about the development of public land grant institutions and the access to higher education provided by programs such as the G.I. Bill, which provided funding for college to military veterans. These developments are celebrated for making college a possibility for most citizens, regardless of economic class, for the first time in human history. On the other hand, they eschew the elitism that surrounded the founding of America's first colleges. Not surprisingly, their heroes are the "self-made individuals" who, despite disadvantages in life, used a college education to achieve wealth and success. The villains of this fantasy are elitist, esoteric thinkers who seem to "waste" resources pursuing impractical academic ends. The following subsections present fantasy types that construct an individual utilitarian perspective of college learning.

The Self-Reliant Fantasy Type. The notion that a student goes to college to become self-reliant was the most common fantasy type supporting the individual utilitarian vision. Throughout the last century, proponents of this vision claimed that college graduates should attain independence by endeavoring for financial self-sufficiency and by having a successful career. Recently, a number of political leaders articulated the relationship between a college degree and the ability to make a living, thus, avoiding dependence on others. President Clinton, for example, remarked, "to make the American dream achievable for all, we must make college affordable to all."[39] President George W. Bush also perpetuated this fantasy in his 2002 State of the Union when he said, "Good jobs begin with good schools."[40]

Before Presidents Clinton and Bush, the idea that an education makes one a self-reliant individual was offered by leaders such as Allen Crow of the Detroit Economic Club. In 1944, he stated that "Higher education . . . must include among its primary functions, the instruction of folks in how to acquire what they need and what they want, by taking care of themselves."[41]

Interestingly, contemporary critics of education argued that the self-reliant fantasy type became dominant in the second half of the twentieth century. Educator and author Alan Bloom, who is opposed to the individualistic perspective, observed that students primarily embrace individualism in their college lives.[42] That is, most people, he claimed, attended college for self-gain and self-improvement. Despite the motivation underpinning the fantasy type at hand, American egalitarianism embedded in the utilitarians' vision dictated that opportunities for education must be available to all of the nation's citizens.

The Equal Opportunity Fantasy Type. In the twentieth century, the prospect of attending college represented a democratic equalizer meant to erase lines of social class and privilege. Secretary of Education Richard Riley celebrated the fact that "American education has become more open, more diverse, and more inclusive."[43] Politicians such as President Clinton also used the equal opportunity fantasy type to appeal to voters, speaking of college as a privilege to which all citizens are entitled. In a speech given in 1998, Clinton said,

> I have something to say to every family listening to us tonight: Your children can go on to college. If you know a child from a poor family, tell her not to give up—she can go on to college. If you know a young couple struggling with bills, worried they won't be able to send their children to college, tell them not to give up—their children can go on to college . . . we can make college as universal in the twenty-first century as high school is today.[44]

Along with politicians, business leaders and educators identified with America's universal access to higher education. The unprecedented access that Americans have to higher education was often seen as cause for commemoration. In 1953, the Chair of Standard Oil, Robert Wilson, represented this mode of thinking: "One of the noteworthy things about higher education in America is that there is so much of it. . . . Nowhere else has it been possible to offer the advantages of higher education to so many."[45] From this perspective, equality of opportunity translated to economic terms and emphasized the right of all individuals to make a good living and thereby transcend economic and social class distinctions. In 1916, philosopher John Dewey explained, "A society which is mobile must see to it that its members are educated."[46] Indeed, this fantasy type demonstrated that the cherished ideal of all Americans having an opportunity to prosper was linked to the notion of universal access to higher education.

Contemporary educators also recognized that students primarily go to college to improve their professional opportunities. Robert Spaeth of St. John's University commented, "We can do little to influence what sort of students will enroll in our colleges; they will be individualists, and they will expect their individualism to be encouraged by the college they choose."[47] Institutions often indulge this individualism by promising students that a degree will lead to high paying jobs and desirable careers. Professors Robert Solomon and Jon Solomon, authors of a book on their observations and criticism of contemporary education, contended "social mobility in the United States is very largely determined by education. Education is the gateway to the professions and, these days, to managerial jobs in business and other organizations."[48]

Higher education has thus been legitimated as a valuable institution because it provides opportunities for all. From this perspective, it is believed that we diminish class distinctions by providing educational opportunities to anyone who wants to go to college. We now turn to the final component of the individualistic vision, the idea that college develops in students a work ethic and a character suited for personal success.

The Practical Mind Fantasy Type. From an individualistic perspective, a college education was expected to motivate a student to succeed in life, to encourage ambition, and to help a student become the type of person who can fulfill that ambition. In a 1987 commencement address, Robert Spaeth stated, "Students determine for themselves what they 'want to get out of' their college experience."[49] In short, along with the acquisition of specific professional skills, the most successful students were expected to be diligent and practical. Along similar lines, Du Pont executive Chaplin Tyler, in a 1938 speech at Virginia Military Institute, observed that an overall "working philosophy" is far more important than any specific course of study. Such a philosophy includes things like logic and "unswerving faith in cold facts."[50]

The ability to persevere in the face of hardship was also cited as an important characteristic for individual success. The collegiate experience presented students with challenges and exposed them to uncertain experiences, and this strengthened the will to succeed. Some who labeled perseverance as the most important asset for a career saw higher learning as an inferior method of training. In a 1937 speech to a convention of college deans, corporate attorney Robert H. Jackson, asked why we value a college education. He valued the formative years a young person spends in college and wondered if those years should be spent gaining real-world experience. He spoke from personal experience and claimed he learned much when he was "tossed into the strife to sink or swim," while students learn less because they were "removed from the struggle of life."[51] Whether they are successful or not, colleges are expected to transform students, and many individualistic thinkers have called for practical, hard working, and ambitious graduates.

Assembling The Individual Utilitarian Rhetorical Vision. A coherent rhetorical vision of higher education emerges when one assembles the fantasy types we have discussed. This rhetorical vision, called individual utilitarianism, emphasizes the practical benefits a degree gives to individual students. Twentieth and early twenty first century discourse provides evidence that fantasy types emphasizing self-reliance, equal opportunities, and practical mindedness have chained through rhetorical communities and shaped what we expect from our colleges and universities. A variety of empirical studies also verify that this fantasy has chained out in the American public. For example, survey data gathered by researchers at the Lumina Foundation for Education showed strong support for expanded access to higher education, and the research group, Public Agenda, documented the belief that college should be attainable for all economic classes.[52] Researchers at the Ford Foundation and at UCLA's Higher Education Research Institute (HERI) provided evidence that most students expected that their education would provide them with basic skills, career preparation, and better earning power.[53] Annual studies by HERI also showed that faculty embraced such a pragmatic view.[54]

As we have seen, the heroes of this vision are the graduates who use their degree to become independent and successful. These people are revered for their determination, and an education further empowers them to survive in a competitive world. Robert Jackson honored such rugged individualists: "The world has an overabundance of those who paddle pretty well in still water. The world cries for men who can navigate 'white water.' I see plenty of it ahead."[55] Additionally, educators are honored for attempting to provide expanded access to higher learning, and elitists are the villains of the individualist vision. University president James Rosser criticized colleges for "educating the sons and daughters of the already elite, or the already able to aspire."[56] Although educators who provide practical training are granted heroic status, the vision condemns professors who are disconnected from the real world or who pursue studies that do not have tangible, material benefits. Robert Lutz of the Chrysler Corporation complained that students often get a "dumb" education "from silly classes based on trendy theory and from curricula that look like they were designed by a TV game-show programmer."[57]

Public narrative construals provide additional evidence of the utilitarian vision. This vision regards the establishment of America's earliest colleges, the private colleges of the colonial era, as an attempt to provide an education only to the most elite students and to offer an impractical classical curriculum. Therefore, one of the most significant narratives in the history of higher education has been the establishment of large public universities. The establishment of these land grant universities was celebrated by utilitarians because, unlike the elite colleges, they provided expanded access to higher education and provided research and instruction in practical subjects such as business, industry, and agriculture. University of Texas President

Homer Rainey, like many others, identified this as a landmark story in higher education: "In the thirty years between 1830 and 1860 there was waged in this country the battle for free public schools." According to Rainey the result was "the finest system of public education that any society has ever known."[58] Likewise, the founding of Cornell University, which pioneered the elective system, was a story often heralded as a victory for practical education. Cornell claimed to offer instruction to any student in any subject and was seen as a landmark in the struggle to develop curriculum based less on the classical liberal arts and more on the basic needs of contemporary society. Finally, the G.I. Bill was a popular narrative for individual utilitarians. This federal program was credited with making higher education available to the masses. When President Clinton proposed increasing educational funding for working families, he called it the "G.I. Bill for American workers."[59]

The core values of this vision embrace learning as the acquisition of skills for survival; they eschew any intellectual experiences that cannot be shown to make students more employable or independent. For example, graduates are expected to find employment related to their degrees. Faculty research is expected to discover useful information. Accordingly, a college's primary focus must be on serving the needs of undergraduates. The vision would also privilege academic disciplines and curricula that can be clearly linked to practical benefits. One would obviously expect students who hold the individualist view to prefer classes that are linked to their careers and dismiss classes that do not seem to provide such skills. Additionally, schools should offer a large variety of majors to accommodate students who choose diverse professions. A final core value of the vision mandates that a college's constituency be composed of students from all socio-economic backgrounds who are pursuing the opportunities offered by the institution.

The Communal Idealists in Higher Education

Having examined the individual utilitarian vision, we now turn to the opposing rhetorical vision of higher education. Many twentieth century rhetors emphasized the community in legitimating higher education. It was often assumed that an educated citizenry promotes the good of an entire society. From this perspective, speakers depicted higher education as a means of encouraging students to appreciate their communities and to place service to others before self-gain. Put differently, communal idealism views college as a place to retreat from society and to exercise the intellect. This vision expects colleges to prepare graduates for leadership roles in the community. Also, communal idealists view learning as an end in itself and value learning for learning's sake. In this vision, heroes are those contemplative students and professors who seek to develop the intellect for the purpose of creating a more perfect and democratic society. Its villains include those people who selfishly use higher education for material gain.

The Servant-Leader Fantasy Type. The communal idealistic vision of higher education is based on a clearly articulated model of leadership. Rather than encouraging individualistic ends, college teaches students to lead by sharing their talents in service to others. In this servant-leader fantasy type, graduates are seen as a select minority of people who must fill leadership roles for the greater community, and ideal leadership comes in the form of service to the community. In other words, college is thought to take the finest young people and inculcate in them a sense of responsibility to others.

Contemporary statements by leading educators articulated the value of the leader who is committed to service. John Howard of the Rockford Institute suggested that, "although you make a living by what you get, you make a life by what you give."[60] In the language of other recent educational advocates, servant-leaders were very necessary, and they claimed the desire and ability to serve others should be nurtured in college. In an essay published in 1992, history professor Ralph Ketcham defended civic education as a way of training students to participate in democracy: "Human beings do have the capacity to rise above the narrow and self-serving states of mind, and this capacity can be nourished."[61] To encourage service to others, Harvard president Derek Bok argued in 1992 that educators must teach students to "deepen their concern for those who need help, to build within them a strong sense of ethical responsibility, to help them acknowledge that exceptional talent carries with it exceptional responsibility for the welfare of others."[62]

The servant-leader fantasy type has a long history that was seen throughout the early twentieth century. Princeton President Harold Dodds told his graduates in 1949 that they belonged to an elite group of educated leaders. He said, "you are under, and will be under all the days of your life, the heavy responsibility of being qualified for membership in that creative minority which decides the great issues of life."[63] Dodds also argued that members of this elite minority cannot honorably escape the role as leaders and that it would be disgraceful for an educated person to shirk his or her responsibility to lead. He was concerned that educated citizens were often "guilty of the sins of civic indolence, private self-interest and slavery to party spirit. These concerns added up to gross neglect of civic duty."[64]

In sum, colleges have long been expected to teach students a sense of social and civic responsibility, and those who serve the community are those who are most suited to lead. Next, we explore higher education's role as critic in the community.

The Watchdog Fantasy Type. An additional communal function of higher education is the role of the independent watchdog. As this fantasy type chained out, colleges were expected to be critics in the community by checking the power of government and challenging the accepted truths of culture. Essentially, the watchdog fantasy type called on schools to act as an authority that monitors the government, industry, and other powerful institutions.

Fantasy themes envisioning the academy as a watchdog were elaborated throughout the twentieth century, but they were especially powerful during the crises leading up to World War II. President of the University of Wisconsin, Glenn Frank, argued that education provides a democracy with corrective criticism: "To Jefferson the freedom of scholars to examine and the freedom of journalists to express were liberties without which neither the political nor the economic liberty of the people could conceivably be secure."[65] That is, this fantasy type used by Frank suggested that academics should use their insight and influence to keep other powerful groups in check.

Part of higher education's watchdog role also allowed for an independent community of thinkers given time to contemplate freely. In a 1935 speech, Robert M. Hutchins advocated theoretical training and a separation of the academy from every day affairs. For Hutchins, the key to fighting controversial ideas was to debate rather than ignore them: "the American people must decide whether they will tolerate the search for truth. If they will, the universities will endure and give light and leading to the nation."[66] In response to the depression and the rise of fascism in Europe, Glenn Frank also emphasized the value of a system of higher education that was allowed free inquiry and used the results of that inquiry to inform other institutions, such as government. As part of the watchdog role, comes the expectation that university research provides the world with knowledge and wisdom. The discovery and preservation of information has long been recognized as a benefit to the community. "Great universities," Frank claimed, "can prosecute and publish fearlessly objective researches into the living issues of state and nation."[67]

Rhetors in the later decades of the century also observed that education teaches students to think insightfully and to avoid seeing the world uncritically. Recently, in 2002, author and professor John Rodden argued that "such concerns are especially compelling today in light of 9/11" because education allows students to "assess the value of data we consume every day."[68] Bloom further cautioned that people not properly educated lack critical abilities: "Lack of education simply results in students seeking for enlightenment wherever it is readily available, without being able to distinguish between the sublime and trash, insight and propaganda."[69] As revealed in the next section of this essay, the communal idealists expected colleges to provide students with a miniature community that prepares them to function and interact within a larger community.

The University as Microcosm Fantasy Type. A final communal view of higher education embraced the value of schools as small communities, within which students learn to function in larger communities. When he was president of Princeton, Woodrow Wilson emphasized the need for a campus to be a community of scholars who motivate one another. As an administrator on campus, Wilson worked to shape the environment within his school, and he tried to convince students to embrace the academic community. Wilson said, "A college body represents a passion . . . a passion not so much individual as social, a passion for the things which live, for the things which enlighten, for the things which bind men together in unselfish companies."[70] Living in this community provided the student with practical lessons in how to serve his fellow citizens and, more importantly, how to selflessly serve an institution larger than oneself. Wilson elaborated: "A college is a brotherhood in which every man is expected to do for the sake of the college the thing which alone can make the college a distinguished and abiding force in the history of men . . . men shall be ashamed to look their fellows in the face if it is known that they have great faculties and do not use them for the glory of their alma mater."[71]

The notion of a miniature community was recently articulated by philosophy professor Robert Solomon and professor of classics Jon Solomon in a book that examined the current state of higher education. They asserted, "The university should be a model for democracy as well as a training ground for democracy."[72] Through activities such as student government and campus media, including student-run newspapers, television, and radio stations, students learned to assess, shape, and interact with public opinion. Learning to respond to the public discussion and attitudes that invariably exist on a campus will prepare students to function in the public sphere after graduation. This persisted as a key role for colleges and universities.

Assembling the Communal Idealist Rhetorical Vision. The communal idealist vision of higher education emphasizes the servant-leader, the watchdog, and the miniature community. The discourse honors those who approach higher education as a community of scholars left to contemplate freely and to teach students to lead. Robert Hutchins argued that "The greatest university is that in which the largest proportion of scholars are the most competent in their chosen fields."[73] The vision despises the selfish individuals who are interested only in self-gain. Harold Dodds remarked, "All history teaches that struggle for power and influence divorced from unselfish ends is self-destructive and in the end unsatisfying."[74] More recently, Willard Butcher of the Chase Manhattan Corporation contended that "A total commitment to personal gain—'meism'—at the expense of society's overall well-being, even if it gets you to the top, will ensure you are *not* a leader."[75]

While the communal idealist fantasy can be seen chaining out in public discourse, empirical data provides further evidence of its popularity. Annual HERI surveys indicated support for increased interaction between students and faculty to establish a more robust academic community, and data gathered by Pew Charitable Trust showed a preference for the traditional classroom experience over nontraditional online classes.[76] Studies by HERI have shown that faculty believed a college education ought to help a student develop moral character, commitment to community service, and responsible citizenship.[77] Likewise, students hoped their schooling would help to develop leadership skills.[78] In sum, communal visions have chained through the public, and, although they are not as popular as individualistic visions, research documents their persistence at the grass roots level.

Central to the communal vision are many of the same narratives that the utilitarians dramatized. Yet those narratives take on a decidedly different form. The communal idealists edified the founding of the colonial colleges. This was seen as a story in which the success of the American Revolution and the establishment of a democratic government was due to the availability of leaders who were trained in American colleges.[79] In 1938 Harvard President James Conant recognized the ongoing role of those early colleges in preparing the elite to be leaders: "Thomas Jefferson in the early days of the last century spoke of the necessity of 'culling the natural aristocracy of talent and virtue from every condition of the people, and educating it at the public expense for the care of the public concern.' In the great wave of enthusiasm for universal schooling, this principal of Jefferson's has tended to become submerged."[80] Because it values the establishment of the colonial colleges, this vision is highly suspicious of the establishment of the land grant universities and the G.I. Bill. These events represented a move away from the style of education that best prepared the finest students to lead and a loss of community which was found in smaller, less bureaucratic institutions. In a 1984 commencement address Harold Logan of W. R. Grace and Company questioned the contribution made by large state universities: "I submit that one of the things we have gotten is a weakening of the private-education system in this country by the rapid growth of our State-subsidized university which has grown to such a size as to lose all personal touch."[81]

The vision's core values downplay the practical benefits of learning and emphasize the intellectual and spiritual benefits. The ideal college prepares its students for responsible participation in the community. Its mission includes forming an educated citizenry, inculcating a sense of citizenship, and nurturing the moral character of students. The curriculum of this college is not based on practical value but on intellectual merit, and the student body is composed of an academically elite group of students who will provide leadership after graduation. Unlike the individual vision, which could accommodate nontraditional learning, the communal idealist vision would prefer the traditional experience of a residential college. Finally, faculty research would include not just the discovery of practical data. Research would promote the contemplation of the values that shape the community. Having described opposing visions of higher education, the next section examines their consequences.

IMPLICATIONS FOR EDUCATIONAL INSTITUTIONS: STRIKING A BALANCE

The goal of this study is to use fantasy-theme analysis to identify the purposes of higher education, as they are expressed in twentieth and early twenty-first century American rhetoric. Fantasy theme analyses "illuminate how individuals talk with one another about their here-and-now concerns until they come to share a common consciousness and create a sense of identity and community."[82] The public discourse we examined suggests that this symbolic convergence process has occurred among audiences with an interest in higher education. Americans have assembled fantasies into two competing rhetorical visions, and, as a result, there is not clear consensus on its purpose. Derek Bok explained, "the bonds of understanding between our universities and the nation have not grown stronger . . . neither educators nor community leaders share a clear, compelling view of what universities can do for the society."[83]

As demonstrated in this study, rhetorical visions shape public expectations for and sentiments about organizations. To maintain legitimacy, then, higher education must be sensitive to both the individual utilitarian and communal idealist visions, as they characterize beliefs exhibited by Americans. The key to success for higher education may lie in accommodating both visions. Too often, colleges help students develop utilitarian skills while downplaying the importance of the community. The communal fantasy themes identified in this study, however, can provide a foundation for restoring the communal idealistic vision.

The ability to participate in a vital community has diminished in the twentieth century, and this breakdown in community has led to severe problems. Many educators lament the belief that the individualistic model dominates contemporary higher education. Robert Spaeth of St. John's remarked:

> Individualism is so rampant in American higher education today that it goes unnamed and often unnoticed. It is, I believe, our way of life . . . it has produced the very failures that critics are constantly bringing to our attention. Individualism has infected both student bodies and faculties, and the two groups encourage it in one another. Students by and large come to college today to major in a field that will lead to a career—their own career—by means of which they hope to become successful and at least materially comfortable.[84]

Examples from other spheres of public discourse also reflect concern for a lack of community. Robert A. Nisbet, in his book *The Quest for Community,* observed that "Despite the influence and power of the contemporary State there is a true sense in which the present age is more individualistic than any other."[85] Likewise, the themes identified as characteristic of the institutional environments surrounding higher education in the twentieth century seem to be individualistic. Nisbet argued that the release from the contexts of community have not led to freedom and rights but "intolerable aloneness and subjection."[86] Furthermore, he saw individualism as the defining characteristic of twentieth-century thought: "it is by no means unlikely that for our own age it is alienated or maladjusted man who will appear to later historians as the key figure of twentieth century thought."[87]

To truly serve contemporary culture, higher education should provide communal experiences that help students to overcome the individualism of the current age. A balanced rhetorical vision will present higher education as an enterprise for equipping students for individual success, but it will also demonstrate that higher education is an enterprise for equipping students to selflessly serve the community. Assuming that the American public craves community, colleges and universities must protect the communal idealist vision or risk becoming ineffectual. Too often, educators fail to demonstrate this to the public. Harvard President Derek Bok argued, "Today, universities need new ways to serve the public . . . we must associate ourselves prominently once again with efforts to solve problems that really concern the people of this country."[88] Put simply, if the communal idealistic vision is to continue to resonate with the public, advocates must make it appealing.

To conclude, fantasy theme analysis has helped us to recognize the meaning that rhetorical communities have given to a college education. Schools have very specific expectations that must be met for them to survive and maintain legitimacy. Over the years, fantasies have chained out in the public and have crystallized into vivid rhetorical visions. Understanding those visions will help explain why so many people feel obligated to attend college, why colleges behave as strangely as they do, what a student can expect from his or her degree, and why colleges should be preserved, revolutionized, or both. In short, we better understand our institutions and what it will take to succeed within them.

PERSONAL COMMENTS ON THE ESSAY

We chose to write our critical essay on higher education because of the natural link between fantasy themes and institutional theory, which suggests that public opinion influences life inside organizations. As we tried to show in our theoretical considerations section, fantasy theme analysis helps us better appreciate organizations such as school, work, church, and government.

Furthermore, the purpose of a college degree is an especially relevant topic. We hope that the questions raised in this essay are questions that you have already thought about. At some point, you might have talked with parents, classmates, or professional colleagues about what you expect to get from your college years. Perhaps this essay will help you to deal with these questions in a new way. Effective rhetorical criticism will often raise questions and provide solutions to problems in our everyday lives. Criticism should provide useful insights that help us to better understand and interact with our world.

The next step in this line of study might be to compare and contrast different approaches associated with different types of rhetors. For example, we might have looked at the difference between educators and those outside of education. It would also be useful to conduct studies on various campuses to determine the extent to which these fantasies have chained out. A close examination of conditions on our campuses might help to determine the ways that students, faculty, and administrators apply the two rhetorical visions. Although the study originally consisted of more observations on public discourse about higher education, we limited the essay to the most common and influential fantasy types.

POTENTIALS AND PITFALLS

Although fantasy-theme analysis is a serviceable, as well as fashionable, critical tool, it is not without its detractors. Prominent protests may be found in essays written by G. P. Mohrmann. In these works, he strikes two significant blows against Bormann's method. First, Mohrmann claims that fantasy-theme analysis is not an appropriate extension of Bales's work on small-group interaction. In this context, fantasies can be used as mere jokes or as manifestations of individuals' needs to enhance their "self-picture, to feel more attractive and powerful, to discharge aggression, or dispel anxiety."[89] Put simply, fantasies may be used as a buffer against reality, not as a creation of it. If this is the case, one possible pitfall of fantasy-theme analysis may include a critic's inability to discern "meaningful" fantasies that do, in fact, chain out in the public realm. Second, because Bormann allegedly misconstrues Bales's work, Mohrmann claims fantasy-theme analysis does not show us much about human interaction. That is, he asserts Bormann's technique is simply a process of naming, with terms such as fantasy themes and fantasy types, revealing "the presence of agile minds" of critics, but tellling "us little about communication, little about the human condition."[90] In short, in some cases, fantasy-theme analysis might be little more than labeling device.

Nevertheless, used adeptly, fantasy-theme analysis boasts noteworthy potentials. For instance, Bormann claims discursive logic and fantasy themes are interrelated, despite Mohrmann's protestations to the contrary. That is, people in public settings do, indeed, make choices based on attitudes formed by the sharing of dramatizations. Bormann writes that "Discursive argument requires a common set of assumptions about the nature of reality and proof."[91] Without rhetorical visions that are produced by the sharing of fantasy themes, a community would have no common set of assumptions upon which to base the premises of their arguments. Put differently, some rationalists may posit that fantasies are not verifiable and, therefore, not remarkably influential. However, for those who subscribe to a narrative perspective, fantasies may be central to understanding human communication.

Another potential of fantasy-theme analysis is that it assumes a multi-step flow of information, rather than a conventional two-step flow. Benoit et al. explain the difference between the two: "Instead of moving simply from the media to opinion leaders and to the public, information flows in all directions between all agents creating a web of interaction and making possible a unified rhetorical vision."[92] Therefore, students who hope to attend college may not get all of their information about higher education solely from newspapers or from literature produced by colleges. Rather, students may also construct their impressions of college from a variety of informal sources, including friends and coworkers. If this instance is representative of the way people formulate beliefs, then fantasy-theme analysis accounts well for the means by which messages spread from small groups to larger publics and back.

FANTASY-THEME ANALYSIS TOP PICKS[93]

Ball, Moya A. *Vietnam-On-The-Potomac*. (New York: Praeger, 1992). To examine the escalation of the Vietnam War, Ball investigates the role of small-group communication in President Kennedy's and Johnson's administrations. Ball scrutinizes declassified documents and interviews with Presidential advisors with Bormann's critical method.

Bormann, Ernest G. *The Force of Fantasy: Restoring the American Dream*. (Carbondale: Southern Illinois Press, 1985). This is the acme of Bormann's work. Using fantasy-theme analysis, he traces changes in American political discourse from colonial Puritanism to Abraham Lincoln's "romantic pragmatism." More than that, Bormann spells out the basics of his method and provides rich examples.

——. "The Symbolic Convergence Theory of Communication and the Creation, Raising, and Sustaining of Public Consciousness" in *The Jensen Lectures: Contemporary Communication Studies*, ed. John I. Sisco (Tampa: The University of South Florida Press, 1983), 71–90. As the title of this essay indicates, Bormann focuses on how usage of fantasy themes develops public consciousness. Moreover, Bormann provides a remarkably lucid and concise account of the principles that underpin fantasy-theme analysis.

——. "Fantasy and Rhetorical Vision: Ten Years Later." *Quarterly Journal of Speech* 68 (1982): 288–305. Here, Bormann responds to his critics, including G. P. Mohrmann and Rod Hart, who question the theoretical foundation of fantasy-theme analysis. In his response, Bormann refines the method's technical terms and discusses its growing body of literature.

Bormann, Ernest G., John F. Cragan, and Donald C. Shields. "An expansion of the Rhetorical Vision Component of the Symbolic Convergence Theory: The Cold War Paradigm Case." *Communication Monographs* 63 (1996): 1–28. The authors explain the "life" of a rhetorical vision. More specifically, they claim the life cycle of a rhetorical vision is shaped by three kinds of communication, including consciousness raising, raising, and sustaining, and by three rhetorical principles, including novelty, explanatory power, and imitation.

——. "In Defense of Symbolic Convergence Theory: A Look at the Theory and Its Criticisms after Two Decades." *Communication Theory* 4 (1994): 259–294. "Two Decades" provides readers with an elaborate response to critics of symbolic convergence theory. Also, the essay provides an extensive literature review of studies utilizing symbolic convergence theory and fantasy-theme analysis.

Bormann, Ernest G., Roxann L. Knutson, and Karen Mulsof. "Why do People Share Fantasies? An Empirical Investigation of the Symbolic Communication Theory." *Communication Studies* 48 (1997): 254–276. To address the question posed in the essay's title, the authors explore characteristics of dramatized narratives. Along the way, they provide clear explanations of kinds of rhetorical visions (i.e., pragmatic, social, and righteous) and of dimensions of dramatized messages (i.e., reality, time, moral, and emotional).

Cragan, John F. and Donald C. Shields. "The Use of Symbolic Convergence Theory in Corporate Strategic Planning: A Case Study." *Journal of Applied Communication Research* 20 (1992): 199–218. This essay boasts two enticing features. First, it provides clear explanations for terms associated with fantasy-theme analysis. Second, it provides a case study that demonstrates how Bormann's theory guided the reconstruction of a company's shattered identity.

Endres, Thomas G. "Rhetorical Visions of Unmarried Mothers." *Communication Quarterly* 37 (1989): 134–150. In this essay, Endres investigates unmarried mothers, an infrequently studied group, with both fantasy-theme analysis and Q-methodology. Q-methodology, a kind of factor analysis, allows rhetorical criticism to be fortified with social-scientific inquiry.

Rarick, David L., Mary B. Duncan, and Laurinda W. Porter. "The Carter Persona: An Empirical Analysis of the Rhetorical Visions of Campaign '76." *Quarterly Journal of Speech* 63 (1977): 258–273. The authors of this essay explore audience perceptions of Jimmy Carter's personality during his campaign for the White House. In their investigation, they reinforce the notion that fantasy-theme analysis is an audience-centered method.

NOTES

1. Ernest G. Bormann, "The Symbolic Convergence Theory of Communication and the Creation, Raising, and Sustaining of Public Consciousness" in *The Jensen Lectures: Contemporary Communication Studies*, ed. John I. Sisco (Tampa: University of South Florida Press, 1983), 74.

2. Moya A. Ball, "Ernest G. Bormann: Roots, Revelations, and Results of Symbolic Convergence Theory" in *Twentieth-Century Roots of Rhetorical Studies*, eds., Jim A. Kuypers and Andrew King (Westport, CN: Praeger, 2001): 221.

3. Sonja K. Foss, *Rhetorical Criticism: Exploration and Practice* (Prospect Heights, IL: Waveland Press, 1996), 123.

4. Ernest G. Bormann, *The Force of Fantasy: Restoring the American Dream* (Carbondale, IL: Southern Illinois University Press, 1985), 9.

5. Ernest G. Bormann, Roxann L. Knutson, and Karen Mulsof, "Why do People Share Fantasies? An Empirical Investigation of the Symbolic Communication Theory." *Communication Studies* 48 (1997): 255.

6. See, for example, William L. Benoit, Andrew A. Kluykovski, John P. McHale, and David Airne, "A Fantasy-Theme Analysis of Political Cartoons on the Clinton-Lewinsky-Starr Affair," *Critical Studies in Media Communication* 18 (2001): 377–394.

7. Ernest G. Bormann, "Fantasy and Rhetorical Vision: The Rhetorical Criticism of Social Reality," *Quarterly Journal of Speech* 58 (1972): 398.

8. Bormann, *The Force of Fantasy*, 7.

9. Benoit et al., 380.

10. Foss, 125.

11. Bormann, "Fantasy and Rhetorical Vision," 398.

12. Bormann, *The Force of Fantasy*, 8.

13. Thomas G. Endres, "Rhetorical Visions or Unmarried Mothers," *Quarterly Journal of Speech* 37 (1989): 139–141.

14. Ernest G. Bormann, "Symbolic Convergence Theory: A Communication Formulation, *Journal of Communication* 35 (1985): 133.

15. Ball, 222.

16. Bormann, "The Symbolic Convergence Theory of Communication and the Creation, Raising, and Sustaining of Public Consciousness," 72.

17. Karen A. Foss and Stephen W. Littlejohn, "The Day After: Rhetorical Vision in an Ironic Frame," *Critical Studies in Mass Communication* 3 (1986): 320.

18. Bormann, "Symbolic Convergence Theory: A Communication Formulation," 132.

19. Ball, 222.

20. Bormann, Knutson, and Mulsolf, 257.

21. Ernest G. Bormann, "Fantasy and Rhetorical Vision: Ten Years Later." *Quarterly Journal of Speech* 68 (1982): 134.

22. Bormann, "Symbolic Convergence Theory: A Communication Formulation," 132.

23. Ball, 221.

24. Bormann, "The Symbolic Convergence Theory of Communication and the Creation, Raising, and Sustaining of Public Consciousness," p. 129.

25. Bormann, "Fantasy and Rhetorical Vision: Ten Years Later," 305.

26. Robert F. Bales, *Personality and Interpersonal Behavior* (New York: Holt, Rinehart, and Winston, 1970).

27. Bormann, "Fantasy and Rhetorical Vision: Ten Years Later," 292.

28. Quoted in Robert L. Scott, "On Viewing Rhetoric as Epistemic," *Central States Speech Journal* 18 (1967): 15.

29. A recent *Chronicle of Higher Education* survey shows that Americans have extremely high confidence in higher education, ranking it with institutions such as the military and local police forces. However, this high ranking comes with criticism of tenure, affirmative action, big-time athletics, and ambiguity on the purpose of education. Americans seem to agree on the importance of general education and leadership training in colleges, while they place less value on the research role of higher education. Findings are presented in Jeffrey Selingo, "What Americans Think About Higher Education." *Chronicle of Higher Education* 49.34 (2003): A10.

30. Ernest G. Bormann, "Fantasy and Rhetorical Vision: The Rhetorical Criticism of Social Reality," 397.

31. Ibid., 398.

32. Ernest G. Bormann, *The Force of Fantasy*, 8.

33. Ernest G. Bormann, "Fantasy Theme Analysis and Rhetorical Theory" in James L. Golden, Goodwin F. Berquist, and William E. Coleman, eds., *The Rhetoric of Western Thought* 5th ed. (Dubuque, IA: Kendall Hunt, 1993), 368.

34. Linda L. Putnam and George Cheney, "Organizational Communication: Historical Development and Future Directions" in T. W. Benson, ed., *Speech Communication in the 20th Century* (Carbondale, IL: Southern Illinois University Press, 1985): 146.

35. Bormann, "Fantasy and Rhetorical Vision," 406.

36. W. Richard Scott, *Institutions and Organizations* (Thousand Oaks, CA: Sage, 1995), 41.

37. W. Richard Scott, "Unpacking Institutional Arguments" in Walter W. Powell and Paul J. DiMaggio eds., *The New Institutionalism in Organizational Analysis* (Chicago: University of Chicago Press, 1991), 181.

38. Robert A. Francesconi, "James Hunt, The Wilmington 10, and Institutional Legitimacy," *Quarterly Journal of Speech* 69 (1982): 50.

39. Bill Clinton, "2000 State of the Union," *Vital Speeches of the Day* 66 (2000): 260.

40. George W. Bush "2002 State of the Union" *Vital Speeches of the Day* 68 (2002): 260.

41. Allen B. Crow, "Higher and H-I-R-E Education," *Vital Speeches of the Day* 11 (1944): 379.

42. Allan Bloom, *The Closing of the American Mind* (New York: Simon and Schuster, 1987), 91.

43. Richard Riley, "The State of American Education," *Vital Speeches of the Day* 66 (2000): 323.

44. Bill Clinton, "1998 State of the Union," *Vital Speeches of the Day* 64 (1998): 259.

45. Robert E. Wilson, "A Businessman Looks at Higher Education," *Vital Speeches of the Day* 20 (1954): 213.

46. John Dewey, *Democracy and Education,* (New York: Macmillan, 1916): 103.

47. Robert L. Spaeth, "Individualism vs. Liberal Arts Education," *Vital Speeches of the Day* 54 (1987): 24.

48. Robert Solomon and Jon Solomon, *Up the University* (Reading, MA: Addison and Wesley, 1993), 61.

49. Spaeth, 24.

50. Chaplin Tyler, "Industry and You: The Field for College Graduates" in Lew Sarrett and William Trufant Foster, eds., *Modern Speeches on Basic Issues* (Boston: Riverside Houghton Mifflin, 1939), 401.

51. Robert H. Jackson, "Why a College Education?" in Lew Sarrett and William Trufant Foster, eds., *Modern Speeches on Basic Issues* (Boston: Riverside Houghton Mifflin, 1939), 401.

52. A study conducted by the Lumina Foundation for Education ranked schools by how selective and affordable they are for average students from low income families. The study concluded that nearly all private and most four-year public institutions are "too selective" or "too costly." Such a conclusion reveals a general belief that college ought to be widely accessible and affordable. For a discussion of the study see Stephen Burd, "Report on College Access Angers Private Institutions." *Chronicle of Higher Education* 48.19 (2002): A27. See also Sara Hebel, "Poll Shows Value Americans Place on a College Education," *Chronicle of Higher Education* 46.36 (2000): A38. This article presents a public opinion survey prepared by Public Agenda which finds that "Most Americans now believe that there cannot be too many people going to college" (A38).

53. The Higher Education Research Institute at UCLA conducts annual nationwide surveys of the attitudes and aspirations of incoming freshmen. In the Fall of 2000, for example, this well-known study found that 70 percent of freshmen identified the ability to make more money as a reason for going to college, and 71 percent identified training for a career as a reason for attending college. Results were published in Thomas Bartlett, "Freshmen Pay, Mentally and Physically, as They Adjust to Life in College." *Chronicle of Higher Education* 48.21 (2002): A35–A37. In a national poll on diversity in higher education by the Ford Foundation, 85 percent of voters felt that it was very important for education to provide basic skills and 72 percent felt that career training was very important. Results are available at www.pbs.org/als/race/media/poll

54. The Higher Education Research Institute at UCLA also conducts a national survey of faculty attitudes. In their 1998–1999 findings, 70 percent of faculty saw the purpose of higher education as preparation for employment and 99 percent thought it was important for students to learn to think clearly. Results are published in Denise K. Maguer, "The Graying Professoriate" *Chronicle of Higher Education* 46.2 (1999): A18–A21.

55. Jackson, 59

56. James M. Rosser, "Universal Access and Entrance and Exit Requirements," *Vital Speeches of the Day* 47 (1981): 368.

57. Robert A. Lutz, "The Higher Education System," *Vital Speeches of the Day* 62 (1996): 651.

58. Homer Rainey, "Are Too Many Youth Going to High School and College?" *Vital Speeches of the Day* 5 (1939): 461.

59. Bill Clinton, "A Bridge to the Future," *Vital Speeches of the Day* 62 (1996): 707.

60. John A. Howard, "Ennobling Obligations," *Vital Speeches of the Day* 54 (1987): 317.

61. Ralph Ketcham, "A Rationale for Civic Education," *Current* (November 1992): 12.

62. Derek Bok, "The Social Responsibilities of American Universities," *Representative American Speeches* 64.6 (1992): 114.

63. Harold Willis Dodds, "The Cultivation of Individual Excellence," *Vital Speeches of the Day* 15 (1949): 555

64. Ibid.

65. Glenn Frank, "The Critical Function in Democracy" in Ashley H. Thorndike, ed., *Modern Eloquence* Vol. 7 (New York: PF Collier and Son, 1936), 199.

66. Robert M. Hutchins, "What is a University" in Lew Sarrett and William Trufant Foster, eds., *Modern Speeches on Basic Issues* (Boston: Riverside Houghton Mifflin, 1939), 56.

67. Frank, 202

68. John Rodden, "But Professor, What are the Humanities For?" *Vital Speeches of the Day* 68 (2002): 346.

69. Bloom, 64.

70. Woodrow Wilson, "The American College," in James Milton O'Neill, ed., *Modern Short Speeches* (New York: Century, 1923), 203.

71. Ibid., 204.

72. Solomon and Solomon, 89.

73. Hutchins, 51

74. Harold Willis Dodds, "The Art of Living" in Ashley H. Thorndike, ed. *Modern Eloquence,* Vol. 7, (New York: PF Collier and Son, 1936), 137.

75. Willard C. Butcher, "Applied Humanities," *Vital Speeches of the Day* 56 (1990): 623.

76. Annual surveys of faculty by the Higher Education Research Institute at UCLA indicate that more interaction between students and faculty outside the classroom is a rising priority. The HERI has observed a steady increase in this desire for community since its inception. Findings of the survey are discussed in Robin Wilson, "A Kinder, Less Ambitious Professoriate," *Chronicle of Higher Education* 49.11 (2002): A10–A11. See also "Students Embrace the Internet, but not as a Replacement to Classrooms, Study Finds," *Chronicle of Higher Education* 49.5 (2002): A47 which discusses a survey sponsored by Pew Charitable Trusts' Pew Internet and American Life Project. In the study, 79 percent of the respondents said the internet had a positive impact on their classes, but most did not see it as a replacement for traditional classes.

77. Although a much higher number of faculty in the Higher Education Research Institute's annual surveys link higher education with career preparation, a significant number in 1998–1999 recognized that higher education could be important for character development (57.5 percent), building commitment to community service (36.2 percent), and preparation for responsible citizenship (60 percent). And, only 26.7 percent agreed that the chief benefit of college is to increase earning power. Results for 1998–1999 are presented in Denise K Maguer, "The Graying Professoriate," *Chronicle of Higher Education* 46.2 (1999): A 18–A21.

78. Freshmen in the Higher Education Research Institute's studies have also indicated recognition of communal utilitarianism. In the fall of 2000, for example, 32 percent identified becoming a community leader as a reason for attending college, and 42 percent wanted to become cultured. Results are presented in Thomas Bartlett, "Freshmen Pay, Mentally and Physically, as they Adjust to Life in College," *Chronicle of Higher Education* 48.21 (2002): A35–A37. The findings of the 2001 HERI freshman study indicated that students may not be interested in politics, but they do wish to make a difference in their local communities. Findings are presented in Alex P. Kellogg, "Looking Inward, Freshmen Care Less About Politics and More About Money," *Chronicle of Higher Education* 47.20 (2001): A47, A50. Again, although overshadowed by career training, 56 percent of voters in the Ford Foundation's survey on diversity in higher education felt that preparing for effective civic participation and leadership was very important for colleges. Results are available at http://www.pbs.org/als/race/media/poll

79. John F. Roche. *The Colonial Colleges in the War for American Independence* (New York: Associated Faculty Press, 1986), 73

80. James B. Conant, "Education For American Democracy," *Vital Speeches of the Day* 4 (1938): 420.

81. Harold R. Logan "A Case for Preserving Higher Education," *Vital Speeches of the Day* 50 (1984): 287.

82. Bormann, *The Force of Fantasy,* 3.

83. Bok, "The Social Responsibilities of American Universities," 109–110.

84. Spaeth, 24.

85. Robert A. Nisbet, *The Quest for Community* (New York: Oxford University Press, 1971), 9.

86. Ibid., 25.

87. Ibid., 10.

88. Derek Bok, "Reclaiming the Public Trust," *Current* (November 1992): 7.

89. G. P. Mohrmann, "An Essay on Fantasy Theme Criticism, *Quarterly Journal of Speech* 68 (1982): 111.

90. Mohrmann 131.

91. Ernest G. Bormann, "Fantasy and Rhetorical Vision: Ten Years Later," *Quarterly Journal of Speech* 68 (1982): 292.

92. Benoit et al., 379.

93. The authors of this chapter are ultimately responsible for compiling this list. However, we are grateful to Dr. Bormann himself for providing his suggestions.

14

The Mythic Perspective

Janice Hocker Rushing and Thomas S. Frentz

If you are like most people, you probably already have lots of experience with myths. Perhaps a parent read you fairy tales when you were young, maybe you found the war stories from the *Iliad* and the *Odyssey* exciting when you were older, or possibly you were enchanted by the film *The Princess Bride*, or even by television series such as *Hercules, Xena: Warrior Princess*, or *Buffy the Vampire Slayer*. But experiencing myths is one thing; writing mythic *criticism* is another.

Basically, mythic criticism means using myths, as well as theories about them, to understand communicative events. If you have read published essays of mythic criticism, you may think this is a formidable set of skills to acquire. We think, however, that anyone with the motivation and resolve to give it a try can learn to do mythic criticism. We also think it helps if you are "called," like Luke Skywalker was when Obi Wan Kenobi first appeared to him. If you accept this call, you will embark upon a journey complete with challenging quests, potentials and pitfalls, ritual tutors and, if you're lucky, some personal insights.

We thought it might be interesting to speak about mythic criticism as if you have been called to such a journey. Now if we get real here, your "call" may simply be an assignment to write a mythic criticism, and if you want to complete the course successfully, you'll have to accept it. Whatever. One way to hear this call is to put yourself in the shoes of "Jane," our mythical heroine, who, like many such heroes, is what Kris Kristofferson once called "a walking contradiction/partly truth and partly fiction."[1] That is, as storytellers we take some liberties in developing her character, but she's based on a real person, and she goes through many of the trials our students have gone through on this path called "mythic criticism." We are her tutors, like Merlin for King Arthur, Kyle Reese for Sarah Conner, or Karl Rove for George W. Bush. That doesn't mean that we know all there is to know about being mythic critics, it just means that we've been down this road before. We tell this story in the voice of Tom, who tends more toward the dramatic in public than does Janice, although she often sets up his best lines, like Paul Schafer does for David Letterman.

At any rate, we develop Jane and ourselves as characters on a journey, because all myths have such characters. And we divide the quest, or the plot, into three phases—"Departure," "Initiation," and Return"—mimicking those that mythologist Joseph Campbell finds present in myths about the hero. This way, you can see myths in action—not only in the critical essay we offer on *The Matrix*, but also in this chapter as a whole.

So let's get started, and see where this Yellow Brick Road leads.

DEPARTURE

I am just spreading the paper napkins for our microwaved lunch when Janice walks in from her Rhetorical Criticism class.

"So Janice. Have you analyzed your last fantasy theme?"

"We certainly did," she answers with a tired smile. "We just 'chained out' all over *Blade Runner*."

"That's a weird choice! What could fantasy theme analysis possibly have to say about that?"

"Well, they had a lot of fun with the 'character' fantasy type—especially the obsession with *eyes*."

"Oh, I get it," I start to perk up. "'Eyes, I just do *eyes*.' 'Not an easy man to *see* . . . I guess.' 'I've *seen* things you people wouldn't believe. Attack ships on fire off the shoulder of Orion. I've watched C-beams. . . .'"

"Get a new movie," Janice cuts me off before I get fully revved. Since this film came out, a lot of my conversation is replicant-speak. And the movie debuted in 1982.

"So what's next?" I ask, conceding to her preference for human talk.

"Our stuff," she answers. "I begin 'myths to critique by' next week."

"And that must mean that Jane's coming in for spring training."

"You got it. But since this is a form of criticism that you supposedly know something about, why don't you hang around and help for a change?" Janice says, trapping me with a turkey sandwich.

Jane is an honors student with a double major in English and Communication. Like most honors students, she has this irritating habit of actually wanting *to learn* what is being taught in her classes. Before Janice begins any new unit in criticism, Jane makes an appointment for an "overview." What she really wants is extended time to ask all those annoying questions that garner her evil looks from students who just want to get on with it. Because Jane is quirky, bright, and possessed of a wonderful set of critical sensibilities, Janice indulges her. And now, apparently, so will I.

I hear an insistent knock on Janice's door and, sure enough, there's Jane—right on time.

"Come on in," Janice says, "you remember Tom from the film course you took two semesters ago?"

"Yeah, sure," she says, shooting me an 'I'm-not-sure-why-you're-here' glance as she grabs a fistful of our WOW potato chips.

Jane's a piece of work. There's an odd symmetry to her. The right side of her hair is a hot pink buzz cut, while the left sports a wild mass of lime green curls. She balances the Medusa side with three thin, silver rings through her right eyebrow. This creates a sort of diagonal line down her face, as my eye travels from the lime green to the three silver things and back again. "I think she's trying to make a statement here," I catch myself thinking, as I silently hum the line in the song from the old musical, *Bye-Bye Birdie*: "Kids these days. Why can't they be like we were, perfect in every way, oh what's the matter with kids, today?" But in most ways, there's nothing at all the matter with Jane, today or any other day. She's just being, well, just being Jane.

"So Dr. Jan, what's up next?"

"Mythic criticism."

"What's that?"

"That's where we'll try to generate some non-obvious insights into a text by using myths as our interpretive framework. You know—we've tried to do this with situations, classical modes of rhetorical proofs, narratives, the strange and wonderful world of Kenneth Burke, genres, and just today through fantasy themes. Myths just give us another way to unlock the communicative secrets of texts," Janice leads off.

"So—what do you mean by 'myths'?" Jane prods. "You mean, like Zeus and Venus and all that?"

Time for me to earn my keep. "Sure. Myths are just big stories," I say, knowing that's not going to satisfy her.

"Sorry Dr. Tom, but we've already done big stories. They're called narratives. Are we simply splitting semantic hairs here?" she asks, with a bit of an edge.

"No," Janice replies, trying to repair my Sesame Street opening. "All myths are narratives, but not all narratives are myths. If you say to me, 'today I got up at 6:30, brushed my teeth, took a shower, ate breakfast, read the paper, and came to school,' that's a brief narration of your first few hours. But that's not a myth. See, myths are long-enduring stories, often anonymously created, that dramatize a culture's deepest beliefs and dilemmas. They tell of origins and destinies, are filled with heroes and villains, and educate the young into the society's values. So when Tom says, 'myths are just big stories,' that's probably what he had in mind," she concludes.

Jane still looks unconvinced, so Janice presses on a bit. "Remember Tom's film class?"

"Vaguely."

"Do you recall watching *Meshes of the Afternoon*, the great American avant-garde film by Maya Deren?"

"That bizarre movie with lots of keys and big flowers? Are you saying *that* was a myth?" Jane looks puzzled, but intrigued.

"Not exactly," Janice cautions, "although it certainly has mythic elements in its dreamlike form and evocative symbols. The reason I brought it up is that Deren once defined myth for her close friend, Joseph Campbell, as 'facts of the mind made manifest in a fiction of matter.'[2] This suggests that although myths are at least partially fictional, they also tell us something 'factual' about the state of our minds. In fact, Campbell goes on to say that we misunderstand the communicative functions of myth when we expect them to tell us 'truths' about the objective world in which we live. Myths can tell us 'truths' all right, but they're truths about our psyches, our interior minds, not about our historical conditions."

"OK—I got it." A light bulb seems to go off over Jane's head. "That's why people are always writing things like, 'Four Myths of Mental Health Care,' or 'Five Myths of the Perfect Marriage.' When we think that narratives should accurately represent the outside world, and then discover that they don't, we call them 'myths,' by which we mean 'falsities' or 'lies.' Right?"

"Absolutely," we say in unison. "And that's why myths are so often placed in opposition to science, which *is* supposed to represent accurately the outside world," Janice adds.

"So that's the reason people dump on myths? Because they don't accurately represent external reality?"

Janice and I look at each other, knowing it's time to introduce "the big one"—the aspect of myth that really sets academics off.

"Yes, but there's a little more to it than that," I begin slowly. "Some people believe that myths are oppressive because they legitimate existing power structures or privilege one group at the expense of another. While the American frontier myth is, on the one hand, an inspiring story of American optimism and adventure, it has, on the other, justified the genocide of countless Native American peoples. It celebrates freedom and rugged individualism, but it also is still used to defend bully-ish foreign policies and irresponsible management of natural resources."

"And myths can gloss over important differences in social class, gender, and race, implying that 'one story fits all,'" Janice interjects. "To take another example, the 'self-made man' myth teaches that in America, you can 'pull yourself up by your bootstraps' and get rich if you just work hard enough and have a few breaks. But the reality is, those 'breaks' are much more likely to come your way if you're a white male from a 'good family' who puts you in 'good schools' than if you're an African-American female born into poverty. The 'self-made man' usually has quite a bit of help from his friends."

"And just to make things even more complicated," I add, "myths are sometimes self-effacing."

"What on earth do you mean by that?" Jane demands, showing no tendencies toward self-effacement herself whatsoever.

"He means that they hide the fact that they're 'myths' and not 'reality,'" Janice explains. "Check out some of Roland Barthes's fascinating little essays on myths in 1950s French culture. He writes about everyday activities, like wrestling and travel, and texts, like advertisements for soap and margarine, as 'mythic' because they present things that have a cultural *history* as if they were timeless and 'natural'—'just the way things are.' Like, who's to say that the only landscapes that are 'scenic' are ones with lots of vertical variations? How come plains are not interesting and don't get good press? It's travel guidebooks that do this, he suggests, and that notion is all tied up with mountains having come over time to signify religious experience. But mountaintops aren't just 'naturally' spiritual. It's their mythic history—how they're *represented* in language—that associates them with God."[3]

"So whenever you discover people talking about what's 'natural' or 'essential,' like when we say, 'women are naturally more nurturing than men,' you might want to ask if there are myths that support that belief and also erase the fact that they are myths," I summarize with a flourish.

"Geez," Jane says, "are myths good for *anything*?"

"Well, many people think they are," I say. "Mythologists like Joseph Campbell and depth psychologists such as G. G. Jung think that myths can give us important information about the cultural psyche, information that's easy to miss if we don't believe that cultures have any inner life, or if we discount myths because they don't do what science does or because they can be oppressive. We have found this analogy between myths and dreams to be useful: *Dreams are to the personal unconscious what myths are to the cultural unconscious.* Dreams and myths—often depreciated as trivial—can tell us something valuable about ourselves. Of course, the authors of a mythic text, such as a speech or a film, get the chance to shape it more than you do your dreams, so the analogy between dreams and myths isn't perfect. There is a conscious element to many mythic expressions that you don't find in dreams."[4]

"Well, going back to that analogy, do you mean that myths, like dreams, bring up all that Freudian sex and aggression stuff?" Jane asks.

"Sure, they can," Janice explains. "Critics can use a Freudian or Lacanian perspective to show how a text reveals something about the unconscious at the same time as it conceals it. That is, its symbols express a wish for sexual or aggressive gratification—that's the 'Id' talking—but they also distort this wish so that our conscious minds won't recognize it. Check out some of film critic Vivian Sobchack's work, like this great piece called "The Virginity of Astronauts," where she argues that although it seems like sex is missing from most science fiction films, it's there if you 'read between the lines,' so to speak. It's just that it's projected onto the aliens and into space."[5]

"Really?" Jane's getting interested. "I'm not sure I buy that." I noticed she was taking down the reference in her notebook.

"But mythic texts can also bring up more than the Id," I pick up the thread. "If Campbell and Jung are right that some myths have universal or 'archetypal' symbols, then they express meanings that originate in the collective unconscious as psychic potentials, not merely those that are repressed because they are socially taboo. Such myths can point the way to cultural growth and individual self-actualization because these psychic potentials represent moral possibilities for a culture. However, that can only happen if they are interpreted carefully and acted upon consciously."

"Whoaaa, that's pretty heavy. I'm not sure I follow you. Can you put this in English?" Jane asks.

"Well," Janice hesitates, and I can tell she's scrolling through the countless bibliographic references on her mental hard drive. "Did you ever see Stanley Kubrick's film *The Shining*? Way back in the 80s, Robert Davies, James Farrell and Steven Matthews did an overlooked piece of criticism on it that really opened it up for me. They argued from a Jungian perspective that the Overlook Hotel was Jack Torrance's psyche, and that he represented the typical western tendency to work real hard (remember the 'self-made man myth'), to concentrate only on his conscious self, and to ignore everything that was going on in his unconscious."[6]

"Which was considerable," I throw in. "Remember Danny Torrance's friend Tony?" I crook my index finger and croak, "Redrum, redrum!"

"Yeah!" Jane says, "and that horrible woman in that hotel room . . ."

"Room 237," Janice recalls with a shudder. "She was Jack's *anima*, or unrecognized 'feminine side.' Anyway, these critics think the movie made a compelling case that our culture needs to balance its one-sided focus on *progress* with attention to our unconscious, or we'll end up like Jack at the end."

"Heeerrree's *Johnny*!!!" I grin in my best demonic Jack Nicholson imitation.

"OK, I think I get you," Jane says, her light bulb glowing. "Myths or mythic texts can actually help us to face things we need to face in order to be more, more. . ."

"Whole," Janice fills in. She likes that word, perhaps a tad too much.

"That seems important. But it also seems important to be suspicious of myths because they can lie or oppress people. I'm confused," Jane complains.

"Well, you aren't alone," Janice says. "Many mythic theorists and critics tend toward one 'camp' or the other—they *either* think we should ruthlessly unmask myths because they distort, lie, and oppress, or they think of myths as psychological or spiritual revelations from 'the other side' that are crucial for living a meaningful life."

Jane mulls that one over a bit, polishes off the last of our WOW's, and then ventures somewhat cautiously, "it sounds to me like some myths are tied up with religion somehow."

"Well, all myths have a 'religious' or 'sacred' dimension, in the sense that they provide meaning for those who believe them," I clarify.

"But the question for a critic is whether this meaning provided by the myth is oppressive or liberating," Janice pushes the ambiguity a bit further.

"Well, which is it?" Jane demands. She always seems to want the bottom line on complex questions before she opens up to multiple perspectives.

"Both," Janice says with finality.

"So is there at least a list somewhere of Important Myths Rhetorical Critics Should Know? I mean, I don't know all that many myths. Give me a handout," Jane taunts.

"Well, I don't exactly have a handout," Janice looks pained; she is prone to "Bad Teacher" dreams, and I figure I'd better rescue her quick.

"There isn't any great list in the sky," I say. "But there are some helpful places to turn.[7] A great reference book is Mark Morford and Robert Lenardon's *Classical Mythology* if you want to know all about the Greeks and Romans. Or if you want to know specifically about *hero* myths, Campbell says that most myths about a hero . . ."

"Which would be most myths," Janice says, relieved.

"Yeah, most myths about heroes conform to the same general structure, which he calls a *monomyth*. This structure—a plot line really—unfolds in three phases: *Departure*, in which the hero-to-be is 'called' to a quest and leaves home; *Initiation*, in which the hero endures trials, dangers, and often captivity as a prelude to acquiring wisdom; and *Return*, when the hero comes back to share his or her newfound wisdom or 'boon' with the family, tribe, or culture."[8]

"Now there are endless spin-offs on this general structure," I continue, going for the Gold. "In her helpful book, *The Hero and the Perennial Journey Home in American Film*, Susan Mackey-Kallis identifies three variations. *Creation/Re-Creation Myths* tell of origins—of the cosmos, of our earth, and of people and creatures. Mackey-Kallis sees films like *2001: A Space Odyssey*, *The Lion King*, and *Contact* as falling within this pattern. She also speaks of *coming-of-age myths*, which chart different kinds of human initiation—from child to adolescent, adolescent to adult, adult to elder, and even elder to ashes. Films like *The Natural*, *Bull Durham*, *Thelma and Louise*, and *The Piano* are cast in this vein. Finally, she identifies *the grail myth*, which tells of redemption from evil, sin, or death. The King Arthur legends epitomize this variant, as do aspects of Christ's journey and, somewhat transparently, films like *Indiana Jones and the Last Crusade*."[9]

While I take a deep breath, Janice continues our musing on good myths to know.

"Now many myths fit nicely under Mackey-Kallis's three variations of the monomyth, but we can identify at least three more that seem particularly relevant to American culture. First, there are the myths of romantic love that chart the agonies and ecstasies of erotic intimacy. These include classic love stories like 'Eros and Psyche,' 'Tristan and Isolde,' 'Romeo and Juliet,' updated film versions like *West Side Story*, and all the variations found in daytime soap operas. We even examined James Cameron's *Titanic* in terms of how the romantic love myth clashed with its myth of technological progress."[10]

"Then there's the American frontier myth," Janice perseveres. "We've already spoken of the potential of this tale to legitimate environmental irresponsibility and American colonization, but there are many variations as the myth evolves. In 1983, I argued that, during the 'Urban Cowboy' era, the western hero was forced into artificiality when his scene got transposed from the open range to the city. Later I traced how, once the land-based frontier has been settled and civilized, the myth simply continues in space, especially in films like *Star Wars* and the *Alien* series. Even though the infinity of space seems more conducive to spiritual wisdom than environmental exploitation, the frontier myth often prefers 'search and destroy' to 'search,' and simply continues to colonize and exploit planets and moons in outer space."[11]

"Hey," I chime in, "I'm feeling left out here. Let's turn to *our* stuff for a moment. For us, a mythic motif that is especially relevant to today's world involves technological progress, what has been called 'The Frankenstein Myth.' This story tells of the gradual separation of humans from their tools up to and even beyond the point where the tools become free from human control. Born in the ancient myth of Prometheus, who stole fire (the root of technology) from the gods, through Mary Shelley's *Frankenstein*, and up through countless films, like *The Terminator* trilogy, *The Matrix* trilogy, and *A.I.*, this story continues to evolve in our cultural psyche."[12]

"We think this myth is important because it expresses our ambivalence about all the technology we think we can't do without," Janice elaborates. "On the one hand, we love it—think of all those cool gadgets James Bond uses, like a cigarette that knocks out his enemy with a puff of gas. But we're also really scared of it . . ."

"I'll be back," I say in my best Arnold Schwarzenneger impression.

Jane is writing furiously now, looking a bit like a cyborg herself.

"Now," I continue, "Robert Jewett and John Shelton Lawrence offer an intriguing twist on Campbell's monomythic structure. They note that in the American version of the monomyth, the hero starts out *separated* from family, tribe, or community, *comes into these groups* to save them from some peril, but then *leaves again* to be on his own (it is usually a 'his' here). Although this structure is not at all limited to the western genre, countless American westerns do honor it. Think of *Shane*, *High Noon*, *The Magnificent Seven*, and *High Plains Drifter*, just to name a few. Apparently, the American monomyth prefers its heroes to be iconoclastic individuals rather than civic-minded community leaders. Lawrence and Jewett expose how the American monomyth forsakes democracy and prefers a superhero who'll get the job done *for* us"[13]

"Almost all of your examples come from film. So is mythic criticism limited to movies?" Jane asks reasonably.

"Absolutely not," Janice jumps back in. "Like Mackey-Kallis, we happen to be interested in films, but other forms of public address can clearly be interpreted mythically. Take Martin Luther King's 'I Have A Dream' speech, for example. Almost everybody can recognize how he brilliantly tries to expand the myth of the American Dream to include his race. Or look at what Walter Fisher does with the American Dream in political elections, or John Arthos does with Louis Farrakhan's use of the shaman-trickster myth in the Million Man March, or what Randall Lake does with notions of mythic time in Native American Protest Rhetoric. Or you can analyze magazine articles mythically, as Farrel Corcoran does with news magazine stories about Soviet funerals, or . . ."[14]

"OK, I think I've got a vague inkling of what myth is, but I've got a paper to write. *What's mythic criticism?*" she demands, cutting us no slack, even though the lunch 'hour' has come and gone forty minutes ago.

This has been invigorating, but Jane is younger than Janice or me and the old folks are wilting here. Somebody's got to end this deal.

"How about we take a breather," I say, instituting what I hope to be the rhetoric of good-bye. "Why don't you go to Janice's class next week, read the examples on the syllabus, and then come back if you want, and we'll take up that question."

INITIATION

Exactly one week later, I'm unpacking Janice's battered, but still functioning NFL lunchbox. A colleague of ours gave that to her back in 1984 as consolation for all the football talk she had to endure when the departmental rhetoricians gathered for lunch. Janice knows absolutely nothing about the NFL, but she inexplicably regards this lunchbox as a priceless treasure.

"Don't nuke the lunches just yet," she cautions. "Jane's on her way up the stairs and she's carrying a big brown paper sack."

"And that can only mean we're about to begin 'Round 2' on mythic criticism?"

Jane walks in without knocking, sporting an ensemble that blends at least three contradictory life styles. "Lunch!" she announces triumphantly, ripping open the bag, passing out giant Snickers bars to me and a bag of baby carrots to Janice. "OK now, listen up. I've got to write this mythic criticism paper, and I'm lost."

"Didn't you pay attention in class?" I chide her.

"Probably as much as you ever did," Jane says.

"Well," Janice begins, "how does a piece of criticism usually start?"

"With some mystery or anomaly in a text that my review of the literature can't make go away," Jane answers dutifully.

"Guess there's a reason why you're an honor's student," I say.

"Yeah, well, sure, I've got plenty of questions about movies and politics and rock music, etc., etc., but how do I know when some *mythic* approach will help to unscramble my intrigue?"

"That's a great question," Janice says. Always begin with positive reinforcement, she maintains, but somehow I've never gotten the hang of it. "Sometimes the text makes overt references to a myth. If a movie's name is *Excalibur* or *Merlin*, it's pretty obvious we're dealing with mythic material here. Or, as in one of my favorites—*The Princess Bride*—the title tells you up front it's going to be a fairy tale."

"'My name ees Imigo Montoya. You keelled my father, prepare to die,'" I say, rolling my R's quite impressively, if I must say so myself.

"Later," Janice replies, refusing to get distracted. "The question is, are the mythic elements so up-front as to present no problem for you to explore, in which case you probably don't have a criticism, or is there something puzzling that a criticism will help you work out? With this movie, does it make any difference that the fairy tale is "book-ended" by the old man reading the story to his grandson? Or that the usual themes of romance and adventure are presented comically?"

"Or you may just have a fragment that gets you started," I offer, "an allusion to a myth but not the whole thing. Like when George W. Bush said of Osama bin Laden that he wanted him, 'Dead or Alive.' You could ask yourself whether the Bush administration reacted to September 11 in other ways that recall the mentality of the Old West—act decisively, shoot straight, and take 'em out."

"'A man's gotta do what a man's gotta do'?" Jane gets into the act.

"Precisely," Janice replies. "Or you could be dealing with a text that is another episode in a myth that is still evolving, so you want to show what this latest installment says about where the culture is now. Take a look at how Karen Rasmussen and Sharon Downey analyze Vietnam War films such as *Platoon* and *Full Metal Jacket*. They deal with a long history of war mythology in America, but show how it gets subverted in films about this war. Or, consider what Constance Penley has to say about *The Terminator* and *La Jetée*—she thinks both films use the time-travel theme of science fiction to develop that technology myth we mentioned earlier; these films comment on how our dependence on technology could bring about an apocalyptic future."[15]

"Maybe you sense that one of those large mythic themes we talked about last week is present, and you want to see how this text acts it out," I add. "Perhaps you think *Fight Club* is a coming-of-age myth, and you want to explore what kind of lessons it teaches about what it means to be a 'man' in a super-materialistic society."

"Hmm," Jane muses. "You mean, like, what did it mean that that Edward Norton character was so interested in buying all the perfect things and then his apartment building got blown up?"

"Yeah," I say, getting excited. "That might have something to do with the materialistic aspect of the American Dream myth."

"You might have two myths going here," I add. "The American Dream and coming-of-age."

"And the Brad Pitt character . . ."

"Tyler Durden!" Janice shouts.

"Yeah, Tyler Durden is the other guy's 'tutor' in initiating him into manhood," Jane enthuses. "I wonder what it means that he does his mentoring with his fists."

"*Voila!*" I cheer, giving Jane a thumbs-up. "You better sit right down at your PC and get started on this one."

Janice now provides the summing-up I usually do. "Any or all of these approaches might get you started. The point is that you want to show how myth functions in a text or a set of them to tell us something important we didn't know. Your purpose could be to show how the myth helps make this text persuasive. Or you could show how the text employs myth to make a statement about the condition of the cultural psyche—remember, this is how the myth functions as a collective dream. Or you might want to show how the existing power structure is reaffirmed or undermined in the text. Or maybe you do all of those things, and . . ."

"Wait, slow down, I can't write that fast," Jane implores. "Say that again—slowly."

"I thought you were an honors student," I rebuke her.

Jane smiles, forgetting her semi-alienated counter-culture pose for a moment. "This doesn't sound all that hard."

POTENTIALS AND PITFALLS

"It's actually quite fun," Janice enthuses. "Myths are inherently entertaining. They catch people up emotionally, not just intellectually—and that includes us when we act as critics, as well as when we're the audience."

"And that can be a plus or a minus," I add.

"Yeah," Jane says, "because people may get behind some horrible social policy because it's cast in mythic terms, and it's our job to point that out."

"It's very important to do that—as well as to point out how myths can enrich our lives by symbolizing possibilities we hadn't thought of," Janice says.

"Of course, there *are* pitfalls," I throw in, not wanting this to be *too* easy. "Like confusing renaming and/or retelling with interpretation."

"'Just when you thought it was safe to go back in the water,'" Jane replies wearily. "Go figure."

"That's where you just rename the characters with mythic terms and retell the text's story using mythic language, and think you've done a mythic interpretation," I expound. "For example, let's say you decide to do a mythic analysis of the film *The Empire Strikes Back*. So you say something like: 'Well, Luke Skywalker is the hero-to-be, Princess Leia is the heroine, Yoda is the spiritual mentor, and Darth Vader is the enemy. This film is a heroic initiation myth where to become a full-fledged hero, Luke must leave his friends, learn how to use the Force from Yoda, get captured and suffer, break free and defeat Darth Vader, and finally save his friends.' Can you see how this 'mythic analysis' doesn't really do much more than rename the characters and retell the story in mythic language?"

"Yeah I can see that," Jane nods, "but how can I be sure I'm not just doing this renaming, retelling thing?"

"The best way," Janice cuts back in, "is to talk through your idea with someone before you write. You'd be amazed what can occur to you in the midst of a good conversation."

"Or, as a second choice, have someone read what you've written," I say. "If you've just reworked the characters and story using mythic terms, your reader, if she or he is being honest with you, might say something like, 'Yeah, so? What's the point?' Take those kinds of reactions as signs that you've done more categorizing than analyzing."

"If, on the other hand," Janice continues, "your reader says something like, 'Really? Huh, I never thought of that,' this should tell you that you've teased your reader with something that s/he didn't see, and that what you've said is intriguing enough to check what you've said against the text. If you get that kind of response, hand the paper in."

"Just a sec," Jane says. "Are there some texts that simply resist a mythic interpretation—no matter how intriguing I find them?"

"Sure," I reply. "Some texts are just better analyzed using another perspective; maybe there aren't any discernible references to myth."

"And it would be challenging, if not impossible, to use myth to analyze a text that is trying to undermine conventional narrative structure," Janice amplifies. What could you do with *Pulp Fiction*, for example, or the film *Momento*, which both try to tear down the way we normally think stories unfold?"

"Or disco music," I contribute, "which imitates the beat of techno-culture, but doesn't have a story line?"

"So what do you do then?" Jane asks.

"Nothing," I laugh. "Turn those over to critics whose specialty is interpreting anti-structure."

"Unless you want to show how these texts work to *undermine* myth. But that's probably too complicated."

"Fair enough," Jane answers, grabbing her backpack. "Can you guys give me an example or two of mythic criticism that I can use as a model of what I should be trying to do? Anything come to mind?"

Janice and I look at each other. Jane seems initiated enough into her journey into the heart of mythic criticism for something a bit challenging. Janice rummages on her bookshelves and pulls out a reprint of a recent essay we wrote.

"Here," she says, "see what you can make of this. It's from *Critical Studies in Media Communication*, on the 1999 film *The Matrix*."[16]

"Good choice," I say. "It should illustrate some of the things we've been talking about—it relies somewhat on Campbell's monomyth, it's an episode in the still-evolving myth of technology, and it deals with both the psychological and the ideological aspects of that myth."

"You may have to enter the 'belly of the whale,' as Campbell says, but you'll fight your way out," Janice cautions.

"Geez, thanks," Jane says, "that was a cool film."

"'Guns . . . lots of guns,'" I drone in my best Keanu Reeves zombified monotone.

"Can we talk about this next week?" Jane asks, ignoring me.

"Why not?" Janice and I say.

"But let's everybody bring their own lunch," I add, feeling suddenly a little queasy about my next class.

The next week at lunchtime, I'm expecting Jane to pop in, and secretly looking forward to it.

"Something's up," Janice says. "Jane was quiet and sullen in class today, and that's not her style."

As if cued to prove Janice right, Jane slouches in, tosses the reprint on Janice's desk, and slumps down in her chair. "All right. You guys win. If you gave me this article to put me on a 'road of trials,' it worked. I thought I left here last week with a pretty decent grasp of what mythic criticism was all about, but this thing is damn near incomprehensible! Myths I've never heard of, theories about male gazes, mothers as mathematical grid systems, something called *puers* and *puellas*. . . . I'm sorry, but this example has put me back to ground zero," she concludes in defeat.

Janice and I just sit there. Big mistake. At the end of last week's session, we were both tired and, with too little thought, gave her something that was written for academic professionals, not beginning students of rhetorical criticism. Now it looks as if our own insensitivity has undone all our good deeds.

"Don't you have something simpler?" she asks a bit more softly. "I'm sorry I said those things about your work, but I was just so frustrated."

"Look," Janice soothes, "it's our fault, not yours. Sometimes professors just lose sight of how tedious their published stuff can be—even when it's on 'fun' texts like *The Matrix*. We'll rework this piece so that you can understand it, and maybe even use it as a model for your own piece of mythic criticism. Is that fair?"

"So how long do you figure it will take you to dumb this one down?" Jane asks, still not sure there isn't a professorial conspiracy against hard-working students like herself.

"We don't need to 'dumb anything down' for you," Janice insists. "We'll just streamline the analysis a bit so that you can see how this perspective works, OK?"

"Two weeks?"

"Two weeks," Janice promises.

As Jane leaves, I turn to Janice. "What could you possibly have been thinking? How are you going to have time to rewrite that article!?"

"I'm not," Janice smiles. "You are. I'll do the second draft, of course, but if I'm teaching the class, the least you can do is supply the examples. Besides, this article needs your 'essential self.'"

"And that would be?" I ask.

"Total transparency."

"Be afraid, be *very* afraid." But I exit with the reprint clutched tightly in hand, knowing 'a man's gotta do what a man's gotta do.'

Two weeks later, here's what we give Jane:

CRITICAL ESSAY: MYTH AND SPECTACLE IN THE MATRIX

When would-be hero Neo finally meets his mentor Morpheus in 1999s heavily hyped film, *The Matrix*, Morpheus offers him the choice of a blue pill or a red one. If he takes the blue, he will wake up the next morning having conveniently forgotten they ever met. If he downs the red, his familiar reality will be shattered forever as he enters a totally alien world. Although as critics we like to regard ourselves as open-minded, we now think we saw the film initially through the comforting haze of the "blue pill." As many know, the story line tells of a computer-generated reality that programs people's minds to live out a virtual, pacified existence while their bodies lie captive, hidden from awareness, reduced to battery cells that recharge the computers. We must have replicated this internal plot in our viewings. Just as the sleeping people within the Matrix see only their virtual existence while remaining blind to their embodied slavery, we too, sitting captivated in our snug theatre seats, were initially so benumbed by the visual style of this film that we failed to appreciate an important mythic advocacy amidst the surface glitter.

Apparently, we weren't alone. Many critics deride *The Matrix* as an overwrought spectacle. Like us, they may share the guilty pleasures of an exhilarating ride, but are incensed that the film's innovative ideas get ground into narrative dust by the visual pyrotechnics of its special effects. "Part of me wants to dismiss 'The Matrix' as a loud and empty spectacle, 1999s apex of dazzling technological style over substance," Andrew O'Hehir complains. "It lacks anything like adult emotion, and its themes and images arrive at a dizzying, stupefying pace, as if vomited up by some voracious creature that ate the last twenty years of sci-fi and action-movie history and only partially digested them."[17] Lisa Schwarzbaum isn't much of a fan either. "[T]he real soullessness here is built into the production . . . and groundbreaking special effects . . . 'The Matrix' sells itself as a gaudy chopsocky concoction with expensive Hollywood action details—a blast of Holly-Kong glitz that never approaches the stylistic cohesiveness of, say, John Woo's 'Face/Off' or the charisma of the propulsive star John Travolta."[18] And Bob Graham seems to speak for many when he says, "It's astonishing that so much money, talent, technical expertise and visual imagination can be put in the service of something so stupid. . . . So this is what more than 100 years of cinematic history has come to: special effects with no movie."[19]

But at least some see past this movie's exhibitionism toward a tale worth telling. Roger Ebert glimpses its worth despite his irritation: "It's kind of a letdown when a movie begins by redefining the nature of reality, and ends with a shoot-out. We want a leap of the imagination, not one of those obligatory climaxes with automatic weapons fire."[20] Stuart Klawans detests the excess precisely because there is substance to squander: "Like a guest at a potlatch, laughing to see his host's worldly goods go up in flames, I roared at *The Matrix*—roared and at the same time was humbled, knowing that Warner Bros. had such magnificence to burn."[21] Anthony Ferrante is actually intrigued by the fractured narrative that typically draws guffaws for its retrofitted "second coming" theme: "[T]he pleasure of THE MATRIX is how complex the story really is. Once you think you've got it all figured out, it throws another surprise into your face."[22] Even O'Hehir, so disdainful of the film's brandishments, still admits to some intrigue over the plot: "[I]n a limited and profoundly geeky sense, this might be an important and generous film."[23] Perhaps there is more here, such comments suggest, than meets the eye.

Forced back to the theatre several times by honors students outraged at our dismissal of what was fast becoming a canonical text for the post-*Blade Runner* generation, we began to see a few of the geeky ways in which *The Matrix* might be profound. Eventually, we recognized that this film was extending, in some culturally significant ways, a technological myth that others and we have called the "Frankenstein complex."[24] A still-evolving tale, this myth warns of our enslavement to technology; as in Mary Shelley's original *Frankenstein*, the tools of our own making become "monstrous" and come to haunt us.[25] But in film, this same technology, materialized as spectacular visual effects, often hides the very warning implicit in the myth.[26] Our critical task is thus identical to the initiation ritual of the hero—namely, to break free from our addiction to technology and "wake up" to how dependent we have become on its devices. What Neo must do within *The Matrix* is thus a microcosm of what we must all do in everyday life to prevent becoming totally controlled by our own artifice.

Like Neo at the outset of *The Matrix*, we are already pretty well caged within our technology-defined cells. Lots of people find life on the Internet much more fulfilling and exciting than anything in the clunky old world of material reality. Cell phones, once a curious novelty for the yuppie technophile, are fast evolving into pacemakers for the psyche. Look around anywhere—in supermarkets, on street corners, in the aisles of airplanes, at tables in expensive restaurants, in college classrooms, even in public restrooms. It's hard to find anybody nowadays either *not* talking on a cell phone or with one, like some handgun from the old West, strapped to his or her belt waiting for the next "beep" to trigger a quick draw. We are so intent on multi-tasking that we drive a car, talk on a cell phone, listen (presumably in the other ear) to a CD. The boundaries of technological activities are blurring as well. Where once we could speak confidently of watching television or surfing the web, these two activities have now merged so that we can do either on our television set and/or our home computer. The myth of technology is not an archaic story about knights in armor, damsels in distress, and fire-breathing dragons, but rather something that impacts our daily lives in important ways.

If *The Matrix* extends the technology myth through its fragmented but innovative plot line, while at the same time it retards it through its spectacular visual effects, then it seems reasonable to place ourselves within this myth/spectacle tension and look a little more closely at what is going on. Because the myth in this movie follows quite closely the three general phases of Joseph Campbell's monomyth,[27] we use his general framework as an organizing schema. However, because the visual effects and action sequences of *The Matrix* often work against this very framework, we pause, from time to time, to examine how the cinematic technology subverts the myth of technological evolution.

Departure

The first time we see the young protagonist— Thomas Anderson" in his day job at a computer software firm and "Neo" the notorious hacker at night—he is asleep in the depressing urban pod he calls home. The numbing ads that scroll down his computer screen suddenly give way to these stark words:

Wake up Neo . . .
The Matrix has you . . .
Follow the white rabbit.

While he struggles to comprehend this strange command from nowhere, his monitor spells out, "Knock, knock, Neo," just as there is a rapping at his door. It is a be-metaled set of poster children for postmodernism enlisting his nocturnal services. Though he still struggles to shake off sleep, this "doubting Thomas" must already suspect something is wrong with his life picture; he retrieves a disk from a fake book entitled *Simulacra and Simulation*, as if he conceals his piracy beneath a darkly skeptical Baudrillardian cover. Warned not to get caught, Troy, the bored leader of this brat pack, hints obliviously at Neo's condition: "Yeah, I know, you don't exist." As if picking up the clue, Neo muses, "You ever have that feeling where you're not sure if you're awake or still dreaming?" Attributing it to "mescaline; it's the only way to fly," Troy persists in his *idiot savant* vein, "Hey, it just sounds to me like you may need to unplug, man. You know, get some R & R?"[28]

At first refusing an invitation to do just that, Neo reconsiders when he sees the white rabbit tattooed on the left shoulder of the woman who is draped over Troy. At this film's revision of *The Terminator*'s (1984) "Tech Noir" nightclub, a slicked-back woman-in-black confronts Neo with, "I know why you're here." Introducing herself as "Trinity," she alerts Neo that the legendary hacker whose fame he well recognizes is female. "I just thought, um . . . you were a . . . guy," he confesses, too self-contained to see past his own nose. "Most guys do," Trinity retorts. There will be many more surprises, but Neo suggests he may be up to them when he answers her query with another. Trinity whispers in his ear: "It's the question that drives us, Neo. It's the question that brought you here. You know the question, just as I did." Like the riddle put to mythic heroes such as Parsifal in his search for the Grail ("Whom does the Grail serve?"), it is only asking the right question—not having the right answer—that indicates a frame of mind receptive enough to see an alternative reality. "What is the Matrix?" he replies. "The answer is out there, Neo. It's looking for you, and it will find you—if you want it to," she responds, and with this acceptance of his "call," Neo joins the long narrative history of heroic attempts to lift the veil of technology from their eyes.

Though Neo wants to answer his own question, he will have to awake to the fact that his everyday life is only a mental construct detached from his body—a rather tall order for someone who has heretofore had little reason to question that his physical sensations were real and his analytical talents were effective. However, the senses, this film repeatedly implies, deceive and pacify. Cypher, the Judas in this tale and in digital terms the "0" to Neo's "1," knows that the taste of a juicy steak he is eating while inside the Matrix is supplied by his virtual programming, but he relishes it anyway because he decides, as many of us would, to trade in the blight of authenticity for the euphoria of illusion. Dark glasses, worn here by the freedom fighters and the mechanized agents, do more than quote *The Terminator* or *Men In Black* (1997); they shield the eyes from the mirage of the Matrix. As Thomas Anderson, Neo is upbraided by his boss for not taking his job seriously enough. This isn't really the problem, and a window washer hangs outside, cleaning Neo's view.[29] He is not yet ready to see clearly, though, and when he receives a cell phone via Fed Ex and the occult Morpheus warns him that he is in danger and must escape by leaping off his skyscraper onto a scaffold, he exclaims to himself in disbelief, "No way! No way—this is crazy!"

But, of course, it's not crazy. For when Neo finally meets Morpheus, he is told, "You have the look of a man who accepts what he sees because he's expecting to wake up. Ironically, this is not far from the truth." Neo is veiled from the truth, Morpheus explains, because he is enthralled by his own projected image which, unknown to him at this point, is merely a mental construct and not the complete self he believes it to be. "Unfortunately, no one can be told what the Matrix is," Morpheus continues, "you have to see it for yourself." "But what *is* the Matrix?" Neo insists, and Morpheus replies, "It's the world that has been pulled over your eyes to blind you from the truth." It is Neo's initiatory task to pull that veil from his eyes.

Initiation

Meeting the Mother

Neo has no clue that his body is wrapped in a techno-placenta in a dark underworld baby ward—umbilical tentacles attaching him to what must be both his source of sustenance and theirs. Webster's locates the origins of "matrix" in the Latin *ma* for "womb," and the French *matr-* or *mater* for "mother."[30] Chad Eby notes that William Gibson uses "matrix," a synonym for cyberspace, as "mother" or "womb" in *Neuromancer*, and that "this analogy evokes a spatial feminine structure that is complete in itself—the turned on by itself parthenogenic womb . . . as the pre-oedipal 'archaic mother'. . ."[31] Similarly, James Beard says that Gibson's characters "*embrace* it erotically (after all, technophilia means 'love' of technology), even oedipally," and that the main character, Case, "penetrates ('jacks in' is Gibson's pun) the 'mother.'"[32]

Although it is usually coded masculine, as opposed to nature as feminine, technology as mother is not foreign to science fiction, particularly when it emphasizes humans' extreme dependence on the machine. The astronauts in *2001: A Space Odyssey* (1968), *Alien* (1979), and *Aliens* (1986) are pictured sleeping like infants in the uterine spaceship, and in *Alien* they refer to the ship's computer as "Mother." The Matrix is indeed a false mother who, as *Psycho*'s Norman Bates might say, "isn't quite herself today." As machine-made, she can't be, and she is monstrously alien because she results from the reduction of the mother's plenitude to the electronic world of "0's" and "1's."

Throughout the technology myth, the typically male hero must relate not only to his mother, but to a feminine "love interest." Everything not artificially woman is generally repressed in this myth, so it often falls to a feminine "other" to help the masculine hero to wake him up to his over-dependence on technology, whether or not that technology is teamed up with a dominating "mother." That is, whatever the hero has *not* seen clearly is in the best position to help him to see now.[33] Although Trinity occupies this role of the female romantic partner, we do not think their relationship ever catches fire. If we wonder what has happened to the erotic feminine in this film, however, we need look no further than the mother Matrix herself. As the scenic backdrop for everything that isn't, this is where the action is. By contrast, what occurs in "reality" aboard the Nebuchadnezzar, unless produced by a program simulating the Matrix, is dull and bleak. The John Woo-style cadences of Neo, Trinity, Morpheus, and Agent Smith—a seamless stitchery of high technology and balletic Kung Fu—are air-borne courting rituals in which the characters gaze at and repeatedly penetrate each other with bullets.[34] Myth and spectacle, often at odds in this film, merge here in a technologized mother upon which we as spectators can gaze for a visual feast of displaced erotic desire.

Descending to the Body

At a mythic level, Neo's most urgent task is to get his body back. After self-assuredly popping the red pill Morpheus offers him, he immediately spirals down an *Alice in Wonderland* rabbit hole to Hell. Morpheus explains that it will disorient Neo's simulated programming so that the rebels can locate his body among the fields of indistinguishable pods where all bodies are encased for the keeping. As Cypher warns, "buckle your seat belt, Dorothy, 'cause Kansas is goin' bye-bye." But just before his mythic descent begins, our attention shifts to a remarkable special effect. As Neo waits for whatever is going to happen, he catches sight of himself in a cracked mirror and, fascinated by his own image, reaches out to touch it. The mirror liquefies and begins to coat him with its substance. "It's going into replication," cautions Trinity, who is monitoring Neo's vital signs; "we've got a fibrillation!" Neo's reflection seems bent on destroying its source, which is itself a simulation of the "real" Neo.[35] In like manner, we are captivated by this oozing mercurial takeover of Neo's body, a stand-in for our own, as this spectacle evokes the typical "how do they *do* that?" awe. Thus, while Neo's plight warns of humanity's technological co-optation, the technological pleasures of spectacle themselves screen us from the prophecy.

Not a moment too soon, Tank gets a connection and Neo drops out of his virtual world where people program computers into its "real" negation where computers program humans. Whereas once humans planted, raised, and harvested crops for their sustenance, in a cannibalistic inversion of the food chain, computers now puree the dead to feed newborn babies, who in turn fuel the computers. In his chilling metaphor of evolution, Agent Smith later turns the humans' "safety valve" argument—that over-population and ruin of one frontier justifies expansion into the next—against Morpheus. By colonizing and destroying their own environment, humans act more like viruses than like the mammals they take themselves to be. Thus humans must be supplanted by the agents' higher life-form. "You are the disease . . . ," he articulates with measured finality, "we are the cure."

The scene of Neo in his pod with feeding lines protruding obscenely from his spine all the way up to the back of his neck is undeniably horrific. Bolting upright in his mechanical womb, hairless and covered with natal slime, Neo takes his first look at "the real world." What he sees, and what we see, are thousands of "pod cribs" housing indistinguishable bodies that provide the computers with an endless supply of energy. Filmed with extreme long shots, from high angles, and through red-tinted filters, this is an impressively gooey technological Hell. Flashes of electricity dance among the pods, perhaps to animate the inert bodies to perform their nutritional function. A high-tech nursemaid, no doubt sensing a waking body, buzzes in, hovers over Neo, rips this problem child from his life-support lines, and flushes him down a "toilet" into a sewer far below. This is one of those scenes people remember for its high "yuck factor," like the Terminator cutting out his eyeball with an exacto knife. More than likely, we will tell our friends about this gore rather than assimilate the narrative importance of Neo's captivity. Once again, the film's spectacle competes with its mythic message. Morpheus and his crew quickly rescue Neo and land him on their ship.

Mythically, however, this scene is crucial. Neo has to get his body back if he is going to grow out of his non-seeing house of mirrors. This task reiterates the task of the traditional mythic hero, who must endure being swallowed into the "belly of the whale" or other symbols of the Devouring Mother's womb, where his former self is consumed.[36] In the Frankenstein myth, the hero's plunge is often into captivity, where he must recognize and identify with the "other"—such as an "inferior" race or gender—that he has oppressed.[37] The oppressed "other" in this part of the story is his own split-off biological, unreflected body, and he must, quite literally, get himself together.

Spiritual Mentoring

Initiation rituals correct excessive individual pride, when the elders take the novice back to the deepest level of mother-child identity, forcing a symbolic death through temporary dismemberment or dissolution, and then ceremonially rescue him. In these moments, the group acts as a kind of "second parent" at his rebirth.[38] Once back in the good mother ship, a much-atrophied Neo lies prone on a surgical gurney, every square morsel of his body pierced with needles. Although these are apparently acupuncture tools needed to summon his fragile unity back to strength, the impression is one of woundedness. He has lost his hair, mythic symbol of masculine strength, he is punctured by lesions that once bound him to the mother Matrix, and he is completely dependent upon his adoptive tribe for nourishment.

In most hero myths, the initiate undergoes prolonged and often grueling instruction from those who already possess the wisdom and skills he must acquire to accomplish the task at hand.[39] Because that task will demand inner resolve as well as outer resources, his central guides may be supernatural, or if human, they must be acquainted with the interior life of the spirit. In the Frankenstein myth, the spiritual realm is also a part of what the hero has repressed in order to progress technologically, for he has been playing God himself. Thus, his spiritual tutor commonly appears in the form of an "other," often a woman or a person of color.[40] Here, the spiritual elder is a rebellious black man whose name means, paradoxically, son of sleep and god of dreams. His name also suggests his ability to morph between two worlds, and recalls the historical Orpheus, who descends to Hell and back on his own "road of trials." Morpheus's spiritual guide in turn is an earthy, yet mystical black woman.[41] It is Morpheus's job to lift the dreamy veil of illusion from Neo's eyes.

Neo must learn how to deploy his considerable physical talents in a virtualized form. At first, Neo is completely ineffective in the sparring program Morpheus has created to mimic the Matrix because he is still relying on the Matrix's temporal and spatial *a priori*'s which, as we have found, are deceptive—mother as the mythical Maya, or veil of illusion. Mid-battle, Morpheus mocks, "Come on! Stop trying to hit me and *hit* me!" With this, Neo kicks into Kung Fu warp speed, presumably by projecting all of his physical skills into his residual self-image, and by ceasing to think the way he has been programmed to think in his false reality. He freezes his fist an inch from Morpheus's face. Back at the control monitors, an awestruck Mouse whispers, "I don't believe it."

Once again, this scene in which Morpheus teaches Neo to fight with his entire being and not just his mind is central to understanding Neo's mythic quest. But once again, visual effects blunt the mythic point, for the scene unfolds as one of the film's most impressive action spectaculars. Shot in slow motion, Morpheus's and Neo's martial arts savagery is magically transformed into something resembling an underwater ballet. As they walk up walls and beams, doing flips and somersaults in flight, the training lesson comes across more as a romanticized dance than a rehearsal for combat. As in so much of this film, the sexual tension is displaced into the spectacular effects rather than located in the relationship between the hero and the feminine "other."

Even with his impressive new skills, becoming one in mind and body is not the same as becoming "the One." If Morpheus's martial arts instruction leads Neo to the door, the Oracle shows him how to walk through it. It is significant that the Oracle embodies two kinds of "otherness"—she is black and female. The scene with Neo and the Oracle is unsettling because the extraordinary unfolds within the ordinary—as often occurs in myth—and because the Oracle's lessons come cloaked in koan-like paradoxes, themselves embedded in chit-chat about baking cookies and breaking vases. But Neo encounters the Oracle within the Matrix, and so it is not surprising that even here, in the den of "Truth," spectacle leaves its traces, as the visual effects of the monk-like child bending a spoon with his or her mind linger longer than the intricacies of spoken dialogue.

In fact, both Trinity and the Oracle hold the keys to Neo's Oneness, even more than Morpheus, who prepares him to meet them. As conductor of the pre-Christian Orphic tradition that not only stresses death and descent into the underworld as a prelude to resurrection, but worships the Goddess TriVia, Morpheus places the Oracle's truth ahead of his own. As far back as the Stone Age, the Great Goddess was a trinity, venerated in her three forms as a young woman, a birth-giving matron, and a wise old woman, and serving as the prototype for countless threefold goddesses.[42] Trinity as Virgin-Mother-Crone seems far more apropos to this film than the too-easy allusion to Father-Son-Holy Spirit, a trio that, though it does emphasize embodiment and transformation, is a patriarchal takeover that represses its feminine roots, a crucial source of redemption for a technological hero. Trinity herself clues us into the right mythic framework when she aborts Neo's masculine presumption in the nightclub. By herself, Trinity may appear primarily as a sleek-and-chic virginal love object who, by the way, kicks butt, but in the context of the whole myth, "the Trinity" is also Mother—as in the second mother of the Nebachudnezzar crew, and Crone—as in the Oracle who taunts Neo with his destiny.

Oracle: So—what do you think? Do you think you are "the One?"
Neo: Honestly, I don't know.
Oracle: You know what that means [pointing to a plaque over her door]? Latin. Means "Know thyself." I'm gonna let you in on a little secret. Being the One is just like being in love. No one can tell you you're in love. You just know it, through and through, balls to bones.

With this declaration, the Oracle invalidates all instruction, including her own. If and when Neo comes to know that he is the One, he will learn it through bodily intuition, from an impassioned commitment of the heart, not a rational decision of the mind.

Reintegrating the Feminine

Whereas Neo is insufficiently aware of Trinity throughout most of the story, as Cypher notes, she watches him right from the beginning scene. Later, although Trinity in her strapless outfit at the nightclub may invite the gaze of others, it is she who again looks at Neo, not the other way around.

When Agent Smith "kills" Neo, which in the rules of the Matrix does away with his body as well, Trinity leans over Neo's limp form inside the rebels' ship, insisting with quiet desperation:

> Neo? I'm not afraid anymore. The Oracle told me that I would fall in love, and that that man, the man that I loved, would be the One. So you see—you can't be dead—you can't be—because I love you. You hear me? I love you.

She kisses Neo, he stirs, and she commands, nearly pilfering Sarah Connor's line to Kyle Reese in *The Terminator*, "Now get up!" In this moment, Trinity's love bequeaths *empathy* to Neo, the singular relational quality that no amount of spectacular action can impart. The virtual Neo who rises from the dead is not the same construct Agent Smith ostensibly blew away.

Although she is a compelling visual icon and goes through the required motions to awaken Neo, something seems peculiarly off-center with the Trinity-and-Neo duo. This kiss has no sizzle. Their relationship, in fact, never approaches the complexity of Molly and Case in *Neuromancer* or the sexual intensity of, say, Kyle Reese and Sarah Connor or Rick Deckard and Rachael Tyrell in *Blade Runner*. Instead, when Trinity emerges from watching Neo from off to the side, she fights with him side-by-side. Trinity relates to Neo as his buddy or sibling, a fairly conventional way, according to Sobchack, to contain female sexuality in science fiction films.[43]

In their fight scenes, Neo and Trinity reflect one another in their sleek black leather, their measured, in-your-face attitudes, and their karate-kicking *machismo*. When the two of them step into the lobby of the building where Morpheus is imprisoned, we see them in full frontal assault mode, Neo on the right, Trinity on the left. They sport the same dark glasses, the same slick hairdos, and nearly the same clothes. As a Matrix security guard yells, "freeze!" the two turn to gaze at each other, forming a near-perfect mirror image that moves in sync as they spring to opposite sides of the frame. In the precisely choreographed mayhem that follows, quick cuts back-and-forth between Trinity and Neo catch each in hang-time gymnastics, their black coats floating incongruously amidst a barrage of bullets. One might be the other—it doesn't seem to matter—as they step tranquilly onto the elevator, the door closing over the dyad, now Neo on the left and Trinity on the right.

Throughout *The Matrix*, as we have noted, Trinity's eroticism is displaced onto the special effects. Desire is directed not to her body, but literally "up there" on the screen. Whereas she helps Neo get his body back, in a way that is as disquieting as it is grand, she loses her own in the bargain. It is difficult, however, to recognize this loss because we're so captivated by the reign of bullets, the shattering of (styrofoam) pillars, and the carnage of killing, which, we can quickly rationalize, is not "really" killing because those being blown away are, after all, just mental contructs generated by the Matrix. Here, as elsewhere in this film, extreme violence becomes indistinguishable from the innocent mayhem committed in computer games all over America.

Claiming Insight

To gain the boon of insight in the myth of technology, the hero must trade in his ego for a larger sense of himself in relation to others.[44] The final struggle between Neo and the agents is, in fact, two battles, the first dominated by sight before Neo's "death," the second permeated by insight after his "resurrection." It does not end in a gun battle, even though it starts with one, and even though the multitudes of spent shell casings drifting languidly through the air with the actors invite us to read it that way. Initially, Neo comes armed with nothing more than his preprogrammed martial arts training plus weapons. "So what do you need besides a miracle?" Tank asks when Neo announces he is re-entering the Matrix to free Morpheus. "Guns," Neo answers decisively, "lots of guns," as an awesome rack of weaponry sure to quicken the pulse of NRA members everywhere slides before him. He must still believe that he can defeat the agents from the outside in, by shooting or karate-kicking them into virtual oblivion. But as long as Neo relies exclusively on his physical skills and Luddist weapons, he lacks the Oracle's in-the-marrow consciousness that would complete his initiation and set him apart from his virtual antagonists. Every time Neo or Trinity blasts one away, the agent simply rematerializes in another virtual human and takes up the fight again. Reiterating the lesson of Frankenstein's bride that technological cures for technological problems merely make those problems worse,[45] this film asserts, at least on the narrative level, that guns can't kill machines.

When Neo arises after Trinity's kiss, though he is still projecting his mind into the Matrix, he does so with full consciousness. He is shot cinematically so that he dominates the space that used to dominate him, and an intensified natural coloring contrasts his new image from the Matrix and its agents, which are always seen through a green filter.[46] When an incredulous Agent Smith attacks with renewed fury, Neo slowly turns away and fends him off with one arm as calmly as an adult might bemusedly repel the flailing of a petulant child. Then, in a blur, Neo boots Smith at least thirty feet away. Trinity has enabled Neo to see the inner reality of the Matrix, to move in and out of its virtual constructs, knowing that the entire thing is a complex mirror of himself, as all of technology-as-menace is a projection of our human "shadows" (a feared extension of our senses that we have "auto-amputated" from awareness).[47] This knowledge is prefigured by the mystical child in the Oracle's foyer who shows Neo that it is not the spoon s/he is playing with that bends, it is one's self.

Thus, when in the second phase of the battle all three agents empty their weapons at him, Neo realizes Morpheus' earlier prognosis that when he's ready, he will not have to dodge bullets. He simply raises his hand and transforms the virtual slugs back into their digital forms as "0's" and "1's"; as displacements of himself, they are not really all that terrifying. Finally, when a visibly shaken Smith stands up to a charging Neo, Neo digitalizes his self construct, passes into Smith's circuitry, and incarnates within him—fracturing him back into disconnected electrical impulses. But as so often happens in this film, even this mythic denouement is overshadowed by the computer generated effects of Neo entering and "moving" through Agent Smith's destabilized personage.

The Return

The film's ending completes the circle of its beginning: as the frame fills with fluid green digits, a phone rings, and we hear but do not see a voice—Neo this time instead of Trinity. Having vanquished their best agents, Neo is calling the computers. The screen warns of danger—the call is an anomaly—but Neo speaks with confidence:

> I know you're out there. I can feel you now. I know that you're afraid. You're afraid of us, you're afraid of change. I don't know the future. I didn't come here to tell you how it's going to end. I came here to tell you how it's going to begin. I'm going to hang up this phone, and then I'm going to show these people what you don't want them to see. I'm going to show them a world without

you, a world without rules and controls, without borders and boundaries. A world where anything is possible. Where we go from there is a choice I leave up to you.

The last scene thus begins not with spectacular display, but with embodied speech. It is not Luddist, as were Neo's actions before his death, but revelatory, promising to see and to show. We might well ask what kind of sight he advocates. Neo's "world without rules and controls, without borders and boundaries . . . where anything is possible," sounds suspiciously reminiscent of the limitless technological frontierism of which Agent Smith accuses the humans.

But given what he has learned, and especially his empathy with the machines' fears—which directly reverse our fears about them—it seems more likely that his descent into Hell and back has taught him to identify with the "other," whether that be his captive body or the technological extensions of himself. If he does indeed "show these people what you don't want them to see"—undoubtedly that their bodies are enslaved—the machines' "choice" is whether to sever them from their life supports, which would kill not only the people but the machines that feed on them, or to realize their ultimate interdependence. Such connection is what Neo has learned from the Oracle and from Trinity. The "other" is in fact him. Neo must be looking inward to his self rather than outward to his image, then, speaking from insight, not sight. With this hard won perspective he is able to stand up to the false Mother as no mere boy can.

Neo's voiceover concluded, the phrase "System Failure," superimposed over the numbers, grows until it fills the frame. The digital array implodes through a dissolve to Neo hanging up the phone, and he flies off over the Matrix's illusion of a cityscape. Soaring literally upward, once more he might evoke the uninitiated hero's hope for limitless flight as an escape from his duty to return to his people.[48] But given the way the story has evolved, we read Neo's ascendance as cutting the umbilical chord to mother Matrix, as he apparently no longer needs material telephone lines to transport himself between worlds. Perhaps as "the One," he has gotten the fragments of his self together.

Conclusion

Neither an array of spectacular effects nor a seamless extension of the myth of technology, *The Matrix* seems to occupy an uneasy middle ground between the two. By entering that contested center, we have tried to reconstruct this mythic tale by stitching its fragments together, all the while noting how the film's state-of-the-art technology tries to break them back apart. But perhaps there is a subtle inevitability at work here, for movies without spectacular effects, particularly when they are *about* technology, are unlikely to snag our attention. Yet this attention is also prone to disembody us. It may well be that any significant cultural statement about our technological predicament must entail an irony of myth and spectacle, for an omission of spectacle defies at least one reality and a compromise with awareness defiles another. If so, then perhaps seeing what there is to see in such films requires, as Morpheus teaches Neo, that we "free our minds" so as to feel our way simultaneously through worlds that are paradoxical.

PERSONAL COMMENTS ON THE ESSAY

"Sheee's baaackkk," I whisper, as Jane strolls confidently into Janice's office the next week.

"Yessss!!!" she proclaims. "I couldn't do that thing you gave me originally, but I can do this. Well, more realistically, I can do something like this," she says, emitting a miraculous memory trace of the modesty expected of a student.

"Well, let's see what you got," I say, cutting her no slack. "What do you take to be our central critical point?"

"That *The Matrix* is an important film because it extends the myth of Frankenstein narratively, but the special effects and action sequences deflect our attention away from that contribution," she answers, with the sort of memorized self-assurance that comes from guessing your professors would ask something like this.

"You go girl!" Janice applauds.

"See, we're not effete snobs after all," I say.

"Well, it's not like it's perfect," she adds, showing the edge we've come to consider charming. "I do have a few questions."

"Why doesn't that surprise me?" I ask.

"Like, for one thing, I remember you saying a couple weeks ago that a common error in mythic criticism is to retell the story using mythic language, instead of using a myth to come up with some non-obvious insights into the text, right?" "That's right," Janice agrees, and I can see that "Bad Teacher" sign reappear on her forehead.

"But it seems to me that your initial section, the one you call 'Departure,' is pretty much plot summary in mythic terms. You don't do that much with the tension between myth and spectacle there."

"You're right," Janice admits, trying not to sound defensive, "but that's because we took out the theoretical perspective of . . ."

"Naa, come on, you can't pull that number, Janice," I interrupt. "But there is more going on there than just plot summary. Remember that in this particular film, the mythic story is pretty fragmented from the get-go. Many of the critics we cite complain about that very thing. And so part of what we're trying to do in that first section is to reconstruct the narrative coherence to the overall story line, so that when, in the next section, we alert you to how the effects often undermine the myth, you'll have a feel for what's being undercut."

"So retelling a story in mythic terms is all right if it furthers your overall critical objective?" she asks.

"Sure," Janice says, "as long as that's not *all* you do. Do you see how we use the reactions of other film critics?"

"I think so," Jane responds. "You use them to set up what you intend to do. One set of critics is hung up on the special effects, while the other is all torqued out because the story, which might be important, doesn't make much sense. But neither group examines the effects *and* the story together—that's where you two come in. Right?"

"Right as rain," I say. "That's one way to *use* literature as part of an argument justifying what you intend to do in your critique. I've always found that using literature argumentatively, to justify your own critical posture, is hard for students to grasp. I'm not sure why, but part of the difficulty may be the connotation of the phrase, 'review of literature.' That suggests a *summary* more than an *argument*." "One thing bothers me, though," Jane says, ignoring my mini-lesson in research methods, as Janice is getting that concerned look again. "You guys cite so many sources that I don't know. Everything from some science fiction novel called *Neuromancer*, to lots of mythic sources I've never even heard of, to tons of old science fiction movies I've never seen. If I have to know all that to do this, I'm back to square one again!"

"Don't worry about that," I say. "We know all that stuff because we're old and we don't have lives . . . ."

"Speak for yourself, geezer guy," Janice cuts me off.

"You do need to do some reading, of course. But to do your version of what we've done here," I plow ahead, "all you really need, in addition to the reviews, is two central texts: Joseph Campbell's *The Hero With A Thousand Faces* and a video or DVD of *The Matrix*. Now, you would need to have read Campbell thoroughly, and you would need to have watched the film until you begin to use its dialogue in your everyday conversations, so it's not a piece of cake."

"I'll go with that, but I think she also needs some sources on the technology myth, so she'd know what's been said already about how this myth has evolved," Janice suggests.

"Yeah, do that in your spare time," I agree.

"Whew! Thanks, guys, this really eases my mind," Jane says, as she heads toward the door.

"So have you picked a text to write about?" Janice asks.

"*Fight Club*. I'm going to knock your socks off."

"I have no doubts. You can borrow my copy and watch it tonight," I say magnanimously.

"I'll take you up on that, but not tonight. Some of us from the class are getting together."

"To pop a few brews?" I query.

"They want me to talk about what I've been doing in here the last three weeks," she answers sheepishly. She's now at the head of the stairs, and she shouts back, "go read Campbell on 'The Ultimate Boon'—I'll expect a report tomorrow."

"She's like the Terminator," I whisper to Janice. "She'll be back."

"I know," Janice smiles. "Some kids these days are like we were. They just *are* 'perfect in every way.'"

Just as I'm heading off to class, Jane returns to stick her head in the door. "What kind of criticism do we do next?"

"Don't even *think* about it!" I say, catching her grin as we gently close the door behind her.

MYTHIC CRITICISM TOP PICKS

Barthes, Roland. *Mythologies.* Trans. A. Lavers. (New York: Wang and Hill, 1957). One of the most influential books on mythology for cultural studies, this book is a brilliant collection of short essays on myth in French life of the 1950s. It is one of "the" works that illustrates how myth works ideologically in everyday life. The long concluding essay, "Myth Today," lays out Barthes's semiological method of analysis, and is as difficult as it is important. But the short essays can be read by a novice, and are fascinating.

Campbell, Joseph. *The Hero With a Thousand Faces* (Princeton: Princeton University Press/Bollingen Series 17, 1949/1972). Referred to throughout this chapter, this book is one of the most-used and best-known sources on the hero myth.

Freud, Sigmund. *A General Introduction to Psycho-analysis* (New York: Pocket Books, 1920/1952). Reissued as *Introductory Lectures on Psycho-analysis.* Trans. and Ed. James Strachey. Intro. Peter Gay. (New York: W. W. Norton Co., 1989). A comprehensive overview of Freud's theories of the unconscious, including his ways of thinking about errors ("Freudian slips"), individual pathologies, dreams, folklore, art, and myth.

Jung, Carl G., Marie-Louise von Franz, Joseph L. Henderson, Jolande Jacobs, and Aniela Jaffe, eds. *Man and his Symbols* (Garden City, New York: Doubleday and Company, 1964). A good introduction to Jung's "archetypes" and how they occur in art and myth. This is a "coffee table book," beautifully illustrated and written for the lay person rather than the theorist. It includes chapters by Jung and several of his followers.

Lawrence, John Shelton and Robert Jewett. *The Myth of the American Superhero* (Grand Rapids, MI: Wm. B. Eerdmans Publishing Co., 2002). Extends their first book, *The American Monomyth*, into popular culture in the current era, arguing that the most typical American hero myth differs from Campbell's monomyth in significant ways.

Mackey-Kallis, Susan. *The Hero and the Perennial Journey Home in American Film* (Philadelphia: University of Pennsylvania Press, 2001). Adapts Perennial Philosophy and mythic frameworks such as Joseph Campbell's to the analysis of many American films.

Morford, Mark P. O. and Robert J. Lenardon. *Classical Mythology*. 7th ed. (Oxford: Oxford University Press, 2003). A great reference for classic Greek and Roman mythology. It includes the stories themselves, plus interpretations, as well as a comprehensive review of mythology in literature, art, music, dance, and film. For classical mythology, this is that "list in the sky" referred to in the chapter.

McGee, Michael C. "In Search of 'The People': A Rhetorical Alternative." *Quarterly Journal of Speech* 61 (1975): 235–249. This article, along with several of McGee's essays, helped push the field of Communication into thinking about rhetoric in a Marxist vein. Here, McGee considers how myths form, decay, and compete with one another through rhetorical processes.

Murdock, Maureen. *The Heroine's Journey: Woman's Quest for Wholeness* (Boston: Shambhala, 1990). An important companion piece to Joseph Campbell's *The Hero With a Thousand Faces*, because Murdock argues that Campbell's monomyth does not generalize well to women. She builds an alternative mythic framework for heroines by adapting and changing crucial aspects of Campbell's monomyth.

Rushing, Janice Hocker and Thomas S. Frentz. *Projecting the Shadow: The Cyborg Hero in American Film* (Chicago: University of Chicago Press, 1995). This book integrates archetypal and ideological aspects of myth so as to examine the Frankenstein myth of technology in popular films. The analysis of *The Matrix* in this chapter depends upon the framework developed in this book.

NOTES

1. Kris Kristofferson, "The Pilgrim: Chapter 33," Perf. Kris Kristofferson. *The Austin Sessions* (Atlantic Recording Corporation, 1999).

2. Joseph Campbell, *Myths to Live By* (New York: Bantam Books, 1972), 10.

3. Rowland Barthes, *Mythologies*, trans. A. Lavers (New York: Wang and Hill, 1957).

4. Campbell, *Myths to Live By*; Anthony Storr, *The Essential Jung* (Princeton: Princeton University Press, 1983).

5. Vivian Sobchack, "The Virginity of Astronauts: Sex and the Science Fiction Film," in *Alien Zone: Cultural Theory and Contemporary Science Fiction Cinema*, ed. Annette Kuhn (New York/London: Verso, 1990), 103–115. See also Constance Penley, "Time Travel, Primal Scene, and the Critical Dystopia," in *The Future of an Illusion: Film, Feminism, and Psychoanalysis* (Minneapolis: Univ. of Minnesota Press, 1989), 121–139; Sonia Livingstone and Tamar Liebes, "Where Have All the Mothers Gone? Soap Opera's Replaying of the Oedipal Story," *Critical Studies in Mass Communication* 12 (1995): 155–175.

6. Robert A. Davies, James M. Farrell, and Steven S. Matthews, "The Dream World of Film: A Jungian Perspective on Cinematic Communication," *Western Journal of Speech Communication* 46 (1982): 326–343.

7. Mark P. O. Morford and Robert J. Lenardon, *Classical Mythology*. 7th ed. (Oxford: Oxford University Press, 2003).

8. Joseph Campbell, *The Hero With a Thousand Faces* (Princeton: Princeton University Press/ Bollingen Series 17, 1949/1972).

9. Susan Mackey-Kallis, *The Hero and the Perennial Journey Home in American Film* (Philadelphia: University of Pennsylvania Press, 2001), 27–33.

10. Janice Hocker Rushing and Thomas S. Frentz, "Singing Over the Bones: James Cameron's *Titanic*" in *Critical Studies in Mass Communication* 17 (2000): 1–27.

11. Janice Hocker Rushing, "The Rhetoric of the American Western Myth," *Communication Monographs* 50 (1983): 14–32; Janice Hocker Rushing, "Evolution of 'The New Frontier' in *Alien* and *Aliens*: Patriarchal Co-optation of the Feminine Archetype," *Quarterly Journal of Speech* 75 (1989): 1–24; Janice Hocker Rushing, "Mythic Evolution of 'The New Frontier' in Mass Mediated Rhetoric," *Critical Studies in Mass Communication* 3 (1986): 265–296.

12. Mary Shelley, *Frankenstein* (New York: Bantam, 1818/1991); Janice Hocker Rushing and Thomas S. Frentz, "The Frankenstein Myth in Contemporary Cinema," *Critical Studies in Mass Communication* 6 (1989): 61–80; Janice Hocker Rushing and Thomas S. Frentz, *Projecting the Shadow: The Cyborg Hero in American Film* (Chicago: University of Chicago Press, 1995).

13. Robert Jewett and John Shelton Lawrence, *The American Monomyth* (Garden City, New York: Anchor/Doubleday, 1977); John Shelton Lawrence and Robert Jewett, *The Myth of the American Superhero* (Grand Rapids, MI: Wm. B. Eerdmans Publishing Co., 2002).

14. Walter R Fisher, "Reaffirmation and Subversion of the American Dream," *Quarterly Journal of Speech* 59 (1973): 160–167; John Arthos Jr. "The Shaman-Trickster's Art of Misdirection: The Rhetoric of Farrakhan and the Million Men," *Quarterly Journal of Speech* 87 (2001): 25–40; Randall A. Lake, "Between Myth and History: Enacting Time in Native American Protest Rhetoric," *Quarterly Journal of Speech* 77 (1991): 123–151; Farrel Corcoran, "The Bear in the Back Yard: Myth, Ideology, and Victimage Ritual in Soviet Funerals," *Communication Monographs* 50 (1983): 305–320.

15. Karen Rasmussen and Sharon D. Downey, "Dialectical Disorientation in Vietnam War Films: Subversion of the Mythology of War," *Quarterly Journal of Speech* 77 (1991): 176–195; Penley.

16. Thomas S. Frentz and Janice Hocker Rushing, "'Mother Isn't Quite Herself Today': Myth and Spectacle in *The Matrix*," *Critical Studies in Media Communication* 19 (2002): 64–86.

17. Andrew O'Hehir, "Short Attention Spawn," *Salon*, April 2, 1999, n. pag. (online magazine). Retrieved April 6, 1999 from the World Wide Web: http://www.salon.com/ent/movies/reviews/1999/04/02reviewa.html

18. Lisa Schwarzbaum, "The Matrix," *EW Online*, April 2, 1999, n. pag. (online magazine). Retrieved April 8, 1999 from the World Wide Web: http://www.ew.com/ew/review/movie/0,1683,563,matrix.html

19. Bob Graham, "Lost in the 'Matrix,'" *San Francisco Chronicle*, March 31, 1999, E-1. (online newspaper). Retrieved April 29, 1999 from the World Wide Web: http://www.sfgate.com/cgi/bin/article.cgi?file=/chronicle/archive/1999/3/31DD49124.DTL

20. Roger Ebert, "The Matrix," *The Chicago Sun Times*, March 3, 1999, n. pag. (online newspaper). Retrieved March 10, 1999 from the World Wide Web: http://www.suntimes.com/ebert_reviews/1999/03/033101.html

21. Stuart Klawans, "The End of Humanism," *The Nation*, April 26, 1999, n. pag. (online magazine). Retrieved April 30, 1999 from the World Wide Web: http://www.thenation.com/issue/990426/0426klawans.shtml

22. Anthony Ferrante, "The Matrix," *Eonline*, April 2, 1999, n. pag. (online magazine). Retrieved April 28, 1999 from the World Wide Web: http://www.eonline.com/Review/Facts/Movies/Reviews/0,1052,71731,00.html

23. O'Hehir, n. pag.

24. Issac Asimov, "The Myth of the Machine," *Asimov on Science Fiction* (Garden City, New York: Doubleday, 1981), 160–162; Rushing and Frentz, "The Frankenstein Myth in Contemporary Cinema"; Rushing and Frentz, *Projecting the Shadow*, 67; Langdon Winner, *Autonomous Technology: Technics-out-of-control as a Theme in Political Thought* (Cambridge, Mass.: The MIT Press, 1977), 280.

25. Shelley.

26. Rushing and Frentz, *Projecting the Shadow*.

27. Campbell, *The Hero with a Thousand Faces*.

28. Thanks to Roberto Loar for calling our attention to the importance of this dialogue.

29. We are indebted to Tai Estopy for this insight.

30. *Merriam-Webster's New Collegiate Dictionary*, 7th ed. (Springfield, MA.: G. & C. Merriam Company, Webster's, 1967), 522.

31. Chad Eby, *Hacking the Body: The Puer Aeternus in Cyberspace* (Unpublished master's thesis, University of Arkansas, Fayetteville, Arkansas, 1997), 26–27.

32. James S. Beard, *Rhetorical Mapping of Technological Psychosis: A Burkean Reading of William Gibson's* Neuromancer (Unpublished doctoral dissertation, Northwestern University, Evanston, Illinois, 1999), 98.

33. Rushing and Frentz, *Projecting the Shadow*; see also Campbell, *The Hero with a Thousand Faces,* 109–120.

34. Roger Horrocks sees this as a common autoerotic theme in westerns. *Male Myths and Icons: Masculinity in Popular Culture* (New York: St. Martin's Press, 1995), 54.

35. We are indebted again to Roberto Loar for his careful reading of this scene.

36. Campbell, *The Hero with a Thousand Faces*, 90–95.

37. Rushing and Frentz, *Projecting the Shadow*, 213.

38. Joseph L. Henderson, "Ancient Myths and Modern Man" in *Man and His Symbols*, eds. Carl G. Jung, Marie-Louise von Franz, Joseph L. Henderson, Jolande Jacobi, and Aniela Jaffe (Garden City, New York: Doubleday, 1964), 130.

39. Campbell, *The Hero with a Thousand Faces*, 69–77.

40. Rushing and Frentz, *Projecting the Shadow*, 25–27.

41. According to O'Hehir, in Hollywood, "blackness is the universally understood symbol for superior wisdom," n. pag.

42. Ralph Abraham, *Chaos, Gaia, Eros: A Chaos Pioneer Uncovers the Three Great Streams of History* (New York: HarperSanFrancisco, 1994), 84–85; Barbara Walker, *The Woman's Encyclopedia of Myths and Secrets* (San Francisco: Harper & Row, 1983), 1018.

43. Sobchack, 106.

44. Campbell, *The Hero with a Thousand Faces*, 172–192.

45. Rushing and Frentz, *Projecting the Shadow*, 74–75.

46. We are indebted to Grant Florer for this observation.

47. Rushing and Frentz, *Projecting the Shadow*; Marshall McLuhan, *Understanding Media: The Extensions of Man* (New York: McGraw-Hill, 1965). 41–47.

48. Campbell, *The Hero with a Thousand Faces*, 196–207.

15

Feminist Analysis

Donna M. Nudd and Kristina L. Whalen

WHY FEMINISM?

Susan Faludi once said, "all women are born feminists, but most get it knocked out of them."[1] In fact, on most high schools and college campuses professors chronicle the "I'm not a feminist but" phenomenon that suggests Faludi is right. In other words, although most women will not self-identify as a feminist, many will profess agreement with the ideals comprising a feminist agenda. So, we have many women (and men) saying, "I'm not a feminist, but I believe in equal opportunity" or "I'm not a feminist, but I believe women should be treated with dignity and respect." This trend led bell hooks to conclude that a more profitable way to offer feminism is to say "I advocate feminism" rather than "I am a feminist." The first phrase "discourages a focus on stereotyped perspectives of feminism . . . and prompts the question 'What is feminism?'"[2]

Describing feminism is, however, a daunting and complex task since feminism has many different veins of thought. These varying perspectives make talking about feminism, in general, quite difficult. Despite its difficulty, communication scholars Cheris Kramarae and Paula Treichler explain their version of feminism as, "the radical notion that women are people."[3] Although Kramarae and Treichler's definition does not capture the theoretical disagreements that exist in feminism, it does express the common spirit of most strands of feminism. *Feminism is a pluralistic movement interested in altering the political and social landscape so that all people, regardless of their identity categories, can experience freedom and safety, complexity and subjectivity, and economic and political parity—experiences associated with being fully human.*

Feminist advocates argue for the necessity and profitability of their activism and critical inquiry by evidencing the *patriarchal* systems most civilizations have been operating under for several thousand years. Although some critics, even feminist critics, argue that we are now living in a post-patriarchal world[4], the majority of feminist critics believe that patriarchy is still entrenched in our political and value systems. For example, Allan G. Johnson writes that three principles encompass the still present patriarchal system: male domination, male-identification, and male-centeredness. According to Johnson, *male domination* refers to the simple fact that men have populated most positions of authority in major societies. Men head large corporations, nation-states, churches, colleges and universities, and most other positions of social importance. While a few women have temporarily taken these seats of prestige, the exceptions have done little to dismantle male domination. In sum, the exceptions are too infrequent and account for only a small fraction of power positions. Johnson outlines the consequences of male domination by writing, "[Male domination] means that men can shape culture in ways that reflect and serve men's collective interest." Additionally, he adds, "male domination promotes the idea that men are superior to women."[5]

Johnson believes that a critique of patriarchy is incomplete if it simply notes degrees of male domination. He argues that we must also note instances of *male identification*. Male identification locates our cultural values in maleness and masculinity. According to Johnson, in a male-identified society the activities of men underscore what it preferred, normal and desirable. The qualities commonly associated with masculinity, such as competition, individualism, invulnerability, rationality, and physical strength, are honored. The qualities commonly associated with femininity, such as cooperation, nurturing, emotionality, and care, are undervalued or trivialized.[6] Besides being undervalued, feminine identified people in our masculine-identified society are measured by a rigged yardstick. What is deemed desirable is always out of reach. Though competition is valued in our society, being a woman carries expectations of acting feminine; hence, acting aggressively and competitively will often be met with disapproval, if not hostility. However, a woman never exercising qualities associated with masculinity has little chance for advancement, since those are the qualities our society rewards. These basic assertions about male identification are not categorically true. Some women appear to successfully pair feminine traits with a masculine sensibility. A handful of critics point to the rash of recent films and television shows that feature conventional feminine beauty with highly physical and aggressive feats (*Alias, Charlie's Angels, Dark Angel, Tomb Raider*) as evidence that male and female identification are becoming intertwined. However, Mary Spicuzza notes that even these shows deserve our critical attention. She writes, "plenty of butt kicking women on screen are ultimately concerned with being sexy, finding a man to complete their lives, and settling down." Spicuzza, quoting many communication scholars, adds, "women heroines are less concerned with achieving female liberation than satisfying male fantasy."[7] Regardless where one stands on this media issue, it is clear that matters surrounding gender identification are complicated, fluctuating, and ripe territory for the rhetorical critic.

Finally, Johnson advocates a focus on our society's *male centeredness*, meaning that our cultural attention is mainly focused on males. "Pick up any newspaper or go to any movie theater and you'll find stories primarily about men and what they've done or haven't done or what they have to say about either."[8] Sporting activities represent one of many culturally significant areas where men seek and receive acclaim. Large populations of men and women watch men's sporting events. Millions watch the Super Bowl, Monday Night football, the World Series, and the NBA Championship series.[9] Advertisers spent copious amounts of money to market products during these events knowing the viewing audience is large. Although women play sports, they do not attract an equivalent viewing audience. The rise of the WNBA provides evidence for a male centered as well as a male-identified society. Naming the organization the *Women's* National Basketball Association highlights that men play a "normal" game of basketball. If one were to say, "I'm going to watch a basketball game," in most cases the assumption would be that a men's game was about to be viewed. A feminist critic would likely argue that the male centeredness is so seemingly natural in our society it remains unspoken. However, if one were watching a basketball game featuring female players, chances are the sex of the players would be spotlighted: "I'm watching a *women's* basketball game," thus underscoring it's a deviation from the norm.

Feminists argue that the mixture of male centeredness and male identification create enormous disparities in our society. With one sex, and the corresponding gendered system attached to biology, at society's center a systematic disparity is maintained. Females and/or femininity are rendered invisible or marginalized under the patriarchal rubric. Carol Tavris notes the invisibility of women in our patriarchal history: "In history, the implicit use of men as the norm pervades much of what school children learn about American and Western civilization. Was Greece the cradle of democracy? It was no democracy for women and slaves. Was the Renaissance a time of intellectual and artistic rebirth? There was no renaissance for women."[10] Tavris maintains that the stories told in our society about our history, our struggles, our values, are wrapped up in masculine precepts. As such, the experiences following the culturally constructed ideas of femininity receive little attention and thus are given little value. Many feminists argue that this occurs because we have bound biological sex with a narrow set of socially constructed ideas about how that sex operates—those constructed ideas are called *gender*.

However important it is to point out the features of patriarchy, sexist oppression is not the only oppression of interest to feminism. Late twentieth century feminism concerned itself with interlocking systems of oppression, noting that most systems of discrimination share common characteristics and must be seen together if liberation struggles are to gain ground. For these reasons feminist scholars such as bell hooks reference the dominant framework as a *white supremacist capitalist patriarchy*.[11] This term underscores that we not only live in a sexist society but a society that discriminates based on economic circumstances and race. A thorough feminist critique will not fail to interrogate how all these ideological systems work together to marginalize discrete groups of people.

So, we will summarize by answering the question that heads this section: Why Feminism? Most feminists believe that we live in a complex social structure guided by patriarchy. They believe this patriarchal system must change, and that criticism may be used as a tool to help foster change. Moreover, the understanding of patriarchy cannot be a simple calculation. Engaged human beings are likely to identify egregious cases of sexism; however, most feminists believe that much of the sexism of the patriarchal framework remains unchallenged. Feminists therefore are motivated to expose the fundamental ways, the often subtle, taken for granted ways, in which societal members undervalue and diminish women. With that done, feminists propose new ideas, assumptions, and viewpoints allowing for humans to realize a wide range of possibilities and promise. But, as stated before, not all feminists are alike; therefore, different feminists have different priorities and solutions. In the next section, we will explore these differences and their relationship to rhetorical criticism.

AN INTRODUCTION TO FEMINIST RHETORICAL CRITICISM

Feminist thought has always been quite diverse in its theories and practices. One of the main theoretical differences among various feminists surrounds disagreements over gender differences. This disagreement is referred to in feminist writings as the "minimalist/maximalist debate." A feminist *minimalist* believes that men and women are more alike than different; therefore, the policies and social organizations privileging men can easily adapt to women if they are just granted access. *Maximalists* believe that women and men are more different than alike. With that premise in mind, feminist maximalists argue that women will never achieve success and comfort in social institutions created by men for men, and thus our social and political landscape must be altered or transformed to accommodate the distinctions between men and women.

From this theoretical debate, many categories of feminism have emerged. Jill Dolan notes that we can generally see American feminism separated into liberal, cultural, and materialist segments.[12] Liberal feminist approaches locate the oppression of women in the systematic failure to include women in dominant structures and cultural production. A liberal feminist rhetorical critique would be interested in the exclusion of women from systems of representation. Are women given a voice in the political system? Can you find women in recent films you've seen, stories read? If so, how many women were featured in comparison to men? Did the stories showcase the women as competent, able to solve problems, lead others, and champion a cause? Liberal rhetorical feminist critics are diligently employing language strategies within the current structures to increase the stature and number of women in places of political and social power. Liberal feminists are also minimalists.

Cultural feminists, on the other hand, are maximalists. They argue that women's nature, primarily shaped by the ability to give birth, is decidedly different from men's. "Because they can give birth, women are viewed as instinctually more natural, more closely related to life cycles mirrored in nature."[13] Cultural feminists argue that women have a unique and valuable perspective that is not adequately reflected in today's society. This deficit of perspective creates a world of domination and violence. Moreover, some cultural feminists have situated themselves within another subcategory of feminist thought, eco-feminism. Eco-feminists believe that if society adopted the non-dominating feminine perspective, the likelihood of continuing ecological devastation would diminish. But this is just one of many cultural feminist perspectives. A rhetorical critic adopting a cultural feminist perspective is likely to critique current rhetorical practices for their sexist domination as well as suggest ways in which a feminine perspective could rehabilitate the rhetorical situation. Does a given communication artifact convey the largely feminine characteristics of caring, nurturing, cooperation, and intuition? Does it glorify aggression, competition, and individualism to the exclusion of other perspectives? How do the messages around us "normalize" a distinctly masculine perspective? How could we infuse and balance our public discourse by including a feminine perspective? These are some of the many questions guiding the explorations of a rhetorical critic that is also a cultural feminist.

Finally, materialist feminists believe that symbol-using humans are historical subjects that are largely socially constructed, not biologically driven. A materialist feminist is interested in analyzing social conditions, such as the influence of race, sexual orientation, and class that work together to define women and men as categories and seemingly erase the possibility of other categories being established, i.e. intersexed and transgendered. As such, this strand of feminism is also interested in unearthing the symbolic systems of gender that oppress all people, not just women. Materialist feminists may study the way masculinity has been constructed in such a way that men, too, have little freedom and dimension in society. So, while liberal feminists are primarily interested in social representation, materialist feminists reveal how people "have been oppressed by gender categories."[14] A materialist feminist might approach a rhetorical artifact by noting the ways in which a particular rhetorical artifact situates masculinity and femininity as stale categories, instead of giving the concept room for growth and movement. Do movies, or other culturally significant discourse, outfit men and women with retrograde notions of masculinity and femininity? How so? Can we point to messages around us that transform the somewhat rigid categories of gender in positive ways? These and similar questions would be of interest to the rhetorical critic with a materialist feminist perspective.

Positioning materialist feminism along the minimalist/maximalist continuum demands some attention. Since materialists stress the social construction of gender, they very rarely look for "real" differences and similarities. Instead, materialists question the constructed categories of gender and offer the concepts dimension and redefinition if it aids the attainment of freedom, safety, complexity, subjectivity, and equality—the goals of feminism.

Although these categories represent large sects of feminist thought, other feminists strands not covered in this chapter apply a feminist lens to a Marxist perspective, psychoanalytical thought, and global issues; there are even feminists operating from libertarian and conservative political perspectives.[15] Feminists in different academic fields have established a literature base specific to their field of inquiry. Therefore, one is likely to see feminist legal studies, feminist international relations, and feminist medicine as well as feminist literary criticism. Women of color, who have traditionally had a complicated relationship with feminism, are interested in the way their ethnic and racial identities intersect with feminism. So, if one delves into the literature about feminism, one is likely to see discussions about Chicana feminism, Black feminism, Asian feminism, and Native American feminism to name a few.[16] When engaging in feminist rhetorical criticism, consideration should be given to how the critic positions an argument on the map of feminism so that those reading the criticism know the assumptions about gender infused in the analysis.

In this next section we will first briefly outline the history of feminist criticism within the rhetorical tradition. Next, an explanation of the approaches feminist rhetorical critics utilize to analyze our symbolic systems will follow. Alongside these general explanations numerous specific examples from feminist rhetorical critics will be provided.

FEMINIST CRITICISM AND THE CHALLENGE TO RHETORIC

The *rhetorical tradition* tethers itself to a long history of oral argument and public oratory. This tradition also has an equally long history of excluding female rhetors or feminine ways of speaking.[17] Sometimes this was done either by making public address unavailable to women through systematic discrimination or by refusing to recognize the many women who did take the podium. When feminist thought merges with rhetorical criticism it is usually an attempt to foreground how gender is operating or being sculpted in particular ways by language choices. Feminists are also interested in discovering new symbolic strategies, or making visible little known language systems, in an effort to dismantle current gender hierarchies. So, another important part of feminist rhetorical criticism is suggesting that alternative, yet equally valid forms of producing symbolic meaning exist.[18] Although we do know that many women enlisted public address as a vehicle for their ideas, we also know that women's position in society relegated message making to other terrain. Feminist rhetorical criticism reclaims this forgotten rhetorical past. All of these concerns have meant that feminist rhetorical scholars have developed somewhat unique approaches to analyzing rhetorical artifacts.

Since feminists are interested in changing the mainstream value system in which we live, one avenue of feminist rhetorical criticism involves using the techniques of rhetorical criticism (many covered in this book), applying a feminist lens or agenda, and analyzing the text. It should not be surprising, given the activist approach of feminist rhetorical scholars, that many use these techniques to study their own feminist history. For example, Susan Schultz Huxman studied the rhetorical vision of Elizabeth Cady Stanton, Anna Howard Shaw, and Carrie Chapman Catt, early feminist leaders in the late nineteenth and early twentieth centuries. While analyzing the most notable speeches of each revolutionary, Schultz explains that even though the women had disagreements and conflict, when viewed as a rhetorical package the womens' views worked well together and strengthened the larger women's right movement.[19] Knowing how rhetoric functioned in the past gives today's feminists an important body of knowledge from which to work for change.

Feminists working for contemporary social change, using modern technology and sensibilities, also receive ample attention by feminist rhetorical critics. For example, Anne Teresa Demo explored the visual rhetoric of the Guerrilla Girls, a New York activist group that challenges the sexism of the art world. Guerrilla Girls, formed in mid 1980s and still active today, use posters, bill boards, flyers, and press conferences to draw attention to under representation of female artists in galleries, museums, and art history reviews. Guerrilla Girls never reveal their identity; instead, they appear on literature and at press conferences clothed in black garb and gorilla masks. Demo analyzes the group's rhetoric, largely visual in nature, and argues that their techniques of *humorous mimicry* (they mimic traditional femininity by using the color pink, calling themselves "girls," and writing in ultrapolite, feminine tones), *historical revision* (they published their own art history book and take on the persona of overlooked artists in press conferences), and *strategic comparison* (they use quotes given by conservatives to support their progressive agenda) are persuasive because they highlight the tension and incongruity in our social order.

While analyzing speeches and texts particular to the feminist agenda remains essential, today feminist rhetorical scholars analyze a vast array of cultural communication for its relation to gender concepts. Not surprisingly, feminist rhetorical critics tend to focus on mediated communication since it transmits messages about gender widely and quickly.

Brenda Cooper, for example, examines the narrative structure of the film *Thelma & Louise*. By examining the way the movie was filmed and the point of view privileged by the movie's plot packaging and camera angles, Cooper argues that *Thelma & Louise* turns the idea of a "male gaze" on its head and, in turn, constructs a "female gaze." Put differently, the film is framed in such a way that it makes a mockery of violent masculinity and blatant sexism—activities glorified in many other Hollywood films. Cooper provides many examples in which the audience sees "female characters actively challenging patriarchal conventions rarely available in mainstream media."[20]

Feminist rhetorical scholars Kristin J. Anderson and Christina Accomando analyze the 1998 box office smash *Something About Mary* for the way the film normalizes stalking, a crime that disproportionately affects women, and blames the victim, in this case, Mary. They do not, however, end their analysis with the film itself. They also look at the way movie reviews serve to translate the misogynist messages of *Something About Mary*. To support their conclusions, Anderson and Accomando analyze the use of a modern Greek chorus in the film. When another stalker is revealed in the film, the chorus returns to sing, "'There's something about Mary that [those who don't know her] don't know.' That is there's something about Mary that actually causes men to stalk her."[21] Turning their attention to reviews, Anderson and Accomando analyze the description of stalking in major newspapers for the authoritative framing of the criminal behavior. They write, "How is the film described if it isn't described as a woman stalked by five men? Reviews construct the film as, at least in part, a sweet and innocent love story." By constantly referring to the stalking as romantic behavior, the theorist note, "That half the reviews examined here reinterpret illegal surveillance techniques, false identities, and violence . . . to mean courtship."[22]

Having been introduced to some examples of feminist rhetorical criticism, the section that follows concretely outlines some of the more common methods of feminist criticism used by rhetorical scholars. It is not meant to be an exhaustive list, but you should be able to see that many of the approaches discussed in the following section were used in the examples of feminist rhetorical criticism described above.

APPROACHES TO USING FEMINIST CRITICISM

Feminist rhetorical scholars are important to feminism because they see patriarchy as being maintained by a symbolic system, a language that defines gender in narrow and specific ways. Through our communication practices and language choices we have both a poverty and power when it comes to gender. The poverty comes when our language use sculpts masculinity and femininity in ways that are not complex, resulting in disparity and domination. Another poverty of thinking occurs when language and communication practices are used so that masculinity and femininity are seen as the only two gendered choices. In some cultures, Native American cultures for example, more than two genders exist.[23] Many feminists are interested in opening up our symbolic system so that many genders flourish and those wanting to express themselves outside of our current gender codes feel the freedom to do so. Herein lays the power of language. By systematically analyzing our language choices and communication practices, one can in part effectively undermine the patriarchal logic of gender. This is the work of feminist rhetorical critics.

There are perhaps countless ways one could go about analyzing rhetorical artifacts for the meaning produced about gender. However, if one looks over the history of feminist rhetorical criticism, four prominent critical techniques emerge.[24]

(1) Feminists are interested in *redefining* gendered ideals and gendered behavior.
(2) Feminist rhetorical scholars are *recovering* communication practices that have been forgotten or considered unimportant.
(3) Feminist rhetorical criticism is interested in *recording* the cultural production of the rhetorical artifacts we consume so as to uncover the ways in which gender is created (as well as arguing that gender is created, not natural).
(4) Feminist rhetorical theorists engage in a *revisioning* of rhetorical theory; they create new theories of rhetoric that champion feminist ideals.

As mentioned earlier, depending on the type of feminism to which one subscribes, some of the choices will be more or less appealing. For example, liberal feminists are interested in women's representation in the current social world. Therefore, a liberal feminist might be more interested in the second and third critical approach. Liberal feminists particular theoretical interests make showcasing forgotten female rhetors and demonstrating how women are excluded from the communication process a priority. Materialist and cultural feminists, interested in reordering our values and institutions, might favor techniques one and four, since both suggest new ways of thinking. That being said, it is possible that all feminist theoretical perspectives could use any number of these approaches, in any combination, to further knowledge about their feminist argument.

Redefining

While attempting to redefine what it means to be a gendered human being, feminist rhetorical critics generally undertake one of several tasks. First, feminist rhetorical critics note the way language is used to describe gendered ideals in stereotypical ways. Second, they try to create new language that will give nonpatriarchal dimension to people's lives or a language to effectively demystify patriarchy. Third, feminist critics reclaim words used to straightjacket masculinity and femininity and thereby infuse them with new meaning.

Feminist scholars have long held the premise that patriarchy is largely maintained by language. Put differently, male domination, male identification, and male centeredness are stable ideas because the words we use in everyday speech acts to keep them anchored. Dale Spender argues that language is man-made.[25] Men "invented" the words we now use to convey meaning. For much of our rhetorical history, men held center stage; the words they used to generate ideas were disseminated and popularized. Women's words were silence. Man-made words became further entrenched when societies created dictionaries that discerned what a *real* word is. Dictionaries quickly became the definitive authority for what was excluded and included in our language. However, the sources used by dictionary makers were overwhelmingly male authored. The words coined by women to describe their experiences and social situation fell off the map. Kramarae writes, "The dictionary is not designed by women or for women's exercise of imagination. . . . It's not only a hostile system for women, but it is constantly referred to as the only system. It does not encourage ideas or new connections and relationships, or imagination about how we could write and talk our past and future."[26] Every year new words are added to standard dictionaries, but the initial deficit of language, it is argued, still haunts women today. Thus, it is important to note the way language is often used to paint a biased picture of gender. The words we choose often unknowingly privilege a patriarchal perspective. As such, feminists are interested in making visible the current, and inadequate, language systems in our culture. Also, women strive to symbolically represent, and thus legitimate, experiences they could not previously explain. For example, words such as sexual harassment did not exist until the second wave of feminism took root in the 1970s.[27]

Another example of this sort of redefinition can be found when exploring the intersections of oppression. Black American women, and often men, were subjected to a color caste system. Black Americans with lighter skin and European facial features consciously and subconsciously gained more privilege and were considered more attractive in both white and black communities. Today, and this is especially true for black women, some of the most prominently featured sport straight hair, Anglo facial features, and lighter skin shades.[28] This subtextual belief was difficult to talk about until it was given a name: Colorism. Colorism describes the discrimination that many blacks experience, a discrimination that is certainly racist, but also can be a very complicated mixture of racism and sexism. While some prominent athletes that do not fit the Anglo mold have gained the cultural spotlight, here one can see some examples of colorism's influence. *Ebony*, a magazine targeting an African American audience, featured tennis great Serena Williams on its October 2000 issue. Although Serena, and her sister Venus, stormed and transformed the largely Caucasian tennis world with their muscular bodies and beaded hair, *Ebony*'s cover showed Serena with long, blond and straight hair. It is difficult to draw complete conclusions from this example. Serena may have considered the implications of the look and chosen it anyway. Feminists of course believe in personal choice. What this demonstrates is words like colorism and sexual harassment can be controversial because it is not always clear when it is appropriate to use new language. Yet, many feminists believe that a healthy dialogue about such issues will not only legitimate the definitions but also clarify their boundaries.

The second definitional technique used by feminists involves taking words that were once used to diminish femininity and reclaiming them for feminist purposes. Mary Daly notes that under patriarchy, the term "spinster" is a sexist category used to label unmarried women as unfulfilled and useless. No such derogatory word exists for men choosing not to wed. Daly turns the notion of spinster on its head by repeatedly using the term to mean "one who spins." She adds, "A woman whose occupation is to spin participates in the whirling movement of creation."[29]

Riot Grrrls, started by punk rockers in Washington D.C, also use nondeferential language in their own publications (called "zines," as in short, self-published magazines) to reshape and redefine femininity. "Riot grrrls see zine writing and publishing as a basic method of empowerment; zine production is self-motivated, political activism that a girl can do entirely independently. Zines subvert standard patriarchal mainstream media by critiquing society and the media without being censored."[30] The language play involved with naming the group Riot Grrrls should not escape notice. Changing the spelling of "girl" to "grrrl" visually as well as semantically alters the passivity of the word. When a growl is added to the word, it is given force and stature.

Many feminist critics have taken to writing their own dictionary definitions or altogether rewriting the dictionary.[31] While inventing new language is often considered "against the rules," many feminists argue the language rules are rigged and need to be reorganized and reinvigorated. Feminist rhetorical criticism utilizing redefinition (1) explains and names how language functions to regulate femininity and masculinity and/or (2) creates or reinvents language that expands the possibilities of gender.

Recovering

Throughout this chapter, you will hear that women and feminine ways of speaking have been systematically excluded from the public realm for much of the rhetorical tradition. However, this exclusion was not complete. For periods of time, generally around social reform platforms such as suffrage and abolition, women produced rhetorical texts. However, in most compilations of public speeches, women account for a small percentage of speakers. Although the historical exclusion of female rhetors is partly responsible for the disparity, it does not always explain their absence. Regardless of the dearth, the notable absence of women "confirms that men continue to serve as standard for communication performance and that women are peripheral in terms of significant discourse."[32]

Karlyn Kohrs Campbell's anthology *Man Cannot Speak for Her* uses the approach of recovering rhetors lost in a male-centered society. Also, Kohrs Campbell's work recovers the rhetorical options surreptitiously proposed by women facing enormous prohibitions. Despite being discouraged from taking the podium, women such as Christine de Pizan, a 14th century French feminist, wrote books for women that clearly serve as rhetorical theory. Christine de Pizan's books *The Book of the City of Ladies* and *The Treasure of the City of Ladies* provide discursive theory that differs from the dominant traditions of time, but is no less valuable. Kohrs Campbell takes issue with many rhetorical scholars that argue "no woman has added to rhetorical theory during this time."[33] According to Kohrs Campbell, the "practices in *The Book of the City of Ladies* add an important dimension to understanding the power of conversation as performance and, in that sense, embodied discourse."[34]

Not all feminist recovering involves archival investigations of classical texts. In contemporary artifacts, our patriarchal society often pushes women to the margins. Elizabeth Dole, for example, was criticized for stepping down from her office at the Department of Transportation when her husband ran for president in 1996. However, a feminist rhetorical analysis demonstrates that Dole's rhetorical significance should not be overlooked. Gutgold notes that Dole was a groundbreaking rhetor at the Republican National Convention in 1996. Her rhetorical style, infused with stories, personal pronouns, and nonverbal intimacy, had never been seen at a political convention. Although Gutgold ultimately argues that Dole was unsuccessful in transitioning to a Presidential candidate, "Dole's long and varied career makes for an ideal exploration into how a woman modifies her speech with her changing roles."[35] As more women enter the public arena, feminist analysis grows increasingly necessary.

Feminist rhetorical critics approaching a rhetorical artifact by recovering are (1) acknowledging rhetors that patriarchy has erased and/or (2) recovering the lost significance of a visible female rhetor.

Recording

Another analytical approach used by feminists is to record cultural production. This means that the techniques used to create an artifact are scrutinized. An important part of this approach is the understanding that an artifact does not stand apart from the processes that make it. By analyzing these *systems of production* one can understand quite thoroughly how messages about gender are created and sometimes understand why a message is packaged a particular way. In sum, this approach analyzes how the rhetorical artifact was put together, not just the end result.

Communication scholar Sut Jhally's criticism of MTV music videos is a form of feminist criticism utilizing this approach. Jhally's highly regarded video *Dreamworlds II* records the processes comprising sexist music videos. His research reveals that men direct 90 percent of music videos. Additionally, he documents the roles, clothing, and behavior of the men and women performing in the videos to demonstrate that music videos overwhelmingly tell a story about male sexual fantasy. Jhally's analysis also notes the camera angles that place men at the center and women at the periphery. When the camera does focus on women it usually only focuses on one part of her, generally the buttocks, legs, or breasts. These production techniques serve, argues Jhally, to visually dismember women—making women objects, and even more disturbingly, only one part of an object. These are just a few examples of the way that the production of the rhetorical artifact is analyzed.

Jean Kilbourne's work in advertising also functions as a rhetorical criticism that analyzes the production of advertisements. Kilbourne analyzed advertisements for the way women's bodies were arranged in the ads to convey a message of demure femininity or sexualized objectification; how the print or voice copy accompanying the ads reinforce these gendered messages; as well as how the images were produced to flawlessness through airbrushing, thus equating femininity with physical perfection. In sum, the conscious choices of the artifact's production are detailed for the meaning they convey.

A feminist approach to analyzing cultural production (1) uncovers who is behind the rhetorical artifact and (2) closely analyzes how the rhetorical artifact is put together.

Revisioning

Finally, an important part of feminist criticism is creating new theories about rhetoric. This approach analyzes a specific rhetorical artifact or artifacts as part of a larger project that revisions what it means to engage in rhetoric. As mentioned before, the definition of rhetoric was once solely used to describe the written and spoken word used to persuade. Feminist theoretical thought worked hard to expand that definition. This was important feminist work since women, as historical subjects, would be significantly excluded from the rhetorical history if defined so narrowly. The work of Karen Foss and Sonja Foss in this area extrapolates new theories about what constitutes *significant* rhetoric. In their book *Women Speak*, significant rhetoric emanates from ordinary individuals not noted for their historical accomplishments. Females or even groups of females in private as well as public domains create significant rhetoric; significant rhetorical works include ongoing rhetorical dialogues that are dramatically different from speechmaking. This is an important theoretical departure, because as Deirdre Johnson notes, much of the work women do is ritualistic and impermanent[36]; hence, feminist rhetoric should include symbolic activities that are less concrete and finished. Revisioning these theoretical ideas, then, it is possible to see much of what women do as historically significant rhetoric. These activities include baking, children's parties, gardening, letter writing, herbology, and needlework, among others. These activities produce meaning, but have had their significance diminished in the patriarchal world.

Likewise, rhetorical theorists such a Sally Miller Gearhart theoretically question some of the fundamental ideas about the way we disseminate ideas. As a society we have for years believed that trying to persuade somebody through discourse was a rational alternative to violence. However, Gearhart notes that common rhetorical techniques have an ability to produce a personal violation as "real" as violence. Instead of trying to change someone through rhetorical message-making, a feminist rhetorician opposing domination would create a rhetorical situation that makes change possible, but doesn't insist on change. Using both the feminist rhetorical approach of revisioning and redefining, Gearhart brings new language into the realm of rhetoric. For example, she uses the word *enfoldment* to describe a rhetorical process whereby you offer, make yourself available, surround, listen, and create an opening with your rhetoric, rather than "penetrating the mind" of those you engage.[37] Influenced by Gearhart, other theorists have built on this premise. Foss and Griffin, for example, have outlined a theory of *invitational rhetoric*. This theory suggests a rubric for actualizing rhetoric of nondomination that invites participants to a point of view, but does not create a rhetorical imposition.[38]

A feminist rhetorical criticism using the approach of revisioning (1) questions the assumptions underlying desirable rhetoric and (2) offers new rhetorical insights and possibilities as well as frameworks to analyze such rhetoric.

CRITICAL ESASY: A FEMINIST RHETORICAL ANALYSIS OF SHALLOW HAL

In the fall of 2001, Twentieth Century Fox released a film, *Shallow Hal* directed by Bobby Farrelly and Peter Farrelly, the brothers whose previous films include *Dumb, Dumb and Dumber* (1994), *Something About Mary* (1998) and *Me, Myself and Irene* (2000). Their fourth major film, *Shallow Hal*, was lauded by a prominent American critic as one of the ten best of 2001.[39] *Shallow Hal*'s major moral, one we would expect many feminists to embrace wholeheartedly, is that for women, *interior* beauty, not exterior beauty, is what truly counts. A feminist rhetorical analysis of the DVD of *Shallow Hal* allows us to investigate more deeply in what ways the film's proposed moral is both underscored and undermined.

We proceed with two main sections. First, we provide a brief discussion of feminist rhetorical criticism as related to film and television. Feminist criticism is especially interested in the representations of gender in these two mediums because the messages are distributed quickly and widely. As bell hooks notes, "Television and film also are critical texts . . . because they are the primary tools used to socialize oppressed peoples to internalize the thoughts and values of white supremacist capitalist patriarchy."[40] Thus, it is important to understand the ways that feminist rhetorical critics unpack films for their content—how they strive to be critical cultural consumers. Second, we analyze more specifically how this particular film, *Shallow Hal*, was put together and the rhetorical choices made in its production. Doing so allows us to better discern the inherently contradictory messages in this popular Farrelly brother film about what constitutes "a beautiful woman" in our society.

Feminist Rhetorical Approaches to Film and Television Artifacts

We believe patriarchy is maintained by a symbolic system, a language that defines gender in narrow and specific ways. By systematically analyzing our language choices and communication practices, we can, in part, effectively undermine the patriarchal logic of gender. There are numerous ways one could go about analyzing rhetorical artifacts for the meaning produced about gender. However, if one looks over the history of feminist rhetorical criticism as it particularly relates to television and film, three prominent critical techniques emerge: recording, recovering, and revisioning. To each of these we now turn.

Recovering

Many feminist scholars are committed to recovering and documenting the contributions women have made in various fields. For instance, the Women's Film Pioneers Project, spearheaded by Jane Gaines at Duke University, epitomizes this type of archival work.

> The Pioneers project began as a collaborative effort to advance research on the accomplishments and history of women filmmakers from the early years of cinema through to the coming of sound. The original emphasis was on directors, writers, and producers. The interest in directors, writers, and producers has been linked to a large archival project inspired by the need to discover, restore, preserve, exhibit, and distribute extant 35 mm films. However, this emphasis does not exclude the parallel interest in women audiences in the silent period.[41]

Rediscovering the work of early women in the film and television industries and female spectators is not the only type of "recovery" work that interests feminist scholars, however.

That the film and television industry is still male-dominated there can be no doubt. As we move into the twenty-first century, women comprised roughly 20 percent of executive producers, producers, directors, writers, cinematographers, and editors working on the top money making films. In particular fields, such as directing, the percentage is even lower; indeed, only one in ten directors in Hollywood is a woman[42] and one in ten directors of American television shows is a woman.[43] Because of the low number of women in powerful positions in the industry, feminist scholars also seek to make the work of *current* women in the industry more visible.

Beyond recovering and illuminating early and contemporary women filmmakers and their contributions, feminist scholars also at times take a second look at women's genres within the film and television industry that the dominant culture has dismissed as trivial. A prime example here is Tania Modleski's book *Loving With a Vengeance: Mass-Produced Fantasies for Women*.[44] Modleski's sophisticated analysis of women and their complicated relationship to soap operas pioneered the way for feminists to ask questions about other genres such as women's films, which our culture has often dismissed as "chick flicks" or "weepies."[45]

Recording

Feminists interested in studying film and television texts also are interested in recording the cultural production of the rhetorical artifacts we consume and in doing so, shedding light on the complex ways in which gender is created. In this analytical approach, techniques used to create the artifact are intensely analyzed. Most importantly, the artifact does not stand apart from the processes that make it. By analyzing these systems of production we can better understand how messages about gender are created and packaged. In sum, this approach analyzes how the rhetorical artifact was put together, not just the end result.

Exemplifying this approach is the book *From Mouse to Mermaid: The Politics of Film, Gender, and Culture.* In their introduction to this collection, the editors underscore that they view "Disney" in multiple ways.

> *First, Disney is Walt:* the seventeen-year-old who practiced his signature and subsequently wrote it on the title frame of each film his company created; the kindly "Uncle Walt" who addressed us on Sunday evenings as host of *The Wonderful World of Color*; the FBI informant who gave J. Edgar Hoover access to film scripts; the man who died on December 15, 1966, in St. Joseph's Hospital across the street from his Burbank studio; the cryogenically frozen body of urban legend that sleeps somewhere deep in the bowels of Disneyland. *Second, Disney is a Studio:* a production facility that grew from one camera in Disney's Uncle Bob's garage in 1923 to its 1990s multiple incarnations as Walt Disney Pictures, Touchstone, Hollywood, Caravan, the many subsidiaries of Buena Vista Television and the Disney Channel, as well as the recent studio acquisitions Miramax and Merchant/Ivory. *Third, Disney is a canon of popular film:* Between 1939 and 1992, the feature-length productions alone number 245, only seventy-seven of which were produced while Walt was alive. *Fourth, Disney is a multinational corporation:* in 1940, public stock in the Disney Company sold for $5 a share and today Disney is an entertainment and media conglomerate worth an estimated $4.7 billion. *And fifth, Disney is an ideology:* a sign whose mythology and cultural capital is dependent on and imbricated in all the above manifestations of the name "Disney."[46]

The book's essayists encourage readers of "Disney" to be cultural critics, pushing us to ask difficult questions about our own pleasures in watching or experiencing "Disney." Thus, these feminist communication scholars ask us to not just examine a cultural artifact from a particular feminist perspective—e.g., documenting sexist stereotypes in a particular Disney film—but rather to consider Disney film as cultural capital, to think of it in terms of its production, its languages, its audiences, its ideologies.

Revisioning

Perhaps the most important contribution feminists have made to the study of film and television is in their revisioning of cinematic theory. The most referenced work in the history of feminist film theory is undeniably Laura Mulvey's "Visual Pleasure and Narrative Cinema."[47] In her essay, Mulvey reasons that because most filmmakers in Hollywood are male, the voyeuristic gaze of the camera is male; moreover, the male characters on the screen make women characters the object of their gaze. Consequently, the spectator's gaze ends up reflecting the voyeuristic male gaze of the camera and the male characters. In essence, Mulvey theorizes that the dominant male gaze in mainstream American films reflects and satisfies the male unconscious.

Mulvey's revisioning of psychoanalytical film theory in terms of gender construction profoundly influenced the way feminist scholars and others thought about film and television texts. For many feminist media scholars, Mulvey's main thesis rang true, for it appeared that in classic films, such as Hitchcock's, women were consistently made into passive objects of male voyeurism who primarily existed to fulfill the desires and express the anxieties of male spectators.

Mulvey's pivotal 1975 concept of the "male gaze" has been revisited these last thirty-three years by many other feminist communication scholars who have amended or revised or critiqued it in significant ways. For example, some scholars have argued that women spectators may reject the male gaze and instead identify or construct a "female gaze" in reading mainstream television shows, such as *Cagney and Lacey*, or mainstream movies, such as *Thelma and Louise*.[48] Scholars in queer studies, have noted that Mulvey's articulation is problematic because the "male gaze" is premised on heterosexuality. These scholars have reconceptualized the way the gaze works in order to shed light on the ways homosexual as well as heterosexual audiences might be processing various mainstream films, such as *The Fight Club* or *Boys Don't Cry*.[49] Mulvey's theoretical concept of the "male gaze" has also been critiqued by scholars who see the need for the gaze to be both *materially* as well as psychoanalytically constructed.[50] hooks, for example, reminds us that the politics of slavery denied the slave the right to look, so much so that a "critical or oppositional gaze" has long been a strategy of resistance and assertion of agency for black Americans in the face of domination. This gaze complicates the viewing experience in American cinemas in different ways for female and male black American spectators.[51]

A Feminist Rhetorical Reading of Shallow Hal

Shallow Hal is a film that reached and continues to reach a large, young viewing audience. In this essay, we scrutinize the rhetorical choices made by the directors of the film and the producers of the DVD regarding *Shallow Hal*'s representations of women, beauty, and sexuality. As feminist rhetorical critics, we approach this task in the spirit of "recording," as we are most interested in analyzing how the film was put together and the rhetorical choices made in its DVD production. We also approach the film and its DVD, however, in the sprit of "recovery" as we seek to recover some of the lost rhetors of the film.

Specifically, this essay proceeds by summarizing the plot of the film, and then analyzing the film's site gags (overt visual comedy), its portrayal of "inner beauty," and its marketing strategies. We argue that the film *Shallow Hal* ultimately reinforces the discrimination women feel under current definitions of beauty in our society. Second, we examine the extratext in the *Shallow Hal* DVD. After analyzing the brothers' offhand remarks about women in the film as compared to their male counterparts, we conclude that many women's contributions in this film are marginalized and that the rhetorical positioning of the Farrelly brothers suggests that this marginalization will continue in future films. Finally, after analyzing the director's, special effects creator's, and Gwyneth Paltow's take on the "fat suit," we make connections between Hollywood's fascination with the fat suit and other forms of discrimination now deemed unacceptable.

The Plot and Proposed Moral of Shallow Hal

The plot of *Shallow Hal* is rather simple.[52] Before the opening credits, the audience sees a nine-year-old Hal at the bedside of his dying father, a reverend. High on morphine, his father advises the nine-year-old Hal that he should find himself "a classic beauty, with a perfect can and great toddies" because "hot young tail's what it's all about."[53] The film then opens with images of the adult Hal (Jack Black) and his closest male buddy, Mauricio (Jason Alexander) at a dance bar. Here, these two rather dumpy-looking men try pathetically, desperately, and unsuccessfully to pick up only the most gorgeous, sexy women. Similar scenes follow that continue to underscore Hal's shallowness until his chance encounter with Tony Robbins in a stuck elevator. The television guru hypnotizes Hal so that, from then on, he will only see the "inner beauty" of people he encounters. Soon following the hypnosis, Hal and Mauricio return to the dance club. Hal, from his point of view, is seen dancing with three model-perfect women, while from friend, Mauricio's point of view, Hal is seen dancing with a trio of women whom Mauricio describes as a "pack of stampeding buffalo."[54] The next day, Hal meets the woman of his dreams, Rosemary (played by Gwyneth Paltrow and, alternately, by Ivy Snitzer). Even though there are a few moments in which the audience is privy to the "real" 300 pound Rosemary, for the most part throughout the courtship, the audience vicariously sees Rosemary through Hal's eyes, which means seeing Rosemary as the movie star-thin, Gwyneth Paltrow.[55] Rosemary is a volunteer at both the hospital burn unit and a member of the Peace Corps; she also, fortuitously, happens to be the daughter of Hal's boss. Hal's dating of Rosemary and Hal's novel insights for Rosemary's father's corporation, lead to an inevitable and immediate rise in Hal's career. Meanwhile, Hal's friend Mauricio mourns the loss of his immature friend and consequently secures the magic words, from Tony Robbins, to de-hypnotize Hal to his old shallow ways of seeing. The ending of this romantic comedy is rather predictable in that Hal's original, real-world vision is restored; yet Hal *chooses* to see beyond Rosemary's physical characteristics to love Rosemary for who she truly is. He appreciates her humor, her altruistic worldview, and her inner beauty. He is in love and he genuinely sees her as beautiful.

Shallow Hal's repeatedly underscored moral—*that one should not judge people, in particular women, by their physical appearances*—appears to be a rather revolutionary one for Hollywood and one we would expect feminists to truly embrace. For the Farrelly brothers' film strives to argue, as Tony Robbins in the film itself testifies, that everything we "know about beauty is programmed: television, magazines, movies;" media images are all falsely telling us what is beautiful and what is not.[56] And indeed, evidence for this thesis occurs early in the film when the unenlightened Hal explains that he is seeking a woman with the "face" of Paulina in a *Sports Illustrated* layout, the "beams" and "teeth" of Heidi Klum, the "knockers" and "ass" of Britney Spears, the "grille" of Michelle Pheiffer, and the "smile" of Rebecca Romijn-Stamos.[57] So from one angle, it would appear that feminists would rejoice in Hal's transformation in this film from an unenlightened, immature, shallow, middle-aged adolescent to a more complicated man who is genuinely in love with Rosemary, a good-natured, funny, altruistic, plus-size woman.

But what's fascinating to us, as materialist feminists, is the way the Farrelly brothers' movie and the supplementary material on the DVD continuously undermine its intended revolutionary message. In this criticism, we will look closely at the film's rhetorical choices, analyzing the comic gags and its construction of "inner beauty." Then we'll analyze the production of the film by reviewing select material from the DVD, including the cover jacket images, the Farrelly brothers' voice over commentary about the making of the film, and the rhetorical implications of Hollywood's latest craze—the fat suit.

Shallow Hal's Site Gags and Construction of "Inner Beauty"

The Farrelly brothers had a reputation for over-the-top humor prior to *Shallow Hal*. Their lowbrow films testify that no topic or groups of people are immune to their mockery. Anyone who had seen any of the Farrelly brother's previous movies would probably find the humor in *Shallow Hal* rather tame in comparison. Yet, if, by the standards previously established in the other Farrelly brothers' films, the crude, visual humor was *underplayed* in *Shallow Hal*, then why did the film's site gags come under such close scrutiny by reviewers.[58] We believe that's what is the most "off" and therefore the most notable about the site gags in *Shallow Hal* is that they consistently undermine, rather than reinforce the film's intended thesis.

Consider that before Hal met Tony Robbins, Hal would never have given the real Rosemary a second glance since he was a shallow man who was always proverbially judging a book by its cover, a man who would never give a 300 pound woman a second glance. Undeniably, the film's overall message is to prove how shallow and wrong Hal's perspective is. Yet virtually all of the site gags in the film are clichéd jokes that primarily work by reinforcing society's stereotypical, often mean-spirited assumptions about overweight people. The film's visual jokes encourage audiences to judge overweight people by the effects of their weight. Hence, the audience is prompted to laugh when they see Rosemary inhale a huge milkshake she was supposed to be sharing with Hal. Or when we see Rosemary do a cannonball that displaces such a large volume of water in the neighborhood pool that it quenches a barbeque and literally propels a child to the top of a tree. Or when we see a perplexed, "caught-in-a-practical-joke" Hal unfurl Rosemary's sexy, lavender g-string that is literally a yard-wide.

One could counter-argue that the humor lies in the audience NOT seeing the obese Rosemary in each of these instances, but rather seeing, as Hal does, the svelte Gwyneth Paltrow. For example, audience members who empathize with Hal can vicariously smile at the incongruity of seeing a model-thin woman having the freedom to consume a double burger rather than peck at a salad. Or slurp down that jumbo shake for two rather than sip a Perrier.

We do not deny that humor is undeniably complex, but we believe it is important to acknowledge that in general, the site gags only work because as audience members, we see the *reality* that Hal is not privy to. Sometimes, we are given glimpses of the very large Rosemary by the filmmakers. For example, we see glimpses in the film of stand-in Ivy Snitzer or see the slim Paltrow casting a huge reflection in a store window. Thus, the filmmakers continually prompt viewers to see the 300 pound Rosemary, so that we imagine her even when she is not literally in the scene. Hence when a scene features only Gwyneth Paltrow, the viewer projects the large Rosemary into the scene, and, thus, the visual gag becomes no fundamentally different than the tried and true "fat jokes" so pervasive in American culture. There really is no laughing "with" Rosemary, only a laughing "at." In general the humor is sophomoric in both its sexism and weightism.

If the humor in the film is problematic, so is its point of view and its construction of "inner beauty." Like most films, the point of view in *Shallow Hal* allows the audience to have full knowledge. As audience members we see many scenes that Hal is not privy to (e.g., the meeting between Tony Robbins and Hal's friend, Mauricio). But a film can privilege a particular character's perspective and *Shallow Hal* privileges Hal's. Thus, for the vast majority of the film, the audience sees what Hal sees; i.e., Gwyneth Paltrow in all her physical, film star perfection. Indeed, from the time Rosemary is introduced, we visually see Paltrow for most of the film; and we very rarely see the 300 pound Rosemary. On the DVD, one of the Farrelly brothers explains why Gwyneth Paltrow was cast to represent *inner* beauty:

> A few . . . critics have problems with the movie, saying, ultimately why is our idea of beautiful women Gwyneth Paltrow's character. And our defense to that is "well, it's not *our* idea, it's [*Hal's*] idea and that was because of what his father tells him—to go out and look for the perfect girl, with the perfect butt, great toddies, good-looking. . . . He's describing, basically Gwyneth. Not that we don't think Gwyneth is the ideal beauty, but that's not what we were proclaiming. We set up this [first] scene specifically to not have to answer those questions, which of course we had to anyway."[59]

But, of course, the main reason the Farrelly brothers were repeatedly asked to answer this question is because their defense of their choice to cast Gwyneth Paltrow as *inner* beauty, is lame. Everyone knows Gwyneth Paltrow was not only cast but also featured, primarily for her *outer* beauty.

Paradoxically, the filmmakers give us a film whose "revolutionary" moral is for society *not* to judge large people by their appearances *within* a film that is undeniably Hollywood-traditional in starring the ultra-thin, Gwyneth Paltrow, rather than a genuine plus-size actress like Kathy Bates, Carmryn Manheim, or Queen Latifah. And perhaps an even greater irony lies in the fact that even Paltrow's body was not-quite-perfect-enough by Hollywood standards, for in the film's bedroom scene, where the audience sees a full-body shot of the backside of Paltrow as she removes her sexy negligee and bikini underwear is, if we are to take the Farrelly brothers at their word, actually *not* Gwyneth Paltrow, but a "butt double."[60]

Shallow Hal fits neatly into Laura Mulvey's theory that most films are primarily designed to provide pleasure to the male spectator. There are numerous scenes in this film in which women are seen as the objects, not the subjects of the gaze, a gaze in which women's bodies are inevitably eroticized. Hal eroticizes only sexy women before his Robbins-induced hypnosis, and, after his Robbins-induced hypnosis, he eroticizes all inherently "good" women, even unattractive ones. Perhaps if our hero discovered the erotic in a relationship with the 300 pound Rosemary, the film might have broken new ground. But Hal's bedroom scene is not shared with Gwyneth Paltrow in her fat suit, it is a conventional bedroom scene with a not-so-attractive male hero and a stunningly attractive Gwyneth Paltrow. Thus, Hal is typical of the film hero whom theorist Laura Mulvey discusses in her book *Visual and Other Pleasures*. Hal is the active hero who advances the narrative, controlling the events, the women, and the erotic gaze.[61] Gwyneth Paltrow functions primarily as erotic spectacle. In spite of their noble intentions, the Farrelly brothers offer no new language of desire.

Shallow Hal—the DVD

DVDs are enormously beneficial to rhetorical scholars. Not only do they allow critics to replay scenes easily with close-captioned dialogue, but DVDs also provide supplementary materials regarding various systems of production, such as marketing, advertising, costuming, filming or editing. Hence, a DVD differs from a VHS copy of a film; for a DVD is not just a repackaging of a film for distribution, but rather it is, as Brookley and Westerfelhaus note, "a synergistic package comprised of product and promotion."[62] As such, it deserves a close, critical reading. In this section, we will again consider the film's intended moral—*to not judge people by their appearances*—as we review the rhetorical packaging of images on the cover jacket of the DVD, the Farrelly brothers' own rhetoric in the DVD commentary, as well as the technical wizardry and the rhetorical implications of the fat suit.

Visual Images from the DVD

Marketing of DVDs relies in part on the selection of key images that try to capture the essence of the film and strike a chord with the audience (in the case of DVDs, the renter or buyer). Similarly, filmmakers choose a very select amount of photos or jpegs from the actual film to send out in their press packets, photos that ideally capture the essence of the film while simultaneously sparking the imaginations of writers and reviewers in the print media.

The front cover of the *Shallow Hal* DVD, features a curvaceous Gwyneth Paltrow, wearing a very tightly fitted, bright pink t-shirt and small-checkered, pink and white skirt. Her body is positioned mostly profile, so that her what-can-only-be-digitally-manipulated breasts perk out quite nicely. She is holding both hands, in a rather schoolgirl way, with Jack Black. Jack Black is wearing a loosely fitting spotted yellow shirt with oversize brown trousers. The calves of Paltrow's naked legs in her slim, heeled sandals contrast with Black's workman-like boots. Paltrow's two inch heels also make her appear slightly taller than Black. The couple is not looking at each other; rather both appear to be looking directly at the potential purchasers of the DVD—Paltrow with a teasing, lovely smile and the wide-eyed Jack with a smirk that suggests he can't believe he's lucky enough to be holding hands with this leggy blond. Behind the couple is a blue brick wall with the couple's shadows: a slight, realistic shadow of Black and a more-defined shadow behind Paltrow which is not realistically hers, but rather that of a 300 or more pound woman. Above the title, "*Shallow Hal,*" is the film's slogan in smaller print, "True Love is Worth The Weight!"

The DVD's cover jacket, which is also used on the VHS version, epitomizes the same paradox we have been discussing in this essay. The slogan's pun, "True Love is Worth the Weight" alludes to this being both a story of a hero's lengthy quest for romance, while also underscoring his true love of a large or weighty woman. But the main "feel" of the front cover belies the latter reading of the slogan, for the images of the two stars is nothing more than yet another photographic reiteration of a male's pleasure and a female positioned-as-erotic-spectacle. Paltrow's sexual come-on positioning is so strong on the cover jacket, so brightly and digitally enhanced, that the shadows behind the stars seem to just blend into the background. The oversize shadow of Paltrow, like the large Rosemary in the film, is seen in only a negligible way and only to the most conscientious viewer.

That the Farrelly brothers are intent on selling the film as both a stereotypical romance and as an original comedy is also shown in the selection of photos that their marketing department distributed to the press. Consider the three most reoccurring photos accompanying the reviews: the slim Paltrow as Rosemary, sweetly and jointly sipping the jumbo shake with Hal (Jack Black); the slim Rosemary and Hal paddling a canoe, with Rosemary "anchoring" one end and Hal up in the air on the other; or Hal, looking perplexed as he stretches out sexy, lavender-laced, bikini underpants that are literally a yard-wide. Similarly, in the two-minute theatrical trailer for *Shallow Hal* which establishes the slim Rosemary and Hal's courtship, no less then nine site gags are featured; including a scene not in the film, of the slender Gwyneth Paltrow leading/pulling an exhausted horse with a severely bowed back. In another section of the DVD, "Deleted Scenes," there is a scene from the bedroom, in which the bed itself collapses under Paltrow's "weight." In essence, most of the press photos, the theatrical trailer, and the deleted film clip function in much the same vein as the site gags analyzed earlier in this essay. These images are thinly disguised fat jokes embedded in a stereotypical romance, images which are consistently at odds with the film's intended thesis.

Farrelly Brothers' Commentary from the DVD

Robert Alan Brookey and Robert Westerfelhaus have examined how the "extra text" in DVDs function rhetorically. They note that "extra text offers consumers access to commentary by those involved with making the film, and it positions this commentary as authoritative."[63] In doing so, the extra texts in DVDs *direct* viewers' experience of the film. In this section, we'll look closely at the "authoritative" words of the directors of *Shallow Hal* in the DVD's extra text called "Commentary by the Farrelly Brothers" and, in the next section, we'll look closely at the "authoritative" words of the creator of the fat suit, Tony Gardner. In both cases, we'll place the "authoritative" voices of the directors and visual effects creator in a larger cultural context.

In the DVD's "Commentary by the Farrelly Brothers," there are four reoccurring topics of discussion. In the voice over (which accompanies the silent re-showing of the film), the brothers make candid observations about working with the film's major actors, offer brief introductions of many performers who played minor characters, comment about filming in Charlotte, North Carolina, and endorse the film's musicians who did the various songs that were included in the film's score.

In listening to their commentary the first time, we were struck perhaps most profoundly by the major differences between the way the actors playing the male minor characters were introduced as compared to the actresses who were playing the female minor characters. To check the accuracy of our initial impressions, we watched "Commentary by the Farrelly Brothers" two more times. We tallied whether the actors, male and female, were introduced by full names, whether their professional credentials were cited, whether they were noted for having worked previously on Farrelly brothers films or were recently discovered. We did not analyze the brothers' introductions to musicians, crewmembers, or actors playing major characters.[64] The 107 minor characters that were introduced range from those with a few speaking lines, such as Hal's co-workers, to local extras in the background. The length of the Farrelly brothers' improvised commentary is, of course, restrained by the length of time each of the minor characters appear in the film (since the brothers are just conversing as the film runs with no sound). The following table displays the results:

Directors' Introductions of the Minor Characters in the "Commentary by the Farrelly Brothers" on the *Shallow Hal* DVD (shown below).

TABLE 15.1

Total References to actors	Female	Male	Total
Playing minor characters	54	55	109
Actor pointed out, but actor's name not recalled or specifically referenced, or actor only referred to by first name	18	3	21
Actor identified by first and last name	36	52	88
Actor's professional credentials referenced	10	24	34
Actor worked on previous films with the Farrelly Brothers	2	13	15
Actor "discovered"	9	2	11

These tallies served to confirm our initial, more subjective impressions. In the Farrelly brothers' commentary, male actors playing minor roles are more likely, as compared to their female counterparts, to be referred to by their full names, to be identified by their professional credits, and to be re-employed by the brothers.[65]

Our analysis of the Farrelly brothers' commentary strongly suggests the proverbial "good ol' boy network" at work. The Farrelly brothers, unconsciously or consciously, seem to rehire more male actors to play minor roles, than actresses. In securing many of the actresses for *Shallow Hal*, the brothers, instead, seemed to rely heavily on Charlie Weston who auditioned "a hundred women" in New York.[66] Indeed, at one point in the commentary, one of the brothers refers to these women who were "discovered" by Charlie Weston as "Charlie's Angels"[67]

"The Farrelly Brothers Commentary" strongly suggests that the makers of *Shallow Hal* do not uphold the same principles when it comes to the male and female actors. With regard to women, the directors simply do not practice what they preach. *Shallow Hal* contends that we should appreciate people for what they do, for who they inherently are, and not judge them by their outward appearances. *Shallow Hal* seeks to teach its audience to value people who have altruistic occupations, those who take care of a sick grandmother, volunteer at the city's hospital or join the Peace Corp. In "The Farrelly Brothers' Commentary" the directors occasionally underscore a minor male actor's altruism—the male friend who snuck into their apartment and cleaned it up; another male friend, a doctor, who treats their friends without insurance.[68] That the Farrelly brothers value men's talent as well as their altruistic acts is shown in the way directors continually cite male actors' major professional achievements. There is a strong sense, upon listening to the commentary, of the Farrelly brothers' immense loyalty to male actors and their appreciation of their career successes. On the rare occasion that the brothers mention an actress' previous professional credits, most often it is invariably about her appearing in a "*Playboy*" or "*Baywatch*" or having a career as "a model."[69] Male actors playing minor roles are more likely to be introduced by what they have accomplished; while for the actresses, on the rare occasion in which they are introduced by their accomplishments, the Farrelly brothers more often than not highlight a previous occupation that inevitably employs only conventionally attractive women.

But it was not just beautiful women who had to be cast according to the demands of the screenplay, unattractive people also had to be either cast or supplemented by the makeup and special effects department. So let us now briefly examine the Farrelly brothers' commentary on some of those performers who played "unattractive" female characters.

Let us begin with Ivy Snitzer, a very large actress who on some occasions serves as a stand-in for the 300 pound Rosemary in *Shallow Hal*. The audience never sees Snitzer's face in the film, though we see her back, her calves, etc. On the occasions that she does appear in the film and in "The Farrelly Brothers' Commentary," the directors either do not comment on her or they offer unintentionally, yet somewhat problematic comments. Without a doubt, Ivy's longest scene in the film occurs when Hal is avoiding her, after having learned from Mauricio that the hypnosis that made him believe "really ugly girls" were "supermodels" was broken. In Snitzer's longest scene in the film, the audience sees her from the back, seated at the hospital, talking to Hal on the telephone. The voice over in "The Farrelly Brothers Commentary" in this scene is not about Snitzer, rather it centers on the brothers' admiration of the male writer of the detective novel that Hal was reading in the last scene in the film.[70] Like Hal, who in this part of the film is avoiding seeing the large Rosemary, the Farrelly brothers in this scene in "The Farrelly Brothers Commentary" avoid talking about Snitzer. But in all fairness to the directors, they do discuss Snitzer's contribution earlier, and their comments are revealing. Snitzer is commended for her "abundance of inner beauty" and for being the "heart and soul of the crew."[71] That Snitzer is seen as part of the *crew*, not a member of the cast is particularly interesting, for it displaces her as an actress and repositions her as another technician, a crew member who has mastery over an "effect." We can surmise that because Snitzer, of course, holds no mastery of light, sound, camera angles, or props, the "effect" she then must be contributing to the film is that of her "fat."

In "The Farrelly Brothers' Commentary" and on other sections of the DVD, Ivy Snitzer is characterized, in general, as a good egg, a gal who helped Paltrow understand her part, a trouper who endorsed the film and its message, a woman whom everyone liked. And we do not mean to imply here that the Farrelly brothers and others were wrong in these assertions. What we are arguing is that, regardless of her own and the directors' noble intentions, she was still somewhat exploited in the making of this film. In an interview, Ivy Snitzer noted how proud her family is about her appearance in *Shallow Hal:* "I think my mother's whole Girl Scout troop is going to opening night!"[72] Yet, sadly, in *Shallow Hal*'s listed credits, Ivy Snitzer is not credited at all, not as part of the cast, not as part of the crew, not as a stand-in or body-double, not even as a consultant.[73]

To best describe the way that we believe Ivy Snitzer was used in the process of making this film, we might turn momentarily to feminist bell hooks. In *Teaching to Transgress*, hooks notes that, in those of our classrooms that are still predominantly white, a "spirit of tokenism" may prevails. Often if there is one lone person of color in the classroom he or she is objectified by others and forced to assume the role of *native informant*.[74] As an example, hooks provides a classroom setting in which the students have been assigned a novel by a American author of Korean ancestry. White students turn to the sole Korean student in the classroom to explain what they do not understand. According to hooks, this practice places an unfair responsibility on the Korean student and assumes that "experience" makes him or her an expert. In the making of *Shallow Hal*, the filmmakers often put Ivy Snitzer in the position of the "native informant" as they conveniently assume that Snitzer represents all plus-size people. This is not only evident in "The Farrelly Brothers' Commentary" but it is also evident in interviews with Gwyneth Paltrow: "[M]y double, Ivy Snitzer, was really supportive. I was nervous and she was so supportive of it, she said, 'I think it's so great.' She loves it when I'm in the fat suit, and that made me feel good. The only concern I had with wearing the suit was about offending people who are overweight. I was concerned about that, but actually it has been fine."[75] Thus, the Farrelly brothers and Gwyneth Paltrow rely on Snitzer to be their "native informant." The implication is that if Ivy Snitzer embraces the film, its jokes, and Paltrow's impersonation of a large person, then all overweight American audience members will embrace *Shallow Hal*.

In general, "The Farrelly Brothers Commentary" in the DVD is most fascinating to us for what the Farrelly Brothers improvised language unintentionally reveals. Male actors playing minor characters, no matter what they physically look like, are more likely to benefit from the good old Farrelly boy network. In contrast, women, particularly attractive ones, are less likely to be cited by their complete names and more likely to have been recently "discovered" by the Farrelly brothers or Charlie Weston. And on the rare occasion that an actress' professional credits are referenced, it's typically in reference to an industry tied to the beauty culture.

The Fat Suit

Another noteworthy section of the DVD is a mini-documentary, called "Seeing through the Layers," which shows viewers the wizardry behind the creation of very unattractive characters for *Shallow Hal*. "Seeing through the Layers" features a series of brief interviews with the make up effects designers, the Farrelly brothers, actresses, and an actor who were made unattractive for their particular parts in *Shallow Hal*. The thirteen-minute documentary primarily focuses on the makeup artist's skill in transforming very *attractive* actresses into unattractive ones.[76] The documentary is fascinating in that the person mainly responsible, Tony Gardner, is both articulate and thoughtful as he describes the various technical challenges this particular film set forth and how he tried to meet them.

The viewer learns that there was quite a "learning curve" for the makeup artists in designing the fat suit for Gwyneth Paltrow. The major challenge being that they had to design a fat suit that was "comfortable" (multiple, lightweight pieces for the actress to wear in accordance with what was needed for a camera shot); a fat suit that appeared "realistic" and "not too cartoonish" and was "lighthearted" enough to work in a romantic comedy.[77] Moreover, the makeup artists had to create a prosthetically-enhanced "fat" face that would allow enough of Paltrow's facial attributes to be clearly "recognizable" to an audience, while simultaneously being "elastic" enough for her acting to come through.[78] In the documentary, Tony Gardner traces the evolution of the fat suit and Paltrow describes the demands on the performer *prior* to its construction (full body cast so that the makeup artists could construct a fat suit to perfectly fit her frame) as well as *after* its construction (the time-consuming demands to literally put on the fat suit costume and the extensive prosthetics and makeup to create the fat Rosemary's face.) The documentary testifies that makeup artists, such as Gardner, can effectively create realistic fat suits that actors enjoy wearing and performing in, fat suits that meet the directors' and producers' expectations, fat suits that audience members find relatively convincing.

Gardner's fat suits for Gwyneth Paltrow and the actress that played Rosemary's mother is of course one of many recently created in Hollywood. Beyond those featured in *Shallow Hal,* consider some of these examples—Robin Williams in *Mrs. Doubtfire,* Goldie Hawn in *Death Becomes Her,* Martin Lawrence in *Big Momma's House,* Mike Myers in the Austin Powers movies, Eddie Murphy in *Nutty Professor* movies, Martin Short in *Primetime Glick*, and flashback or dream sequences of Julia Roberts in *Americas' Sweethearts.*

The DVD documentary, "Seeing Through the Layers" and the recent proliferation of fat suits prompts us to pose an ethical question: Does the fact that makeup artists have the talent and technical know-how to create fat suits ultimately justify their use in film and television?

A number of reviewers and activists have responded to the use of fat suits in *Shallow Hal* and other films with a resounding "no." In an excellent essay on this subject, Marisa Meltzer discusses how humor aimed at minority groups has changed through the years.

> Over the past several decades, comedy has gradually become less broad and more sensitive to overt racism. . . . We've come a long way since Peter Sellers was cast as bucktoothed Chinese sleuth Sidney Wang in *Murder by Death.* By now, the cardinal rule of humor—you can only make fun of a group if you're part of it—is familiar enough to be a punch line itself. (Remember Jerry Seinfield's outrage over his Catholic dentist's Jewish jokes?) But fat people are the last remaining exception.[79]

To Meltzer's dismay, "Fat people are now America's favorite punch lines." Meltzer, like many others, contends that fat suits are the moral equivalent of blackface.

In calling for a boycott of *Shallow Hal,* the National Association to Advance Fat Acceptance (NAAFA) makes the same claim. The executive administrator, Maryanne Bodolay, explains:

> Putting thin performers in fat suits is no different than putting white performers in blackface. . . . To have these actors become 'fat' and then film them gorging on food and breaking chairs is an insult to the 55 percent of Americans who are deemed 'overweight.' . . . These movies are giving people permission to make fun of fat people. . . . Hollywood is intent upon perpetuating the myth that fat people are miserable and unattractive, and that the path to happiness is through losing weight. In reality, beauty comes in all sizes, and people can find happiness at whatever size they are.[80]

Diane Bliss, the founder and chair of the recently formed Screen Actors Guild's Plus-Size Task Force (PSTF) cites an academic study that documents NAAFA's claim about the media's stereotypical representations.

> Michigan State University did a study of the representations of plus-size people in TV and film and statistically proved what our common sense tells us: people of size are more likely to be portrayed as stupid, lazy, unemployed, a member of an ethnic group, and the target of the joke. Older

plus-size women are fairly frequently portrayed in a positive, non-stereotypical light as nurturing mothers, but we're seldom portrayed as desirable love interests or leading ladies.[81]

Some of the members of the Plus-Size Task Force have expressed in various interviews why they are fighting Hollywood's current depictions of large people. What emerges from these sources first is that the plus-size actresses resent the limited roles available to them. For example, Diane Bliss says, "When I moved to L.A. four-and-a-half years ago, most of the auditions were for the 'fat chick.' Nearly every time someone was described as a plus-size woman, there was always a negative adjective attached."[82] Rebekah Derrick adds, "The main problem is that the roles we're offered have nothing to do with anything but weight."[83] The plus-size activists also resent the industry's double standard for male and female actors of size: "Why is the chunky and average-looking Jim Belushi considered 'leading man material' a star of his own sitcom," Diane Bliss asks, "while his wife is played by the gorgeous Courtney Thorne-Smith, size 2?"[84] In speculating as to why plus-size characters are often caricatures, Sarah Sachs notes "All races, all personalities are overweight; it's always something to be picked on because it's universal—there's someone in each category that could be overweight. That's why it's an easy target."[85] Actress Lisa Brounstein believes it has more to do with capitalism, "Our society says that overweight, plus-size or fat people need to diet to fix themselves. There is a billion-dollar diet industry that's telling us that we need to fix ourselves. I think that's how Hollywood gets away with making fun of us."[86]

With its paucity of interesting roles, its double standard regarding acceptable size for actors and actresses, and its "diet industry" marketing incentives, Hollywood is an industry that clearly discriminates against plus-size actresses. One can easily understand why plus-size actresses, with limited opportunities available, would be taken aback when two roles for large women in *Shallow Hal*—Rosemary and her mother—are earmarked for thin actresses. A number of reviewers concur with the plus-size actresses' observations. For example, a reviewer for the *New Daily News* writes, "Casting a heavy actress in a lead romantic role is still as impossible to imagine as it once was to think of women having the vote or serving in the military. . . . It's good that U.S. movies are giving lip service to the idea that big is beautiful, but it's time they cast those movies from real life and not from the bins of the special effects department."[87]

Essay's Conclusion

All in all, there can be no denying that the moral of *Shallow Hal*—*that one should not judge people, in particular women, by their physical appearance*—is constantly undermined in both the film and in the DVD supplements. The film's site gags, its clichéd idea of "inner beauty," and its predominantly adolescent male point of view, when considered in conjunction with *Shallow Hal*'s iconic marketing images, the rather sexist "Farrelly Brothers' Commentary," and the political perception that Hollywood's fascination with "fat suits" echoes their previous fascination with "blackface," we are hoping that readers of this essay will agree that *Shallow Hal* undermines its intended revolutionary message. Or as, Peter Travers, a reviewer for *Rolling Stone* articulated his experience with *Shallow Hal*:

> There is something condescending, not to mention hypocritical, about asking an audience to laugh uproariously at the spectacle of a fat person being sneered at and dissed as "rhino," or "hippo" or "holy cow," and then to justify those laughs by saying it's society's fault and tacking on a happy ending that allegedly teaches us a moral lesson. It won't wash.[88]

POTENTIALS AND PITFALLS

Feminist rhetorical analysis is well-suited for many communication artifacts that exist in our cultural world. Given that gender is one of the primary ways we determine social behavior, very few artifacts are devoid of gendered implications. It must be stressed again, though, that gender is only one of the many identities that complex humans use to interact with the world. While looking for the gendered implications of a rhetorical artifact, one must be vigilant not to undermine or dismiss the other identities at work in the communication processes and fail to understand their impact as well.

Additionally, we believe that critical work requires equal part critique and equal part solution. It is often easy to point out what is oppressive about a communication artifact and then fail to offer any solutions. Many critics of feminist theory suggest that by pointing out all the ways communication oppresses women, one runs the risk of largely positioning women as victims. A potential pitfall of feminist analysis is failing to offer concrete alternatives to patriarchal order. For example, while the above essay primarily combined the feminist approach of recovering and recording to critically analyze the film, other approaches could be utilized as well. While one part of the feminist project is to critique existing rhetorical practices for their patriarchal logic, the other two approaches offered in this chapter centers on feminist solutions. In sum, feminist rhetorical critics should offer new solutions, new ways of thinking. Therefore, as an alternative or supplement, the essay above could have focused more on creating new definitions for beauty and attractiveness, instead of critiquing the rhetorical contradictions of the directors.

In addition, the essay alludes to the need for new language and new theories of cinematic representation that transcend existing formulas and standards. This too could have been the focus of the paper or should be the focus of other researchers that build on the analysis. With that in mind, a feminist rhetorical critic might take a film such as *Shallow Hal* and compare it to *My Big Fat Greek Wedding,* another romantic comedy featuring a larger lead actress. By comparing the two films, one could argue that *My Big Fat Greek Wedding* achieves where *Shallow Hal* fails. The paper could detail the specific ways in which *My Big Fat Greek Wedding* provided a positive, transformative character, a character decidedly more interesting than Paltrow's. Additionally, *My Big Fat Greek Wedding* provides a point of analysis about ethnicity. The film *Shallow Hal* deals with definitions of beauty, but the definitions are largely Caucasian in their orientation. Other ethnicities and subcultures have different standards of attractiveness and a wider acceptance of different body types. One has to be careful not to entrench assumptions that undermine a critique of race, class, heterosexism, etc., while striving to analyze gender.

In sum, a feminist critic puts together the analytical rubric that works best to elucidate all the strategies of domination made rigid by language and may also suggest new rhetorical paths to take—paths that achieve freedom, safety, complexity, subjectivity, and equality.

FEMINIST ANALYSIS TOP PICKS

Campbell, Karlyn Kohrs. "Rhetorical Feminism." *Rhetoric Review* 20 (2001): 9–12. A concise essay that provides a survey of the work done by feminist scholars in the field of communication. Beginning critics will find this history very helpful.

Campbell, Karlyn Kohrs. *Man Cannot Speak for Her: A Critical Study of Early Feminist Rhetoric, vol. 1* (New York: Greenwood Press, 1989). This book simultaneous investigates feminist rhetoric and offers news ways of thinking about the rhetorical process. One of the most important works in feminist rhetorical scholarship.

Condit, Celeste M. "In Praise of Eloquent Diversity: Gender and Rhetoric as Public Persuasion." *Women's Studies in Communication* 20 (2) (1997): 91–116. Condit's article is an excellent example of feminist revisioning. She provides a through rationale for new ways of communicating gender. The article also will further a student's understanding of the different positions on gender that rhetorical scholars take.

Hamlet, Janice D. "Assessing Womanist Thought: The Rhetoric of Susan L. Taylor." *Communication Quarterly* 48.4 (2000): 420–437. This essay provides an interesting rhetorical analysis of the former editor of *Essence* magazine. The study is an excellent example of feminist scholarship and furthers understanding of Womanist scholarship.

Hanke, Robert. "The 'Mock-Macho' Situation Comedy: Hegemonic Masculinity and its Reiteration." *Western Journal of Communication* 62.1 (Winter 1998): 74–93. Well done and easy to understand analysis of the television shows Home Improvement and Coach. This essay allows the student to see the ways in which portrayals of masculinity are critiqued in feminist analysis.

Lotz, Amanda D. "Communicating Third Wave Feminism and New Social Movements: Challenges for the Next Century of Feminist Endeavor." *Women and Language.* XXVI (2003): 1–9. This essay provides students with an overview of feminist thought from the perspective of the communication field. This article is helpful for students seeking to understand the complex and contradictory messages about feminism in the media and elsewhere.

Shugart, Helene. "She Shoots, She Scores: Mediated Constructions of Contemporary Female Athletes in Coverage of the 1999 U.S. Women's Soccer Team." *Western Journal of Communication* 67 (1) (Winter 2003): 1–31. Shugarts analysis of famous female athletes unearths the patriarchal strategies used to subordinate these successful and empowered women. Shugart provides theoretical language for understanding these strategies.

NOTES

1. Susan Faludi, "Whose Backlash Is It Anyway?: The Women's Movement and Angry White Men," FSU Student Government Summer Lecture Series, Florida State University, Tallahassee, June 25, 1997.

2. Karen A. Foss, Sonja J. Foss, and Cindy Griffin, *Feminist Rhetorical Theories* (Thousand Oaks, CA: Sage, 1999): 79.

3. This definition appears in Kramarae and Treichler's *A Feminist Dictionary* (London: Pandora Press, 1985).

4. See Christine Hoff Sommers, *Who Stole Feminism,* (Simon & Schuster; Reprint edition, 1995).

5. Allan G. Johnson, *The Gender Knot* (Philadelphia: Temple University Press, 1997), 5.

6. Johnson, 6.

7. Mary Spicuzza, "Bad Heroines," *MetroActive* [online], Available: <http://www.metroactive.com/papers/metro/03.15.01/cover/womanfilm-0111.html>

8. Johnson, 8.

9. For example, http://www.superbowl.com notes that an estimated 131 million viewers watched Super Bowl XXXV and marketing departments spent 2.5 million for each 30-second advertising spot.

10. Carol Tavris, *The Mis-Measure of Woman* (New York, Simon & Schuster, 1992), 18.

11. For a more thorough explanation of the use of this term view *bell hooks: Cultural Criticism and Transformation*, dir. Sut Jhally, Media Education Foundation, 1997.

12. Jill Dolan, *Feminist Spectator as Critic* (Ann Arbor, MI: University of Michigan Press, 1988), 3–16.

13. Dolan, 7.

14. Ibid. 10.

15. For examples of groups that fall into these categories see <http://www.ifeminists.net/> and <http://www.iwf.org/>.

16. For a more thorough listing of the categories of feminism, see Julia T. Wood's chapter 3 of *Gendered Lives* (Belmont, CA: Wadsworth, 2003).

17. Karlyn Kohrs Campbell, *Man Cannot Speak for Her Vol. 1* (New York: Greenwood Press, 1989).

18. For example, see Karlyn Kohrs Campbell, "Three Tall Women: Radical Challenges to Criticism, Pedagogy, and Theory," in *The Carroll C. Arnold Distinguished Lecture*. (Boston, MA: Allyn and Bacon, 2003), 4.

19. Susan Schultz Huxman, "Perfecting the Rhetorical Vision of Woman's Rights: Elizabeth Cady Stanton, Anna Howard Shaw, and Carrie Chapman Catt," *Women's Studies in Communication,* 23 (2000): 307–336.

20. Brenda Cooper. "'Chick Flicks' as Feminist Texts: The Appropriation of the Male Gaze in *Thelma & Louise*," *Women's Studies in Communication* 23 (2000): 277–306.

21. Kristin J. Anderson and Christina Accomando, "Madcap Misogyny and Romanticized Victim-Blaming: Discourses of Stalking in *There's Something About Mary*," *Women & Language* 22 (1999): 27.

22. Anderson and Accomando, 27.

23. *Gender: The Enduring Paradox*, videorecording. Smithsonian 1990.

24. See Krista Ratcliffe, *Anglo-American Challenges to the Rhetorical Tradition* (Carbondale, IL: Southern Illinois University Press, 1995). Ratcliffe's work on feminist rhetorical strategies have been adopted for this section. We have expanded her analysis beyond the Anglo-American tradition and added the examination of cultural production as an option in lieu of re-reading traditional rhetorical texts.

25. Dale Spender, *Man Made Language* (Boston: Routledge & Kegan Paul, 1985).

26. Cheris Kramarae, "Punctuating the Dictionary," *International Journal of Society and Language* 94 (1992): 137–138.

27. Sue Wise and Liz Stanley, *Georgie Porgie: Sexual Harassment in Everyday Life* (New York: Pandora, 1987).

28. Teri Kwal Gamble and Michael Gamble, *The Gender Connection* (New York: Houghton Mifflin, 2002), 354.

29. Mary Daly, *Gyn/Ecology: The Metaphysics of Radical Feminism* (Boston: Beacon, 1978), 3.

30. Jessica Rosenberg and Gitana Garofalo, "Riot Grrrls: Revolution from Within," *Signs: Journal of Women in Culture & Society* 23 (1998): 810.

31. Kramarae and Treichler. See also Mary Daly's *Websters' First New Intergalactic Wickedary of the English Language* (Boston; Beacon, 1987).

32. Karen A. Foss and Sonja K. Foss, *Women Speak: The Eloquence of Women's Lives* (Prospect Heights, IL: Waveland Press, 1991), 10.

33. See James A. Herrick's quote of George Kennedy in *The History and Theory of Rhetoric: An Introduction*, 2nd ed. (Boston: Allyn Bacon, 2001), 152.

34. Kohrs Campbell, *Three* 6.

35. Nichola Gutgold, "Managing Rhetorical Roles: Elizabeth Hanford Dole from Spouse to Candidate 1996–1999," *Women & Language* 24 (2001): 29–36.

36. *Monuments are for Men; Waffles are for Women: Exploring Gender Permanence & Impermanence,* video recording, University of California Extension Center for Media and Independent Learning, 2000.

37. Sally Miller Gearhart, "Womanpower: Energy Re-Sourcement," in *The Politics of Women's Spirituality: Essays on the Rise of Spiritual Power within the Feminist Movement*, ed. Charlene Spretnak (Garden City, NY: Doubleday, 1982), 143.

38. Sonja K. Foss and Cindy Griffin, "Exploring Rhetoric Beyond Persuasion: A Proposal for an Invitational Rhetoric," *Communication Monographs* 62 (1995): 6.

39. A list of Richard Roeper's (of Ebert and Roeper) ten best films of 2001 can be found at http://www.reel.com/reel.asp?node=features/awards/awards01/critics

40. Foss, Foss, and Griffin, 89.

41. http://www.duke.edu/web/film/pioneers/ (Accessed August 24, 2002.)

42. Sarah Ebner, "Culture, Television & Radio: Breaking the Celluloid Ceiling; There are Fewer Women Film Directors Than Ever Before," *Birmingham Post* 24 June (2003): 12.

43. Elizabeth Guider, "Little Progress in TV," *Daily Variety*, 27 June (2003).

44. Tania Modleski, *Loving With a Vengeance: Mass-Produced Fantasies for Women* (New York: Routledge, 1984).

45. Flo Leibowitz, "Apt Feelings, or Why 'Women's Films' Aren't Trivial," in *Post-Theory: Reconstructing Film Studies*, edited by David Bordwell and Noël Carroll, 219–229, (Madison: U of Wisconsin Press, 1996).

46. Elizabeth Bell and Laura Sells, *Mouse to Mermaid: The Politics of Film, Gender, and Culture* (Bloomington and Indianapolis: Indiana University Press, 1995). Italics ours.

47. Laura Mulvey, "Visual Pleasure and Narrative Cinema." *Screen* (16.3) (Autumn 1975): 6–18.

48. See for example, Cooper, "'Chick Flicks.'"

49. See Robert Alan Brookey and Robert Westerfelhaus, "Hiding Homoeroticism in Plain View: The *Fight Club* DVD as Digital Closet," *Critical Studies in Mass Communication* 19 (2002): 21–43.

50. See Jane Gaines, "White Privilege and Looking Relations: Race and Gender in Feminist Film Theory" *Screen* 29 (1988): 4.

51. Sue Thorman, "Feminism and Film," in *The Routledge Companion to Feminism and Postfeminism*, edited by Sarah Gamble, 102 (New York: Routledge, 1998).

52. *Shallow Hal.* Dir. Bobby Farrelly and Peter Farrelly. Perf. Gwyneth Paltrow and Jack Black. 2001. DVD. Twentieth Century Fox, 2002. Throughout this section of the essay, we will be citing from the Twentieth Century Fox DVD version of *Shallow Hal.* When citing from the actual film on the DVD, we will note the specific chapter number; for example, (*Shallow*, chapter 3).

53. Ibid., chapter 1.

54. Ibid., chapter 8.

55. In this description and subsequent analysis of the film, we need to distinguish between Gwyneth Paltrow, in her own body, playing the Rosemary character, and the 300 pound Rosemary (played by Paltrow in a fat suit or by Ivy Snitzer). The language available to us to describe these two different bodies of Rosemary is charged. Our cultural construction of beauty in twenty-first century America gives us a multitude of ways to describe Paltrow's body (model-thin, perfect, svelte, normal, beautiful) all of which have positive connotations. Although we try to avoid pejorative adjectives (obese, overweight, fat) to describe the second body type of Rosemary, the adjectives available to us (very large, plus-size, 300 pound) all seem woefully insufficient, in that they do not allow us to provide a laden-free or inherently positive description.

56. *Shallow*, chapter 20.

57. Ibid., chapter 6.

58. For easy access to over thirty reviews of *Shallow Hal*, proceed to the following website http://www.metacritic.com

59. "Commentary," chapter 1.

60. Ibid., chapter 16.

61. Laura Mulvey, *Visual and Other Pleasures* (Basingstoke: Macmillan, 1989).

62. Brookey and Westerfelhaus, 25.

63. Ibid., 24.

64. Comments about the actors who played major characters were not included in the analysis for our table; these include Rosemary, Hal, Hal's friends—Mauricio and Walt, Hal's neighbor—Jill, and the TV guru—Robbins.

65. Again, these claims are made only based on the brothers' improvised comments, they do not account for the actors and actresses as cited in the actual film credits for *Shallow Hal,* nor do they represent the Farrellys' actual hiring practices.

66. "Commentary," chapter 11.

67. Ibid., chapter 8.

68. Ibid., chapter 13 and 9.

69. Ibid., chapter 18, 7, and 8.

70. Ibid., chapter 23.

71. Ibid., chapter 9.

72. "Gwyneth's Double Breaks Her Silence," Interview with Ivy Snitzer, *Entertainment Tonight Online* (November 9, 2001). October 7, 2002 http://www.etonline.com/celebrity/a7536.htm.

73. *Shallow, c*hapter 28.

74. bell hooks, *Teaching to Transgress* (New York: Routledge, 1994), 43.

75. "Gwyneth Gets Heavy!" Interview with Gwyneth Paltrow. *Entertainment Tonight Online.* November 9, 2001. October 7, 2002. http://www.etonline.com/celebrity/a3291.htm

76. Although there is a brief section on Ivy Snitzer, the three, we presume, conventionally unattractive actresses who were made even more unattractive for their scenes in the dance bar—Bonnie Aarons, Lisa Brounstein, and Fawn Irish—are *not* interviewed in this thirteen-minute documentary. Nor is Nan Martin who played Nurse Tanya Peeler.

77. "Seeing Through the Layers," *Shallow Hal.*

78. Ibid.

79. Marissa Meltzer, "Hollywood's Big New Minstrel Show," *Bitch* (Winter 2001). http://www.bitchmagazine.com

80. "Fat Rights Organization Boycotts 'Shallow Hal,'" Press Release. NAAFA. November 7, 2001. http://www.nafaa.org

81. Interview with Diane Bliss. *Big Fat Blog.* n.d. 8 October 2002. http://bigfatblog.com/interviews/bliss.php

82. "ET's Exclusive—Plus-Size Panel." Interview with Lisa Bounstein, Susanne Wright, Tess Borden, Rebekah Derrick, Sharon Sachs, Megan Cavanagh, Diane Bliss, and Alex Alexander. *Entertainment Tonight Online.* November 27, 2001. October 8, 2002 http://www.etonline.com/celebrity/a7755.htm

83. "ET Exclusive—Plus Size Panel."

84. For a review in the *Philadelphia Inquirer* that echoes these women's concerns see, Carrie Richey, "'Shallow Hal' Tries to Have it Both Ways," Rev. of *Shallow Hal. Philadelphia Inquirer* (November 9, 2001). October 7, 2002 <http://ae.philly.com/entertainment/ui/philly/movie.html?id=49495&reviewId=5945>

85. "ET Exclusive—Plus Size Panel."

86. Lisa Brounstein is the actress who played one of the "ugly" women dancing at the bar in *Shallow Hal.* She is a "staunch defender" of *Shallow Hal.* She is also an active member of the Screen Actors Guild's Plus-Size Task Force. "ET Exclusive—Plus Size Panel."

87. Bernard, Jami. "Thin on Respect." Review of *Shallow Hal. New York Daily News.* November 11, 2001. October 8, 2002, http://nydailynews.com

88. Travers, Peter. Review of *Shallow Hal. Rolling Stone* (December 6, 2001), <http://www.rollingstone.com/reviews/movie/5947659/review/5947660/shallow_hal

16

Ideographic Criticism

Ronald Lee

For most students, communication is a pragmatic discipline. It provides methods of analysis, a storehouse of strategies, and tried-and-true techniques for aiding an advocate in effectively advancing a cause. Whether in public speaking, argumentation, public relations, or persuasion, the paradigm of an advocate moving a specific audience toward a pre-determined end dominates undergraduate communication pedagogy. When students first approach rhetorical criticism, they typically bring this orientation with them.

For several years, I was assigned to teach COMM 201. This course had a daunting title, *Introduction to Research Methods in Communication Studies*. Given the makeup of my department, the other faculty members expected me to prepare sophomores for upper-division courses in both the social-science and humanist traditions. So, I set out to cover experimental, survey, ethnographic, and *critical* methods. How precisely was I supposed to provide a useful introduction to rhetorical criticism in two-and-a-half weeks (five 75-minute class periods)? Moreover, how was I supposed to prepare students to fulfill an assignment to write their first critical paper? Well, I did what I suspect almost every communication professor does. I presented a highly pragmatic approach of criticism. This is a critical methodology that I rarely use in my own scholarly work.

By presenting such a model, however, I introduced students to a clear point of departure for much of contemporary rhetorical criticism. Understanding the commitments of the pragmatic model, along with its limitations, provides a vocabulary of concepts that other approaches to criticism radically re-characterize. Of particular note is the so-called "ideological turn" in rhetorical criticism. Although the phrase "ideological turn" captures a particular attitude toward criticism, it includes under its umbrella a constellation of different perspectives and methods.

This chapter focuses on Michael Calvin McGee's *rhetorical materialism* (theoretical perspective) and *ideographic criticism* (how that perspective is used in criticism). Beginning in the 1970s, McGee wrote a series of essays that changed the way a generation of critics think about, talk about, and do criticism. Even those who reject his program have been obliged to enter an ongoing conversation with his vision of rhetoric and the critical perspective he has promulgated.

McGee taught at the University of Memphis, the University of Wisconsin-Madison, and for the twenty years before his death at the University of Iowa. Beyond his own writing, he influenced a generation of Iowa graduate students, a number of whom now rank among the most influential rhetorical theorists and critics in the field.

In what follows, I outline, as a point of departure, a pragmatic approach to criticism. Second, I explain the ideological turn in criticism by contrasting it to this pragmatic approach. Third, I detail the particular commitments of McGee's rhetorical materialism. Fourth, I explain how this rhetorical materialism is expressed in the doing of ideographic criticism. Finally, for my critical essay, I illustrate the use of ideographic criticism in an analysis of Senator Edward Kennedy's "Truth and Tolerance in America" speech delivered at Liberty Baptist College on October 3, 1983.

POINT OF DEPARTURE

In 1968, Lloyd Bitzer wrote a very widely read essay entitled, "The Rhetorical Situation." This article served as the initial perspective of my COMM 201 class. It is the classic presentation of an approach that focuses on understanding the strategic way an advocate may overcome obstacles to success. All of its component parts are defined in terms that point the critic toward an instrumental effect. By instrumental effect I mean the persuasive influence that messages, deliberately employed, have on a targeted audience.

As Bitzer approaches a text for critical analysis, his attention is drawn to the situation that called forth the discourse. In adopting this focus, he views a work of rhetoric as "pragmatic," because it "functions ultimately to produce action or change in the world." "The rhetor," Bitzer writes, "alters reality by bringing into existence a discourse of such a character that the audience, in thought and action, is so engaged that it becomes a mediator of change."[1]

Bitzer's view presupposes a particular epistemology. It takes for granted that objective conditions in the external world call forth discourses. "Nor should we assume," he argues, "that a rhetorical address gives existence to a situation; on the contrary, it is the situation which calls the discourse into existence."[2] There is a brute presence to situations; these situations present exigencies (problematic circumstances); and these exigencies can be "completely or partially removed if discourse, introduced into the situation, can so constrain human decision or action as to bring about the significant modification of the exigence."[3]

Assume for a moment that you are taking a class in corporate advocacy. During the semester, the instructor presents you with a series of case studies. In these cases, you are reading about organizations that have run into trouble. One of these cases involves the 1992 charges brought against Sears Auto Centers. Sears was accused of systematically pressuring customers into buying parts and services they did not need. Customers from across the country complained of having paid hundreds of dollars for unnecessary repair work. Former Sears' employees revealed to government investigators that intense pressure to boost revenue, due to a commission pay system and unrealistic sales goals, forced them to oversell. Various states brought suit against the corporation. The story sparked a firestorm of highly negative publicity and, ultimately, threatened the health of one of Sears' most important retail sectors.

In addition, you are given materials that describe Sears' public-relations response to this crisis. You are asked by the instructor to evaluate Sears' public messages based on what you have been told about the situation. You follow Bitzer's approach to criticism. First, you identify the exigencies (loss of business and profit, civil and criminal prosecution). Second, you locate the audiences that can be mediators of change and thus ameliorate the exigencies (Sears' customers, relevant law enforcement agencies). Third, you examine the constraints that limit the range of possible rhetorical responses (for instance, offering every regular, automotive-center customer a free set of tires would be financially infeasible). Finally, you evaluate the rhetorical strategies that Sears did enact and make judgments about their wisdom. Evaluating the "wisdom" of these choices will almost certainly be preoccupied with judgments of their effectiveness.

IDEOLOGICAL TURN IN CRITICISM

Notice how narrow the range of judgment is in this pragmatic model of criticism. The critic is limited to assessing the skills of the advocates in meeting their pre-determined ends.[4] Other questions, especially those concerning competing values or the veracity of the discourse, are left aside. As a result of not posing such questions, criticism takes on a decidedly establishment bias. The danger is that conventional wisdom and tradition, typically determined in concert with entrenched interests and institutions, become equated with truth. In the present case, our student critics may feel restricted to looking at the world through the eyes of Sears' corporate officials. "We can clarify this issue," Philip Wander, himself an important figure in the ideological turn, has remarked, "by asking ourselves what in everyday language we would call the person . . . who examines or rewrites drafts of . . . statements so that their impact on specific audiences can be ascertained or improved; for whom policy, audience, and situation are a given and the overriding question is how to assess the effectiveness of the speech?" His answer is "not . . . a critic." "We would," Wander concludes, "be more inclined to call him or her a 'public relations consultant.'"[5] Once critics begin to ask, "Whose interests are served by these messages that construct this particular version of the truth?" they are dealing with ideology. So, before we can continue, we must come to some workable understanding of this troublesome concept.

Ideology in the most general sense is "any system of ideas . . . directing political and social action."[6] The questions swirling around ideology ask: To what extent are these ideas true or false? What forces perpetuate these particular ideas? What groups benefit from and what groups are disadvantaged by these ideas?

The underlying assumption is that ideology "usually does not mirror the social world . . . but exhibits some transformation of it."[7] We generate concepts, myths, images, and stories about the nature of our world. These ideas are used to interpret social reality. These interpretations may create falsehood and distortion. Importantly, these distortions are not neutral in their effect for they work to the advantage of some groups and to the disadvantage of others.

For example, there are two broad perspectives on poverty in America.[8] One perspective focuses on poor people as the cause of their own condition. They lack education; they have an inadequate work ethic; they form unstable families often headed by unwed mothers; they frequently have criminal records and are part of the illegal drug culture; and they fail to manage their money wisely. A second perspective focuses on poverty as the consequence of an economic and political system. On this view, capitalism has created an economic system that requires surplus workers to assure an abundance of cheap labor. The social effects of this system are viewed as having fostered racism, urban ghettoes, and a dramatic and unfair skewing of the distribution of material resources.

Each perspective warrants very different political actions. The first justifies programs to help the poor improve themselves. These efforts typically include job training, education, counseling, and strict law enforcement. The second view justifies structural changes in the system that will lead to the redistribution of resources. These efforts might include a steep progressive tax structure, generous government spending on housing and medical care, and the federal regulation of business to assure fair and equal treatment of employees. In addition, these perspectives are advocated with quite different discourses. The first uses messages that talk of "markets," "merit," "competition," and "opportunity." The second talks of "equal treatment" "compassion," "exploitation," and "profiteering."

The example of poverty brings us to the heart of the matter. At root, ideology concerns the relationship among discourse, power, and truth. If we spend a few moments with each term, we should arrive at a workable understanding of ideology.

(1) Discourse. The term "discourse" refers to "language in use, or more broadly, the interactive production of meaning."[9] This definition highlights a distinction between contextual and abstract uses of language. For the sake of illustration, consider the phrases "moral language" and "moral discourse." As I turn around in my chair to look at my bookshelves, I see several works of moral philosophy. These include A. J. Ayer's *Language, Truth and Logic*, R. M. Hare's *The Language of Morals,* and Charles Stevenson's *Ethics and Language.* These authors chose to feature the word "language" in their titles because they are interested in the linguistic properties of ethical propositions. Each of these scholars provides a unique account of the meaning of the word "good" in the statement "X is good." Their treatment of this statement is apart from any consideration of any actual utterances of the word "good." They do not examine any particular speakers, audiences, or contexts. They are not interested in whether any specific object, person, or state of affairs is in fact good. Instead, their interest is wholly theoretical (or what moral philosophers call meta-ethical).

I also have on my bookshelves books and journals that contain treatments of "moral discourse." The authors of these works explore the moral utterances of actual speakers—Abraham Lincoln, Adolf Hitler, Martin Luther King, Jr., Nelson Mandela, and many others—in order to understand the meaning of their moral talk in historical context. These scholars do examine particular speakers, audiences, and contexts. Although their interest is in part theoretical, it is a theoretical interest grounded in a concern for the influence of specific moral messages in the world of practical affairs.[10]

(2) Power. Once the term "discourse" is substituted for "language," the relevance of power should become more obvious. Actual advocates are trying to influence the course of events in a manner that promotes their interests. Some advocates have more resources (money, access, technology, networks of influential friends) than others. Some advocates are pressing a case on behalf of established institutions and traditional ways of doing things, while others are working for groups with little social or economic standing and who find their interests at odds with the status quo. These disparities in position and resources make a huge difference in the ability to influence audiences.

Let us begin working from the most everyday of examples to grander illustrations of national political life. When I was an undergraduate, I was a participant in a perpetual pinochle game in the student lounge. If a player had to attend class, another student would take the vacated seat. As we started each new game and assigned various responsibilities, someone would always say to the person assigned to tally the points, "It is a poor scorekeeper who cannot win for her team." This aphorism captures one face of power—the illicit power exercised by those in positions of authority. So, in place of the card-game scorekeeper, we might just as well speak about Jeffrey Skilling, the former president of Enron, and David Duncan, the Arthur Andersen partner who oversaw the auditing of the Enron Corporation books. They are accused of profiting mightily from the creation of false reports documenting Enron profitability. They had the power to manufacture an allegedly misleading discourse that persuaded thousands of investors to put money into their enterprise.

Power, of course, is often exercised without any tinge of corruption. The President describes the crisis of terrorism, uses his authority as commander-in-chief to mobilize the armed forces, and urges the nation's citizens to sacrifice for the common good. Like the previous cases, this is an example of a powerful individual making an explicit decision that alters some state of affairs. And also like the other cases, it is done largely through the use of discourse. The President characterizes a situation as a "crisis," calls forth the historic precedents for the use of military force, and exhorts the citizenry to unite behind his leadership.

In the examples we have used thus far, a person or group who possesses power makes an explicit decision to exercise that power to bring about a particular result. Yet, many of the most interesting discursive expressions of power are far more subtle and commonplace. Such cases are not the result of a single decision, but rather the product of power that is exercised by a way of talking that constitutes social and political culture. These forms of power go under a number of different names depending on the particular theorist and circumstance, including socialization, legitimation, domination, and hegemony. Each term suggests that belief systems are perpetuated by powerful political, social, and economic interests. Yet, it would be impossible to locate a set of decision makers that consciously decide on such matters. In advanced industrial societies, the apparatus of indoctrination is hidden and often denies its own existence.

For instance, Americans do not think of their children's education as an exercise in political propaganda. Instead, the schools are viewed as quintessentially democratic institutions governed by local communities.[11] Education is seen as the critical and objective study of the world. Yet, upon reflection, it is obvious that stable societies must have an efficient way to pass on values and customs to each new generation. The fact that we interpret this process as education rather than indoctrination exemplifies the masking of power.

When I teach political communication, I title the second day of class discussion, "All I Really Needed to Know about Politics I Learned in Kindergarten"[12] My purpose is to draw my students' attention to the subtle ways in which Americans are socialized into a particular view of the political world. There are some obvious patriotic lessons passed on in the early years of elementary schooling, such as reciting the Pledge of Allegiance and singing "My Country 'Tis of Thee," but there are also a host of subtle, supposedly nonpolitical, and yet critically important beliefs inculcated in children during these formative years. For instance, children learn that they are required to go to school and that school officials have power over them. Importantly, this power appears sweetly benign as personified by kindergarten teachers. This benevolent image of power is reinforced in the stories of the Founding Fathers, children's paternal conception of the President, and classroom visits by Officer Friendly. Students also learn the importance of order, the value placed on finishing work in a timely matter, and the rewards that are passed out to the best and most obedient students. These are beginning lessons about the merit system in a capitalist economy.[13] As these pupils continue on in their education, they come to understand the country through the positive meanings associated with liberty, freedom, equality, tolerance, and democracy. These concepts are then organized into larger stories such as the American Dream.[14]

The school is not the only institution socializing the citizenry. The media present powerful representations of national life. Advertising, for example, bombards viewers with the values of consumerism. Industrialization and urbanization weakened the traditional sources of socialization—church, family, and ethnic community. Commercial messages filled this void by switching their focus from the features of goods (product-based advertising) to selling consumers a lifestyle that they may purchase by selecting particular products.[15] Now, advertising rather than religion and tradition have become the dominant source of individual identity. Notice, we do not think of beer and automobile advertising as political. Yet, thousands and thousands of commercial messages construct for us a particular view of the country. It is a place where men and women are beautiful; it is a place where everyone is affluent; and it is a place where consumption makes people happy.

To put this point about power in yet another way, I would remind you of what instructors tell all students of argumentation and persuasion. Those who have the power to define the terms of the controversy have a tremendous rhetorical advantage. For instance, if I am an opponent of preferential systems of college admission, I can shape the terms of discussion if I get to define affirmative action as an attack on the impartial and objective standard of merit. After all, if John has a higher SAT score than Jose, then John should be admitted and Jose should be turned away. What could be fairer than to make a decision on the color-blind criteria of merit? On the other hand, if I am a supporter of affirmative action, I generally prevail if the evidence of merit, especially standardized test scores, is defined as the byproducts of privilege. Of course Jose, whose parents are first-generation, working-class immigrants, is not going to have the same kind of elaborated vocabulary as John, whose professional parents both had the advantage of advanced graduate educations. From this point of view, the accident of birth explains John's 95th percentile verbal score on the SAT far better than some concept of merit. In fact, Jose's very respectable 85th percentile score, given his social and economic position, may be the more "meritorious" achievement.

On a larger scale, this is what examining the relationship between discourse and power makes evident. Powerful interests, through the communication apparatuses of an advanced society, define the very terms of discussion. Yet, if you have a vision of some cabal sitting in a room pulling the strings that determine what the public will believe, then you have a terribly oversimplified view of power. The United States is a democratic republic; it has an advanced capitalist economy; and it is a predominantly Christian nation. These traditions and institutions together create a set of belief systems that shape our view of the world. They are perpetuated by political, economic, and social interests. Their domination of our thinking is virtually invisible because it is not imposed by some identifiable thought police. Rather, it merely appears as the American way of life.

(3) Truth. From what I have already said about power, I suspect that it is obvious that "truth" is dependent upon standpoint or perspective. There are often various versions of the truth. Each version may be sponsored by those who represent a different set of interests.

In an earlier life, I spent a summer attending law school. One of my courses was Torts. Tort law concerns civil action taken by a plaintiff in order to receive compensation for the wrongful act of a defendant. This is the form of the law that is derisively characterized as "ambulance chasing." If you were to slip, fall, and break your leg on a patch of ice in front of a retail store, then you might bring a civil action in order to receive compensation for your injury. You would argue that the proprietors had been negligent because they failed to clear the ice away from the store entrance.

My law professor was especially good at disabusing students of any simple positivist view of the law. As naive outsiders, we may think of the application of the law as a relatively straightforward and rational procedure. First, the facts are discovered. Second, the relevant law is found. Third, an objective decision is made about the match between the facts and the law. The law, on this view, either applies to these facts or it does not. Supposedly, it is this predictable, rational procedure that assures justice.

As my law professor told us, the lawyer's job is to *characterize* the facts and the law in ways that are to the advantage of our client. The law is a rhetorical enterprise that pits opposing interpretations of the facts and the law against one another. The more persuasive version of the "truth" wins the verdict. Neither the law nor the facts are settled matters, but rather objects that may be differently constructed in discourse.[16]

In our slip-and-fall case, the facts may be complicated. Perhaps at the time you came to the store an ice storm was in progress. The defendant's lawyer argues that it was impossible for anyone clearing sidewalks to keep up with the rate of ice formation. Moreover, you were inappropriately dressed in high-heeled shoes. No reasonable person would venture out in these conditions wearing that type of shoe. So, the plaintiff was the one who was negligent and the defendant did everything a reasonable person could expect. Both the facts and the law may be persuasively characterized.

What I have said about the law is equally true of nearly any enterprise concerned with the construction of social reality. For example, many histories are written of the same event. Even when the relevant facts are generally agreed upon, the placement and characterization of those facts within a larger narrative may radically change the meaning of events.[17] So, taken together, discourse and power may create persuasive versions of the truth. These versions may be widely accepted and serve as the basis for decisions in the world of practical affairs.

I fear that the work we have done so far creates too inclusive a domain for ideology. If we define ideology "as any discourse bound up with specific social interests," then it becomes hard to think of any discourse, at least in some remote sense, which does not fall under its umbrella.[18] There is no simple way out of this problem. We might try to distinguish "social interests" from all possible human interests, but this exercise does not get us very far. Eating is a human interest (a bodily need), but certainly the production, selling, marketing, and meaning of food is tied up with serious economic and political interests. All we might say is that as the social interest is better organized, more powerful, and its relationship to dominant cultural discourses more obvious, we can be more confident in calling such affected discourses ideological. Conversely, as the social interest appears disorganized, lacking in influence, and its relationship to dominant cultural discourses is unclear or weak, we may view these discourses as relatively nonideological.

Remember that discourses that meet these criteria may resist the label "ideology." Americans do not typically refer to the public school curricula, advertising, or the law as examples of ideological discourse. Yet, these discourses are paradigm cases of ideology. This quality of ideology denying itself is a central characteristic of the concept. In summary, on this view, ideological discourse is a "discourse bound up with specific social interests." It produces a version of the truth and perpetuates belief systems on behalf of powerful interests. This account has set aside many thorny theoretical issues, but for our purposes it is enough to recognize that discourse, power, and truth are bound up in the concept of ideology.

RHETORICAL MATERIALISM

Michael Calvin McGee's participation in the ideological turn is based on his construction of a particular theoretical perspective on rhetoric, which underwrites a method of critical analysis. I will begin with an explanation of McGee's theory, rhetorical materialism, and then proceed to his method, ideographic criticism.

McGee identifies himself as a "rhetorical materialist." He uses this self-identifier to distinguish his program from traditional critical-theoretical approaches that had largely dominated the field into the 1970s. This is an important point to grasp. McGee was not theorizing in a vacuum; he was instead providing a perspective that stood in opposition to what was then the prevailing disciplinary paradigm.

McGee was reacting against a regime of rhetorical theory built on the authority of revered figures and texts. At that time, communication scholars largely thought about rhetoric through the ideas and theoretical prescriptions of such great thinkers as Aristotle, Isocrates, Cicero, Quintilian, St. Augustine, Francis Bacon, George Campbell, and Richard Whately. The result of this approach was "a 'rhetoric' which is on its face uninformed by historical or immediate contact with actual practice." "The theory and technique of rhetoric," McGee writes, "come less from human experience than from the metaphysical creativity and inspiration of particular writers." "What has been called 'rhetorical theory,'" McGee contends, "through much of our tradition is not theory at all, but a set of technical, prescriptive principles which inform the practitioner while, paradoxically, remaining largely innocent of practice."[19]

Under this old regime, accounts of rhetoric come down as commandments from on high. They were frequently divorced from any actual discussion of how people do, in fact, engage in the practice of public persuasion. A speech was determined as eloquent and effective based on the application of classical theories. So, if the speaker was found to follow the advice of Aristotle, then the speech must have been both worthy and successful. Not surprisingly, the discourse surrounding contemporary social upheavals, especially the antiwar, civil rights, and women's movements, did not resemble the speeches given by the ancients. I suspect it is obvious that the mediated age of celebrity and fifteen-second ads operates on different principles than addresses to the Athenian Assembly, the Roman Senate, or the British Parliament.

By contrast with this earlier tradition, McGee is committed to the exploration of actual rhetorical encounters. McGee's sense of materialism is captured in the definition he offers of rhetoric. "Rhetoric," he writes, "is a natural social phenomenon in the context of which symbolic claims are made on the behavior and/or belief of one or more persons, allegedly in the interest of such individuals, and with the strong presumption that such claims will cause meaningful change."[20] From this definition, we may proceed to unpack the dimensions of rhetorical materialism.

First, the "natural social phenomenon" is the recurring human experience of the relationships among "speaker/speech/audience/occasion/change." You cannot live in the social world without being impacted by these relationships. Each time you are addressed as an audience—for instance, as the reader of this chapter, as a student in a class, or as a citizen of the republic—you enter into this confluence of relationships. You cannot avoid it. It is not simply an idea but an unavoidable part of living in the social world.

Second, the phrase "in the context of which" features for McGee the problematic relationship between "discourse" and "rhetoric." Rhetoric represents the entire experience of the complex social relationships among speaker/speech/audience/occasion/change. Discourse is residue that is left behind. It is the copy of the "speech" which has been saved. McGee uses an analogy to explain the rhetoric-discourse distinction. "We can construct," he writes, "the nature, scope, and consequence of a nuclear explosion by analyzing its residue when the raw matter and even the energy inherent in its occurrence have dissipated. Thus it is possible to reconstruct the nature, scope, and consequence of rhetoric by analyzing 'speech' even when 'speaker,' 'audience,' 'occasion,' and 'change' dissipate into half-remembered history." So, from a particular discourse we have the tracings that will permit a "reconstruction *of the whole phenomenon . . .* for it is the *whole* of 'speaker/speech/audience/occasion/change' which impinges on us."[21]

Third, the phrase "symbolic claims" suggests, for McGee, that "*every* interactivity of society contains or comprises a claim on some human being's belief and/or behavior."[22] Unlike conventional accounts of rhetoric, McGee does not distinguish rhetoric from coercion. He understands rhetoric as a species of coercion. It is, he writes, a "coercive agency," but certainly one that is preferable to other physical forms of coercion. He suggests that it is preferable in two different senses. First, when an audience acquiesces to rhetoric, it does so feeling that some more personal account was given for imposing the speaker's will. Second, the symbolic is preferable because it sublimates the "pain" of more violent forms of coercion. So, rhetoric may be thought as a preferable, more ethical form of coercion, but it is a form of coercion nonetheless.

Fourth, the phrase "behavior and/or belief" should draw the reader's attention to the complexities of moving from a change in belief to altering behavior. The scholarship in persuasion and social psychology is filled with the difficulties inherent in the process of changing beliefs to influence attitudes in order to ultimately create new behaviors. This process is complex even in the simplest of direct transactions (speaker—message—target audience), but considerably more difficult to account for in the intricate communication environment of contemporary society. Beliefs and attitudes are shaped by ideology and other diffuse discourses that influence the tenor of an entire society.

Fifth, the phrase "allegedly in the interest of the audience," McGee explains, "calls to attention the relationship between 'speaker' and 'audience' as 'leader' to 'follower.'"[23] The relationship between leader/follower and speaker/audience is a continuing theme in McGee's work. "Every 'audience,'" he writes, "comes together with an interest and the expectation that the 'speaker' will aid in procuring that interest. And every 'speaker' comes to 'audience' with the desire to accomplish an otherwise impossible task by mobilizing a collective force."[24] As you can imagine, the tension of interests between leader and follower, speaker and audience is at the center of any ideological criticism. For the rhetorical creation of a sense of collectivity among audience members requires the invention of messages that appear to harmonize the interests of the leader and the people.

Finally, the phrase "the strong presumption that such claims will result in meaningful change" draws our attention to the issue of rhetorical effects. Few social-science models of any stripe have much success at predicting cause-effect relationships. Certainly, any retrospective claim of a direct effect between a particular feature of a message and a specific historical outcome is foolhardy. The message variable is at best one among a bundle of other forces (economic, demographic, political, cultural, and so forth) and to try to draw specific causal connections is impossible. Yet, in the everyday world we "conduct a continual deliberation based on our ability to model the environment and to predict the consequences of changing it."[25] Even though we can neither explain nor control all the factors that influence change, our public discourse is filled with such talk. We do speak as if speech is a powerful agency to control the environment. This talk creates a sense of the collective and then speaks as if the collective will can shape meaningful social change. In these rhetorical transactions, we create a discourse that reveals the world in which we live. It is powerfully shaped by the ideological commitments that we share. As these commitments are modified, the messages reflect these changes. We can map the ideological shifts in our society by paying attention to these messages.

Up to this point, I have introduced you to ideology and materialism. I suspect many of you have recognized the influence of Karl Marx on the ideological turn in criticism. Marxism certainly creates the intellectual background against which many ideological critics work.[26] Yet, at the same time, the last twenty years have witnessed the collapse of communism and, at least in some respects, the repudiation of Marxism. So, one might naturally be led to wonder if ideological criticism itself is not a spent intellectual enterprise. This is why Michael McGee is such an interesting and important intellectual figure in rhetorical studies. Although admittedly influenced by Marxism, his commitments to this tradition have always been tempered.

McGee describes himself as a *Marxissant* and his politics as planted firmly in the tradition of Anglo-American liberalism.[27] "A *Marxissant*," McGee explains, "is one who accepts the fundamental categories and logic and maybe even methods of Marxist analysis, but is not a party member and is not committed to the social state or the dictatorship of the proletariat." "A *Marxissant*," he continues, "believes that theory is alive, not frozen or sterile or orthodox, and it needs to be developed and moved forward. But most fundamentally . . . *Marxissants* are more nationalistic, in that they tend to deny the international aspects of Marxist theory."[28] These sentiments have introduced a number of commitments that may at first appear confusing. Upon reflection, however, I actually think you will find them quite straightforward.

First, McGee finds the intellectual approach of Marxism useful for understanding society, but he does not ascribe to its political program. Second, McGee does not accept Marxist theory (or any theory) as orthodoxy. So, the fact that Marx made a claim in the 19th century pertaining to the British Empire does not mean that it should be taken as holy writ by 21st century theorists trying to understand liberal democracies and advanced capitalism. Instead, Marxism is an interesting point of departure for thinking about society. Third, McGee does not accept the universalistic aspects of Marxism. In saying that he is a nationalist, he means that he believes that national culture is a critically important element in explaining society. "Marxist theory holds," he observes, "that if you are a worker living in Cleveland, you have more in common with a worker in Gorki than you do with a banker in Columbus. And this is not true."[29]

What does it mean to say that McGee is a liberal in the Anglo-American liberal tradition? It means that McGee's work is focused on the tradition and language of the English and American political experience. "If we're going to have a true politics of the left in Anglo-America," McGee argues, "it must be liberal politics. There's no choice, because liberal politics is all that will fly here. If we cannot talk about what we want to accomplish in the terms of liberalism, then we are condemning ourselves to a life of marginality."[30] So, a commitment to liberal/progressive, conservative, or even radical politics must be articulated in the language of Anglo-American liberalism. To use any other political vocabulary, for instance the terminology of Marxism or Fascism, dooms the advocate to irrelevancy. Only liberal discourse can form a collectivity that can make a significant difference. The important social movements in American history have made their way by appeals to the core commitments of liberalism—liberty, equality, property, rule of law, and so forth.

Given the commitments of rhetorical materialism, how does McGee proceed as a rhetorical critic? What critical apparatus does he mobilize to glean the ideological commitments that are present in a text? The answers to these questions revolve around the concept of the "ideograph."

IDEOGRAPHIC CRITICISM

Critics need a way to move between discourse and ideology; they need a rhetorical window on the exercise of power and the accompanying promulgation of truth. In Dana Cloud's words, critics require a methodology that provides "an analytical link between rhetoric—understood as situated, pragmatic, instrumental, and strategic discourse—on one hand, and ideology—the structures or systems of ideas within which individual pragmatic speech acts take place and by which they are constrained—on the other."[31]

Michael McGee's concept of the "ideograph" provides just this link between rhetoric and ideology. The definition of "ideograph" is surprisingly complex, given its very ordinary and everyday nature. So, let us begin with a list of ideographs and then move to their formal characteristics. In the American context, the following words and slogans are examples of ideographs: <equality>, <freedom>, <freedom of speech>, <law and order>, <liberty>, <national security>, <privacy>, <property>, <rule of law>, and <separation of church and state>.[32]

McGee lists the "characteristics" (in italics) that would constitute a "formal definition of 'ideograph.'"[33] I have commented on each of these seven characteristics below:

1. *"An ideograph is an ordinary language term found in political discourse."*[34] Ideographs are not technical terms, words used by experts or privileged insiders; rather they are terms that appear regularly in ordinary public talk. These are words that you will encounter on the news, hear on talk radio programs, find in the texts of political speeches, encounter in grade school classrooms, and use in everyday conversation.
2. *"It is a high-order abstraction representing collective commitment to a particular but equivocal and ill-defined normative goal."*[35] On the highest level of abstraction, ideographs are ambiguous, although they have a high emotional affect. For instance, the words <liberty>, <freedom>, and <equality> are emotionally evocative, but they have little cognitive meaning unless tied to specific situations. They are general enough in their meaning that they may be used in a wide variety of contexts. The ideograph <liberty> might be employed by either side in the abortion debate or it might be evoked by either side in the controversy over the meaning of separation of church and state. Ideographs are "normative" because they are value terms that are used to make judgments. Ideographs are "goals" because they represent something to be obtained or a path to follow. So, political candidates might urge their audiences to pursue the path of <freedom>.
3. *"It warrants the use of power, excuses behavior and belief which might otherwise be perceived as eccentric or antisocial, and guides behavior and belief into channels easily recognized as acceptable and laudable. Ideographs such as 'slavery' and 'tyranny,' however, may guide behavior and belief negatively by branding unacceptable behavior."*[36] The essential function of an ideograph is to warrant the exercise of power. Taking or not taking action is justified in the name of ideographs. Some ideographs are positive (<liberty>, <freedom>, <equality>) and behaviors that can be justified by positive ideographs are regarded as socially acceptable. Some ideographs are negative (<tyranny>, <socialism>, <censorship>) and behaviors that further these values are branded as unacceptable.
4. *"And many ideographs ('liberty,' for example) have a non-ideographic usage, as in the sentence, 'Since I resigned my position, I am at liberty to accept your offer.'"*[37] Ideographs "signify and 'contain' a unique ideological commitment."[38] They are the public vocabulary of ideology. So, when terms such as "liberty" and "freedom" are used in non-ideological contexts, they do not function as ideographs.
5. *"Ideographs are culture-bound, though some terms are used in different signification across cultures."*[39] Ideographs are universal because they exist in all societies. Specific ideographs are culture bound. The Anglo-American liberal tradition features a defining set of ideographs—the focus on <liberty>, for instance—that would not appear, or at least not appear with the same significance, in other cultures.

6. *"Each member of the community is socialized, conditioned, to the vocabulary of ideographs as a prerequisite for 'belonging' to the society."*[40] Becoming a member of a culture requires understanding the society's ideographs. As part of being socialized as an American, every school child learns to respect <property>, to love <liberty>, and to guard <freedom>.

7. *"A degree of <tolerance> is usual, but people are expected to understand ideographs within a range of usage thought to be acceptable: The society will inflict penalties on those who use ideographs in heretical ways and on those who refuse to respond appropriately to claims on their behavior warranted through the agency of ideographs."*[41] These penalties may range in severity. Speaking in ways that use ideographs inappropriately may result in political marginalization. Absent the appropriate language, advocates will simply fail to find an audience. Rhetorical sanctions may be imposed as deviant rhetors are labeled "traitors," "demagogues," or "extremists." This may result in public scorn and rhetorical exile. Finally, legal and economic sanctions may be inflicted on those who are determined to be guilty of "subversion" or "treason." This can result in prosecution or loss of employment. During the Red Scare of the 1950s, Joseph McCarthy employed many of these terms to punish the American Left. Likewise, since the rise of the Christian Right in the late 1970s, religious conservatives have been charged with possessing an insufficient commitment to <tolerance> and <pluralism>. Critics on the Left have punished them with accusations of "racism," "homophobia," and "sexism."

Ideographs are especially important for understanding the relationship between leaders and citizens. They are the storehouse of words and phrases from which leaders select appeals to warrant exercises of power. These are the terms that are used when leaders claim to be acting in the name of <the people>.[42] "Ideographs represent in condensed form," Condit and Lucaites explain, "the normative, collective commitments of the members of a public, and they typically appear in public argumentation as the necessary motivations or justifications for action performed in the name of the public."[43]

Remember ideographs are abstract terms that take on more specific meaning as they are placed in given contexts. Like other terms of value, ideographs are often in tension with one another. "An ideograph," McGee writes, "is always understood in its relation to another."[44] So, <freedom> is always understood in relationship to <order>, <responsibility>, and the <rule of law>. In any given circumstance, advocates may argue that one ideological commitment is more important than another. For instance, in the civil rights struggles of the 1950s and 1960s, segregationists and integrationists battled over the preeminence of particular sets of ideographs. Segregationists held that <property> rights permitted proprietors of restaurants, motels, retail stores, and other <private> businesses to decide whom they would serve. If owners of apartment buildings did not want to rent to black families, they should have that prerogative as controllers of private property. Integrationists held that the ideological commitment to <equality> demanded that businesses who served the <public> had an obligation to treat each customer alike. The resulting public accommodation and opening housing legislation put into law regulations that elevated, in this context, <equality> over <property>.

In brief, this example depicts the synchronic and diachronic dimensions of ideographic analysis. The *synchronic dimension* explores the tension among ideographs at a particular time. In the civil rights illustration, there were advocates posing differing ideological constructions of segregation in an effort to influence passage of specific legislation. The *diachronic dimension* explores a society's changing ideological commitments through time. In America, <equality>

has become an ever more important ideological commitment and its prominence has come at the expense of other ideographs, including <property>.[45]

I want to return for a few moments to the "point of departure" at the beginning of the chapter. Recall that I contrasted a pragmatic model of criticism (Bitzer's rhetorical situation) with ideological criticism. With the introduction to McGee's ideographic criticism, I want to spend a little time contrasting the two approaches. I draw your attention to three specific differences: the nature of effects, the concept of audience, and assumptions about reality.

Effects. In the pragmatic model, the critic is interested in evaluating the instrumental impact of a particular speaker's message on a target audience. The effects are quite narrow in conception. Did the message have the particular effect that the speaker desired? For instance, did the Sears' public relations campaign bring customers back to its Auto Service Centers?

In ideographic analysis, the critic is interested in examining the discourse as a symptom of changes in ideology and, thus, public consciousness. Put differently, the discourse itself is understood as the effect rather than the cause. When ideographs change, for instance <equality> displaces <property>, this reflects a change in ideology. The society has begun to justify political actions in new ways and warrant the exercise of power in different ideological terms.

What caused these changes in ideology? This is a very difficult question and is beyond the scope of rhetorical analysis. Typically, such changes are the result of economics, demographics, conflict, or some other social malady. The result of such forces change social reality—the way Americans think about race has changed dramatically over the last century—and these changes are then reflected in the society's rhetoric. These rhetorical changes are marked by new relationships among the culture's ideographs.

Audience. In the pragmatic model, the audience is often assumed to be a fixed target. The audience pre-exists the message. Thus, the advocate adapts the message to a set of audience predispositions and behaviors. The critic's work is to assess the choices that the rhetor made.[46]

In ideographic analysis, the audience itself is taken to be rhetorically constructed. Power is exercised and political actions are justified in the name of <The People>.[47] The audience does not pre-exist the message, but is actually constituted by it. Adolf Hitler constructed the German people as a superior Aryan race. Martin Luther King, Jr. constructed a people who were judged by the "content of their character" rather than the "color of their skin." Ronald Reagan characterized ordinary Americans as "heroic." In each case, these definitions of <The People> become ideological premises upon which to justify taking particular forms of political action. Understanding the changing ideological construction of <The People> is at the center of doing ideographic criticism.

Reality. In the pragmatic model of criticism, there is an implicit assumption that an objective situation (circumstances, audiences, constraints) is present which may be instrumentally altered by the strategic use of discourse. The situation pre-exists the discourse. In ideological criticism, there is an explicit assumption that rhetoric constitutes reality. As I mentioned earlier, ideological criticism concerns the relationship among discourse, power, and truth. The constellation and relationship among ideographs maps the shape of this rhetorically constituted reality.

FINAL THOUGHTS

All criticism involves making arguments on behalf of judgments. "When a . . . critic," Wayne Brockriede writes, "states clearly the criteria he has used in arriving at his judgment, together with the philosophic or theoretic foundations on which they rest, and when he has offered some data to show that the rhetorical experience meets or fails to meet these criteria, then he has argued." Confronted with this form of critical argument "a reader has several kinds of choices: he can accept or reject the data, accept or reject the criteria, accept or reject the philosophic or theoretic basis for the criteria, and accept or reject the inferential leap that joins data and criteria."[48]

Using Brockriede's notion of criticism as a template, let us think through how a critic may use ideographic criticism to form an argument on behalf of a judgment. First, ideographs are a kind of *data*. They direct the critic to look for the presence of ideographs in a text. The critic looks both for the tension among ideographs at a single point in time as well as for changing patterns of ideographic tensions over time. These patterns are the critic's data.

Second, the *theoretical foundation* of ideographic analysis is rhetorical materialism. It is the commitments of rhetorical materialism that underwrite the relationship among rhetoric, discourse, and ideology. It is only when rhetoric and ideology are understood in particular ways that ideographic criticism becomes compelling. The data provided by ideographs represent patterns of public consciousness. These patterns are maps of changing ideological commitments. As a result, the critic reveals the changing patterns by which power is justified.

Third, ideographic criticism does not present any single set of *criteria for evaluation*. Rather, the results of ideographic criticism provide data that underwrite several different forms of evaluation.

(A) An ideographic criticism documents progressive or regressive ideological-rhetorical trends. Celeste Condit and John Lucaites, in their book *Crafting* <equality>, have documented the increasingly important role <equality> has played in American public consciousness. By and large, they tell an affirming story of an improving and more just America. The ascendancy of <equality>, they argue, has had positive consequences on the moral quality of our national discourse. Used in this way, the reader is asked to judge the positive and negative quality of the ideographic trend.

(B) Ideographic criticism believes ideology is false consciousness. For these critics, public rhetoric often rationalizes political acts that help the powerful and disadvantage the powerless. The acceptance of these explanations accounts for why the people who have the least complain the least. The poor, for instance, have been led to believe that the cause of their deprived circumstances is their own failings.[49] Dana Cloud, in her ideographic analysis of family-values discourse, draws precisely this type of conclusion. "<Family values> talk," she writes, "functioned during the [1992 Presidential election campaign] to scapegoat Black men and poor Americans for social problems." She continues, "Ultimately, in constructing the family as the site of all responsibility and change, the rhetoric of <family values> privatizes social responsibility for ending poverty and racism."[50] Employed in this matter, readers are asked to accept or reject the discourse as a distortion promulgated for the purpose of established interests.

(C) Ideographic criticism reveals political irony. Irony lies in the incongruity between the actual result and the normal or expected result. Kenneth Burke's general formula—"what goes forth as A returns as non-A"—captures this sense of this trope.[51] A particularly good illustration of irony is the famous postulate by the nineteenth-century economist Thomas Malthus. He reasoned that "population, when unchecked . . . tends to increase up to the limits of 'the means of subsistence.'"[52] Given this premise, one could then reason that helping the poor (A) actually hurts the poor (non-A). The compassionate (A) are really those who appear to lack compassion (non-A). "It did not hurt the Malthusian theory," Mark Blaug argues, "that it justified resistance of the upper classes to all efforts to reform social and political institutions: for if poverty had its roots in the unequal race between population and subsistence, only the working class itself, by practicing prudential restraint could improve its own conditions."[53]

Irony is not limited to the discourses of poverty and welfare. For example, Celeste Condit and Ann Selzer explored the newspaper coverage of a Kansas murder trial. They found, ironically, that the journalistic standards of <objectivity> lead "to a prosecution bias in the reporting of criminal trials."[54] Objectivity (A) led to bias (non-A). In the critical essay that accompanies this chapter, I explore the ironic function of <tolerance> in Senator Edward Kennedy's "Tolerance and Truth in America" address. I argue that the force of <tolerance> is to limit rather than enlarge the acceptable means of political expression. Tolerance (A) leads to intolerance (non-A).

Irony is a complex form of evaluation. By exposing inconsistencies of ideological warrants, it opens up semantic space for resistance. These terms begin to lose some of their positive emotive force and, ultimately, these justifications for the exercise of power become less compelling. This form of ideographic criticism suggests lines of counterargument and alternative political narratives. The reader is left to judge the merits of these new ways of looking at the world.

CRITICAL ESSAY

For my critical essay, I have written an analysis of Senator Edward Kennedy's 1983 "Tolerance and Truth in America" speech, which was delivered to an audience of faculty members and students at Liberty Baptist College. Senator Kennedy's discussion of religion, politics, and public discourse demonstrates the ironic consequences that an ideological commitment to <tolerance> entails. In promoting civility in the public square, a society may often silence the citizenry's most cherished moral beliefs.

You may wonder why I chose a twenty-one-year-old speech for analysis. My selection had motivations beyond the text's usefulness as a schoolroom illustration. In the aftermath of September 11th, the tension between religious conviction and public speech has produced tears in the fabric of American civil society. It did so in two related ways. First, Osama bin Laden issued a fatwah on February 23, 1998 calling on Muslims to "kill the Americans and plunder their money wherever and whenever they find it."[55] His justification, in large part, rested on the depiction of the United States as a "pagan" nation. Americans are "pagan" because they have formed a society in which the place of religion is proscribed in national life. The commitment to religious pluralism has no place in the ideal theocratic state envisioned by followers of al-Qaeda.

Second, within the United States, 9/11 led to acts and statements of religious intolerance. Some American Muslims suffered through frequent and often severe episodes of harassment. Incidents ranged from ethnic profiling to verbal and physical assault. During the twelve months following attacks, the American-Arab Anti-Discrimination Committee alleged over 700 violent incidents targeting Arab Americans, including several murders; over 80 cases of illegal and discriminatory removal of passengers from aircraft; a 400 percent increase in employment discrimination; and numerous instances of denial of service.[56]

Beyond individual acts of bigotry, American public discourse was littered with intemperate remarks by prominent religious and political leaders. For instance, the Reverend Franklin Graham, son of evangelist Billy Graham, said during a November 16, 2001 interview on the NBC *Nightly News* that Islam was "a very evil and wicked religion." "It wasn't Methodists flying into those buildings, it wasn't Lutherans," Graham told NBC. "It was an attack on this country by people of the Islamic faith." In a recently published book, entitled *The Name*, Graham writes, "The God of Islam is not the God of the Christian faith. The two are different as lightness and darkness." "Much is said and published today about how peace-oriented Islam is," he continues. "A little scrutiny reveals quite the opposite."[57]

In another example, Dr. Jerry Vines, former President of the Southern Baptist Convention, as quoted by reporter Jim Jones, said in a widely reported public speech that "Christianity was founded by the virgin-born Lord Jesus Christ. Islam was founded by Muhammad, a demon-possessed pedophile who had 12 wives, and his last one was a 9-year-old girl." "Allah," he continued, "is not Jehovah. Jehovah is not going to turn you into a terrorist that'll try to bomb people and take the lives of thousands and thousands of people." In saying this, he drew the lesson that the contemporary American commitment to religious pluralism had gone too far. "Today, people are saying all religions are the same. They would have us believe Islam is just as good as Christianity. But I'm here to tell you . . . that Islam is not as good as Christianity."[58]

In a last troubling example, Cal Thomas, a widely syndicated political columnist, wrote on May 21, 2003, that the United States was threatened by the presence of Muslim citizens within its borders. He argued that "when Muslims gain political power, the historical and contemporary record is not encouraging for people who hold democratic values and are of the 'Judeo-Christian' persuasion."[59]

Beyond the stresses of 9/11, the mingling of the religious and the political have been prominent in a whole host of recent controversial issues. These would include debates over the morality of stem cell research and the prospects of legalizing homosexual civil unions. Over and over again in contemporary national life the country struggles with the proper relationship between faith and politics.

Edward Kennedy's 1983 speech at Liberty Baptist College is a very good text with which to think. You will find in reading the analysis that I am quite critical of this vision of religious tolerance. Yet, I find Kennedy's presentation of the essential issues a vivid portrait of what is at stake.

CRITICAL ESSAY: REFLECTIONS ON <TOLERANCE>: AN IDEOGRAPHIC ANALYSIS OF EDWARD KENNEDY'S SPEECH AT LIBERTY BAPTIST COLLEGE

American elected officials fill their discourses with phrases emphasizing their subordinate relationship to the public. They call themselves "public servants" and in meeting regularly with constituents, standing for election, and in countless other acts of deference they recognize their "public accountability." In defending any legislative or executive act, the democratic script requires our political leaders to offer justifications in terms of the "public good."

Though this word "public" appears everywhere in the discourse of American national life, its meaning is far from a settled matter. Like all important political symbols, it has high affect and low cognitive specificity.[60] Put differently, the citizenry reacts emotionally to the term, as it does to "liberty," "freedom," "equality," and other important American symbols, but its meaning is ambiguous and subject to considerable change as it moves among differing contexts. Michael McGee has called such terms "ideographs." "An ideograph," he writes, "is an ordinary language term found in political discourse. It is a high-order abstraction representing collective commitment to a particular but equivocal and ill-defined normative goal." Ideographs function to "warrant the use of power."[61]

As with all ideographs, the changes in the meaning of "public" are marked by altered relationships with other ideographs. <Public> and <private> are in a dialectical tension that shifts with context and history. In the segregated world of the Old South, the prerogatives of

<private property> permitted landlords, innkeepers, and business owners to turn away patrons on the basis of race. With the passage of Title II of the Civil Rights Act of 1964, discrimination in places of public accommodation because of race, color, religion, or national origin was prohibited. As a result, the sphere and privileges of <private property> were diminished by the demands of <equality>. The <public>, in this context, became more important than the <private> in the hierarchy of American values.

By mapping such discursive shifts, the critic may illuminate important changes in ideology and the concomitant alterations in public consciousness. With the passage and eventual general acceptance of the premises of the 1964 Civil Rights Act, the acceptable rhetorical choices open to speakers changed. To invoke now the rights of <private property> to justify turning away a customer of color is to announce oneself a racist. Three generations ago, such an argument would fit comfortably inside a particular political tradition. Today, this tradition has no respectable members.

Beginning in the 1970s, a series of events led to another deep division over the proper relationship between <public> and <private>. The grounds of this controversy were very different, but once again the fundamental character of the <public> was at issue. This time it was not a matter of which groups in America were entitled to full citizenship (the issue of civil rights), but rather which <private> beliefs could be responsibly brought to bear in discussions of <public> issues. Where <equality> mediated the dispute between <public> and <private property> in the case of segregation, the ideograph <tolerance> was at the center of this dispute.

In the 1970s and 1980s members of conservative religious congregations began to organize politically and through this organization sought to influence the outcome of elections, the appointment of federal judges, the passage of legislation, and the general ideological direction of American politics. This emerging coalition of religious conservatives went under a number of names and organizational titles. Generally, it was known as the New Christian Right. Although initially, the name of the Reverend Jerry Falwell's political organization—the Moral Majority—was widely used to identify the movement.

Beyond the traditional liberal/conservative disagreements over policy issues, these religious conservatives hoped to reverse the trend toward what they saw as an increasingly coarse and debased culture. This divide was called by some commentators a "culture war"—a war that drew battle lines along an orthodox-progressive rift. "Orthodoxy," James Hunter explains, "is the commitment on the part of adherents to an external, definable, and transcendent authority." "Progressivism," on the other hand, holds that "moral authority tends to be defined by the spirit of the modern age, a spirit of rationalism and subjectivism."[62] Those holding orthodox religious views pressed a social-conservative agenda into the center of the American political dialogue. Over a period of years and in many different contexts, vigorous debates sprung up over family values, regulation of pornography, the wisdom of overturning *Roe v. Wade*, government funding of the arts, the provision of gay rights, the distasteful language and images in popular media, and a host of other cultural issues. Although religious conservatives also tended to favor fiscal constraint, low taxes, market economics, and a large military, they often did so for cultural reasons. For instance, representatives of the New Christian Right have frequently argued that high taxes and inflation force both parents to work. A fiscally disciplined government, they believe, would create a tax policy that would permit mothers to stay at home with their young children.

The progressive/orthodox cultural divide was in an important sense about the theory of democratic public communication itself. Very different views of moral authority guide the inventional choices that advocates on each side of the cultural divide have made. These divergent moral commitments create two different rhetorical styles. Their differing systems of belief demand a certain form of expression and the forms of expression themselves have become elements of controversy. The certainty of religious faith may lead to the articulation of political principles grounded in moral absolutism. Such an approach clashes with a deliberative legislative style built on the virtues of political bargaining. It is one thing to disagree with the utility of a particular policy, but it is quite another to argue that those on the other side are immoral, blasphemous, or un-Christian.

At the pitched height of this "culture war," Senator Edward Kennedy of Massachusetts, the living embodiment of the Democratic liberal tradition in contemporary American politics, accepted an invitation to deliver an address at Liberty Baptist College.[63] The Reverend Jerry Falwell, pastor of Thomas Rhodes Baptist Church and Chancellor of the college, was the personification of the New Christian Right. He had founded the Moral Majority and he had articulated the argument justifying the entrance of Christian evangelicals into the secular world of national politics.[64] Senator Kennedy had often been the target of the Moral Majority's attacks. No two individuals in 1983 were better representatives of the progressive and orthodox voices in the American "culture war."

The Senator's speech is particularly interesting because it is so self-reflexive. The very fact of the event itself—Kennedy speaking to the students and faculty at Liberty Baptist College—is the subject of the talk. There is something utterly American about offering an invitation to a speaker with whom you strenuously disagree and then for the speaker to accept an invitation to speak before a group which is so hostile to his ideological orientation. It is a ritual embodying American political <pluralism> and <tolerance>. Such rhetorical moments run deep in American democratic mythology, for they recall the unfettered exchange of ideas in the New England town meeting and the American commitment to protect the voice of minority opinion against the power of the majority.

Moreover, this is a self-reflexive religious occasion. It recalls the 1960 election in which John Kennedy's Catholicism was an overriding issue. In JFK's famous address to the Houston Ministers, he provided the most memorable contemporary statement on religious toleration. The tension here is even more complex. In 1960, Protestants feared the influence of the papacy on a Catholic president. John Kennedy had to convince the Protestant majority that his membership in the Roman Catholic Church was consistent with American pluralism. In 1983, it is not the influence of Church hierarchy that threatens pluralism, but religious orthodoxy. Interestingly, many conservative Catholics were quite sympathetic with the Moral Majority. Edward Kennedy, although well known as a Catholic, was hardly in good standing with the Church. His pro-choice position on abortion, for instance, made him an anathema to many faithful Catholics. This tension between Church teachings and the politics of Catholic politicians was a constant refrain during this period. These clashes were particularly memorable for Governor Mario Cuomo of New York and Vice Presidential candidate Geraldine Ferraro.

If we think of this address as the second part of the Kennedy discourse on religious tolerance—John Kennedy's Houston Ministers address as the first—then the younger brother got the more difficult assignment. This assertion requires some elaboration. John Kennedy's challenge was more difficult politically and certainly the stakes were higher, but Edward Kennedy's task is more difficult rhetorically and philosophically. John Kennedy had to do two things: first, he had to dispel unfounded Protestant fears by making known the real position of the American Catholic Church; and, second, he had to explain that anti-Catholic bigotry had no place in the American creed.[65] Put differently, this was essentially a speech about civil rights. American Catholics had a right to be full-fledged citizens in the United States. He asked Americans to write Catholics fully into a broad and inclusive sense of <the people>.

By contrast, Edward Kennedy was not coming to ask for religious inclusion, but rather requesting restraint on religious expression. From the perspective of the Moral Majority, this circumstance was filled with irony. At least in one sense, Kennedy's mission may be interpreted as an attempt to exclude evangelical, fundamentalist Christian participation in electoral politics. This exclusion is based on the uncomfortable moral message brought as a critique to Kennedy's own progressive politics.

All of this points to the complexity of <tolerance>. Certainly, as John Kennedy maintained in 1960, <tolerance> does not permit a religious litmus test for public office. But what requirements does <tolerance> place on the style of religious expression when it enters the political arena? One would assume that a commitment to <tolerance> would stop short of reducing moral argument to mere pronouncements of taste or preference. American <pluralism> is not supposed to result in a "naked public square" in which citizens cannot bring serious moral/religious argument to bear on the important issues in national life.[66]

This is not the first time that this address has been the subject of an academic rhetorical analysis. Robert Branham and Barnett Pearce were also struck by the use of "<tolerance>" as a means of negotiating between, what they called, the "incommensurability [of] worldviews."[67] Their interest was quite different than mine. Branham and Pearce went about explaining Kennedy's negotiation among competing audiences and how this negotiation was to the benefit of both the Senator and Reverend Falwell. "Kennedy offered Falwell," they contended, "legitimacy and respect as a rhetor in the public arena, and Falwell offered Kennedy arenas in which he could revise his image and defuse what had to be anticipated as his most strident opposition. The means of accomplishing this was 'civility,' that elusive melody best sung in duet."[68] Branham and Barnett explained Kennedy's address and Falwell's participation in the occasion in terms of effectively managing a set of situational exigencies.[69]

By contrast, I have an ideological interest that drives my analysis of the speech. Kennedy's rhetorical characterization of important ideographs—<public>, <private>, <tolerance>—warrants a particular use of power. It dismisses certain forms of political expression as unreasonable and unwelcome in the public square, while commending other utterances as reasonable arguments that elevate public debate. These forms of political expression, at least by implication, are tied to particular groups. Although billed as a "nonpolitical" speech, the language of the address has the profoundest consequences for empowering some parties and viewpoints and silencing others. Although I do not carry out a thoroughgoing diachronic analysis, I am yet interested in documenting how significantly this discourse departs from the rhetoric of civil rights. Many of its references—slavery and abolition, anti-Semitism and anti-Catholicism, Pope John XXIII and Martin Luther King, Jr.—recall earlier appeals for inclusion based on <equality>, but this address instead uses <tolerance> as a means of exclusion. Unpacking this ideological complexity is the purpose of this critical analysis.

In what follows, I provide an overview of the themes in Senator Kennedy's address, "Tolerance and Truth in America." Second, I examine the speech's construction of the public, private, and technical spheres. Third, I explore how the tension between Kennedy's construction of <public> and <private> shapes the meaning of <tolerance>. Finally, I argue that there is an erupting irony of exclusion in Kennedy's treatment of religion that is symptomatic of democratic liberalism.

THE THEMES IN "TRUTH AND TOLERANCE IN AMERICA"

The speech, "Truth and Tolerance in America," is a sophisticated rhetorical effort. As such, it does not fall conveniently into discrete parts, for sections of the speech perform multiple tasks. Nonetheless, for simplicity's sake, I have divided the text's forty-four paragraphs into six functional sections.

Section 1: Civility Ritual. The immediate events leading up to the speech and the opening of the speech itself were exercises in the American ritual of civility. Both Reverend Falwell and Senator Kennedy, although political opponents, paid homage to the nation's commitment to listen respectfully to others ideas and then engage in spirited debate. For instance, Reverend Falwell hosted a dinner for the Kennedy family before the address.[70]

At the beginning of the speech, Senator Kennedy thanked Reverend Falwell for his "generous introduction." He joked with the students, "In honor of our meeting, I have asked Dr. Falwell, as your chancellor, to permit all students an extra hour next Saturday night before curfew. In return, I have promised to watch 'The Old Time Gospel Hour' next Sunday."[71]

I refer to this opening as ritualistic because it is a common, oft-repeated rhetorical gesture that is underwritten by the American culture.[72] The host warmly welcomes the speaker and thanks him for coming. The speaker thanks the host for his hospitality and for the invitation to speak. Even if the two parties have serious disagreements, they engage in a rhetorical dance that highlights the civil and respectful nature of their disagreement. In this particular speech, this commonplace takes on added importance because it is itself central to the topic of the address.

Section 2: Characterization of Topic and Construction of the Audience. Kennedy tells the audience that he has come to Liberty Baptist College to "discuss my beliefs about faith and country, tolerance and truth in America." He says, "We cannot turn and should not turn aside from a deeper, more pressing question—which is whether and how religion should influence government."[73]

He defines his address as a "nonpolitical speech."[74] In this context, "nonpolitical" means nonpartisan. "Since I am not a candidate for president," Kennedy says, "it certainly would be inappropriate to ask for your support in this election—and probably inaccurate to thank you for it in the last one."[75] Kennedy implies that the topic of this "nonpolitical speech" should not divide the audience along party lines, because he is going to speak to the basic ideological commitments that unite Americans.

The immediate audience for this address was made up of "students, faculty, administrators, and residents of Lynchburg."[76] However, the mediated audience was a good deal larger. This speech was widely covered by the national press.[77]

In the speech itself, Kennedy constructs the students of Liberty Baptist College as representatives of an American religious people. They embody a conservative political view with which he disagrees, but they are a people who listen carefully to argument and accept the American pluralist tradition of respecting differences. "I know," he tells the audience, that "we begin with certain disagreements . . . But I also hope that tonight and in the months and years ahead, we will always respect the right of others to differ—that we will view ourselves with a sense of perspective and a sense of humor."[78]

Section 3: History of Religious Intolerance and the Separation of Church and State. In this section of the address, Kennedy provides examples of religious intolerance in America. These include the exile of Roger Williams and his followers from Massachusetts, the anti-Catholic laws in colonial Maryland and Pennsylvania, the discrimination faced by Jews in all thirteen colonies, and the harassment of Baptists in Virginia.

Kennedy provides an interesting example of religious intolerance within the coalition of believers that make up the Moral Majority. "[B]ecause the Moral Majority has worked with members of different denominations," Senator Kennedy explains, "one fundamentalist group has denounced Dr. Falwell for hastening the ecumenical church and for 'yoking together with Roman Catholics, Mormons, and others.'"[79] Kennedy argues that on "this issue, [Falwell] himself has become the target of narrow prejudice."[80]

With this background of religious discrimination, Kennedy enters into a short history of the American commitment to religious freedom and the separation of church and state. During the revolution, he tells the audience, "Catholics, Jews and nonconformists all rallied to the cause and fought valiantly for the American commonwealth—for John Winthrop's 'city upon a hill.'" After the war, "when the Constitution was ratified and amended, the framers gave freedom for all religion—and from any established religion—the very first place in the Bill of Rights."[81] He refers to Thomas Jefferson's pronouncement that "his proudest achievement was . . . drafting the Virginia Statute of Religious Freedom."[82] Kennedy lists the various religious traditions that could be found among the founders.

Then, Senator Kennedy moves to a key section of the address. Here he introduces the value of <pluralism>. As a prelude to offering a definition of this pivotal concept, he says, "In 1789 their fear was of factional strife among dozens of denominations. Today there are hundreds—and perhaps thousands—of faiths and millions of Americans who are outside any fold."[83] "Pluralism," Kennedy continues, "does not and cannot mean that all of them are right; but it does mean that there are areas where government cannot and should not decide what is wrong to believe, to think, to read, and to do."[84]

Kennedy recognizes that the "separation of church and state can sometimes be frustrating for women and men of deep religious faith." "They may," he explains, "be tempted to misuse government in order to impose a value which they cannot persuade others to accept." This is the "temptation," which can start us down a "slippery slope where everyone's freedom is at risk." "Let us never forget," he warns, "today's Moral Majority could become tomorrow's persecuted minority."[85]

Section 4: Public and Private. A meaningful <pluralism> demands a workable boundary between <public> and <private>. "The real transgression," Kennedy argues, "occurs when religion wants government to tell citizens how to live uniquely personal parts of their lives." "Some questions," he continues, "may be inherently individual ones or people may be sharply divided about whether they are. In such cases—cases like Prohibition and abortion—the proper role of religion is to appeal to the conscience of the individual, not the coercive power of the state."[86]

There are other circumstances that may be deemed <public>. The <public>, for Kennedy, is determined by questions "which we must decide together as a nation, and where religion and religious values can and should speak to our common conscience."[87] Kennedy uses the "issue of nuclear war" as a "compelling example." "It is," he says, "a moral issue; it will be decided by government, not by each individual; and to give any effect to the moral values of their creed, people of faith must speak directly about public policy."[88] For instance, "the Catholic bishops and the Reverend Billy Graham have every right to stand for the nuclear freeze—and Dr. Falwell has every right to stand against it."[89]

Section 5: Imposed Will and Essential Witness. The terms of the entire argument are now stated. On the one hand, "no religious body should seek to impose its will"; and, on the other hand, religious leaders should "state their views and give their commitments when public debate" involves "ethical issues."[90] Kennedy describes this distinction as "drawing the line between imposed will and essential witness."[91] In different language, Kennedy tells the audience, "we keep church and state separate—and at the same time, we recognize that the city of God should speak to the civic duties of men and women."[92]

Senator Kennedy proposes four tests "which draw the line and define the difference" between imposed will and essential witness. He spends the next 17 paragraphs elaborating on these tests. The first test is that "we must respect the integrity of religion itself."[93] We should remember that religion has often been wrongly invoked to "sanction prejudice and even slavery, to condemn labor unions and public spending for the poor."[94] "God," Kennedy argues, "has taken no position on the Department of Education—and that a balanced budget amendment is a matter for economic analysis, not heavenly appeals."[95] In short, "religious values cannot be excluded from every public issue—but not every public issue involves religious values."[96]

The second test holds that "we must respect the independent judgments of conscience."[97] People of good will often disagree on matters of public policy. "Those who proclaim moral and religious values can offer counsel," Kennedy argues, "but they should not casually treat a position on a public issue as a test of fealty to faith."[98] When we do "apply moral values to public life, let all of us avoid the temptation to be self-righteous and absolutely certain of ourselves."[99] The "respect of conscience" implies a willingness to respect the moral disagreements of others as sincere and well-intentioned. The application of religious teachings to the practical world of politics is hardly a certain matter without room for differences.

The third test commands that "in applying religious values, we must respect the integrity of public debate." "Faith," Kennedy says, "is not substitute for facts."[100] Even if privately one's faith makes him certain of the correct position on a public issue, this private certainty does not excuse this person from engaging in public debate. Religious-based conviction cannot permit the use of unreasonable means of advocacy. There is a temptation, when so sure of one's position, to use whatever rhetorical means necessary to succeed. This kind of demagoguery undermines serious public debate, which is at the center of a pluralist democracy.

The fourth and final test demands that "we must respect the motives of those who exercise their right to disagree."[101] "The more our feelings diverge," Kennedy advises, "the more deeply felt they are, the greater is our obligation to grant the sincerity and essential decency of our fellow citizens on the other side."[102] As an example, Kennedy argues that those "who favor E.R.A. are not 'antifamily' or 'blasphemers' and their purpose is not 'an attack on the Bible.'"[103]

Section 6: Conclusion. Kennedy concludes the speech with an appeal for peace. "For as the apostle Paul wrote long ago in Romans, 'If it be possible, as much as it lieth in you, live peaceably with all men.'"[104]

Public, Private, and Technical Spheres

This speech has a remarkably pleasing quality. We could all get along if we observed the rituals of civility, the conventions of fair debate, and the rules of sweet reason. All this trouble started when some among the religious sought either to "impose their will" on areas of purely personal concern or to bring their harsh judgmental language to bear on public policy matters. To use Roderick Hart's terminology, Senator Kennedy is arguing that some religious leaders have violated the rhetorical provisions of the "church-state contract."[105] They did so by straying out of their own sphere of influence—spiritual matters related to the church and public matters related to ethics—and strayed into the world of politics. If we could just keep everything in its rightful place—follow the dictates of civic decorum and say the right thing at the right time—the nation would be a more peaceful place.

Recall that Senator Kennedy framed this event as "nonpolitical." He acknowledged a disagreement with his audience on partisan matters of policy and sought common ground on the American commitment to "tolerance" and "pluralism." After all, freedom of religion and the nation's subsequent religious diversity are matters of first importance to the faithful. I think it is fair to assume that Kennedy hoped this speech would be received as a philosophical statement of common national values.

Among the most valuable lessons one can learn about ideology is that it often comes wrapped in discourses that deny its very existence. When someone tells you that a message is "nonpolitical," you should be on guard for the implicit introduction of ideological warrants. In this case, the boundary between Kennedy's "imposed will" and "essential witness" is hardly a matter that can be understood apart from ideology, for it demands attention to two of the central ideographs in the liberal democratic tradition—<public> and <private>. As I noted earlier, in the civil rights struggle these two terms mediated the tension between <equality> and <property>. By limiting the domain of the <private> in such areas as housing, employment, and customer service, the commitment to <equality> became more central to American society.

In this text, <private> and <public> are reified into three apparently separate spheres of activity—private, public, and technical. These distinctions are drawn from the history of liberal thought. The changing boundaries among these spheres, what Jurgen Habermas has called "colonization,"[106] have received a good deal of scholarly attention in the last fifteen years.[107] Kennedy has vested interests in maintaining a particular set of boundary lines and these interests have real consequences.

Rhetorical Construction of the Private Sphere

To begin, let us catalogue, as best we can, those things that appear to fall within the private sphere in Kennedy's address. This cataloguing is rather tricky, for each item does not imply the private in the same way nor does it get placed in this sphere on the same grounds. Some items were labeled private because they were personal, others are subjective, and still others are said to have limited force in civic discussion. The Senator's speech mentions nine items that appear to belong inside the private domain:

- *Conscience:* "[W]e must respect the independent judgments of conscience. Those who proclaim moral and religious values can offer counsel, but they should not casually treat a position on a public issue as a test of fealty to faith."[108]
- *Motive:* "We sorely test our ability to live together if we too readily question each other's integrity. . . . [T]he more our feelings diverge, the more deeply felt they are, the greater is our obligation to grant the sincerity and essential decency of our fellow citizens on the other side."[109]
- *Nonmajority values:* "[W]omen and men of deep religious faith . . . may be tempted to misuse government in order to impose a value which they cannot persuade others to accept."[110] "Some questions may be inherently individual ones or people may be sharply divided about whether they are."[111]
- *Personal lives:* "The real transgression occurs when religion wants government to tell citizens how to live uniquely personal parts of their lives. The failure of Prohibition proves the futility of such an attempt when a majority or even a substantial minority happens to disagree."[112]

- *Prohibition and abortion:* "In such cases—cases like Prohibition and abortion—the proper role of religion is to appeal to the conscience of the individual, not the coercive power of the state."[113]
- *Religion:* "When people agree on public policy, they ought to work together, even while they worship in diverse ways."[114]
- *Truth:* "I believe there surely is such a thing as truth, but who among us can claim a monopoly on it?"[115]
- *Voting:* "John Kennedy said at that time, 'I believe in an America where there is no (religious) bloc voting of any kind.'"[116]

In this collection of words and phrases, at least three different senses of <private> emerge. They certainly overlap in their use, but for our task they may be separated for purposes of analysis.

1. Private as Independent or Nonconsensus Judgment or Choice: Any individually held view, which is apart from a national consensus, is in the domain of the private. The term "conscience" designates the source of independent judgment. Such independent judgments deserve respect, meaning the speaker should not be criticized for offering them in an open forum, but there public force is to be severely circumscribed. Decision makers should listen respectfully to such appeals but should not be bound by them. As a rule of decorum, advocates should refrain from questioning the private motives of those who speak in the public sphere. Instead, they should presume the decent intentions of their opponents.

2. Private as Personal Conduct: There are certain parts of life and forms of conduct that are understood as "personal." In the context of this address, religious devotion, the drinking of alcoholic beverages (Prohibition), and the decision to terminate a pregnancy (abortion) would all fall under the rubric of the <private>. Voting is a special case of personal conduct. Organizing others into voting blocs based on beliefs rightly assigned to the personal sphere (such as religious devotion), is a violation of the liberal-democratic boundary between <public> and <private>.

3. Private as an Unverifiable Claim: The dimensions of private captured in (1) and (2) all point to a largely subjective view of truth. Kennedy believes that "there surely is such a thing as truth," but no one "among us can claim a monopoly on it."[117] Many claims to truth, especially those based on the transcendent, may exist above and apart from the person, but they cannot be established through any agreed upon public methods of verification. This explains the distinction in the address between "facts" (publicly verifiable) and "truth" (not publicly verifiable). As a result, when religious truth is brought to the public square, it must come as a private moral commitment and not as a claim that binds public decision makers.

Rhetorical Construction of the Public Sphere

Following a parallel procedure, I have identified six items that appear to fall within the public domain in Kennedy's address. Again, the Senator's discourse is more suggestive than explicit. It is the evident tension between <public> and <private> that permits me to make these judgments with some confidence.

- *Debate:* "In applying religious values, we must respect the integrity of public debate."[118]
- *Facts:* "In [public] debate, faith is no substitute for facts."[119]
- *Government office:* "Respect for conscience is most in jeopardy—and the harmony of our diverse society is most at risk—when we reestablish, directly or indirectly, a religious test for public office."[120]

- *Issues requiring collective action (e.g., the Nuclear Freeze proposal):* "[T]here are other questions which are inherently public in nature, which we must decide as a nation . . . the issue of nuclear war is a compelling example." Kennedy elaborates, "It is a moral issue; it will be decided by government, not by each individual."[121]
- *Peace:* "As fellow citizens, let us live peaceably with each other; as fellow human beings, let us strive to live peaceably with men and women everywhere."[122]
- *Standards of civility:* "I hope for an America where we can all contend freely and vigorously, but where we will treasure and guard those standards of civility which alone make this nation safe for both democracy and diversity."[123]

In this collection of words and phrases, different senses of <public> emerge. I have identified three dimensions of <public> life.

1. Public as Collective Action to Regulate Other-Regarding Actions. There is a distinction between issues that require collective action—<public>—and issues that require individual moral suasion—<private>. So, for example, only the will of the collective <public>, as expressed in government action, can adopt policies that will lessen the likelihood of a nuclear war. By contrast, through moral suasion, one could influence a pregnant woman to forego an abortion or induce an alcoholic to stop drinking. Less obvious, but I believe lurking in the intellectual background, is an appeal to John Stuart Mill's distinction between "self-regarding" and "other-regarding" actions. "But neither one person, nor any number of parsons," Mill wrote, "is warranted in saying to another human creature of ripe years that he shall not do with his life for his own benefit what he chooses to do with it."[124] However, "[a]s soon as any part of a person's conduct affects prejudicially the interests of others, society has jurisdiction over it."[125] Kennedy appears to believe that there is a distinction between those activities that primarily impact the individual who decides to engage in them and those activities that threaten the interests of others. The self-regarding actions should be considered a matter of private choice and the other-regarding actions as a matter of public jurisdiction and regulation.

2. Public as Official Office and Action: Officials who hold government office must be evaluated in terms of <public> rather than <private> standards. So, no candidate for elected office or nominee for appointed office should be disqualified on the basis of religion. Kennedy does not make clear how other criteria may fall out across this boundary. On occasion, distinctions have been drawn between <public> and <private> conduct. So, for instance, an official may be a poor family member (e.g., adulterer or neglectful parent) and, yet, carry out official duties in an exemplary manner (e.g., eschew interest-group contributions or standup for the poor).[126]

3. Public as Civic Debate: The notion of public debate appears to be equated by Kennedy with civic discussion. In this sense, public has quite a narrower meaning than merely speaking in front of an audience. Churches, for instance, are public places and ministers speak from the pulpit to large audiences. Yet, this occasion would only become public, in the sense Kennedy appears to imply, if the minister's homily took up civic matters. Religion, after all, is conceived by the Senator as private. Moreover, there are rules of <public> conduct that differ from rules of <private> behavior. In this speech, the rules of <public> conduct focus on the code of "civility" and the requirements of "public debate." The implication is that one might conduct a <private> discussion in quite a different way from a <public> one. In speaking with my wife about an issue of national importance, I certainly may call into question the other side's motives. In discussing whom we might vote for, we certainly may entertain issues that have to do with the candidate's <private> conduct. However, if we were invited to take part in a <public> debate about these matters, the demands of civility would preclude raising such issues in front of a wider audience.

Rhetorical Construction of the Technical Sphere

Lurking behind the grand liberal clash between <private> and <public> is a more prosaic sphere—the technical realm. In the twentieth century government has become more and more complex and with that complexity has evolved an ever-growing reliance on specialized expertise. Areas of decision that were once the object of public debate and legislative deliberation have increasingly been relegated to regulatory agencies or other technical offices for determination.[127] Expertise has two related appeals: professional judgment is supposed to examine issues objectively without the undue influence of politics; and experts are supposedly able to unwind the complexities of issues and thus reach more rationally considered judgments.[128]

The technical emerges from the tension between <public> and <private>, although here these terms take on somewhat different meanings. The tension is between the general public and its representatives and the expertise of specialists. Public comes to mean something close to "lay public." The public's representatives are thought to be involved in partisan politics. So, in this sense, the technical is an oasis of expertise and objective judgment. Yet, the technical is hardly private. Judgments are not made based on individual or subjective consideration. Judgments are made following standardized procedures promulgated by a professional community. There is, as a result, a form of accountability that extends beyond the consequences of private decisions.

In Kennedy's speech there are only hints of items that may fall within the technical sphere. When I mention them, they may well appear to the reader as merely another part of the public debate. Yet, I am confident that there is here another strain in the <public>/<private> tension.

- *Law:* "As Professor Laurence Tribe, one of the nation's leading constitutional scholars has written, 'Law in a nontheocratic state cannot measure religious truth'—nor can the state impose it."[129]
- *Economic analysis:* "[A] balanced budget constitutional amendment is a matter for economic analysis, not heavenly appeals."[130]

In these brief examples, two different dimensions of the technical emerge.

1. The technical as governmental institutions shielded from politics: In this sense of technical, the courts are the preeminent institution in the technical sphere. In the paragraph following the quotation from Laurence Tribe, Senator Kennedy identifies abortion as a private issue. Of course, the abortion question was settled by the Supreme Court. The point of clash between left and right on questions of reproductive freedom has to do with the proper site of decision. Liberals argue that the availability of abortion is tied to a woman's right to privacy. This right was promulgated by the Court in *Roe v. Wade.* Conservatives argue that the issue of abortion should be correctly left to the legislature, for it is the representatives of the people that ought to make such moral choices. In this context, the Court is a technical sphere because it brings learned judgment to the reading of the Constitution and because it is sheltered by the structure of the judicial branch from the influence of partisan politics.

2. The technical as objective policy analysis. In distinguishing "economic analysis" from "heavenly appeals," Kennedy is making an observation about objectivity. The findings of economic analysis are credible because they must meet the standards of professional practice. When policymakers make appeals based on economic analysis, they are calling on a disciplinary ethos to underwrite their claim.[131] The findings of the Court and the conclusions of professional economists are certainly used in public debate, but much of their authority comes from their gestation in the technical sphere.

THE MEANING OF <TOLERANCE>

For Senator Kennedy, the commitment to <tolerance>, properly understood, serves as a regiment of border guards around the perimeter of the <public>. The terms of entry are found in the eight dimensions I have listed in the analysis of the three spheres. These dimensions in turn become, for Kennedy, the operational meaning of <tolerance> in a liberal democratic society.

Ironically, given the ordinary meaning of "tolerance"—the sense of allowing something or of indulging beliefs or practices differing from one's own—<tolerance> as a border guard tolerates very little. Crossing this boundary requires a quite extensive list of documents—it is hardly an easy crossing.

What does Kennedy's <public> look like? It appears to have two dominant features. First, this <public> has limited the agenda of items that may be subject to open discussion and debate. Second, this <public> has restricted the list of *topoi* (topics) that may serve as resources for the invention of argument. Let me take up each in turn.

The <public> agenda is restricted to civic debate about other-regarding actions that require collective deliberation in order to regulate. Conversely, any self-regarding action, which may be influenced by individual moral suasion, is a <private> rather than <public> matter. Even if a consensus on this principle existed, which it may, the constitutive terms of this axiom are so ambiguous that their meaning will certainly change with each advocate's application of the criteria.

We know from the illustrations in Senator Kennedy's address that abortion is a paradigm case of a "personal" and thus self-regarding action. We also know that nuclear war, racism, and poverty are paradigm cases of public and thus other-regarding action. Notice how Kennedy labels abortion as outside the public sphere by definition. Whether abortion is a self- and other-regarding action is the essential question at issue. This is precisely the point at which people of faith want to introduce religious-moral argument.

Interestingly, there are those who have characterized racism as essentially a personal issue. The argument that the rights of <private property> permitted landlords, motel operators, store-owners, and restaurateurs to make personal decision about serving African Americans was a viable argument in America less than forty years ago. Likewise, the same argument that what was necessary was the moral suasion of individual consciences rather than collective public action was offered. So, Southern segregationists could talk about how they felt or their personal moral outlook or their independent judgment of conscience.[132]

My point is that the invoking of <tolerance> always comes with serious ideological consequences because there is no objective standpoint from which to draw the <public>/<private> line. What stands inside the public sphere, as other-regarding action, and what stands outside, as self-regarding action, is always based on a process of persuasive definition. These definitions have everything to do with the exercise of power. Senator Kennedy wants to use his political power to assure the legal provision of abortions; forty years before George Wallace and Bull Connor wanted to exercise their political power to maintain American apartheid.

The second feature of Senator Kennedy's <public> is even more troubling. The first feature restricted what could be talked about in public, but the second restricts how citizens may argue and deliberate over issues of civic importance. Only an argument warranted by *consensus values* and supported by *verifiable evidence* is permitted into the public realm.

In listening to Senator Kennedy, he appears as someone who is merely calling for more civility in the cause of producing a dignified and serious public dialogue. Think for a moment about how ideologically loaded such calls to civility inevitably are. Those with power—those who enjoy the presumption of the settled present—have always chastised the subordinate class for its failure of decorum.[133] There is an enormous rhetorical advantage if your opponent must speak on your terms and follow your rules.

Kennedy's restriction on the *topoi* of public debate goes to the very heart of the function of the <public>. Ideally, the public stands between the intimate sphere and the official sphere. It is a place where people bring moral views, gestated in the intimate sphere of the family, to bear on public issues. The resulting debate and discussion becomes a recognizable public opinion. This public opinion then asserts influence on government officials and makes a difference in the exercise of state power. Notice, on this view, the public is the place of mediation between private values and state action.[134]

If the public does not convert private values into public opinion, then what is the meaning of democracy? What would the will of the people comprise if not the amalgam of private morality? The answer, I suppose, and the one apparently offered by Senator Kennedy is that public values and private values are different in kind. The values of the public are not grounded in the life histories of private citizens, but rather they are of a wholly different type that does not require that choices be made among competing private values. The liberal fear is that if you begin to make such choices, the peaceful civic order will be disturbed.

So, if private values are set aside, what language of value can be used in public discourse? I see only two rhetorical choices: appeals to rights and appeals to utility. Interestingly, rights and utility are largely the discursive domain of the technical. Courts settle matters of rights and the appropriate subject-matter experts calculate the costs and benefits, in other words the utility, of various policy options.

Rights talk is the rhetoric of drawing lines in the sand. Over this line you shall not cross.[135] So, for example, *Roe v. Wade* posited a right to privacy and said that the state may not interfere with the privacy of a woman's body and, therefore, may not prevent her from terminating a pregnancy. The concept of separation of church and state draws a line—for instance, prayer in the public schools—over which the state may not step. Notice the rhetorical similarity between the language of rights and Kennedy's boundary drawing around the public sphere. In each case, the force of the discourse is to draw a line and post a guard. Notice that rights do not make substantive moral claims. To say that a woman has a right to choose is far different than saying that abortion is a moral good.

To speak of utility is to talk pragmatically about the respective effectiveness of various alternatives. Utility is the calling card of the technical sphere; experts can calculate the respective costs and benefits of various alternatives. As Senator Kennedy put it, "a balanced budget constitutional amendment is a matter for economic analysis."[136] Notice, too, how explicitly the speech favors "facts" over "faith." It is only the objective, observable, and verifiable material of the sciences that should influence public opinion and official action.

Religious discourse is essentially about human purpose. What is our purpose and given that purpose how should we live? This is the moral tradition of virtue not of rights and utility. "The virtues," Alasdair MacIntyre writes, "are precisely those qualities the possession of which will enable an individual to achieve *eudaimonia* and the lack of which will frustrate his movement toward the *telos*." By *eudaimonia*, Aristotle meant a state "of a man's being well-favored himself and in relation to the divine."[137] The God who said, "Only the man who says goodbye to all his possessions can be my disciple" (Luke 14:33), is no utilitarian. The apostles who left the upper room to convert the world largely by their own martyrdom hardly engaged in an objective cost-benefit analysis.

I draw your attention to these implications not for the purpose of advocating a religious morality, but rather to illustrate how deeply <tolerance> is implicated in the American cultural divide. In the way it is evoked here, an entire moral tradition is denied its voice. This situation has been characterized by Richard Neuhaus as the "democratic paradox": "We insist that we are a democratic society, yet we have in recent decades systematically excluded from policy consideration the operative values of the American people, values that are overwhelmingly grounded in religious belief."[138]

The ultimate irony is that <tolerance> is the most effective ally of intolerance.

PERSONAL COMMENTS ON THIS ESSAY

My own background influences my views on the place of religion in the public square and affected the shape of this essay. Like most other critics working in the tradition of the "ideological turn," I readily acknowledge that my construction of the truth is a product of my standpoint. To do otherwise would be hypocritical. Having said this, I still have a responsibility to make arguments that my readers will find convincing. I am not merely asserting this as my unsupported opinion.

I am a practicing Roman Catholic and I do not believe that there is any easy distinction between private piety and public advocacy. The notion of citizen is only meaningful when individuals can bring their private morality to bear on public issues. Yet, as a Catholic, I am well aware of the long record of American discrimination against those of my faith. I am familiar with much of the grubby history of Catholic bigotry that polluted the nation's public discourse. To put this differently, I believe that <tolerance> is a two-edged sword. There is no easy set of rules for assuring simultaneously both the robustness and the civility of the public dialogue.

I took as my task the explication of these complications. Tolerance begets intolerance. Anglo-American Liberal discourse is fraught with irony. We are left to muddle our way through as best we can. Another critic, with a different background and other ideological commitments, would have made other choices. My essay was driven by theorizing on the relationship among the public, private, and technical spheres. Another critic, calling on different theoretical literature, would have approached <tolerance> quite differently. The ideological predispositions of the critic will always influence the nature of the criticism.

POTENTIALS AND PITFALLS

Ideographic criticism is especially powerful when applied to discourses that celebrate particular values. This is so for three reasons: (1) Ideographic criticism links the celebration of particular values to the justification of power. (2) Ideographic criticism demonstrates the ways in which a particular celebrated value subordinates and organizes competing values. (3) Ideographic analysis can map alterations in value orientation over time and thus show the changes in a society's public discourse, which reflect changes in citizenry's public consciousness.

The critic must be careful in generalizing from ideographic analysis. A single speech or a small set of messages may not represent anything particularly important about the public. In fact, official pronouncements from government leaders may be resisted by the citizenry. One lesson we should learn from the fall of the Soviet Union and the communist regimes of Eastern Europe is that a regime's justifications for power are often not accepted by the populace. Kept in line by the brute force of the state, the citizens apparently never bought into the government's propaganda. When given an opportunity, they quickly seized the chance to topple their countries' leaders.

In my short essay on Edward Kennedy's "Truth and Tolerance" speech I tried to demonstrate that he articulates an influential strain in liberal thinking. His speech is important because it represents a significant segment of the American political culture. If it is merely an idiosyncratic expression of <tolerance> by one lone Senator, then it is of little consequence.

IDEOGRAPHIC ANALYSIS TOP PICKS

Condit, Celeste and John Lucaites. *Crafting <equality>: America's Anglo-African Word* (Chicago: University of Chicago Press, 1993). This prize-winning book is an excellent example of a diachronic analysis of ideographs. The authors trace the development of <equality> through American history.
Condit, Celeste and J. Ann Selzer. "The Rhetoric of Objectivity in the Newspaper Coverage of a Murder Trial." *Critical Studies in Mass Communication* 2 (1985): 197–216. This essay explores the ideological commitment of journalism to the ideograph <objectivity>. In exploring the coverage of a Kansas murder trial, they demonstrate the ironic effect of <objectivity>. The commitment to <objectivity> leads to reporting that is biased toward the prosecution.
Cloud, Dana. "The Rhetoric of <Family Values>: Scapegoating, Utopia, and the Privatization of Social Responsibility." *Western Journal of Communication* 62 (1998): 387–419. This essay explores the phrase <family values> as an ideograph. It examines the ideological force of this ideograph and concludes that it works to victimize the poor. It has the force of blaming the poor for their own circumstances. It also works to absolve the fortunate of any responsibility for society's disadvantaged.
Martin, Martha. "Ideologues, Ideographs, and 'The Best Men': From Carter to Reagan." *Southern Speech Communication Journal* 49 (1983): 12–25. This essay argues that the aftermath of the Watergate scandal provided Jimmy Carter with an opportunity to create a presidential image of "good moral character," "intelligence," and "competency"—an ideographic cluster that mirrored the nineteenth century's definition of "best men."
McGee, Michael Calvin. "An Essay on the Flip Side of Privacy" in *Argument in Transition: Proceedings of the Third Summer Conference on Argumentation*, edited by David Zarefsky, 105–115. (Annandale, VA: Speech Communication Association, 1983). This essay illustrates the ideological complexity of the abortion debate. McGee demonstrates that the abortion debate implicates a series of underlying ideographic tensions. These are tensions among <public>, <private property>, <liberty>, and <equality>.

For a theoretical grounding in ideographical analysis, read in the following essays:
McGee, Michael Calvin. "In Search of the 'People': A Rhetorical Alternative," *Quarterly Journal of Speech* 61 (1975): 235–249.
———. "The 'Ideograph,' A Link between Rhetoric and Ideology," *Quarterly Journal of Speech* 66 (1980): 1–16.
———. "A Materialist's Conception of Rhetoric." In *Explorations in Rhetoric: Studies in Honor of Douglas Ehninger*, edited by Raymie E. McKerrow, 23–48. (Glenview, IL: Scott, Foresman, 1982).

NOTES

1. Lloyd F. Bitzer, "The Rhetorical Situation," *Philosophy and Rhetoric* 1 (1968): 3–4.
2. Bitzer, 2. In a later essay, Bitzer clarifies his theory and allows for greater participation of the agent using rhetoric within the situation. See, Lloyd F. Bitzer, "Functional Communication: A Situational

Perspective" in *Rhetoric in Transition: Studies in the Nature and Uses of Rhetoric,* ed. Eugene E. White (University Park: Pennsylvania State University Press, 1980), 21–38.

3. Bitzer, 6.

4. Philip Wander makes this same point in commenting on the alledged sterility of neo-Aristotelian (Traditional) criticism, which shares many of the same commitments as Bitzer's situational approach. In making his remarks, Wander refers to Forbes Hill's essay on President Richard Nixon's speech of November 3, 1969. See Philip P. Wander, "The Ideological Turn in Modern Criticism," *Central States Speech Journal* 34 (1983): 1–18; and Forbes I. Hill, "Conventional Wisdom—Traditional Form: The President's message of November 3, 1969," *Quarterly Journal of Speech* 58 (1972): 373–386.

5. Wander, 9.

6. Antony Flew, "Ideology" in *A Dictionary of Philosophy* (New York: St. Martin's Press, 1979), 150.

7. Edward B. Reeves, "Ideology" in *Encyclopedia of Religion and Society* (Walnut Creek, CA: Altamira Press, 1998), 234.

8. This example is laid out in great detail in Murray Edelman, *Political Language: Words that Succeed and Policies that Fail* (New York: Academic Press, 1977).

9. Robert T. Craig, "Communication" in *Encyclopedia of Rhetoric* (New York: Oxford University Press, 2001), 135.

10. Michael McGee draws much the same contrast in his discussion of "instantiation." See Carol Corbin, ed, *Rhetoric in Postmodern America: Conversations with Michael Calvin McGee* (New York: Guilford Press, 1998), 144–151.

11. See Ronald Lee and Karen K. Lee, "Multicultural Education in the Little Red Schoolhouse: A Rhetorical Exploration of Ideological Justification and Mythic Repair," *Communication Studies* 49 (1998): 1–17.

12. My lecture title is a take off of the best seller by Robert Fulghum, *All I Really Needed to Know I Learned in Kindergarten: Uncommon Thoughts on Common Things* (New York: Villard, 1988).

13. See David Easton and Jack Dennis, *Children in the Political System: Origins of Political Legitimacy* (New York: McGraw-Hill, 1969); and Fred I. Greenstein, *Children and Politics* (New York: Yale University Press, 1965). Interestingly, they are also the same lessons used about merit systems in communist countries.

14. See H. Mark Roelofs, *Ideology and Myth in American Politics: A Critique of a National Political Mind* (Boston: Little, Brown, 1976); and John K. White, *The New Politics of Old Values*, 2nd ed. (Hanover, NH: University Press of New England, 1990).

15. See Stuart Ewen, *Captains of Consciousness: Advertising and the Social Roots of Consumer Culture,* 25th anniversary ed. (New York: Basic Books, 2001); and William Leiss, Stephen Kline, and Sut Jhally, *Social Communication in Advertising: Persons, Products and Images of Well-Being*, 2nd ed. (London: Routledge, 1997).

16 This may explain why so many theorists have been preoccupied with the law as a paradigm for understanding rhetoric more generally. See, for example, Chaim Perelman and L. Olbrechects-Tyteca, *The New Rhetoric: A Treatise on Argumentation* (Notre Dame, IN: University of Notre Dame Press, 1969); Stephen E. Toulmin, *The Uses of Argument* (Cambridge, England: Cambridge University Press, 1958); and James Boyd White, *Heracles' Bow: Essays on the Rhetoric and Poetics of Law* (Madison: University of Wisconsin Press, 1985).

17. See Hayden White, *Metahistory: The Historical Imagination in Nineteenth-Century Europe* (Baltimore: Johns Hopkins University Press, 1973), 1–42.

18. Terry Eagleton, *Ideology: An Introduction* (London: Verso, 1991), 9.

19. Michael Calvin McGee, "A Materialist's Conception of Rhetoric" in *Explorations in Rhetoric: Studies in Honor of Douglas Ehninger*, ed. Ray E. McKerrow (Glenview, IL: Scott, Foresman, 1982), 24.

20. McGee, "A Materialist's Conception of Rhetoric," 38.

21. Ibid., 39.

22. Ibid.

23. Ibid., 41.

24. Ibid.

25. Ibid., 43.

26. See James A. Aune, *Rhetoric and Marxism* (Boulder, CO: Westview, 1994).

27. Carol Corbin, ed., *Rhetoric in Postmodern America: Conversations with Michael Calvin McGee* (New York: Guilford Press, 1998), 94–100.

28. Corbin, 95.

29. Ibid.

30. Ibid., 94.

31. Dana L. Cloud, "The Rhetoric of *Family Values*: Scapegoating, Utopia, and the Privatization of Social Responsibility," *Western Journal of Communication* 62 (1998): 389.

32. Placing a term or slogan inside angle brackets, *liberty*, has become the conventional way of identifying an ideograph within the communication literature.

33. Michael Calvin McGee, "The 'Ideograph': A Link between Rhetoric and Ideology," *Quarterly Journal of Speech* 66 (1980): 15.

34. Ibid., 15.

35. Ibid.

36. Ibid.

37. Ibid.

38. Ibid., 7.

39. Ibid., 15.

40. Ibid.

41. Ibid., 15–16.

42. See Michael Calvin McGee, "In Search of the 'People': A Rhetorical Alternative," *Quarterly Journal of Speech* 61 (1975): 235–249.

43. Celeste M. Condit and John L Lucaites, *Crafting Equality: America's Anglo-African Word* (Chicago: University of Chicago Press, 1993), xii–xiii.

44. McGee, "The 'Ideograph,'" 14.

45. See, Condit and Lucaites.

46. Other rhetorical scholars have critiqued Bitzer's objective view of the rhetorical situation. They have suggested that situations do not pre-exist discourse, but instead are largely constituted by it. See, for example, Richard Vatz, "The Myth of the Rhetorical Situation," *Philosophy and Rhetoric* 6 (1973): 154–161; and Robert J. Branham and W. Barnett Pearce, "Between text and context: Toward a Rhetoric of Contextual Reconstruction," *Quarterly Journal of Speech* 71 (1985): 19–36. For an overview of Situation Theory see, Marilyn J. Young, "Lloyd F. Bitzer: Rhetorical Situation, Public Knowledge, and Audience Dynamics," *Twentieth-Century Roots of Rhetorical Studies*, Jim A. Kuypers and Andrew King, eds. (Westport, Connecticut: Praeger, 2001), 275–302.

47. See Maurice Charland, "Constitutive Rhetoric: The Case of the *Peuple Québécois*," *Quarterly Journal of Speech* 73 (1987): 133–150; and Michael Calvin McGee, "In Search of the 'People': A Rhetorical Alternative," *Quarterly Journal of Speech* 61 (1975): 235–249.

48. Wayne Brockriede, "Rhetorical Criticism as Argument," *Quarterly Journal of Speech* 60 (1974): 167.

49. See Edelman.

50. Cloud, 387.

51. Kenneth Burke, *A Grammar of Motives* (Berkeley: University of California Press, 1969), 517.

52. Mark Blaug, *Economic Theory in Retrospect*, 4th ed. (Cambridge, England: University of Cambridge Press, 1985), 550.

53. Blaug, 551.

54. Celeste Condit and J. Ann Selzer, "The Rhetoric of Objectivity in the Newspaper Coverage of a Murder Trial," *Critical Studies in Mass Communication* 2 (1985): 197.

55. "Jihad Against Jews and Crusaders: World Islamic Front Statement" (February 23, 1998), 2. http://www.efreedomnews.com/News%20Archive/Terrorists/Fatwah2_BinLaden.htm

56. ADC Research Institute, "Executive summary," *Report on Hate Crimes and Discrimination against Arab Americans: The Post-September 11 Backlash* (2003). http://www.adc.org/hilal/web/executive.htm.

57. Michael Wilson, "Evangelist Says Muslims haven't Adequately Apologized for Sept. 11 Attacks," *New York Times*, (August 15, 2002): A14; Fred Jackson, Jim Duke, and Jody Brown, "Evangelist Graham in Presidential Hot Water over Comments: White House Hosts Ramadan Gathering," Agape Press (November 20, 2001). http://www.familypolicy.net/nf/franklin-11-20-01.shtml; Hanna Rosin, "Younger Graham Diverges from Father's Image," *Washington Post* (September 2, 2002): A3.

58. Jim Jones, "Baptist Calls Islam Founder 'Pedophile'; Church Leaders Agree, Muslims Outraged," *Pittsburgh Post-Gazette* (June 13, 2002): A5.

59. Cal Thomas, "It's Time to Confront the Threat from within," *Baltimore Sun* (May 21, 2003): 19A.

60. See Roger W. Cobb and Charles D. Elder, "The Political uses of Symbolism," *American Politics Quarterly* 1 (1973): 305–338; Murray Edelman, "Symbols and Political Quiescence," *American Political Science Review* 54 (1960): 695–704; and Richard M. Merelman, "Learning and Legitimacy," *American Political Science Review* 60 (1966): 548–561.

61. McGee, "The 'Ideograph,'" 15.

62. James Davison Hunter, *Culture Wars: The Struggle to Define America* (New York: Basic Books, 1991), 44.

63. The college has since been renamed Liberty Baptist University.

64. See Jerry Falwell, *Listen, America!* (Garden City, NY: Doubleday, 1980).

65. See Harold Barrett, "John F. Kennedy before the Greater Houston Ministerial Association," *Central States Speech Journal* 15 (1964): 259–266; Beryl F. McClerren, "Southern Baptists and the Religious Issue during the Presidential Campaigns of 1928 and 1960," *Central States Speech Journal* 18 (1967): 104–112; and John M. Murphy, "Comic Strategies and the American Covenant," *Communication Studies* 40 (1989): 266–279.

66. The phrase "naked public sphere" was coined by Neuhaus. See Richard John Neuhaus, *The Naked Public Square: Religion and Democracy in America* (Grand Rapids, MI: Eerdmans, 1984).

67. Robert J. Branham and W. Barnett Pearce, "A Contract for Civility: Edward Kennedy's Lynchburg Address," *Quarterly Journal of Speech* 73 (1987): 428.

68. Branham and Pearce, 440.

69. For a discussion of the situational perspective on criticism, see Bitzer. Also, see Robert J. Branham and W. Barnett Pearce, "Between Text and Context: Toward a Rhetoric of Contextual Reconstruction," *Quarterly Journal of Speech* 71 (1985): 19–36.

70. Owen Peterson, ed., *Representative American Speeches 1983–1984* (New York: H. W. Wilson, 1984), 53.

71. Edward M. Kennedy, "Tolerance and Truth in America" in *Representative American Speeches 1983–1984*, ed. Owen Peterson (New York: H. W. Wilson, 1984), 55. "The Old Time Gospel Hour" was the name of Reverend Falwell's nationally syndicated radio broadcast.

72. See Eric W. Rothenbuhler, *Ritual Communication: From Everyday Conversation to Mediated Ceremony* (Thousand Oaks, CA: Sage, 1998).

73. Kennedy, 56.

74. Ibid., 55.

75. Ibid.

76. Peterson, 53.

77. For example, stories about the speech appeared in the following major newspapers: C. Bohlen, "Kennedy Visits the Falwell Empire," *The Washington Post* (October 4, 1983): A1, A4; J. Margolis, "Teddy Goes to Moral Majority Country to Praise and Condemn," *The Chicago Tribune* (October 4,

1983): sec. 1, 14; and E. Randolph, "Kennedy Warns Falwell on Perils of Religious Zealotry," *The Los Angeles Times* (October 4, 1983): part 1, 6.

78. Kennedy, 55.
79. Ibid.
80. Ibid.
81. Ibid., 56–57.
82. Ibid., 57.
83. Ibid.
84. Ibid.
85. Ibid.
86. Ibid., 58.
87. Ibid.
88. Ibid.
89. Ibid.
90. Ibid., 58–59.
91. Ibid., 59.
92. Ibid.
93. Ibid.
94. Ibid.
95. Ibid.
96. Ibid.
97. Ibid.
98. Ibid.
99. Ibid., 60.
100. Ibid.
101. Ibid., 61.
102. Ibid.
103. Ibid., 62.
104. Ibid., 63.
105. Hart argues that the implied contract states that the United States government's "rhetoric will refrain from being overly religious and [organized religion's] rhetoric will refrain from being overly political." Roderick P. Hart, *The Political Pulpit* (West Lafayette, IN: Purdue University Press, 1977), 44.
106. See Jürgen Habermas, *The Theory of Communicative Action*, vol. 2 (Boston: Beacon, 1987).
107. See, for example, Craig Calhoun, ed., *Habermas and the Public Sphere* (Cambridge, MA: MIT Press, 1992); Frank Fischer, *Technocracy and the Politics of Expertise* (Newbury Park, CA: Sage, 1990); G. Thomas Goodnight, "The Personal, Technical, and Public Spheres of Argument: A Speculative Inquiry into the Art of Deliberation," *Journal of the American Forensic Association* 18 (1982): 214–227; Ronald Lee and Shawn J. Spano, "Technical Discourse in Defense of Public Virtue: Ronald Reagan's Explanation of the Iran/Contra Affair," *Political Communication* 13 (1996): 115–129; Robert Patterson and Ronald Lee, "The Environmental Rhetoric of 'Balance': A Case Study of Regulatory Discourse and the Colonization of the Public," *Technical Communication Quarterly* 6 (1997): 25–40; and Charles A. Willard, *Liberalism and the Problem of Knowledge: A New Rhetoric for Modern Democracy* (Chicago: University of Chicago Press, 1996).
108. Kennedy, 59.
109. Ibid., 61.
110. Ibid., 57.
111. Ibid., 58.
112. Ibid.
113. Ibid., 58.
114. Ibid., 55–56.
115. Ibid., 55.

116. Ibid., 56.

117. Ibid., 55.

118. Ibid., 60.

119. Ibid.

120. Ibid.

121. Ibid., 58.

122. Ibid., 63.

123. Ibid., 62.

124. John Stuart Mill, *On Liberty* (Indianapolis: Bobbs-Merrill, 1956), 93.

125. Mill, 92.

126. This distinction between an exemplary public life and a checkered private one has been applied to Senator Kennedy himself. Likewise, his brother John Kennedy was a notorious womanizer, but yet arguably one of America's ablest presidents.

127. See Habermas, *The Theory of Communicative Action*; Theodore Lowi, *The End of Liberalism: The Second Republic of the United states*, 2nd ed. (New York: Norton, 1979); and Patterson and Lee.

128. See Walter Lippmann, *Public Opinion* (New York: Free Press); and Willard.

129. Kennedy, 57.

130. Ibid., 59.

131. In rhetorical studies, Stephen Toulmin has grounded an informal logic on the appeal to argument fields and Charles Willard has developed what he calls a "rhetoric for modern democracy" based on technical argument within and between disciplines. These projects are much in the same spirit as Kennedy's appeal to the expertise of the judiciary and to the objectivity of economic analysis. See Stephen E. Toulmin, *The Uses of Argument* (Cambridge, England: Cambridge University Press, 1958); and Willard.

132. See James J. Kilpatrick, *The Sovereign States: Notes of a Citizen of Virginia* (Chicago: Henry Regnery, 1957); and James J. Kilpatrick, *The Southern Case for School Segregation* (New York: Crowell-Collier, 1962).

133. See Ronald Lee, "Language and Political Power: A Perspective on Radical/Revolutionary Rhetoric," *Current Continental Research* 3 (1981): 155–64.

134. See Jürgen Habermas, *The Structural Transformation of the <Public> Sphere: An Inquiry into a Category of Bourgeois Society*, trans. Thomas Burger and Frederick Lawrence (Cambridge, MA: MIT Press, 1989).

135. See Ronald Beiner, *What's the Matter with Liberalism?* (Berkeley: University of California Press, 1992).

136. Kennedy, 59.

137. Alasdair MacIntyre, *After Virtue: A Study in Moral Theory* (Notre Dame, IN: University of Notre Dame Press, 1984), 148.

138. Neuhaus, 37.

17

Critical Rhetoric and Continual Critique

Raymie E. McKerrow and Jeffrey St. John

What is meant by "critical rhetoric" and what does it mean to use it as a way to understand or analyze rhetorical practice? If critique is "continual" does that mean that one never can decide what one thinks about past rhetoric—as the project of criticism unfolds anew with each moment? What's the point of criticism if judgment is not reached in some sense—so that we know what we think an event? What, then, does it mean to "continually critique?" As another way of introducing this subject: How should one frame critical rhetorical practice? Is it best conceived as a formalized *method* of rhetorical analysis, as Norman Clark has suggested?[1]

In what follows, we respond to the questions introduced above in underscoring the thesis that critical rhetoric is best viewed as a fluid and flexible *orientation*, not a formal, rule-governed method. We argue in this essay that critical rhetoric has never been intended to serve—either primarily or secondarily— as a conventional rhetorical perspective. Believing this, we present a reading of critical rhetorical practice *qua* orientation precisely because we are not convinced that the kinds of rhetorical artifacts that the critical rhetoric project engages are best evaluated through method-based means. We hold, rather, that the adoption of an orientation—in all that we conceive that term to embody—toward the analysis of those phenomena is the best way to ensure that critical rhetoric is applied to the fullest of its emancipatory potential. In our view, a method-based critical rhetoric can be neither truly a "critical rhetoric" nor the optimal venue for evaluating rhetorical phenomena in an increasingly fragmented and destabilized social world.

Before taking up these matters in greater detail, we think it is important to revisit the putative "starting point" for the critical rhetoric project. From a traditional perspective, the starting point for criticism focuses on an active *agent* who seeks to effect change in his or her environment through suasive speech, symbolic expression, or other stylized means of broadcasting an idea, creating an event, or taking a public stand. Examples from the last century abound: Picasso's *Guernica*; self-immolating Buddhist monks in the early years of the Vietnam War; the silent candlelight vigils of women and men symbolically protesting domestic abuse. Each of the persons involved in these kinds of protests is, of course, identifiable as a sentient actor, and may certainly be evaluated rhetorically for the words or deeds he or she has said or done at a particular time and place. Picasso painted; morally impassioned monks lit themselves on fire; this much is clear. Criticism that begins with the focus on the agent is a worthwhile endeavor, but is not the only approach that might be useful in answering specific questions.

Thus, while acknowledging the value of an agent-centered approach, we wish to stress that there exist other means of achieving answers to questions one might have about events, and that such means are sometimes grounded upon conceptions of public space, power relations, and the nature of public speech and action which are not as accessible to analysis from an agent-centered approach.

The starting point for the critical rhetoric project is not the active agent seeking change, though as noted above, we do not deny the efficacy or reality of agency as an ever-present persuasive force in human affairs. Rather, we simply choose to begin elsewhere. As McKerrow indicated in 2001:

> Two forms of critical analysis comprise the critical practice. A critique of domination has as its aim an emancipatory purpose, and can best be styled as a "freedom from" (McKerrow, 1991) that which otherwise limits its potentiality. A critique of freedom has as its aim a reflexivity which grounds its actions in a constant reflection on the contingency of human relations, and can best be styled as a "freedom to" (McKerrow, 1991) move toward new relations with others. In the former instance, the recognition of power in its repressive role is paramount; in the latter, the recognition of power as productive is paramount. In both instances, the assumption is that a critique may move beyond mere criticism (McKerrow, 1991) and incorporate an interrogation of the assumptive ground from which critical analysis arises. . . . Thus, if one is working within the constructs of a democratic state, the assumptions that ground democracy are as open to critique as are the actions that emanate from that state. Whether one is focusing attention on a critique of domination or of freedom, as originally set forth, the "telos" which animates both reflects a commitment to change: "Whether the critique establishes a social judgment about 'what to do' as a result of the analysis, it must nonetheless serve to identify the possibilities of future action available to the participants" (McKerrow, 1989, p. 92). The commitment to recursivity or a constant critique does not imply a dismissal of a commitment to change.[2]

In promoting an analytic perspective that underscores this commitment, our starting point lies in an understanding of *form* in the sense offered by Kenneth Burke. Taking up his injunction that the "symbolic act is the *dancing of an attitude*,"[3] we would claim a similar perspective for critical rhetoric. Following Burke, we would note that form does not necessarily (or even mainly) entail the study of phenomena that are "formal" in the sense of a series of one-to-one epistemic correspondences, though the degree of formality in the discursive formation may surely vary. Rather, form suggests to us something about 1) the relational properties that inhere in a particular event, or, to frame it more expansively, in a particular discursive formation; and 2) the effect(s) that form may have on the rhetorical choices and interventions which it may or may not be possible to achieve in light of form's influence on artifacts, discourses, and contexts. With this much in mind, we would stress that what the individual agent can or cannot do assumes a much different flavor when precise questions of form are brought to bear. In particular, within the critical rhetoric project as we are articulating it the rhetorical emphasis does not hinge on an agent's ability to perform certain rhetorical acts. Rather, the emphasis is on those seen or unseen relational properties within which the agent—as agent—is contained and with which he or she must contend in the social world.

To use Jim Kuypers's language in his essay in this volume, we might say that the critical rhetoric project re-frames a re-framing of rhetorical analysis.[4] This is not at all to dismiss other modes of analysis, or other starting points. As we alluded above, different questions require different foci on the influence of the agent-as-agent; we take the validity of that proposition to be self-evident, but worthy of reproduction in this space nonetheless. To argue, for example, that an agent-centered point of departure is *the* premier analytic frame for all analyses of public action is as wrongheaded as arguing that the same distinction in fact belongs to critical rhetoric. Both assertions are or would be fatuous, nondemonstrable, and unhelpful. As we see it, what prompts the adoption of a particular perspective is not the critical frame itself but *the questions one seeks to answer* (and this is just as true under more traditional formulations as it is for the critical orientation advanced here). The chosen rhetorical mode is informed by the phenomenon, not the reverse. For this reason, critical rhetoric is (or should be) as open to embrace or dismissal as any other frame of inquiry.

We have yet to support our initial claim that *orientation* is the preferred frame within which critical rhetoric operates. To establish that claim, we will work to connect our assertion above (about the primacy of the *phenomenon*—as opposed to *rhetorical agent*—under investigation) with some claims about social actors and their actions. In what follows, we examine first the relationship among critical rhetoric, social action, and orientation. This is accomplished by using, as a prime illustration of theory's role as a container within which criticism operates, a specific essay that may direct one's understanding of the critical rhetoric project in ways we would not prefer. Consistent with the "inventional" or "fragmentary" nature of the project, as ably outlined by Michael Calvin McGee,[5] we offer several brief analyses or cases in order to show what we think is actually at work within a critical rhetoric orientation. We seek, then, to explain both 1) the ground of our starting point; and 2) our claims about orientation as a modality; in both cases, through a discussion of the relationship among critical rhetoric, social action, and orientation itself. As suggested above, we begin with one scholar's call for an adaptation of critical rhetoric in the promotion of a "critical servant," subjecting it to analysis to illustrate a principal of criticism: if the theoretical frame is cloudy or unclear, the critical act that follows from it will be less useful.

CRITICAL RHETORIC AND SOCIAL ACTION

Norman Clark has linked his framing of the rhetorician as "critical servant"[6] to Raymie McKerrow's original statement of the critical rhetoric project.[7] In so doing, we believe that Clark has 1) tried to turn McKerrow's critical rhetor into a social actor who acts in certain contexts that are not necessarily of his or her own making[8]; and that he has 2) described his own "the critical servant" in a way that does not significantly distinguish that "servant" from McKerrow's "rhetor."

In his essay, Clark first identifies a contrasting pair of options that he claims are available to every citizen in a community. As Clark reads it, a social actor may either A) freely and usefully serve the public good (the *opheleia*); or B) work against his or her own will in servitude or subjugation (the *douleia*). Clark understandably embraces the former category and tries to infuse his critical servant with the aims and outcomes of a selfless civic engagement. In Clark's view, a person's decision to serve the public in a spirit of *opheleia* must be accompanied by an enthusiasm for real action. A practical outlook is key here. The philosopher Isocrates' "conception of the role of rhetors in society" was for Isocrates—and is for Clark as well— "inextricably linked to an understanding of practical, useful political service."[9] Clark calls his critical servant's brand of public service an "orientation," not a method, a point we would ask the reader to keep in mind.

Clark's critical servant serves his or her community and its members by doing good; by combining beauty and virtue; and in general by adopting an attitude that becomes a "purposive and artistic act."[10] The critical servant functions as the kind of person whose commitment to serving the public is constantly directed toward doing what is best for the community. His or her service is freely offered, because slavery and forced labor are antithetical to the ideals of *opheleia*. It is, in fact, the very threat of one's slide into *douleia* that provides the social actor with a powerful internal check against the rise of pride and other human failings. Though idealistic in its premises, relying as it does on what would seem to be a rare mix of discipline, selflessness, and dedication, Clark's argument is mainly consistent to this point in its development.[11] Less persuasive, however, are 1) Clark's claims about the relationship between knowledge and community; and 2) his view of the critical servant's role as the source of a community's wellspring of good judgment and good will.

At this stage in his argument, Clark rejects McKerrow's[12] suspicion of universal truth, charging McKerrow with standing in "binary opposition" to Plato; and, Clark accuses both McKerrow and Plato of a critical nearsightedness. Clark then works to show how his critical servant overcomes the problems that he (Clark) has outlined. Clark claims—and the insertion of numbers here is ours—that

> [1] Critical servants situate their knowledge of possible actions within the history of the community. [2] Some of the knowledge found in the history of the community may lay claim to universality. [3] It is not a service to the community to render this knowledge *a priori* inaccessible, as Plato would have it, or *a priori* suspect, as some postmodern theorists would. [4] Instead, critical servants work to ground this knowledge in the present community, as a resource for social critique. [5] Since the knowledge is tied to the community, it retains its persuasive force. [6] However, it is always temporally relative, always situationally contingent, and always subject to further critique and revision.[13]

We argue that Clark's claims here—at the heart of his case—seem difficult to sustain. To be as fair to his position as possible, we will address each of Clark's six sentences above in turn.

We do not object to Clark's first sentence [1], other than to note that the phrase "Critical servants" here could be replaced with no change of meaning by "Aristotelians," "Platonists," "Ramists," "Benthamites," "Southern Agrarians," or "standpoint feminists." In other words, we think that there is almost no group of critical thinkers for whom "knowledge of possible actions within the history of the community" is *not* a crucial element of its understanding of how communities solve their problems. In this respect, the "critical servant" appears to us to be no different than other social actors.

In his second sentence [2], Clark attempts to assign agency to "knowledge," as if "knowledge" were a person capable of thinking and acting. There appears to be no other possible agent in his sentence to whom thought and action might be ascribed. We do not understood how "knowledge" can be understood to act self-consciously on its own behalf and toward its own ends.

In his third sentence [3], Clark clears conceptual space for his critical servant by jettisoning almost all current players from the rhetorical stage. Plato on the one hand and all postmodernist theorists on the other are invited to leave.

In Clark's next two sentences [4–5], "knowledge," which he had previously depicted as self-aware and self-originating, is now made to stand in the service of the critical servant, who is called to apply it to his or her community in a manner that somehow (we are not told) transforms it into a "resource for social critique." We are not convinced that knowledge can function in this dual role.

It is the sixth and final sentence [6], however, that we take to be the most damaging to Clark's overall argument. Clark has sought to root his position in a set of local knowledge claims whose practical outcomes prove their own value. In other words, he seems to be arguing that a community knows itself best and may therefore govern itself best (with the aid of its critical servants). But he now offers up a postmodernist description of how knowledge itself should be handled—that is, with a healthy suspicion. Knowledge, he asserts, is "always temporally relative, always situationally contingent, and always subject to further critique and revision."[14] What does this claim mean for social action by a critical rhetor?

We worry that Clark seems to be offering his critical servant the best of both worlds, without any of the drawbacks. His servant is allowed to act confidently in clearly "good" ways, but is at the same permitted to be insightfully skeptical about things that are not so good. We think there is a problem with that arrangement. Clark's ideas about service are based on the ability of the servant to work with(in) the community's values, and to seek change consistent with what that agent sees as being 'good for the community.' But how does the servant know what is good? Who gets to offer a counterclaim if what the servant says is good really isn't? Clark provides important checks and balances on the agent's sense of self in its refusal to operate from a place of pridefulness or personal aggrandizement, but neither pride nor aggrandizement can be lasting categories if the community is forever "subject to further critique and revision" and if, at the same time, its ethical decision-making functions as a kind of independently objective standard of evaluation.

Clark alleges that ensuring that the servant acts appropriately is what "critical rhetoric ought to do: reclaim or re-use the knowledge of the historically-situated community to propose change."[15] This ideal is laudable. But we question the way in which Clark seeks to get to where we think he is going. Recall that his entire argument for the agent-doing-good-in-the-community is modeled on a framework that Clark argues is explicitly *critical*. Is the task of a person operating within a critical rhetoric orientation to "propose change" by individual agents? If so, what is the status of the change proposed? How will it be enacted? McKerrow has addressed similar questions in the context of how the rhetorical critic perceives and evaluates *time*. Within what he terms the "postmodern polity," McKerrow argues that

> the obligation of the critic is to determine how time functions, and then to work from that knowledge to an interpretation of its role in the discursive event. That the interpretation may include a critique of the culture's conception of time as inappropriate to its objectives is one possibility among many that may be enjoined in the performance.[16]

Keep in mind that critical rhetoric does not deny the possibility of an individual acting. But critical rhetoric *does* pursue a re-framing of the basis for that action, and it understands action's meaning(s)— in a sphere of social action— very differently than do formulations for rhetorical inquiry grounded in Clark's assumptions.

Critical Rhetoric's Agents and Actions

We contend that the basis for action within a critical rhetoric framework hinges on the relational properties underlying the production of discourse by the agent. We reverse the order of Clark's evaluations of agency, examining the agent (i.e., his critical servant) initially not as a cause but as an effect. It is on an agent's agency *understood as an effect* that the critical rhetoric project focuses its primary attention. An agent's becoming a cause, in the sense of his or her doing or saying something, or an agent's taking of a position: neither of these is somehow automatically precluded from critical rhetoric's scope. Far from it, for change—of the very kind Clark is hoping for—would be almost impossible to consider if one were blinded to either agent or agency. But there remains for us here a crucial caveat. Wouldn't it serve the critic to consider the broader *rhetorical* possibilities for freedom (or limitation) of action that might exist in a given discursive formation—either through its denial or resistance, or through its refashioning into an unfamiliar form— *prior* to essaying a formal evaluation of a particular action itself? If so, and we think it does, then a different kind of language is needed. What is needed is a set of terms that are not susceptible to being interpreted as the effects of prior social practices or prior social action.

Let us be as clear as possible in our meaning here. We are asking: Can a social actor be both an *effect* and a *causal agent* at the same time? We believe that he or she can, but we qualify that claim by noting that *the claim itself* muddies the waters of its own evaluation. McKerrow is careful to establish this point in his first account of critical rhetoric.[17] The evaluation of an agent's influence influences both the agent and the evaluation. To better frame a context for continual critique, the critic must insistently acknowledge that rhetorical power lies in whatever social activities ground the discursive act under investigation.[18] The power to do and say things in or for a community, for example, is not necessarily something the critical rhetor could arbitrarily "share . . . with the audience,"[19] as that sharing presumes that power is both a discrete possession that the speaker controls and one that may be distributed as he or she chooses. Once again, we do not suggest that the power to act is an illusion; but once again: the starting point for critical rhetoric is not with the agent as *rhetor*. It lies with a careful study of the social or communal situation out of which the rhetor acts.

What, if any, are the specific consequences of our concerns for Clark's argument? First, we think that Clark's willingness to embrace "orientation" is itself a type of restraint on potential action, given the intermingling of assumptions about whether or not the critical servant is truly free to act as he or she would like (see our discussion above on this point). Recall that the role of the critical servant is to serve the communal good. On this logic, our objections to Clark's formulation are basic but, we think, no less potent. We ask: who is to say that what the community deems the "good" is in fact the good in all or even most instances? What external standard is that good checked against (if any)? How do those who would enact the good monitor their own progress toward that end? To operate within Isocrates' frame (if we may step away for a moment from the specifics of Clark's argument) is not necessarily to argue only for what the community already accepts as prevailing social relations. We have already offered three examples of agents' crafting of powerful symbolic objections to extant cultural or political conditions (Picasso, Monks, and vigils). To develop this point further would detract from our central claims, but we would at least suggest that for Isocrates, understanding the community's values is not the same as faithfully preserving those values in an unaltered form. We do not see how this proportion could be any less true of Clark's critical servant.

From our perspective, the question here is not one of protecting a preferred version of the needs (or the good) of the community, but is rather one of being open to the possibility of any and all avenues toward *freedom*, for two reasons. First, a "critical rhetoric" is by definition one that seeks to liberate. As noted earlier, "a [critical rhetor's] critique of freedom . . . has as its aim a reflexivity that grounds its actions in a constant reflection on the contingency of human relations and can best be styled as a 'freedom to' move toward new relations with others."[20] Second, we think that to begin with the presumption that the rhetor knows best, particularly in the absence of even partial knowledge of those formation(s) which may inform, restrain, or enable other options, is shortsighted. What are needed are opportunities for a critical rhetor's engagement with the community that permit the broadest array of choices for action—but with the clear and minimal understanding that whatever action is proposed or undertaken may well make for social or communal relations that are not as good or efficient or desirable as one might have hoped, or which are simply wrong for that society at that time. Commitment to change, even when selfless and well-intended, cannot be enacted in a single-minded way. Improving the social arena requires a comprehension of that arena that we think *is* unavailable to the "critical servant" as that social actor is presently formulated by Clark.

THE CRITICAL RHETOR: ACTION AND ORIENTATION

Critical rhetoric functions as a form of critique, one committed to the analysis of moments of the integration of power and knowledge.[21] It is informed by a fluid *telos*—purpose, goal, end state—one for which the phenomenon observed, in the cultural and power-based conditions in which it occurs, is precisely the field of operation itself; moreover, this is not an independent or putatively fixed *telos*, and not one of a static rhetorical observer. The critique is *telos*-driven, but in a way that acknowledges the unseen or unexplored influences of power and knowledge in the equation. It is a critique of "a relativized world" that does not take itself so seriously as to believe that once instantiated, any change in the world is thus "finished" and complete.[22]

Commitment to a critical rhetoric does not preclude the naming of an oppressor or an oppressee, nor of taking a contextualized stance about the truth or falsity of a claim. What one can say is that the oppression thesis (that is, domination within the context of a 'freedom from' oppression) allows for a coexistence of oppressor and oppressed within a discursive formation that is not in every sense their own making. Once identified and altered in some way, the formation that otherwise perpetuates one set of power relations is inescapably immersed in yet another set—and thus a new relation may come into being. The point, patently, is that one does not escape from the conditions or conditioning of culture. The material reality of lived experience may or may not require changes in particular power relations. In part, what critical rhetoric does is examine the impact of particular discursive formations on the lived conditions of a people, and at the same time raises the question of social change. With respect to truth and falsity, one can say what it is that the community believes to be true, as those beliefs are expressed through language and action. To say a discourse is permanently "false" is to presume an independent stance or privileged position of one who speaks from within the truth. To say that a particular discourse does not work to achieve its ends, or that the ends achieved have deleterious consequences, is not to engage the truth or falsity of a discourse per se; it is rather to engage that discourse's meaning at the level of experience and to critique various implications for the possibilities of freedom that it enjoins.

Second, and relatedly, it is not the case that a critical rhetoric, as a transformative practice, removes itself from the recognition of the material force of rhetoric. That force is simply exercised in a contingent realm rather than within a deterministic world. Materiality *is* recognized: rhetoric itself may have material force; it may invoke change in the lived conditions of a people through its expression. The province of critique, the possibility of taking a position on the expression of materiality, is not lost from within a critical rhetoric position. The meaning and efficacy of that critique, and the position it privileges at the moment of response to the effects of material rhetoric, is transformed from one of perceived permanence—i.e., this is the way it is going to be—to one cognizant of and responsive to an otherwise relativized world. That which becomes will remain other than it is.

As McKerrow has observed, "the subject, as citizen and social actor, is capable of acting. . . . While not wholly formed through discourse, it is through that discourse that the subject gives expression"[23] to its being-in-the-world. The fixation on the role of the rhetor as active agent in modernity is transformed, in this perspective, into a concern for the role of a subjectivity that is itself formed through the very discourse to which it gives expression. As speaking subject, it expresses judgment in the form of critique—a position on the world as it exists, leading to a world that it might yet become. What is implicit is that in and through its expression, the becoming world is once again subject to reflexive judgment as to its well-suitedness in the lives of those it engages. As was already suggested above, the work in this formulation is to seek to remain within a more traditional focus on the speaking subject as the source that effects all change. While that may well be advantageous, the focus of a critical rhetoric is on its rendering the present formation into being, and from that analysis, what the potential avenues for change are that might be further explored.

Orientation versus Method[24]

This analysis brings us to an assessment of the role of "method" in relation to a critical rhetoric project. To select any one artifact as an exemplar of the approach is to increase the potential for reifying that artifact as the "way to do this sort of criticism." The recurring (though inexact) parallel to Burkeian criticism may be instructive. Burkeian criticism takes an orientation toward events and creates a frame of response where none existed. Burke did not write critical essays from stylized headings (i.e., Agent, Scene, Agency, Act, Purpose)—much less from the later addition, Motive. Rather, he suggested these critical elements as ways of thinking through the event in question. Conversely, we have used the "orientation" as a "method" in essays that stand as exemplars for future students of discourse. The conceiving of critical rhetoric not as method but as an orientation serves to keep one's options open with respect to more "methodological" approaches. There is no denying that certain critical terms or concepts, such as examining discourse through an understanding of a "scene-act" ratio, or by "perspectives by incongruity," might well add to an understanding of how that discourse came into being at this time rather than at another time, or how it functioned in relation to changes in the social order. We assume that the orientation provided through critical rhetoric does not preclude the adoption of a critical vocabulary, or even a more precise ethnographic approach in unpacking discursive formations, or in seeking answers to specific questions. But conceiving critical rhetoric in terms of a formal "method" robs it of the flexibility it otherwise possesses in being responsive to certain questions. Even more importantly, it potentially robs critical rhetoric of its salience. As McKerrow argues, "[a] critical practice must have [social and cultural] consequences."[25] Such practice also opens up the analytic frame to what Michael Calvin McGee has appropriately termed the "inventional" process of doing criticism, in operating from an assessment of "fragments"—in which the goal is to gain an understanding of how certain fragments coalesce around particular themes or values, and what that then means in terms of understanding how one engages "freedom from" domination or "freedom to" become in ways not yet considered or deemed possible.[26]

If the above is not sufficient as an explanation of the choice of orientation as opposed to method, three additional reasons for making this choice may assist in grounding our rationale. First, the critical opportunity invites the possibility of critique rather than mere criticism. In other words, the "opportunity" goes beyond what "method" would normally imply or even entail in seeking to promote questions about the fundamental assumptions on which the current good is grounded. For example, while those who responded to government propaganda in the early "critical thinking" movement were (appropriately enough) highly critical, they did not seek to go beyond their criticism to question the fundamental nature of democracy. Rather, they acted fully within the assumptive framework of what was understood in their time as the appropriate means of engaging the public in a democratic state.[27] This is not to say that one's method might not invoke critique, but rather that the orientation expressly invites such an attitude at the outset of engaging a critical question in a fully fleshed out context of critique.

Second, the "opportunity" is one that is focused on the possibility of a critical inventive act on the critic's part, rather than the shaky assumption that the speaker is the source of invention. The critic's role is best understood through and within and amid what has been constructed by the discourse: the discourse into which the critic enters and the discourse emerging from the critic's engagement with the same. What this means is that the opportunity exists to go beyond any single artifact or expression to "invent" a formation that helps to explain how any one fragment comes into being at a certain moment. We've long understood that prior rhetoric impinges on future possibilities; what the orientation toward invention suggests, contrary to a narrow focus on method, is that there is more than meets the eye in one's appraisal of an artifact, and that the role of the critic is not simply to *reflect* a given reality, but to partake in the *creation* of a reality heretofore unavailable to the mind's eye.

Finally, the inventive act, whether in the context of a critique of domination or a critique of freedom, requires the analytic and political flexibility necessary to ensure that invention is possible. We would argue that this flexibility is not available within the confines of a (formal) prescribed method.

CRITICAL ESSAY:
CRITICAL RHETORIC AS ORIENTATION:
TWO EXERCISES IN INVENTION

In seeking to parallel other essays in this volume by putting into practice the critical lens we have articulated in the preceding discussion, we have focused our attentions on the inventional nature of the critical act. In so doing, our purpose is not to capture the "essence" of how one practices critical reflection, but rather to suggest an *attitude* toward criticism.

In fulfilling the "exercise" we will focus attention on two primary themes in contemporary discourse. First, we will examine the discourse surrounding civility, which is fully ensconced within the democratic judgment that for deliberation to be true to its goals, it must be rational. Second, we examine a rational argument that goes against the grain—that articulated by "race traitor" rhetoric.

Part One: Civility

There are several theories demarcating what it means to be part of a civil society. The common perception is that one participates as a qualified citizen within a society that is at once part of the "state apparatus" (in that one is never far removed from oversight by a central authority) and simultaneously exists apart from the state—or is antithetical to the state.[28] Our formulation will not follow this standard separation, because we believe it to be a convenient fiction masquerading as a natural artifact of the collectivizing impulse. This is not to deny the convenience of maintaining the fiction, especially when the interests of civil society and the state are at odds with one another—but what of the relation when they are in concert? Where is the dividing line between state and society when the two are in league with each another, embracing the same normative values, and with the people complicit (in Gramsci's sense) in creating and maintaining the "rules for conduct" that govern the state-as-society's everyday affairs? As noted elsewhere,[29] the primary problem when both are in league is that "who is invited to the table"—who is determined in advance to be rational and reasonable, or capable of adhering to civility standards—is established in advance by whomever is in control, with the cooperation of those who in theory are part of a separate body inscribed as "civil society." It makes little sense, in this arrangement, to consider these entities as separate and autochthonous, since they subscribe to a discursive formation that undergirds both, and in giving expression to its dictates generally perpetuates the normative guidelines inherent within the formation. The power relationship is acknowledged and accepted as unexceptional in its force with respect to "maintaining the peace"—a goal of the state that the community (civil society) fully endorses.

To consider a counterforce to the above prized "possession," consider the following observations on the nature of civility:

- Civility may well be a virtue. But, it probably is not a virtue that will be of much help in deciding the political questions that ultimately matter.[30]
- When civility becomes a sensitivity that, like indiscriminate tolerance, casts aside regard for the truth, it bears little resemblance to civility understood as liberal learning, manners and morals, behavior appropriate to the discourse of civilized people, or even plain courtesy.[31]
- ... 'more' civil society in the contemporary Middle East could well mean increased symbolic and practical burdens for women.[32]
- [T]he social totality shaping civil society is a sphere of inequality and conflict—and ... maybe revitalizing civil society requires heightened levels of political struggle over state policy rather than good manners and 'civil discourse.'[33]
- Nothing is written in stone or is true by definition; a 'robust' civil society can serve all sorts of purposes, and the presence or absence of bowling leagues proves nothing by itself.[34]

Taken together, we believe the above sentiments about civility capture two "truths" for the present moment. First, it is surely the case that those voices immersed in the controversy over what constitutes civil society and its essential component, civility, are at least somewhat cognizant that merely "being civil" in contributing to "civil society" may not be sufficient to advance the rights or interests of citizens. Second, as Rabo notes in reference to Middle Eastern societies—and the same could be said as applied to some subcultures within the United States—more 'civilness' in society may simply mean that the present normative standards for behavior toward others are strengthened, not reformed.[35]

What these disparate voices also suggest, from the perspective of an "inventional" process, is that discursive power relations must be factored in when the intricate relationship between the state and civil society is under analysis, and moreover, whenever the nature of what in fact constitutes "civil discourse" within a civil society is addressed. If only those who are already deemed "civil" are invited to a conference dedicated to examining the decline of civility in a society, what might one expect in the way of the conferees' contributions and perhaps the meeting's outcome? If the discursive formation that is fashioning who can say what in what circumstance is not challenged by the inclusion of those who might effortlessly violate its strictures through their mere presence (and through their discourse), what chance is there for social change that redresses the balance of "who gets to be civil?" As Ehrenberg argues, the presence of social inequalities within a community makes seeing "civil society" as necessarily "anti-state" problematic.[36] What force more effectively reproduces injustices than a civil society that is already complicit with the dictates of a state that does not have that society's best (or even ancillary) interests at heart? Would it seem inappropriate for those who are in the "lower" social position with respect to inequalities, however measured, to be suspicious of the claims of a civil society that it *does* have their interests at heart? We unfortunately have no confidence that a formal method of analysis could insightfully answer these queries or others like them.

Part Two: Race Traitor

"Treason to whiteness is loyalty to humanity." With this as their constantly repeated slogan, a group of self-proclaimed "race traitors" has sought to redress the privileges that accrue to a dominant race within the United States by seeking to "dissolve the forces that hold whiteness" within that privileged status. As the creators of the magazine that carries their creed, *Race Traitor*, argue, "if it becomes impossible for the upholders of white rules to speak in the name of all who look white, the white race will cease to exist."[37] A primary reason for focusing on this discourse is that those who proclaim that the rest of those who are white (as are the authors) are wrong in the failure to cease an enjoyment of the privileges of whiteness would not be among those whom we might consider "civil" or worthy of a place at the table when discussing race relations. After all, they have essentially "opted out" by virtue (or vice?) of their very discourse, or so it would seem were one to operate from within normative standards for civil talk. And that is precisely the point: there may be times in civil society when saying "no" is critical—and saying so in a manner that alerts other members of society to the existence of wrongs that have been committed in their name. There is an old expression about hitting a mule on the head with a two-by-four to get its attention. While we abjure the injury this expression implies, we would note that just as there is some truth to the folk wisdom it conveys, there is also some truth to the need for civil society to be hit on the head, if only metaphorically. This does not mean that paradigm-shifting action is inevitably more "right" or "truthful" than the torpor secured by its obverse. But it *does* suggest that a forced compliance with the prevailing norms of civil discourse will preclude the allowance for such shifting—to the potential detriment of the society that precludes conflictual expression.

The strength and limitation of the race traitor "movement" has been well-chronicled.[38] Rather than repeating these analyses, we would like to reflect on the primary argument, as it underscores what a critical rhetoric perspective promotes. A key element in these analyses is that marginal discourses like those evinced within the *Race Traitor* movement are not always facile. In fact, in light of our argument, we think the *Race Traitor* phenomenon is a prime example of the very thing it says it seeks to avoid. By making race a fixed ontological determinant, it reifies that which should not be used to target populations as a criterion of significant difference. Race is a social, not a purely biological construct, and as such, may be altered through the kind of "dismissal" argued for by the *Race Traitor* advocates. As Flores and Moon point out, the argument promoted by this group is not particularly helpful because it promotes a binary vision of race—in being a traitor to whiteness, one must extol blackness: "the claim that whiteness is 'evil' is often directly contrasted with the glory of blackness."[39] Other "races" or ethnicities are "folded into" this mix by dint of their participation in varying degrees of "in-betweenness," as persons who are either more or less white or more or less traitors to whiteness through their adoption of a "reverse oreo" mentality. To the contrary: a stance that does not value the individuality of difference brought forward through Asian ethnicity or any other non-white/non-black cultural influence is simply re-naming the power relation in the guise of blackness— you are "with us" or "against us" becomes the default polarized position. Whether blackness ought to be valorized and re-privileged over whiteness is not the question here: that any other group would not have the same possibility as would members of the valorized "color" is merely to renew a racist argument from a different vantage point.

It would appear, from the critique above, that not counting by race—whether in terms of population census, the presence or absence of students of color on college campuses, or in other ways—would be a preference. To avoid race by not counting would be a good thing. At least that is another "fragment" that needs to be considered in the context of this discussion. Flores and Moon do indeed raise the question, and their argument is instructive. When their argument about "the elimination of racial categories in local, state, and government agencies" is raised, "the racial paradox reminds us that questions of whether or not we 'count' race are not the same as questions of if and how we can eradicate racism."[40] As they later ask, if particular minorities were in need of special services, how would that be known, if not through extant methods of inquiry? "Most vulnerable," they observe, "are traditionally disenfranchised peoples who often depend on targeted monies and social programs."[41] In other words, it is not sufficient simply to stop counting—as if that would by itself render color invisible. What is not as compelling is the impression one is left with that we stop there—that exposing "race traitors" as racist and continuing to support "counting by race" is at all sufficient to end the argument. From a critical rhetoric perspective, what may also be said is that this is an opportunity for critique, not of domination by the state with respect to continuing a dependence on its programs, but rather a critique pointing to a possible freedom to become something other than we are at present. To enhance civil society through a process whereby the *difference* is acknowledged for what it brings to the conversation, as it is relevant to, or important in the consideration of events would seem to be a *telos* toward which we might aim. That "counting" per se would no longer be the chief determinant of when *color* matters would allow for the full play of difference, including color. The aim, as McKerrow has argued,[42] is not to make color invisible, but instead to allow for its contribution when and where it does make a difference in the conversation.

How one accomplishes this new set of social relations (and the corresponding critique it would invite) is beyond the scope of this analysis. But the point we wish to make is that discursive and artifactual fragments, as an invitation to invention, lead us to the possibility of wondering what the world would be like if those depending on governmental social programs were no longer dependent; or if the color of their skin were no longer a contributing factor in that dependence (or cultural perceptions thereof). Flores and Moon are correct in their caution: to do away with racial categorization in the present would likely disadvantage those for whom such "counts" count. But to leave it as "this is the way it is" is insufficient; a call for a different future is simultaneously a call for a different "civil society" in which color matters, but not by virtue of its count. It matters for what it brings to the dialogue, wherein difference is respected as a valued commodity or as a resource for resolving society's ills.

CHAPTER CONCLUSION

This chapter has sought to reframe and remind: to reframe critical rhetoric's practice as an *orientation*, and to further the explanatory power of an inventional, critical modality in its engagement of discursive and artifactual fragments in the social world. How one carries the impetus to utilize its perspective forward remains open. There is a danger in citing examples of the kind of criticism we envision, as in citing particular approaches one risks the reification of that approach as the prime exemplar of "how to do critical rhetoric." We are rather content with the more ambiguous, yet potentially more fruitful, charge to our readers: *consider placing yourself inside an orientation that asks questions about the nature of language as it reveals particular formations between and among people, and the productive capability of power in enhancing social action.* Opening one's attitude toward events by considering the context whereby the event has come into being will go a long way toward realizing the potential of this critical perspective. Just as Kenneth Burke eschewed using critical markers (e.g., the "Pentad") in advancing critical judgment, we would remind readers that critical rhetoric functions as an intellectual backdrop to the critical act—it enjoins asking questions related to how the context forms discourse rather than how discourse effects publics. While recognizing the power accorded the speaker in traditional analyses of public oratory, it yet suggests that there is more to the story. By asking questions of the speaker as a product of the discourse that produced him or her, we hope to understand how the discourse came to be in this rather than another time, and what possibilities for freedom it hinders or makes available. Intervention as a means of remedying social ills demands no less from us than understanding how we come to be in this time and place, with these sets of attitudes toward events, ourselves, and others. Critical rhetoric is but one starting point in the path toward social action.

PERSONAL COMMENTS ON THE ESSAY

Exercising one's voice is about choices, whether responding to another person who has asked a question, or writing a scholarly essay. There are, of course, differences in the nature of each response, but the fact remains that one could choose several different ways to "style" one's commentary. That was the situation we faced when asked by the Editor to compose a chapter related to Critical Rhetoric. To make it possible to compare different approaches, the Editor has had a marked influence on the structural components of each chapter, but has left what is said, and how it is argued, to each author's choice. So, why did we make the choices we made, and what problems did that create for us?

We chose to focus on one particular essay (Clark's) as an object of critique for two reasons. First, because the essay, if interpreted as we have, moves the critical rhetoric project in directions that we see as less profitable or useful in maintaining the focus and hence promise of the perspective. Second, because it gave us an opportunity to provide an illustration of a narrowly focused critical response to particular expressions. In this latter instance, the approach is as important as the argument being advanced: we wanted to show students how critical reflection might work in actual practice. In making this choice, the primary difficulty is in accurately reflecting what the original author intended (as near as we can determine—knowing intention is a problem in itself) prior to subjecting that intention (as we interpret it) to critical commentary. Once that problem is resolved to our satisfaction (and we didn't ask the original author if there was agreement), the second problem is making the case clear to readers who have not participated in the conversation about critical rhetoric. Whether we have been successful in this latter goal is left to the reader's judgment.

We also, for our "critical essay," chose two critical "case studies" as illustrative of what it means to take this perspective seriously and apply the "mind-set" or "attitude" toward particular objects of inquiry. Civility and Race Traitors would seem an odd duo to consider, but their very difference made sense to us in illustrating what it means to take "fragments" of contemporary discourse, and through critical reflection, comment on the nature of the discourse and its influence. Here, the problem is to be clear about the nature of an "orientation" toward the object, as differentiated from a "method" of analysis. The latter, borrowing from science, works "methodically" through a set of criteria or questions in seeking answers. The former is not as "neat and clean," hence is both more problematic (how do we know the "answer" is right?) and more open (possibilities are not foreclosed by methodological constraints). We consider the advantage (openness) to outweigh the disadvantage, in part because we are not sure any "answer" will be right for all time.

POTENTIALS AND PITFALLS

In writing theoretical essays, one hopes to have an influence on the work of other scholars. With respect to what has become known as the "critical rhetoric project," it appears that the initial ideas have had a heuristic impact. As the following "critical bibliography" suggests, several scholars have provided new avenues from which to explore the notion of Critical Rhetoric. These have taken form as extensions of the theory, corrections of what are perceived to be shortcomings or critical weaknesses, or the creation of oppositional views in order to illustrate the fundamental flaws in the approach.

If you begin with the recognition that traditional rhetoric has a history of emphasizing the "great man speaking well," de-centering the role of the speaker as the origin of thought, words and action raises significant questions. What becomes of the object of criticism if the focus is not on the person speaking?

When you add to this purported "removal" of the active speaker/rhetor a commitment to a recursive or continual critique, a question about the possibility of criticism itself competes for attention. If critique is never-ending, what can we say about any specific instance of communication as to its value in achieving specific goals?

If you then suggest that the nature of critique does not rest in "method" but rather exists as an "orientation" toward an object, the negative reaction becomes even more strident. How can you possibly know what it is you have, or can argue, if you cannot rest your argument on the mantle of objective, methodical assessment of an object or event?

In short, these are the kinds of problems or pitfalls that arise when advancing the "critical rhetoric project." There are others, to be sure, but one could argue that they all can be reduced, in essence, to the issues just delineated.

> Issue One: The existence of a subject. McKerrow attempted to deal with this "flaw" in assessing the possibility of a subject or speaker within a critical rhetoric perspective: If the subject is decentered . . . can there be a role for the speaker as agent of social change? I answer this question in the affirmative. Resituating the subject does not necessitate the destruction of the speaker. . . . By giving voice to critique, the subject renews self.[43]

What is implied in this response to the issue is that the speaker, though de-centered, is not "dead" to the issues involved. At the same time, it also means that we are already immersed in a set of social practices and rituals that are not of our own making—and that we speak from within a conversation that has already pre-figured for us the possibilities of expression as well as the range of interpretations that might be most likely. This does not mean everything is "fixed" and determined ahead of time—but it does mean that the discursive formation is not open-ended and infinite with respect to who can say what to whom with what effect. You can yell "Fire" in a crowded room—but in so doing, you already know the possible impact of giving voice to that expression—if there were no fire, nor a possibility of one, what would happen to you as a consequence of people's believing you and acting on that belief? Kuypers does an eloquent job of considering this issue, arguing in part that the role of critical rhetoric "diminishes" the speaker's contribution.[44] Although we wouldn't use that label, it is the case that critical rhetoric changes the landscape within which speakers act and react. In aiming for the retention of what is termed "prudence" or "practical wisdom," which in turn actively engages ethical conduct or action, Kuypers argues that a critical rhetoric perspective may fail to contain prudence or "prudent action." Ethics is not automatically removed when adopting a critical rhetoric perspective. Rather, the "scene" (to use a term from Burke's pentadic orientation toward criticism) shifts from the speaker to the context in which the speaker acts. Prudence, as reflective of moral conduct or right action, is still possible within the rhetorical moment. The critical concern is not in "not accounting for the agent as the causative force" but rather lies in "accounting for ethical action or its absence in the rhetorical context." Reminding us of the importance of ethical considerations is a valuable contribution to the project; hence, Kuypers's points are well-taken—and accommodated within a slight shift from a focus on the speaker as active agent to the speaker as part of a larger context in which rhetorical action is taken.

Issue Two: The Possibility of Criticism. We might start with the observation that criticism and critique are different objects. Criticism is the shallower, narrower term—with a focus on "making things better." Critique, on the other hand, goes deeper and broader—its focus, while on "making things better" is also on the assumptions that ground the very object of critique. As McKerrow has noted, the propaganda critics of the early twentieth century certainly were focused on improving democracy.[45] But, they did not go beyond that to actively suggest that the very assumptions on which democracy was premised were themselves subject to revision. When invoking "critique" as the operative term, we are suggesting that not only do we want to improve our lot, but we want to subject the foundations underlying our social relations to scrutiny. Critique does not mean "everything we find is wrong"—that is, it is not inherently fault-finding. We may decide, after examination, that for now at least, specific social practices are fine the way they are. That isn't always likely, but it is at least a logical possibility—and one we need to retain in order not to fall into an irreversible litany of 'this is wrong, this is wrong,' ad infinitum.

Dana Cloud argues, among other things, that the critical rhetoric project may well rob us of the possibility of critique.[46] If we can never finish, how do we say anything is ever "wrong" or in need of correction? Consider the possibility that rhetoric is a moral and material force: it acts on us at every moment of our lives. If that were not the case, we would not be able to affirm such phrases as "a child who lives with criticism learns to criticize." Living in a social relationship bound by the continual expression of one's flaws may well have an impact on how one sees oneself. Kent Ono and John Sloop's articulation of a "telos" (purpose/goal) for a "sustained critical rhetoric" adds immeasurably to the power of the theoretical stance to make a difference. What is suggested is simply this: we do act with purpose within discrete historical moments, and we do judge the social worth of our actions at that moment as hopefully positive. What the critical rhetoric orientation suggests is not that we can't decide anything in the moment, but that once decided, once acted on, as we move on we can't just rest on our laurels. We can't just brush the dust off our hands, say the job is done, and assume all is now right with the world. It may be for then, and for always, but we owe it to ourselves to ask: what changes in power relations does this action portend, and how do those changes affect others? Does the correction of one inequity produce another down the road—one that also should be remedied? What the orientation commits us to is not indecision in the moment, but the realization that action is never final. There is no "fini" to the play of human life.

Issue Three: Orientation *re deviva*. Revisiting this issue at the end of an essay devoted to suggesting its merits may seem overkill. Hopefully, we have addressed the primary concerns raised with respect to this issue. Consider Burke's dramatism and the role of the pentad—Scene, Act, etc. function as a rough equivalent to "who-what-when-where-how." Just as you do not see a newspaper article with subheads identifying the discussion of "who" or "what" you will not see Burke's own critical works identifying "Scene" as distinguished from a discussion of "Act." (The chapter by Anderson, King, and McClure exemplifies this.) Rather, the terms function as a framing device—serving to give the journalist or the critic a set of tools with which to understand an event. Forgetting to mention 'scene' might be dumb or it might be equally irrelevant to the story or event. But forgetting to think about whether it is or not would be foolish. Critical rhetoric is oriented toward questions of power and their influence in framing social actions—what is or is not possible to express or do in specific settings. Forgetting to ask, in the process of examining rhetoric's material force, whether scene or act were somehow implicated would not be wise. Thus, critical rhetoric is not itself a "method" but saying that does not mean one is solely committed to whimsy in reflecting on an event. One can appropriate method in the act of examining a rhetorical context—while mindful of the broader issues that critical rhetoric brings to bear on the examination.

CRITICAL RHETORIC TOP PICKS

The following lists are not exhaustive, but reflect work done in advancing the "critical rhetoric project" in both theoretical and critical terms. We have moved beyond the editor's request and provided three lists. The first contains essays that owe their impetus to the original McKerrow essay in 1989. The second contains our top picks for theoretical contributions and extentions. The third contains our top picks for analyses using a critical rhetoric orientation.

WORKS ON CRITICAL RHETORIC BY REYMIE E. MCKERROW

"Critical Rhetoric: Theory and Praxis." *Communication Monographs* 56 (1989): 91–111.

"Critical Rhetoric in a Postmodern World." *Quarterly Journal of Speech* 77 (1991): 75–78.

Critical Rhetoric and Propaganda Studies." In *Communication Yearbook*, 14, edited by J. Anderson, 249–55. Newbury Park, CA: Sage, 1991.

"Critical Rhetoric and the Possibility of the Subject." In *The Critical Turn: Rhetoric and Philosophy in Postmodern Discourse*, edited by J. Anderson, 51–67. Carbondale, IL: Southern Illinois Univ. Press, 1993.

"Corporeality and Cultural Rhetoric: A Site for Rhetoric's Future." *Southern Communication Journal* 63 (1998): 315–328.

"Space and Time in a Postmodern Polity." *Western Journal of Communication* 63 (1999): 271–90.

"Critical Rhetoric." In *Encyclopedia of Rhetoric*, edited by Thomas Sloane, 619–622. NY: Oxford University Press, 2001.

"Coloring Outside the Lines." *Southern Communication Journal* 67 (2002): 290–294.

PRIMARILY THEORETICAL WORKS RELATED TO CRITICAL RHETORIC

Hariman, Robert. "Critical Rhetoric and Postmodern Theory." *Quarterly Journal of Speech*, 77 (1991): 67–70. This essay, along with Charland's below, is an invited response to the critical rhetoric essay. In part, it suggests that McKerrow's essay is written in a modernist vein, hence does not separate itself as a truly postmodern contribution. The essay also notes the problematic status of the rhetor as active agent affecting a specific audience if one adopts the orientation provided by a critical rhetoric perspective.

Charland, Maurice. "Finding a Horizon and Telos: The Challenge to Critical Rhetoric." *Quarterly Journal of Speech* 77 (1991): 71–74. Although finding much to commend in the perspective, it raises concerns about the potential for 'continual critique' to turn into an infinite process, with no end in sight. Also raises concerns about the role of the active agent. McKerrow's response to these two pieces is "Critical Rhetoric in a Postmodern World" cited above.

Ono, Kent. A. and John. M. Sloop. "Commitment to 'Telos'—A Sustained Critical Rhetoric." *Communication Monographs* 59 (1992): 48–60. This essay is sympathetic to the project, and responds directly to the criticism that continual critique makes it impossible to ever "take a stand" for some specific change, as one is always in the mode of critic rather than acting to create change. By crafting the role of "telos" as the purposeful act of an agent, Ono and Sloop advance the theoretical power of critical rhetoric as a means of enacting change in the world.

Gaonkar, Dilip P. "Performing with Fragments: Reflections on Critical Rhetoric." In *Argument and the Postmodern Challenge*, edited by Raymie E. McKerrow, 149–155. (Annandale, VA: Speech Communication Association, 1993). This essay critiques the alleged absence of reason as a hallmark of deliberative discourse that is a consequence of assuming a critical rhetoric stance.

Cloud, Dana L. "The Materiality of Discourse as Oxymoron: A Challenge to Critical Rhetoric." *Western Journal of Communication* 58 (1994): 141–163. This essay chronicles the shift toward a discussion of discourse as material. In particular, McGee and McKerrow's work is critiqued for its alleged shortcomings in advancing ideological criticism. Cloud proposes an alternative perspective in remedying the problems inherent within McGee's and McKerrow's formulations.

Murphy, John M. "Critical Rhetoric as Political Discourse." *Argumentation and Advocacy* 32 (1995): 1–15. This essay interrogates McKerrow's penchant for creating dichotomies (in this case—disassociations between opposites, as in permanence/change or domination/freedom) and critiques the absence of an active subject seeking change through the power of the word. Murphy proposes an alternative to the study of public discourse, based in Mikhail Bakhtin's concepts.

Clark, Norman. "The Critical Servant: An Isocratean Contribution to Critical Rhetoric." *Quarterly Journal of Speech* 82 (1996): 111–124. This essay has been subjected to extensive analysis within the present essay. It alleges that critical rhetoric does not observe or properly credit the relationship between the rhetor and the audience. Drawing on Isocrates, a classical Greek rhetorician, Clark offers a theoretical replacement for the missing pieces of a critical rhetoric perspective in suggesting that Isocrates' approach provides for a "contingent good" serving the interests of the community.

Kuypers, Jim A. "Doxa and a Critical Rhetoric: Accounting for the Rhetorical Agent through Prudence." *Communication Quarterly* 44 (1996): 452–462. As the title suggests, this analysis provides a "correction" to the absence of a central agent enacting change by recasting the sense of doxa and its corollary, "prudence" or "practical wisdom" (e.g., doing the right thing). The changes place responsibility for ethical action within an understanding of the community's will to action.

Greene, Ronald. W. "Another Materialist Rhetoric." *Critical Studies in Mass Communication* 15 (1998): 21–40. This study extends beyond Cloud's critical analysis, in arguing for a new understanding of what it means to theorize rhetoric as "material." In the process, it critiques McGee, McKerrow, and Cloud, and offers a rationale for replacing their formulations with a new definition of rhetoric as material that will better account for the use of rhetoric in changing power relations.

NOTES

1. Norman Clark, "The Critical Servant: An Isocratean Contribution to Critical Rhetoric," *Quarterly Journal of Speech 82* (1996): 111–124.

2. Raymie E. McKerrow, "Critical Rhetoric" in *Encyclopedia of Rhetoric*, ed. Thomas Sloane (NY: Oxford University Press, 2001), 619–622.

3. Kenneth Burke, *The Philosophy of Literary Form* (Berkeley, CA: University of California Press, 1941/1973), 9.

4. Jim A. Kuypers, "Framing Analysis." Chapter 12 of this volume.

5. Michael Calvin McGee, "Text, Context, and the Fragmentation of Contemporary Culture," *Western Journal of Speech Communication 54* (1990): 289.

6. Clark, 114.

7. Raymie E. McKerrow, "Critical Rhetoric: Theory and Praxis," *Communication Monographs 56* (1989): 91–111.

8. Clark, 116.

9. Ibid., 113.

10. Ibid., 114–115.

11. Ibid., 116–118.

12. See McKerrow, 1989, and Raymie E. McKerrow, "Critical Rhetoric and the Possibility of the Subject" in *The Critical Turn: Rhetoric and Philosophy in Postmodern Discourse,* ed. I. Angus and L. Langsdorf (Carbondale, IL: Southern Illinois Univ. Press. 1993), 51–67.

13. Clark, 118.

14. Ibid.

15. Ibid., 122.

16. Raymie E. McKerrow, "Space and Time in the Postmodern Polity," *Western Journal of Communication 63* (1999): 287.

17. McKerrow, 1989.

18. Ibid., 98.

19. Clark, 112.

20. McKerrow, "Critical Rhetoric," 2001, 619.

21. McKerrow, 1989, 91.

22. Ibid.

23. McKerrow, 1993, 64.

24. The manner in which we use the term "method" is very similar to the way this book's editor uses the term "perspective." We mean a formalized approach toward performing criticism.

25. McKerrow, 1989, 92.

26. McKerrow, 1990, 279.

27. Raymie E. McKerrow, "Critical Rhetoric and Propaganda Studies," in *Communication Yearbook, 14,* ed. J. Anderson (Newbury Park, CA: Sage, 1991), 249–55.

28. See Nicanor Pelis, *Shaping Globalization: Civil Society, Cultural Power and Threefolding* (Queson City, Philippines, Center for Alternative Development Initiatives, 1999) and Sam Eisenstadt and Wolfgang Schluchter, "Introduction: Paths to Early Modernities—A Comparative View," in *Public Spheres and Collective Identities*, ed. Samuel N. Eisenstadt, Wolfgang Schluchter, and Bjorn Wittrock (New Brunswick, NJ: Transaction Publishers, 2001), 1–19.

29. Raymie E. McKerrow, "Coloring Outside the Lines: The Limits of Civility," *Vital Speeches of the Day*, (February 15, 2001), 67, 278–281, and Raymie E. McKerrow and Jeffrey St. John, "Legitimizing Public Discourse: Civility as Gatekeeper," in *Proceedings of the Fifth Conference of the International Society for the Study of Argumentation*, ed. Frans H. van Eemeren, J. Anthony Blair, Charles A. Willard, and A. Francisca Snoek-Henkemans (Amsterdam: Sic Sat Press, 2002), 747–751.

30. James Schmidt, "Is Civility a Virtue?" in *Civility*, ed. Leroy S. Rouner (Notre Dame, IN: University of Notre Dame Press, 2000), 37.

31. Edwin J. Delattre, "Civility and the Limits to the Tolerable" in *Civility*, ed. Leroy S. Rouner (Notre Dame, IN: University of Notre Dame Press, 2000), 164.

32. Annika Rabo, "Gender, State and Civil Society in Jordan and Syria," in *Civil Society: Challenging Western Models*, ed. Chris Hann and Elizabeth Dunn (London, Routledge, 1996), 174.

33. John Ehrenberg, *Civil Society: The Critical History of an Idea* (NY: New York University Press, 1999), 249.

34. Ehrenberg, p. 249.

35. Rabo, p. 174.

36. Ehrenberg, p. 249.

37. Noel Ignatiev and John Garvey, eds., *Race Traitor* (NY: Routledge, 1996), 10, 36.

38. Dreama Moon and Lisa Flores, "Antiracism and the Abolition of Whiteness: Rhetorical Strategies of Domination among 'Race Traitors,'" *Communication Studies*, 51 (2000): 97–115, and Lisa A. Flores and Dreama G. Moon, "Rethinking Race, Revealing Dilemmas: Imagining a New Racial Subject in *Race Traitor*," *Western Journal of Communication*, 66 (2002): 181–207.

39. Moon and Flores, 189.

40. Ibid., 200.

41. Ibid., 200.

42. McKerrow, "Coloring Outside the Lines," 2001.

43. McKerrow, "Critical Rhetoric and the Possibility of the Subject," 64.

44. Jim A. Kuypers, "Doxa and a Critical Rhetoric: Accounting for the Rhetorical Agent through Prudence," *Communication Quarterly* 44 (1996): 452–462.

45. McKerrow, "Critical Rhetoric and Propaganda Studies."

46. Dana L. Cloud, "The Materiality of Discourse as Oxymoron: A Challenge to Critical Rhetoric," *Western Journal of Communication* 58 (1994): 141–163.

18

Conceptually-Oriented Criticism

Stephanie Houston Grey

Over the past three decades debates over methodology have become increasingly problematic for the practice of rhetorical criticism. While the existence of standardized frameworks (like some of the templates you have been reading in this volume so far) for understanding and evaluating discourse provide a certain intellectual consistency within the field, this consistency, some suggest, comes with a price. Rhetorical critics are often seeking dynamic approaches to criticism that allow for more flexibility in practicing their craft. James Jasinski, in two essays, undertook the task of providing some contours and vocabulary to these trends, encouraging discussion over the methodological consequences of this shift.[1] Rather than identify themselves with one methodology or template, many critics now prefer to allow texts of cultural or political significance to suggest interesting conceptual questions. These critics are eclectic entrepreneurs of critical templates, theory, and cultural practice. At stake in these discussions is the heuristic value of methodology itself as a guiding principle in critical practice, leaving the rhetorical critic to cast a broader net. Here critical perspective becomes a guiding principle. Then these critics pursue the act of criticism as a means for understanding how ideas, symbolic strategies, and cultural patterns evolve. Jasinski notes that "this emerging pattern of interconnected trends—decline of method and development of conceptually-oriented criticism—may be one of the most significant recent developments in rhetorical studies."[2] Note that Jasinski uses the terms "conceptually-oriented criticism" rather than "conceptual criticism." The conceptual approach is not to be confused with a methodology, but represents a trend that moves away from methodology in the traditional sense. As this perspective departs from the creation and replication of methodological frameworks, the rhetorical critic is provided greater freedom—yet, in most cases—this freedom comes with increased responsibility.

Perhaps it is worthwhile to review the goals of rhetorical criticism before unpacking the intricacies of the conceptual orientation. In chapter 2 Jim A. Kuypers explains that rhetorical criticism is designed to enhance and expand our understanding and appreciation of particular communicative acts as well as the rhetorical process itself. It is shared with audience members who themselves are shareholders in the endeavor to understand language and representation—producing insights that improve our ability to consume these texts with an informed awareness. This process is one that is both intellectual and audience driven. To extend this discussion, Jasinski identifies three main purposes that animate critical practice. This list is by no means exhaustive, but offers a meaningful starting point. First, criticism "is seen as a force for educating

342 Stephanie Houston Grey

its audience and helping those audience members to become better judges and/or consumers of various types of practices."[3] The problem with both cultural and political discourse is that, to the untrained mind, they often become an unchallenged reality—a social or empirical truth. It is the responsibility of the rhetorical critic to insure that consumers of his or her work will be equipped with the tools necessary to reflect on these symbolic realities in an informed fashion. Second, criticism "contributes to the development of theory within its respective spheres of practice"[4] Within the field of rhetorical criticism theory and practice enjoy a mutually influential relationship, with one shaping the contours of the other. It should be noted that theory-building—in the sense of building universal models—is not the imperative of the conceptual orientation, or of all criticism in general.[5] On a more practical level, rhetorical theory is what constitutes the lexicon that allows rhetorical scholars to create a shared disciplinary history rather than a universal body of accumulated knowledge. Conceptually oriented criticism may add or subtract from this lexicon, but it does not seek to offer some ultimate framework or final word on rhetorical practice. Finally, a "growing number of critics, in rhetorical studies as well as in other academic disciplines, believe that criticism must play a role in both exposing and fighting various forms of oppression and injustice in the world."[6] As noted in the chapter on critical rhetoric in this volume, the evaluative component of a criticism—the part where the critic offers some judgment—has also become increasingly complex and at times problematic. Now, rather than simply tracing the rhetorical effect of a text, the critic can actively engage the text, suggesting how its reinforcement of a particular social reality shapes the lives of those who follow or are marginalized by it and offer a verdict of sorts. While this goal is sometimes contested, language always involves hierarchical relationships and it is the orientation of the critic that leads them to either highlight or ignore these relationships.[7] One of the strengths of the conceptual orientation, as we shall see, is that it provides the critic with the opportunity to address each of these goals if he or she chooses to do so. The following sections will outline, elaborate, and expand upon the conceptual orientation in rhetorical criticism.

Before moving on, let us take a moment to understand how the conceptual orientation itself orients the critic to the text and the practice of criticism itself. In 1947 Earnest Wrage drew a connection between rhetorical criticism and the "history of ideas." This piece would suggest a deceptively complex relationship between the text, the critic, and the conceptual frameworks used to explore these "ideas." He writes that "the word idea, therefore, is not restricted here to a description of the great and noble thoughts uttered by accredited spokesmen for the edification of old and young. It is employed in a more inclusive sense and refers widely to formulations of thought as the product and expression of social incentives, which give rise and importance now to one idea, then another."[8] There are two important points to understand here. First that discourse expresses ideas that continue to circulate and influence other symbolic activities. Second, that these "ideas attain history in process, which includes transmission. The reach of an idea, its viability within a setting of time and place, and its modifications are expressed in a vast quantity of documentary sources."[9] As ideas are expressed and become commonplace in the cultural vocabulary, they are deployed in discourse over and over again, and each instance where it is used changes that idea (sometimes slightly, sometimes radically). It is often these modifications that become the stuff of the rhetorically oriented mindset. You may be familiar with Kenneth Burke's idea of social frameworks and the dramatistic approach. In his *Grammar of Motives*, Burke suggests that the entire arc of human history can be understood as a series of symbolic frameworks that shape human consciousness through the process of identification.[10] As they shape consciousness, they subsequently shape human action. The conceptual orientation examines the way that particular concepts that shape or inform symbolic activity are expressed in significant texts and using this exchange to explore shifts in human consciousness and standards of judgment. If you can identify a core principle for the conceptual orientation, this is it.

Once one begins to examine the fluid exchange between historical context, concept, and text, the entire practice of rhetorical criticism takes on a new depth. Take for example the idea of "rhetoric." In his intellectual history of the field of rhetoric, Victor Vitanza argues that rhetoric is, at once, something that people practice while also being a concept which philosophers and practitioners alike have debated.[11] Thus it derives its meaning both from how it is done and how it is talked about. This process extends Wrage's notion that rhetoric allows people to negotiate ideas, and suggests that the field of concepts through which individuals come to understand their universe both shape and reflect their collective ethos.[12] Allan Megill recently suggested that this process is further complicated by the forces of globalization as ideas circulate in ever-widening bandwidths and the local assimilates these modes of thought.[13] In short, as a critic, you exist at a complex interchange of concepts, the texts that influence these concepts, and the critic who develops these critical frameworks from what he or she perceives in operation during these key moments. For Jasinski, these concepts influence the standards of judgment both for those individuals who have consumed a text, and the critic who is writing to the larger audience of rhetorical critics. As new ideas emerge that influence how we judge texts, the critic must remain flexible in the face of this ever-altering landscape. Conceptually-oriented criticism is thus both playful and a serious business.

The Concept as Mediator between Text and Historical Context

Historical context has been one of the more vexing questions for rhetorical critics, particularly when one considers what it is that constitutes a "text." This question came to the forefront of the field in the 1980s, culminating in a disciplinary debate. Two of the primary interlocutors in this discussion were Michael Leff and Michael McGee. A brief glance at this exchange—with a modest dose of oversimplification—is instructive. The crux of this discussion focused on the way that texts were to be understood in relationship to their historical context. Michael Leff, arguing for the integrity of the text, noted that the field was at a point where "critical attention had drifted away from particular discourse and toward such complex *intertextual* phenomena as social movements, genres, and ideologies."[14] This trend suggested an entangled vision of text and context—kind of like blurring the lines between your primary and secondary sources in a research paper. Concerned about the focus upon broad cultural or historical forces, Leff cautioned that "when not grounded in particulars, efforts at rhetorical interpretation rigidify along the axis of the form/content dichotomy, since interpretation finds its end in abstract regularities rather than in the complex interplay among representational content, discursive form, and the context of situation."[15] In other words, the dynamics that one sees in texts, are often more intricate and complex than the abstract assumptions that emerge in the theories about these texts. Leff's concern that rhetoric was in danger of losing its disciplinary integrity to fields such as history or sociology is well-founded. When one is too focused upon broad historical frameworks, the text gets lost in these regularities and the practice of rhetorical criticism loses that which distinguishes it from other manifestations of art and science. Another outcome of this trend was the construction of theory-for-theory's-sake, creating universal abstract models that eventually lost their connection to the way that discourse is actually performed from situation to situation and by differing actors.

In a somewhat different perspective, McGee suggested that discussing a text in relationship to its historical context necessitates that the critic understand that texts are never delivered to them as self-contained wholes. McGee identified three dynamics that complicated this relationship. First, texts are constructed from borrowed fragments from other texts that have come before, meaning that a text is simply generated out of a larger cultural vocabulary of commonplaces and strategies. Second, texts have a complex relationship with their larger culture. When the text is consumed (which may differ from its point of creation), it may be judged differently by subgroups within a particular culture. Finally, the text will itself be dissected and appropriated by future political or cultural actors. Much like Wrage suggests, the text articulates ideas that will become the fodder for future symbolic actions, transmissions and judgments. McGee cautions that if "you can't chase down the fragments from which an argument was constructed (if you can't find the prosecution's case in the trial of Socrates, for example), you use the discursive equivalent of the theory of spontaneous generation and treat the argument *ex nihilo* philosophy and/or literature, words without history, or words with only an intellectual or literary history."[16] In other words, McGee importantly asserts that the text cannot emerge fully finished from a symbolic vacuum, but must be recognized as part of a larger social dialogue.

Which esteemed critic is right? From a conceptual orientation, the answer is both. Jasinski writes that "conceptually oriented criticism proceeds more through a process of *abduction* which might be thought of as a back and forth tacking movement between text and concept or concepts that are being investigated simultaneously."[17] Leff is correct that the textual dynamics and interplay must remain the unique domain of rhetorical criticism. It is within the text that one sees concepts articulated and brought together in a coherent whole, allowing a brief snapshot of the cultural universe at that time and providing a legitimate and meaningful point of departure for criticism. McGee is also correct that the larger frameworks generated by symbolic action such as ideologies, power relationships, and ideographs that generate shared meaning exist as a series of fragments that are constantly un-seaming and reemerging in other contexts. At the junction between Leff and McGee resides the concept—a framework or idea that informs our reception of a text—allowing for future rhetorical action. The conceptual orientation recognizes that each text can generate new and creative meanings that challenge the generalized assumptions of model builders, while also examining the way that these texts shape the larger historical consciousness and can have a profound influence on the social dynamics of an entire culture far beyond the time and place of its own enactment. There is no set process for how this occurs. The critic must understand history at both a literal and an intellectual level. The concept is a product of the text, the context in which it is judged, and the critic that must organize these ideas into a meaningful whole. The concept is identified through the critic's reading of a text or collection of inter-related texts that informs the way that it/they and, potentially, future texts will be consumed. The primary domain of the conceptual orientation is the sphere in which communicative practice meets larger historical, strategic, aesthetic, or ideological frameworks that shape human consciousness and standards of judgment. Limiting the critic to one particular methodology is, from this standpoint, bound to lead to failure because practice is always more complex than the theoretical frameworks that scholars create to describe them. Texts are generative. This means that they create and replicate the larger fields of reference that are used to define them. The critic who approaches the text with a conceptual orientation must remain open to this dynamic.

A Brief Touchstone

An extended exploration of a benchmark illustrating the conceptual orientation can serve to outline this perspective. In 1992 Robert Hariman published an essay over the relationship between decorum, style, and power that has become one of the most cited pieces of criticism published in recent decades.[18] This piece highlights the performances that define the court of Haile Selassie, the emperor and religious leader of Ethiopia for over forty years, particularly how seemingly aberrant or illogical behaviors can be made to seem natural by well-entrenched rules of decorum. Jasinski notes that Hariman's piece "illustrates a growing trend in rhetorical criticism—decreased emphasis on questions of critical method and increased emphasis on criticism as a means of engaging questions of conceptual significance."[19] The central concept of Hariman's essay, style, is one that has been traditionally associated with mere ornamentation by Enlightenment thinkers who sought to place logic and science at the center of human thought. When one thinks about style, one might think about Martha Stewart's suggestions for holiday decorations or the paramilitary design of the Hummer. The insight of Hariman's piece is that he identifies style not as design afterthought, which has no relationship to function, but as a powerful constitutive force that mandates human conformity. Jasinski notes that Hariman is not interested in creating a new methodology and that his "study is an effort to unpack central terms within the rhetorical tradition in a way that allows them to speak to issues in contemporary social thought."[20] Style, often relegated to the margins of the rhetorical canon, becomes intertwined with power.

The piece deploys the court and the activities that mark it as a text. It is here that the King becomes the symbolic center of spectacle—a symbolic body representing authority. In this place dogs of one gender bear names of the opposite gender and palace courtiers are admired for allowing court pets to pee on their feet. The question this raises is why, given the illogical nature of these behaviors and judgments, do the courtiers continue to obey these rules. In the context of the court rules of decorum have evolved to such an extent that they can become powerful tools in the management of identity and human action. Hariman writes that as "political life is styled, it will be a life lived on the surface of things, and stylistic analysis should contribute to the task of understanding how that specific surfaces are seen or not seen at all. In short, understanding the aesthetic dimension of political experience requires that one uncover what is in full view."[21] Here the ornamentation of the surface, with its idiosyncrasies as illustrated by the court, run deep and shape human consciousness at a profound level. Hariman articulates his critical role in the following way: "To capture this sense of how power is both represented and generated by particular rules of appropriateness, and how the critic has to bridge the gap between fragmentary text and comprehensive appeal, I have introduced the additional concept of a political style and illustrated this concept by examining one such style briefly."[22] Here the concept of style becomes a mediating force between the critic, the text, and the larger frameworks that shape human action. Using the concept of style, Hariman is able to articulate the "extent that power is constituted by processes of communication, [and that] every political act requires a political culture that can be identified in part by its rules for appropriate communication."[23] The goal of this piece is not to create a new critical methodology or to train the next generation of students to be "stylistic critics," but to demonstrate how frameworks of decorum can become so rigid that exaggerated, even aberrant behaviors, begin to seem natural.

One can see how the three goals articulated by Jasinski are addressed by Hariman's piece. First the audience is asked to think critically about the way that style may function to reinforce conformity in a highly substantive way. Perhaps Martha Stewart's rules for holiday decor becomes a cultural mandate of sorts and the design of the Hummer, particularly in a time of war, extend military consciousness throughout the entire culture. This dovetails into the second goal of insuring that theoretical insight is gleaned from the text. Here the canon of style moves to the forefront alongside invention and arrangement as key elements in the rhetorical lexicon. Finally, the dictates of style can be demonstrated to reinforce the traditional boundaries of power and reinforce political ideologies that mandate problematic social hierarchies. For Jasinski the key to understanding the concept is how it influences or "thickens" judgment. He concludes that "the nexus of rhetoric and judgment is perspective; advocates craft arguments and appeals that shape the way audiences perceive and, in turn, act in the world. Criticism contributes to or thickens our grasp of political and rhetorical judgment as it reveals the way perspectives are crafted, circulated, and subverted."[24] The conceptual orientation is one that thickens our understanding of the way that consciousness is shaped by a host of social, epistemic, and aesthetic frameworks that mark society. These include touchstone political events, campaigns, aesthetic practices, scientific discourse, consumer society, and of course the critical act itself.

Since symbolic action is ubiquitous, the critic's only limitation is his or her own ability, knowledge base, and imagination. The concept becomes a mediating device between the critic, text, and historical frameworks that influence judgment, allowing a unique glimpse into the evolution of thought and its impact on concerted social and political action. Here are a few quick suggestions. Is the United States now in an era dominated by a paramilitary style with the emergence of vehicles like the Hummer and online recruiting tools disguised as civilian video games? Can this paramilitary style be used as a concept to unpack the forces that drive countries into a state of complacency during a protracted war? Perhaps the concept of social geography might be used to explain why victims of Katrina were deemed unworthy and disposable by the federal government. In this case, the map of the United States is not an objective description of spatial boundaries, but a subtle explication of the expendable and impoverished. Does the concept of *thanatos* (the cultural representation of death) help us to understand how those who suffer with AIDS use art as a means of shifting cultural stigma surrounding this disease? In each case, the text summons forth a culturally recognizable concept that allows the critic to explain its rhetorical dynamics in a way that contributes meaningfully to the larger cultural dialogue. With this overview of conceptually-oriented criticism complete, we can now turn our attention to a specific case. I have provided a condensed version of one of my own previously published essays for analysis.

CRITICAL ESSAY: REPRESENTING GROUND ZERO: TRACING NARRATIVES OF ROMANTIC REGENERATION IN THE HIBAKUSHA LITERATURE[25]

When communities undergo profound spiritual or psychological trauma, the discursive rituals that maintain cultural stability must respond to these shifting circumstances. These emergent histories reconstruct the traumatic moment, representing the past through vocabularies capable of both revision and selective repression of portions of this history. One particularly acute trauma for U.S. culture, as well as the international community, resulted from the attacks on Hiroshima and Nagasaki in August 1945. Because the world's first exposure to nuclear weapons was manifest as an act of war against military targets that included large civilian populations, accounts of the bomb and its aftermath continue to reverberate throughout our collective memory. A key ideological challenge for many American advocates following the war was to create a moral narrative that repressed the fear and anxiety the acts provoked, resulting in a worldview in which the presence of atomic weapons seemed natural. Robert Lifton and Greg Mitchell suggest that the one-sided nature of these renderings promote moral pathology, repressing both fears of potential retribution and guilt at the expense of recognizing the true threat that these weapons present.[26] This selective memory was further necessitated by a mythology Thomas Englehardt describes as "victory culture," a constellation of discourses that reaffirmed armed conflict as an ethical endeavor and that persisted until the cultural disillusionment resulting from the Vietnam conflict.[27] As one probes the history of nuclear consciousness, one finds a discourse rife with sublimations and contradictions that seek to protect the American ethos.

Symbolic and historical accounts of Hiroshima and Nagasaki remain sites of particularly acute political contest in American culture. Traditional histories often provide a technical description of the bomb's development and a narrative describing the flight of the Enola Gay. This viewpoint was vividly demonstrated in 1995 when the Smithsonian constructed an exhibit to commemorate the bomb on the fiftieth anniversary of its deployment. While the original exhibit dealt with the entire history of WWII, many historians vigorously protested the depiction of the bomb's effects including photos and accounts of/from the victims of the blast. This debate was so contested, the museum capitulated and simply displayed the Enola Gay with the flight recorder. Michael Sherry refers to this strategic amnesia as "patriotic orthodoxy," a process that uses history to heighten American nationalism by limiting internal moral reflection.[28] Criticism of this orthodoxy usually originates in the work of historians pejoratively labeled "revisionists," a description applied to scholars who view traditional justifications of Hiroshima and Nagasaki as a rationale for preserving nuclear weapons as justifiable instruments of war in an attempt to reduce the fear and anxiety these weapons provoke. Given the contentious exchange between orthodox and revisionist actors, it is not surprising that displays such as the Smithsonian Exhibit become battlegrounds over censorship. In the Smithsonian exhibit, the elements that raised the most objections by orthodox historians were the exhibition of casualty photos and the inclusion of accounts from survivors. The presence of a potentially authentic Japanese identity within the Western recollections represents a challenge to the creation of an ethically seamless enactment of national identity, and thus survivor discourse has come to play a unique role in atomic history. Yet, one sees upon closer examination, the survivor accounts play a much more complex role in this process. Foregrounding themes of retribution and regeneration, survivors' accounts constitute the point at which conflicting ethics in the collective psyche of both national cultures are resolved and ultimately authenticated. This directly impacts the way that nuclear weapons are subsequently judged.

Eyewitness accounts of Japanese survivors represent a central component of atomic culture. These individuals, refereed to as *hibakusha* (bomb-effected persons), constitute a lasting memory that mark both boundaries and zones of permeation between American and Japanese memory. The most popular western account dealing with the bomb remains John Hersey's *Hiroshima*, written for the *New York Times* in 1946.[29] Selling more than seven million copies, this text is considered the quintessential bomb testimonial in America. In this text, Hersey distills the Japanese experience from interviews with six *hibakusha*, translating these accounts for an American audience. The prolific Takahashi Nagai produced a work with similar influence in Japan, *The Bells of Nagasaki*.[30] Published in 1949 and later reprinted in the U.S., this text launched Nagai as an inspirational representative of the *hibakusha*. As a devout Christian, he grapples with the spiritual implications of nuclear technology and the suffering it produced. Michihito Hachiya's *Hiroshima Doctor* marked the bomb's tenth anniversary and was published in anticipation of the Hiroshima Maidens arrival in America, a group of Japanese women scarred by the bomb who visited the U.S. to receive plastic surgery and tour the country, bringing a message of peace and mutual forgiveness.[31] As a physician, Haychiya records his frustrations in treating radiation illness and his struggle to resolve his sense of nationalism with the reality of surrender and come to terms with human nature and creation of such destructive technology. Masuji Ibuse's *Black Rain*, the docu-novel that many literary critics call the most significant text in twentieth century Japan, was published in 1965 and translated into English the following year.[32] Crossing the boundaries between documentary and fiction, this text synthesizes the diaries of real *hibakusha* to create the character Shigematsu, a traditional Japanese man confronted with a niece suffering from radiation sickness. These four key texts represent significant political actions in the development of nuclear consciousness, employing interrelated literary forms in a ritualistic manner to justify the presence of the bomb, shaping how its meaning is established, and the manner in which these representations shape perceptions of this technology.

In a series of literary transformations, these texts inscribe the *hibakusha* as the true witness and the central actors in the atomic drama, allowing western audiences to manage nuclear weapons as agents of moral regeneration. Understanding the way that the *hibakusha* narratives ultimately regenerate nuclear weapons requires understanding the unique role that romanticism plays in the rise of technological culture. In traditional understandings of romanticism, it is held in opposition to science. Yet, in their analysis of President Reagan's "Star Wars" speech, Kenneth Zagacki and Andrew King note that romantic narratives of individual enlightenment and achievement play a crucial role in rehabilitating nuclear weapons.[33] If one examines the developing relationship between realism and romanticism, one finds that heroic narratives of creative and poetic insight permeate virtually every technological transformation experience within western society. Jonathan Taylor notes that "in this way twentieth-century science is shot through with assumptions from nineteenth-century Romanticism and its stress on the imagination, intuition, and individualism."[34] Even going back to novels that warn of the dangers of science such as Mary Shelley's *Frankenstein*, romanticism has come to define science for nearly two centuries.[35] The *hibakusha* give a meaning to the bomb that transcends the technical description of the weapon and its effects.

The vocabularies of sacrifice, technical mastery, and cultural transformation define these key texts, marking fundamental transitions in the collective memory of Hiroshima and Nagasaki. This case study will proceed through three major phases of the *hibakusha* literature spanning two decades from the 1940s to the 1960s: first Hersey and Nagai's use of religious terminology, second, Haychiya's reliance on scientific realism, and third, Ibuse's embrace of aesthetics. Although each of these accounts is marked by a shift in terminology for understanding the bomb, each returns to the common romantic form of personal quest where the bomb erases a fraudulent system and provides those who experienced it with a higher order of truth. In this way the bomb becomes an agent of moral regeneration rather than one of destruction. In short, as the audience comes to know the bomb through these accounts, this process of knowing becomes one where the bomb is transformed into an object of moral redemption rather than an object of destruction. This analysis will thus trace the concept of romanticism through these texts and explore the relationship between literary form and the development of historical consciousness.

The Concept of Romanticism

Among the most significant literary forms to mark the last two centuries has been romanticism. Charles Taylor notes that beginning in the eighteenth century, European romanticism affirmed individual perception in contrast to Enlightenment empiricism and scientific abstraction.[36] As a literary form that uses human experience to generate poetic truth, romanticism locates moral insight within individual interpretation of nature rather than empirical observation. Lionel

Trilling traces a unique American form of romanticism into the twentieth century, arguing that modern romantic writers created an authenticity designed to naturalize existing cultural viewpoints through literature.[37] While often described as a literary form, the following analysis suggests that romanticism plays a significant role in the formation of nuclear consciousness through the collective history generated by the *hibakusha*.

In *hibakusha* literature this romantic impulse mingles with documentary realism to create story where the bomb plays a redemptive role. The manner in which this is accomplished resonates with what Frank Kermode calls the "naive apocalyptic," a romantic form that presents certain ethical interpretations and then willfully dismantles them for transcendent insight.[38] Thus, the romantic depiction places the hero within a fraudulent system, forcing him or her to draw closer to a coveted truth by initiating a quest for personal enlightenment. For the *hibakusha*, the bomb not only eradicates artifice but also provides the narrator with moral redemption. Texts that span a relatively broad historical period and two different languages present both difficulties and opportunities. While interpreting their cultural context becomes a complex process, one can identify shifts in competing ethical vocabularies that delineate cultural authority. In other words, texts tell stories that ask the audience to identify with narrators who must overcome some challenge or obstacle. In these texts, the narrators develop a unique relationship with the bomb since they, in a way, have been closer to it than most people. Given that the bomb is described in many different ways—as anything from just retribution to a war crime perpetrated by the United States—these accounts are meaningful in that they shape the way we interpret and morally represent nuclear technology. Dispersed across a wide range of contexts, *hibakusha* literature represents the performance of an atomic allegory that maintains the ethical coherence of nuclear weapons. Rather than simply challenging Western narratives as orthodox historians might suggest, the relationship of the survivors to the bomb is more complicated.

The Rise of Nuclear Theology

In a 1946 report from the Federal Council of Churches on the atomic bomb a number of ministers endorsed the statement that "all men and Christians in particular are required to search their hearts and minds, to reexamine their principles and practices, and to seek with the greatest diligence for effective ways to abolish the diabolical horror."[39] With one side supporting the attack as a form of just punishment and the other criticizing the action as an irresponsible use of apocalyptic technology, an authentic standpoint from which to morally judge the bomb seemed necessary. In an historical context where even the President of the United States used biblical terminology to explain the scope and effects of nuclear technology, the *hibakusha* began to justify their experience in terms of religious redemption, a theme common to romantic genres. In his analysis of prophetic rhetoric, James Darsey notes that the primary script for the martyr is one in which great suffering is endured for spiritual ends, an act marked by moral regeneration.[40] Similarly, the *hibakusha* were initially transformed into an international symbol of penance and salvation, thus reaffirming traditional narratives of Christian sacrifice and transcendence.

The significance of this allegory stems from its capacity to make trauma and suffering meaningful through spiritual enlightenment, allowing the initial representations of Hiroshima and Nagasaki to provide ethical cohesion to an otherwise distant and terrifying event. Hersey's *Hiroshima* and Nagai's *Bells of Nagasaki* lead readers through the intense physical and spiritual devastation of the Japanese bomb survivors, undergirding the horror of their accounts with themes of religious transformation and salvation. This journey is sparked by the *Kyodatsu*—a state of demoralization that swept across Japan following its surrender. American strategists anticipated this demoralization, projecting the bomb's capacity to psychologically eliminate the enemy's will to fight. In *hibakusha* literature, however, the *Kyodatsu* exceeds the short-term panic American strategists anticipated, striking at the core of Japanese culture and ethics. In accounts such as Hersey's, the *Kyodatsu* becomes a more expansive experience where the *hybakusha* emerge as a universal symbol for explaining and alleviating this sense of displacement. Not surprisingly, these narratives direct significant attention to the erasure and regeneration of Japanese culture as one of the primary conflicts addressed by the larger atomic drama.

Close inspection of early *hibakusha* literature reveals that the degradation embodied by the *Kyodatsu* is remedied through spiritual transformation. This quest for spiritual meaning is often initiated when the bomb detonates. In many eyewitness accounts from Hiroshima and Nagasaki, the flash that accompanied the detonation, the *pika*, is usually followed by images of damnation. Nagai conveys his initiation into the cataclysm in a decidedly Christian tone, writing that "I felt, as I looked around, as if the end is near. For a moment I kept my ear cocked for the blast from the trumpets from heaven, so convincing was the devastation."[41] Following the logic of divine retribution, punishment stems from guilt. When an act is perceived to have divine mandate, those harmed by the act are harmed for a justifiable reason and the cataclysm may even have a beneficial end. Hersey, for example, draws on members of the Christian ministry such as Tanimota, a protestant minister, and Kleinsorge, a Catholic priest, as his primary eyewitnesses. Given the spiritual orientation of these individuals, it is not surprising that the bomb is seen as an avenue into the mind of God.

While the works of Hersey and Nagai avoid the overt language of divine retribution, the infiltration of this vocabulary nevertheless emerges, particularly in the religious conversions of the *hibakusha*. Yasumasa Sato points out that conversion to Christianity was one of the most significant themes in postwar literature, helping the Japanese people to accept both defeat and moral responsibility for their crimes.[42] After the young file clerk, Ms. Sasaki, is crushed during the blast and permanently disfigured, her fiancé's subsequent rejection initiates her quest to find meaning in a seemingly immoral universe. Father Kleinsorge interjects to remind her that God sometimes punishes the wicked in order to teach them wisdom and that she must learn to accept her suffering without bitterness. Ms. Sasaki is so moved by Kleinsorge's explanation that she eventually becomes a nun. William Hamlin notes that in romantic visions involving cultural exchange, the pagan value system absorbs and is regenerated by the "truth" of the Christian culture.[43] Here, Hersey's status as a mere translator of the *hibakusha* experience as well as his reliance on Westerners and English-speaking Japanese, seems highly problematic. Yet, the acknowledgement of Western cultural superiority seems even more explicit in Nagai, a Japanese native who rejects indigenous religions such as Shinto. Living in the ruins of Nagasaki, he is visited by a group of angry young soldiers who express indignation at Japan's surrender and declare their allegiance to the native religious images. Nagai replies that "those Gods were created by our ancestors whose knowledge of philosophy and theology was more primitive than ours. Those were really just paper gods. And in this way we came to believe in the invincibility of our country and in legends about the divine wind and the like. We were paying homage to dead images."[44] Some contemporary critics dismiss Nagai's work because of his portrayal of native religious icons. John Dower, for example, argues that the popularity of Nagai stemmed from his generosity and the sympathy generated by the patient child who stood by his side.[45] This interpretation may comfort contemporary critics, yet Nagai's narrative was consistent with the postwar *Kyodatsu* and the mass disillusionment with traditional culture, a phenomenon more extensive that modern historians sometimes suggest.

Perhaps the most counterintuitive aspect of these narratives is the way in which they construe the bomb as an agent of spiritual progress and transformation. Nagai, for example, suggests that the bomb should be welcomed for awakening the spirit of Christ in Japan, erasing pagan traditions the same way that it had erased the two cities. This is graphically illustrated in *Bells* where the bomb becomes a regenerative force after the Urakami (a Christian shrine) is reconstructed: "The bells are ringing! These are the bells of the Angels ringing out from the ruined cathedral, echoing across the atomic wilderness and telling us that the dawn has come."[46] The atomic age signals the next stage of cultural evolution. Rather than a locus of violence and barbarism, the West instead becomes a force for moral regeneration. This dynamic figures prominently in Nagai's funeral oration for those who perished in the initial attack: "Blessed are those who mourn for they shall be comforted. We must walk this way of expiation faithfully and sincerely. And as we walk in hunger and thirst, ridiculed, penalized, scourged, pouring with sweat and covered with blood, let us remember how Jesus carried his cross to the hill on Calvary."[47] This allegory of redemption through martyrdom characterizes many initial *hibakusha* responses to the atomic bomb.

Nagai universalizes this sacrifice by describing "how noble, how splendid was that holocaust of August 9, when flames soared up from the cathedral, dispelling the darkness of war and bringing peace! In the very depth of our grief we reverently saw here something beautiful, something pure, something sublime. Eight thousand people, together with their priests, burning with pure smoke, entered into eternal life."[48] This encomium connects this spiritual sacrifice to the international order: "Joyfully we have hated one another, joyfully we have killed one another. And now at last we have brought this great evil war to an end. But in order to restore peace to the world it is not sufficient to repent. We had to obtain God's pardon through the offering of great sacrifice."[49] The embrace of what is perceived as authentic religion in the face of physical and psychological suffering elevates the *hibakusha* and authorizes them to embody the growing nuclear conscience expressed by liberal historians while simultaneously venerating the bomb. Certainly, *Hiroshima* and *Bells* participate in this dynamic, with one tracing the redemptive tension from the outside and the other from the inside. With Hersey's narratives of religious conversion and Nagai's embrace of martyrdom, these texts portray the bomb as a harbinger of spiritual progress. Within the contemplation of Hiroshima and Nagasaki, one can intuit a universal truth that has direct relevance to all humanity. As long as one maintains faith and properly understands the bomb as a redemptive object, its initial use could be justified as a product of divine providence.

Hachiya and the Scientific Quest

As nuclear war became a genuine threat in the 1950s, the discursive rituals of spiritual sacrifice began to erode, leading to supplementation through realist vocabularies of physics and medicine. In America, civil defense campaigns familiarized the public with nuclear technology, a propaganda strategy that functioned to educate the populace about atomic attack while also reducing nuclear anxiety.[50] If the public could be convinced that the bomb was a natural outgrowth of a benevolent science, perhaps it would adapt to the presence of the atom as it had done with other technologies. Given that romantic authors often sought in nature a special spiritual or philosophical insight, the perceived conflict between nature and technology was one that had to be resolved. Recall that in 1955 the dramatic exhibition of the Hiroshima Maidens illustrated the power of medicine to cure the cosmetic effects of heat and radiation. While the success of these campaigns is debatable and civil-defense drills derived from this period are often used as a source of contemporary humor, science clearly attempted to "know" the atom as a means to control fear and anxiety. With their focus on deep description and immediacy, the *hibakusha* were uniquely poised to participate in this political campaign and the desire to resolve the atom with the natural order.

Marking the tenth anniversary of the bombing, Hachiya's *Hiroshima Doctor* confirms this mandate for technical objectivity by literally reproducing the physician's diary. As Treat points out, "writings about the atomic bombings have two themes—the violence itself and the act of writing about the violence."[51] Indeed, a note in the introduction to Hachiya's work suggests that the author intends to avoid literary embellishment. This type of immediacy is augmented by the fact that Hachiya can be described as an "indigenous ethnographer," an individual who, while remaining a member of the exotic culture under investigation, nevertheless portrays this alien terrain in objective terms. Hachiya, for example, describes the surreal, alien behavior exhibited by those searching for medical attention after the *pika*, writing that their "reactions astonished outsiders who reported with amazement the spectacle of long files of people holding stolidly to a narrow, rough path when close by was a smooth road going the same way."[52] Hachiya's is imbued with special knowledge because of his unique role as both survivor and scientist. Ultimately, however, his medical ethic must reduce the *hibakusha* to objects of study, inspiring intense fascination with the bomb's physical effects. In Rene Girard's theory of triangulation he emphasizes the process of identification, where desire for a coveted object drives the narrator to pursue the traits it embodies, whether by worshiping a virtue possessed by some great individual or endeavoring to conform to an institutional ideal.[53] Following a similar logic, Hachiya's sense of confidence and certainty in his profession is shaken by these experiences, leading him to speculate upon the latent inferiority of his own culture and the elevated mind that must have spawned such a creation.

This is accomplished in a framework that blends romanticism with realism. This embrace of realism can be seen in the thick description of the *pika*, where the *hibakusha* anticipate the catastrophe with daily routines that are followed by the narrator's struggle to interpret the ensuing chaos. Although religious conversion remains one possible outcome of this suffering, in *Hiroshima Doctor*, Hachiya—who professes no religious belief other than an occasional embrace of Buddist tolerance—is transformed not by Christianity but by a transcendent scientific quest.[54] Paul de Man suggests that the romantic hero often begins a quest in an initial state of ignorance that is disrupted by an extraordinary event, forcing a sudden maturation and shift in consciousness where wisdom is gleaned from nature. He writes that this "second self exists as a single moment, an apocalyptic flash of lightening that concludes a book which, up until now, has consisted of nothing but falsehood and deceit."[55] For Hachiya, this apocalyptic flash occurs when be begins his pursuit of truth by explicating the physical and the psychological effects of the catastrophe. In studies of enlightenment discourse, light often represents knowledge. The *pika* is an extreme example of this metaphor—a hyperbole for the ultimate act of scientific mystery and explanation. For Hachiya, it signals the moment when he must exit the falsehood of his native reality and enter the realm of discovery.

After the blast, Hachiya provides unembellished descriptions of his surroundings, assuming epistemic authority over the carnage by distancing himself from the event psychologically. Although he initially empathizes with the survivors' suffering, he writes that eventually "my capacity to comprehend the magnitude of their sorrow, to share with them the pain, frustration, and horror became so dulled that I found myself accepting whatever was told me with equanimity."[56] Indeed, much of Hachiya's work is heavily reliant on pure scenic descriptions—a style that functions to distance the observer from the blast while reinforcing his ability to know and understand it. This method allows him to present his observations as pure. He writes in one instance that "a panorama spread before me: tired war victims, demobilized soldiers, old people leaning against burnt pillars, people walking aimlessly, heedless of all around them."[57] He apprises the reader of the physical deterioration of the burn victims, reducing them to a collection of grotesque symptoms—bodies that emit strange odors and chemicals. Yet, Hachiya's recurrent, emotionally-charged nightmare is quite telling: "I saw an eye sitting on the palm of a girl's hand. Suddenly it turned and leaped into the sky and then came flying back towards me, so that, looking up, I could see a great bare eyeball staring point blank at me. I was powerless to move."[58] The visual nature of science reduces individuals to items of interest or study, and Hachiya seems acutely aware of his own detachment. As he examines the victims, he also examines his own interior.

The images of technological inferiority reach their peak in Hachiya's work as well. At one point he concludes that "damage of this order could have no explanation. All we had were stories no more substantial than the clouds from which we reached to snatch them."[59] While Hachiya is sometimes critiqued for being a Japanese nationalist, even stories that attempt to express patriotism turn out to be ill-founded, such as the false report that counterstrikes had been launched against the Americans in response to the attacks on Hiroshima: "At last Japan was retaliating! The whole atmosphere of the ward changed, and for the first time since Hiroshima was bombed, everyone became cheerful and bright. Those who were hurt the most were the happiest."[60] While this elation might be interpreted as a moment of resistance that illustrates the will to fight, these emotions are clearly founded on illusion and misinformation. Shamed by both this ignorance and the helpless degradation of his culture, Hachiya attempts to describe the symptoms of radiation sickness as a means to psychologically control the bomb and, in much the same way that American scientists attempt to reduce public fear during the 1950s, to dispel superstitions using a technical vocabulary to mask his intense anxiety.

Rather than critiquing the link between science and progress in nuclear discourse, Hachiya creates a text with stylistic elements that makes it an object of speculation and awe. Given the context in which the text emerged, particularly attendant on the spectacle of the Hiroshima Maidens, this empirical vocabulary helped mollify nuclear anxiety be creating psychological distance from the bomb, rendering it nothing more than another tool of technological wonder. Here it is not set in contrast to nature nor is it viewed as aberrant, but becomes a natural outcome of the individual will to advance and strive. Knowing the bomb becomes a stepping-stone on the road to redemption not only for the individual, but for his entire culture.

Ibuse and the Nuclear Sublime

In the years following Hiroshima and Nagasaki, *hibakusha* poets published widely, developing a rich and controversial history in Japan. The efforts of those who portrayed the attack using verse and associative imagery soon became known for the creation of the "nuclear sublime." This transition from realist documentation to aesthetic interpretation drew considerable fire from polemicists such as Sadako Kurihara who critiqued the burgeoning Hiroshima Literature Society, a collection of critics and intellectuals who sought to apply systematic aesthetic standards to this growing literary genre. Kurihara argued that the standards of judgment that this group embraced violated the spirit of *hibakusha* literature by subjugating it to the modernist impulse that had produced atomic technology.[61] Despite this criticism, the shift away from documentary realism was underway. Literary critics sanctioned writers such as Kenzaburo for being too ideologically driven and attempting to score "anti western points with vivid descriptions of suffering.[62] The rise of the nuclear sublime within prose literature became evident in 1966 with the publication of Ibuse's *Black Rain*, a book that would become the most widely read Japanese novel both domestically and internationally. The crux of Ibuse's text was not to portray the bomb as an empirical reality, but to translate the nuclear experience into a universal cultural vocabulary. Ibuse synthesizes real *hibakusha* accounts to create Shigematsu, a traditional Japanese man, and transform him into a universal "everyman." Through Shigematsu, Ibuse seeks wisdom through poetic insights in the pastoral lives of many Japanese of the time and their perceptions of the atomic experience.

Employing a pastoral style to share his insights, Ibuse elaborates on Shigematsu's bomb experience and his subsequent struggle with radiation sickness, a disease that has left him weakened and unable to engage in hard physical labor. He eventually finds peace by raising fish with a group of friends, escaping from the toil of his previous life into the realms of nature, reflection, and traditional heritage. The primary strategy Ibuse uses to present the remembrances of Shigematsu stem from the Japanese artistic tradition known as *beijoshim*, a style marked by poetic simplicity and unperturbed thought. This literary impulse presents subjects in plain, unadorned terms and then juxtaposes them with other objects or ideas, thus producing literary insight. Like prior *hibakusha* narratives, Shigematsu's journal becomes the focus of the narration as he transcribes it for his niece's (Yasuka) suitor, who wishes to document her radiation exposure and, hence, fitness for marriage. The novel moves back and forth between a period some years after the bomb and the days depicted in his journal where he has recorded his family's struggle to survive. As Shigematsu confronts his niece's growing illness in the present and reflects on the days immediately following the blast, Ibuse uses the perceptions of his narrator to represent Japan's postwar experience.

Ibuse frequently uses associative imagery to capture the aesthetic essence of his narrator's memories. In these passages he often juxtaposes common images from everyday life against images detailing the excesses of nuclear war. In one passage he compares a cluster of corpses to a garden of tulips, conflating the ravages of decay with rare, simple beauty. Later, Shigematsu sees three naked, female corpses floating in a shallow pool, one with a length of intestine forced from her buttocks—presumably extracted by a shockwave. Ibuse relates the grotesque image of looped entrails drifting in water to a child's balloon lofting in the breeze.[63] While *Black Rain* offers some of the most graphic accounts of blast wounds and radiation illness, Ibuse is spared the critique of excessive realism because the text's graphic horror is diluted by playful and often perverse images. As Leon Chai notes, romantic poets often use the objective world to reveal "the internal subjective reality of the self."[64] In one passage, for example, Shigematsu's friends discover a body that is flash-burned in a standing position, mistaking it for a blackened scarecrow woven on a South Sea Island or perhaps a store mannequin.[65] This charring effect, one well-documented in prior accounts, serves to illustrate the sense of wonder and alienation experienced by those who inhabit this atomic wasteland. These images do not derive their meaning from their material nature or historical significance, but rather exist to illustrate the state of consciousness of those who see them.

Given this focus on the interior, *Black Rain* often reverses the relationship between nuclear experience and moral allegory present in early accounts. In *Bells of Nagasaki*, Nagai ruminates over the blast by asking questions: "In which direction was this atomic cloud floating? Toward good or evil? Toward justice or wickedness?"[66] Here, the primary ethical question focuses on bomb technology and its philosophical ramifications for humanity. Even Hersey, who claimed journalistic objectivity, could not resist transforming Ms. Sasaki, herself crushed by books, into an allegory for those literally crushed by knowledge. Unlike these earlier texts, Ibuse's moral insights in *Black Rain* have a more complex relationship to the bomb and its future use. Throughout his journey in the nuclear wasteland, Shigematsu remembers poems and stories that help him assign meaning to the events he has witnessed. When he sees a group of soldiers burning corpses, he recalls the story of Pinnochio and the idea that once the strings are cut, down fall the puppets: "The poor plaything of metal and wood and metal pins was supposed to have felt no pain in his own wooden limbs when he banged his shin against something, what of the dead who had once been human beings."[67] Here, the author's concern lies with the dehumanizing nature of death—how death leaves the body rigid, devoid of traits and feelings that once animated it once its link with authority is cut—yet another simple insight gleaned through the contemplation of the bomb.

To argue that Ibuse's work is devoid of political critique would be misleading. As a reluctant participant in Japan's wartime ministry, he became known in the years following the war for anti-military satire and a profound suspicion of patriotism. This stands in stark contrast to Nagai, who created a Japanese flag with his own blood, and Hachiya, who dramatically saved a portrait of the emperor from a fire. It is this nationalistic spirit that falls prey to Ibuse's satire. One commonplace in early *hibakusha* literature involves schoolgirls trapped in a burning building who begin singing the national anthem as they each succumb to the fire.[68] Few more romantic gestures can be imagined. This nationalistic pride is parodied in *Black Rain* when a group of students sing "Lay me Beneath the Waves" a song dedicated to the war effort. As the bomb detonates, the singers are left charred and without clothing, but manage to finish the last chorus while standing at attention, then jumping into the river to drown in the cool water.[69] The comic nature of this image expresses incredulity toward blind nationalism, pointing to the absurdity of such an act, as well as the overwrought pathos of earlier accounts. Perhaps one of the most poignant symbols for the fallen nation emerges when Shigematsu finds a scorched, dying horse lying in shallow water alongside the remains of a brightly adorned rider: "How immeasurable the pain it must have felt, with the west-dipping sun beating down unmercifully on its burnt flesh. How immeasurable its loss for the man in the boots! But pity eluded me! I felt only a shudder of horror!"[70] One of the humiliations that the Japanese were subjected to after the surrender occurred when American officials took the liberty of riding the Emperor's horse before the newsreels. By evoking the humiliation of the dismounted Emperor, Ibuse represents a prideful nation now reduced to degradation through his own internal insight.

While the *hibakusha* remain uniquely Japanese, they also embody certain principles that transcend national boundaries, a characteristic that eventually led to the appropriation of their experiences to represent atomic war. Interestingly, in *Black Rain*, this begins with the reinvigoration of traditional, rural Japanese culture, a process facilitated by excavating the life of Shigematsu. John Dorsey, for example, concludes that the Shigematsu of the present, who learned to raise fish since he can no longer engage in proper labor for fear of relapse into atomic sickness, seems "reassured about his way of life."[71] Ibuse's detailed descriptions of Shigematsu's cultural practices make *Black Rain* one of the more extensive descriptions of Japanese society to reach Western audiences. The text is as much about pickled radishes, loaches, and trefoil root as it is about the ethics of war. This cultural encyclopedia seems most evident when Ibuse elaborates on the quaint peasant festivals such as the River Imp Festival, the Mass for Dead Insects, and Bamboo Cutting Festival. He writes that as "the horrors of that came back to him ever more vividly, it seemed to him that in their very insignificance these farmers' festivals are something to be loved and cherished."[72] In one instance, the classic mushroom cloud metaphor, an image resonant among

Western audiences, is supplanted by a jellyfish dangling from its tendrils.[73] Thus he alters the aesthetic terrain of war. The bomb becomes a gateway back to nature, leading Shigematsu to reject prior values for those that bring the individual closer to the pastoral setting.

The final irony becomes evident when Shigematsu realizes that Yasuka, affected by radiation despite being quite distant from the blast, is not showing sings of recovery. He initially had pondered her predicament and even contemplated lying to her suitor in order to facilitate marriage. The issue becomes irrelevant when she experiences a relapse and it becomes probable that severe, long-term tissue damage has taken place. She describes the day when she walked outside her house and into a small "cheat of a shower" that stained her clothing black, leading her to joke that as a commercial dye, it would be an unparalleled success. As she begins to deteriorate and it becomes clear that she will become yet another casualty of the war, it is his contact with nature that sustains Shigematsu and allows him to accept the changes that the bomb has wrought in his life. In the last passages of *Black Rain*, Shigematsu returns to his fish farm, hoping for the rainbow that would signal his niece's recovery, yet knowing that these are mere fantasies. He and his wife are left to grow closer to the land, accepting the bomb not as that which has subverted their lives, but as an entity that has brought them to this place in a gradual fulfillment of their family's destiny.

Final Thoughts

Since World War II, the *hibakusha* have remained integral to the performance of atomic history in American culture. One of the most widely published critics in the study of nuclear consciousness, Brian Taylor, suggests that depictions of the *hibakusha* remain critical to the nuclear debate.[74] While this literature is essential to understanding the effects of nuclear war, the desire to achieve authenticity within both the American and Japanese context has led to a tendency to valorize the bomb as an object that provides great insight. This suggests that both the orthodox and revisionist historians mentioned in the introduction have perhaps oversimplified the *hibakusha*'s role in history. Narratives of romantic redemption, at their most benign, represent the subjective desire to understand one's self. When literary form is coupled with narratives of moral enlightenment and hierarchy, it heightens nationalistic tendencies and potential conflict by producing texts that draw links between violence and progress. For each narrator, the bomb functions to lead them to a higher order of truth. The desire to gain authenticity by appropriating certain ethical vocabularies such as religion, science, and aesthetics, creates shifts in the way that the bomb is perceived and judged. In many cases, moral enlightenment is achieved by linking redemptive experience and cultural apocalypse to forge an acceptable symbol for nuclearism. Therefore, debates over the inclusion/exclusion of these texts from nuclear memory are more complicated than one might think.

Exploring the replication of this cycle in literature is crucial to understanding how the bomb can become a usable weapon by conceiving of it as a vehicle for regeneration. Anne Tomiche notes, the *hibakusha* continue to impact perceptions of nuclear power by "reliving the event with all the intensity of the first time, by repeating it in the present."[75] It is their proximity to the bomb that grants *hibakusha* a special authenticity in these accounts. Hence, their power as an atomic symbol should not be underestimated. After recognizing that history is a performance and that this performance is shaped by certain frameworks, it becomes clear that the stability of an increasingly complex international order remains dependent on the evolving relationship between romantic redemption and nuclear war.

PERSONAL COMMENTS ON THE ESSAY

In the preceding essay we have seen how many traditional and cultural historians have talked about the *hibakusha*. In this piece, the *hibakusha* are not so much important as a distinct social group, but how they are represented as a mass-witness to the first use of atomic technology. The conceptual field of the piece is literary form—a framework through which the atomic experience is rendered visible for the international community. Upon a careful reading of the texts within their historical and intellectual context, the concept of romanticism emerges as a means for describing the ways that the *hibakusha* create a backdrop against which the bomb is subtly venerated. These accounts are very ambivalent about the role of the bomb since they suggest that the bomb, as well as being an object of destruction, also functions as an agent of regeneration (at both the individual and cultural levels). With its focus on intense personal enlightenment, the concept of romanticism places the bomb in the context of spiritual or natural elevation of consciousness. It is a teacher, not a brutal weapon of war that has no other purpose other than to kill people on an unprecedented scale. The *hibakusha* are thus constituted through this conceptual field. Rather than simply accept the verdict of orthodox historians that these accounts challenge our national culture, a careful scrutiny of the literary form reveals that they may in fact complicate this simple standard of judgment by venerating the bomb through the form in which the story is told. This might stand as a cautionary tale warning critics and historians alike to pay attention to the narrative forms that guide these stories and the relationship between the *hibakusha* and the bomb. Just because they suffered does not mean that they are uniformly critical of the bomb itself.

A friend of mine once noted that if you know exactly how a rhetorical criticism is going to turn out, what is the use in writing it? Well, not to diminish the importance of careful outlining and preparation, she had a point. When I first initiated this project, I visualized going in a much different direction. Given the way that bomb-survivor discourse had been talked about in the dominant histories, I expected to be discussing how the *hibakusha* functioned to challenge the dominant nuclear narratives of orthodox historians. While continuing to study the literature itself, I was surprised to find that another strategy would be necessary. The paradigm of critical rhetoric, while somewhat relevant to the present study, would not be the key or guiding feature of the essay. One of the strengths of the conceptual orientation is that it allows the critic to respond to what Leff refers to as the particulars of the discourse. If I had continued to approach it with the approach I had expected to use, this would have led to a completely different form of criticism and actually the piece would have lost part of its critical insight. It was, in part, the recognition that the dominant readings of survivor discourse had been incomplete, if not misleading, that gave the piece a breath of originality. Once a common set of themes had been identified, it was only then that I turned to Romanticism as the key concept that would guide the dynamics of the critique. Once I took this turn the other ideas fell in place like a line of dominoes. Hopefully, this concept is at once illuminated by the texts just as the texts are themselves illuminated by the concept.

In returning to Jasinski's goals of the rhetorical critic I would pose that all three goals are met. If the bomb is being cast as an agent of moral regeneration at key points in the evolution of nuclear consciousness, consumers of this discourse can reflect upon these ideas and explore for themselves the resonance of these claims. As far as the second goal is concerned, remember that McGee notes that the text is never "finished." Likewise, the rhetorical criticism is never finished either. This piece is not the last word on the *hibakusha* or nuclear consciousness. In fact, it would be the height of hubris to suggest otherwise. The piece is purposefully "suggestive" and invites other readings. Criticism, like politics and culture, is an ongoing dialogue. For the conceptual orientation, the concepts under scrutiny are not templates to be enshrined in positivistic theory, but might be thought of as additions to the storehouse of wisdom accumulated over time—ideas that both develop and subvert our understanding of what it is rhetorical critics do. Finally, the piece attempts to comment upon the very real hierarchical positions played by very real people. Can a true *hibakusha* voice emerge when they are being deployed to support various political or cultural agendas? Can they be said to even have a true voice? These are good questions. From a conceptual orientation these goals are not viewed as distinct, but are almost always mutually implicated in this type of work. In the end, the concept of romanticism, a traditional literary form, is used to demonstrate how the *hibakusha* literature has effected judgments about nuclear weapons while the criticism itself, using this concept, attempts to alter the judgments of scholars interested in these types of questions.

After reflecting upon the piece four years later, some of its failures are certainly evident. While the significance of the texts is established, their direct connection to the cultural context might have been more overtly accomplished through the citation of more political and cultural sources. Perhaps most problematic is the use of an explicitly Western literary genre to describe in most cases distinctly Japanese writing. It is here that perhaps more overt reference to the post-colonial theories of cultural exchange, where Western forms of thought are exported then appropriated by other cultures might have been useful. Perhaps a more nuanced explanation of the *hibakusha* as a social movement might have given the essay a bit more texture. The difficulty that any rhetorical critic runs into is that there is always more to say and, at some point, you must put pen to paper. Symbolic activity possesses an almost infinite complexity and the critic is attempting to halter and channel this discourse for one moment. If a critic ever finds him or herself stepping back and admiring his or her work, marveling at its perfection, it is at this point where the critical voice is lost and the critical mind is frozen in stone.

POTENTIALS AND PITFALLS

The conceptual orientation presents a series of larger issues for the field of rhetoric as a whole. Think about some of the other disciplines that one might study in school. What is it that keeps them together? For the hard sciences—geology, astronomy, biology, etc.—their content areas seems to be a good starting point, but a shortsighted stopping point. What keeps these researchers functioning as a cohesive institutional force are the methodologies that they use to determine the truth-value of their work and the viability of one another's research. As a practitioner of hard science, you know that everyone in your field is playing by the same rules and if they are not, their work will be devalued or perhaps even silenced. Jasinski foreshadows this question when he asks "if criticism no longer is methodologically driven or oriented around the development and application of specific methods, then how is it currently organized?"[76] If every rhetorical critic pursues differing concepts, "how can they build on each other?"[77] Even in the fields of the social sciences the methodology sections where researchers demonstrate statistical significance and the validity of their findings, it is the method that binds them—not the object of study. This is no idle navel gazing (though those who study rhetoric are prone to these lapses into sometimes crippling self-reflection). If this orientation persists, how then do the essays build on one another? If not, what have we lost? Is this even the best goal for scholarship?

Another issue raised by this mode of criticism is the difficulty one might have in identifying it. How does one know it when one sees it? Take an analysis of war metaphors for example.

The critic uses the concept of metaphor to enlighten a text, while also commenting upon how the analysis informs our understanding of the concept of metaphor itself and how it shifts our standards of judgment. Often metaphoric investigations are seen as a distinct genre of criticism, but it could be argued that it also has many of the same components of conceptually-oriented criticism. Let's say that Hariman's article had bred a generation of young critics who applied his unique vision of style using a more formulaic methodology to a host of other texts. Has his work now morphed into a completely new methodology? This question is vexing because most disciplines that gain authority within the academy do so through the acceptance of their methods for producing insight. If it loses sight of methodology as a guiding premise, will the discipline survive or be relegated to a historical footnote? As rhetorical critics, though, it is incumbent upon each of us to reflect on the methods that we use, never simply accepting their authority.

The conceptual orientation is difficult if not, perhaps, impossible to teach. It proceeds in an intuitive fashion. Critics must fully immerse themselves in their own intellectual history and develop an understanding for the critical evolution of their discipline. From this standpoint, the conceptual orientation is a more advanced critical perspective. Given that it does not have an abstract critical methodology or can be judged on its capacity to build theory, it is often difficult to evaluate. Through the critical process of abduction, the movement back and forth between text and concept requires a developed understanding of the diversity of potential symbolic forms that can encapsulate an idea. The increased responsibility placed on the shoulders of critics is generated by the fact that it is they who must guide the ship through the channel. When critics become consumed with one or two methodologies, this will shape the types of texts that they are drawn to and the range of observation that they can make. The conceptual critic, always in danger of being labeled a dilettante, must remain aware of numerous standards or fields of judgment to make critical decisions. It is also this ability to swim freely in the field of symbols that raises the most troubling questions about the future of rhetorical criticism.

Perhaps one answer to this question is that it is not the objects of study or the methodology that binds rhetorical critics, but their shared orientation. This *rhetorical orientation* is what binds the fields of rhetorical criticism and theory. No other field of study does more to encourage skeptical inquiry than the field of rhetoric. The realm of human symbolic activity is vast, but with each individual insight, every stone that is overturned, a new dialogue is enacted. Perhaps this is the price of exploring symbolic exchange in all of its complexity—that rigid or codified perspectives, while comforting, ultimately obscure as much as they reveal. When one discards simplicity, one is left with uncertainty. Much like the text the critique is never a finished product. The "conceptual orientation," something that you may see running throughout a number of chapters in this text, encourages us to understand the field in the same way. This shared understanding stems from the recognition that symbolic activity shapes perceptions and standards of judgment. The dialogue is never over. No theory or model is ever complete. They exist to be redeployed and in each deployment emerge altered in a way that hopefully provides some new perspective that is then reincorporated into the field. This, like it or not, is a discipline of critical practitioners and not a constellation of models. And, as in most cases, this is its strength as much as its weakness.

CONCEPTUALLY ORIENTED CRITICISM TOP PICKS

Browne, Stephen, "*Like Gory Spectres*: Representing Evil in Theodore Weld's *American Slavery As It Is*," *Quarterly Journal of Speech*, 80 (1994): 277–292. This criticism examines the idea of sentimental representation in the manner in which slavery, as an institution, is depicted in public discourse.

Bruner, M. Lane. "Carnivalesque Protest and the Humorless State." *Text and Performance Quarterly*, 25 (2005): 136–155. Bruner uses the concept of the carnival to explore the relationship between aesthetic forms of social resistance to dominant hegemonic orders.

Darsey, James. *The Prophetic Tradition and Radical Rhetoric in America.* (New York: New York University Press, 1997). This book examines the way that differing groups seek to change or radically shake the existing American system of thought using the concept of prophecy.

Grey, Stephanie. "The Statistical War on Equality: Visions of American Virtuosity in *The Bell Curve*." *Quarterly Journal of Speech*, 85 (1999): 303–329. This piece looks at the way that ethics are visually represented in pseudo-scientific discourse using both geographical location and linear time in the concept of the bell curve.

Hariman, Robert. "Decorum. Power, and the Courtly Style." *Quarterly Journal of Speech*, 78 (1992): 149–172. This essay explores the relationship between power, style, and decorum with the royal court.

Hariman, Robert and John Louis Lucaites. "Public Identity and Collective Memory in U.S. Iconic Photography: The Image of Accidental Napalm." *Critical Studies in Media Communication* 20 (2003): 35–66. This piece examines how particularly historical ideologies can be inscribed through visual, iconic formats, focusing upon the ways that this vision impacts social judgment.

Jasinski, James. "Constituting Antebellum African American Identity: Resistance, Violence, and Masculinity in Henry Highland Garnet's (1843) *Address to the Slaves*." *Quarterly Journal of Speech* 93 (2007): 27–57. Jasinski uses the image/idiom of the avenging messiah/suffering servant in the vivid anti-slavery discourse of Henry Garnet and its impact on African-American identity.

NOTES

1. James Jasinski, "The Status of Theory and Method in Rhetorical Criticism," *Western Journal of Communication* 65 (2001), 249–270; and James Jasinski, *Sourcebook on Rhetoric: Key Concepts in Contemporary Rhetorical Studies* (New York: Sage, 2001), 138–141. During the course of my elaboration of Jasinski's essays I have engaged in what he might call "thickening." While attempting to remain true to his original vision, the current discussion expands the general terminology into territories that may or may not have been previously envisioned.

2. Jasinski, "Status of Theory," 254.

3. Jasinski, *Sourcebook*, 140.

4. Ibid.

5. On this point, see James Darsey, "Must We All Be Rhetorical Theorists?: An Anti-Democratic Inquiry," *Western Journal of Communication* 58 (1994): 164–181.

6. Jasinski, *Sourcebook*, 140.

7. For an explanation of the contested nature of criticism as activism see, Jim A. Kuypers, "The Rhetorical River," *Southern Communication Journal* 73.4 (2008): 350–358; and Jim A. Kuypers, "Must We All Be Political Activists?" *The American Communication Journal* 4.1 (2000) http://acjournal.org/holdings/vol4/iss1/index.htm

8. Ernest Wrage, "Public Address: A Study in Social and Intellectual History," *Quarterly Journal of Speech* 33 (1947): 451.

9. Wrage, 452.

10. Kenneth Burke, *Grammar of Motives* (Berkeley: University of California Press, 1968).

11. Victor Vitanza, *Negation, Subjectivity and the History of Rhetoric* (New York: State University of New York Press, 1997), 46.

12. Anthony Grafton, "The History of Ideas: Precept and Practice, 1950–2000 and Beyond," *Journal of the History of Ideas* 67 (2006): 1–32.

13. Allan Megill, "Globalization and the History of Ideas," *Journal of the History of Ideas* 66 (2005): 179–187.

14. Michael Leff, "Words the Most Like Things: Iconicity and the Rhetorical Text," *Western Journal of Communication* 54 (1990): 254–255. Italics mine.

15. Leff, 255.

16. Michael McGee, "Text, Context, and the Fragmentation of Contemporary Culture," *Western Journal of Communication* 54 (1990): 274–289.

17. Jasinski, "Status of Theory," 256.

18. Robert Hariman, "Decorum Power, and the Courtly Style," *Quarterly Journal of Speech* 78 (1992): 149–172.

19. Jasinski, *Sourcebook*, 139.

20. Jasinski, "Status of Theory," 256.

21. Hariman, 152.

22. Ibid., 163

23. Ibid.

24. Jasinski, "Status of Theory," 262.

25. An older version of this piece can be reviewed. See Stephanie Houston Grey, "Writing Redemption: Trauma and the Authentication of the Moral Order," *Text and Performance Quarterly* 22 (2002): 1–23.

26. Robert Lifton and Greg Mitchell, *Hiroshima in America: Fifty Years of Denial* (New York: Putnam, 1995), 302.

27. Thomas Englehardt, *The End of Victory Culture: Cold War and the Disillusionment of a Generation* (New York: Basic, 1995), 45.

28. Michael Sherry, "Patriotic Orthodoxy and American Decline," in *History Wars*, eds. Edward Linenthal and Tom Englehardt. (New York: Metropolitan, 1996), 26.

29. John Herscy, *Hiroshima* (New York: Vintage, 1946).

30. Takahashi Nagai, *The Bells of Nagasaki*, trans. William Johnstone (Tokyo: Kodasho, 1949).

31. Michihito Hachiya, *Hiroshima Diary*, trans. Warren Wells (Chapel Hill: University of North Carolina Press, 1955).

32. Masuji Ibuse, *Black Rain: A Novel*. trans. John Bestor (Tokyo: Kodansho, 1969).

33. Kenneth Zagacki and Andrew King, "Reagan, Romance and Technology: A Critique of Star Wars," *Communication Studies* 40 (1989): 1–12.

34. Jonathan Taylor, *Science and Omniscience in Nineteenth-Century Literature* (Sussex: Academic Press, 2007), 68.

35. Nancy Yousef, *Isolated Cases: The Anxieties of Autonomy in Enlightenment Philosophy and Romantic Literature* (Ithaca: Ithaca University Press, 2004), 152–159.

36. Charles Taylor, *The Ethics of Authenticity* (Cambridge: Harvard University Press, 1992), 32.

37. Lionel Trilling, *Sincerity and Authenticity* (Cambridge: Harvard University Press, 1971), 97–101.

38. Frank Kermode, *The Sense of an Ending: Studies in the Theory of Fiction* (London: Oxford University Press, 1967), 18.

39. Quoted in Gar Alpervitz, *Atomic Diplomacy: Hiroshima and Potsdam* (London: Pluto, 1994).

40. James Darsey, *The Prophetic Tradition and Radical Rhetoric in America* (New York: New York University Press, 1997), 32.

41. Nagai 167.

42. Yasumasa Sato, "Modern Japanese Christian Literature After the Second World War," *The Chesterson Review* 14 (1988): 413–19.

43. William Hamlin, "Attributions of Divinity in Renaissance Ethnography and Romance: Or, Making Religion of Wonder," *Journal of Medieval and Renaissance Studies* 24 (1994): 415–47.

44. Nagai 102.

45. John Dower, "The Bombed: Hiroshimas and Nagasakis in Japanese Memory," *Hiroshima in History and Memory*. Michael J. Hogan (ed.). (Cambridge: Cambridge Univeristy Press, 1996), 130.

46. Nagai, 117.

47. Ibid., 109.

48. Ibid., 108.

49. Ibid.

50. Elizabeth Mechling and Jay Mechling, "The Campaign for Civil Defense and the Struggle to Naturalize the Bomb," *Western Journal of Communication* 55 (1992): 105–33.

51. John Treat, *Writing Ground-Zero: Japanese Literature and the Atomic Bomb* (Chicago: University of Chicago Press, 1995), 35.

52. Hachiya, 55.

53. Rene Girard, *Deceit, Desire, and the Novel: Self and Other in Literary Structure*, trans. Yvonne Freccero, (Baltimore: Johns Hopkins University Press, 1961), 9.

54. Hachiya, 229.

55. Paul de Man, *Romanticism in Contemporary Criticism* (Baltimore: Johns Hopkins University Press, 1993), 15.

56. Hachiya, 24.

57. Ibid., 193.

58. Ibid., 115.

59. Ibid., 25.

60. Ibid., 48.

61. Treat, 103.

62. Ibid., 267.

63. Ibuse, 159.

64. Leon Chai, *The Romantic Foundation of the American Renaissance* (Ithaca: Cornell University Press, 1995), 7.

65. Ibuse, 7.

66. Nagai, 48.

67. Ibuse, 162.

68. Hersey, 88; Nagai, 24.

69. Ibuse, 10.

70. Ibid., 109.

71. John Dorsey, "Literature Related to the Atomic Bomb from Hiroshima to the End of the War," in *Aesthetics and the Literature of Ideas*, edited by Francois Jost (Newark: University of Delaware Press, 1990), 112.

72. Ibuse, 112.

73. Ibid., 54–55.

74. Brian Taylor, "Our Bruised Arms Hung Up as Monuments: Nuclear Iconography in Post-Cold War Culture," *Critical Studies in Media Communication* 29 (2003): 1–34.

75. Anne Tomiche, "Repetition: Memory and Oblivion," *Revue de Literature Comparee* 3 (1991): 276.

76. Jasinski, *Sourcebook*, 138.

77. Jasinski, "Status of Theory," 266.

19

Eclectic Criticism

Jim A. Kuypers

"I have tried to be as eclectic as I possibly can with my professional life, and so far it's been pretty fun."

Roland Barthes

Eclectic and eclecticism are sometimes misused terms. They have been used to call attention to differences not easily categorized or perhaps recognized by a person looking for a common thread. For instance, consider this use of eclectic:

> Typically off-year elections are used for two things: one is a sort of testing ground, as a dry run for the next year. And two: you get a real eclectic mix of issues that don't have an overarching theme but that's a little different this year.[1]

What the author actually describes is not an eclectic mixture, but a hodgepodge, which is a confusing or a heterogeneous mixture. A more accurate use of eclectic would be to label as eclectics those who derive their sense of style or taste from a wide variety of sources. While seemingly diverse, the common link among the sources is the person who puts them all together. For an eclectic, there is a theme. The task for the eclectic critic is to make that theme apparent to others.

When I speak of eclectic criticism, I am not speaking of a jumbled mess of viewpoints presented in an unwieldy manner. The best eclectic criticism takes components of various rhetorical theories, blends them together into a comprehensive whole, all to better explain the workings of an intriguing rhetorical artifact. Pauline Kael writes that "Eclecticism is the selection of the best standards and principles from various systems of ideas. It requires more orderliness to be a pluralist than to apply a single theory. . . . Criticism is exciting because you must use everything you are and everything you know that is relevant."[2] Although some, particularly those who use single perspectives to guide their criticism, might take issue with Kael, eclectic critics would agree with Kael's depiction of excitement.

Beyond excitement, though, there often lies a sense of exploration. Eclectic critics are frequently drawn to extremely diverse rhetorical artifacts, and analysis of these diverse forms of rhetoric necessitates the development of nuanced, flexible, and diverse perspectives of analysis. On this note theatrical director and producer David Esbjornson says,

> I have an eclectic past . . . but I intentionally have pursued that because there are so many interesting points of view that I want to explore. I think I'm not quite as all over the map as maybe people

think. There's a certain reason that I have done all those plays. I tend to gravitate to the writers that I think are trying to say something, or who are outside of the center a bit and who are trying to break in and get their point of view expressed.[3]

Eclecticism has a long history. The term is often used to describe ancient philosophers who followed no particular philosophical school, but instead sought to take what was to them the best of established doctrines in order to construct a new system. The original Greek term, *eklektikos*, simply means choosing the best. Diogenes of Appolonia (fifth century B.C.) was one of the first eclectics. By the first century B.C. the term eclectic was in common use. One of the better-known examples of eclectic philosophers was Cicero, who blended the Stoic, Peripatetic, and New Academic doctrines. As an approach to philosophy and to rhetoric, eclecticism eschews single perspectives and draws its power instead from insights gained from combining multiple theories or perspectives into a blend used for a specific purpose.

Writing of the eclectic critic in particular, Bernard L. Brock, Robert L. Scott, and James W. Chesebro remarked that

> the conscientious eclectic is apt to be more interested in the immediacy of experience than the abstract integrity of a system or method. Such a person will argue that [perspectives] are but more-or-less-complete sets of tools with instructions by which to build scaffoldings and frameworks. They will argue that when what is made is made, the tools are laid aside, the scaffolding torn down, and the framework absorbed. When the eclectic critic does use a [perspective], it is an "open-ended" one that does not force or prescribe a specific [plan] and provides the critic with a great deal of creative decision making. The eclectic approach stresses the critic's ability to assemble and absorb ways of working, subordinating these to the task at hand.[4]

The last sentence is especially noteworthy in that it reinforces the critic's dominant role in producing good criticism. Good critics "absorb" or assimilate theory into their personal perceptions, and then bring to bear their eclectically enhanced point of view to bear on the rhetorical artifact. Eclecticism stresses the personality and critical capacities of the critic. On this point Ed Black wrote that it "is inevitable that any expositor will approach a work from a certain point of view. His frame of reference may be subconscious and unsystematized, but it will assuredly be present, shaping the bias of his interpretation by influencing the direction of his attention, selectively sharpening some and sulling others of his sensibilities, and molding the nuances of his judgment in a thousand imperceptible ways."[5] In some ways, eclecticism turns the tables, allowing first the critic to influence the perspective and then the perspective to influence the critic.

As with the other perspectives covered in this book, eclecticism has both strengths and weaknesses. When it works well, it certainly offers the critic a great deal of flexibility, and its potential to allow for nuanced insights and new theoretical understandings is quite high. The critic has great freedom to explore, and the potential for allowing greater personality into the criticism certainly exists. However, if a critic does not fully develop the new point of view before undertaking the criticism, the results could be scattered and meaningless observations in place of genuine criticism. In short, the effort to produce criticism instead devolves into a hodgepodge of poorly related theoretical tidbits and unrelated insights. Another concern is that it is particularly easy for a critic to construct a point of view that will find exactly what the critic wants to find. Then there is the burden of acquiring enough knowledge in order to practice eclectic criticism. By this I mean that if a critic wishes to use parts of several different perspectives in order to derive a new point of view, that critic must first obtain a healthy working knowledge of all of the perspectives that will be used.

Eclecticism is not for everyone, and despite its strengths, only a minority of critics blend and develop their own framework from which to proceed with criticism. What follows below are four examples of eclectic work published in communication journals. The authors of each essay explains in their own words the eclectic nature of their work.

"CARNIVALESQUE PROTEST AND THE HUMORLESS STATE," BY M. LANE BRUNER. PUBLISHED IN *TEXT AND PERFORMANCE QUARTERLY* 25.2 (2005): 136–155

Revolutionary discourses are interesting things to study. Thomas Jefferson once famously remarked that "a little rebellion" now and then was a good thing, "as necessary in the political world as storms in the physical."[6] Only the people's stormy uprisings, he believed, ensured a continued focus on republican virtue. But what are these storms? Are they all alike? What is their relationship to the virtuous state? How do we know, for example, when rebellions produce more or less freedom? How can we recognize the best kind of rebellions?

An excellent opportunity to study rebellion was provided in the late 1980s, as people rose up in communist regimes from China to East Germany to demand more political and economic freedoms. As a rhetoric scholar interested in the relationship between discourse and politics, and how different patterns of communication create different types of political communities, I was eager to study how these rebellions worked (or not). I was especially curious to learn why the rebellions against the Soviet Union were generally nonviolent, productive of more freedom, and helped to develop the rule of law, while those against communism in China were violent, did not produce more political freedom, and made no impact on authoritarian rule.

The methods and theories most appropriate for scholars are driven by the questions they pursue, and those who want to study the world-historical relationship between the rhetorical and the political can hardly rely on one theory or method, or even a small combination of theories and methods. Instead, the *eclectic* critic is also required to be well-versed in political, economic, cultural, and philosophical matters as well. This is where an eclectic critic's strengths come into play: their relatively broad theoretical and historical background enables them to study the broader relationships between the ways people talk and behave and the kinds of communities they create as a result of that talk and behavior.

To be an eclectic critic, in the sense expressed here, one must follow the sage advice of Cicero and Quintillian, two famous rhetoricians concerned with the development of the virtuous orator: they must be *highly eclectic* in their learning.[7] The virtuous rhetor persuades to improve the community, but a person cannot improve the community unless they are exceptionally wise. To be truly eloquent, according to Cicero, the virtuous rhetor must be able to distinguish good from evil, the desirable from the undesirable, the profitable from the unprofitable, all the virtues and vices and how they arise and are transformed, the difference between just and unjust states, as well as understand the common sense of mankind, the laws of nature, moral duties, and more. One can hardly expect to be a good *critic* of persuasive acts if unfamiliar with the learning required of virtuous persuaders themselves. Nor can the eclectic critic risk being a *dilettante*, knowing just a little bit about everything. As Quintillian noted, "a little learning is a dangerous thing."[8] Instead, the responsible eclectic critic must seriously study the history of ideas, comparative law, aesthetics, and any other number of similarly important subjects. The guiding principle behind all of the work of the eclectic rhetorical critic is this: what theoretical, historical, and methodological tools must be brought to bear to investigate the world-historical question at hand.

To prepare for my study of rebellion, for example, I first had to decide what my objects of study and guiding research question would be. I then had to decide what I needed to know in order to engage in such a study. I decided that, building upon my prior research on Russia (i.e., on public memory and national identity in Russia during the collapse of communism, and on the rhetorical and political dimensions of the subsequent transition to capitalism), I would limit my study to the rebellions against the Soviet Union.[9] My larger research question, however, led me to expand this initial plan: I wanted to know *why* those rebellions were so successful, so I decided to compare them to a failure. Thus, I also studied the tragic 1989 rebellion against communism in China.

I started exploring this question about productive rebellions by obtaining numerous accounts and histories of the political, economic, and cultural histories of the Soviet Union and China, and then of the rebellions in the old Soviet states and the massacre at Tiananmen Square in Beijing in 1989. One thing became immediately clear, other than the obvious fact that the political, economic, and cultural conditions in both countries were quite different: the protests against the Soviets were generally comic, while those against Chinese communists were anything but. I learned that in Poland, East Germany, Ukraine, the former Czechoslovakia, etc. resistance against the state, when most successful, was "carnivalesque," that the carnivalesque was a public and comic way of reversing "normal" social roles, and that the carnivalesque had a long and interesting history in Europe.

Not yet deeply understanding the carnivalesque, I next had to obtain the very best studies related to that concept. Here I learned that, from at least Ancient Rome up until the nineteenth century, it was a European custom to have official days set aside when community norms would be comically turned upside down. The master would be the servant and the servant the master. Some scholars saw this strange discursive practice as a means for the powerful to strengthen their grip on society by providing well-managed opportunities to release social tensions; others, however, argued that moments of carnival were excellent opportunities for disempowered people to send serious political messages under the protective cover of "just joking!"

As an eclectic critic, I first enjoyed studying the political, economic, and cultural histories of Russia and China, then studying accounts of the protests themselves, then studying the carnivalesque, and then studying performance theory and social movement theory. If I wanted to study these comic and serious public performances and understand how and why they worked (or not), these were simply parts of the puzzle I sought to solve.

Here is what the picture looked like once the pieces were in place. In the states attempting to separate themselves from a crumbling Soviet Empire, the initially funny thing was the overly serious communist state officials themselves. Here is an illustrative example. In Poland, during the crackdown on the Solidarity movement, which paradoxically was a workers movement against a communist state that purportedly represented the interests of the working classes, state employees went around the major cities painting big circles over pro-Solidarity graffiti, a practice that seemed especially ridiculous to some Polish dissidents. The dissidents decided, therefore, to go out at night and repaint the circles as elves, with little feet, hands, and a hat. Over the next couple of years, little elves began to appear everywhere, but the significance of the elf was unclear to state officials. Dissidents would do other silly things such as go in groups to the local zoos and demand "freedom for the bears" while singing communist songs and giving out candy to children. When arrested—though the police had no idea what these crazy people were doing—the news images of happy young people ironically singing communist songs and demanding freedom for the bears were clear enough to everyday citizens: the Soviet Union has always been symbolized by the bear.

Months later, on Children's Day, thousands of children came out of their houses dressed like elves! What was the state to do? The people identified themselves as comic characters, like Smurfs, defending the ethical state, and protesting for everything from clean air to inexpensive toilet paper. Eventually, and without directly confronting the state, but instead using abstract symbols to communicate comically, the revolutions against the Soviet Union were, for the most part, peaceful and successful. This is not to say that they were *only* successful because of this widespread comic tactic. Still, the tactic worked in large part because of the cultural, economic, and political contexts in which it was used.

There was nothing "funny," however, in China, when dissidents gathered on the central public square in Beijing to demand more political liberty. The Chinese situation was quite different from the situation in the former Soviet territories. The Chinese state was economically and politically stronger. The communist leadership was already preparing to turn the country toward capitalism, but certainly not toward greater political liberties. Ultimately the protest was crushed. Tanks and gunmen opened fire on the protestors, killing thousands. Today, the vast majority of people in China have no memory of the massacre, since it has been erased from their public memory (e.g., the event is not taught in schools, memorial images or tapes are not shown on television, and references to the massacre are consistently filtered out of Chinese Internet search systems).

My initial investigation concluded, therefore, that carnivalesque tactics were best employed under specific political, economic, and cultural conditions, which I outlined in my study. When deployed in most of the former Soviet territories, they helped to transform them into more economically and politically liberal states. Conversely, I concluded that comic tactics were not used in China, and serious strategies did not work at all.

When this study was concluded, I attempted to describe the specific tactics that were most successfully used, and in what specific contexts, in order to apply them to present day protests against present day injustices in other political contexts. Today, for example, groups are using carnivalesque tactics against large corporations, transnational organizations such as the World Bank, and in support of environmental protection and nuclear disarmament. On the whole, however, they have not often been successful. Why? How can we apply the lessons learned by the anti-communist protests to fight for greater social justice today, so that these "storms" can indeed lead to more just states?

In sum, to answer my initial research question (i.e., what constitutes a successful rebellion), as we have seen, I first had to rely on my prior work on political transformation and public memory in the former Soviet Union, as well as histories and personal accounts of the rebellions of the late 1980s, and they, in turn, led me to study the carnivalesque. Then, however, I actually had to closely study the protest tactics themselves, for these were my "texts." Yes, I was also interested in what the protesters would say, and what others would say about them, but I was also interested in the way the protesters communicated their messages through embodied performances. This required studying performance theory and social movement theory to better understand how the comic wave gained momentum. This, as if to complete the research circle, required knowing a lot about economic and political policies in the former Soviet Union and China, and how shifting economic and political policies contributed to varied social and political conditions. Only within this larger context was the function of the rhetorical artifact, the variously situated protest tactics, clear.

Of course, not all rhetorical criticism explores world-historical questions, nor does it try to improve the human condition. For scholars seeking to understand, for example, the dominant tropes and figures in a speech, or the principal metaphors in an advertisement, or the generic expectations in an Inaugural Address, one primary method and a handful of theoretical concepts may suffice. To critique the discursive construction of national, racial, gendered, or class identities, however, the critic must begin to move into a wider range of methods and theories, as well as broader cultural, political, and economic matters. In the same manner, to critique the larger world-historical relationship between identity and statecraft, and to determine the most virtuous forms of rhetoric, requires even more, just as it would were one to wish to become a virtuous orator. One can never feel completely successful in such an endeavor, given the limits of human understanding, but the potential payoff for the attempt can be great.

"TEXAS VERNACULAR ROCK HOUSE STRUCTURE: DEFINING 'HOME' THROUGH RHETORICAL DEPICTION," BY MARY EVELYN COLLINS. PUBLISHED IN THE *AMERICAN COMMUNICATION JOURNAL* 9 (2007)

I have always been intrigued with a particular style of house that is very common in the Southwestern United States, from Missouri to New Mexico, but most especially in Texas. This interest was prompted by the fact that the only house that my parents actually built was a bungalow in the "rock house" style. It was a transitional time in their lives and this was perceived to be the house that would become their retirement home. I was not quite three when we moved in, but my older brothers were teenagers, the eldest in college. Less than two years later, with a better retirement plan promised, there was a job change and a move to another town. That house still stands, with the pecan trees my parents planted looming high above its roof, a survivor of Texas storms, a flood, and assorted families with active children.

What began to interest me in recent years was, that with the return of the bungalow in popular new home building, there was also a return to Arts and Crafts Movement elements used in the new "retro" look homes. So much reminded me of the charming front porches and roof lines of the Texas rock houses.[10] The version of the Arts and Crafts, or Craftsman, bungalow in America emerged in the eastern United States with stucco walls and river stone columns or brick walls with river stone or stacked stone trim elements. In the far west, California particularly, the bungalow had stucco walls and some flat stone trim. Many "California bungalows" had a Spanish look with tile roofs and side or rear patios, rather than front porches. All over America whole neighborhoods of bungalows were built from 1900 to the early 1940s.[11] Their popularity disappeared after World War II when the new ranch style home came into vogue.

The bungalow style in Texas used local stone, usually gathered from fields, pastures, and riverbanks. The stones are arranged vertically rather than horizontally, making the outside wall look like freckles, with the various colors shown on the flat side in irregular arrangement. This arrangement was economical, since fewer stones were needed for the outside wall construction than would be needed for a stacked wall. The style was used in small, humble dwellings and in large, expensive homes, both in the countryside and in the city.

As I continued to explore the history, I was stunned by the loyalty to these rock bungalows and began to notice that elements from the original designs were appearing in new buildings. There had been many examples of this style elongated to look similar to the ranch style house, but in recent years porches, arches, and side patios or terraces appeared in new homes. Even some exterior sections are found in the multicolored flat rock arrangement, although the majority of the exterior might be brick, white limestone, or stucco.

Certainly one can see that this form of architecture has become quite influential, and has been receiving preservation interest. Here the key word is *influence*. For if influential, then rhetorical (or, paraphrasing Kenneth Burke, any good communication is rhetorical). Any influential architecture is rhetorical in its visual form. From this beginning premise, I began to look for some rhetorical means—a perspective—to help in the analysis process in order to better understand how this type of home is influential and why.

My first thought was of Burke's cluster criticism, because this type of criticism has been used very successfully in analyzing visual elements in art, architecture, and photography.[12] Looking at the history of the Texas Rock House led me to believe that the house itself was highly identified with the values and concerns of those trans-South emigrants that made their way to Texas in order to start a new life in a new place. Burke's idea of identification as consubstantiality,[13] when some individual and some property share a substance, seemed very applicable to emigrants' intention to build a home in the new place that was "solid," "permanent," and connected with the very soil that would bring them their livelihood: the rock being the substance and the values the personal intention. However, this identification was only part of the problem to be addressed in the rhetorical analysis. The question of regionality or the influence of locale and culture on the nature of the house style and the choice of building materials made it necessary for me to look for additional tools with which to analyze the influence of this particular style.

This brought to mind the notion of rhetorical depiction developed by Michael Osborn in a seminal essay in the collection *Form, Genre, and the Study of Political Discourse*.[14] Rhetorical depiction as explained by Osborn has five functions: presentation, intensification, identification, implementation, and reaffirmation. Each one of these functions must be addressed in the analysis in order to have a successful discussion of rhetorical depiction and the ultimate outcome of the rhetoric. In the case of the Texas Rock House there seemed to be some very appropriate questions to pose from each of the five functions.

First, presentation can be repetitive, that is, showing us what we already know, or innovative, which shows us a new way of knowing when the past no longer works for us.[15] Innovative presentation depends on the use of metaphor to connect to the new way of knowing. Intensification is the expression of heightened feeling, that is, how we see the rhetoric as instigating reaction.[16] Identification, as in Burke, is a sharing of characteristics, but with a narrative quality, identification with the community story.[17] Implementation is the "what do we do" question. How is the message of the rhetoric put into action? Osborn adds, "Implementation includes the classical idea of deliberative rhetoric for it has to do with the designs of the future."[18] Osborn also asserts that "Implementation can be defined as applied identification."[19] The last function of rhetorical depiction is reaffirmation, which means that the rhetoric brings the community back to its identity with its values in a common "appreciation." "Reaffirmative depiction guards the sacred fire around which a nation or a subculture gathers periodically to warm itself in recognition of its being."[20]

The Texas Rock House is evidence that families, most new to the state and region, had deliberately decided to establish homes in order to make a new start in new communities. Herein began a new subculture with its shared values. By incorporating insights gained from both Burke and Osborn, I was better able to share with others the fascinating rhetorical strength of the Texas Rock Houses. My approach was eclectic in that I had to blend rhetorical perspectives in order to better appreciate the hidden rhetorical dynamics that were enbedded in the architecture of these houses. In the visual form, such as architecture, there are various elements that connect with values and purpose for those who live within the dwelling. This form of eclecticism is not a jumble or hodgepodge, but an evolved process that began with the classical scholars who highly influenced Kenneth Burke and then Burke influenced Michael Osborn. A close reading of either Burke or Osborn will reveal a developmental path of true eclecticism: the ability to see the influential elements in all of communication, no matter the form or genre.

"FROM SCIENCE, MORAL POETICS: DR. JAMES DOBSON'S RESPONSE TO THE FETAL TISSUE RESEARCH INITIATIVE," BY JIM A. KUYPERS. PUBLISHED IN *THE QUARTERLY JOURNAL OF SPEECH* 86.2 (2000): 146–167

Years ago I came across a letter written by James Dobson, president of Focus on the Family. The letter was distributed to over 2 million constituents of Focus on the Family, and concerned the 1993 Fetal Tissue Research Initiative, which allowed for scientific experimentation on aborted fetuses. Dobson spoke out against this initiative, in particular calling attention to the immoral nature of the practice, making Biblical analogies, and making predictions of eventual cloning of humans for spare body parts.[21]

The letter intrigued me on several levels and I wanted to study it further. First, Dobson had an enormous potential impact. The audience for his monthly letters was then over 2 million, but his potential radio audience, to which he read the entire letter, approached 200 million in North America and 550 million worldwide. What were these audience members being asked to believe? Dobson's detractors had called him a televangelist and doctrinal speaker in the past, but this seemed simplistic criticism of someone with such a large multinational and diverse audience. I was interested in discovering if his letters contained elements of indoctrination, or if he were communicating truly to a worldwide audience, attempting persuasion rather than indoctrination. Dobson's letter was also noteworthy because it successfully brought together the resources of scientific and moral language. The letter seemed to be using science to argue against a scientific practice; moreover, it appeared to be asking for individual moral action in the face of an impersonal science. I was curious to discover how all of this was being accomplished. Just why did this letter have so much power as I read it? Finally, it simply interested me, having elements of science, Jewish history, God's wrath, individual morality, futuristic predictions, and charismatic appeal.

As I pondered how to go about exploring my questions, I soon realized that no single perspective would do the job I wanted it to do. So, to understand the rich moral culture Dobson's letter represents and reached out to, I examined it in three stages: first, I performed a judgmental analysis of the letter in order to determine what Dobson's potential reading audience was being asked to believe. I sought also to understand how Dobson met the needs of his regular readers, and was able to appeal to other than his usual audience, even while eschewing the type of discursive strategies often employed by doctrinal speakers. Second, using Kenneth Burke's distinction between semantic and poetic meaning as a starting point, I examined Dobson's discourse as a moral-poetic response to the amoral stance of scientific discourse. Finally, I undertook an inquiry of the motive underpinning Dobson's discourse that allowed me to better understand the actions of Dobson's envisioned moral agent.

The end result was a *method* of analysis (criticism) that blended *perspectives* (judgmental analysis and Burkean dramatism—namely, moral-poetic language and motivational analysis) into a critical point of view. This flexible combination allowed me to study the letter on three different levels, thereby more fully explaining the inner and outer workings of the letter better than if I had used any one perspective alone.

What I found amazed me. Judgmental analysis allowed me to discover that Dobson based his initial argumentative appeals upon the language of science (factual, secularly authoritative); however, halfway through his letter he resorted to a different strategy and shifted to adjudicative appeals (judgments relying upon some type of code) based upon the factual evidence he had already submitted as true. This new strategy took on a moral-poetic dimension that acted in opposition to the scientific discourse: scientific discourse (that allows for fetal tissue research) gave way to a moral-poetic discourse designed to allow for individual moral action. The moral-poetic and motivational portions allowed me to discover how Dobson pitted medical research (Science) against moral action; used what Kenneth Burke called "poor semantics" (scientism: what society believes to be science; science given the status of a public philosophy) as support for his moral interpretation; and then provided a way out of the moral quagmire science has placed humans in by highlighting our ability to morally act, thereby initiating an individual-moral redemptive cycle.

"THE RHETORIC OF EXORCISM: GEORGE W. BUSH AND THE RETURN OF POLITICAL DEMONOLOGY," BY JOSHUA GUNN. PUBLISHED IN THE *WESTERN JOURNAL OF COMMUNICATION* 68.1 (WINTER 2004): 1–23

In the months that followed the attacks on U.S. soil on September 11, 2001, "we the people" were traumatized and frightened. In the fall of that year and the spring of the next, I remember I was frequently flying across the country in search of my first academic job. Like everyone else I encountered in an airport, I was an anxious traveler. In early 2002, I vividly recall sitting in an airport bar in Dallas on a layover when President George W. Bush delivered one of his many, many speeches on 9/11. All of us in the bar were staring at the television set, transfixed, disturbed, worried. Bush's speech was designed to comfort us, especially the folks in that bar, who were waiting to board an airplane. But I was unnerved by the speech, which used a number of biblical metaphors and the kind of language I remembered in church growing up. I was also startled that, as of yet, few media commentators were discussing the religious overtones of Bush's speechcraft.

I was raised in an evangelical Baptist church in a congregation that—I realize in retrospect—was inching toward Pentecostalism. I vividly remember the fiery sermons delivered by Brother Snooks (yes, that was his name). I remember the discussions we had in church about "spiritual warfare," about battling demons on a daily basis, about how listening to rock music was an invitation for demonic possession. Spiritual warfare is a concept, now fully formed in many evangelical and charismatic religious systems, that refers to the idea that mortal human beings must do battle with demons on a daily basis through prayer and various religious rituals, such as exorcism. When I heard Bush deliver his speeches after 9/11, I couldn't help but think of the language of spiritual warfare.

One day, out of simple curiosity, I decided to research who Bush's speechwriters were. I discovered Michael John Gerson was Bush's chief speechwriter from 2001–2006. Gerson is an evangelical Christian who was responsible for penning many of Bush's more memorable, religious statements. It then occurred to me that the charismatic language of spiritual warfare was quite deliberate in Bush's speeches. Over lunch meetings and casual conversation I began sharing my ideas with friends. I argued that Bush's speeches spoke to two audiences: those who got the religious warfare references, and those who did not. I was surprised to learn that most of those who I shared my ideas with resisted my argument. I recall at one lunch meeting a colleague laughed aloud at the suggestion that Bush's speechwriters were employing the language of demonology. Few bought my argument that my personal background in evangelical religious beliefs gave me the authority to make arguments. In other words, if I was going to convince people that Bush's speeches since 9/11 were about spiritual warfare, I couldn't appeal to my own authority and experience, as valid as both were to me. I had to appeal to something in the speeches themselves.

When I was thinking about these ideas—and as Bush continued to make religious references in his speeches—I was invited to interview for a job in California. Part of the interview consisted of a guest lecture in a rhetorical criticism class. I decided I might try out my arguments on Bush's speeches. I wanted to offer an argument to the students about what I saw in these presidential addresses, but I also needed to teach them something about rhetorical criticism. I cannot detail exactly how or why I landed on the approach that I did: it just came to me. Up to that point, I had studied speech genres with my professors but had only found the concept of genre useful for talking about popular music. It occurred to me, however, that I was thinking about genres too narrowly for speeches. I thought: what if a genre could be much bigger than a speech? What if a genre is something like a certain religious experience?

Genres are patterns that are repeated in discourse of all kinds. Most of us are familiar with film or music genres: "romantic comedy," "hip-hop," "horror," and "alternative rock" are just some examples. Speeches also have genres: a eulogy or presidential inaugural addresses, for example, are just two of many types of speech genres. Regardless of the kind of discourse, though, all genres have patterns that create expectations in people. So, if I was going to go to a funeral, I would *expect* to hear a eulogy, and that eulogy would praise the deceased. My expectations would be violated if I went to a funeral and a speaker began attacking the dead person as a liar and criminal.

Bush's post-9/11 speeches were designed to meet expectations, so there had to be some generic norms. I printed out and read all of Bush's speeches from September 11, 2001 until November 11, 2002. As I read the speeches, I looked for repeated patterns that might form expectations in those who heard them. What I found were not so much formal patterns—that is, what a president should do and say to a general audience—as I did informal or indirect patterns that closely modeled an experience that religious people know well: the conversion experience. If you are an evangelical, you are probably familiar with this story (quite literally embedded in the song, "Amazing Grace"): a lost soul meets misfortune and woe until, having discovered Jesus and accepted Him as one's own "personal savior," one is "born again." Or to put the pattern alternately, "I was blind/but now I see."

I noticed something else about Bush's speeches too. He used a lot of demonic metaphors to describe "the enemy." He kept talking about "smoking [the enemy] out of their holes" and purging other countries of "evil." What I had already unconsciously noticed at the Dallas airport bar suddenly became clear to me: Bush's speeches repeated a religious conversion narrative, but one that premised conversion on the casting out of evil. I was reminded immediately of the film *The Exorcist*, in which a couple of priests cast a demon out of a girl in order to save her soul. I concluded that Bush's speeches were rhetorical exorcisms.

When I went on my job interview, I taught the students about genre, and then presented them with information about Spiritual Warfare, and in particular, about the casting out of demons. In charismatic literature, to cast out demons one has to name the demon, argue with it, battle with the demon, and then cast it out. I provided the students with a copy of Bush's 2002 State of the Union address and asked them to locate the pattern of exorcism in the speech. They did, without much difficulty. At that moment I knew that I was on to something that others could see also if I just presented the argument in the right way. After my presentation, one of my colleagues urged me to write up the lecture as an article and publish it. So I did.

Writing criticism and teaching it, however, are two different things. I knew that the generic approach to criticism would not be enough, as more was going on in Bush's speeches. It seemed to me that Bush's speeches were not just patterned, but that the pattern was highly emotional and perhaps worked at levels we are not consciously aware of. So in writing up my criticism, I also decided to discuss *myth* (deep, culturally based patterns we all absorb as members of a community) and psychoanalysis (the idea that patterns repeat in our heads, not just out there in texts). The resulting rhetorical criticism was "eclectic" in its approach: by combining close textual analysis with generic, mythic, and psychoanalytic criticism, I offered a reading of many of Bush's speeches as an exorcism. Had I done a simple generic criticism, or not thought about how the speeches work emotionally, my reading of Bush's rhetoric would have been much less insightful. It was only by "thinking outside of the box" and using the approach that best got at the dynamics of the speech that I could make a compelling case. To me, this is the key to eclectic criticism: you must let the object you are criticizing help you determine the type of analysis that you use.

NOTES

1. "Kristina Wilfore Quotes," ThinkExist.com, http://en.thinkexist.com/quotation/typically-off-year-elections-are-used-for-two/984893.html

Wilfore is the executive director of the ballot Initiative Strategy Center http://www.ballot.org/index.asp?Type=B_DIR&SEC=%7BF3E1F9CD-E021-4103-8258-180C7FD1AA7F%7D&DE=%7B4B311291-3444-4C64-8C55-D1331C758500%7D

2. Pauline Kael, *I Lost It at the Movies* (Boston: Little, Brown, 1964) 309. I first came across this quotation in Bernard L. Brock, Robert L. Scott, and James W. Chesebro, eds. *Methods of Rhetorical Criticism: A Twentieth-Century Perspective* 3rd ed. (Detroit: Wayne State University Press, 1989), 89.

3. "David Esbjornson Quotes," ThinkExist.com, http://en.thinkexist.com/quotation/i-have-an-eclectic-past-but-i-intentionally-have/737562.html.

4. Brock, Scott, and Chesebro, 89.

5. Edwin Black, "Plato's View of Rhetoric," *Readings in Rhetoric*, Lionel Crocker and Paul A. Carmack, eds. (Springfield, IL: Charles C. Thomas Publisher, 1965), 68.

6. Jefferson's opinions, expressed in a letter to Colonel Edward Carrington on January 16, 1787, proved to be controversial in the wake of the French Revolutions and Shays Rebellion, two rebellions against the upper classes. Cited in Gerald Stourz, *Alexander Hamilton and the Idea of Republican Government* (Stanford, CA: Stanford University Press, 1970), 34.

7. See, for example, Cicero's daunting list in *De Oratore*, in *Cicero: On Oratory and Orators*. Trans. J. S. Watson (Carbondale, IL: Southern Illinois University Press, 1986), 100. Quintillian wrote that the ideal orator must be a good person whose character is shaped by philosophy, for rhetoric is a *virtue*. See the *Institutio Oratoria*, Vol. I. Ed. Charles E. Little (Nashville, TN: George Peabody College for Teachers, 1951).

8. *Institutio Oratoria*, 23.

9. See M. Lane Bruner, *Strategies of Remembrance: The Rhetorical Dimensions of National Identity Construction* (Columbia, SC: South Carolina University Press, 2002); and *Market Democracy in Post Communist Russia*. Coeditor Viatcheslav Morozov (Leeds, England: Wisdom House, 2005).

10. This particular movement of revived interest is well-documented in several publications. The most comprehensive is *American Bungalow*, published by the John Brinkmann Design Office, Santa Monica, CA.

11. Chicago is know for its bungalow neighborhoods, featuring houses that are narrow to facilitate more house on a narrow lot, with the front door on the side of the house, with the front room window

wall nearest the street. Denver features bungalow neighborhoods with brick bungalows, both single story and story and a half, with front porches and garages.

12. See the discussion in Sonja K. Foss, *Rhetorical Criticism,* 4th edition, (Waveland Press, 2009), 63–96.

13. Kenneth Burke, *A Rhetoric of Motives,* (1950; rpt. Berkeley: University of California Press, 1969), 41.

14. Herbert W. Simons and Aram A. Aghazarian, eds. (Columbia, SC: University of South Carolina Press, 1986), 79–107.

15. Osborn, "Rhetorical Depiction" in *Form, Genre, and Political Discourse*, 82–86.

16. Ibid., 86.

17. Ibid., 89–92.

18. Ibid., 93.

19. Ibid., 92.

20. Ibid., 95.

21. Just five years later, all that Dobson suggested materialized in science circles. For example, see the December 8, 1998 BBC News article, "Human spare-part cloning set for approval," http://news.bbc .co.uk/1/hi/sci/tech/230002.stm. By 2004, British scientists were given formal approval to clone human embryos for "therapeutic purposes." Antony Barnett and Robin McKie, "UK to Clone Human Cells," *The Observer* (June 13, 2004). http://www.guardian.co.uk/society/2004/jun/13/health.research

Index

Biographical Sketches of the Authors

Matthew T. Althouse is Associate Professor of Communication at the State University of New York (SUNY) College at Brockport, where he teaches courses in public address, rhetoric and religion, and qualitative research methods. He has published essays in *Communication Quarterly* and in a volume titled *Comics & Ideology*.

Floyd D. Anderson is Professor of Communication at the State University of New York College at Brockport. He is the author or coauthor of numerous articles on rhetorical theory and/or criticism. He is a Past President of the Eastern Communication Association, and was the 2001 recipient of the Donald H. Ecroyd and Caroline Drummond Ecroyd Teaching Excellence Award. His research interests include the history of rhetoric and public address, meta-theory and meta-criticism, dramatistic rhetorical theory and criticism, and political rhetoric.

Moya Ann Ball is recently retired as Associate Professor of Speech Communication and Associate Vice President for Academic Affairs at Trinity University, San Antonio. As well as chapters and articles, she has authored *Vietnam-on-the-Potomac*. Her research focuses on the Vietnam decision-making activities of Presidents Kennedy, Johnson, Nixon, and their advisors.

Edwin Black was Professor of Communication Arts at the University of Wisconsin, Madison. He was the author of the seminal book, *Rhetorical Criticism: A Study in Method* and a host of landmark essays of criticism. He twice received the Speech Communication Association Golden Anniversary Award. He died early Saturday morning, January 13, 2007.

William L. Benoit is Professor of Communication at the University of Missouri. He has published over 120 journal articles and book chapters, and is the author or editor of eight books including *Accounts, Excuses, and Apologies* and *The Clinton Scandals and the Politics of Image Restoration*. He was selected as the American Communication Association's Outstanding Teacher at a Doctoral Institution. He is also the recipient of the American Communication Association's Gerald M. Phillips Mentoring Award and also the University of Missouri Gold Chalk Award for graduate mentoring. He has served as the editor for the *Journal of Communication*. His primary interests are rhetorical theory and criticism and political communication.

Stephen H. Browne is Professor of Rhetorical Studies at The Pennsylvania State University. He teaches courses in rhetorical theory, rhetorical criticism, and social protest rhetoric. Browne is the author of *Jefferson's Call For Nationhood*, *Angelina Grimke: Rhetoric, Identity, and the Radical Imagination*, and *Edmund Burke and the Discourse of Virtue*. His book on Angelina Grimke received the National Communication Association's Diamond Anniversary Book Award, and he has received the Karl R. Wallace Award from the Speech Communication Association.

M. Lane Bruner is Associate Professor of Critical Political Communication and Graduate Director of the Doctoral Program in Public Communication in the Department of Communication at Georgia State University. He is the author of *Strategies of Remembrance, Democracy's Debt, and Market Democracy in Post-Communist Russia* (coedited), as well as over two dozen scholarly essays and book chapters on rhetoric and politics. His current research focuses on artful resistance to corporate globalization, global constitutionalism and the history of statecraft, and critical theoretical approaches to the relationship between subjectivity and materiality.

Thomas R. Burkholder is Associate Professor and Chair at the Hank Greenspun School of Communication, University of Nevada—Las Vegas. He teaches courses in rhetorical criticism, rhetorical theory, history of United States public address, and college teaching in communication. His research interests include nineteenth-century U.S. public address, the rhetoric of woman suffrage, political rhetoric, and presidential rhetoric. His scholarly work has appeared in *Communication Studies*, the *Southern Communication Journal*, the *Western Journal of Communication,* and in various book chapters. He is coauthor, with Karlyn Kohrs Campbell, of the second edition of *Critiques of Contemporary Rhetoric*.

Mary Evelyn Collins is an Associate Professor of Speech Communication at Sam Houston State University. Her research interests include Folk Speech and Cowboy Humor; Child and Family Advocacy; Rhetorical Depiction and Culturetype as a Critical Tool in Rhetorical Analysis; and the intersection of cultural tradition and popular culture forms. She is a past president of the Southern States Communication Association.

Kathleen Farrell is Professor and Chair at the Department of Communication, St. Louis University. She teaches and researches instances of contemporary and historical public argument, argument theory, and argument pedagogy. Her work includes studies of the rhetoric of the American Left, public discourse of the American Cold War era, arguments about the relationship between politics and aesthetics in the 1930s, and the South African Truth and Reconciliation Commission. She has published in numerous scholarly journals, edited volumes, and proceedings. She is the author of *Literary Integrity and Political Action*.

Thomas S. Frentz is professor of Communication at the University of Arkansas, Fayetteville. He is the coauthor of *Projecting the Shadow: The Cyborg Hero in American Film* and *The Communicative Experience*, and has published over two dozen articles. He received the Golden Anniversary Monograph Award from the National Communication Association, and the Michael M. Osborn Teacher-Scholar Award from the Southern States Communication Association. He teaches classes in film, rhetoric, cultural studies, and qualitative methods, while his research interests include language use, rhetorical theory, film criticism, and personal narratives.

David Henry is Professor at the University of Nevada. He teaches courses in rhetorical theory and criticism, political communication, persuasion, and argumentation. His scholarship focuses on presidential rhetoric, nuclear politics, social movement studies, and scientists as political advocates. He has published in the *Quarterly Journal of Speech*, *Communication Monographs*, the *Rhetoric Society Quarterly*, *Communication Education*, *Communication Studies,* and the *Southern Communication Journal*. He received the 1998 University Distinguished Teaching Award at Cal Poly State University, San Luis Obispo, and shared with all contributors to *Eisenhower's War of Words: Rhetoric and Leadership* (Michigan State University Press) the 1995 Marie Hochmuth Nichols Award for Outstanding Scholarship in Public Address. Henry was the editor of the *Western Journal of Communication* and the *Quarterly Journal of Speech*.

Stephanie Houston Grey is an Assistant Professor of Rhetoric in the department of Communication Studies at Louisiana State University. She researches and teaches in the areas of Rhetoric and Culture, Epistemology and Aesthetics, Trauma, and Interdisciplinarity. Her research has appeared in journals such as *The Quarterly Journal of Speech*, *Communication and Cultural/Critical Studies*, *Text and Performance Quarterly*, *Communication Yearbook* and *The American Communication Journal*. She received the Rainmaker Award 2008, designating her a top 100 faculty at LSU.

Joshua Gunn is an Assistant Professor of Communication Studies at the University of Texas at Austin. He has published essays in the *Quarterly Journal of Speech*, *Western Journal of Communication*, *RSQ: Rhetoric Society Quarterly*, *Rhetoric and Public Affairs* and others. He conducts research at the intersection of rhetorical and cultural studies, currently in pursuit of two, interrelated projects: (1) the integration of psychoanalysis and rhetorical/textual theory; and (2) a demonstration of the relevance and ubiquity of theological forms in public culture and daily life.

Forbes I. Hill was Emeritus, Queens College of the City University of New York. He has published in the field of history of rhetoric and public address. He is the author of "Aristotle's Rhetorical Theory," in James J. Murphy and Richard Katula's volume, *A Synoptic History of Classical Rhetoric*. Hill passed away on November 5, 2008.

Andrew King is Professor at the Department of Speech Communication at Louisiana State University. He is the author of *Postmodern Political Communication*, *Power and Communication*, and coeditor of *Twentieth-Century Roots of Rhetorical Studies*. He is the former editor of the *Quarterly Journal of Speech* and the *Southern Communication Journal*. He was selected as the American Communication Association's Outstanding Teacher at a Doctoral Institution in 1998. Professor King's academic interests lie in the areas of communication and power, and medieval and Renaissance rhetorical theory. He is a past president of the Kenneth Burke Society.

Jim A. Kuypers is an Associate Professor at Virginia Polytechnic Institute and State University. He is the author of six books, including *Bush's War: Media Bias and Justifications for War in the Terrorist Age* and (with Robert E. Denton) *Politics and Communication in America: Campaigns, Media, and Governing in the 21st Century*. He is a former editor for the *American Communication Journal*. He is the recipient of the American Communication Association's Outstanding Contribution to Communication Scholarship Award, the Southern States Communication Association's Early Career Research award, and Dartmouth College's

Distinguished Lecturer Award. His research interests include political communication, meta-criticism, and the moral/poetic use of language.

Ronald Lee is Professor of Communication Studies at the University of Nebraska-Lincoln. He teaches and writes about contemporary rhetoric and political culture. His work has appeared in the *Quarterly Journal of Speech*, *Political Communication*, *Western Journal of Communication*, *Communication Studies*, *Southern Communication Journal*, *Argumentation and Advocacy*, and *Technical Communication Quarterly*. He is presently completing a book on the rhetorical negotiation of presidential legacies.

Kevin R. McClure is Associate Professor of Communication Studies at the University of Rhode Island. His work has appeared in *Communication Quarterly* and the *Western Journal of Communication*. He teaches and writes about rhetorical theory and criticism.

Ramie McKerrow is Professor in the School of Communication Studies at Ohio University, Athens, Ohio. He has published in the areas of modern rhetoric, argumentation theory, and critical/cultural approaches to contemporary rhetoric. He is past president of the Eastern Communication Association and the National Communication Association, and received the Charles H. Woolbert Research Award from the National Communication Association.

Donna Marie Nudd is Professor of Communication at Florida State University. Her essays have appeared in *Text and Performance Quarterly*, *Bronte Society Transactions*, *Communication Education*, and the *Modern Language Association Series*. As a practitioner in performance, she has served as director and dramaturge for Terry Galloway's one woman shows which were shown in Edinburgh, London, New York, Toronto, Mexico City and alternative venues throughout the U.S. In 2001, Donna Marie Nudd and Terry Galloway, long-time collaborators, won NCA's Irene Coger award for lifetime achievement in Performance. Her major areas of interest include feminist criticism, pedagogy, radical performance, and adaptation for film and theatre.

Robert C. Rowland is Professor and Chair of the Department of Communication Studies at the University of Kansas. He is the author of *Israeli and Palestinian Symbol Use* (with David Frank), *Analyzing Rhetoric*, *The Rhetoric of Menachem Begin: The Myth of Redemption Through Return*, and more than thirty published essays on rhetorical criticism, argumentation, and narrative. A recent study found that he was one of the thirty most published scholars in the field. Professor Rowland's research interests include critical methodologies, public argument, argumentation theory, and political communication.

Janice Hocker Rushing was Professor in the Department of Communication at the University of Arkansas, Fayetteville. She was the author of *Erotic Mentoring: Women's Transformations in the University*, coauthor of *Projecting the Shadow: The Cyborg Hero in American Film*, and of many articles on the rhetorical criticism of the media. She was the recipient of the Michael M. Osborn Teacher-Scholar Award from the Southern States Communication Association in 2001 and the NCA Douglas W. Ehninger Distinguished Rhetorical Scholar Award in 2005. Her writing interests included mythology, gender, and values in contemporary media and in American academia. Rushing succumbed to cancer in 2004.

Thomas J. St. Antoine is Associate Professor of Communication at Palm Beach Atlantic University. His work has been published in the *Florida Communication Journal* and in *Research on Christian Higher Education*. He has also presented papers at numerous conventions and is a former editorial assistant for the *Quarterly Journal of Speech*. His teaching and research interests include the rhetoric of higher education and organizational rhetoric.

Jeffrey St. John is Associate Professor in the School of Communication Studies at Ohio University, Athens, Ohio. He publishes in the areas of legal and political rhetoric, communication theory, and public argument. His work has appeared in journals such as *Rhetoric & Public Affairs* and the *Quarterly Journal of Speech*. He teaches classes in public advocacy, free speech, argumentation, communication theory, and public deliberation.

Kristina L. Whalen is an Assistant Professor and Director of Forensics in the Speech Division of the English Department at City College of San Francisco. Her work has been published in *Text and Performance Quarterly* and *Women's Studies and Communication*, among others. Her research explores the intersection of feminist argument and performative protest.

Marilyn J. Young is the Wayne C. Minnick Professor of Communication, Emerita, at Florida State University. She has published numerous articles and book chapters and authored two books, *Flights of Fancy, Flight of Doom: KAL 007 and Soviet-American Rhetoric* and *Coaching Debate*. With David Marples she edited *Nuclear Energy and Security in the Former Soviet Union*. Her research interests are in argumentation; rhetorical theory and criticism; and political (particularly international) rhetoric, especially the development of political language and argument in newly emerging democracies.

CPSIA information can be obtained at www.ICGtesting.com
Printed in the USA
LVOW111350030712

288728LV00005B/80/P